THE ART OF PROGRAMMING

Computer Science with C++

Steven C. Lawlor
Foothill College

PWS Publishing Company

I(T)P

An International Thomson Publishing Company

Boston • Albany • Bonn • Cincinnati • Detroit • London • Madrid • Melbourne • Mexico City •
New York • Pacific Grove • Paris • San Francisco • Singapore • Tokyo • Toronto • Washington

PWS Publishing Company
20 Park Plaza, Boston, MA 02116-4324

Sponsoring Editor: *David Dietz*
Marketing Manager: *Nathan Wilbur*
Manufacturing Buyer: *Andrew Christensen*
Production Editor: *Pamela Rockwell*
Cover Designer: *Eileen Hoff*
Composition/Interior Design: *The Curtis Company*
Cover Printer: *Phoenix Color Corp.*
Text Printer and Binder: *West Publishing*
Cover Illustration: *Lee Krasner, "Composition," 1943. National Museum of American Art, Washington, DC/Art Resource, NY. © 1998 Pollock-Krasner Foundation/Artists Rights Society (ARS), New York*

I(T)P International Thomson Publishing
The trademark ITP is used under license.

Printed and Bound in the United States of America
97 98 99 00 — 10 9 8 7 6 5 4 3 2 1

For more information contact:
PWS Publishing Company
20 Park Plaza
Boston, MA 02116

International Thomson Publishing Europe
Berkshire House 168-173
High Holborn
London WC1V 7AA
England

Thomas Nelson Australia
102 Dodds Street
South Melbourne, 3205
Victoria, Australia

Nelson Canada
1120 Birchmont Road
Scarborough, Ontario
Canada M1K 5G4

International Thomson Editores
Campos Eliseos 385, Piso 7
Col. Polanco
11560 Mexico D.F., Mexico

International Thomson Publishing GmbH
Konigswinterer Strasse 418
53227 Bonn, Germany

International Thomson Publishing Asia
221 Henderson Road
#05-10 Henderson Building
Singapore 0315

International Thomson Publishing Japan
Hirakawacho Kyowa Building, 31
2-2-1 Hirakawacho
Chiyoda-ku, Tokyo 102
Japan

ISBN: 0-534-95135-X

Library of Congress Cataloging-in-Publication Data

Lawlor, Steven C.
 The art of programming: computer science with C++ /
Steven C. Lawlor.
  p.   cm.
 ISBN 0-534-95135-X (alk. paper)
 1. C++ (Computer program language) 2. Electronic digital
computers--Programming. I. Title.
QA76.73.C153L394 1997
005. 13'3--dc21   97-22065
                                                    CIP

CONTENTS

Chapter 2

THE C++ LANGUAGE   41

Chapter 4

THE SELECTION STRUCTURE   105

Chapter 8

ARRAYS   261

Chapter 12

MEMORY ACCESS   443

Chapter 13

THE PREPROCESSOR AND OTHER FEATURES   493

PREFACE

Is computer programming an art or is it a science? If done well, the answer is yes—to both questions. The scientific basis of computer programming is demonstrated in the constant application of the scientific method. We are faced with a problem; we formulate hypotheses—programs—to solve the problem; and we test the programs to prove their effectiveness in solving the problem.

Art, though, plays at least as important a part in the programming process. In almost any kind of situation that can be dealt with using computers, there is more than one possible solution—more than one program that will do the job. The programming artist will find the most effective solution, the one that not only satisfies the elements of the problem but also does so most efficiently and with greatest ease of use. Equally importantly, the artist will present the solution in a manner that is easily understood by the rest of the programming community.

With this book, students learn not only the science of programming—algorithm development and testing—but also the art of programming—proven techniques for program development and presentation.

THE OBJECTIVES OF THIS BOOK

Programming courses must combine two objectives that do not always overlap. One is to teach language syntax and usage—which words perform what actions on the computer. The second is to teach program development—how to efficiently and cleanly develop a computer solution for a problem. There must always be some tradeoffs between these objectives. The trick is to cover both objectives with the fewest tradeoffs, and to do so in a manageable and teachable unit.

The major objective of this book is the latter—program development—but in order to fulfill that objective, the student must have a working mastery of the former—language syntax and usage. The book combines these objectives by introducing programming concepts and immediately reinforcing them with the C++ constructs needed to implement them. The student learns a programming concept and is able to practice it immediately. By the end of the book, the student should be comfortable with good programming practice, and will have been exposed to much of C++.

PROGRAMMING FUNDAMENTALS

The book is an introduction to programming. No previous programming experience or knowledge of computers is required or expected. The student is introduced to proper and accepted techniques of structured program development—top-down design, modularity, encapsulation, and data abstraction. Examples throughout the book show the entire development process clearly traced through the five major steps in program development:

1. **Task**. Identification of the problem to be solved.

2. **Analysis**. An in-depth analysis of the task including outputs and inputs, internal data requirements, and data relationships and formulas.

3. **Design**. The process for designing the solution including the statement of an overall algorithm and the stepwise refinement of that algorithm to a detailed solution.

4. **Implementation**. Translating the design into a computer program, clearly keyed to the design with comments and structure.

5. **Test**. Deciding on testing procedures and showing the results of the program, including execution charts for detailed analysis of the solution.

Structured, modular programming is always stressed. Too often it is tempting to forget structure in simple processes, but if good habits are not developed from the outset, the bad habits developed by default will be hard to break later.

THE PROGRAMMING LANGUAGE

C++ is a good language for a first course in computer programming for a number of reasons. The language is at a high enough level to allow implementation of proper structure and clear modularity, but it can access the computer at a low enough level to utilize some of the more basic features of the computer. Abstraction, of both data and processes, is not just an abstraction with C++; it is an integral part of the language. Object orientation is becoming the dominant methodology in software engineering, and C++ fully utilizes it.

C++ is also a commercially popular language. The student will not have to learn a language simply to demonstrate programming techniques and then never see it again in the real world. In addition, many C++ implementations have effective integrated development environments that make programming easier and less daunting for the beginner.

Standards

The ANSI standard for C++ has not yet been set, but many of the popular compiler vendors are following the November, 1996, working papers from the ANSI X3J16 committee. This book follows that proposed standard. Some parts of the standard have not been universally implemented, so we step gingerly around them. For example, we mention the `bool` data type, but all examples and problems will operate without it. We use `string` objects beginning with Chapter 2 and continuing throughout the book. The `string` class has yet to find its way into some compilers, but that is rapidly changing.

To accommodate those whose compilers do not have the `string` data type, or who wish a traditional treatment of strings (null-terminated arrays) we have included Appendix D, *C Strings*, which can substitute for or enhance Chapter 9, *Strings*.

PEDAGOGICAL ELEMENTS

This text is meant to be accessible and nonthreatening for the student. To that end a number of pedagogical features are built into the book.

In-Chapter Features

- **Writing Style.** The writing style is purposefully informal, designed to be open and friendly.

- **Chapter Previews.** Each chapter starts with a preview informing the students of the kinds of knowledge they should be expecting from the chapter.

- **Memory Diagrams.** A solid understanding of C++ requires a solid understanding of the interaction of the language with the computer's memory. These diagrams show sections of memory and the changes that take place as a result of a program's actions.

- **Object Summaries.** These charts show the various objects required by the process. With each object, we show its behaviors and properties. They appear at the end of each chapter, and at key points within the chapters.

- **Execution Charts.** These charts trace the execution of programs line by line, variable by variable. Students can look at the code presented, and be led carefully through its execution with all the features and pitfalls clearly outlined. They appear at the end of each chapter, and at key points within the chapters.

- **Margin Notes.** All important points are addressed within the flow of the text, but concepts of special note are referred to in short margin notes alongside the paragraphs that contain the full explanation. This allows a smooth text flow, sharp highlighting of key points, and efficient review.

  Heads Up. These margin notes focus on key points of program design and implementation. They exist on almost every page.

  Traps. Possible programming problems and common errors are addressed within the text flow, but highlighted by the *Traps* in the margin.

- **Your Turn.** At the end of each logical section—two to seven times per chapter—there are reading-reinforcement questions. The answers to these are collected at the end of each chapter.

- **Nuts 'n' Bolts Boxes.** These are optional boxes on the underpinnings of the C++ language.

- **C++ Plus Boxes.** These optional boxes show C++ features that complete the standard language but are not necessarily needed for demonstrating basic programming concepts. *Nuts 'n' Bolts* and *C++ Plus* boxes allow the student to delve into the language in more detail, and allow the instructor greater flexibility to adjust the depth of the course.

- **Putting It Together.** At the end of each chapter, and at other key points within some chapters, *Putting It Together* sections show complete examples of the materials just covered. These features follow a program through the full development process—task, analysis, design, implementation, and test—and always include detailed *Object Summaries* showing the objects and their properties and behaviors called for in the design, and *Execution Charts* for the code produced.

End-of-Chapter Features

- **Key Terms.** These are collected in their order of appearance at the end of each chapter.

- **New Objects, Functions, and Statements.** Brief descriptions of new objects, functions, and statements introduced in the chapter are collected here.

- **Concept Review.** Important concepts are summarized at the end of each chapter.

- **Traps** and **Heads Up** Summaries. All the *Traps* and *Heads Up* margin notes are gathered in this one place at the end of each chapter.

- **Exercises.** Student exercises at the end of each chapter require not just regurgitation of the material but the ability to effectively apply the chapter's concepts.

- **Programs.** Programming problems reinforce the chapter's materials. Most of the programs show expected outputs and give a list of suggested variables.

End-of-Text Features

- **Operators in Precedence.** Appendix B pulls together all the ANSI C++ operators, in precedence, with examples of their usage. This one-page appendix may become the most dog-eared page of the student's textbook.

- **Function Reference.** Appendix C contains a reference to all the functions introduced in the book. For each function it shows the function prototype, outlines the purpose and parameters of the function, and gives the possible return values.

- **Quick-Reference Card.** The last page of the book is a two-sided, card-stock, tear-out page containing one-line prototypes for all the functions introduced with the header file that contains the declaration for each function. This card can be used by the student during programming sessions, and some professors may allow the students to refer to it during tests.

MODULARITY AND FLEXIBILITY

Just as modularity is an important part of programming, it is an important part of this book. Courses vary considerably in the depth and in the order in which they cover language elements; therefore, the book is organized with maximum flexibility. A course of instruction may be tailored to the individual needs and tastes of a professor or academic situation by assembling the modules of the book in a variety of forms. Almost any type of presentation can be accommodated in a smooth, orderly format.

Optional Features

Many of the sections of the book may be excluded from an individual course without loss of continuity. These sections fall within four categories:

1. **Boxes.** Any of the *Nuts 'n' Bolts*, and *C++ Plus* boxes may be included or excluded at the professor's discretion.

2. **Optional Modules.** Four of the modules within the chapters are marked as optional. Any or all of these may be excluded:

    How We Got Here: A Brief History (Chapter 1)
    Hexadecimal Numbers (Chapter 1)
    Incrementing and Decrementing in Expressions (Chapter 5)
    Recursion (Chapter 6)

3. **Appendix D, *C Strings*.** Chapter 9, *Strings*, discusses string usage in terms of the `string` data type (actually an object). Since this concept is new to C++, and since it does not make use of the efficiency of traditional "C strings" (null-terminated arrays), we have included an appendix that can be used in addition to or in place of Chapter 9.

4. **Modular Chapters.** See the description that follows.

Modular Chapters

Two of the chapters, Chapter 12, *Memory Access*, and Chapter 13, *The Preprocessor and Other Features*, are entirely modular. Each module within these chapters is self-contained, with its own *Putting It Together* section and *Your Turn* reading-reinforcement questions. There are *Exercises* and *Programs* at the end of each chapter to support these modules. In some cases, the modules include submodules, each of which may be assigned by the professor or not, according to the demands of the individual course. Following are the modules and submodules in each chapter:

Chapter 12, *Memory Access*
    Basic Pointers
        Addresses and Pointers
        Pointers, References, and Functions
    Pointers and Arrays
    Pointers and Objects
    Allocating Memory
        `new()` and `delete()` Functions
    Linked Lists

Chapter 13, The Preprocessor and Other Features
    The C Commenting Style
    Basic Preprocessor Features
        The Preprocessor
        File Inclusion
        Character Replacement
        Macro Replacement
    Advanced Preprocessor Features
        Conditional Compilation
        Preprocessor Error Messages
        Renaming Data Types
    Other Language Features
        The Enumeration Data Type
        The Conditional Expression
        Combining Expressions (the comma operator)
    Nonstructured Program Flow
    Unions

Order of Presentation

Many of us emphasize different topics in our courses, and have different orders of presentation to support these emphases. To accommodate these differences, the topic modules within modular Chapters 12 and 13 may be treated in three different ways. Any one or a combination of these treatments will maintain a smooth flow of subject material.

1. The modules within Chapters 12 and 13 may be presented in their place in chapter order. In other words, the presentation would flow from Chapter 11 to Chapters 12, and 13.

2. Any or all of the modules within Chapters 12 and 13 may be left out entirely without loss of continuity.

3. The modules within the two chapters may be assigned at earlier points in the course. Following is an order of presentation in which the individual modules are moved to the earliest appropriate places within the other chapters. Introducing the modules any point at or after the suggested places below will ensure a smooth flow.

Chapter 1, *Computers and Programming*
Chapter 2, *The C++ Language*
    Forming a C++ Program
    Comments (Chapter 13)
    Assignment
    Addresses and Pointers (Chapter 12)

THE PACKAGE

The Art of Programming: Computer Science with C++ includes a wealth of
ancillary materials so that the instructor can tailor the teaching and learning environments to the particular situation. Included with the supple-
ments are:

Student Compiler Handbook

The *Student Compiler Handbook* is a unique concept. It contains intro-
ductions to a number of different C++ programming environments (Borland,
Code Warrior, Symantec, Visual, and UNIX) as well as a number of demonstration programs. The demonstration programs may be used as a supple-
ment to class lectures, for extra examples for the students, or assigned to
the students for analysis.

Program Listings

All the program examples in the text are available via ftp download from *www.pws.com/pwsftp.html*. Having these listings allows the students to read about a concept and immediately reinforce the reading by running and experimenting with the example. In addition, listings for any programs in the *Exercises* sections are accessible from the same site. Since many of these are debugging exercises, this allows the students to quickly see the results of their changes.

Also available on-line are source code files for all the demonstration programs in the *Student Compiler Handbook*. Whether or not the students have the *Student Compiler Handbook*, the program examples should provide more breadth for them.

Instructor's Manual

The *Instructor's Manual* contains for each chapter:

1. Answers to the end-of-chapter Review Questions and Exercises.

2. Listings for suggested solutions for each of the programming problems at the end of the chapter.

3. Test questions (60–75 per chapter). These questions include a mixture of different testing formats: multiple choice, true/false, fill-in-the-blank, short answer, program tracing, code debugging, and code segment writing.

4. Transparency masters—copies of diagrams, illustrations, and sample code from the text in easily reproducible form.

ACKNOWLEDGMENTS

A package such as this can never be the work of just one individual. My name is on the cover, but it would require a huge cover to list all those who were instrumental in making this text and its companion products a reality. We have come to expect superior quality from PWS, but that quality is no accident. Those people are smart and they work hard! I would especially like to thank David Dietz, the sponsoring editor, and Susan Garland and Katie Schooling, for their help, encouragement and insight; Richard Mixter, who was involved in the earlier stages of the project; Pamela Rockwell, Production Editor, a wizard at pulling all the right strings to get things done; and Nathan Wilbur, Market Development Manager, and his staff for presenting it to you.

The Art of Programming: Computer Science with C++ was extensively reviewed. I felt that I was constantly on the hot seat, but the process was fruitful and made a much more useful final product. For their thoughtful reading and insightful comments, I wish to thank, in alphabetical order:

Thomas Ahlborn, *West Chester University*
Farrokh Attarzadeh, *University of Houston*
Dale Bryson, *Umpqua Community College*
Buster Dunsmore, *Purdue University*
Rhonda Ficek, *Moorehead State University*
Steven Leach, *Florida State University*
Dieter Schmidt, *University of Cincinnati*
Cliff Sherrill, *Yavapai College*

One of the most important factors in the development of this book was extensive class testing, of both the current book and its predecessor *The Art of Programming: Computer Science with C*, by the author and by many of his colleagues. I would like to thank professors John Berry, Elaine Haight, and Roberta Harvey for using it in their classes and providing invaluable feedback. Perhaps most of all, I would like to acknowledge my debt of gratitude to the hundreds of students who suffered, with amazing tolerance and good humor, through the early test editions, and provided the most important commentary.

Steven C. Lawlor
Cupertino, California

Chapter 1

COMPUTERS AND

PROGRAMMING

PREVIEW

The computer is an undeniable part of daily life today. Those who read this book have decided not just to accept the computer, but to take an active role in how the computer is used—not just to use it, but to direct its use. This chapter takes you on your first steps down that road. It gives you a basic understanding of the computer system and how it operates. After reading this chapter, you will know:

- The historical background of today's computers.
- What a computer system is and how its functional components work together.
- The overall types of instructions that direct the computer.
- How data appear within the computer.
- How computer instruction sets are designed.

Almost all of us are involved with computers on a daily basis in some fashion. They are in the cars we drive, the televisions we watch, the clocks that tell us the time, the microwave ovens that heat up our leftovers, and, of course, the machines that populate many of our desktops. Computers typically write our paychecks . . . and send us our bills.

Without computers, life would certainly be different. However, computers are relatively new on the human scene. We can measure civilization in thousands of years and the industrial revolution in hundreds. Yet computers have only been around for tens of years. This relative newcomer has been quick to take hold, dig in, and proliferate.

What is this machine, anyway? A simple definition of a **computer** is a machine that, given instructions, can manipulate data by itself. Calculators and typewriters can manipulate data, but they need a constant stream of instructions—someone constantly pushing the keys—to get any work done. With a computer, give it the data and a set of instructions—a **program**—and you can leave it alone to do its job.

Let's spend a little time looking back to see how these machines developed.

HOW WE GOT HERE: A BRIEF HISTORY (Optional)

Three basic needs drove humankind to develop the computer: the need to perform calculations faster and more accurately, the need to control processes consistently, and the need to handle ever increasing amounts of data.

Early Efforts

We have been using mechanical aids for calculations for thousands of years. Evidence indicates that the Asians have been using the abacus (shown in Figure 1–1), relatively unchanged, for almost 3,000 years.

FIGURE 1–1

Abacus

Photo Courtesy of IBM Corporation

FIGURE 1–2
Pascaline

Photo Courtesy of IBM Corporation

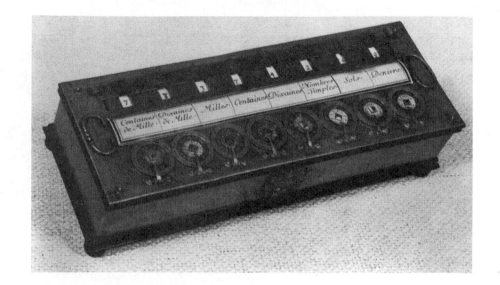

Taxes played an important part in the development of one of the first mechanical calculators. Blaise Pascal, a French mathematician and child prodigy, wanted to help his father in his tax work. So in 1642 the younger Pascal designed a box full of gears, ratchets, and wheels, eventually called the Pascaline, shown in Figure 1–2. The Pascaline could add, subtract, multiply, and divide. In all, about 50 of them were built, yet the venture was never a commercial success; the calculators had an unfortunate tendency to break down and make mistakes.

Over the following two centuries, a number of people attempted to go into the calculator business. A principal stumbling block was not the design of the gadgets, but the ability to make the parts with enough precision to perform accurately. It was not until 1820, when Thomas de Colmar introduced his Arithmometer, that calculating machines became commercially viable.

Some of the first attempts at process controls were based on the spiked drums that are the heart of the music box. From the early 1600s there were mechanically controlled organs that would play various selections and even move figurines in dancing patterns. In the early 1700s various people experimented with mechanically controlled weaving looms to produce consistent patterns in cloth. By the early 1800s Joseph Marie Jacquard was using punched cards to successfully control looms. The Jacquard loom became the standard of the weaving industry.

These two paths, calculation and process control, were brought together by Charles Babbage in the 1830s and 1840s. Charles was a brilliant and imaginative thinker, although he seemed always to move on to bigger and better thoughts before his previous ones had been realized. His first mental creation, the Difference Engine, was more a sophisticated calculator than a computer. It was designed to calculate mathematical tables and directly create the printing plates for them. Babbage made some unsuccessful attempts at actually building a Difference Engine (with financial support from the British government), but soon lost interest and moved on. His ideas proved sound, however. A few years later, based on those ideas, George and Edward Scheutz actually built a Difference Engine.

FIGURE 1–3
Analytical Engine
Photo Courtesy of IBM Corporation

Babbage proceeded on to an even more ambitious project, the Analytical Engine, shown in Figure 1–3. This was to be an automatically sequenced (essentially a programmed) machine that could perform various calculations. Its sequencing would be controlled by punched cards similar to Jacquard's. Babbage spent years planning, designing, and developing solutions for various programming problems, but he never actually built the machine. Much of what we know about Babbage's work is through the diligence and keen interest of Augusta Ada Byron, Countess of Lovelace and daughter of the poet Lord Byron. Having a sharp intellect herself, she appreciated the possibilities of Babbage's ideas and both translated and significantly added to his notes. In cooperation with him, she developed a number of sophisticated sequences for the Analytical Engine, and is often given credit for being the first computer programmer. It is truly unfortunate that, within her lifetime, her programs never had a machine on which to run.

The third path, handling large amounts of data, was the next to be explored. Every 10 years the United States takes a census—a count of its people and their various characteristics. Today's census consists of an absolute mountain of data. The mountain is reduced to a figurative molehill, however, by computers. In 1880 the data mountain was not as high, but it took 12 years to compile the census results. This meant that the 1880 census information came out two years *after* the next census was taken. In 1890, Herman Hollerith adapted the Jacquard card idea by punching the raw census data into cards. Using a machine (such as the one in Figure 1–4)

FIGURE 1–4
Tabulating Machine
Photo Courtesy of IBM Corporation

to sense the holes in the cards, he was able to tabulate the data in various ways. The census results were produced in only three years. In fact, the complete 1890 census information came out shortly after the 1880 information.

Hollerith's data-handling ideas were used in a number of successful tabulating and accounting machines over the next half-century. Hollerith's company eventually formed part of what is now IBM.

The truly programmable computer, combining rapid and accurate calculation, program control, and large data-handling characteristics, did not start to become a reality until the 1940s. There is a lot of argument over which was the first actual "computer," but we could probably pick from among the Atanasoff-Berry machine (created by John Atanasoff and Clifford Berry of Iowa State University) and the Z3 program-controlled calculator (created by Konrad Zuse in Germany), both introduced in 1941, or ENIAC. The latter was a 30-ton monster containing almost 19,000 vacuum tubes and occupying a 1,500-square-foot room. ENIAC was built by the University of Pennsylvania and first operated in 1945. Zuse's machine, unfortunately, did not survive World War II. The other two are currently in museums.

Modern Computer Generations

Since the 1940s, advances in computers have come rapidly. The general trends have been faster processing, smaller size, more storage capacity, and lower cost. We typically look at modern computer development in terms of generations. Figure 1–5 shows examples of the technology that separates the generations.

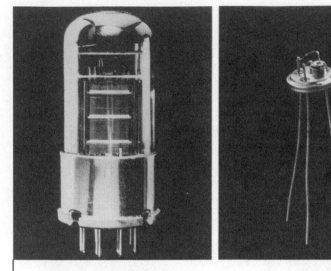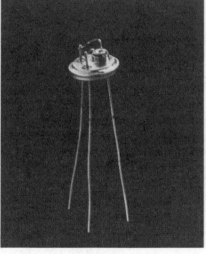

First—Vacuum Tube **Second—Transistor** **Third and Fourth—IC**

FIGURE 1–5

Generations of Computer Components

Photos of vacuum tube and transistor courtesy of IBM Corporation. Photo of Pentium Processor courtesy of Intel Corporation.

- *First generation.* The first generation of computers used vacuum tubes as their principal components. The Atanasoff-Berry, Z3, and ENIAC were first-generation machines.

- *Second generation.* In the second generation vacuum tubes were replaced by transistors, making computers smaller, faster, more reliable, and cheaper. The transistor was invented in 1947, but it was not until the introduction of the IBM 709TX in 1958 that second-generation computers became commercially viable.

- *Third generation.* The individual transistor is tiny compared to a vacuum tube, but when we put many transistors together with other components on a single chip of silicon, size decreases dramatically again. This integrated circuit, or IC, forms the basis for the third generation of computers. The IBM 360, introduced in 1964, was one of the first of this generation.

- *Fourth generation.* The line marking the fourth generation of computers is a bit fuzzy. It is characterized by large-scale integration—putting thousands, now millions, of components on a single chip. Digital Equipment Corporation's minicomputer, the PDP-11, and IBM's 370 mainframe, introduced in 1970 and 1971, respectively, were among the first fourth-generation machines. Today's personal computers, from desktop size down to palm size, are the latest flowering of the fourth generation.

- *Fifth generation.* Whatever it is, we are anxiously awaiting it.

Advances in computers are still coming rapidly. As soon as a new product is released, its replacement is in the design or testing phase. If the auto industry had experienced the same technology explosion, a Volkswagen today would be able to carry 100 passengers, go 500 miles per hour, be the size of an ant, and cost 29 cents.

YOUR TURN 1–1

1. What is a computer?
2. What is a program?
3. What three needs provided the incentives to develop the computer?
4. Name three important early calculators.
5. What do music boxes, weaving looms, and computers have in common?
6. Name some early uses for punched cards.
7. When were the first electronic computers developed?
8. What four general trends accompanied the development of the modern generations of computers?
9. What differentiated the four generations of modern computers?

THE COMPUTER SYSTEM

The word *system* is important in a discussion of computers. An effective computer system is an interconnected set of components working toward a common end. The system consists of two main categories—hardware and software. **Hardware** consists of the actual pieces of equipment—keyboards, screens, the components inside the boxes, printers, and so forth. To use a noncomputer example, a car, your Ferrari, is hardware.

Software is the instructions that direct the hardware—telling it how to perform tasks for us. One is not much good without the other. Take your Ferrari, for example. To use it for its intended purpose, getting from here to there, you must drive it—instruct it by pushing the pedals, turning the wheel, working the shift lever, and pressing the buttons. Without those instructions, your Ferrari is nothing but an expensive driveway ornament. Similarly, without software the computer is nothing but an expensive paperweight.

HARDWARE

Computers come in all sizes, from pocket-sized to building-sized. While the larger systems can process more data at a faster rate, all computers are functionally quite similar. They have roughly the same categories of components that operate in about the same ways.

Access to Data

Almost any operation in the computer involves accessing data. There are two, and only two, types of data access: read and write. A computer **read** operation is similar to reading a book. You look at the words on the page and copy them to your mind, but they are not removed from the page. Playing back an audio-or videotape is a read operation. You may play it back as many times as you want; the data are not destroyed. A read access, then, simply makes a copy of the data while leaving the original intact.

FIGURE 1–6

Moving Data

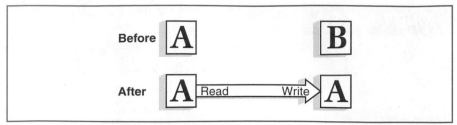

A data move consists of a read and a write. The read copies the data from the location being read and the write replaces the data at the location being written.

A computer **write** operation is similar to writing on a sheet of paper, except that a computer write operation actually erases what was there before. Recording an audio- or videotape is a more complete example of a write operation. The previous data are erased, and new data are recorded. A write access, then, replaces data where the write occurs.

As shown in Figure 1–6, any movement of data in the computer involves a read and a write. Data are read from here and written there.

The CPU

The heart of any computer system is its **central processing unit** (**CPU**). The CPU has three main functions: control, arithmetic operations, and logical operations. In its **control** function the CPU takes your instructions, one at a time, and, following each, directs the rest of the computer system. It is your supervisor inside the system. You are the ultimate boss. You either write the instructions or load some other prewritten ones, but you give those instructions to the CPU and it carries them out.

Once you give a set of instructions to the CPU and direct it to follow them, you are no longer in control of the computer; the CPU is. Control will be returned to you only after those instructions are finished or some error condition forces the CPU to halt them. It is important to remember that the CPU is not some intelligent being but a brainless machine. It handles one instruction at a time, looking neither forward nor back, and never

HEADS UP!

Any movement of data is a combination of a read and a write.

HEADS UP!

The CPU directs the rest of the computer system.

FIGURE 1–7

A Computer System

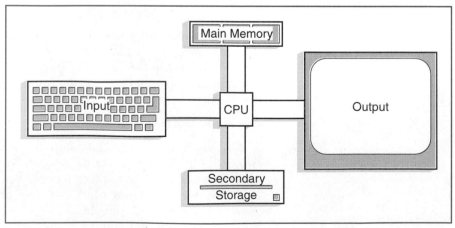

A computer system consists of a number of functional components, all controlled by the CPU, which, in turn, follows program instructions.

evaluating the propriety or outcome of the instruction. *You* would know to subtract deductions from an employee's paycheck; the CPU would just as happily add them if it were so directed. It would throw itself off a cliff if that were one of the instructions.

Analyzing the computer's output and making sure it has the proper instructions is, of course, up to you. You cannot expect any intelligent help from the CPU.

Many of the operations done by the computer are actually performed within the CPU. For these operations, it directs itself. For example, **arithmetic operations**—addition, subtraction, multiplication, and division—are performed within the CPU. Obviously, a computer must perform arithmetic. Calculating a paycheck by multiplying the employee's hours by that employee's pay rate and subtracting various deductions is a typical example.

Logical operations—comparisons—are also performed within the CPU. Is this larger than that? Are these two items equal? You would probably also use logical operations in producing a paycheck. To determine whether to pay overtime, you would compare the employee's hours to 40. To find the data on the employee's deductions, you would compare the employee's name to the names in your file of employees.

Main Memory

Having a CPU is a start, but you still need other components in your computer system. For example, where do the instructions that the CPU is following come from? Where does the CPU put the data it is processing or the results of its efforts? As shown in Figure 1–7, the CPU is connected to a **main memory**—a temporary working storage area. Main memory stores two types of things: the current set of instructions that the CPU is following and the data that these instructions manipulate.

Physically, main memory is made up of thousands or millions of **locations**—sets of components that store these individual pieces of data. As illustrated in Figure 1–8, each location has an **address**—a unique number that the CPU can use to refer to the location. This address is similar in

HEADS UP!

Main memory is temporary working storage.

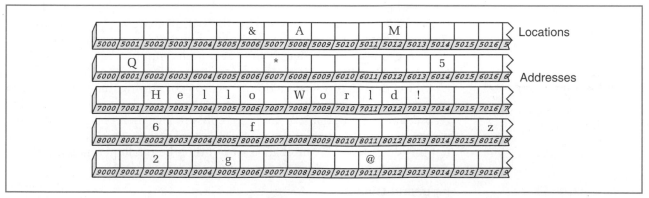

FIGURE 1–8
Main Memory

Main memory consists of individual locations, each of which has an address. In this example, the character *A* is stored in location 5008, *2* in 9003 and *Hello World!* in locations 7002 through 7013.

concept to our street addresses. There is only one 45 Oak Street in our town and there is only one location 721365 in main memory. This construction allows **random access** to main memory; the CPU can reach any single location in memory—one letter, one number, or one instruction. That sounds reasonable and, in fact, it is necessary that the CPU be able to do that to get anything accomplished. Yet some other storage systems, as we shall see, will not allow this individual access. Main memory is all electronic—no moving parts—so it is very fast; a piece of data might be accessed in a twentieth of a millionth of a second. This makes it hundreds or even thousands of times faster than other storage systems.

Main memory has its limitations, however. It is both relatively expensive and volatile, meaning that when the power is turned off, it forgets. Therefore, you use main memory only for active, current storage—the program with which you are currently working and the data associated with it. When you finish with a program, you replace it in main memory with a new one.

Secondary Storage

Disks, both hard and floppy, are the most common examples of **secondary storage**. Unlike main memory, secondary storage is permanent. You can change the data there any time you want, but unless you do, the data will remain forever. Secondary storage is also relatively cheap; therefore, you typically have lots of it connected to the system, often hundreds of times the main memory capacity.

This sounds so good that perhaps you should forget main memory and work only with secondary storage. However, secondary storage is slow—hundreds of times slower than main memory. More important, secondary storage is only accessible in chunks called physical records, or sectors or blocks, depending on the device. These physical records may be from about 80 to thousands of characters long. In order to work with data effectively you must be able to access individual characters, numbers, or instructions, which you can only do in main memory.

You use both storage systems, then, in the computer. You do your work using main memory. The data or instructions you need are loaded into main memory and processed. If you wish to save these things permanently, you read them from main memory and write them to secondary storage, typically hard or floppy disks. This then allows you to write the instructions and data for the next project into main memory and process them.

For example, if you had data in secondary storage that you wished to change, a payroll record perhaps, your instructions to the CPU would direct it to read the physical record or records containing that payroll record into main memory, write the change to the individual characters in the record (the copy in main memory, of course), and then write the physical record back to its original space in secondary storage, replacing the original physical record. Your change would then be made permanent.

Input and Output

Even with all this, the system still lacks some essential items—ways for us humans to communicate with it. The most common type of input device is the keyboard, although there are others, such as the mouse, the optical scanner, and so forth. Screens and printers are the most common types of output devices.

Following Instructions

The instructions controlling the CPU and the data the CPU works with must be stored in main memory. If they are in secondary storage, they must be read from there and written to main memory. The CPU has a number of small storage circuits called **registers**. One of these registers, the **instruction register**, is capable of holding a single computer instruction— only one. The instruction currently being followed must be there so that the CPU can react to it.

The CPU has a few (perhaps 4 to 16, depending on the CPU) other registers called **data registers**. These store the data that the CPU uses in arithmetic or logical operations. There are only a few of these registers, so data must continuously be moved in and out of them.

To perform a single instruction, the CPU must fetch the instruction from main memory, put it in its instruction register, interpret it, and perform it. That instruction is then replaced in the instruction register by the next instruction. Since only a copy of each instruction is written to the instruction register, the original is not destroyed—it is still in main memory—but it is no longer visible to the CPU. The CPU can "see" only one instruction at a time.

That fact, or limitation, will be very important to you as you program. Humans can see the "big picture"—what led up to this action and what actions will follow. Computers cannot. They can see only the present, which to them is about a fifty-millionth of a second. If you could instruct your computer to take a step forward, it could not see that the result of that action might be to plunge off a thousand-foot cliff; it would simply step forward. Directing the hardware to perform some useful, reasonable task is up to you. The computer cannot help you.

A Simple Addition Operation

To us, adding two numbers, such as 12 and 25, is a simple operation. To the computer, it involves at least three instructions and a number of operations. The added complication, though, is more than made up for in speed and accuracy.

Figure 1–9 takes a graphical look at how the computer might do the addition. This is only part of a program; somehow the numbers must have been placed in main memory, and something must be done with the result after it is calculated.

HEADS UP!

The CPU has only one instruction register and can see only one instruction at a time.

SOFTWARE

Hardware you can touch; software you can't. Software may be stored on various media, disks or paper perhaps, but it is simply ideas—instructions

1. Fetch the first instruction and put it in the CPU's instruction register.
2. That instruction directs the CPU to fetch the value from location 6016 and put it in a data register.

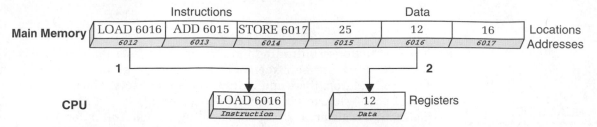

3. Fetch the second instruction and put it in the CPU's instruction register, replacing the first one.
4. That instruction directs the CPU to add the contents of location 6015 to the contents of the data register.

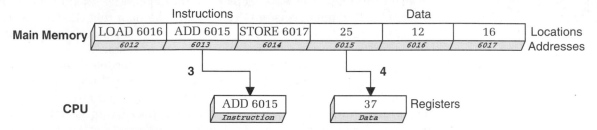

5. Fetch the third instruction and put it in the CPU's instruction register, replacing the second one.
6. That instruction directs the CPU to move the contents of the data register to location 6017, replacing the value there.

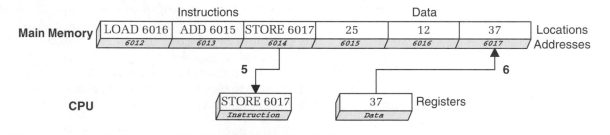

FIGURE 1–9

A Simple Addition Operation

to make the hardware perform for you. A set of instructions is called a program. Some programs figure out the payroll, others fly aircraft, still others assist you in writing reports or books. Software is divided into two categories: system and application. You are probably most familiar with **application software**—that written to perform specific tasks for individual users of the computer system. Some examples are accounting, spreadsheet, word processing, and game programs. Most of the programs you write (and all that you will write from this text) will be applications.

System software provides services for all the users of the computer system. It has two main objectives. The first is to deliver the hardware's resources to you in a relatively simple manner. For example, to print some characters at the printer, the CPU must know to which wires the printer is connected, in what fashion and at what speed it should send the characters, whether the printer is currently busy printing characters previously sent to it (and if so, to wait until it is free), and how to react to error conditions in the printer channel. All these details must be considered for each character printed, and doing so involves many computer instructions.

FIGURE 1–10

The Operating System

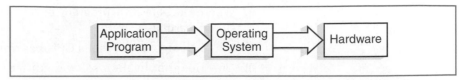

To make programming easier and systems more compatible, an application program sends general instructions to system-program routines in the operating system. These routines translate and expand the general instructions into the specific ones needed to drive the hardware.

Since printing is such a common activity, you do not want to have to write those instructions into every program that uses the printer. Instead, the system designers have written printing routines into the system software that we all use. Our application program designates a set of characters and passes them along to the system-software printing routine. When that routine is finished, it passes control back to our application program, which continues on with its task.

The second main objective of system software is to provide compatibility between different hardware configurations. Computers within the same family, Apple Macintoshes or PC clones, for example, often have different printers or screens. A single configuration of the system software will allow the same set of application-program instructions to accommodate the different hardware. This facilitates **portability** of application software—the ability to run the same application software on different hardware configurations.

Operating Systems

HEADS UP!

Your application software sends instructions to the operating system.

An **operating system**, described in Figure 1–10, is a set of system-software programs. Your application program will have to make use of, and be compatible with, the operating system in use on your computer. Unfortunately, there is not just one operating system. Life would be too simple if you could write application software that would run on any machine. Some of the popular operating systems are MS-DOS, OS/2, Macintosh, Windows, and XENIX on microcomputers; and UNIX on micros, workstations, and midrange computers. Many manufacturers of midrange and mainframe computers supply their own operating systems. IBM, for example, has OS/400 for its AS/400 line of midrange computers, and Digital Equipment Corporation (DEC) has VMS on its VAX machines.

YOUR TURN 1–2

1. What are hardware and software and how do they differ? Why is one useless without the other?
2. Explain how data are moved from here to there using reads and writes. Which data are erased and which are duplicated?
3. What is the CPU? What are its three main functions?
4. How does main memory differ from secondary storage?
5. What is the significance of individual locations and addresses in main memory?

6. Where do data or a program have to reside to be worked on? to be stored permanently?
7. Why is it significant that a CPU has only a single instruction register?
8. How does application software differ from system software?
9. What is an operating system?

THE NATURE OF DATA

Humans and computers are different. One look at a representative sampling of each group will tell you that. Humans and computers also process and store data differently. We do not fully understand how the human brain works, but we know exactly how the computer operates, and the way the computer stores and works with data is significantly different from the human way.

In many cases we are shielded from those differences because data are automatically translated to computer form on the way into the computer and are translated back on their way out to us. We never really see data in their pure computer form. We do, however, have to understand something about that form in order to appreciate what happens to our data inside the computer, as well as to ensure that we can make the most efficient use of the computer.

NUMBER SYSTEMS: OURS AND THE COMPUTER'S

Our **decimal number system** is based on 10 number symbols, 0 through 9 (*decem* means 10 in Latin). We have all grown up with numbers like 6 or 49 or 3,017, which are combinations of our 10 basic symbols. It would be hard for us to imagine those values expressed in any other way. Our 10-symbol system developed quite naturally because our earliest counting machinery had only 10 different elements—the 10 fingers on a human's hands.

FIGURE 1–11

Decimal Positional Notation

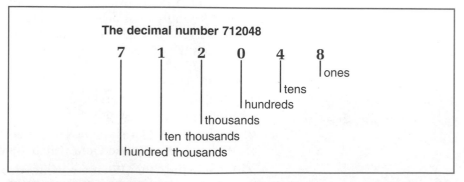

The decimal number 712048

7 1 2 0 4 8
| |ones
| |tens
| |hundreds
| |thousands
| |ten thousands
| |hundred thousands

Positional notation determines a number's magnitude. Notice that in a decimal number system each higher position is 10 times the position before it: 1 times 10 is 10, 10 times 10 is 100, 100 times 10 is 1,000, and so forth.

FIGURE 1–12

The Human's Versus the
Computer's Counting
Machinery

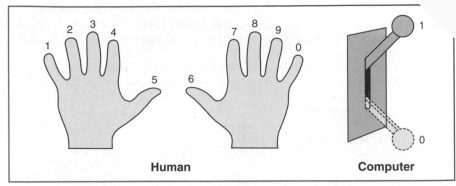

The computer's number system differs from the human's because of a fundamental
difference in natural counting machinery. The human's system has 10 positions while
the computer's has only 2.

Each of the values 0 through 9 can be expressed with one symbol. To
express numbers greater than 9 in the decimal system, we use combinations of symbols and positional notation. As shown in Figure 1–11, a
symbol's position determines its magnitude. In decimal, the first (rightmost)
position tells how many ones, the second (to its left) tells how many tens,
and so forth. The value 24 is two tens and four ones. Similarly, 4,680 means
four thousands, six hundreds, eight tens, and no ones.

Binary Numbers

The computer's basic counting machinery consists mainly of large sets or
arrays of transistors acting as switches. These switches have only two possible states: off and on. Therefore, the computer is capable of working only
with those states. We symbolize them with the digits 0 and 1. This means
that instead of using the decimal system with 10 digits, the computer must
express numbers in a **binary number system**—one with only two symbols,
0 and 1. Though humans express the value nine as 9, the computer must
express it with a series of zeros and ones, 1001.

HEADS UP!

All data must be translated to
offs and ons to be processed
by the computer.

FIGURE 1–13

Binary Positional Notation

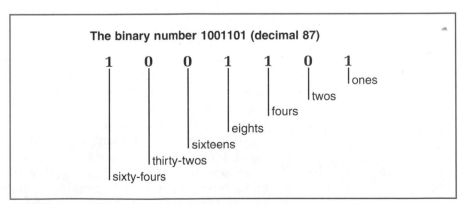

The binary number 1001101 (decimal 87)

Positional notation works the same in binary as it does in decimal, except that each
succeeding position is 2 times the position before it, rather than 10 times, as in decimal.

ecimal number to binary, divide the decimal number by 2; the remainder becomes the rightmost binary
... the process using the quotient, the next remainder becoming the next binary digit to the left. Keep this up
... the quotient is zero.

For example, 77 divided by 2 is 38 with a remainder of 1, so our rightmost binary digit is 1. The quotient 38 divided by 2 is 19 with a remainder of 0 so our next binary digit to the left is 0. (Our binary number is now 01.) Dividing 19 by 2 gives us 9 with a remainder of 1 (101). Dividing 9 by 2 gives us 4 with a remainder of 1 (1101). Our 4 divided by 2 gives us 2 with a remainder of 0 (01101). The 2 divided by 2 gives us 1 with a remainder of 0 (001101). Finally, 1 divided by 2 gives us 0 with a remainder of 1 (1001101). The process stops here because the quotient is 0. Decimal 77, then, is binary 1001101.

Decimal 77

$$
\begin{array}{ccccccc}
0 & 1 & 2 & 4 & 9 & 19 & 38 \\
2\overline{)1} & 2\overline{)2} & 2\overline{)2} & 2\overline{)9} & 2\overline{)19} & 2\overline{)38} & 2\overline{)77} \\
0 & 2 & 2 & 8 & 18 & 30 & 76 \\
\hline
1 & 0 & 0 & 1 & 1 & 0 & 1
\end{array}
$$

Binary 1001101

Binary 1001101

$$
\begin{array}{ccccccc}
1 & 0 & 0 & 1 & 1 & 0 & 1 \\
\times & \times & \times & \times & \times & \times & \times \\
64 & 32 & 16 & 8 & 4 & 2 & 1 \\
= & = & = & = & = & = & = \\
64 & + 0 & + 0 & + 8 & + 4 & + 0 & + 1 = 77
\end{array}
$$

Decimal 77

Going the other way, from binary to decimal, we add up the decimal values of the positions in the binary number that contain 1 digits. For example, from the right, 1001101 has a 1, no 2, a 4, an 8, no 16, no 32, and a 64. Adding this up, 1 + 4 + 8 + 64, we end up with 77 again.

FIGURE 1–14

Conversion Between
Decimal and Binary
(Optional)

In decimal notation, the highest numeric value we can express with a single digit is nine (9). If we want to express the value 10, we have to start the current position over at zero (0), move to the next position, begin that with one (1), and write the value as 10. If we want to count beyond 99, we must start those two positions over and begin a third, to give us 100.

In binary notation, shown in Figure 1–13, the highest numeric value we can express with a single symbol is 1. To express values greater than one we also use positional notation, but we must use more number positions because we can express fewer numbers, only one of two, in each position. To express the value one, we would use the symbol 1, the same as in decimal, meaning one 1. But since 1 is as high as we can go in binary notation, to express the decimal value two we would have to use the next binary position. Binary 10 (read *one oh* or *one zero*, never *ten*) means one decimal two and no ones, the equivalent of decimal 2. Following this logic, we would express decimal three as binary 11, one two and one one. Decimal four would require yet another binary position, 100, meaning one four, no twos, and no ones. Decimal 9 would be 1001 (one eight, no fours, no twos, one one) and decimal 77 would be binary 1001101. In the decimal system, each position is 10 times the position to the right of it because there are 10 symbols to use in each position. By contrast, there are only two symbols in the binary system; therefore, each position is only two times the position to the right of it.

To work with large numbers, computers use large combinations of zeros and ones. This takes a lot of transistor switching, but what the computer loses in numerical efficiency, it more than makes up for in speed. A human can add 9 to 19 in perhaps half a second. The computer would have to add 1001 to 10011, but it can do it in about a millionth of a second.

FIGURE 1–15

Hexadecimal Positional
Notation

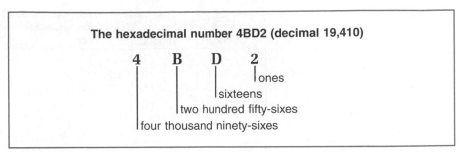

In hexadecimal notation, each succeeding position is sixteen times the position before it, rather than ten times as in decimal or two times as in binary.

Hexadecimal Numbers (Optional)

Binary numbers tend to be long and cumbersome. The two-digit decimal number 99, for example, is binary 1100011. Still, in many applications we must refer to the individual switch settings stored in the computer—in other words, to the individual binary digits such as 11010100. To do so, we typically use the **hexadecimal number system**, numbers with the base 16, because one hexadecimal digit represents exactly 4 binary digits—11010100 can be represented with just two hexadecimal digits.

A base-16 number requires 16 number symbols, so we borrow 0 through 9 from the decimal system and add A, B, C, D, E, and F for the values above 9 (see Figure 1–15). Decimal 10 is A in hexadecimal ("hex" for short), and hex F is decimal 15. Decimal 16 is hex 10.

To convert from binary to hex, group the binary digits in fours beginning from the right and convert each group to the appropriate hex digit. For example, we would separate binary 1101100 as 110 1100. The first group is decimal 6 or hex 6, and the second is decimal 12 or hex C. The complete hex number is 6C. The binary number 11010100 is D4 in hex. See Figure 1–16 for another conversion.

Table 1–1 shows the decimal numbers 1 through 20 together with their binary and hex equivalents.

FIGURE 1–16

Conversion Between
Decimal and Hex

Going from decimal to hex uses the same process as going from decimal to binary except that we divide by 16 and keep track of our remainder in hex digits. Hex to decimal follows the same pattern as binary to decimal except that the positions are powers of 16—1, 16, 256, 4,096, 65,536, and so forth.

Decimal 19410

$$
\begin{array}{cccc}
0 & 4 & 75 & 1213 \\
16\overline{)4} & 16\overline{)75} & 16\overline{)1213} & 16\overline{)19410} \\
\underline{0} & \underline{64} & \underline{1200} & \underline{19408} \\
4 & 11\,(B) & 13\,(D) & 2
\end{array}
$$

Hexadecimal 4BD2

Hexadecimal 4BD2

$$
\begin{array}{cccccccc}
4 & & 11\,(B) & & 13\,(D) & & 2 & \\
\times & & \times & & \times & & \times & \\
4096 & & 256 & & 16 & & 1 & \\
= & & = & & = & & = & \\
16384 & + & 2816 & + & 208 & + & 2 & = \ 19410
\end{array}
$$

Decimal 19410

In the decimal to hex conversion, as in the decimal to binary conversion, the rightmost number is determined first, moving to the left with each subsequent calculation.

TABLE 1–1	Number System Conversion Table				
Decimal	Binary	Hex	Decimal	Binary	Hex
1	1	1	11	1011	B
2	10	2	12	1100	C
3	11	3	13	1101	D
4	100	4	14	1110	E
5	101	5	15	1111	F
6	110	6	16	10000	10
7	111	7	17	10001	11
8	1000	8	18	10010	12
9	1001	9	19	10011	13
10	1010	A	20	10100	14

Notice the extra digits it takes to express a number using only the two symbols available in the binary system.

CHARACTERS IN THE COMPUTER

HEADS UP!

Characters are represented in the computer by coding schemes composed of sets of offs and ons.

A numeric value remains the same no matter which symbols we use to express it. A typical car has four wheels whether we call it 4 (decimal), 100 (binary), or IV (Roman). We saw that computers can handle numeric values easily with their two-symbol binary system. However, we know that computers work with more than just numbers. We have seen bills, advertising letters, and grade reports with *A*s, *B*s, and *C*s on them. In fact, most computers can work with a set of at least 96 different printable characters.

How can computers work with 96 different character symbols when they can only store and understand 2? They do so by using various **coding schemes** that combine binary digits in definite patterns to represent different characters. One such scheme is the **American Standard Code for Information Interchange** (**ASCII,** pronounced *ask'-key*), shown in Table 1–2. A single ASCII code requires seven binary digits (zeros or ones), allowing for 2^7 or 128 different combinations. The ASCII system is used in almost all personal and desktop computers, as well as in most midrange and large computers. An *A* in the ASCII coding scheme is 1000001; an *N* is 1001110.

The **extended binary-coded-decimal interchange code** (**EBCDIC,** pronounced *eb'-see-dick*) uses eight bits, which allows 2^8 or 256 possible code combinations, about half of which are actually used. EBCDIC is used on many minicomputers and mainframes. Most computers could use either coding scheme; the choice really depends on the scheme for which the software was written. Since both schemes represent essentially the same group of characters, software is available to translate one code to the other so that ASCII computers can communicate with EBCDIC computers and vice versa.

The sets of binary digits that represent characters look to the computer just like binary numbers. For example, the characters *A* and *N* in ASCII are 1000001 and 1001110, which, if interpreted as binary numbers, would have the decimal values 65 and 78. If we could see inside the computer's memory, we would find only offs and ons and we would not be able to tell whether they were supposed to represent numeric values or characters. To use a human analogy, holding up a hand could mean "5," "Hi," or "Stop."

TABLE 1–2 Some ASCII Codes

Char	Decimal	Binary		Char	Decimal	Binary		Char	Decimal	Binary
Blank	32	0100000		A	65	1000001		a	97	1100001
,	44	0101100		B	66	1000010		b	98	1100010
.	46	0101110		C	67	1000011		c	99	1100011
;	59	0111011		D	68	1000100		d	100	1100100
?	63	0111111		E	69	1000101		e	101	1100101
				F	70	1000110		f	102	1100110
0	48	0110000		G	71	1000111		g	103	1100111
1	49	0110001		H	72	1001000		h	104	1101000
2	50	0110010		I	73	1001001		i	105	1101001
3	51	0110011		J	74	1001010		j	106	1101010
4	52	0110100		K	75	1001011		k	107	1101011
5	53	0110101		L	76	1001100		l	108	1101100
6	54	0110110		M	77	1001101		m	109	1101101
7	55	0110111		N	78	1001110		n	110	1101110
8	56	0111000		O	79	1001111		o	111	1101111
9	57	0111001		P	80	1010000		p	112	1110000

ASCII is a seven-bit coding scheme used by most micros, as well as by many midrange and large computers. See Appendix A for a complete table.

How does the computer know whether a given set of binary digits is a number or a character? It really doesn't. Our program will tell the computer what to do with the set of digits, and that will determine whether they are used as characters or numbers. If we instructed the computer to perform a mathematical operation, it would use the digits as numbers rather than as characters. If we instructed it to print text, those binary digits would be interpreted as characters.

The ASCII (and EBCDIC) schemes were designed with this in mind. Notice that the alphabet is also in numerical order. The bits that represent the character *A* (in ASCII) have the numeric value 65 (in decimal), *B* is 66, *C* is 67, and so forth. Sorting characters alphabetically is just a matter of ordering the numeric values of their codes. Notice also that in the ASCII code, all the lowercase letters have greater values than any of the upper-case letters. This causes a bit of a sorting problem, but we shall see that there are some easy ways to handle the problem.

UNITS OF DATA STORAGE

Humans store data in many different formats. In this book, for example, most of the data are stored in text form, with the character (a single letter, space, number, symbol, or punctuation mark) being the smallest unit. Characters are combined into words, which are combined into sentences, which are combined into paragraphs, which are combined into sections (under a heading), and so forth. Because the computer is not as flexible as the human brain, much more attention must be given to the machinery to have the data come out right. Let us examine the computer storage units that contain that data.

The Bit

We have called each symbol in a binary number a binary digit or, in computer terms, a **bit**. The number 11001110 (decimal 206) has eight bits (from right to left, no ones, 1 two, 1 four, 1 eight, no sixteens, no thirty-twos, 1 sixty-four, and 1 one hundred twenty-eight). To store this value, the computer would use eight switches. The right one would be off, the next three on, the next two off, and the left two on. The bit, the setting of one switch, is the smallest unit of computer storage. However, bits never sit alone in the computer, but are grouped into larger units.

HEADS UP!

The bit is the smallest unit of data.

Bytes

Having the computer process data one bit at a time would be like putting sugar in your coffee one grain at a time; it is easier to use lumps. The computer processes bits in lumps called bytes, which saves computer instructions and time. Think about directing someone to put sugar in your coffee. It is much easier and faster to say, "Put in one lump," than "Put in one grain, another grain, another grain, another grain. . . ."

The **byte** is the smallest unit of data on which the computer can operate. If you instruct the computer to move data from here to there, it will move at least one byte at a time. If you instruct it to add, it will add at least one byte to another to make up a resultant byte. The addition may be done a bit at a time in the CPU, but the single instruction will direct the CPU to add all the bits in each byte involved.

In virtually all modern digital computers the byte contains eight bits, not because of some mysterious electrical property, but for convenience. It makes sense to process data a character at a time, and a character, in either ASCII or EBCDIC, will fit within eight bits. (EBCDIC is an eight-bit code. ASCII is seven bits, but by adding an extra, meaningless bit it will fill an eight-bit space.)

If our computer uses binary notation for numeric values, these binary values will be forced to fit within whole bytes. It would take only one bit to express the binary value zero (0), but when we store it in the computer we use at least an entire byte in memory (00000000). Decimal 23 would be stored as 00010111. In fact, all our memory circuits are organized in bytes. Numbers with values above 255 (eight bits, 11111111) require two or more bytes of storage and, depending on the computer, might take two or more sets of instructions to process. (There are instructions in C++ that refer to individual bits. However, these instructions still force the CPU to take in full bytes even though the operations are bit-specific.)

HEADS UP!

The byte is the smallest unit of data on which the computer operates.

Words

Even a small computer processes eight bits concurrently to save time and instructions. Larger machines process more bits concurrently (16, 32, or 64, for example) for the same reasons. We call the number of bits a computer can actually process simultaneously a **word**. Since each character occupies eight bits (one byte), words are often multiples of eight. Even though many word lengths are multiples of whole bytes, they are always expressed in bits. We refer to a 32-bit rather than a 4-byte word.

HEADS UP!

The word is the unit of data that the computer can actually operate on.

YOUR TURN 1–3

1. Why is the computer limited to a binary number system?
2. Why is hexadecimal notation often used to represent binary numbers?
3. How are characters represented in the computer? Why?
4. What is the smallest unit of data storage?
5. What is the smallest unit of data the computer can operate on? How many bits does it have?
6. What is the unit of data that a CPU actually operates on? How many bits does it have?

COMPUTER LANGUAGES

Computers don't understand C++—or Basic or COBOL or Pascal or any of the other common programming languages. Each CPU has a set of instructions manufactured into it. The instructions differ for different brands and models of CPUs, yet they all have two things in common: they each consist of sequences of offs and ons (because that is the internal alphabet of the computer), and each one by itself doesn't do much. Displaying some characters on the screen is usually simple for you to do using a typical programming language, but it may require a dozen or more instructions to the CPU.

Language Levels

This manufactured-in language is referred to as the computer's **machine language**, a term also used to describe the entire category of built-in CPU languages. It is the lowest level of computer languages—easily understood by the computer but almost impossible for humans to comprehend. When you write programs in high-level languages like C++, you can understand them, but they have to be translated to the computer's own machine language before the computer can execute them.

Writing a program in machine language might offer some advantages. Since it is the actual language of the computer, you could direct the computer to do anything it is capable of and in the most efficient manner. If a generalized language has to be translated into a specific machine language, compromises must be made. The job will get done but perhaps not with the greatest efficiency.

Nobody, however, programs in machine language. Trying to keep track of all those offs and ons (even if you use zero and one as symbols) would drive you nuts.

People can realize the advantages of machine-language programming by using **assembly languages**, the second level of languages. They are so called because a program called an assembler translates the assembly-language instructions into machine language to be executed. Simple assembly languages are merely symbolic machine languages. Instead of referring to an instruction as 0111010110110011, you use the word ADD, considerably easier on us humans. Programs must still be written in the same painstaking detail, though, because you are still dealing with the CPU's own instruction set. The trade-off between assembly and high-level

 **HEADS UP!**

To execute, a program must be in machine language.

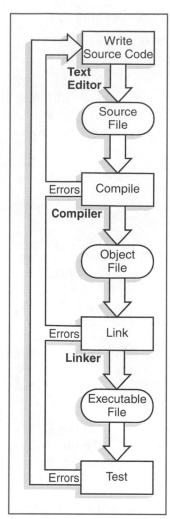

FIGURE 1–17

From Source to Execution

HEADS UP!

A program goes through many steps from source to execution.

HEADS UP!

Errors must be corrected in source code.

languages is that a program in assembly executes as efficiently as possible but takes a long time to write, whereas a program written in a high-level language may not execute as efficiently, but it will take less time to write.

High-level languages are meant to be easy for humans to work with. They are more similar to English (or some other human language), and one high-level-language instruction translates into many machine-language instructions, making high-level-language programs considerably shorter than machine-language programs. This does not mean that you can simply chat with the computer; strict vocabulary and syntax (construction of the instructions) are essential because the computer is nothing more than a machine and cannot understand our often relaxed and colorful way of speaking. Can you imagine what the very literal and precise computer would make of the expression "raining cats and dogs"?

From Source to Execution

A program written in C++ (or any other high-level language) is simply text—readable by humans but worthless to the computer. Let us follow the process of writing a C++ program and see how it turns into executable machine language. We can see it graphically in Figure 1–17.

You start by creating **source code**, the text program written in C++. Since this is just text, you will use some kind of text-editing or word-processing program to aid you in the writing. Once it is completed, you will save (copy) the source program to secondary storage.

The next step is to create **object code**, the program translated to machine language. A **compiler** program performs this operation. You execute the compiler, you tell it which source file you want translated, and the end result is an object program . . . or a batch of error messages. If there are errors at this stage, they must be corrected in the source code, so you must return to the previous stage—use the text editor, make the changes, resave the source code, and then compile again.

The compiled program is not ready to run yet. C++, like most high-level languages, has libraries of prewritten routines that you as a programmer may use. You refer to them in the source code, and the references are embedded with the object code. Your object code must now be **linked** with the object code for the prewritten routines. Similar to the compiling stage, you execute a linker program, tell it the object files (yours and the libraries') , and it produces a file of **executable code**, the program that will actually run on the computer. Of course, if there are any errors at this stage you must return to the source code for corrections and go through the process again.

The process is not finished yet. The computer only considers as errors things that it cannot execute. It has no understanding of what you want to do or whether an executing program will do it. You must test the program by running it and comparing it with known results. If there are errors here (referred to as logical errors), they must be corrected in the source code and the process repeated.

Integrated Development Environments

Many C++ compilers are available in **integrated development environments** (**IDEs**) that combine the processes we just described into one package. The

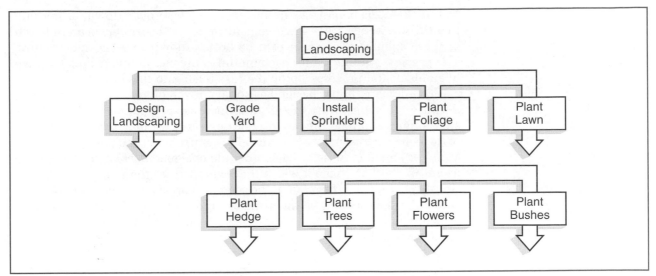

FIGURE 1–18
Modular Design

Almost any process can benefit from modular design. Here we show part of the stepwise refinement used in designing a landscaping project.

packages from different vendors differ in their features, yet all of them allow you to work in one "desktop" environment that provides a source code editor in which to write the program plus a one-command process that compiles, links, and runs the program (if it can get that far without serious errors); lists errors and warnings; and returns you to the source-code editing environment. All of these environments have some kind of "debugging" facilities that help you find the errors in your program.

MODULAR DESIGN

Attacking a huge, complicated task can seem as daunting and impossible as moving a mountain. But the mountain can be moved if we take it one shovelful at a time. Likewise, the huge project is easier if we break it down into small pieces, or **modules**, and attack each module separately. This process is known as **modular design**. Once the individual modules are completed, we can combine them to complete the huge task.

But how do we break this huge task down into modules? By using **top-down design**. At the top layer is a single, concise statement (just a few words) of the overall objective of the project. In the second layer, the objective is broken down into a few major modules, perhaps two to five, which define the parts of the project needed to achieve the objective. Further layers break down each of these modules into the submodules needed to perform that module, and so forth until the whole system is described in detail. This process is called **stepwise refinement**.

For example, if we had a yard with nothing but weeds, our first-level overall objective might be to landscape the yard (see Figure 1–18). This project can be broken down into a number of second-level modules: design the landscaping, grade the yard, install the sprinklers, plant the foliage, and plant the lawn. Each of those second-level modules can be refined

 **HEADS UP!**

Top-down modular design makes the programming process easier.

further. Planting the foliage, for instance, can be broken down further into planting the hedge, trees, lawn-edge flowers, and accent bushes. And each of these submodules can in turn be broken down into sub-submodules. The process continues until each module and submodule is broken down to an elemental process—"plop the rose bush into this hole."

Top-down modular design has some not-so-coincidental side benefits. Because the submodules are all described as separate tasks, they can be split among a number of people. For our yard, we may hire different experts to design the landscaping, install the sprinklers, and plant the bushes. Modules are often reusable. A submodule designed for one project may be useful in another. Since it was fully developed for the first project, it can simply be lifted and inserted in the second. For example, grading the front yard for a lawn would be the same as grading the back yard for a patio. This use and design of submodules leads us to one of the principal advantages of C++: the creation of objects.

OBJECTS

Take apart a microwave oven. If you don't have a one, borrow your neighbor's. Now go ahead—bash it with an ax and find out what's inside. Do you see all those wires, circuit boards, integrated circuits, and other stuff? How does all that junk actually work? You say you don't care as long as the food gets cooked? Now you get the idea behind object-oriented programming.

We can view the microwave, before bashing, as an **object**, something that we can manipulate to perform some task for us. The object is **encapsulated**—self-contained. All of its working parts are inside it. We need not add anything to it to make it perform. We have no idea what goes on inside the object, nor do we even care, but the object has an **interface**—some connections with the outside world that allow us to make use of it. We know what it can do for us—cook our food—and we know how to direct it—set the timer and so forth.

An object has **properties** (or *attributes*)—various characteristics. Some of them are **public**—the part of the interface that we are allowed to manipulate—and some **private**—hidden from our view. On the microwave we can set the cooking level, low to high. This is a public property. The bias voltage to integrated circuit U12 is another property, but we cannot adjust it, nor do we even know what it is; it is private.

An object can have **behaviors** (or *methods*)—things that it can do. As with properties, some of these behaviors are public—we can initiate them. Starting the oven on its cooking cycle is a good example. Other behaviors are private—part of the inner workings of the object. We do not control the actual generation of the microwaves or the running of the oven's clock.

Properties and behaviors, both public and private, work together to perform tasks. We know that it takes 55 seconds on medium high to properly cook a hot dog. Any less and it will be only a warm dog; any more and the ends will explode. We will set the cooking-level property to medium high and the timer property to 55 seconds. Then we will initiate the cook

HEADS UP!

We can use objects without knowing exactly what is inside them.

HEADS UP!

Properties are characteristics of objects.

HEADS UP!

Behaviors are things that an object can do.

behavior. This public behavior will set a number of private properties and initiate some private behaviors.

For example, the oven will read the cooking level and set the power-level property of the microwave generator accordingly. It will start the microwave-generating behavior and begin the timer-countdown behavior that constantly reduces the timer property. It will set off another behavior that will continually read the timer property (perhaps hundreds of times per second) until that property reaches zero. That condition will stop the microwave-generating behavior and initiate the buzzer behavior. All of this is happening within the oven object while we are over at the refrigerator object getting the mustard and relish.

Object Orientation

Object-oriented thinking comes naturally to humans. In fact, we use objects all the time without really considering them. We drive our cars, use the lawn mower, make telephone calls, and wear shoes. Cars, lawn mowers, telephones, shoes, and, of course, microwave ovens are all objects. They have properties and can exhibit behaviors. They become **abstract**. We know what they are, what they do, and how we can make use of them, but we do not know, nor do we care, what is inside them.

Most objects are **reusable**. All of those mentioned above certainly are. Dinner, however, is not; nor should it be. Reusability wherever possible, though, is one of our goals. Think about wanting to drive to the supermarket and having to design and construct an automobile beforehand.

Some objects, such as microwave ovens, we acquire in a fully functional condition. Other objects we must assemble ourselves. It might be possible to purchase a living-room object fully assembled, but typically we want to put it together ourselves. We spend some time thinking about what we want to do in our living room and how we want it to look, and then we acquire and assemble the pieces to fit our design. Once we have our living-room object constructed, we will reuse it. We won't build a new living room each time we want to sit down and relax.

Most of the pieces of our living-room object are actually other objects—couches, chairs, lamps, carpet, and so forth. If we could not find a coffee table to fit our design, we might have to build one, assuming we had the proper skills. Even this object that we built "from scratch" would use other objects—screws, bolts, brackets, and such.

"Assuming we had the proper skills. . . ." This isn't a book on carpentry, so that might be a big assumption. This *is* a book on computer programming, however, so you *will* acquire the proper skills to build your own computer-program objects.

HEADS UP!

Object orientation is a way of thinking.

HEADS UP!

Objects may be acquired or built.

YOUR TURN 1–4

1. Of the three language levels, which is required by the computer? Which is easiest for humans?
2. Trace the process of going from a program that you write to a program capable of controlling the computer. Identify both the files produced along the way and the programs needed to produce them.

3. What is modular design, and how does it interact with top-down design and stepwise refinement?
4. What is an object?
5. In reference to objects, what do we mean by *encapsulation* and *interface*?
6. What are object properties and behaviors?
7. What do we mean by *object orientation*?

THE PROGRAMMING PROCESS

The purpose of a program is to instruct the computer to perform some task. In writing the program you must, of course, give the proper instructions so that the task is completed as required. But there are many ways to write a program and things to consider other than just completing the task. In your programming you should always keep these objectives in mind:

- *Execution efficiency.* Will the program execute in a reasonable amount of time?

- *Programming efficiency.* Can you write, test, and complete the program in a reasonable amount of time?

- *Maintainability.* After the program is written and operating, can you or some other programmer easily make changes in it?

- *Reusability.* Code lifted from previous programs forms 93.86 percent (or thereabouts) of any new program. Is the code from this program written in a cleanly encapsulated object so that these objects can easily be used in future programming projects?

Often these objectives involve trade-offs. For example, it usually requires more programming effort to make a program that executes more efficiently. Since human time is much more expensive than computer time today, it might be economical to sacrifice some computational efficiency for ease of programming (except in time-critical applications such as screen updates, when waiting for the screen to fill would be frustrating for the user). You should always take extra care to ensure that your program is maintainable. Conditions and situations constantly change, and your program will have to change to keep up. In designing your program objects you must consider not only the needs of the current project but also those of future projects. Proper encapsulation—making sure that the object is entirely self-contained—usually handles this requirement.

In any case, all these factors indicate the need for planning.

Writing computer programs can be fun. Certainly seeing the result of your correctly written program is fun. The tendency for new programmers is to try to reach this pinnacle of fun too quickly. When faced with a programming situation, they immediately sit down at the computer keyboard and start banging out computer code—computer instructions—without laying the proper groundwork. The result is 30 minutes of typing in this ill-conceived program and 30 hours of debugging—cleaning out the mistakes and getting it working. That is *not* fun. Nor is it time-efficient for you or, if you work as a programmer, cost-efficient for anyone employing you.

Not spending enough time in the planning stages.

In addition, you often end up with a program that does not really satisfy anyone's needs. The programming process has dictated the end result. A program exists to do something useful for some user. The end result, what the program will do for the user, should be firmly in mind before the first line of program code is even written. The end result dictates the programming process.

Programming Stages

In this section we will examine a process for writing successful computer programs. At first it may seem cumbersome and overly formal, but it is effective, it works, and it is the process that virtually all good programmers follow either formally or informally. The process can be divided into five distinct stages, each of which should be completed before moving on to the next.

1. **Task.** Investigate the situation to find out what solution the situation requires. Symptoms of the problem won't do. "It's taking too long to tabulate these chemical analyses" is insufficient. "Create a system to accept chemical sample readings, tabulate them, and print the results" is more to the point. The result of this step is to have a short, but clear, definition of the task to be performed.

2. **Analysis.** Look at the task from the user's point of view. What information or action do we need from the system? How should that information be presented or action taken? What data will have to be fed into the system to produce the information or action? Are there additional factors or constraints affecting the task? The result of the analysis should be a **logical plan**—how the completed system should appear to the person using it.

3. **Design.** Develop the procedures—the **algorithm**—to execute the logical plan. How do we give the data to the system? What steps are required to turn the data into the required information or action? The result of the design should be a detailed description of the behaviors needed for the task and the objects that exhibit these behaviors—not in computer terms yet, but in terms that people (the most important person being you) can understand.

4. **Implementation.** The completed design can now be coded—translated to a computer language. The result of this stage is a computer program.

5. **Test.** Make sure your coded program works. Before actually testing, you should develop a **test plan** that verifies that each object works as intended, and that collectively these objects work together to satisfy the logical plan. The test plan should include all foreseeable situations in which the program might be used.

Let us follow a simple task through to completion. Our company, MegaTurbo, Incorporated, provides computer systems consulting services as well as computer products to our clients. Since we spend all of our time on clients' projects, we haven't computerized our billing processes. Our hand-created bills are not only time-consuming, they are often wrong. We need to fix this situation.

Mistaking symptoms for the task.

HEADS UP!

Testing must also be planned carefully.

The fact that our billing process takes too long and is error prone does not define our task. It is just a symptom of the problem. What we must do is create a computer program to take billing data and, in a timely fashion, turn them into a final, correct bill.

ANALYSIS

Now that we have a simple statement of the task, we must develop a logical plan—look at the situation from the users' point of view. In the analysis phase, we should work very closely with the users, the people who are actually responsible for the billing in this example. We start with the output. Seems backward? Not really. We must look at what the system is supposed to accomplish, its outputs, and then work backward to see how we get there. We should be quite specific at this point, showing actual samples of how the outputs should appear. The output for our example should be a bill showing the total amount for services, product sales, sales tax, and a grand total. At this point we should design the actual output format. In consultation with the users, the people who actually do the billing, we decide it should look like the following:

```
                    MEGATURBO,  INCORPORATED

  To: Customer


  ------------------------------------------------

  Services                                $12345.67

  Product                                  12345.67

  Sales tax                                  123.45
                                          ---------

  Total                                   $23456.78
                                          =========
```

(In a real-world situation, the outputs would probably consist of a more fully itemized bill in addition to outputting data to various files such as one that keeps track of each customer's billings.)

From the output we can determine our data requirements. From the user the system will require the name of the customer, the amount for services, and the amount for the product. The system can calculate the sales tax from the amount of the product (services are not taxed in this state) and add everything together to determine the total bill.

Here again, we want to design the actual input in consultation with the user. We decide that it should look like the following (the data the user types are shown in boldface):

```
Customer name: Customer
Amount for service: 12345.67
Amount for product: 12345.67
```

Our next step is to design the process for the computer. Here we will follow top-down design using stepwise refinement to build a modular program of behaviors.

The overall process consists of three major behaviors:

1. Gather sale data from keyboard
2. Generate billing data
3. Produce bill

The first step is concise enough as it stands. The second and third steps can use some refinement. We can divide the second step into two parts:

2.1 Calculate sales tax
2.2 Calculate total bill

We can also divide the third step into two parts:

3.1 Produce heading
3.2 Produce body

In fact, we could even divide step 3.1 into two parts:

3.1.1 Display company information
3.1.2 Display customer information

For the total project, then, the process would be

1. Gather sale data from keyboard
2. Generate billing data
2.1 Calculate sales tax
2.2 Calculate total bill
3. Produce bill
3.1 Produce heading
3.1.1 Display company information
3.1.2 Display customer information
3.2 Produce body

 HEADS UP!

Anyone should be able to read your pseudocode.

We have shown the design in a **pseudocode**, literally a "false code," which is basically plain English in **outline form** with the minor modules indented within the major modules of which they are a part. Step numbers such as 3.1.2 are often used to make discussion of the steps easier. It is much easier to refer to step 6.2.9.3 than the step 26 lines down on the second page.

Now we must describe the objects that exhibit these behaviors. Each object's description will include a name, the behavior we wish to use, and each of the object's properties. Property descriptions are often more useful if we identify each of the properties as it relates to things outside the object. There are four possibilities:

- *Required.* The value of these properties must be supplied to the object. We will use the abbreviation *(req)*.

- *Provided.* The object provides the values of these properties to the rest of the process. We will use the abbreviation *(pro)*.

- *Internal.* These properties are used only within the object—neither required nor provided. We will not use an abbreviation for these properties.

OBJECT SUMMARY		
Object Name	**Behavior**	**Properties**
1. Sale data	Gather sale data from keyboard	customer (pro) service (pro) product (pro)
2. Bill data	Generate billing data	
2.1 Sales tax	Calculate sales tax	tax rate (con) product (req) sales tax (pro)
2.2 Total bill	Calculate total bill	service (req) product (req) sales tax (req) total (pro)
3. Bill document	Produce bill	
3.1 Heading	Produce heading	
3.1.1 Company heading	Display company information	company (req)
3.1.2 Customer information	Display customer information	customer (req)
3.2 Body	Produce body	service (req) product (req) sales tax (req) total (req)

- *Constant.* These properties are simply constant values. For example, we may use *pi* defined as 3.1416 in our program. We will use the abbreviation *(con)*.

A complete description of the component objects in the process, then, is shown in the Object Summary.

Notice that the terms *required* and *provided* refer to data that go into or out of an object, not necessarily data going into or out of the computer. For example, the *Sale data* object's behavior accepts data from the keyboard, input into the computer. The important thing is that data are not being input into the object; it is the object's behavior that takes the data from the keyboard and makes them available to other objects—*provided* in our terms. The purpose of the *Sale data* object is to provide customer, service, and product data to the rest of the process.

Similarly, all the objects within the *Bill document* object exhibit behaviors that produce something on the screen, output from the computer, but it is the behavior that produces the output. The values of the properties that the behavior must use to produce the bill are *required* by *Bill document* and must be *provided* by other objects. In other words, those data must be supplied to the *Bill document* object for its behavior to work.

It may seem that we are carrying stepwise refinement and objects too far for this simple project but it does serve to illustrate the process, and if we get used to object-oriented thinking now, it will come easily to us when our programming projects get tough.

Once the design is completed, it should be tested. Step through it or, better yet, have somebody else step through it to see if it really works. Time spent in the design stage is invariably well compensated for in time *not* spent in the coding and especially the testing stages. If problems occur later, you will have a solid design to fall back on. If it was possible to pick the most important step in the programming process, it would probably be the design step.

HEADS UP!

Plan before you start writing code.

Program 1–1

```cpp
#include <iostream>                                // May require <iostream.h>
#include <iomanip>                                 // May require <iomanip.h>
#include <string>
using namespace std;                      // Required for only some compilers

const float taxRate = 0.05;

int main(void)
{   float services, product, salesTax, total;
    string customer;

    //-------------------------------- Input Customer, Services, Product
        cout << "Customer name: ";
        cin >> customer;
        cout << "Amount for services: ";
        cin >> services;
        cout << "Amount for product: ";
        cin >> product;

    //---------------------------------- Calculate Sales Tax and Total
        salesTax = product * taxRate;             // Sales tax on product only
        total = services + product + salesTax;    // Total includes services,
                                                  // product, and sales tax

    //------------------------------------------------------------ Print Bill
      //---------------------------------------------------------- Print Heading
        //------------------------------------- Print Company Information
          cout << "\n\n             MEGATURBO, INCORPORATED\n\n";
        //--------------------------------- Print Customer Information
          cout << "To: " << customer << "\n\n";
          cout << "-------------------------------------------\n\n";
      //--------------------------------------------------------- Print Body
        cout << setprecision(2) << setiosflags(ios::fixed);
        cout << "Services                           $"
             << setw(8) << services << "\n\n";
        cout << "Product                            "
             << setw(8) << product << "\n\n";
        cout << "Sales tax                          "
             << setw(8) << salesTax << "\n";
        cout << "                                  ---------\n\n";
        cout << "Total                              $"
             << setw(8) << total << "\n";
        cout << "                                  ========" << endl;
    return 0;
}
```

IMPLEMENTATION

HEADS UP!

If the pseudocode is well written, translating to computer language should be easy.

In the implementation step, we simply translate the pseudocoded design into instructions that the computer will understand. Here we will use the C++ language, although the design could be translated into any other programming language. The actual C++ code for this task is shown in Program 1–1. Don't worry about the particulars of the language at this point; we will be spending the rest of the book learning the language. Do, however,

Output

```
Customer name: TechnoMagnum
Amount for services: 42304.8
Amount for product: 5612.43


        MEGATURBO, INCORPORATED

To: TechnoMagnum

-------------------------------------------

Services                          $42304.80

Product                             5612.43

Sales tax                            280.62
                                  ---------

Total                             $48197.85
                                  =========
```

notice how the modular design was translated into C++ code and is shown using blank lines and indenting.

Even without knowing C++ or any other computer language, you should be able to understand much of what the program is doing because of the programmer's choice of words and the program's layout. We will be discussing program style and readability throughout this book. A wise programmer once said, "You should write your program so that a four-year-old can read it." We are not quite sure which four-year-old she was referring to, but if your program is easily readable, not only will others be able to understand it, but you, too, after not looking at it for a time, will be able to remember and see clearly what you did.

TEST

At this point, if we have done our job correctly, the programming process should be finished. No matter how confident we are, though, we will still have to prove it to others. We must have a test plan for the program. The plan should exercise the program in the situations likely to be encountered in actual use. One method for developing test data is to take data being used by the current system, manual or computerized, and see if they work in the new one.

Be sure to use data that stretch the situation to its limits—the largest purchase likely to be made, or billing for services but no product, or the different customer names we deal with. A test using "International Amalgamated Hypercircuits, Incorporated" or a total that exceeded $99,999.99 would turn up shortcomings in this program. You will see why as we examine the C++ language in more detail.

A program may fail for any number of reasons. In correcting the errors and retesting, we should be careful to stick to our design. Too often, the tendency is to experiment with code, neglecting the original design. If we finally get something working, it probably won't do the right thing. Always check your program against the design when trying to correct the errors.

YOUR TURN 1–5

1. What are the five stages of the programming process, and what is the end result of each stage?
2. What is pseudocode, and why is outline form important?
3. What are the differences between required, provided, internal, and constant property values in an object?
4. What is the difference between an input and a required property value?

SUMMARY

- **KEY TERMS** (in order of appearance)

Computer	Machine language
Program	Assembly language
Hardware	High-level language
Software	Source code
Read	Object code
Write	Compiler
Central processing unit (CPU)	Link
Control	Executable code
Arithmetic operation	Integrated development
Logical operation	environment (IDE)
Main memory	Module
Location	Modular design
Address	Top-down design
Random access	Stepwise refinement
Secondary storage	Object
Register	Encapsulate
Instruction register	Interface
Data register	Property
Application software	Public
System software	Private
Portability	Behavior
Operating system	Abstract
Decimal number system	Reusable
Binary number system	Task
Hexadecimal number system	Analysis
Coding scheme	Logical plan
American Standard Code for	Design
Information Interchange	Algorithm
(ASCII)	Implementation
Extended binary-coded-decimal	Test
interchange code (EBCDIC)	Test plan
Bit	Pseudocode
Byte	Outline form
Word	

• CONCEPT REVIEW

- A computer is a machine that, given a program, can manipulate data by itself.

- Driving the development of the computer were needs to calculate faster, control processes more consistently, and handle large amounts of data.

- Calculation aids have been in use for almost 3,000 years—since the introduction of the abacus. Pascal introduced the Pascaline in 1642, and others experimented with mechanical calculators, but it was not until de Colmar's Arithmometer in 1820 that such devices were commercially successful.

- Process controls of musical instruments and animated figurines have existed since the early 1600s, but Jacquard's successful punched-card-controlled loom marked a turning point in that field. In the 1830s and 1840s Babbage combined the two paths with the design of the Analytical Engine.

- Hollerith, in 1890, applied the punched card to the task of handling the massive amounts of data from the U.S. census. Electronic computers, the forerunners of today's machines, did not appear until the 1940s with equipment like the Atanasoff-Berry computer, Zuse's Z3, and the ENIAC.

- Modern computers are divided into four generations: the first generation principally used vacuum tubes; the second, transistors; the third, integrated circuits; and the fourth, large-scale integrated circuits. The fifth generation lies in the future.

- Computer systems contain hardware, the equipment, and software, the instructions that direct the equipment.

- Much of what a computer does involves moving data from here to there. A move requires reading, copying data from here, and writing, replacing data there.

- The central processing unit (CPU) controls the rest of the system in accordance with our instructions. It also performs arithmetic and logical operations. Main memory consists of thousands or millions of data locations, each with a unique address. Main memory allows random access, and it is here that we store the programs and data with which we are currently working. Secondary storage is accessible only in chunks and is used for permanent storage.

- The CPU makes use of registers in executing instructions. It has only one instruction register, so it can see only one instruction at a time, and very few data registers, so it must continually move data in and out of them.

- Software is divided into application software, for tasks for individual users of the system, and system software, to provide common services for users and application software. Common system software facilitates portability of application software. An operating system is a collection of system-software programs.

- Computers do not store data the way humans do. Because the computer uses off-on switches as its main data-storage method it cannot directly use the decimal number system; instead, it must store everything in the binary system. Although hex numbers cannot be directly

- stored, we often use the **hexadecimal** number system to refer to numeric values.

- Characters must also be stored using only offs and ons (or zeros and ones, as we usually refer to them). Various **coding schemes** are used, the most popular of which are the **American Standard Code for Information Interchange** (**ASCII**) and the **extended binary-coded-decimal interchange code** (**EBCDIC**).

- The units of data storage in the computer are based on its construction. The smallest unit of storage, the **bit**, is a single binary digit—the setting of one switch. To actually process data, bits are combined into larger units. The **byte**, eight bits, is the smallest unit that the computer can operate on, and the **word**, possibly consisting of many bytes, is what the computer actually processes.

- A programming language is one we use to communicate our instructions to the computer. The lowest level of computer language is **machine language**, the one actually used and understood by the CPU. Since machine language is extremely difficult for humans to use, we have developed other languages more suitable for us, but they still must be translated into machine language to control the computer. **Assembly language** is the next level, using human symbols but still quite detailed instructions. **High-level languages** were meant to be easier for humans to use.

- To create a usable computer program in a high-level language, you must first write **source code** in the high-level language; translate it to **object code** with a **compiler**; and then **link** that object code to other preexisting object code to form an **executable program**. Integrated **development environments** (**IDE**s) wrap these processes in one package.

- It is easier to design and write programs in smaller **modules** rather than in one big piece. This is the principle behind **modular design**, which is usually implemented by using **top-down design** and **stepwise refinement** to break the task into manageable modules.

- **Objects** are things we use to perform tasks for us. It should be **encapsulated** so that all we need be aware of is its **interface**. Its **properties**, or characteristics, can be either **public**, part of the interface, or **private**, used only within the object. An object's **behaviors** are the things that it can do. They too may be public or private.

- Object orientation is a way of thinking in which objects become **abstract**. Most properly formed objects are **reusable**.

- The overall programming process is usually thought of in five different stages. The **task** definition is a short statement of the job to be performed. The **analysis** develops a **logical plan** from the user's point of view. The end result of the **design** is the **algorithm**, showing the program's design in **pseudocode** in **outline form**, to execute the logical plan.

- It is often useful to develop an object summary outlining each object, its behaviors, and its properties. We can label the property values as required *(req)* for the object to operate, provided *(pro)* to the rest of the process, internal to the object, or constant *(con)*.

- The programmer will then **implement** the algorithm by coding it into a computer program. The final stage is to **test** the program using a predetermined **test plan**.

- Any movement of data is a combination of a read and a write.
- The CPU directs the rest of the computer system.
- Main memory is temporary working storage.
- Secondary storage is permanent storage.
- To work on data in secondary storage, you must first move them to main memory.
- The CPU has only one instruction register and can see only one instruction at a time.
- Your application software sends instructions to the operating system.
- All data must be translated to offs and ons to be processed by the computer.
- Characters are represented in the computer by coding schemes composed of sets of offs and ons.
- The bit is the smallest unit of data.
- The byte is the smallest unit of data on which the computer operates.
- The word is the unit of data that the computer can actually operate on.
- To execute, a program must be in machine language.
- A program goes through many steps from source to execution.
- Errors must be corrected in source code.
- Top-down modular design makes the programming process easier.
- We can use objects without knowing exactly what is inside them.
- Properties are characteristics of objects.
- Behaviors are things that an object can do.
- Object orientation is a way of thinking.
- Objects may be acquired or built.
- Testing must also be planned carefully.
- Anyone should be able to read your pseudocode.
- Plan before you start writing code.
- If the pseudocode is well written, translating to computer language should be easy.

• TRAPS: COMMON PROGRAMMING ERRORS

- Not spending enough time in the planning stages.
- Mistaking symptoms for the task.

• YOUR TURN ANSWERS

• 1–1

1. A computer is a machine that, given instructions, can manipulate data by itself.

2. A program is a set of instructions.

3. The three needs that provided the incentives to develop the computer are the need to perform calculations faster and more accurately, the need to control processes consistently, and the need to handle large amounts of data.

4. The abacus, the Pascaline, and the Arithmometer are three early calculators.

5. Music boxes, weaving looms, and computers all have a method to consistently control their processes—programs in various forms.

6. Weaving looms, such as Jacquard's, and Babbage's Analytical Engine were controlled (or intended to be controlled) by punched cards. Hollerith's tabulating machines stored data on punched cards.

7. The first electronic computers were developed in the early to mid-1940s.

8. Faster processing, smaller size, more storage capacity, and lower cost all came with the development of modern computers.

9. Through the four generations of computers, the principal component shifted from the vacuum tube to the transistor to the integrated circuit and finally to the large-scale integrated circuit.

● **1–2**

1. Hardware is the equipment and software is the instructions to direct the equipment. Equipment that doesn't know how to operate is useless, as are instructions with nothing to instruct.

2. When data are moved, they are read (copied) from one location and written to another, replacing what was there.

3. The central processing unit, in response to our instructions, controls the computer system and performs arithmetic and logical operations.

4. Main memory allows random, fast access, but is volatile and relatively expensive. Secondary storage is slower and can access data only in blocks, but it is permanent and cheaper.

5. Individual pieces of data are stored in locations in main memory. Since each location has a unique address, the CPU can access any of these locations.

6. Both data and programs must be in main memory to be worked on, but they must be in secondary storage to be stored permanently.

7. Because a CPU has only one instruction register, a computer can look at only a single instruction at a time. It cannot look forward or backward.

8. Application software performs specific tasks for individual users of the computer system. System software provides services for all the users of the computer system.

9. An operating system is a set of system-software programs.

● **1–3**

1. The computer's basic counting machinery, the switch, has only two states, off and on, which we usually represent with the symbols 0 and 1, so it is limited to a binary number system.

2. A single hexadecimal digit represents exactly four binary digits, so a byte can be represented by two hex digits, requiring less space.

3. Characters must be represented in the computer with offs and ons—0s and 1s. We use various character coding schemes, the most popular being ASCII, to represent the characters.

4. The bit, the setting of one switch, is the smallest unit of data storage.

5. The byte, eight bits, is the smallest unit the computer operates on.

6. The word is the actual unit of operation for a CPU. Its number of bits depends on the computer.

• **1–4**

1. The computer can run programs only in machine language, which is almost impossible for humans to understand. High-level languages are easier for people, but must be translated to machine language for the computer.

2. Source code, the program in C++, is written using a text editor and producing a source file. The source file is compiled into an object file, which is linked with other object code to produce an executable file.

3. Modular design refers to designing a large project in small pieces or modules. The project is broken down, from the top down, by stepwise refinement—expanding each module into submodules, and then doing the same for each submodule until each one is an elemental process.

4. An object is something we can use to perform tasks for us.

5. A properly formed object should be encapsulated—its workings are contained within it, not usually visible from the outside. We use the object through its interface, those connections to things outside the object.

6. Properties are characteristics of an object; behaviors are things that the object can do.

7. Object orientation is a way of thinking. It involves taking abstract objects—that we have designed or obtained from another source—and using them by concentrating only on their interface and not on what is inside them.

• **1–5**

1. The first step of the programming process produces a clear definition of the task to be performed. The analysis results in the system stated in logical, human terms. The design produces the algorithm to execute the logical plan using the computer. Implementation translates that design into a computer program. Testing, the fifth stage, verifies that the code works as it should.

2. Pseudocode is a way of expressing a process in easily readable form. Outline form is used to clearly show modules and objects and their submodules and subobjects.

3. Required property values are needed for an object to perform; provided property values are supplied to the rest of the process; internal property values are used only within the object; and constants are fixed values.

4. An input typically comes from outside the program—the keyboard or a data file. An object's behavior will set up the mechanism for the input and the value that was input may then be used internally within the object or provided to processes outside the object. Required property values must come from some other source within the program, such as a provided property of another object.

EXERCISES

1. What was the *first* electronic computer? Research the topic, make your choice, and defend it.

2. Compare a third-generation computer, such as an IBM 360, to a typical desktop computer of today. How do they match up in calculation speed, as well as in main memory and secondary storage capacity, size, and cost? Your library should contain data on historical computers and a local computer store will provide data on the current ones.

3. What will herald the arrival of the fifth generation of computers? Is it here yet?

4. Examine the inside of a computer. (Please don't disassemble your school's mainframe.) See if you can identify the CPU, main memory, secondary storage devices, and various input and output devices.

5. Identify the operating system and the version of the C++ language available on your computer.

6. What are the binary equivalents of these decimal numbers?
   a. 5   b. 21
   c. 42   d. 227

7. What are the decimal equivalents of these binary numbers?
   a. 1101   b. 10110
   c. 100011   d. 1101101

8. What are the hexadecimal equivalents of these decimal numbers?
   a. 10   b. 51
   c. 147   d. 688

9. What are the decimal and binary equivalents of these hexadecimal numbers?
   a. B   b. 2C
   c. E84D   d. 143F

10. Write your name in the ASCII code. (Refer to Appendix A.)

11. What is the relationship between upper- and lowercase letters in the ASCII code?

12. What is the word size of the computer you will be using in this course? Is it the same as the assumed word size of the implementation of C++ you will be using?

13. All other things being equal, a CPU with a 32-bit word usually will not execute a typical program twice as fast as a 16-bit CPU. Why not?

14. Was a program ever written in machine language?

15. Make a top-down-design chart similar to Figure 1–18 (page 23) showing your preparations to go to school or to work in the morning. Show the design in outline form. Create an object summary for it.

16. Make a top-down-design chart similar to the one in the text for reconciling and balancing your checkbook. Show that design in outline form. Create an object summary for it.

17. Make a top-down-design chart similar to the one in the text for a program that plays poker with the person at the keyboard. Show that design in outline form. Create an object summary for it.

PROGRAM

1. Familiarize yourself with your own C++ environment by typing in and executing the following program:

Program

```
#include <iostream>              // May require iostream.h
using namespace std;             // May not be needed

int main(void)
{
    cout << "Hello world!" << endl;
    return 0;
}
```

Output

```
Hello world!
```

Chapter 2

THE C++ LANGUAGE

PREVIEW

In Chapter 1 we examined the computer system and the process of programming it. Now we will concentrate on our chosen programming language, C++. From this chapter you should learn:

- The advantages and background of the C++ language.
- How a C++ program is formed.
- How values and variables are represented in C++.
- The differences between data types.
- Declaration of both values and variables in those data types.
- The arithmetic operators and how arithmetic expressions are formed in C++.
- The differences in operations with different or mixed data types.
- How to assign values to variables.

In many ways the C++ language is as simple as its name—yet that very simplicity gives it an elegance and efficiency available in few other programming languages. Many languages take great pains to shield the programmer from the inner workings of the computer. They are designed to be "intuitive" and "user friendly." Because of this isolation, however, the programmer cannot take advantage of all the computer's inner mechanisms. Compromises must be made. The job gets done, but perhaps not in the most efficient manner.

C++ sets up few such barriers. You can dive right into the heart of the computer and manipulate its pieces directly and efficiently. This does not mean that you must be a computer hardware expert; the description of the computer's functional components from Chapter 1 should be sufficient. With that understanding you will find that C++ becomes intuitive at a more elementary level and it, too, becomes user friendly.

THE LANGUAGE

The C++ programming language has recently exploded in popularity. It started out as the "fad" language of the day. But unlike other fads that have emerged, blossomed, and then withered, C++ seems destined to be in flower for a long time. It has a number of advantages. A major one is its ability to write programs that execute quite efficiently. Many system programs are written in C++, as are many programs that depend on screen graphics such as computer-aided design. Execution speed is extremely critical in these areas.

Another advantage is its portability, in large part the result of C++ programmers themselves enforcing and demanding consistency in various implementations of the language. Yet another advantage is that C++ continues to grow with the advent of new techniques and greater demands on languages.

How did C++ get its name? Was there a B++? an A++?

There was no A++ or B++. The seed language was the Basic Combined Programming Language (BCPL), developed in 1967. It was refined into a language called, simply, B, which Dennis Ritchie enhanced to form the original C language in 1972. In 1983 a group of computer-industry people got together to set some official standards for C. They formed the X3J11 committee under the **American National Standards Institute** (**ANSI**), and by 1988 they had completed the standards for the C language. Before this standard, the de facto standards were contained in Appendix A of a book by Brian Kernighan and Dennis Ritchie called *The C Programming Language*. Their version is often referred to as **K&R** C.

In the late seventies the concept of objects and object-oriented programming had begun to take hold. Bjarne Stroustrup, an early proponent of objects, set about the task of enhancing the C language to implement this new concept. He came up with C with Classes, which, by about 1983, was further enhanced—one of the enhancements being a shorter name: C++. (We will see in Chapter 5 where the "++" comes from.)

ANSI standards for C++ are currently under development by the X3J16 committee. The latest prerelease version of the standard is December 1996, and this book adheres to that standard. The C++ standard incorporates the C standard but makes some specific changes to it. For the benefit of the C programmers who are upgrading to C++, we will note those differences in the text. We often refer to *ANSI Standard C++* in this book, which is meant to include the existing ANSI C standards and the ANSI C++ prerelease standards mentioned above.

It would be impossible for the ANSI standards to cover everything; there is too much that is nonstandard about the various hardware and system-software configurations in existence. ANSI provides standard methods of displaying characters on the screen, for instance, but graphic screen controls differ so widely on various systems that graphics are not covered by the standard. The standard does, however, provide the solid core. Each compiler adds extensions to it to take advantage of the special capabilities of the hardware and system software for which it is destined.

FORMING A C++ PROGRAM

C++ was designed to be a modular language, and the format of the actual program supports these features. Actually, although the C++ compiler is not very particular about the physical appearance of the program, it allows you, through proper design and tradition, to make your programs neat, readable, and understandable. For example, **whitespace**—spaces, tabs, line endings, and blank lines—is, for the most part, irrelevant to the compiler. But you can, and should, add it in specific places to indicate the outline of your program.

Let us examine the listing in Program 2–1 to see some of the characteristics of a properly formed C++ program.

Outline Form

The finished program should end up looking like the design we developed in Chapter 1—in outline form with main topics to the left and subordinate topics indented within the main topic. Here we have a number of main topics including `int main(void)`, which has a number of subordinate topics within it, all of which are indented one level (three spaces in this example) to the right.

Since line endings are mostly irrelevant, the material for the first `cout` line is continued on the next line. We clearly indicate that by starting the second line immediately below similar material in the first line. Notice, however, that the line is not split within the quoted material. Line breaks are not allowed inside quotes. The C++ compiler would not look kindly on the following statement:

```
cout << "A perfect quiz                              // Displays on screen
        is " << quiz  << " points.\n";
```

Program 2–1

```
// Name: Steven C. Lawlor        Source file: ch02p01.cpp
// A Sample Program
// Illustrates the format of a C++ listing

#include <iostream>                              // Compiler directive
using namespace std;                // Statement needed by some compilers

int main(void)                      // Beginning of function definition
{  int quiz;                              // Declaration of a variable

   quiz = 20;                                  // Assignment statement
   cout << "A perfect quiz "                    // Displays on screen
           "is " << quiz  << " points.\n";
   cout << "Will I get perfect scores?" << endl;     // Note the endline
   return 0;
}
```

Output

```
A perfect quiz is 20 points.
Will I get perfect scores?
```

Comments

Almost every language has a method of including **comments**—notations that appear in the program listing but do not become part of the final executable code. In C++ everything from // to the end of the physical line is ignored by the compiler and so becomes a place to put comments. Line endings, remember, are mostly irrelevant, but this is an exception. Once the compiler reaches the end of the line, it "turns itself back on," so to speak, and processes whatever follows. If you want a comment to extend to more than one line, you must put // at the beginning of the comment on each line.

The first three lines of the following are ignored by the compiler, as is the end of the last line.

```
// Name: Steven C. Lawlor        Source file: ch02p01.cpp
// A Sample Program
// Illustrates the format of a C++ listing

#include <iostream>                              // Compiler directive
```

As far as the compiler is concerned, this:

```
   cout << "A perfect quiz is " << quiz          // Displays on screen
           << " points.\n";
```

is the same as this:

```
   cout << "A perfect quiz is " << quiz << " points.\n";
```

The compiler ignores the comment and all the whitespace, including the line ending.

Directives

The elements known as **directives** do not immediately become part of the compiled code; instead, they are instructions to the compiler (or, in many C++ implementations, to a separate program called a *preprocessor*, which is run just before compiling). These instructions tell the compiler to temporarily change the source code in some way or, in some cases, determine which part of the source code is to be compiled. The changes may or may not become part of the compiled code, depending on the directive. The `#include` in the sample directs the compiler to insert the source code found in the file `iostream` at this point in the source code before compilation.

```
#include <iostream>                          // Compiler directive
```

HEADS UP!

Directives finish at the end of the line.

Directives always start with a pound sign (#) and finish at the end of the physical line in the source code. This is another exception to the "line endings are irrelevant" rule. Notice that the comment at the end of the line is still ignored. Some non-ANSI compilers require that directives begin at the left margin; ANSI C++ (C++ that follows the ANSI C standard) has no such restriction, although in any C++, the # must be the first nonwhitespace character on the line. We will look at `#include` and a few other directives in more detail later.

To recap on line endings, they are significant in the following situations:

- In quoted material—they are not allowed here.
- At the end of a comment—the line ending ends the comment.
- At the end of a directive—the line ending ends the directive.

Statements

A **statement**, when compiled, becomes an instruction or group of instructions that performs a specific operation. The line

```
quiz = 20;
```

HEADS UP!

Statements end with a semicolon.

in the sample program is an assignment statement. It places the value 20 in the memory location labeled `quiz`. All single statements end with a semicolon and may be contained within the same physical line or may extend over many lines, as with the first `cout` in the sample.

```
cout << "A perfect quiz is " << quiz       // A single statement that
     << " points.\n";                      // displays on  the screen
```

Objects

Some people call C++ a simple language because of the limited number of statements available. Others call C++ a complicated language (they use the euphemism "rich") because of all the operators, functions, and objects available in it. What C++ lacks in statements, it more than makes up for in objects. Remember that an object has properties and behaviors. For now we will use only a very few objects and are most concerned with their behaviors—what they can do for us. Later we will make up our own objects, with behaviors and properties.

The **cout** object, for example, displays things on the screen. We follow cout with an **insertion operator** (<<) and then all the things we want to display, separated by other insertion operators. The statement

```
cout << "A perfect quiz is " << quiz          // Displays on screen
     << " points.\n";
```

displays three things on the screen: the words *A perfect quiz is*, the value of the variable *quiz*, 20 in the example, and the word *points*, followed by a period and that funny \n thing.

HEADS UP!

Newline characters drop the display to the next line.

The \n is called the **newline** character. It indicates that the output should drop to the beginning of the next line at that point. The end of the cout object's behavior does not end a displayed line. Without the newline, whatever displayed next would be right next to *points*. Wherever a newline appears in the code, the display drops to the next line when the code is executed. For example,

```
cout << "A perfect\nquiz is";
```

would produce

```
A perfect
quiz is
```

on the screen when executed.

Newline is seen as a single character by C++ but, because it does not show as a distinct character symbol on the screen, we represent it in our source code with two characters, backslash and *n*.

The **main()** Function

A **function** is a set of instructions that performs an operation—often a much more complicated operation than is performed with a single statement. A function may include statements, references to other functions and objects, machine-language instructions, and a host of other things. It may have been written by someone else and included with your compiler, or you may make it up yourself. Many preexisting functions are ANSI standard (you will see many of them in this book), while others are peculiar to a given compiler.

C++ is designed to be a modular language, and modules are typically implemented in most languages by functions or procedures. A C++ program is written almost entirely in functions—one or more depending on the complexity of the program. When you execute a C++ program, it starts its execution in the main() function. Therefore, every C++ program must have a main() function, but only one. C++ does not care where the main() function appears in the program; the compiler will find it.

In the sample program you see this function defined starting with int main(void) (more on the int and void later). Note that there is no semicolon after this line—it is not a statement but the beginning of a function definition. The statements below it, between the opening brace ({) and closing brace (}), are the operations in the function.

Declarations

In C++, as in many other languages, before you use almost anything you must declare it. The **declaration** tells the compiler that a variable or a function can be a valid part of your program and specifies how it may be used. Among other things, it allows the C++ compiler to check your source code for proper usage and to verify the spelling of variables and functions. In the sample program, the variable *quiz* is declared as containing an integer (whole number).

```
int quiz;                          // Declaration of a variable
```

Although you do not see it in the source code, `cout` is also declared. Its declaration is contained in the included file `iostream`. This is called a **header file**; it contains declarations and definitions that would normally be found at the beginning, or head, of a program. Except for `main()`, every function and object that you use *must* be declared, whether you make an explicit declaration in your source code or include a file with the declaration in it. All ANSI-standard functions and objects (and those that are supplied with the compiler) are declared in various header files.

Since C++ is relatively new and its standards are still in process, we may find some differences in language requirements between compilers. The new standards have adopted new names for some of the header files. Some compilers will still use the old names. The declarations in `iostream`, for example, were previously in the header file `iostream.h`. If your program does not compile using

```
#include <iostream>
```

try using

```
#include <iostream.h>
```

The compilers that use `iostream` should also require the statement

```
using namespace std;         // Be sure to type the semicolon
```

near the beginning of the program. Most do, some do not. If your program will not compile with it in, take it out.

YOUR TURN 2–1

1. What are the advantages of the C++ language?
2. What group is establishing the common standards for C++?
3. Of what significance is whitespace in a C++ program?
4. How do we put comments in a C++ program?
5. What is the difference between a directive and a statement? What punctuation difference is there?
6. What are functions?
7. What does a declaration tell the compiler?

VALUES IN C++

In Chapter 1 we looked at various number systems and at characters as they are stored in the computer. Now we must look specifically at how we express those values (or *literals* or *constants*, as they are often called when they are written directly in a program), in C++.

Numeric Values

We divide numeric values into two categories: **real numbers**, those that allow decimal points, and **integral**, or whole, **numbers**. In C++, decimal numbers in either category can be expressed exactly as in normal math. The real number 47.3908 means exactly the same in C++ as it does anywhere else. The same applies to the integer 253.

Character Values

Besides decimal, there are other ways of expressing numbers in C++; one is ASCII (or EBCDIC if we happen to be using that type of computer). By enclosing a character in single quotes (apostrophes) we are really referring to its ASCII code. The notation 'A' is the same as 65. The notation ' ' (a space) is the same as 32. We could, for instance, add 32 + 65 or ' ' + 'A' or ' ' + 65 or any combination of representations and, depending on how we wish to display the result, show 97 or the character a (whose ASCII code is 1100001 or decimal 97). Remember, once it's stored, it's just a set of bits.

Calling a character a number is a bit foreign to most of us, and differentiating between a numeric value and a character can seem even worse. Consider the character '4', for example. Its numeric value is 52—the value of its ASCII code. The '4' is just a symbol—the one we have chosen to represent the numeric value of, say, the number of wheels on your car. We could have referred to that value as 100 (4 in binary notation), IV (Roman numerals), or even §, as long as we agreed that the symbol represented that particular numeric value. We would typically say that 4 + 2 = 6, using the symbols to represent numeric values. In C++ we might also say that '4' + '2' = 'f', specifically using character notation, because '4' (52) + '2' (50) = 102 ('f').

Some characters in ASCII (as well as in EBCDIC) are not on the keyboard and therefore are difficult to show in character notation. An example is the form-feed code sent to a printer to tell it to go to the next page. In C++ we represent these characters with **special characters**, each of which consists of a backslash (\) followed by a keyboard character. Even though two characters are shown, they represent, and are stored as, one single character. Here is the standard list:

\0	Null (absence of a character)	\t	Horizontal tab
\a	Audible alarm (bell)	\v	Vertical tab
\b	Backspace	\'	Apostrophe (single quote)
\f	Form feed	\"	Quote (double quote)
\n	New line	\?	Question mark
\r	Carriage return	\\	Backslash

HEADS UP!

A single character is actually a number.

HEADS UP!

The character value '4', whose ASCII code is 52, is different from the numeric value 4.

SPECIAL CHARACTERS

The use of special characters is a case in which ANSI C++ offers compatibility among various hardware configurations. Take the form feed (\f) for example. This is typically the ASCII code with a decimal value of 12, so we should be able just to use the number 12. But "typically" is a key word here; not all computer systems use the same codes to represent things. ANSI C++ has a list of special characters that represent certain functions that may be implementation dependent. The compiler will translate these to the proper code for that implementation. Newline (\n), for instance, is the character that returns the printer or cursor to the beginning of the next line. In some systems it is ASCII 10, but in others it is ASCII 13 followed by ASCII 10—actually two characters. It is still stored as one character but, depending on the implementation, it may represent the output of two.

Using only a single backslash in a string to represent a backslash.

Notice that we need a special character to represent the backslash since we use that character to create other special characters.

String Values

A **string** is a set of characters. In C++, as in most languages, we indicate its string status by enclosing the set of characters in quotes—double quotes, not apostrophes.

```
"This is a string."      or      "12345"
```

The notation `'String'` would be meaningless in C++; there can only be a single character within single quotes.

The string `"12345"` adds to the confusion about characters versus numeric values. This is not the numeric value that we would express in decimal as 12,345; it is simply a set of characters—ASCII codes. Trying to perform mathematics on the string would be impossible. We can add two single numbers, `'4'` + `'2'` (52 + 50), but trying to add `"12345"` + `"67"` (49, 50, 51, 52, 53 + 54, 55) makes no sense at all.

Remember to use the proper special characters in strings. For example, we represent the string *old\new* with `"old\\new"` and *"What's up?"* with `"\"What\'s up\?\""`.

SIMPLE OUTPUT

To write useful programs, we must have a way of printing out the results. In Chapter 1 and at the beginning of this chapter we saw that by using `cout`, we displayed data on the screen. The `cout` object works with any standard type of data including strings (in double quotes), single-character values (in single quotes), and integral and real numbers. Program 2–2 shows `cout` in more situations. We use the insertion operator (<<) to separate the object name from the first value, and more insertion operators to separate subsequent values. Remember that `cout` does not automatically drop down to the next line. We use the special character newline (\n) for that purpose.

Program 2–2

```
#include <iostream>
using namespace std;

int main(void)
{   cout << "Here are the characters " << 'X' << " and " << '\n';
    cout << "and the numbers " << 46 << " and " << 12.345 << ".\n";
    cout << "Remember, it is the newline\ncharacter "
         << "that drops output to the next line.\n";
    return 0;
}
```

Output

```
Here are the characters X and
and the numbers 46 and 12.345.
Remember, it is the newline
character that drops output to the next line.
```

Let us examine the newlines a bit more. In the first cout, newline was printed as a single-character value. In the second, it was printed as part of a set of characters beginning with the period. In the third, it was right in the middle of a set of characters, and appears again as the last character of that two-line cout.

Another way to output a newline is to use the **endline** manipulator **endl**. To increase efficiency, C++ does not send one character at a time to the output device (in this case, the screen); instead, it *buffers* characters, saves them up, and outputs a bunch at a time. (We will discuss buffering further in Chapter 10, *Files*.) The endline manipulator not only outputs a newline character, but also directs the system to "dump the buffer"—to send all its saved-up characters to the output device before the newline.

It's a good idea to make endl the last output of a program. That way you are sure to send all the saved-up characters to the screen and leave the cursor on a new line. Whatever is displayed next, by whatever program, is sure to start on its own line and not next to your program's output.

Many programmers use the endl instead of a single newline in their code. It's the same number of keystrokes as '\n', and if the program crashes (fails), they are sure to see the entire output up to that point.

Remember, endl is not a character; it does not belong within quotes, unless you simply want to display the characters e, n, d, and l. The couts in Program 2–2 can be rewritten this way:

TRAP

Putting endl within quotes.

```
cout << "Here are the characters " << 'X' << " and " << endl;
cout << "and the numbers " << 46 << " and " << 12.345 << ".\n";
cout << "Remember, it is the newline\ncharacter "
     << "that drops output to the next line." << endl;
```

YOUR TURN 2–2

1. What is the difference between an integral and a real number? How are both types represented in C++ using decimal notation?

2. How are characters represented in the computer? How are they related to numbers?

3. In a C++ language using the ASCII code, how is the storage of values represented as `'A'` and `65` similar?

4. Why do we have special characters such as `\n` or `\a`? How do we represent the backslash?

5. What is a string? How do we represent a string value in C++?

6. Can we interpret string values as numbers, as we do with character values?

7. What is the fundamental output object in C++ and with what data types does it work?

8. How do newline and endline differ?

VARIABLES

In any language, a **variable** represents a location or set of locations in the computer's main memory. We put values in these spaces so that we may use the values elsewhere in the program. The space is "variable" because we may change the value stored there at any time. When we refer to that space we use its current value.

Variable Names

HEADS UP!

Use variable names that indicate the purpose of the variable.

HEADS UP!

Variable names cannot contain spaces.

HEADS UP!

You can't start a variable name with a number.

Don't start normal variable names with an underscore.

Wrong case in a variable name.

To reasonably refer to that space in memory, we must give it a **variable name** (or in ANSI C++ terms, a *variable identifier*). We are relatively free in naming variables in C++. This allows us to use names that might have some meaning for us. For example, if we are going to store someone's pay in a variable, we would probably call it *pay* rather than *x* or *fp* or *iq*. There are, however, a few basic rules that we must follow:

- We can use any number of characters in a variable name.

- We can use only alpha characters (*A* through *Z* or *a* through *z*), numeric characters (*0* through *9*), or the underscore (_) in variable names. Notice that a space in a variable name is not allowed. To specify a two-word variable name for "gross pay," for example, we can use the underscore in place of the space: *gross_pay*.

- Variable names must begin with an alpha character or an underscore, not a number. *farley* and *_bluto* are valid names, *2bad* is not. Typically, application programmers do not start variable names with an underscore. These are traditionally reserved for variables or functions defined with the compiler or other libraries.

- C++ is case-sensitive; upper- and lowercase characters are not treated the same. *Total*, *total*, and *TOTAL* would be three different variables. It is not considered good form to have in your program variables whose names differ only in case. Variable names in C++ are traditionally lowercase. An uppercase character is often used instead of an underscore to denote a two-word variable name; for example, *grossPay*.

- The C++ compiler looks for certain key words, words with special meanings, when it compiles a program. They are treated as **reserved words**—set aside for use by the compiler. We use them in program statements for their intended purposes, but we may not use them as variable names. Following is the list of ANSI C++'s reserved words:

and	false	signed
and_eq	float	sizeof
asm	for	static
auto	friend	static_cast
bool	goto	struct
break	if	switch
bitand	inline	template
bitor	int	this
case	long	throw
catch	mutable	true
char	namespace	try
class	new	typedef
compl	not	typeid
const	not_eq	typename
const_cast	operator	union
continue	or	unsigned
default	or_eq	using
delete	private	virtual
do	protected	void
double	public	volatile
dynamic_cast	register	wchar_t
else	reinterpret_cast	while
enum	return	xor
explicit	short	xor_eq
extern		

Your compiler probably adds some capability to the ANSI standards, so it is likely that you have to avoid extra reserved words. Also, to prevent confusion, avoid naming variables with the same names as objects or functions. For example, *cout* and *main* are poor choices for variable names.

DATA TYPES AND DECLARATIONS

As in most other languages, C++ can store data in various forms, or **data types**. The major differences between C++'s data types are the size, in bytes, of each type, and whether or not each allows a decimal point. Which data type you choose depends on whether your value might have a fractional component, as well as the sizes of the values you might use. With regard to size, your choice is often a trade-off between the amount of memory used and execution speed. Smaller data types take up less main memory and secondary storage, but C++ often must convert them to larger ones to perform calculations, and the extra conversion slows execution.

A single program may have many data types within it, and your operations may combine values of different types—for example, you may add values of two different types together for a meaningful result. We shall see, however, that there is a penalty to be paid for mixing data types that must be weighed against the advantages of storage size.

Forgetting to declare a variable.

Declarations

Whenever we use a variable, we must declare it. Declaration of a variable performs a number of functions:

- It introduces a new identifier, the name of the variable, into your program.

- It identifies the data type of the variable, which directs C++ as to how to store the variable's value—whether it can have a fractional component or whether it is allowed to be negative as well as positive, for example.

- It **defines** the variable—meaning that the appropriate amount of main memory is allocated to the value or variable.

- It may also **initialize** a variable—assign a meaningful value to that space in memory. Memory is never empty; there is always something lying about in it, which we colorfully refer to as "garbage" because we can't predict its value. A value used in a program should, of course, replace this garbage. A variable declaration allocates memory to the variable, but, at least with the variables we will be using, it does not replace the leftover value. As part of our declaration, we can replace this garbage with a specific initial value.

Variable declarations follow this general form (the underlined material is optional):

datatype variable = initialization;

For example:

```
int frequency;
int startValue = 14;
```

Notice the semicolons at the end of the declarations; they are statements and therefore must end in semicolons.

We can declare more than one variable of a single type in one declaration statement by separating the declarations with commas.

```
int total, counter, interval;
int begin_range = 0, end_range = 100;
```

We can mix initialized and noninitialized declarations in the same statement (as long as they are of one type), but many consider it improper form. Notice that in the following declaration, *end_range* is initialized to 100, but *begin_range* is not initialized at all; it contains garbage.

```
int begin_range, end_range = 100;
```

Variables must be explicitly declared, in statements such as those above, before they are used. On the other hand, values such as 47 or 12.098 or

Leaving a semicolon off the end of a declaration.

"Hello" are implicitly declared wherever they appear in the program. C++ knows a value's data type by the manner in which we write it.

Integral Data Types

Integral data types allow only integral, or whole, numbers—no decimal points. The numeric values are stored in straight binary form, padded with leading zeros to fill the appropriate size allocated to the data type. Decimal 13 would be stored as 1101 with enough leading zero bits to make it the right size. There are two basic integral types: char for "character" and int for "integer."

The **char** data type is eight bits long. Some people pronounce it as in the first four letters of "charm," others as "care" like the beginning of "character." The basis for the name, "character," is somewhat misleading. Yes, we do store in it what we humans understand as characters, but we can also store numbers there. In fact, the computer can't tell the difference. Remember, a character is simply a set of bits, just like a number.

In a single char space we can store the code for *A* or perhaps the number 65. Because the ASCII code for *A* consists of the same bits as the binary representation for decimal 65 exactly the same value, 01000001, is stored. (Note the leading zero bit to make up eight bits.) Once that set of bits is established, we may instruct the computer to treat it as a character (print it out, for example) or as a number (add it to another, for example).

Either integral data type may have one of two modifiers, signed or unsigned. The **signed** modifier means that the value may be either positive or negative. The **unsigned** modifier means that the number may only be positive. An unsigned char may have values from 0 to 255 (the decimal equivalent of 11111111); signed chars, because the sign takes up one bit, may have values ranging from −128 to 127. By convention, we do not use signs with hex or character notation (such as 'A'); they may only be positive.

Some valid char declarations are:

```
char letter;
signed char bread;
unsigned char index;
char topGrade = 'A', bottomGrade = 'F';
char topGrade = 65, bottomGrade = 70;
```

All of these declarations allocate 8 bits per variable, but the second one allows both positive and negative values; the third treats the stored value as positive only. The fourth and fifth declarations have exactly the same effect because the ASCII codes for *A* and *F* are 65 and 70. The two declarations could not exist in the same section of the program, of course, because we may not duplicate variable names.

The first declaration, just plain char, is treated as either signed or unsigned depending on your particular version of C++. Most treat it as signed.

Remember, char is a numeric data type. The declaration

```
char num = 4;
```

declares the variable num and initializes its value to 4.

HEADS UP!

The char data type is numeric.

```
char num = '4';
```

declares the variable `num` and initializes its value as 52, the ASCII code for the character *4*.

The `int` data type has more bits than the `char`, but its size is not precisely defined by ANSI. It is often the word size of the machine for which the compiler is designed; however, there are a number of exceptions to that guideline. For example, most newer PC-compatible computers have 32-bit word sizes, but many older C++ compilers for these PCs use a 16-bit `int`.

The `int` data type may have a `signed` or an `unsigned` modifier, but `signed` is the default under the ANSI rules. Just plain `int` will be treated as a `signed int`. The `int` data type may also have a **short** or a **long** modifier. ANSI tells us only that a `long int` has at least as many bits as a `short int`, but in most implementations a `short int` is 16 bits whereas a `long int` is 32. Notice that the data type `int` is the same size as either a `short int` or a `long int`. It supposedly depends on the word size of the machine, but that guideline is so often violated that it could depend on the type of computer the compiler is designed for, the phase of the moon, whether Jupiter is in Capricorn. . . . Know your compiler!

To enhance portability (being able to recompile unchanged source code for use on another type of machine) it is a good idea to declare your `int`s as either `short` or `long`.

The data type `int` is the default. If a declaration has modifiers but no data type, it is assumed that it is an `int` of some kind. Just `short`, for example, means `short int`. Here are some valid `int` declarations:

```
int currentPage, lastPage;
short age;                          // Equivalent to short int age
unsigned volts = 110;       // Equivalent to unsigned int volts = 110
unsigned volts = 'n';           // Equivalent to declaration above
unsigned long national_debt;              // An unsigned long int
signed short variance;        // Modifier signed not needed under ANSI
```

The **bool** data type is integral, but it does not store anything we would think of as numbers. It can take on one of two values: **true** or **false**. We usually use variables of the `bool` data type to keep track of some condition in our program. For example, if our program is charging things to our credit card and we have reached the card's limit, we might set the `bool` variable *maxedOut* to `true`. Each time the program considers another charge, then, it should check to see if *maxedOut* is `true`. (*Note:* The `bool` data type is new; it may not exist on older compilers.)

Integral Values

The data types of values are declared by the form in which we write them in a program. Character values such as `'A'` are `chars`, an integral data type. If a value has no decimal point, such as −386, it is integral. Integral numeric values default to type `int` (remember, that may be the same size as either `short` or `long`, depending on your machine).

Decimal-notation integers are stored as `signed`; whether one is `short` or `long` depends on the value. If the value exceeds the size of a `short int`, it is stored as a `long int`. For example, if the default `int` on your machine

FIGURE 2–1

Data-Type Designations

	Integral		Floating Point
Signed	**Unsigned**		**Signed**
`char ["A"]`	`unsigned char`		`float      [4.2F]`
`short`	`unsigned short`		`double     [4.2]`
`int   [4]`	`unsigned       [4U]`		`long double[4.2L]`
`long  [4L]`	`unsigned long[4UL]`		
`bool  [true]`			

The ANSI C++ numeric data types (except `enum`) with their key words and, in brackets, examples of explicit declarations of values, where such declarations are allowed.

is 16 bits (with a maximum decimal value of 32,767) and you put the number 145832 in your program code, the compiler stores it in a `long int`—32 bits.

We may also explicitly declare values by following the value with an `L` or a `U` (or `l` or `u`) or both. The postfix `L` forces the value to be stored as a `long` and `U` as `unsigned`. The value `56UL` is stored as an `unsigned long`.

Floating-Point Data Types

Real numbers, those with decimal points, are stored as **floating-point data types**. They are stored not in simple binary notation but in a binary form of scientific notation (typically IEEE—Institute of Electrical and Electronics Engineers—floating-point notation). In scientific notation we use a **mantissa** of significant digits multiplied by some power of 10. For example, 7,146 might be expressed as 7.146×10^3. The two values are the same; 10^3 is 1,000, and $7.146 \times 1,000$ is 7,146. In our C++ program we can write the number as `7146.0` or `7.146e3`, that is, a mantissa of 7.146 and a power-of-10 **exponent** of 3. The latter form is referred to as **E notation**.

For floating-point values, then, the computer stores the mantissa and the exponent. (Actually, since the computer works exclusively in binary, it stores a binary mantissa and the exponent as a power of two, but we will look at it in decimal to keep it simple.) The memory space allocated to the number is fixed, depending on the data type we declare, and is divided between mantissa and exponent. This means that there are limits on the sizes of both the mantissa and the exponent. The data type we choose should take those limits into account.

There are three different floating-point data types: `float`, `double`, and `long double`. In terms of the size of each, all ANSI guarantees is that a **double** is greater than or equal to a **float**, and a **long double** is greater than or equal to a `double`. In many microcomputer C++s, a `float` is 32 bits, a `double` is 64, and a `long double` is 80. Unlike integral data types, floating-point data types always allow positive or negative values, and so cannot have the modifiers `signed` or `unsigned`.

Following are some examples of floating-point-variable declarations:

```
float wageRate = 12.75;
double area, volume;
long double humongous;
```

HEADS UP!

There is no such thing as an `unsigned float`.

When declaring a `long double`, be sure to state `long double`, not just `long`, because that would default to a `long int`.

A value with a decimal point is normally stored as a `double`. We may explicitly declare it as a `float` with F or f, or a `long double` with L or l. A number written as `3.806e-3F` (or `.003806F`) is stored as a `float` instead of a `double`. A value with a large number of significant digits or a large exponent is automatically stored as a `long double`.

The String Data Type

C, the predecessor to C++, did not have a string data type. Compared to other languages (Basic, for example) C's string handling, while efficient for the computer, was clumsy for the programmer. C++ has implemented a string data type. It is not as a native data type such as `int` or `float`, but an object, with properties and behaviors. At this point the distinction makes little difference to us except for a couple of details. (*Note:* The `string` data type is a relatively new part of the proposed standard. Many compilers have not yet implemented it.)

The **string** key word is not a language key word (it does not appear on the list on page 52); it is the name of a class of objects (`cout`, for example, is the name of an object within a class of objects—not a key word). To use string objects, we must declare the class of them by putting

```
#include <string>
```

in our program, much like our requirement for putting

```
#include <iostream>
```

in the program to use the `cout` object.

ANSI C++ declares `string` to be usable within a *namespace* called *std*. We will not go into namespaces here, but some compilers get nasty if you do not put

```
using namespace std;
```

in your program. Other compilers will object to it. Compile Program 2–3 on your computer. If it objects, take the statement out and recompile it. Be sure

Program 2–3

```
#include <iostream>
#include <string>
using namespace std;                        // Required by some compilers

int main(void)
{   string message = "Hello world!";

    cout << "The message: " << message << endl;
    return 0;
}
```

Output

```
The message: Hello world!
```

to notice the semicolon after this statement. The directive #include <string> does not need one; the statement using namespace std; does.

The quotes are not part of the string; they just serve to tell the C++ compiler where the string begins and ends. For example, the statement

```
cout << "This is a bunch of characters";
```

displays

```
This is a bunch of characters
```

on the screen.

To include quotes as part of the string, we must use the special character \". (We must use the backslash with any of the special characters except the apostrophe and question mark, although the backslashes also work there.)

```
"He said \"I\'m drowning in a sea of C++!\""          // \' not necessary here
```

would be stored as

```
He said "I'm drowning in a sea of C++!"
```

(The \" must be used within double quotes, "\"", so that C++ can differentiate between the quotes that mark the beginning and end of the string and those that are meant to be within the string. There is no such problem with the apostrophe. However, the \' is necessary when showing the single character value apostrophe, '\'', because single character values are enclosed in apostrophes.)

This statement:

```
cout << "Her name\nis \"Henrietta.\"");
```

would produce

```
Her name
is "Henrietta."
```

The character \n starts a new line and \" is a quotation mark.

The compiler **concatenates** (connects together end to end) adjacent strings. For example

```
"This is just "  "one string."
```

is stored as

```
This is just one string.
```

Remember, whitespace, such as a space, tab, or line ending, is ignored by the compiler (unless it is inside quotes), so this concatenation property is often used to write a single long string using two lines in C++ code.

```
"This is just "
"one string."
```

is stored the same.

Since we cannot put line endings between quotes, the following would not work.

```
"This is just
  one string."
```

HEADS UP!

Two strings separated by whitespace are concatenated.

Putting a line ending within a string.

We will cover strings in much greater detail, including looking at a number of handy ways of manipulating them, in Chapter 7.

Constants

When is a variable not variable? When we declare it to be **constant**. By using a `const` qualifier in front of a variable declaration, we are telling C++ that this variable may not be changed. Since the term "constant variable" is somewhat contradictory, we usually refer to them simply as "constants."

```
const float pi = 3.1416;
```

The `float`, *pi*, may now be used in our program, but nothing can change it.

Another question might be "Why not just put the number where we need it in the program?" One reason is that constants improve the readability of our program. For example, our process may have a low limit of −35.769 and a high limit of 849.325. If someone read those two numbers buried in the source code, it would not immediately be obvious what they meant. We often refer to such numbers as "magic numbers." Seeing the words `low` and `high` instead, though, would provide an instant clue.

```
const float low = -35.769, high = 849.325;
```

```
cout << "Process goes from " << low << " to " << high;
```

Another reason is so that we may easily change the values. Perhaps we want to rewrite the process so that the low is −22.445 and the high 942.86. There may be many places in the program where we refer to these two figures. If we declare them as constants, and then use the constants instead of the numbers, we need to make the change only in one place in the program.

To facilitate both of the reasons above, we traditionally declare constants near the beginning of the program—after the `#include` directives but before the `main()` function. That way the constant declarations are easy to find, and the constants are assigned before we actually start our process. Common sense, not just tradition, tells us that we should always initialize a constant. If we don't give it a value when it is declared, there is no way to give it a value later!

YOUR TURN 2–3

1. Which characters can be used in C++ variable names? What can the name start with?
2. Are *books* and *BOOKS* the same variable?
3. What does the data type say about a value or a variable?
4. What does a variable declaration do in a program?
5. Which data types are integral? Which are floating-point?
6. What characters do we use at the end of numbers to declare values unsigned? `long`? `unsigned long`? `float`? `long double`?

7. What must we put at the beginning of our program to use `string` variables?

8. How do we put a quotation mark in a string value?

9. How does C++ interpret two string values separated only by whitespace?

10. Why do we use constants in our programs?

ARITHMETIC EXPRESSIONS

An **expression** is anything that can be reduced to a single value. Under this definition a single value, say 14, qualifies as an expression, as does a single variable, say *pounds*, which has a value in memory. We are more interested in expressions that require some evaluation by the computer—those that are made up of more than one value or variable, for example, 26 + 17. We have all done arithmetic and so have evaluated arithmetic expressions, but we must examine the strict rules that C++ applies to arithmetic expressions.

An arithmetic expression consists of values and/or variables connected by **arithmetic operators**, which tell the computer how to combine the values. The expression 26 + 17, for example, uses an operator, +, indicating that the values on either side, 26 and 17, are to be added together. The resultant value of the expression is 43.

Many expressions, such as 12 + 9 / 3, have more than one operator. A simple "chain" calculator would evaluate the expression by taking each of those operations in turn: 12 + 9 is 21, 21 / 3 is 7. C++ (or, for that matter, almost any other computer language) is not so simple. There are strict rules about which operation is to be done first no matter where it occurs in the expression. The rules involve **precedence**, a hierarchy or ranked order of operations that dictates the types of operations that are to be performed before other types; and **associativity**, which dictates order if two operations have the same level of precedence. Table 2–1 shows the arithmetic operators in precedence, highest first, and their associativity. Appendix B shows all the operators.

The same calculation, 12 + 9 / 3, would have a different result in C++. Since the division operation is higher in precedence than addition, it would be performed first—9 / 3 is 3, 3 + 12 is 15.

We can force calculations to be in any order we choose by enclosing some of them in parentheses. Inner parentheses will be evaluated before outer parentheses and before no parentheses. The same expression can be forced to the order that the simple calculator would follow by putting the addition operation in parentheses—(12 + 9) / 3.

The associativity rule applies when two operations are on the same precedence level. In the expression 12 / 6 / 2, the two division operations are on the same level, but they associate from left to right, so we have 12 / 6 is 2, then 2 / 2 is 1.

The easiest way to make a C++ expression from a handwritten arithmetic expression is to spread the handwritten expression out in a straight

TABLE 2–1

Level	Type	Associativity	Operator	Symbol	Example
1	Unary	Right to left	Negate Plus	– +	–4 +4
2	Multiplicative	Left to right	Multiply Divide Remainder	* / %	6 * 4 6 / 4 6 % 4
3	Additive	Left to right	Add Subtract	+ –	6 + 4 6 – 4
4	Assignment	Right to left	Equals	=	x = 4

line with the proper operators and then, referring back to the original hand-written expression, add parentheses to ensure that the C++ expression is evaluated in the same order as the handwritten one. Let us examine the following handwritten expression, translate it to C++, and show how it will be evaluated by the computer. The first C++ expression was written without parentheses to illustrate precedence and to show that, without parentheses, many expressions will not evaluate as we had intended.

Handwritten Expression

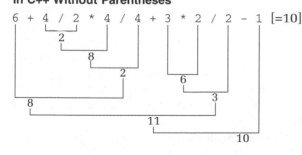

$$\frac{\frac{6+4}{2} \times 4}{4 + \frac{3 \times 2}{2-1}} [= 2]$$

In C++ Without Parentheses

6 + 4 / 2 * 4 / 4 + 3 * 2 / 2 – 1 [=10]

In C++ With Parentheses

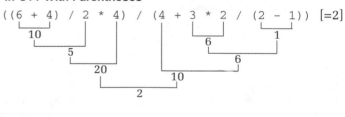

((6 + 4) / 2 * 4) / (4 + 3 * 2 / (2 – 1)) [=2]

Note that in the second C++ expression (the one with parentheses), the inclusion of the parentheses around the top of the fraction

    ((6 + 4) / 2 * 4)

does not change the result. The parentheses are, indeed, unnecessary, but if they improve the readability or understandability of the program, they can certainly be included.

The code in Program 2–4 illustrates precedence and associativity.

Most C++ compilers require that when an arithmetic expression is used with a cout object the entire expression be enclosed in parentheses. For purposes of illustration we have shown the expressions in Program 2–4 without the enclosing parentheses, but our compiler gave us a bunch of

HEADS UP!

Parentheses can often improve the readability of an expression.

HEADS UP!

In cout, enclose arithmetic expressions in parentheses.

Program 2–4

```cpp
#include <iostream>
using namespace std;

int main(void)
{
    cout << "Without parentheses: " << 12 + 9 / 3
         << ", with: " << (12 + 9) / 3 << "\n";
    cout << "Without parentheses: " << 6 + 4 / 2 * 4 / 4 + 3 * 2 / 2 - 1
         << ", with: " << ((6 + 4) / 2 * 4) / (4 + 3 * 2 / (2 - 1)) << endl;
    return 0;
}
```

Output

```
Without parentheses: 15, with: 7
Without parentheses: 10, with: 2
```

warning messages. The two cout statements should more properly be written as follows:

```cpp
cout << "Without parentheses: " << (12 + 9 / 3)
     << ", with: " << ((12 + 9) / 3) << "\n";
cout << "Without parentheses: " << (6 + 4 / 2 * 4 / 4 + 3 * 2 / 2 - 1)
     << ", with: " << (((6 + 4) / 2 * 4) / (4 + 3 * 2 / (2 - 1)))
     << endl;
```

HEADS UP!

An operation on integers produces an integer result.

TRAP

Exceeding the limits of the data type.

TRAP

Watch integer division.

HEADS UP!

The remainder operator works only with positive integers.

Integer Arithmetic

C++ performs its arithmetic according to the data types on which it is currently operating. If the data types in a particular operation are integer, the result is also integer. This typically causes no problem except when the result exceeds the maximum capacity of an integer or when you are dividing. If you exceed the limits of an integer, you get a meaningless result because many of the bits are not stored—they are thrown away. For example, 32000 * 10 (in a C++ implementation that defaults to a short int) yields the result −7680.

When dividing an integer by an integer the result is an integer—a truncated version of what a floating-point division would yield. The result of the expression 3 / 2 is 1, not 1.5. Since both 3 and 2 are integers (they have no decimal points), an integer calculation is done, producing an integer result. Note that this is not a rounding off but a truncation; the result is not 2, but 1.

The **remainder** (or *modulo* or *modulus*) operator deserves special attention. It is valid only with positive integers, and the result is the remainder after dividing the value before the operator by the value after the operator. The result of the expression 5 % 3 is 2 because 5 divided by 3 is 1 with a remainder of 2. As the following long division shows, 762 / 35 is 21, but 762 % 35 is 27. Other remainder examples are shown as C++ expressions at the right.

```
        21
    35)762
        70
        ──
        62
        35
        ──
        27
```

```
13 % 3 = 1
1 % 5 = 1
8 % 3 = 1
14 % 362 = 14
```

Be careful when using the remainder operator with negative numbers; the results vary with the particular implementation of C++.

Mixed Arithmetic

HEADS UP!

Each calculation is performed at the highest data type.

In general, when data types are mixed in an expression, each operation is performed at the highest data type involved in the expression—"highest" meaning the one that takes up the largest amount of memory. Since there is some overlap, floating-point types are considered higher than integral. It is important to recognize that the calculations are not all performed at the highest data type included in the expression; each operation is evaluated separately and performed at the highest data type involved in just that operation. Eventually the result will be of the highest data type in the entire expression, but it may take a while to get there.

For example:

$$8.3 + 5 / 2 \qquad [=10.3]$$
$$\underset{2 \,[\text{int}]}{\underline{}}$$
$$\underset{10.3 \,[\text{double}]}{\underline{}}$$

The expression 5 / 2 was performed first, and since both the 5 and the 2 are integers (they have no decimal points), 5 / 2 was performed as type int with a result of 2 (not 2.5). Compare that with this:

$$8.3 + 5 / 2.0 \qquad [=10.8]$$
$$\underset{2.5 \,[\text{double}]}{\underline{}}$$
$$\underset{10.8 \,[\text{double}]}{\underline{}}$$

NUTS'N BOLTS

MIXED ARITHMETIC

Most C++ compilers don't do arithmetic on all the standard data types; this would require too many built-in routines and conversions. Typically, the smallest size for calculations for integers is type `int`. Remember, this might be equivalent to `short` or `long`, depending on your compiler. `char`s are promoted to `int`s and, if the standard `int` is a `long`, `short`s are also promoted. `long int` calculations on a `short int` compiler are naturally done using `long int` calculations. For floating-point types, nothing less than `double` is calculated. `long double`s are, of course, calculated at `long double` size.

What does all this mean to you? Computing is a series of trade-offs. If you declare variables as type `float` rather than `double` (perhaps to save memory space), calculations on these `float`s will be done as `double`. In other words, the computer will have to go through extra conversions—`float`s to `double`s and then back to `float` for the result. The trade-off is storage space versus execution speed.

Program 2–5

```cpp
#include <iostream>
using namespace std;

int main(void)
{   cout << "Without the decimal point: " << 8.3 + 5 / 2
         << ", with: " << 8.3 + 5 / 2.0 << endl;
    return 0;
}
```

Output

```
Without the decimal point: 10.3, with: 10.8
```

In this case 2.0 (or even just 2.) is a floating-point value (actually a `double`; see the *Nuts 'n' Bolts: Mixed Arithmetic* box, page 63) so 5 / 2.0 was calculated as a floating-point expression, with a result of 2.5. Program 2–5 illustrates the differences in these calculations.

ASSIGNMENT

As we said, variables identify spaces in main memory. These spaces are variable because they can contain various and changeable values. Putting a value into one of these spaces is known as **assignment**. We usually refer to "assigning a value to a variable," but technically we are writing a value into the memory space identified by the variable.

We have seen how initial assignments can be included as part of declarations, but we must also make assignments as part of our program. For example, we may wish to store the results of a calculation in a variable, or to change the value of a variable we had assigned previously. There are many ways to assign values to variables, but all of them follow this fundamental rule:

HEADS UP!

Fundamental rule of assignment.

A variable may have only one value at a time.

We may assign many different values to a variable, but each time we do, we write to the memory space reserved for that variable and, as we saw in Chapter 1, a write operation replaces data. If the variable *checkers* had the value 137.93 and you assigned 6.2 to it, the 6.2 overwrites, or replaces, the 137.93, and the value of *checkers* is then 6.2. What happens to the 137.93? Unless you specifically copied it elsewhere in memory beforehand, it is lost.

The standard assignment operator is the equal sign (=). Referring to Appendix B or Table 2–1 we can see that, in precedence, it follows all the arithmetic operators, which means that after all the arithmetic is done, the assignment is made. The general form of an assignment is

variable = expression

Program 2–6

```cpp
#include <iostream>
#include <string>
using namespace std;

int main(void)
{   float principal, rate, time, interest;
    string instrument;

    principal = 1000;
    rate = .075;
    time = 3.5;
    instrument = "bond";
    interest = principal * rate * time;
    cout << "For this " << instrument << ", the interest on $" << principal
         << " at " << (rate * 100) << "%\n";
    cout << "for " << time << " years is $" << interest << "." << endl;
    return 0;
}
```

Output

```
For this bond, the interest on $1000 at 7.5%
for 3.5 years is $262.5.
```

where *variable* identifies a space in memory and *expression* evaluates to a single value. The following are valid assignment statements:

```cpp
x = 14;
y = (x + 15) / 12.7;
interest = principal * rate * time;
name = "Clyde Sniggle";
```

Notice that in each case there is a single variable to the left of the equal sign—something to which to assign the value. (The variable is often referred to in references as a *modifiable lvalue*—an identifier that can properly be used at the left of the assignment operator.) The spaces in the statements are not actually necessary in C++, but they tend to make the statements a little more readable. It is common practice to use spaces around most operators other than the unary ones. Program 2–6 shows assignment statements.

The resultant value of an assignment expression is the value of the assignment. Since the assignment operator's associativity is right to left, this allows more than one assignment to be made in a single statement. For example,

```cpp
x = y = z = 17 + 9;
```

would calculate 17 + 9 first (the + is higher in precedence than =) and assign the value 26 to *z*. The value of the entire expression $z = 17 + 9$ is the assignment value 26, so that value would be assigned to *y*. The value of $y = z = 17 + 9$ is now also 26, so that value would be assigned to *x*.

HEADS UP!

For better readability, put spaces around all except unary operators.

Program 2–7

```
#include <iostream>
using namespace std;

int main(void)
{  short number;

   number = 30000.9;                                // Floating-point value
   cout << "The number is " << number << ".\n";
   number = number * 2;                   // Make the value to large for a short
   cout << "The number is now " << number << "." << endl;
   return 0;
}
```

Output

```
The number is 30000.
The number is now -5536.
```

HEADS UP!

The assigned variable (or any other, for that matter) can never change data type.

Forced Conversions

Any numeric value may be assigned to any type of numeric variable. Whether that value is actually stored in its original form is essentially up to you and how you write the assignment. A value assigned to a variable is always of the type of that variable. It has to be; there is a specific memory space allocated and a specific form (integer or floating point) to be followed.

If a floating-point value is assigned to an integer variable, the decimal part is dropped. If a value is assigned to a data type that will not hold it, as many bits as possible are stuffed in, but the result will be unrecognizable. Program 2–7 shows examples of these phenomena.

Most C++ programmers get into the habit of explicitly declaring their data types so there are no forced conversions. Some variants of the language require this explicit typing and produce weird results if you depend on forced conversions.

YOUR TURN 2–4

1. How does precedence differ from associativity? Which is considered first?

2. Of the operators covered in this chapter, which are highest in precedence? Which are the lowest?

3. How do we change the normal order of operations?

4. What happens if an arithmetic operation involving two integers yields what we would think of as a fractional result (such as dividing 3 by 2)?

5. What is the result of a remainder operation?

6. If dissimilar data types are involved in an arithmetic operation, of what data type is the result?

7. How many values may a simple variable have at one time?

8. Of what data type will an assignment be?

PUTTING IT TOGETHER

Let's look at an example to illustrate what we have learned up to this point. We will develop this example just as we would any other program—by going through the five steps of program development.

TASK

The people at Sticky Molasses Company need to know how much a trailer fully loaded with molasses weighs and would like us to write a program to tell them.

ANALYSIS

The total weight of the molasses trailer is an accumulation of various things. The weight of the trailer alone is 7,540 pounds. Molasses weighs 78.2 pounds per cubic foot. It is packaged in drums that are 2 feet high and a foot in diameter. The drums alone weigh 16 pounds. They are packed eight to a pallet. The empty pallets each weigh 22 pounds. Finally, the trailer holds 24 pallets. Our process must calculate the weight of each drum filled with molasses, calculate the weight of a full pallet, multiply that by the number of pallets per trailer, and add the weight of the trailer.

For our calculations, the formula for the volume of a drum (a cylinder) is:

$$\pi \left(\frac{diameter}{2} \right)^2 \times height$$

We can round off the pallet weight to the nearest pound for these purposes.

We want the computer to show us the results of some of the interim calculations as well as the final total. The output should be similar to:

```
Each drum weighs:        ###.###### lbs.
(Pallet exact weight:    ####.###### lbs).
Pallet approx. weight:   #### lbs.
Total trailer weight:    ##### lbs.
```

DESIGN

This task is a relatively straightforward sequence of behaviors as follows:

Calculate and display the weight of a full drum
Calculate and display the weight of a full pallet
Calculate and display the weight of the full trailer

Since we must display the exact weight of a pallet as well as calculate and display the rounded weight of a pallet, let us expand the second module, for the following result.

Calculate and display the weight of a full drum
[Calculate and display the weight of a full pallet]
    Calculate and display the exact pallet weight
    Calculate and display the rounded pallet weight
Calculate and display the weight of the full trailer

The Object Summary describes the objects that exhibit these behaviors.

OBJECT SUMMARY

Object Name	Behavior	Properties
Drum	Calculate and display the weight of a full drum	drum, empty (req) pi (con) diameter (con) height (con) lbs/cu ft (con) drum, full (pro)
Pallet	Calculate and display the weight of a full pallet	
Exact pallet	Calculate and display the exact pallet weight	pallet, empty (req) drum (req) drums/pallet (con) pallet, exact (pro)
Rounded pallet	Calculate and display the rounded pallet weight	pallet, empty (req) drum (req) drums/pallet (con) pallet, rounded (pro)
Trailer	Calculate and display the weight of the full trailer	trailer, empty (req) pallet (req) pallets/trailer (con) trailer, full

EXECUTION CHART

Line	Explanation	drum	pallet	trailer
1	Allocate space for and declare the constants in the statement. (Note that *drum*, *pallet*, and *trailer* do not yet exist.)	—	—	—
2	Allocate space for and initialize *pallet*. (Note that *drum* and *trailer* do not yet exist.)	—	22	—
3	Allocate space for and initialize *trailer*. Although *trailer*'s initial value is only 7540, its eventual value will be larger than a `short` can hold in this C++.	—	22	7450
4	Allocate and initialize *drum*. Although *drum*'s initial value can be accommodated by a `short`, it must eventually hold a `float`.	16.000	22	7450
5	Since C++ has no exponentiation operator, diameter / 2 must be multiplied by itself to square it. The 2.0 in each division forces the calculation to `double`. Without the decimal points 1 / 2, an integer operation, would be 0 rather than 0.5.	170.724	22	7450
6	*drum*'s actual value should be 170.7238. The stored value is as much as this C++ can fit in a `float`.	170.724	22	7450
7	Since we don't have to store the value for future use, we calculated the actual pallet weight in the `cout` statement. Notice the parentheses around the arithmetic expression.	170.724	22	7450
8	Since *drum*, which is involved in the first calculation in the expression, is `float`, all the calculations will be done at type `double`. *pallet*, the variable to be assigned, is `short`, so the part of the result after the decimal point will be discarded and the integer component assigned to *pallet*. By adding .5 to the result before truncating, the value will be rounded.	170.724	1388	7450
9	*pallet* is displayed as an integer.	170.724	1388	7450
10	Both *pallet* and *pallets_trailer* are `short`. Multiplying them together might exceed a `short`'s capacity in this C++ (32767), so we forced the calculation to a `long` by multiplying *pallet* by 1L.	170.724	1388	40852
11	The total trailer weight is displayed.	170.724	1388	40852

Program 2–8

Note: The line numbers shown with this program are there only for reference in the Execution Chart; they are not part of the code. By looking at the Execution Chart you can follow the process and changes in variable values as the program produces the Output shown below.

```
   #include <iostream>
   using namespace std;

1  const short diameter = 1, height = 2,         // Diameter and height of drum
                drums_pallet = 8, pallets_trailer = 24;
   const float lbs_cu_ft = 98.5, pi = 3.1416;

   int main(void)
2  {   short pallet = 22;
3      long  trailer = 7540;                      // May be greater than 32767
4      float drum = 16.0;                         // Must store a real value

       //------------------------------ Calculate and display weight of full drum
5          drum = drum + pi * (diameter / 2.0) * (diameter / 2.0) * height
                   * lbs_cu_ft;
6          cout << "Each drum weighs:        " << drum << " lbs.\n";

       //------------------------- Calculate and display weight of full pallet
          //----------------------- Calculate and display exact pallet weight
7            cout << "(Pallet exact weight:     "
                   << (pallet + drum * drums_pallet) << " lbs).\n";
          //--------------------- Calculate and display rounded pallet weight
8            pallet = pallet + drum * drums_pallet + .5;          // Round off
9            cout << "Pallet approx. weight:  " << pallet << " lbs.\n";

       //------------------------ Calculate and display weight of full trailer
10         trailer = trailer + 1L * pallet * pallets_trailer;    // Force long
11         cout << "Total trailer weight:   " << trailer << " lbs.\n";
       return 0;
   }
```

Output

```
   Each drum weighs:        170.724 lbs.
   (Pallet exact weight:    1387.79 lbs).
   Pallet approx. weight:   1388 lbs.
   Total trailer weight:    40852 lbs.
```

IMPLEMENTATION

In the *Drum* object properties we look at the weight of a drum both empty and full. To follow a human analogy, let us use the same property, *drum*, and have the object fill it. The object will receive the *drum* empty, calculate its weight including contents, and change the *drum* property to reflect its full weight. We will follow the same pattern for the *pallet* and *trailer* properties in the *Pallet* and *Trailer* objects.

Choices of variables to implement our properties are very important here, as they are in any program. The data types of the variables must reflect the nature of the data and must be large enough to accommodate the data. For example, the empty drum is an integer value, 16, but it must eventually accommodate a real value, so we declare it as float.

The design is implemented in Program 2–8.

TEST

We find that the values in the output match our hand calculations.

SUMMARY

- **KEY TERMS** (in order of appearance)

American National Standards Institute (ANSI)	char
	signed
K&R	unsigned
C++	int
Whitespace	short
Comment	long
Directive	bool
Statement	true
cout	false
Insertion operator	Floating-point data type
Newline	Mantissa
Function	Exponent
Declaration	E notation
Header file	double
Real number	float
Integral number	long double
Special character	string
String	Concatenate
Endline	Constant
endl	const
Variable	Expression
Variable name	Arithmetic operator
Reserved word	Precedence
Data type	Associativity
Define	Remainder
Initialize	Assignment
Integral data type	

- **CONCEPT REVIEW**

  - C was first developed in 1972 by Dennis Ritchie, and its initial, *de facto*, standard was in a book by Kernighan and Ritchie (**K&R**). In 1988, the **American National Standards Institute** released the standard for **ANSI** C.

  - In the early 80s, C was enhanced by **C++**. ANSI standards are currently in development.

  - C++ lends itself to modular design by allowing the use of **whitespace**, which is largely ignored by C++. With it, you can make your program visually represent its organization in outline form. Elements of a C++ program include **comments**, which are ignored by the C++ compiler; **directives**, instructions to the compiler rather than the computer; and **statements**, the instructions for the computer.

  - Objects include cout for display. The **insertion operator** separates cout and the values to display. The **newline** character drops the display to the beginning of the next line. The **endline** manipulator, `endl`, outputs the contents of the buffer as well as a newline.

- **Functions** are sets of statements that perform operations. One of the most important is `main()`.

- Most things in C++ must be **declared** before they are used. Most of the declarations for the standard functions and objects are contained in **header files**.

- Decimal numeric values, **real** or **integral**, are represented in C++ just as they are in handwritten math.

- Characters are stored in ASCII (or EBCDIC) form and, inside the computer, are indistinguishable from numbers. The character `'A'` is stored like the decimal value 65 (the numeric value of its ASCII code). We can put characters in our C++ code that do not exist on the keyboard by using **special characters** such as \t for tab or \n for newline.

- **String** values are sets of characters. We show them in C++ code by enclosing them in double quotation marks.

- Simple output is performed using the `cout` object separating the various output items with the insertion operator.

- A **variable** is a space in the computer's memory. **Variable names** can be multicharacter combinations of alpha, numeric, or underscore characters, and are case-sensitive. None of ANSI C++'s **reserved words** can be used as a variable name, nor can a variable name begin with a numeric character.

- When we use data, either as values or in variables, they must be declared as a specific **data type**. The declaration tells C++ whether the data are stored in straight binary fashion or IEEE floating-point notation; specifies how many bytes to allocate to the data; and **defines** the value or variable by allocating memory to it. A variable may also be **initialized** in a declaration.

- The **integral data types**, `char` and `int`, use straight binary notation and may be **signed** or **unsigned**. The `int` data type may be **short** or **long**. The `bool` data types can only be **true** or **false**. The **floating-point data types**, `float`, `double`, and `long double`, use IEEE E notation, storing a **mantissa** and an **exponent**. All floating-point data types are signed.

- The **string** data type is implemented as an object in C++. Adjacent strings values, those separated only by whitespace, are **concatenated** by C++.

- **Constants**, declared using the **const** qualifier, give a value to a variable that cannot be changed in the program. We usually refer to such "constant variables" as simply constants.

- An **expression** is anything that reduces to a single value. Arithmetic expressions are made by combining values or variables together using **arithmetic operators**. The expressions must be carefully constructed because the order of operation is determined by the operators' **precedence** and **associativity**. The order of operations may be altered by enclosing operations in parentheses. Operators include not only the standard ones but also some special ones such as **remainder**.

- The results of arithmetic operations depend on the data types. An operation on two integers produces an integral result, truncating any fractional part. Operations mixing integers and floating-point values will produce floating-point results. Generally speaking, in mixed arithmetic lower data types are promoted to higher before the operation is performed.

- **Assignment** is the process of putting a value in a variable. A variable may have only one value at a time, so an assignment replaces any value that was there before. An assignment will always be of the data type of the assigned variable. C++ performs conversions automatically if it needs to.

• HEADS UP: POINTS OF SPECIAL INTEREST

- The ANSI C++ standards are still in process.
- Whitespace is used to enhance the readability of programs.
- Directives end at the end of the line.
- Statements end with a semicolon.
- Newline characters drop the display to the next line.
- A single character is actually a number.
- The character value '4', whose ASCII code is 52, is different from the numeric value 4.
- Use variable names that indicate the purpose of the variable.
- Variable names cannot contain spaces.
- You can't start a variable name with a number.
- Don't start normal variable names with an underscore.
- The char data type is numeric.
- There is no such thing as an unsigned float.
- Be sure to put the needed lines at the beginning of your program.
- Two strings separated by whitespace are concatenated.
- Constants look like variables but may not be changed.
- Parentheses can often improve the readability of an expression.
- In cout, enclose arithmetic expressions in parentheses.
- An operation on integers produces an integer result.
- The remainder operator works only with positive integers.
- Each calculation is performed at the highest data type.
- Fundamental rule of assignment.
- For better readability, put spaces around all except unary operators.
- The assigned variable (or any other, for that matter) can never change data type.

• TRAPS: COMMON PROGRAMMING ERRORS

- Splitting a line inside quotes.
- Using only a single backslash in a string to represent a backslash.

- Putting `endl` within quotes.
- Wrong case in a variable name.
- Forgetting to declare a variable.
- Leaving a semicolon off the end of a declaration.
- Declaring a `long double` as a `long`.
- Putting a line ending within a string.
- Exceeding the limits of the data type.
- Watch integer division.

• YOUR TURN ANSWERS

• 2–1

1. Among the advantages of C++ are efficiently executing programs, portability, and its continued growth.

2. ANSI (the American National Standards Institute), specifically the X3J16 committee, is establishing standards for C++.

3. In most places whitespace is ignored by the C++ compiler, so you can use it to make your programs more readable.

4. Characters after `//` on a physical line are ignored by the C++ compiler, so that becomes a place for comments.

5. Directives are instructions to the compiler or preprocessor. Statements directly become part of the executable code. Statements always end with a semicolon; directives end at the end of the physical line.

6. Functions are ways of modularizing a program. They perform sets of operations.

7. Declarations tell the compiler that the object declared can be a valid part of the program and specify how it can be used.

• 2–2

1. Real numbers allow decimal points; integral numbers are whole numbers. The decimal notation for both types of numbers is the same in C++ as it is in math.

2. Characters are represented in the computer using coding schemes such as ASCII. These schemes represent characters with sets of bits, which, as far as C++ is concerned, are numeric values.

3. `'A'` and `65` are both stored as integral numbers.

4. Special characters represent those that we cannot produce on the keyboard. The backslash is represented by two backslashes in a row, `\\`.

5. A string is a set of characters. It is represented by enclosing it in quotation marks (not apostrophes).

6. Each individual character of a string is a numeric value, but it rarely makes sense to work with dissimilar sets of numeric values.

7. The fundamental output object in C++, `cout`, works with all standard data types.

8. The newline character directs the output device to drop to the next line. The endline manipulator directs the system to send all the saved-up characters to the output device and then outputs a newline character.

• 2–3

1. A–Z, upper- or lowercase, 0–9, and underscore (_) can be used in C++ variable names. A name can start with anything but a number.

2. C++ is case-sensitive, so *books* and *BOOKS* are not the same variable.

3. The data type indicates whether a value or a variable is represented by straight binary or exponential notation, and how many bits it occupies.

4. A variable declaration directs C++ how to store values in the variable, allocates space in memory, and, possibly, initializes the variable.

5. `char` and `int` (with the possible modifiers `signed`, `unsigned`, `short`, and `long`), and `bool` are integral; `float`, `double`, and `long double` are floating-point data types.

6. To specifically declare the data type of a value, at the end of the value we use U for `unsigned`, L for `long`, UL for `unsigned long`, F for `float`, and L again for `long double`. The decimal point differentiates the `long double` from a `long int`.

7. We must put `#include <string>` and usually `using namespace std;` at the beginning of the program to use `string` variables.

8. We use the special character \" to put a quotation mark in a string value.

9. C++ interprets two string values separated by whitespace as one continuous string value.

10. Constants improve readability by avoiding "magic numbers." They also allow us to easily change values that are used in more than one place in the program.

• 2–4

1. Precedence determines the order of operators of different levels; associativity determines the order of operators on the same level.

2. Unary operators are highest in precedence; assignment is lowest of those discussed in this chapter.

3. We change the order of operations by enclosing them in parentheses.

4. If an arithmetic operation involving two integers yields a fractional result, the result is truncated to an integer.

5. The result of a remainder operation is the remainder when the first value is divided by the second.

6. The result of an arithmetic operation involving dissimilar data types is the data type that takes the largest amount of memory, with floating-point higher than integral.

7. A simple variable may have only one value at a time. Any new assignment will replace the old value.

8. An assignment can only be the data type of the assigned variable. An expression result of another data type will be converted, perhaps creating a garbage result.

EXERCISES

1. Compare C++ to either another high-level language or to an assembly language. Which language will require less programming time to create the same program? Which program, once written, will operate more efficiently?

2. Rewrite the following program in proper form and then compile and run both programs to see if they do the same thing.

```
#include <iostream>// Here it comes
using namespace std;int main(void){int number;number
=2;cout<<"We had "<<number<<". ";number=number*2;cout
<<"Now we have "<<number<<"."<<endl; return 0;}
```

3. Add documentation to the code in Exercise 2. Include the documentation required for your class and that which tells what each statement does.

4. In an implementation of C++ using ASCII, to what characters would the following expressions evaluate? (Refer to the complete table in Appendix A.)

   a. 'J' + ' '   b. '4' + '5'
   c. 'p' - '?'   d. '~' - '<'

5. Write cout statements to produce the following output. All numbers should be embedded in the output using the appropriate codes.

```
2, 4, 6, 7.9,
This program is definitely mine!
```

6. Of the following, which are invalid variable names? Why are they invalid?

   a. *Gnash*   b. *union*
   c. *9Times*   d. *too_many*
   e. *thisIsIt*   f. *WhatEver*

7. Of the following, which are invalid declarations? Why are they invalid?

```
a. unsigned float zip = 46;
b. Double Dip;
c. short stuff, pants = 12.6;
d. long double disaster
e. string spaghetti = 'pasty pasta';
```

8. In the C++ that you use, in what data types would the following values be stored? In what data types could they actually fit?

   a. 91   b. 40265
   c. 45.   d. 1657.39854

9. What are the values and data types of the following expressions?

   a. 7 / 4   b. 9 / 2. + 25 / 3
   c. 6 + 4.8 / 2 * 3   d. 25 % 5 + 12.5 * 2 / 5

10. If $x = 5$ and $y = 2$ and both are integers, what are the values of the following expressions?

    a. x % y + 14.6 / y   b. y = 1. * x / 2 + 3.5
    c. y = y * x   d. y = 16.2 * x / 3

11. Make up ten expressions of your own, each with at least three operators and two data types. Evaluate them by hand, and verify your results by putting them in a computer program.

12. Fill out an execution chart for the following program. (*Note to future programmers:* Wouldn't this program be a lot easier to understand if it were well commented?)

Program

```
1 #include <iostream>
  using namespace std;

  int main(void)
2 {   int bytes, code, dollars, pennies;
3       float cost, per_byte = 1.42;

4       code = 3;
5       bytes = code * 17 * 2;
6       dollars = bytes * per_byte + .5;
7       cout << code << " code segments cost " << dollars << " dollars.\n";
8       code = code + 1;
9       bytes = code * 17 * 2;
10      cost = bytes * per_byte;
11      pennies = cost * 100 + .5;
12      cout << code << " code segments cost " << cost << " dollars.\n";
13      cout << "  This time we count the " << (pennies % 100) << " pennies.\n";
14      return 0;
  }
```

Output

```
3 code segments cost 145 dollars.
4 code segments cost 193.12 dollars.
  This time we count the 12 pennies.
```

PROGRAMS

1. Enter and execute Program 2–1 (page 44).

2. Enter and execute Program 2–6 (page 65).

3. Write a program to give some information about yourself. It should produce something like the following:

```
NAME:  your name
MAJOR:
OTHER COMPUTER COURSES TAKEN:
OCCUPATION:
HOBBIES AND ACTIVITIES:
REASONS FOR TAKING THIS COURSE:
COMMENTS:
```

4. Find the value of each of the following expressions, being sure to pay attention to data type. Write a program that confirms your answers.

    a. 3.5 + 8 / 3
    c. 7.5 − 38 % 7 * 2 + 10

    b. 4 * 11.5 / 2 + 16
    d. 25 / 2. + 13 / 3

5. Write a program that assigns $a = 4$, $f = 9$, $b = -6$, $x = 4$, and $h = 7$ and prints out the results of the following expressions. All the variables are integers but the results should be as shown. Your output should have the same form and the same values as shown. (The last digit may vary according to your C++ implementation)

    1. $a + f \dfrac{b^2 + h}{3}$

    2. $x + 6f \dfrac{h + 9}{4 - b}$

    3. $\dfrac{(a+b)^2}{f - \dfrac{x+1}{h-4}}$

    4. $\dfrac{\dfrac{(1+h)(1-f)}{3f}}{h^2 - x}$

    Output

    ```
    1 = 133
    2 = 90.4
    3 = 0.545455
    4 = -106.667
    ```

6. There are 12 inches in a foot. Write a program in which you initialize the integer variable *inches* to a value, 46, assign the number of feet to *feet*, and print the result.

    Variables

    ```
    inches, feet
    ```

    Output

    ```
    46 inches is 3.83333 feet.
    ```

7. Write a program to find the average of the four values 4, 42, 16.7, and .0045.

    Variables

    ```
    v1, v2, v3, v4
    average
    ```

    Output

    ```
    The four numbers are:
    4 42 16.7 0.0045
    The average is:
    15.676126
    ```

8. You are given a sphere with a radius of 25. Find the circumference, the largest cross-sectional area, and the volume of the sphere. Remember, the fractional numbers you get may not agree exactly with those below.

    Variables

pi	π (3.1416)
radius	25
circumference	($2\pi r$)
area	largest cross-sectional area (πr^2)
volume	$\left(\dfrac{4}{3}\pi r^3\right)$

Output

```
Radius:              25
Circumference:       157.08
Cross-sectional area: 1963.499878
Volume:              65449.996094
```

9. Rewrite Program 8 to work with a radius of 14.

Output

```
Radius:              14
Circumference:       87.964798
Cross-sectional area: 615.753601
Volume:              11494.066406
```

10. Change the value of π in Program 9 to 3.1415926535987632. Compare the two results.

11. Write a program that produces a bill and coin breakdown for an amount of money. Initialize the amount in the float variable *dollars* and use the *pennies* variable to keep track of the amount not yet converted to bills and coins. You will have to make use of integer arithmetic and the remainder operator in this program.

Variables

```
dollars   float
pennies   int
```

Output

```
The coin breakdown for 7.73 dollars is:
Dollar bills: 7
Half dollars: 1
Quarters:     0
Dimes:        2
Nickels:      0
Pennies:      3
```

Chapter 3

BUILDING A C++ PROGRAM

PREVIEW

Now that you have been introduced to the C++ language, you are ready to look at issues of style, usability, and readability. In this chapter, we will examine:

- The elements that contribute to a program's style and readability.
- Using prewritten source code, header files, in a program.
- Getting data from the keyboard.
- Controlling your output's appearance.

Programs don't just happen. They are very carefully crafted and, when completed, should not only do the job but also be a work of art. In Chapter 1 you looked at the steps in developing a program in any language, and in Chapter 2 you were introduced to the specific language, C++. Here we will look at some of the elements that make your C++ program that work of art, including programming style and the basics of its human interface—input and output.

DEVELOPING A STYLE

A student asked the lecturer, "Should my program have a specific style?" "Yes," answered the lecturer, "most definitely!" and turned to the next question, leaving the student a bit baffled.

The lecturer's point was that a program must have a definite, cohesive, readable style, but that not all styles will be the same. Your style will depend on a number of things, among them your own personality and, probably more significantly, the demands of the environment in which you find yourself. As a student, you will find that your school or professor may demand certain style elements. As an employee, you will be required by your employer to use the company's style. The reason for the style demands in either environment are the same: *communicability*. The people in each environment must deal with a number of programs from a number of programmers. If all the programmers use the same style, they will be much more able to read and understand each other's work.

It is important that you develop an appreciation for style. Even though the style demands may change in the next environment to which you move, the habit pattern you develop will make it easy for you to accommodate the changes. The programs you see in this book follow a consistent style; if there are no other style demands made on you try following this style.

There are certain style elements that are almost universal, and we will mention these in this chapter and in subsequent chapters as new concepts are introduced. Other elements differ from place to place. In Chapter 2 we mentioned our preference for lining up opening and closing braces in the same column. The "K&R" style opens the brace at the right end of the line preceding the statement block and closes it in the column under the left end of that line. As we see in Figure 3–1, either style works, but if you mix them or have no consistent way of treating braces and blocks, your programs will be confusing.

Modularity

Top-down modular design is a universally accepted program-design method, so your program should reflect its modularity. The beginning and end of a program module should be obvious and clearly marked. The typical way of doing this is by using outline form, as we saw in Chapter 2. The beginning of the module should be a comment that identifies the module or, in appropriate cases, a statement (properly commented) that begins a module. Statements within the module should be indented one level

HEADS UP!

You are probably not the only one who will have to read your programs.

HEADS UP!

Keep your style consistent.

HEADS UP!

Outline form shows modularity.

Text Style

```
#include <iostream>

int main(void)
{   int quiz;

    quiz = 20;
    cout << "Perfect is " << quiz
        << " points.\n";
    cout << "Will I be perfect?";
        << endl;
    return 0;
}
```

"K&R" Style

```
#include <iostream>

int main(void){
    int quiz;

    quiz = 20;
    cout << "Perfect is " << quiz
            << " points.\n";
    cout << "Will I be perfect?";
            << endl;
    return 0;
} // End of main()
```

No Style

```
#include <iostream>
int main(void){int quiz;quiz=20;cout<<"Perfect is "<<quiz<<" points.\n";cout<<
"Will I be perfect?"<<endl;return 0;}
```

FIGURE 3–1

Programming Styles

underneath the beginning line. Submodules should be indented further within their containing modules, as shown below.

At this point our program objects are being implemented in modules. Later we will create objects as separate entities and use them by referring to them in modules. At that time we will look at specific object style.

```
statement; // Begins module
{   statement;
    statement;
    // Submodule starts here
        statement;
        statement;
    statement; // Back in the containing module
    statement;
}
```

Whitespace

Proper use of whitespace—spaces, indenting, and line breaks—is important to program design. Most programmers put spaces around operators, such as the insertion and the assignment operators, as well as around almost all arithmetic operators. The exception to this is unary operators—those that refer to only one thing. The multiplication symbol is a binary operator; it refers to the two values to be multiplied together.

```
apples * oranges
```

The minus sign can be used as a unary negate operator as well as the binary subtraction operator. In its unary form, we would not leave space between it and what it affects.

```
apples * -oranges            // Negates oranges, then multiplies by apples
```

When a line is too long and must be broken, the turnover line should be indented so that it lines up with similar things in the line above. In the `cout` statement in Figure 3–1, lining up the insertion operators clearly shows that the second line is part of the `cout` above.

Many programmers advocate including blank lines before program sections. Notice that the program in Figure 3–1 has a blank line between the `#include` directives (in this case only one) and the `main()` function.

Documentation

HEADS UP!

Documentation is a constant process.

In Chapter 1 we looked at the five-step program-development process. Many programmers add a sixth step, **documentation**—all those written things that describe the program and what it does. Documentation is not really a sixth step, to be done after the first five are completed; it is an ongoing process that begins with the first statement of the task. It includes the task statement, the logical design, the program design laid out in outline form, the program itself (including the proper comments), and manuals or written instructions on how to use the program.

As you can see, the documentation produced with each step of the development process is the basis for the next step. For example, coding a program is simply a translation of the program design produced in the analysis step.

Commenting

HEADS UP!

Comment things that aren't obvious.

Just like handwriting styles, commenting styles differ. In the style in this book you will notice that the program code in its outline form is clearly identifiable from the left side of the program. Comments are always lined up at the right margin. This is one style; there are many others. Two general rules of commenting are always to comment those parts of the code that are not obvious from looking at the code itself, and never to comment on those that are obvious. The following comment is reasonable:

```
taxable = gross - retirement      // Must occur before income tax calculated
```

This comment only gets in the way:

```
cout << "Total weight: " << totalWeight;        // Display the total weight
```

Since comments are ignored by the compiler, they do not end up in the executable code. In other words, you can add comments freely to your source code without making your executable program larger.

Much of the documentation and commenting for the programs in this book are in the text and Execution Charts. The programmer generally does not have a text to go along with the programs (although paragraphs and even pages can be put in comments), so the code, including comments, must be self-explanatory.

Readability

A program must, of course, do the job for which it was intended. Beyond that, the most important criterion for a program is **readability**. That should be the objective for your programming style. Two groups of people must be able to easily read and understand your program: other people, and you. You know that your program is not readable when, while you are working in one section of it and must refer to another section that you wrote last week, it takes you 20 minutes to figure out what you did in that section.

A number of factors contribute to readability:

- *Preliminary documentation.* Looking at the task statement, logical design, and program design will give the reader a quick overview of what the program does and how it does it. It forms an introduction to the program.

- *Modular outline form.* The outline form from the program design should be carried over into the program code itself. Modules and submodules should be easy to identify.

- *Variables.* Choose your variable names so that the name itself indicates the nature of the data in the variable. To store the beginning of a range of values, use *beginRange*, not *br* or *x*.

- *Commenting.* Make your comments count.

- *Consistent style.* Whatever your style, keep it consistent.

INCLUDING HEADER FILES

The #include directive instructs the compiler to temporarily, at the beginning of the compile process, insert the contents of a file at that point in the source code. We will look at the #include directive more fully in Chapter 13, but we will use it now to add some source code supplied by the compiler's publisher to the beginning of our programs. These files, called **header files** (of which iostream is an example), contain, among other things, declarations and definitions for standard ANSI C++ objects, functions, and constants.

The directive has this form:

```
#include <fileid>
```

where the fileid is the identification of the file to be placed in the source code.

Notice that a directive does not end in a semicolon. For the simple directive given here, be sure that it is contained on a single line.

For the first few chapters, all of our programs have

```
#include <iostream>
```

near the beginning because we are using objects, like cout and cin, that are declared in iostream. Remember, some older compilers require iostream.h.

If we use string variables, our programs have

```
#include <string>
```

As we add other objects and functions to our repertoire, we will find many of them declared in other header files, so our programs will have a number of #include directives at the beginning.

1. What should be the objective of programming style?
2. How is modularity demonstrated in program statements?
3. When should the documentation be done?
4. How much commenting should be done in a program?
5. What five factors contribute to readability?
6. What is the difference between a directive such as #include and a program statement? At which point in the process does each one act?
7. What ends a directive?

INPUT

The cout object takes all data types, converts them to characters if they are not already chars or strings, and displays those characters on the screen. The **cin** object does the opposite. It takes a series of characters from the keyboard, converts them to the appropriate data types, and assigns the data to variables. Where we used the insertion operator with cout, we will use the **extraction operator** (>>) with cin.

```
cin >> variable >> variable >> . . . >> variable;
```

For example, assuming *miles* is a float variable, given the keyboard input 47.2 followed by the *Enter* key,

```
cin >> miles;
```

assigns 47.2 to *miles*.

Prompts

HEADS UP!

Always precede an input with a prompt.

The couts before each of the cins in Program 3–1 are called **prompts**. They exist to display something on the screen that tells the person at the keyboard what to type in. Can you imagine this program running without those couts? In almost every conceivable case, a cin should be preceded by a prompt.

Delimiters

As we saw in the generalized form of a statement using cout and the insertion operator, we can input many values in a single statement. There must, however, be something—some **delimiter** or separator character—in our input that tells the computer when one value ends and another begins. To see which characters can act as delimiters, we must understand how the cin takes characters from the keyboard input **stream**, the characters from the keyboard waiting to be processed. For each variable, cin follows these steps:

1. Move past any whitespace (spaces, tabs, and newlines).
2. Convert characters to the appropriate data type until it encounters a character that is inappropriate for that data type.
3. Assign the resulting value to the variable.

Program 3-1

```cpp
#include <iostream>                              // Might be iostream.h
#include <string>
using namespace std;                             // May not be needed

const float taxRate = 0.06;              // Change here when rates change

int main(void)
{   string server;
    float food, drink, tip, total, tax, bill;

    //----------------------------------------------------- Input Charges
    cout << "Server:      ";
    cin >> server;
    cout << "Food total: ";
    cin >> food;
    cout << "Beverages:   ";
    cin >> drink;
    cout << "Tip:         ";
    cin >> tip;
    //----------------------------------------------------- Calculate Bill
    total = food + drink + tip;
    tax = total * taxRate;
    //----------------------------------------------------- Print Bill
    cout << "\nTax:        " << tax << "\n";
    bill = total + tax;
    cout << "Please pay: " << bill << "\n";
    cout << "to your server, " << server << endl;
    return 0;
}
```

Output

```
Server:      Nelda
Food total: 34.82
Beverages:   16.75
Tip:         6

Tax:         3.4542
Please pay: 61.0242
to your server, Nelda
```

According to C++, then, a delimiter is any character that is inappropriate for the data type. Whitespace is the logical choice for a delimiter because it is an inappropriate character for any numeric input, so it stops the conversion for the current and is skipped as the next variable is processed. We can see how delimiters work in Program 3–2.

Notice the nonsense the last two lines produced in Output #2 of Program 3–2. The problem was actually the input for the first cin, where the user at the keyboard put in an int followed by a float instead of the other way around. The 12 was converted to the float, *f*, stopping at the space.

HEADS UP!

Whitespace is the most reasonable delimiter.

Program 3–2

```cpp
#include <iostream>
using namespace std;

int main(void)
{   int i;
    float f, g;

    cout << "Enter a float and an integer: ";
    cin >> f >> i;
    cout << "Enter another float: ";
    cin >> g;
    cout << "\nInteger: " << i << ". Floats: " << f << ", " << g << "."
         << endl;
    return 0;
}
```

Line markers: `1, 2, 3` (cin >> f >> i;), `4, 5` (cin >> g;), `6` (cout << "\nInteger: ...)

Output #1

```
Enter a float and an integer: 1.23 45
Enter another float: 67.89

Integer: 45. Floats: 1.23, 67.89.
```

EXECUTION CHART (Output #1)

Line	Explanation	Stream After Operation	i	f	g
1	Input stream empty, so wait for input of characters followed by newline.	1.23•45\n (• is a space)	??	??	??
2	Skip whitespace—there is none. Convert to first inappropriate character for `float`—the space between the numbers. Assign value to f.	•45\n	??	1.23	??
3	Skip whitespace. Convert to first inappropriate character for `int`—the newline. Assign value to i.	\n	45	1.23	??
4	Skip whitespace, the newline. Input stream empty, so wait for input of characters followed by newline.	67.89\n	45	1.23	??
5	Skip whitespace—there is none. Convert to first inappropriate character for `float`—the newline. Assign value to g.	\n	45	1.23	67.89
6	Print values of i, f, and g.	\n	45	1.23	67.89

Output #2

```
Enter a float and an integer: 12 3.45
Enter another float:
Integer: 3. Floats: 12, 0.45.
```

EXECUTION CHART (Output #2)

Line	Explanation	Stream After Operation	i	f	g
1	Input stream empty, so wait for input of characters followed by newline.	12•3.45\n (• is a space)	??	??	??
2	Skip whitespace—there is none. Convert to first inappropriate character for `float`—the space between the numbers. Assign value to f.	•3.45\n	??	12	??
3	Skip whitespace. Convert to first inappropriate character for `int`—the decimal point. Assign value to i.	.45\n	3	12	??
4	Skip whitespace—there is none. Input stream contains characters, so no need to wait.	.45\n	3	12	??
5	Skip whitespace—there is none. Convert to first inappropriate character for `float`—the newline. Assign value to g.	\n	3	12	.45
6	Print values of i, f, and g.	\n	3	12	.45

```
#include <iostream>
#include <string>
using namespace std;

int main(void)
{   string first, last;

    cout << "Enter your first and last name> ";
    cin >> first >> last;
    cout << "You are " << last << ", " << first << endl;
    return 0;
}
```

Output

```
Enter your first and last name> Mortimer Plutarch
You are Plutarch, Mortimer
```

The next variable, *i*, was an int, so the conversion stopped at the decimal point, which is inappropriate for an int. The next cin found an input stream with valid characters in it, so it did not stop for more input; instead it converted the .45 to a float and assigned it to *g*.

Since whitespace is the most natural delimiter for numbers, it has been defined as the delimiter for strings, as shown in Program 3-3. In Chapter 7 we will look at other functions that allow us to input whitespace as part of a string.

As programmers, we must anticipate possible errors or differences of interpretation on the users' part. Later, when you have been exposed to more of the language, we will examine some techniques for doing that. At this point, though, it is important that you see what happens to a keyboard input and spot where errors may occur.

The Input Buffer

We talked about output buffering in Chapter 2 when we introduced the endline (endl) manipulator. Much the same process is used for input—the system saves up characters typed at the keyboard and sends the bunch of them all at once to our process.

But how big is a bunch? How does the system know when to send the bunch to our process? The user, the person at the keyboard, tells it by pressing the *Enter* or *Return* key. Just as endl is the programmer's way of saying "Send the characters to the output device," the *Enter* key is the user's way of saying "Send the characters from the input device."

This process is usually intuitive . . . usually. But consider Program 3-4. The prompt asks for a character so the user types in *a* . . . and nothing happens. Nothing will happen until the user types the *Enter* key, at which time the system sends the character to the process, the process assigns it to *chr*, and the process continues. Our prompt probably should read *Type a character followed by Enter.*

Program 3-4

```
#include <iostream>
using namespace std;

int main(void)
{   char chr;

    cout << "Type a character> ";
    cin >> chr;
    cout << "Here's your character: " << chr << endl;
    return 0;
}
```

Output

```
Type a character> a
Here's your character: a
```

YOUR TURN 3-2

1. What operator separates the `cin` object and all its variables?

2. What is a prompt, and how do we display one?

3. What is the input stream?

4. Show the three steps `cin` goes through to handle the input for a single variable.

5. What is the typical delimiter for `cin`?

6. If 123.45 were entered for an `int` variable, what would happen?

7. What tells the system to send a batch of characters from the keyboard to our process?

MAKING YOUR OUTPUT LOOK GOOD

We have looked at the fundamental output object, `cout`, which has the general form

```
cout << expression << expression << . . . << expression;
```

Now let us look at how we can exert more control over the appearance of our output.

The Worthington Arms Super-Deluxe Luxury Apartments rent for $95 per month (they may have exaggerated a bit on the name). We must have our computer write a rent check every two weeks, so we have to convert that monthly rent into a biweekly one. The statement,

```
cout << "Rent: $" << (95.0 * 12 / 26) << "\n";
```

produces

```
Rent: $43.8462
```

Writing a check for $43.8462 would probably not be well received by the bank. Obviously, we need ways to better control the appearance of our output.

HEADS UP!

Output form is as important ~~⁀put~~ data.

Program 3–5

```
#include <iostream>
using namespace std;

int main(void)
{
    cout << hex << "The rent is $" << 95 << " per month for a "
        << 12 << " month lease.\n";
    cout << "This amounts to $" << (95.0 * 12 / 26) << " every "
        << 2 << " weeks." << endl;
    return 0;
}
```

Output

```
The rent is $95 per month for a 12 month lease.
This amounts to $43.8462 every 2 weeks.
```

Output Manipulators

We can include various **manipulators** in the objects used with `cout` to change the appearance of the output. Let us start with the simple output from Program 3–5 and play with it to show the effects of some simple manipulators.

To improve readability we have used one `cout` for each output line. As far as C++ is concerned, we could have used four `cout`s or just one `cout` to print both lines.

We can change the base of integers from decimal to hexadecimal (and even octal) and back again using the `hex` and `dec` (and `oct`) manipulators. Like all manipulators (with the exception of one, which we will address shortly), once the condition is set, it remains set until changed by an offsetting manipulator. In Program 3–6, one use of `hex` changes all integers to hexadecimal notation. Notice that it affects only the integers, however, not the real number. The 2 in the last line is the same in hex and decimal notations.

If we change the second line to this:

```
    << dec << 12 << " month lease.\n";
```

the output changes to this:

```
The rent is $5f per month for a 12 month lease.
```

HEADS UP!

Most output manipulators remain set until unset.

HEADS UP!

The numeric base manipulators work only with integers.

Manipulator Functions

The manipulators we just looked at are simple words. Most, however, are functions, which require **arguments**—values we must send to them to specify exactly how they are to change the appearance. To use manipulator functions, we must include the file `iomanip` (or, in some compilers, `iomanip.h`). One important function, **setw()**, sets the minimum width of the output field.

```
setw(minimumWidth)                                          <iomanip>
```

Program 3–6

```cpp
#include <iostream>
using namespace std;

int main(void)
{
    cout << hex << "The rent is $" << 95 << " per month for a "
        << 12 << " month lease.\n";
    cout << "This amounts to $" << (95.0 * 12 / 26) << " every "
        << 2 << " weeks." << endl;
    return 0;
}
```

Output

```
The rent is $5f per month for a c month lease.
This amounts to $43.8462 every 2 weeks.
```

HEADS UP!

setw() affects only the next output.

HEADS UP!

If your output has more characters than specified in setw(), they will all print.

This function is the exception to the "once it is set, it remains set" rule. Setting the width affects only the next field printed.

Notice that in Program 3–7 only the 95 was affected, and it was right-justified in the six-character field—leading spaces were added to position it on the right side of the field. Remember, also, that setw() specifies the *minimum* width. If the value you are printing is longer than the minimum, the result of the formula after the setw(2), for example, the entire value will be printed.

The **setprecision()** function allows us to specify the number of significant digits in a floating-point number. It has no effect on integral numbers.

setprecision(*digits*)   <iomanip>

Adding this statement to the beginning of the program (or anywhere before the formula is printed)

```cpp
cout << setprecision(3);
```

will change the output to this:

```
The rent is $    95 per month for a 12 month lease.
This amounts to $43.8 every 2 weeks.
```

We can change the output appearance in a number of other ways using **ios flags**—output conditions that we can set and unset by using the functions **setiosflags()** and **resetiosflags()**.

setiosflags(*flags*)   <iomanip>

resetiosflags(*flags*)   <iomanip>

HEADS UP!

The ios::fixed flag affects how setprecision() works.

For example, one of the ios flags, **ios::fixed**, allows us to set the number of decimal places for floating-point numbers. When ios::fixed is set, the setprecision() function sets the number of digits after the decimal point instead of the total number of digits. Adding the statement

```cpp
cout << setiosflags(ios::fixed);
```

BUILDING A C++ PROGRAM

Program 3–7

```
#include <iostream>
#include <iomanip>                              // For manipulator functions
using namespace std;

int main(void)
{
    cout << "The rent is $" << setw(6) << 95 << " per month for a "
         << 12 << " month lease.\n";
    cout << "This amounts to $" << setw(2) << (95.0 * 12 / 26) << " every "
         << 2 << " weeks." << endl;
    return 0;
}
```

Output

```
The rent is $     95 per month for a 12 month lease.
This amounts to $43.8462 every 2 weeks.
```

changes the output to

```
The rent is $     95 per month for a 12 month lease.
This amounts to $43.846 every 2 weeks.
```

Values are normally right-justified in a field. The **ios::left** flag will left-justify subsequent fields. We can return to right justification either by using **ios::right** or by using ios::left in resetiosflags() to return to the default right-justified condition.

In Program 3–8 we set up the output in a somewhat columnar fashion using our newfound functions and flags. Notice that we have expressed 95 as 95.0 so that it acts as a floating-point number. Also, we set two flags with one function call:

```
cout << setiosflags(ios::fixed | ios::left);
```

We can set as many flags as we wish in one call if we separate the flags with the **pipe symbol** (|).

The resetiosflags(ios::left) manipulator set the condition back to right justification—the default. setiosflags(ios::right) would have produced the same result.

The full set of manipulators and manipulator functions is listed in Appendix D.

YOUR TURN 3–3

1. What are output manipulators?

2. Which manipulators change the base of numeric outputs?

3. How long does a manipulator's effect last?

4. How does the effect of the setprecision() manipulator differ when ios::fixed is set?

5. What symbol do we use to combine flags together in a single setiosflags() call?

Program 3–8

```cpp
#include <iostream>
#include <iomanip>                              // For manipulator functions
using namespace std;

int main(void)
{
   cout << setprecision(2);
   cout << setiosflags(ios::fixed | ios::left);
   cout << setw(17) << "The rent is $"
        << setiosflags(ios::right) << setw(6) << 95.0
        << " per month for a "
        << setw(3) << 12 << " month lease.\n";
   cout << "This amounts to $" << setw(6) << (95.0 * 12 / 26)
        << setiosflags(ios::left) << setw(17) << " every "
        << resetiosflags(ios::left) << setw(3) << 2 << " weeks." << endl;
   return 0;
}
```

Output

```
The rent is $       95.00 per month for a  12 month lease.
This amounts to $ 43.85 every                2 weeks.
```

PUTTING IT TOGETHER

Gleam and Glitter Jewelers makes jewelry out of gold and diamonds. Before its designers embark on a project, though, they must have an idea of the cost based on the materials and labor involved. Their current manual system of figuring cost is more guesswork than anything else.

TASK

We must build Gleam and Glitter a program to consistently figure cost. The important parameters in the cost calculation must be easy to change as the staff members gain experience or conditions change.

ANALYSIS

The most significant costs for G and G's jewelry are gold, diamonds, and the time it takes to design and create the piece. We want our program to input these factors like this:

```
Gold - weight (oz), carats: 1.864 18
Diamonds - weight (carats), grade: 2.33 4
Design and creation time (hours): 12.5
```

Gold's value is determined by its weight, the cost of pure gold, and its purity (in carats, with 24 being pure gold).

$$value = weight \times cost \times \frac{carats}{24}$$

Diamond value is estimated by weight (in carats), grade (1 through 5), and the cost for grade 5 diamonds according to this formula:

$$value = weight \times \frac{cost}{2} \times \frac{grade}{5}$$

Design time is charged at an hourly rate determined by previous experience.

The program should calculate the value of each component as well as the total, and print a value analysis:

```
Value Analysis
   Gold:        1.864 oz  @  312 (18   carats) $   436.18
   Diamonds:    2.330 cts @ 1640 (4    grade)     1476.00
   Creation:   12.500 hrs @   55                   687.50
      Total value:                             $ 2599.68
```

DESIGN

Overall, we want our program to behave as follows:

> Determine gold value
> Determine diamond value
> Determine design and creation value
> Print value report

Each of the first three objects can be expanded into two steps: inputting the materials and calculating the values.

> Determine gold value
>   Input materials
>   Calculate value
> Determine diamond value
>   Input materials
>   Calculate value
> Determine design and creation value
>   Input hours
>   Calculate value
> Print value report

The cost of gold, diamonds, and labor should be put in constants because these change from time to time, and G and G wants to make it easy to modify the program. All together, then, we will need the objects shown in the Object Summary to perform the process.

IMPLEMENTATION

Program 3–9 shows the final code.

TEST

The output matches the hand calculations for the figures. Our test plan should include runs that validate extreme values for all the factors in the jewelry's cost.

OBJECT SUMMARY

Object Name	Behavior	Properties
Gold	Determine gold value	
Input	Accept weight and purity from keyboard, provide to other objects	gold (pro) carats (pro)
Calculate	Calculate gold value	gold (req) carats (req) gold cost (con) pure gold (con) gold value (pro)
Diamonds	Determine diamond value	
Input	Accept weight and grade from keyboard, provide to other objects	diamonds (pro) grade (pro)
Calculate	Calculate diamond value	diamonds (req) grade (req) diamond cost (con) top grade (con) diamond value (pro)
Creation	Determine design and creation value	
Input	Accept creation time from keyboard, provide to other objects	creation (pro)
Calculate	Calculate design and creation value	creation (req) hourly cost (con) creation value (pro)
Report	Print value report and cost code	gold (req) carats (req) gold cost (con) gold value (req) diamonds (req) grade (req) diamond cost (con) diamond value (req) creation (req) hourly cost (con) creation value (req)

Output

```
Gold - weight (oz), carats: 1.864 18
Diamonds - weight (carats), grade: 2.33 4
Design and creation time (hours): 12.5

Value Analysis
   Gold:      1.864 oz  @  312 (18   carats) $   436.18
   Diamonds:  2.330 cts @ 1640 (4    grade)     3439.08
   Creation: 12.500 hrs @   55                   687.50
      Total value:                          $  4562.76
```

Program 3–9

```
   #include <iostream>
   #include <iomanip>
   using namespace std;

1  const int goldCost = 312;                          // Cost per ounce
2  const int pureGold = 24;                      // 24 carat is pure gold
3  const int diamondCost = 1640;                      // Cost per carat
4  const int topGrade = 5;                         // Grades 1 through 5
5  const int hourlyCost = 55;

   int main(void)
   {
   //-------------------------------------------------------------- Gold
g1    float gold, goldValue;
g2    int   carats;

g3    cout << "Gold - weight (oz), carats: ";
g4    cin >> gold >> carats;
g5    goldValue = gold * goldCost * carats / pureGold;


   //---------------------------------------------------------- Diamonds
d1    float diamonds, diamondValue;
d2    int   grade;

d3    cout << "Diamonds - weight (carats), grade: ";
d4    cin >> diamonds >> grade;
d5    diamondValue = diamonds * diamondCost / 2
                   * (1 + 1.0 * grade / topGrade);        // Force double


   //---------------------------------------------------------- Creation
c1    float creation, creationValue;

c2    cout << "Design and creation time (hours): ";
c3    cin >> creation;
c4    creationValue = creation * hourlyCost;


   //------------------------------------------------------------ Report
r1    cout << setiosflags(ios::fixed);
r2    cout << "\nValue Analysis\n";
r3    cout << "  Gold:    " << setprecision(3) << setw(8) << gold
r4          << " oz  @ " << setw(4) << goldCost << " ("
r5          << setw(3) << setiosflags(ios::left) << carats << " carats) $"
r6          << setiosflags(ios::right) << setprecision(2) << setw(8)
            << goldValue << endl;
r7    cout << "  Diamonds:" << setprecision(3) << setw(8) << diamonds
            << " cts @ " << setw(4) << diamondCost << " ("
            << setw(3) << setiosflags(ios::left) << grade << " grade)   "
            << resetiosflags(ios::left) << setprecision(2) << setw(8)
            << diamondValue << endl;
r8    cout << "  Creation:" << setprecision(3) << setw(8) << creation
            << " hrs @ " << setw(4) << hourlyCost << "              "
            << setprecision(2) << setw(8) << creationValue << "\n";
r9    cout << "     Total value:                    $" << setw(8)
            << (goldValue + diamondValue + creationValue) << endl;
      return 0;
   }
```

EXECUTION CHART

Line	Explanation	Input Stream	gold	carats	goldValue
1–5	Declare constants.				
	Gold object	**Input Stream**	**gold**	**carats**	**goldValue**
g1, 2	Declare variables.		??	??	??
g3	Prompt for input.		??	??	??
g4	Input from keyboard.	1.864 18\n	??	??	??
g4	Skip any whitespace and convert to inappropriate float character (the space between the numbers).	18\n	1.864	??	??
g4	Skip whitespace and convert to inappropriate integer character (the newline).	\n	1.864	18	??
g5	Calculate gold value.	\n	1.864	18	436.176
	Diamond object		**diamonds**	**grade**	**diamValue**
d1, 2	Declare variables.	\n	??	??	??
d3, 4	Prompt and input. Since input of *diamonds* will skip whitespace (the newline) `cin` will wait for input of new characters.	2.33 4\n	2.33	4	??
d5	Calculate diamond value. Since *grade* is integer, must force division to `double`.	\n	2.33	4	3439.08
	Creation object		**creation**		**creatVal**
c1	Declare variables.	\n	??		??
c2, 3	Prompt and input.	\n12.5\n	12.5		??
c4	Calculate creation value.	\n	12.5		687.5
	Report object		**goldVal**	**diamVal**	**creatVal**
r1	Set fixed rather than floating-point notation.	\n	436.176	3439.08	687.5
r2	Print heading.	\n	436.176	3439.08	687.5
r3	Print *gold* in 8-character field with three decimal places.	\n	436.176	3439.08	687.5
r4	Print *goldCost* in 4-character field.	\n	436.176	3439.08	687.5
r5	Print *carats* in 3-character, left-justified field.	\n	436.176	3439.08	687.5
r6	Print *goldValue* in right-justified, 8-character field with 2 decimal places.	\n	436.176	3439.08	687.5
r7	Output diamond information. Notice that to go back to right justification, the `ios::left` flag was reset.	\n	436.176	3439.08	687.5
r8	Output creation information.	\n	436.176	3439.08	687.5
r9	Output total value.	\n	436.176	3439.08	687.5

SUMMARY

- **KEY TERMS** (in order of appearance)

Documentation	hex
Readability	dec
Header file	Argument
Extraction operator	Ios flag
Prompt	ios::fixed
Delimiter	ios::left
Stream	ios::right
Manipulator	Pipe symbol

- **NEW OBJECTS AND FUNCTIONS** (in order of appearance)

```
cin >> variable >> variable >> . . . >> variable;

cout << expression << expression << . . . << expression;

setw(minimumWidth)                                      <iomanip>

setprecision(digits)                                    <iomanip>

setiosflags(flags)                                      <iomanip>

resetiosflags(flags)                                    <iomanip>
```

- **CONCEPT REVIEW**

  - It is important to maintain a consistent programming style. Some elements of style are modularity, whitespace, **documentation**, and commenting. The major objectives in maintaining a style are **readability** and communicability.

  - The #include directive instructs the computer to insert a file of source code at the point of the directive. Typical files to include are the **header files** that come with the compiler.

  - The **cin** object gets characters from the input **stream** and converts them to data types matching the variables in the cin statement. The **extraction operator** separates cin and each of its variables.

  - A keyboard input is typically preceded by a **prompt**, a screen output informing the user of the kind of data expected.

  - To handle an individual item input, cin skips any leading whitespace, converts to the first character in the input stream that is inappropriate for the data type of the variable, and assigns the resultant value to the variable. The most common **delimiter** is whitespace because it is inappropriate for a number and has been defined as such for strings.

  - We can control the appearance of our output with **manipulators**. The numeric base of an integer can be changed using **hex** and **dec** (and oct).

  - Most manipulators are functions requiring **arguments**. **setw()** sets the minimum width for the next output. **setprecision()** specifies the number of digits printed or, if **ios::fixed** is set, the number of digits after the decimal point. **Ios flags**, such as ios::fixed, **ios::left**, and **ios::right**, can be set and reset using the functions **setiosflags()** and **resetiosflags()**. Flags can be joined in one function call by separating them with a **pipe symbol** (|).

- You are probably not the only one who will have to read your programs.
- Keep your style consistent.
- Outline form shows modularity.
- Documentation is a constant process.
- Comment things that aren't obvious.
- Directives act before statements.
- Directives end at the end of a line.
- Always precede an input with a prompt.
- Whitespace is the most reasonable delimiter.
- Output form is as important as output data.
- The numeric base manipulators work only with integers.
- Most output manipulators remain set until unset.
- `setw()` affects only the next output.
- If your output has more characters than specified in `setw()`, they will all print.
- The `ios::fixed` flag affects how `setprecision()` works.

• **TRAPS: COMMON PROGRAMMING ERRORS**

- Writing a program that, after time, even you cannot read.

• **YOUR TURN ANSWERS**

• **3–1**

1. Communicability—being able to communicate your ideas to others and to yourself—is the objective of programming style.
2. Modularity is shown using outline form with indenting to show modules and submodules.
3. Documentation should be done continuously as the program goes through the various stages of development.
4. Comments should be included when they are needed to explain something that is not obvious from the code.
5. The five readability factors are: the preliminary documentation (the task statement, logical design, and program design), modular outline form, choosing meaningful variable names, proper commenting, and consistent style.
6. A directive is an instruction to the compiler or preprocessor. A program statement directly becomes part of the executable code. Directives act before statements.
7. A directive ends at the end of the physical line instead of at a semicolon (as a statement does).

• **3–2**

1. The extraction operator (>>) is used to separate everything in `cin`.

2. Prompts are reminders displayed on the screen before inputs. They are displayed using `cout`.

3. The input stream is the characters waiting to be processed by an input object.

4. In handling the input for a single variable, `cin` skips leading whitespace, converts characters until it reaches an inappropriate character for the data type, and assigns the result.

5. Whitespace is the usual delimiter for `cin`.

6. If 123.45 were entered for an `int` variable, `cin` would convert to the decimal point, inappropriate for an `int`, leaving the `.45` in the input stream for whatever was next.

7. The *Enter* or *Return* key tells the system to send a batch of characters from the keyboard to our process.

● 3–3

1. Output manipulators can be added to a `cout` statement to change the appearance of the output.

2. The base of numeric outputs can be changed using `hex` and `dec` (and `oct`).

3. The manipulator's effect lasts until it is reset, except for the `setw()` function, which lasts only through the next output.

4. Normally `setprecision()` sets the number of significant digits that print. When `ios::fixed` is set, however, `setprecision()` sets the number of digits after the decimal point.

5. By putting a pipe symbol (|) between them, we can use as many flags as we want in a single `setiosflags()` call.

EXERCISES

1. Show the proper preliminary lines to use string variables in a program.

2. Correct the following program so that it works as shown.

```
#include <iostream>
using namespace std;

const taxRate = 0.07

int main(void);
{   string item;
    float price, quantity;

    cout "Item: ";
    cin item;
    cout "Price and quantity: ";
    cin price, quantity;
    total = price * quantity;
    total = total * 1 + taxRate;
    cout "Including tax, your " << item << " cost $" << total << "." << endl;
}
```

Output

```
Item: Widget
Price and quantity: 50 2
Including tax, your Widget cost $107.
```

3. Fully comment the program in Exercise 2 so it fits the requirements of your class.

4. Add the cout statements and manipulators to the following main() function to produce the output shown. Do not print out any spaces.

```cpp
int main(void)
{   string thing = "Word";
    float number = 12.3456;

    cout << "123456789012345\n";
    cout << thing << number << endl;
    return 0;
}
```

Output

```
123456789012345
Word12.3456
   Word  12.3
Word  12.346
Word     12.346
```

5. Fully comment the program in Exercise 4 so it fits the requirements of your class.

6. Add the formatting to the following program so that it produces the output shown.

```cpp
#include <iostream>
#include <string>
using namespace std;

const int methusalah = 969;

int main(void)
{   string name;
    int age;

    cout << "What's your first name and age? ";
    cin >> name >> age;
    cout << "Name            Age\n";
    cout << "Methusalah     " << methusalah << "\n";
    cout << name << age << "\n";
    cout << "You have lived " << (100.0 * age / methusalah)
         << "% of Methusalah's age." << endl;
    return 0;
}
```

Output

```
What's your first name and age? Fred 26
Name            Age
Methusalah      969
Fred             26
You have lived 2.683% of Methusalah's age.
```

7. Fully comment the program in Exercise 6 so it fits the requirements of your class.

8. Rewrite and comment the following program in proper form. Show the output, given an input of 37.

```
#include <iostream>
#include <iomanip>
using namespace std;const float factor = 5.287;
int main(void){int initial;
float result;cout<<"Start with> ";cin>>initial;result=initial*factor;cout<<
"Given " <<setw(5)<<initial<<" and a factor of "<<setiosflags(ios::fixed)<<
setprecision(3)<<factor<<", the result\nis approximately "<<setprecision(2)
<<setw(6)<<result<<"." << endl;return 0;}
```

PROGRAMS

1. Write a program that prints the following pattern. You do not need any variables.

   Output

   ```
      >
      >   >
      >      >
   >>>         >
      >      >
      >   >
      >
   ```

2. Write a program that accepts two numbers from the keyboard and prints the following information.

   Variables

   ```
   first
   second
   ```

   Output

   ```
   First number?  7
   Second number?  2
   The second goes into the first 3 times
   with a remainder of 1.
   The quotient is 3.5.
   ```

3. Write a program to print out a customer bill for Ajax Auto Repair. The parts and labor charges are input and a 6 percent sales tax is charged on parts but not on labor. Be sure to line up the output as shown.

   Variables

   ```
   parts
   labor
   salesTax
   total
   ```

Output

```
PARTS? 104.50
LABOR? 182.15

        AJAX AUTO REPAIR
        SERVICE INVOICE
PARTS                $ 104.50
LABOR                  182.15
SALES TAX                6.27
TOTAL                $ 292.92
```

4. Ajax would like a program to compute an employee's paycheck. The employee's gross pay is the hours worked times the hourly pay. Income tax withholding, FICA tax, payroll savings plan, retirement, and health insurance are subtracted from the gross pay. From time to time the various rates for these deductions change, so these values should be stated as constants.

Constants

fitRate	15% of gross pay
ficaRate	6.2% of gross pay
savingsRate	3% of gross pay
ratirementRate	8.5% of gross pay
healthIns	$3.75 per employee

Variables

hours	
hourlyPay	
grossPay	
fit	Federal income tax withholding
fica	Social security tax withholding
savings	Payroll savings
retirement	
netPay	Gross pay less deductions

Output

```
HOURS? 40
HOURLY PAY? 7.50

GROSS PAY:            $ 300.00

FEDERAL INCOME TAX: $   45.00
FICA:               $   18.60
PAYROLL SAVINGS:    $    9.00
RETIREMENT:         $   25.50
HEALTH INSURANCE:   $    3.75

NET PAY:            $  198.15
```

5. Write a program to calculate interest on a loan. It should allow input of principal, rate in percentage form, and time in days. Use the following variables. Don't add any variables, and don't leave any out. Your output should look like the one following.

$$interest = principal \times \frac{rate}{100} \times \frac{time}{365}$$

Variables	Output
principal	PRINCIPAL? **1450**
rate	RATE, TIME? **14.5 250**
time Integer	
interest	INTEREST: $144.01

6. Write a program to figure out the circumference, cross-sectional area, and volume of a sphere, given a radius. The radius should be input and the rest printed out as shown.

Formulas

$\pi = 3.1416$
$circumference = 2 \times \pi \times radius$
$cross\text{-}sectional\ area = \pi \times radius^2$
$volume = {}^4/_3 \times \pi \times radius^3$

Variables

Choose variables appropriate for the problem

Output

```
RADIUS: 25

CIRCUMFERENCE:            157.080
CROSS-SECTIONAL AREA:   1963.500
VOLUME:                65449.996
```

7. Write a program that will accept keyboard input of various coins and return the total value.

Variables

input   Value from keyboard
total   To accumulate the value of the inputs

Output

```
Half dollars? 3
Nickels?      3
Pennies?      7
Your total is $2.67.
```

8. Write a program that accepts a number of seconds from the keyboard and converts it into days, hours, minutes, and seconds. Use integer arithmetic and the remainder operator.

Variable

seconds

Output

```
How many seconds? 106478
Days:     1
Hours:    5
Minutes: 34
Seconds: 38
```

Chapter 4

THE SELECTION STRUCTURE

PREVIEW

As programs become more complicated, we must do all we can to keep them simple. One simplification method is a technique called structured programming. In this chapter we will examine that technique and concentrate on one of its facets. In particular, we will look at:

- The basic principles of structured programming.
- The simplest of the structures.
- A structure that allows a program to branch in one of two directions.
- Setting up conditions for choosing one branch or another.
- Types of operators used in these conditions.
- The principal statement used to create a selection.
- Extending a selection to more than two branches.
- C++'s special multibranch structure.

Even a well-designed program may be difficult to write and even more difficult to communicate to others. Top-down modular design adds consistency to the design process and makes it easier. Object-oriented programming pulls together data and processes into self-contained units and allows us to reuse code more easily. Yet many programs are thousands of lines long, and the number of different but interconnected processes in the program can be mind-boggling. Wouldn't it be nice if we could reduce the variety of different processes that can be required in a complicated program?

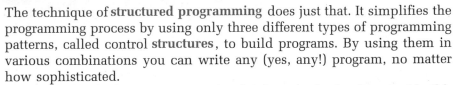

STRUCTURED PROGRAMMING

HEADS UP!

Any program may be built from only three basic structures.

The technique of **structured programming** does just that. It simplifies the programming process by using only three different types of programming patterns, called control **structures**, to build programs. By using them in various combinations you can write any (yes, any!) program, no matter how sophisticated.

The individual structures are simple; they are the fundamental building blocks of programs. These building-block structures are combined to form useful, and sometimes quite complicated, programs. One structure may follow another; be put inside another; be put inside one that is inside another, following another, inside another; and so forth. These simple patterns can be combined in any way necessary to get the job done. While the end result may be a complicated program, it is nevertheless composed of simple pieces.

These three structures are:

- *Sequence.* One operation after another. This is the structure we have been using up to this point.

- *Selection*. A choice between sets of operations. We will discuss this structure in this chapter.

- *Iteration.* Repetition of a set of operations. We will discuss this in Chapter 5.

HEADS UP!

Design your program carefully before writing the code.

A good structured programmer will outline the various structures in the program first in simple, human language as we have been doing in the design stage of our program development. The outline is often done in a slightly more formalized **pseudocode** (literally a false code) that uses a few key words to indicate structures but still employs human instead of computer language. Typically, the programmer will create the pseudocode outline using the same text editor that will be used to write the actual program source code. In fact, the pseudocode will become *part of* the source code.

HEADS UP!

To make pseudocode useful, keep it simple.

Like our designs up to this point, a good structured outline looks like a well-ordered set of class notes. Major topics—in this case structures—are at the left margin; subsidiary topics, the structures inside, are indented within the major ones, and so forth. It is easy to see which structures are within other structures because they are indented within them.

FIGURE 4–1

Weekly Payroll

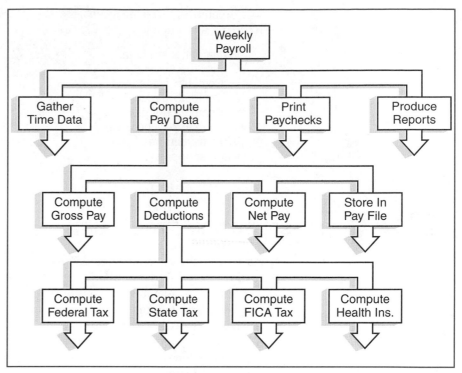

A top-down design for our weekly payroll starts with an overall statement of the task (Weekly Payroll), breaks that down into individual modules (such as Compute Pay Data), and keeps breaking down modules until they become self-contained program segments.

In the top-down design of a weekly payroll, illustrated in Figure 4–1, there are numerous applications of each of these structures; we will use that figure to illustrate both the structures and a structured outline.

The Sequence Structure

Our **sequence structure** consists simply of one operation after another. The four main objects in the payroll example gather timecard data, compute pay data, print paychecks, and produce reports, in that order. Since the sequence is so simple, we have no special format or indenting for it, nor any special pseudocode key words. The sequence in our outline would be written like this:

> Gather timecard data
> Compute pay data
> Write paychecks
> Print reports

In expanding this outline we can put one sequence structure within another. The Compute pay data object, for example, can be expanded into four operations and inserted into the pseudocode, giving us a sequence within a sequence.

```
Gather timecard data
Compute pay data
    Compute gross pay
    Compute deductions
    Compute net pay
    Store in paycheck file
Write paychecks
Print reports
```

THE SELECTION STRUCTURE

HEADS UP!

A program follows only one of the two branches.

HEADS UP!

Be sure your branching structures come back to the same path.

As you might have suspected, this outline will be expanded further and further—top-down modular design at work. **Compute gross pay**, for example, is more complicated because we may figure either regular plus overtime pay using an overtime formula, or simply regular pay. Each of these choices is a separate **branch** of the process—a particular path that the process may take. Notice that each time through the process, the program will follow only one of the two branches, overtime or regular pay, but no matter which branch is followed, the process will end up in the same place—gross pay will be calculated. This last condition, ending up in the same place, is extremely important to the modular programming process. We must be able to replace **Compute gross pay**, a simple statement of the object, with an entire structure, but must always continue on to **Compute deductions**.

The second of the structures, the **selection structure**, shown in Figure 4–2, sets up this branching situation. There must be some reason to take one branch or another—pay overtime or regular pay—so the selection begins with some condition. If the condition is true (the hours are greater than 40), we will perform one branch (**Figure overtime pay**); if they are not, we will perform the other (**Figure regular pay**).

FIGURE 4–2

The Selection Structure

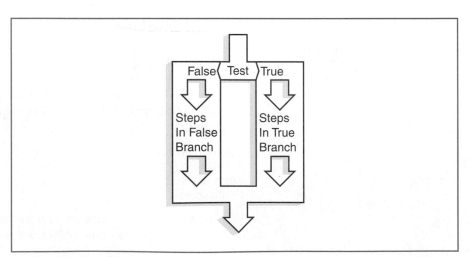

Depending on whether the condition established is true or false, a selection structure performs one branch or the other and then moves on.

```
if hours > 40          [Compute gross pay]
    Figure overtime pay
else
    Figure regular pay
Rest of program
```

Notice the key words and the indenting. The structure starts with *if* followed by the condition. The operations that are performed if the condition is true are indented under *if*. In this example it is only one operation, but it might be many, even including other structures. The false branch is indented under the key word *else*. The entire selection structure ends when the indent level returns to the level of the *if*. This indicates the point at which the two branches come back together. Inserting this module in the outline, we end up with the following:

```
Gather timecard data
Compute pay data
    if hours > 40          [Compute gross pay]
        Figure overtime pay
    else
        Figure regular pay
    Compute deductions
    Compute net pay
    Store in paycheck file
Write paychecks
Print reports
```

Notice that the actual operations are at the left side of the outline and the comments, such as *Compute gross pay*, are at the right. The operations and their indenting should clearly show the various structures in the program; the comments explain what they do. Neither Congress nor the International Association of Programming Gurus has passed a law mandating this style; it is the author's, and others may differ. But this works, and if you haven't already developed your own style, try this one.

Certain key principles are imperatives in top-down modular structured programming, without which the process breaks down.

- *One entry, one exit.* Each structure may have only one entry point and one exit point. This is important so that a single line can be replaced by an entire structure. Structures formed using the guidelines given above will follow this principle.

- *Proper nesting.* To **nest** something is to enclose it entirely within something else. If, for example, a selection is put within a branch of another selection, the selection structure must begin and end within that branch. In the following examples the left one is properly structured; the one on the right would be senseless:

```
if this is true              if this is true
    Something                    Something
    if this is true              if this is true
        Another thing                Another thing
    else                         else
        Yet another                  Still another
    End of the if structure      else
else                                 Yet another
    Still another            End of the if structure
End of the if structure          End of the if structure
```

Try following the one on the right through. It doesn't work!

Programming the paycheck process will not end here, of course. More lines in the outline will be considered as modules and expanded into submodules until each submodule is a small but complete programmable entity. By following this top-down procedure the design stage will be simpler and more manageable. The programming stage will be equally simple and manageable because the final, complicated program may be built from simple, individual subprograms.

Now that we see how the selection structure works, let us apply it in the C++ language.

YOUR TURN 4–1

1. How does structured programming simplify the programming process? *uses only 3 different*
2. How may structures be combined in a program? *Any way. types of prog patterns*
3. What is pseudocode? *false code :! human lang.*
4. Why is indenting important in pseudocode? *which structures are inside which. "outline format"*
5. Which structure have our programs used before this chapter? *SEQUENCE.*
6. What is meant by "branches" in a program? *path process may take*
7. Which structure implements branching? *Selection*
8. In a selection structure, where is the true branch and where is the false branch? *SECOND NEXT   FIRST*
9. What are two imperative principles of top-down modular structured programming? *last condition first condition*

CONDITIONS

There must be some condition set up to tell the computer to take one branch or the other. This condition evaluates to either true or false, and typically is some kind of comparison. For example, let us say that we are at a fork in the road. We have to get to the place beyond, but should we take the high road or the low road? If it's cold, the high road might be blocked with snow. If it's warm, the low road might be uncomfortably hot. It's decision time. If the temperature is over 60 degrees Fahrenheit, we'll take the high road. Otherwise, it's the low.

The condition in the example above is based on comparing the temperature with 60. It is either over 60 degrees—true—or it isn't—false.

A **condition** in C++ typically consists of one or more comparisons that relate one value to another. A comparison has the form

expression comparisonOperator expression

For example:

x + 4 > 9

where we compare the value of the expression *x* + 4 with the value 9. An expression, remember, is anything that reduces to a single value; so, in essence, a comparison always compares two values. The *comparisonOperator*, > in our example, tells the computer how the comparison should be made.

HEADS UP!

Conditions are either true or false; there are no maybes.

HEADS UP!

Comparisons compare values.

TABLE 4–1

Operator	Symbol	Explanation	Example
Unary Right-to-left associativity			
Logical not	!	Make false expression (0) true (1); make true (nonzero) false (0).	`!(time > present)`
Arithmetic Discussed in Chapter 2			
Relational Left-to-right associativity			
Greater	>	First greater than second?	`x + y > z - 19`
Less	<	First less than second?	`cost < maximum - 100`
Greater or equal	>=	First greater than or equal to second?	`load >= limit`
Less or equal	<=	First less than or equal to second?	`testValue <= Norm`
Equality Left-to-right associativity			
Equal	==	First equals second?	`count + 1 == endCount`
Not equal	!=	First not equal to second?	`checkSum != newSum`
Logical AND Left-to-right associativity			
	&&	First and second true?	`val1 && val2`
Logical OR Left-to-right associativity			
	||	First or second or both true?	`val1 || val2`
Assignment Discussed in Chapter 2			

If the value of x is 7, then 7 + 4 is 11, 11 is greater than 9, and the comparison is true.

Relational and Equality Operators

The *comparisonOperator* comes from one of two categories: **relational operators** or **equality operators**. The operators differ in function, of course, but the categories also differ in precedence, with the relational operators being higher than the equality operators. Both sets of operators are shown in Table 4–1. (The entire set of operators is shown in Appendix B.) Be sure to notice that the equal operator (==) is not the same as the assignment operator (=).

Operators of both categories have left-to-right associativity. In precedence, of the operators we have examined so far, all the arithmetic operators come first, followed by the relational operators, followed by the equality operators, and ending with the assignment operators. This order of evaluation is convenient because the arithmetic expressions are reduced to values first, and then the values are compared according to the comparison operators.

HEADS UP!

= is not ==.

HEADS UP!

Parentheses can be added—and are encouraged—to increase readability.

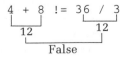

$$4 + 8 \; != \; 36 \; / \; 3$$

12   12

False

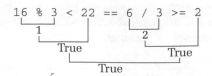

Logical Operators

Our conditions can consist of more than one comparison. We can tie multiple comparisons together with two of the **logical operators**—the **and operator** (&&) and the **or operator** (||). Using the *and* operator, if the comparisons on both sides are true, then the whole condition is true. If even one comparison is false, then the whole condition is false.

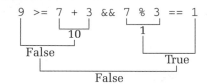

Using the *or* operator, if either or both of the comparisons are true, then the whole condition is true. Both comparisons would have to be false for the whole condition to be false.

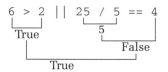

Many comparisons can be combined together using many *and*s and *or*s. The *and* operator is higher in precedence than *or*. Both of them are lower than the comparison operators, but higher than assignment, as you can see in Table 4–1. This means that comparisons are evaluated first and then combined by the logical operators. Order of evaluation can, of course, be adjusted any way we want by using parentheses.

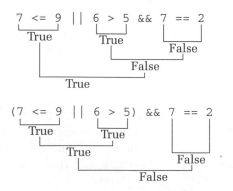

The **not operator** (!) is a logical operator, but it is also unary, acting on only one expression. In precedence and associativity, it falls in with the other unary operators. The logical *not* operator makes what was true false, and what was false true.

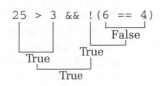

$$25 > 3 \; \&\& \; !(6 == 4)$$

String Comparisons

HEADS UP!

String comparisons are by the numeric values of the character codes.

Often we must compare two strings to see which is greater. But how do we know whether *Murgatroyd* is greater than *Stella*? Let us examine how C++ makes the comparison. A string is a set of characters, and each character value is nothing more than a number—the numeric value of its ASCII (or EBCDIC) code. C++ will compare these individual values character by character, beginning with the first character position in each string and moving toward the end. C++ makes the greater-than, less-than decision the first time it finds a difference in the character position it is currently comparing. If C++ gets to the end of both strings and finds no difference, the strings must be equal.

HEADS UP!

The number of characters in strings to be compared is irrelevant.

Murgatroyd and *Stella* are easy. C++ compares an *M* (ASCII 77) with an *S* (ASCII 83). The *S* is greater, so *Stella* is greater than *Murgatroyd*. Notice that the number of characters in each string is not significant. The first difference ends the comparison.

How about *Aaron* and *Aardvark*? The first three character positions in each string are the same, but in the fourth position are *o* and *d*. The *o* (ASCII 111) is greater than the *d* (ASCII 100), so *Aaron* is greater than *Aardvark*. But *aardvark* is greater than *Aaron* because, in the first character position, *a* (97) is greater than *A* (65). *Bytes* is greater than *Byte* because the *s* in *Bytes* is greater than the null at the end of *Byte*.

HEADS UP!

In ASCII, lowercase characters are greater than uppercase characters.

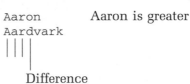

```
Aaron            Aaron is greater
Aardvark
| | | |
      Difference
```

YOUR TURN 4–2

1. What is the typical general form of a comparison? *relate 1 value to another*
2. Name the two classes of comparison operators and list the members of each class. Which class has a higher precedence?

   2) RELATION <, >, <=, >= HIGHER; EQUALITY !=, ==
3. What are the three logical operators and what is their precedence?

   3) not (!) and (&&) or (||)
4. What determines the greater of two characters? *Diff. in ASCII #*
5. How are strings compared? *DIFF IN ASCII # (by first diff found)*

STATEMENT BLOCKS

Modularity is enhanced by allowing statements to be grouped into **blocks**. Any time a statement is called for in a program, you can provide either a single statement or a block of statements. The block begins with an open brace ({) and ends with a close brace (}). Notice that the statements in any `main()` function, such as the one in Program 4–1, are within a block. We will see that C++'s control structures call for a statement within the structure. Very often this statement will really be a block of statements enclosed in braces.

The compiler doesn't care where it finds the braces but you, being human and more visually oriented, will want to place them carefully. In this book the open brace is at the same indent level as the statement or definition of which it is a part; the statements within the block are indented one level further; and the close brace is directly below (in the same column as) the open brace. This format has three advantages:

1. The outline is easy to see because of the indentation.
2. It's hard to forget the close brace because of its alignment with the open brace.
3. Many other C++ programmers follow the same pattern.

THE `if` STATEMENT

The selection structure in C++ is implemented by the `if` statement, which has this general form:

```
if (condition) statement;
```

We can, and usually do, substitute a block of statements for the single *statement* in the general form, giving us the more common form

```
if (condition)
{   statement;
    statement;
      . . .
}
```

The *condition* in the `if` statement is as we have described earlier and, of course, will evaluate as either true or false. If the *condition* is true, the statements within the block will be executed; otherwise, they won't. Notice that the condition is enclosed in parentheses, and there is no semicolon after the condition. To put a semicolon there would end the entire structure at that point.

In our pseudocode the selection structure began with the *if* key word and ended when the indent level came back to that of the *if*. In C++ it begins with the same key word, `if`, and ends at the end of the single statement or at the closing brace at the end of the block of statements. Although C++ will not care, our indenting should match that which we set up for our pseudocode.

Let's look at a simple example, a guessing game. In Program 4–1 we will try to guess a value that was written into the program.

In the first execution, the value of *guess* is equal to 10 (the condition was true), so the statement inside the `if` structure is executed. In the second execution, *guess* is not 10 (the condition was false), so the statement in the structure is skipped.

Program 4–1

```
#include <iostream>                            // How about that .h?
using namespace std;                 // Don't use it if you don't need it

const int secret = 10;

int main(void)
{  int guess;

   cout << "What's your guess? ";
   cin >> guess;
   if (guess == secret)                            // Secret value
      cout << "You guessed that ";
   cout << "the secret number was " << secret << endl;
   return 0;
}
```

Outputs

```
What's your guess? 10
You guessed that the secret number was 10.

What's your guess? 42
the secret number was 10.
```

Using = when you mean ==.

Be careful to notice that the symbol for equality is ==, two equal signs. A single equal sign is the assignment operator. If we change the `if` statement to

```
    if (guess = secret)
```

the output becomes

```
What's your guess? 8395
You guessed that the secret number was 10.
```

NUTS'N **BOLTS**

WHAT'S TRUE AND WHAT'S FALSE?

Could you lie to a computer? Easily. The computer, being a nonthinking machine, has no idea what is true or false, good or bad, nice or nasty. Our human concepts of true and false are translated into strictly numeric terms for the computer. In C++ anything that evaluates to true is assigned the value one; false is assigned zero. The statement

```
cout << (6 == 6) << " " << (3 > 9) << endl;
```

would produce

```
1 0
```

on the screen.

When trying to evaluate true versus false, C++ interprets any nonzero value as true and zero as false. The value of

```
7 > 3 && 14
```

is true, or one.

Program 4–2

```
#include <iostream>
#include <iomanip>
using namespace std;

int main(void)
{   float weight, price = 0.2;

    cout << "Enter weight of apple: ";
    cin >> weight;
    cout << "Eve's ";
    if (weight > 10)
    {   cout << "Premium ";
        price = price + 0.1;
    }
    cout << setiosflags(ios::fixed) << setprecision(2);
    cout << "Apple. $" << price << "." << endl;
    return 0;
}
```

Output

```
Enter weight of apple: 11.3
Eve's Premium Apple. $0.30.
```

Output

```
Enter weight of apple: 7.8
Eve's Apple. $0.20.
```

It did not work as we expected, because 10 (the value of *secret*) was assigned to *guess*, which became the value of the test expression `guess = secret`. C++ interprets anything nonzero as true (see the *Nuts 'n' Bolts* box *What's True and What's False?*), so it executed the statement inside the structure.

Let's look at an example that doesn't involve equality. Eve's Apple Company has an automatic apple scale that weighs each apple and labels it accordingly. Unfortunately, the input interface is broken, so an operator has to type the weights into a keyboard. Apples are normally priced at 20 cents each, but if one weighs more than 10 ounces, it is a premium apple and worth another 10 cents. The program outline is as follows:

> Establish base price
> Enter weight
> Print "Eve's"
> if weight > 10
>   Print "Premium"
>   Add premium to price
> Print "Apple" and price

Program 4–2 translates this pseudocode into C++.

The `else` Clause

A more complete version of the `if` statement has statements in both the true and false branches. The false branch begins with an **else** clause:

```
if (condition) statement; else statement;
```

Program 4–3

```cpp
#include <iostream>
#include <iomanip>
using namespace std;

int main(void)
{   float weight, price = 0.2;

    cout << "Enter weight of apple: ";
    cin >> weight;
    cout << "Eve's ";
    if (weight > 10)
    {   cout << "Premium ";
        price = price + 0.1;
    }
    else
    {   cout << "Juicy ";
    }
    cout << setiosflags(ios::fixed) << setprecision(2);
    cout << "Apple. $" << price << "." << endl;
    return 0;
}
```

Output

```
Enter weight of apple: 9.2
Eve's Juicy Apple. $0.20.
```

Output

```
Enter weight of apple: 10.1
Eve's Premium Apple. $0.30.
```

---

or, more commonly,

```
if (condition)
{   statement;
    statement;
        . . .
}
else
{   statement;
    statement;
        . . .
}
```

The Eve people don't want to call their apples just *Eve's Apples* even if they are only normal apples, so an apple weighing 10 ounces or less will be called an *Eve's Juicy Apple*. Our change in design is evident in Program 4–3.

Bowing to market pressures, the Eve people now have set up four grades of apples.

Weight	> 10	> 8 but <= 10	> 6 but <= 8	<= 6
Grade	Premium	Juicy	Snack	Cooking
Price	.30	.20	.15	.10

Premium Apples still weigh more than 10 ounces and cost an extra 10 cents. *Juicy Apples* are the normal grade at a normal price, but they have to

Program 4–4

```cpp
#include <iostream>
#include <iomanip>
using namespace std;

int main(void)
{   float weight, price = 0.2;

    cout << "Enter weight of apple: ";
    cin >> weight;
    cout << "Eve's ";
    if (weight > 10)
    {   cout << "Premium ";
        price = price + 0.1;
    }
    else
    {   if (weight > 8)                               // Brace necessary?
        {   cout << "Juicy ";
        }
        else
        {   if (weight > 6)                           // Brace necessary?
            {   cout << "Snack ";
                price = price - 0.05;
            }
            else
            {   cout << "Cooking ";
                price = price - 0.1;
            }
        }                                             // Brace necessary?
    }                                                 // Brace necessary?
    cout << setiosflags(ios::fixed) << setprecision(2);
    cout << "Apple. $" << price << "." << endl;
    return 0;
}
```

Outputs

```
Enter weight of apple: 12
Eve's Premium Apple. $0.30.

Enter weight of apple: 9.2
Eve's Juicy Apple. $0.20.
```

Outputs

```
Enter weight of apple: 7.5
Eve's Snack Apple. $0.15.

Enter weight of apple: 5.9
Eve's Cooking Apple. $0.10.
```

weigh more than 8 ounces. Those weighing more than 6 ounces but up to 8 are called *Snack Apples* and cost 5 cents less. All others are *Cooking Apples* and sell for 10 cents less. This leaves us with four branches to deal with, but our selection structure only has two.

The solution is to branch one of the branches. In the Eve case, if the weight is less than 10 ounces, our revised Program 4–4 tests to see if it is more than 8. The first else clause contains a complete selection structure with two branches and the condition weight > 8. The else clause within that selection structure also contains a complete selection structure with two branches and the condition weight > 6.

To be in the *Juicy* category, apples had to weigh more than 8 ounces, but less than or equal to 10 ounces. Why didn't we write that `if` statement as in the following segment?

```
if (weight > 10)
{   cout << "Premium ";
    price = price + 0.1;
}
else
{   if (weight > 8 && weight <= 10)
    {   cout << "Juicy ";
    }
```

We could have, but the test for less than or equal to 10 would have been wasted. If the weight was not less than or equal to 10, the program would execute the statements in the true branch just below `if (weight > 10)`, jump to the end of that selection structure, and never reach the `else` branch and our test.

The Dangling `else`

Let us modify the situation a bit to illustrate a potential problem: the "dangling `else`." For this case, Eve has three categories: apples less than 6 ounces are too small; apples greater than 10 ounces are labeled *Premium*; and those in between have no special label. Rewriting the middle of Program 4–4 this way:

```
if (weight >= 6)
    if (weight > 10)
        cout << "Premium ";
else
    cout << "Apple is too small.";
```

does not work correctly. Apples between 6 and 10 ounces are called *too small* and those less than 6 ounces are unlabeled.

Why? The code looks good; the indenting is nicely structured.

Remember, indenting means nothing to C++. Its rules say that an `else` is attached to the nearest open `if`. The way C++ sees it, the code is structured this way:

```
if (weight >= 6)
    if (weight > 10)
        cout << "Premium ";
    else
        cout << "Apple is too small.";
```

The solution is to enclose the second `if` in braces, closing it, so that the `else` matches the first `if`.

```
if (weight >= 6)
{   if (weight > 10)
        cout << "Premium ";
}
else
    cout << "Apple is too small.";
```

The `else if` Construct

If you examine the sets of braces in Program 4–4 with the comments `//`
`Brace necessary?` beside them you will see that these brace sets are not
really necessary. Each of them encloses the material within an `else` clause,
but that material in each case consists only of an `if` statement. Granted,
the `if` statements contain statements within their clauses, but still they
are single `if` statements. This section of the program could be rewritten:

```
if (weight > 10)
{  cout << "Premium ";
   price = price + 0.1;
}
else
    if (weight > 8)                          // No brace necessary before if
    {  cout << "Juicy ";
    }
    else
        if (weight > 6)                      // No brace necessary before if
        {  cout << "Snack ";
           price = price - 0.05;
        }
        else
        {  cout << "Cooking ";
           price = price - 0.1;
        }
```

Branching of `else` clauses with `if` statements is such a common occurrence that the `else` followed by the `if` is often written on one line
almost as if it were one key word, **`else if`**. It is not, but the indenting that
results outlines a very clear multibranch structure that is actually made of
multiple two-branch `if else` statements. This section could be rewritten
as

```
if (weight > 10)
{  cout << "Premium ";
   price = price + 0.1;
}
else if (weight > 8)
{  cout << "Juicy ";                                    // Brace necessary?
}                                                       // Brace necessary?
else if (weight > 6)
{  cout << "Snack ";
   price = price - 0.05;
}
else
{  cout << "Cooking ";
   price = price - 0.1;
}
```

You might also have noticed that the set of braces commented is not
necessary either. There is only one statement, `cout << "Juicy ";`, within
them. These braces could be eliminated, but to maintain consistency, we
probably should retain them.

What if we had left out some of the other braces? For example, those
after `else`?

```
      else
         cout << "Cooking ";
         price = price - 0.1;
```

It looks fine because of our nice neat indenting. However, C++ will see it this way:

```
      else
         cout << "Cooking ";
      price = price - 0.1;
```

TRAP

Program code that is indented properly but lacks proper punctuation.

Since there are no braces, the else branch ends with the semicolon at the end of cout << "Cooking ";, and price = price - 0.1; will execute after the entire if, else if, else structure is finished, subtracting 10 cents from the prices of *all* the apples.

Let's also compare our nested ifs, using the else if construct, with sequential ifs—one if after another. As an example, let us look at each with *weight* equal to 12.

Nested

```
if (weight > 10)
{  cout <<"Premium ";
}
else if (weight > 8)
{  cout <<"Juicy ";
}
else if (weight > 6)
{  cout <<"Snack ";
}
cout <<"Apple." << endl;
```

Output

```
 Premium Apple.
```

Sequential

```
if (weight > 10)
{  cout <<"Premium ";
}
if (weight > 8)
{  cout <<"Juicy ";
}
if (weight > 6)
{  cout <<"Snack ";
}
cout <<"Apple." << endl;
```

Output

```
Premium Juicy Snack Apple.
```

TRAP

Using sequential ifs when you need nested ifs.

In both cases the first test, weight > 10, was true. Using the nested else ifs, the program printed *Premium*, and then jumped beyond the end of the structure and printed *Apple*. Using the sequential ifs, the program did exactly the same thing, but the end of the structure, since there was no else, came immediately after printing *Premium*, and the next statement to execute was if (weight > 8). This test was also true, so it

NUTS'N BOLTS

MORE ABOUT TRUTH

Remembering that a zero value is interpreted as false and that anything nonzero is true, we might have a program segment like this:

```
cout << "How many extra? ";
cin >> extra;
if (extra)
    cout << "There are " << extra << " extra." << endl;
[and so forth]
```

If *extra* is anything but zero the condition will be true, and the cout will be executed.

Program 4–5

```cpp
#include <iostream>
#include <string>
using namespace std;

int main(void)
{  string name;

   cout << "Who are you? ";
   cin >> name;
   if (name >= "L" && name < "M")
      cout << "You don't have to wait in line." << endl;
   else if (name < "Ho")
      cout << "Line one, please." << endl;
   else if (name < "P")
      cout << "Line two, please." << endl;
   else
      cout << "Line three, please." << endl;
   return 0;
}
```

Outputs

```
Who are you? Homer
Line two, please.

Who are you? Zerch
Line three, please.

Who are you? Lawlor
You don't have to wait in line.
```

---

printed *Juicy*, and moved to `if (weight > 6)`, which was also true, so it printed *Snack*, and finally *Apple*.

Let us apply the `if` and `else` statements to strings. As people come into the building, they type their names into a computer and the computer tells them in which line to stand. We have no idea why they are standing in line. It seems to be a favorite human pastime.

Those whose names begin with *A* up to but not including *Ho* stand in line one; *Ho* through *O* stand in line two; and the rest in line three. If their name begins with *L*, they do not have to wait in line. Program 4–5 shows the code.

YOUR TURN 4–3

1. How do we put more than one statement inside an `if` branch? { } braces
2. Must a selection structure have an `else` branch? NO, if false is to take no action.
3. What is the difference between = and ==? =: ~~comparison~~ ass. ==comparison.
4. Are braces always required around true and false branches? yes, my if more than 1 statement
5. Is there an `else if` key word? NO
6. What is the difference between nested `ifs` using the `else if` construct and sequential `ifs`? 1 struc. only 1 may exe. sep. many may execute

THE switch STATEMENT

The C++ language includes a multibranch alternative to the `if` statement called the **switch** statement. It has some severe limitations, but within these limitations it can be very handy.

```
switch (integralExpression) {statementBlock}
```

The *statementBlock* is a number of statements within the various branches. The beginnings of the branches are distinguished by case identifiers, all beginning with the key word **case**.

```
case integralValue:
```

At the end of each of the branches is a **break** statement, which causes an immediate jump to the statement following a `switch` structure; in other words, to the statement beyond the closing `switch` structure brace.

```
switch (integralExpression)
{   case integralValue:
        statement;
        statement;
          . . .
        break;
    case integralValue:
        statement;
        statement;
          . . .
        break;
    case  as many as are necessary:
          . . .
        break;
    default:
        statement;
        statement;
          . . .
}
```

A simple example is shown in Program 4–6.

The *integralExpression* following the `switch` key word must evaluate to some integral data type, `char` or `int`; floating-point results are not allowed. The value of the expression becomes a case value to be matched to the possible `case` identifiers within the statement block following the `switch`. For example, if the *integralExpression* evaluates to 6, the `switch` looks for `case 6:`.

Each of the `cases` within the block following `switch` has an *integralValue*, which, along with `case` and a following colon, becomes the identifier. For example, two of the cases might be `case 9:` and `case 6:`. The `switch` causes the program to jump directly to the matching identifier; in other words, the next code to be executed will be that immediately following the identifier. In the example, that would be the code following `case 6:`. If there are other `cases` in the execution path, they are ignored.

If there is no matching label, the jump is to the **default** label. The default label is not absolutely necessary and, if it appears, may be in any

HEADS UP!

switches can use only integral expressions.

HEADS UP!

A case must have an integral value; no expressions allowed.

Program 4–6

```cpp
#include <iostream>
using namespace std;

int main(void)
{   int number;

    cout << "Enter a number and see if I am programmed"
         << " to print out two times it: ";
    cin >> number;
    switch (number * 2)
    {   case 6:
            cout << "Six." << endl;              // No braces are necessary for
            break;                               // individual branches in switch
        case 4:
            cout << "Four." << endl;
            break;
        case 12:
            cout << "Twelve." << endl;
            break;
        case 8:
        case 10:
            cout << "Either eight or ten." << endl;
            break;
        default:
            cout << "I don't know that one." << endl;
    }
    return 0;
}
```

Outputs

```
Enter a number and see if I am programmed to print out two times it: 3
Six.

Enter a number and see if I am programmed to print out two times it: 5
Either eight or ten.

Enter a number and see if I am programmed to print out two times it: 1
I don't know that one.
```

HEADS UP!

Make default the last branch.

HEADS UP!

Case identifiers in the normal flow of execution are ignored.

position within the block, but it may appear only once. In practice, there is usually a default label, and it is typically the last one. The last branch, default or otherwise, does not need a break statement because execution would continue out of the switch structure anyway.

In Program 4–7, the Eve Company has modified its apple-labeling program so that the person at the keyboard inputs a character—*P, J, S,* or any other letter—indicating the grade, and the program then prints the name and price.

A jump to a case identifier continues execution from that point on. Subsequent case identifiers in the code are ignored. The Execution Chart for an input of *J* (uppercase) shows the execution pattern. In our example, to allow for either upper- or lowercase letters in the input, two cases are

Program 4–7

```cpp
      #include <iostream>
      #include <iomanip>
      using namespace std;

      int main(void)
      {  float price;
         char grade;

         cout << "Enter grade of apple: ";
   1     cin >> grade;
   2     cout << "Eve's ";
   3     switch (grade)
   4     {  case 'P':
   5        case 'p':
   6            price = 0.3;
   7            cout << "Premium ";
   8            break;
   9        case 'J':
  10        case 'j':
  11            price = 0.2;
  12            cout << "Juicy ";
  13            break;
  14        case 'S':
  15        case 's':
  16            price = 0.15;
  17            cout << "Snack ";
  18            break;
  19        default:
  20            price = 0.1;
  21            cout << "Cooking ";
         }
  22     cout << setiosflags(ios::fixed) << setprecision(2);
  23     cout << "Apple. $" << price << "." << endl;
         return 0;
      }
```

Outputs

```
Enter grade of apple: p
Eve's Premium Apple. $0.30.

Enter grade of apple: s
Eve's Snack Apple. $0.15.

Enter grade of apple: J
Eve's Juicy Apple. $0.20.

Enter grade of apple: Q
Eve's Cooking Apple. $0.10.
```

EXECUTION CHART			
Line	**Explanation**	*price*	*grade*
1	Input apple grade.	??	J
2	Print first part of label.	??	J
3	Look for `case 'J':`.	??	J
9	Found identifier.	??	J
10	Ignore case identifier.	??	J
11	Assign *price*.	.2	J
12	Print "Juicy ".	.2	J
13	Continue execution beyond `switch` block.	.2	J
22	Adjust for dollars-and-cents format.	.2	J
23	Print last part of label including *price*.	.2	J

Program 4–8

```
     #include <iostream>
     #include <iomanip>
     using namespace std;

     int main(void)
     {  float price;
        char grade;

        cout << "Enter grade of apple: ";
1    cin >> grade;
2    cout << "Eve's ";
3    switch (grade)
4    {  case 'P':
5       case 'p':
6          price = 0.3;
7          cout << "Premium ";
8       case 'J':
9       case 'j':
10         price = 0.2;
11         cout << "Juicy ";
12      case 'S':
13      case 's':
14         price = 0.15;
15         cout << "Snack ";
16      default:
17         price = 0.1;
18         cout << "Cooking ";
     }
19   cout << setiosflags(ios::fixed) << setprecision(2);
20   cout << "Apple. $" << price << "." << endl;
     return 0;
     }
```

Outputs

```
Enter grade of apple: p
Eve's Premium Juicy Snack Cooking Apple. $0.10.

Enter grade of apple: P
Eve's Premium Juicy Snack Cooking Apple. $0.10.

Enter grade of apple: J
Eve's Juicy Snack Cooking Apple. $0.10.

Enter grade of apple: s
Eve's Snack Cooking Apple. $0.10.

Enter grade of apple: F
Eve's Cooking Apple. $0.10.
```

put together. If the value of grade is *j*, execution will continue from case 'j':. If grade is *J*, execution will continue from case 'J':, passing right by case 'j':.

Line	Explanation	price	grade
1	Input apple grade.	??	J
2	Print first part of label.	??	J
3	Look for `case 'J':`.	??	J
8	Found identifier.	??	J
9	Ignore case identifier.	??	J
10	Assign *price*.	.2	J
11	Print "Juicy ".	.2	J
12	Ignore case identifier.	.2	J
13	Ignore case identifier.	.2	J
14	Assign *price*.	.15	J
15	Print "Snack ".	.15	J
16	Ignore default identifier.	.15	J
17	Assign *price*.	.1	J
18	Print "Cooking ".	.1	J
19	Adjust for dollars-and-cents format.	.2	J
20	Print last part of label including *price*.	.1	J

EXECUTION CHART

As stated in Chapter 2, character values such as `'P'` are integral numeric values—the ASCII codes for those characters. The program would have run the same had we substituted `case 80:`, using the ASCII value for *P*, instead of `case 'P':`, but we would have sacrificed readability.

A little review of punctuation is in order here. Notice that the *integralExpression* following `switch` is enclosed in parentheses, and that there is no semicolon after the statement. All the statements within the following structure are contained within one set of braces. There need not be separate sets of braces in each branch, although there certainly could be if the structure warranted it. Each case identifier is followed by a colon, which tells C++ that it is a case identifier.

The `break` statements at the end of each `switch` branch are not necessary for C++, but they are necessary for the use of `switch` as a multibranch structure. If we left out the `breaks`, execution would continue from whichever `case` matched through all the rest of the statements in the `switch` structure, as in Program 4–8. Again, we will follow the execution through with a *J* input.

All the apples are priced at 10 cents, even the *Eve's Premium Juicy Snack Cooking Apples*.

TRAP

Using the wrong punctuation in a `switch` structure.

TRAP

Leaving out the `breaks`.

YOUR TURN 4–4

1. What are the major limitations of the switch statement? *Can only compare value of int statement to int values.*
2. After the switch jumps to a particular case, what happens if the program encounters another case? *further case statements ignored.*
3. What is the purpose of a break statement in a multibranch structure using switch? *imm. jump to statement following break statement*
4. Is a default statement necessary? *No, if not to take action.*

PUTTING IT TOGETHER

To tie together what you have learned here, let us consider a problem for a warehouse for computer products. Each computer that comes into the warehouse has a product code that tells something about that particular machine—where it was made, the type of processor, the disk capacity, and the model name. Deciphering these product codes is cumbersome for the warehouse people. They would like us to use the computer to make their jobs easier.

TASK

Our task is to develop a program that allows a warehouse employee to type in a code, and have the computer display the product characteristics.

ANALYSIS

The program should accept input of a product code and display the product's characteristics in a format similar to the following:

```
Enter product code: 4J540Tig
Made in Japan
Processor: 486
Disk: 540 MB
Model: Tiger
```

If the product code doesn't make sense, because of an error in input perhaps, the program should either reject the entire product code or, when possible, decipher anything it can while printing error indications for anything it cannot decipher. A valid product code has a country code consisting of an uppercase alpha character. If that isn't present, the program should print an error message and quit.

The product characteristics in their positions in the product code and the meanings of the characters in those positions are in Table 4–2.

TABLE 4–2		
Characteristic	**Value**	**Translation**
Processor	3	386
	4	486
	5	Pentium
Country	U or A	United States
	J	Japan
	S	Singapore
	K	Korea
Disk	Number	Capacity in GB for Pentiums, MB for others
Model	Tig	Tiger
	Ost	Ostrich
	Pus	Pussycat

The process consists of two main objects in a sequence:

```
Input product code
React to product code
```

The second object does one of two things: it prints an error message or it deciphers the product code. The overall structure of this second object, then, is a selection.

```
Input product code
if country code alpha                    [React to product code]
    Print error message
else
    Decipher code
```

Deciphering the code is a bit more complicated; there are four characteristics of the code to be deciphered in sequence. Expanding that section of the pseudocode, we have:

```
Input product code
if country code not alpha                [React to product code]
    Print error message
else
    [Decipher code]
        Type of Processor
        Country of origin
        Disk capacity
        Model name
```

Deciphering each of the characteristics, except for the disk capacity, follows the same pattern. The character(s) for that characteristic are matched with valid possibilities and the appropriate translation is printed out—multibranch selections. To decipher the disk capacity we check the processor type and multiply the number by 1,000 (for megabytes instead of kilobytes) if the processor is a Pentium—a simple selection.

```
if Pentium processor            [Disk capacity]
    Multiply disk capacity by 1000
```

OBJECT SUMMARY		
Object Name	**Behavior**	**Properties**
Code	Input product code	processor (pro) country (pro) disk (pro) model (pro)
React	Check alpha country code	country (req)
Error	Print error message	
Decipher	Decipher code	
Processor	Determine type of processor	processor (req)
Country	Determine country of origin	country (req)
Disk	Determine disk capacity	disk (req)
Model	Determine model	model (req)

The characteristics in the product code are determined by the positions of the characters in the code. We must have our program look for specific delimiters (separators) and divide the code accordingly. We can use the cin object to separate these character sets and assign them to appropriate variables. Let's modify Table 4–2, creating Table 4–3, to identify the delimiter for each characteristic, the data type of each, and the variable to which we will assign the value.

TABLE 4–3

Characteristic	Delimiter	Data Type	Variable
Processor	Noninteger character (the alpha country code)	int	*processor*
Country	None—only single character long	char	*country*
Disk	Noninteger character (the model code)	float	*disk*
Model	Newline (noninteger)	string	*model*

Since the variables will be used in more than one object, they are declared before any of the objects.

The results are shown in Program 4–9.

TEST

The test involves running many sample codes, being sure that we see that all valid codes work correctly and that all invalid codes are rejected. The single output shown here is one of the tests, the one shown in the Execution Chart. In making your own tests you will probably find any number of ways for a sloppy input operator to mess up the program. Later we will look at some techniques for catching such errors before the program crashes.

Program 4–9

```
    #include <iostream>
    #include <string>
    using namespace std;

    int main(void)
    {   char country;
        int processor;
        float disk;
        string model;

        //----------------------------------------------- Input Product Code
        cout << "Enter product code: ";
1       cin >> processor >> country >> disk >> model;

        //----------------------------------------------- React to Product Code
2       if (country < 'A' || country > 'Z')              // Check for alpha country
3           cout << "    Invalid product code.\n"; //--------------------- Error
```
(Continued)

Program 4–9 *(Continued)*

```
              else
              {  //------------------------------------------------------- Decipher Code
                   //---------------------------------------------------- Type of Processor
                   cout << "Processor: ";
4                  switch (processor)
5                  {  case 3:
6                        cout << "386\n";
7                        break;
8                     case 4:
9                        cout << "486\n";
10                       break;
11                    case 5:
12                       cout << "Pentium\n";
13                       break;
14                    default:
15                       cout << "<Invalid processor>\n";
                   }
                   //---------------------------------------------- Country of Origin
                   cout << "Made in ";
16                 switch (country)
17                 {  case 'U':                    // Both U and A (America) mean U.S.
18                    case 'A':
19                       cout << "United States\n";
20                       break;
21                    case 'J':
22                       cout << "Japan\n";
23                       break;
24                    case 'S':
25                       cout << "Singapore\n";
26                       break;
27                    case 'K':
28                       cout << "Korea\n";
29                       break;
30                    default:
31                       cout << "<Country invalid>\n";
                   }
                   //---------------------------------------------------- Disk Capacity
32                 if (processor == 5)
33                    disk = disk * 1000;
34                 cout << "Disk: " << disk << " MB\n";

                   //---------------------------------------------------- Model Name
                   cout << "Model: ";
35                 if (model == "Tig")
36                    cout << "Tiger" << endl;
37                 else if (model == "Ost")
38                    cout << "Ostrich" << endl;
39                 else if (model == "Pus")
40                    cout << "Pussycat" << endl;
41                 else
42                    cout << "<Invalid model>" << endl;
              }
           return 0;
           }
```

Output

```
Enter product code: 5S3.6Pus
Processor: Pentium
Made in Singapore
Disk: 3600 MB
Model: Pussycat
```

EXECUTION CHART

Line	Explanation	Input Stream	*processor*	*country*	*disk*	*model*
1	Enter line at keyboard.	5S3.6Pus\n	??	??	??	??
	Convert to inappropriate `int` character.	S3.6Pus\n	5	??	??	??
	Convert one character to `char`.	3.6Pus\n	5	S	??	??
	Convert to inappropriate `float` character.	Pus\n	5	S	3.6	??
	Skip space and convert to newline.	\n	5	S	3.6	Pus
2	See if *country* out of range *A–Z*. It isn't.	\n	5	S	3.6	Pus
4	Look for `case 5:`. Find it in line 11.	\n	5	S	3.6	Pus
12	Display *Pentium*.	\n	5	S	3.6	Pus
13	Jump beyond end of `switch` structure.	\n	5	S	3.6	Pus
16	Look for `case S:`. Find it in line 24.	\n	5	S	3.6	Pus
25	Display *Singapore*.	\n	5	S	3.6	Pus
26	Jump beyond end of `switch` structure.	\n	5	S	3.6	Pus
32	*processor* equals 5.	\n	5	S	3.6	Pus
33	Adjust *disk*.	\n	5	S	3600	Pus
34	Display *disk* specs.	\n	5	S	3600	Pus
35	See if *model* equals *Tig*. It doesn't.	\n	5	S	3600	Pus
37	See if *model* equals *Ost*. It doesn't.	\n	5	S	3600	Pus
39	See if *model* equals *Pus*. It does.	\n	5	S	3600	Pus
43	Display *Pussycat*.	\n	5	S	3600	Pus

SUMMARY

- **KEY TERMS** (in order of appearance)

Structured programming	Relational operator
Structure	Equality operator
Pseudocode	Logical operator
Sequence structure	*And* operator
Branch	*Or* operator
Selection structure	*Not* operator
Nest	Block
Condition	`else if` construct

- **NEW STATEMENTS** (in order of appearance)

```
if (condition) statement;
if (condition) statement; else statement;
switch (integralExpression) {statementBlock}
case integralValue:
break
default:
```

- **CONCEPT REVIEW**

- **Structured programming** simplifies the programming process by limiting programs to combinations of only three control **structures**. Structured programs are often designed using a slightly more formalized **pseudocode**.

- The **sequence structure**, one operation after another, is the simplest of the structures.

- The **selection structure** contains two **branches**. Which branch the execution takes depends on a **condition** consisting of one or more comparisons. Comparisons are made of expressions connected by **relational operators** or **equality operators**.

- Branches may contain any statement or **block** of statements, including other structures, in which case the structures are said to be **nested**.

- Comparisons can be tied together with the **logical operators and** and **or**. The **not operator** is a unary operator that makes what was true false, and vice versa.

- Strings are compared by looking at the numeric values of the character codes that make up the string. The comparison starts at the first character position in each string and continues, position by position, until a difference is found. That difference determines which string is greater.

- A single statement can always be replaced by a statement **block**, a set of statements enclosed in braces.

- The `if` statement implements the selection structure. It may contain only one true branch, in which case the false branch is to do nothing; or it may have an `else` clause where the false branch is stated.

- To form a multibranch structure, one branch of an `if else` statement may contain another complete `if else` statement. It is so common to branch the `else` branch of the selection structure that most programmers treat the **else if** construct as a single multibranch structure.

- The `switch` statement sets up a more limited multibranch structure by allowing the program to jump to any of a number of **case** identifiers. The integral expression following `switch` is evaluated, and C++ searches for a corresponding value following any number of `case` statements. If it finds no match it looks for a **default** label. Execution resumes at the appropriate `case` or `default`. Subsequent `case`s are ignored.

- A **break** statement causes the execution to transfer to the statement following the end of the `switch` structure. These `break`s are typically used to separate the `switch` structure into individual branches.

- Any program may be built from only three basic structures.
- Design your program carefully before writing the code.
- To make pseudocode useful, keep it simple.
- The sequence is the simplest structure.
- A program follows only one of the two branches.
- Be sure your branching structures come back to the same path.
- Indenting is extremely important.
- Style is just as important in pseudocode as in the actual program.
- Conditions are either true or false; there are no maybes.
- Comparisons compare values.
- = is not ==.
- Parentheses can be added—and are encouraged—to increase readability.
- String comparisons are by the numeric values of the character codes.
- The number of characters in strings to be compared is irrelevant.
- In ASCII, lowercase characters are greater than uppercase characters.
- Indenting means something to us, but not to C++.
- An entire `if else` structure is considered one statement.
- `else if`, although not a key word, is a common construct.
- Braces may make a program more readable.
- `switch`es can use only integral expressions.
- A `case` must have an integral value; no expressions allowed.
- Make `default` the last branch.
- Case identifiers in the normal flow of execution are ignored.

• TRAPS: COMMON PROGRAMMING ERRORS

- Leaving out the closing brace in a block.
- Leaving the parentheses off the condition.
- A semicolon after the condition in an `if`.
- Using = when you mean ==.
- Program code that is indented properly but lacks proper punctuation.
- Using sequential `if`s when you need nested `if`s.
- Using the wrong punctuation in a `switch` structure.
- Leaving out the `break`s.

• YOUR TURN ANSWERS

• 4–1

1. Structured programming simplifies the programming process by building even complicated programs of combinations of three simple patterns.

2. Structures may be combined in a program in any way needed to do the job.

3. Pseudocode is a language only slightly more formal than a plain-English outline that is used to represent a structured program.

4. Indenting in pseudocode shows the structure of a program by clearly outlining which structures are within which, and which follow which.

5. Our previous programs (before this chapter) have all followed the sequence structure.

6. Branches are different paths a program might take according to some conditions.

7. The selection structure implements branching.

8. The true branch begins at the line following (and indented within) the *if* key word and condition; it ends before the *else* key word or at the end of the structure if there is no *else*. The false branch begins at the line following (and is indented within) the *else* key word and ends at the end of the structure. The end of the structure is shown when the indent level returns to that of the *if* and *else* key words.

9. The two principles of top-down modular structured programming are that a structure should have only one entry point and one exit point, and structures must be properly and completely nested.

● 4–2

1. A comparison is usually two expressions separated by some comparison operator.

2. Of the two classes of comparison operators, relational operators, >, <, >=, and <=, are higher in precedence than equality operators, == and !=.

3. The logical operators, in order of precedence, are *not* (!), *and* (&&), and *or* (||).

4. The greater of two characters is the one whose ASCII code has the higher numeric value.

5. Strings are compared, character by character, until a difference is found. If none is found, the strings are equal.

● 4–3

1. We put more than one statement inside an `if` branch by enclosing the statements within braces.

2. A selection does not have to have an `else` branch if the false branch is to take no action.

3. The = operator makes an assignment; the == operator makes a comparison.

4. Braces are required only if there is more than one statement in the branch.

5. There is no `else if` key word, but the two key words are often used together to create multibranch structures.

6. The entire set of nested `if`s is one structure; if it is set up using `else if`, only one branch will execute. Sequential `if`s are separate structures, and many may execute.

1. The `switch` is limited in that it can only compare the value of an integral expression to a number of integral values.

2. If the program encounters another `case` after the `switch` jumps to a given `case`, further `case` statements are ignored.

3. The `break` statement used at the ends of branches effectively separates the branches by sending execution to the end of the `switch` structure.

4. A `default` statement is not necessary if the `default` branch is to take no action.

EXERCISES

1. In mathematics we might state a range for x as $1 < x < 5$. Show how we should write the following range expressions in C++.

   a. $1 < x < 5$ b. $16 \geq x \geq -7$

   c. $22.6 \geq x > 12.03$ d. $36 < x \leq y < 115$

2. Correct the errors in the following program segment:

```
if y > 25
    x = 2;
    cout << "x is " << x << endl;
else
    y = 19
```

3. Write the condition that is true if $6 \leq x \leq 25$ or $x > 100$.

4. If $a = 1$, $b = 2$, and $c = 3$, are the following conditions true or false?

```
a. a >= c - b
b. b / 2 == a || c < 3
c. b < c -2 || a * 3 >= c && b > a
d. 5 || !b && c
```

5. Write a short program to test your answers to Exercise 4.

6. Which in the following sets of strings is greater?

   a. *Windows* or *Unix*   b. *Abigail* or *About*

   c. *Phred* or *fred*   d. *%$*&!?/* or *&#$%*

7. Write a short program to test your answers to Exercise 6.

8. The following code segment compiles without error, but it prints *That's it* no matter what the value of x is. What's wrong? Fix it.

```
if (x = 4)
    cout << "That's it" << endl;
else
    cout << "Wrong number" << endl;
```

9. The following code segment displays nothing if x is not positive and *We only want positive numbers* if x is between zero and five. What's wrong? Fix it.

```
if (x > 0)
   if (x > 5)
      cout << "x is big enough" << endl;
else
   cout << "We only want positive numbers" << endl;
```

10. Put the following program segment in proper structured format using nested `if`s.

```
if (p >= 6) {x = 25; cout << "High p value" << endl;}
else if (p >= 2) {x = 50; cout << "Minimal p value" <<
endl;} else {x = 100; cout << "p below minimum" <<
endl;}
```

11. Repeat Exercise 10 but use the `else if` construct.

12. With traffic lights, *R* (for red) means "stop," *Y* means "caution," and *G* means "go." Any other color letter means "weird." Given the statements below, write the program segment that prints what the color letter means. Use the `else if` construct.

```
cout << "Color letter: ";
cin >> color;
```

13. Repeat Exercise 12 using the `switch` statement.

14. What is wrong with the following program segment?

```
float p, x, y;

Switch p + 14 / y
   case 12.6
      cout << "1" << endl;
   case x
      cout << "2" << endl;
   else
      cout << "0" << endl;
```

15. What is the difference between the following two program segments? What value of *x* is produced if its initial value is 2?

```
if (x > 0)        if (x > 0)
   x = x + 2;        x = x + 2;
else if (x > 2) if (x > 2)
   x = x + 4;        x = x + 4;
```

PROGRAMS

1. Write a program to compare two numbers with executions similar to the following.

Variables

```
number1, number2
```

Outputs

```
Enter two numbers 37.589 24
37.589 is greater than 24.
```

```
Enter two numbers 26.3354 47.2
47.2 is greater than 26.3354.

Enter two numbers 84 84
They are equal.
```

2. Adams County has a 7 percent sales tax rate; the rest of the state has a 6 percent rate. Write a program to print out the amount owed on a purchase including sales tax, given the amount of the purchase and the county.

Variables

```
purchase    Amount of purchase
county
taxRate     Determine using selection
```

Outputs

```
AMOUNT OF PURCHASE? 15        AMOUNT OF PURCHASE? 26
COUNTY? Baker                 COUNTY? Adams
TOTAL BILL: $ 15.90           TOTAL BILL: $ 27.82
```

3. Write a program that changes 12-hour, A.M.-P.M. time into 24-hour time. It should execute like the samples. (*Hint:* Input a dummy char variable to move the input stream past the colon.)

Variables

```
hours
minutes
suffix    a - a.m.; p - p.m.; n - noon; m - midnight
dummy     To pass by the :
```

Outputs

```
Enter time (H:Mx): 6:42p
1842 hours

Enter time (H:Mx): 9:5a
0905 hours

Enter time (H:Mx): 12:00m
0000 hours

Enter time (H:Mx): 12:0n
1200 hours
```

4. A truth table shows the results of values when combined in certain ways. Write a program to show truth tables for combining true and false values using the *and* operator and the *or* operator. Print out the results as the values of the *and* or *or* expressions (0 or 1).

Variables

```
T   Variable with true value
F   Variable with false value
```

Output

```
AND Truth Table      OR Truth Table
      T   F                 T   F
 T    1   0            T    1   1
 F    0   0            F    1   0
```

5. The Ace Courier Service charges $10 for the first pound or fraction thereof and $6 per pound for anything over one pound. Write a program that figures the charges.

Variable

```
weight
```

Outputs

```
WEIGHT? .7          WEIGHT? 2.5         WEIGHT? 4.2
CHARGE: $10.00      CHARGE: $19.00      CHARGE: $29.20
```

6. All good people have last names that begin with the letters *G* through *L*; all others are bad. Write a program that differentiates the good people from the bad.

Variable

```
name
```

Outputs

```
Name? Atilla                 Name? G
Atilla is a bad person       G is a good person

Name? Farnsworth             Name? M
Farnsworth is a bad person   M is a bad person

Name? Harvey                 Name? Lawlor
Harvey is a good person      Lawlor is a good person
```

7. Social Security (FICA) tax is currently 7.65 percent of earnings up to $50,400 for the year. Write a program that accepts earnings for the current week and previous cumulative earnings up to the current week and returns the amount of FICA tax to be withheld.

Variables

```
currentEarnings
prevEarnings
```

Outputs

```
This week's pay? 700         This week's pay? 1850
Previous pay? 12600          Previous pay? 50200
FICA to withhold: $ 53.55    FICA to withhold: $ 15.30
```

8. Write a program to assign grade points according to a letter score. An *A* is 4 grade points; *B* is 3; *C*, 2; *D*, 1; and *F*, 0. Use the `else if` construct.

Variables

```
grade
gradePoints
```

Outputs

```
Letter grade: B        Letter grade: F
Grade points: 3        Grade points: 0

Letter grade: a        Letter grade: Q
Grade points: 4        Grade points: Invalid letter grade.
```

9. Rewrite Program 8 using the `switch` statement.

10. The HiRisq Insurance Company determines auto insurance rates based on a driver's age, the number of tickets the driver received in the last three years, and the value of the car. The base rate is 5 percent of the value of the car. Drivers under 25 years of age pay 15 percent over the base, and drivers from ages 25 through 29 pay 10 percent over. A driver with one ticket pays 10 percent over the rates already figured. Two tickets draws a 25 percent extra charge; three tickets adds 50 percent; and drivers with more than three tickets are refused. Write a program to show a driver's insurance premium.

Variables

Choose appropriate variables

Outputs

```
DRIVER'S AGE? 35           DRIVER'S AGE? 19
NUMBER OF TICKETS? 1       NUMBER OF TICKETS? 3
VALUE OF CAR? 10000        VALUE OF CAR? 850
PREMIUM: $ 550             PREMIUM: $ 73.3125

DRIVER'S AGE? 29           DRIVER'S AGE? 81
NUMBER OF TICKETS? 2       NUMBER OF TICKETS? 4
VALUE OF CAR? 15000        VALUE OF CAR? 12500
PREMIUM: $ 1031.25         COVERAGE DENIED
```

Chapter 5

THE ITERATION STRUCTURE

PREVIEW

Iteration is the last of the three structures and completes our knowledge of the control patterns. In this chapter you will learn:

- How to set up the basic iteration structure.
- Two different places in the loop to put conditions for staying in the iteration structure.
- Some common concepts usually applied within the iteration structure.
- The special case of controlling the iteration structure with a counter.
- Putting iterations within iterations.

One major reason for using a computer rather than doing things by hand is that many of our tasks are repetitive. With only the two structures we have covered so far, the sequence and selection, to repeat a set of operations, we would have to either execute the program a number of times or rewrite the same code over and over in the same program. Neither solution sounds entirely satisfactory, so in this chapter we will introduce the mechanism for directing the computer to repeat a set of operations.

THE ITERATION STRUCTURE

HEADS UP!

Loops must have conditions.

This repetitive pattern is called an **iteration structure** or a **loop**. Under the structured-programming guidelines there must always be an end to the repetition—some condition set up to tell the computer whether it should perform the operations in the loop again or go beyond the loop to the rest of the program. This condition may be tested either before the loop operations are performed (at the beginning of the loop) or after (at the end of the loop).

In our payroll example (shown in Figure 4–1 in the previous chapter), computing the pay must be done for each employee; the same operation must be done many times. The overall structure of the payroll process was:

Gather timecard data
Compute pay data
Write paychecks
Print reports

Following the top-down modular procedure, we can expand the **Compute pay data** module with an iteration structure:

Begin loop   [Compute pay data]
    Compute employee pay
End loop

HEADS UP!

True conditions continue the loop.

This would not be good programming practice, however, because we have stated no conditions for continuing the loop or for exiting it. The program would compute pay forever. In C++, the test condition is always for continuing the loop—when the condition is true, the operations are repeated. If we choose to test at the beginning of the loop, we might write the outline this way:

while more employees
    Compute employee pay

Alternatively, we may wish to test at the end of the loop as follows:

do
    Compute employee pay
while more employees

We have used the word *while* to state our test and, if the test was at the end of the iteration structure, the word *do* to begin the loop. These are the

FIGURE 5–1
The Iteration Structure

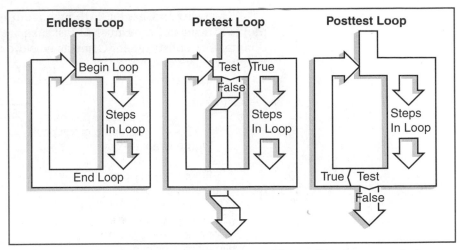

The iteration structure, or loop, repeats a process. The endless loop repeats forever; obviously it is not good programming practice because it allows no way to end the process. In a pretest loop the conditions are tested at the beginning of the loop. A posttest loop tests for the conditions at the end of the loop.

same key words you will use later when you actually program the loop in C++, so we might as well use them for our informal outline here.

Notice the difference between testing at the beginning of the loop (a **pretest loop**) and testing at the end (a **posttest loop**). The difference isn't much except for the first time through. In a pretest loop, if the conditions are not true when the program reaches the loop, the operations within the loop are never performed. Perhaps this section figures the pay for temporary employees and there might not be any in a given week.

In a posttest loop the operations are performed at least once, no matter what the conditions, because the test is not made until the program reaches the end of the structure. In many bank payroll systems there must be some activity every payroll period, even if it is a void check. To accommodate this, we must go through our loop at least once—a posttest loop.

Most of the time it doesn't make any difference whether you choose a pre- or a posttest loop, but you still must examine each situation carefully. If there is a possibility that you may not want the program to execute the operations within the loop, you should choose a pretest loop. If the operations must be performed at least once no matter what, choose a posttest loop.

The top-down design is progressing. We will replace the single line Compute pay data with the structure above. The *do* form was chosen because we must produce at least one check, even if it is void. We have kept the original line at the side to explain what the structure does.

HEADS UP!

Choose pretest or posttest according to the situation.

```
Gather timecard data
do                                          [Compute pay data]
    Compute employee pay
while more employees
Write paychecks
Print reports
```

We now have an iteration structure within our sequence.

As we saw in Chapter 4, though, computing the pay for a single employee consists of a number of tasks, so we will use our expansion from Chapter 4 to substitute for Compute employee pay and include it within the iteration.

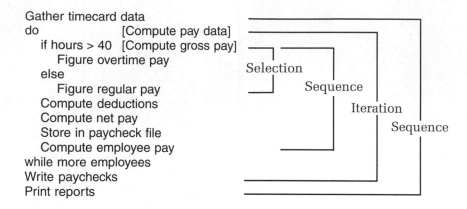

```
Gather timecard data
do                    [Compute pay data]
    if hours > 40   [Compute gross pay]
        Figure overtime pay
    else
        Figure regular pay
    Compute deductions
    Compute net pay
    Store in paycheck file
    Compute employee pay
while more employees
Write paychecks
Print reports
```

Program 5–1

```cpp
#include <iostream>              // Remember the '.h' if your system requires it
#include <iomanip>
using namespace std;                            // Do you need it?

int main(void)
{   float price;
    short quantity;
    char answer;

1   cout << setiosflags(ios::fixed) << setprecision(2);        // Remains set
    cout << "Do you wish to enter a purchase (Y/N)? ";
2   cin >> answer;
3   while (answer == 'Y' || answer == 'y')              // Upper- or lowercase Y
    {   cout << "Enter price and quantity: ";
4       cin >> price >> quantity;
5       cout << "The total for this item is $" << (price * quantity) << endl;
        cout << "Another (Y/N)? ";
6       cin >> answer;
7   }
8   cout << "Thank you for your patronage." << endl;
    return 0;
}
```

Output

```
Do you wish to enter a purchase (Y/N)? y
Enter price and quantity: 1.98 6
The total for this item is $11.88
Another (Y/N)? Y
Enter price and quantity: 4.29 15
The total for this item is $64.35
Another (Y/N)? n
Thank you for your patronage.
```

Structurally speaking, the overall program is a sequence. Within the sequence, the steps from do to while form an iteration; within the iteration is another sequence; and within that sequence is a selection with the two methods for figuring pay as its branches.

LOOPS IN C++

In Chapter 4 we looked at conditions in C++—those expressions that evaluate to either true or false. The conditions we use for the iteration structure will be formed in the same way. In C++, the iteration structure condition is always that for continuing rather than exiting the loop. When the condition is true, C++ will repeat the statements in the loop.

Pretest Loops

A pretest loop begins with the keyword **while**. The general form of this configuration of the iteration structure is:

```
while (condition) statement;
```

For the *statement* referred to above, we can substitute a block of statements—a group of statements enclosed in braces—which leads us to the most common form of the structure, as shown on the following page.

EXECUTION CHART

Line	Explanation	price	quantity	answer
1	Set numeric output format. Since this remains set, it need be done only once, so it is put outside and before the loop.	??	??	??
2	The cin object with the char data type answer variable will take one character from the input stream.	??	??	y
3	This is the beginning of the loop and also the test. Since this is a pretest, there must be something to test; this was provided by line 2. As with all pretest loops, the condition might be such that we would never execute the loop at all, but go directly beyond the closing brace to line 8. In this case, however, the value of answer is y. Because of the or operator (||), the condition will be true with either upper- or lowercase Y.	??	??	y
4	Input price and quantity separated by a space.	1.98	6	y
5	Display the result in dollars and cents.	1.98	6	y
6	This input gives the program something to test when it goes back to the beginning of the loop. The cin object will skip the newline left at the end of the stream by the previous cin and request that the system wait for a new input.	1.98	6	Y
7	End of the block that makes up the body of the while loop. The program will go back to the test in line 3.	1.98	6	Y
3	Condition true, continue with loop.	1.98	6	Y
4	Input new values.	4.29	15	Y
5	Display result.	4.29	15	Y
6	Ask the question.	4.29	15	n
3	Neither relation is true, so the condition is false.	4.29	15	n
8	The program is now beyond the loop and, since this is the last statement, it finishes.	4.29	15	n

```
while (condition)
{   statement;
    statement;
     . . .

}
```

Notice the punctuation and indenting. The *condition* is enclosed in parentheses; each statement in the block is indented one level and ends with a semicolon; there is no semicolon after the condition or after the block's closing brace. The punctuation is required by the C++ compiler. The indenting and line endings are for us; they make the program more readable.

Program 5–1 allows a customer to type in the price of an item and the quantity being purchased and get the total amount for that item. The customer can do this over and over until there are no more items. Notice the initial input of the *answer* before entering the loop. This is a pretest loop and must have something to test at the loop's beginning.

Posttest Loops

We could have set this up as a posttest loop if we assumed that a person who did not wish to make a purchase would not have run the program. In

---

Program 5–2

```
#include <iostream>
#include <iomanip>
using namespace std;

int main(void)
{   float price;
    short quantity;
    char answer;

    cout << setiosflags(ios::fixed) << setprecision(2);          // Remains set
    do
    {   cout << "Enter price and quantity: ";
        cin >> price >> quantity;
        cout << setiosflags(ios::fixed) << setprecision(2);
        cout << "The total for this item is $" << (price * quantity) << endl;
        cout << "Another (Y/N)? ";
        cin >> answer;
    }while (answer == 'Y' || answer == 'y');                      // Upper- or lowercase Y
    cout << "Thank you for your patronage." << endl;
    return 0;
}
```

Output

```
Enter price and quantity: 2.45 12
The total for this item is $29.40.
Another (Y/N)? y
Enter price and quantity: .99 4
The total for this item is $3.96.
Another (Y/N)? n
Thank you for your patronage.
```

other words, the body of the loop would be executed once no matter what. The posttest loop begins with a **do** statement and has this general form:

```
do statement; while (condition);
```

with our usual implementation of it looking like this:

```
do
{   statement;
    statement;
      . . .
}while (condition);
```

Not putting a semicolon after the condition in a posttest loop.

There was no semicolon after the closing brace in the pretest loop but there is, and must be, one at the end of the *condition* in the posttest loop. Program 5–2 is a rewrite of Program 5–1 using a posttest loop.

Sentinel Values

HEADS UP!

A sentinel value should be something weird.

In Program 5–2 the person at the keyboard is asked a separate question about whether to continue. We could eliminate that question by interpreting special responses to the other question about price and quantity not as normal data but as a signal to the program to do something different. We call the value of this special response a **sentinel value**. The sentinel value must be something that would not occur in the normal course of operations—for example, a price and quantity of zero.

Program 5–3

```cpp
#include <iostream>
#include <iomanip>
using namespace std;

int main(void)
{   float price;
    short quantity;

    cout << setiosflags(ios::fixed) << setprecision(2);        // Remains set
    cout << "Enter 0 0 to quit.\n";
    do
    {   cout << "Enter price and quantity: ";
        cin >> price >> quantity;
        cout << "The total for this item is $" << (price * quantity) << endl;
    }while (price != 0);
    cout << "Thank you for your patronage." << endl;
    return 0;
}
```

Output

```
Enter 0 0 to quit.
Enter price and quantity: 2.45 12
The total for this item is $29.40
Enter price and quantity: 0 0
The total for this item is $0.00
Thank you for your patronage.
```

Simply removing the *answer* input and testing for a *price* not equal to zero, as in Program 5–3, is insufficient. The sentinel value, zero, is assigned to the sentinel variable, *price* by the `cin` object, then used to calculate the total for the item (which should not really be an item), and then tested in the `while` statement. Notice that the output is a little silly.

The sentinel value must be tested for immediately. One structured solution is shown in Program 5–4.

The `cout` and `cin` objects are repeated, but that is necessary so that the `while` has something to test and we don't print a meaningless result.

The **sentinel-value-controlled loop**, as in Program 5–4, is one of the most common forms of loop.

Program 5–5 makes Program 5–4 just a little cleaner by asking the user to type only one zero to exit the loop. It does not make any difference to C++ if we input *price* and *quantity* in one `cin` or two.

```
cin >> price >> quantity;
```

is equivalent to

```
cin >> price;
cin >> quantity;
```

Program 5–4

```cpp
#include <iostream>
#include <iomanip>
using namespace std;

int main(void)
{   float price;
    short quantity;

    cout << setiosflags(ios::fixed) << setprecision(2);          // Remains set
    cout << "Enter 0 0 to quit.\n";
    cout << "Enter price and quantity: ";
    cin >> price >> quantity;
    while (price != 0)
    {   cout << "The total for this item is $" << (price * quantity) << endl;
        cout << "Enter price and quantity: ";
        cin >> price >> quantity;
    }
    cout << "Thank you for your patronage." << endl;
    return 0;
}
```

Output

```
Enter 0 0 to quit.
Enter price and quantity: 3.75 2
The total for this item is $7.50
Enter price and quantity: 10.59 6
The total for this item is $63.54
Enter price and quantity: 0 0
Thank you for your patronage.
```

Program 5–5

```cpp
#include <iostream>
#include <iomanip>
using namespace std;

int main(void)
{   float price;
    short quantity;

    cout << setiosflags(ios::fixed) << setprecision(2);          // Remains set
    cout << "Enter price of 0 to quit.\n";
    cout << "Enter price and quantity: ";
    cin >> price;
    while (price)                                                // Nonzero is true
    {   cin >> quantity;
        cout << "The total for this item is $" << (price * quantity) << endl;
        cout << "Enter price and quantity: ";
        cin >> price;
    }
    cout << "Thank you for your patronage." << endl;
    return 0;
}
```

Output

```
Enter price of 0 to quit
Enter price and quantity: 6.35 8
The total for this item is $50.80
Enter price and quantity: 2.5 10
The total for this item is $25.00
Enter price and quantity: 0
Thank you for your patronage.
```

In either case the two values are delimited by whitespace—space, tab, or newline. If the user responds to the *price* input with a value and newline, that newline will make the input available to our process, so we can test for it immediately. If the user responds to the *price* input with a value, a space, and a value, followed by newline, `cin >> price;` assigns the first value to *price*, leaving the space and the second value in the input stream. The `cin >> quantity` finds the stream with characters, so it skips the space and assigns the value to *quantity*.

We also simplified the `while` statement. Remember from Chapter 4 that anything nonzero is true, so

```cpp
    while (price)                                                // Nonzero is true
```

is equivalent to

```cpp
    while (price != 0)
```

YOUR TURN 5–1

1. What is the purpose of an iteration structure? *repeats operations.*
2. When the condition in a C++ iteration structure is true, does the execution of the loop continue or stop?

3. What is the difference between a pretest and a posttest loop? How is each implemented in C++?

4. How are sentinel values used to control loops?

ACCUMULATING AND COUNTING

Accumulating, adding (or multiplying, or whatever) values to a variable to keep a running result, is a common operation in loops. The accumulation process takes the value of the variable in which we are accumulating, adds another value to it, and stores the result in the accumulator variable. Using *total* as our accumulator variable and *extra* as a value we want to add to the accumulator, an accumulation statement looks like this:

```
total = total + extra;
```

HEADS UP!

An assignment statement is not an equation.

As an algebraic equation, that makes no sense at all—but this is a statement representing a sequence of instructions to the computer, not an equation. Remember also, from our discussion in Chapter 4, that = does not mean equality, it means assignment. Let us suppose that the value of *total* is 100 and of *extra* is 5. Since addition (+) is higher in precedence than assignment (=), the addition expression is evaluated first. The computer will add the value of *total* (100) to the value of *extra* (5), giving the result 105. The assignment operator is next, so the value 105 is assigned to *total*, replacing the 100.

```
total = total + extra;
         100       5
              105
```

We can use any arithmetic operator. In the previous example we accumulated by adding to the *total* variable. Below, starting with the same values, we will use the multiplication operator. The new value of *total*, of course, will be 500.

```
total = total * extra;
         100       5
              500
```

To work effectively, the accumulator variable, *total* in this example, must have a reasonable value before an accumulation operation is performed. If we had declared *total* as:

```
int total;
```

Not initializing an accumulator.

without any other assignments to *total*, garbage times anything is still garbage. Variables to be used as accumulators must be **initialized**, given a first value, somehow, whether it is in the declaration:

```
int total = 100;
```

or in some other assignment operation:

```
cout << "What do you want to start with? ";
cin >> total;
```

Accumulation Operators

Since accumulation is such a common operation, the designers of C++ gave us shorthand notation for it: a set of **accumulation operators** formed by the arithmetic operator for the type of accumulation we are doing, followed by an equal sign. For example, the statement

```
total = total * extra;
```

could be rewritten

```
total *= extra;
```

This operator does not represent some new kind of mathematical operation; it simply indicates two separate operations. When evaluating an expression, C++ takes the variable before the operator (*total* in the example), copies both it and the arithmetic operator following it to the other side of the equal sign, and then compiles the result. There is no execution advantage to the accumulation operator; it just saves a little typing in the source code.

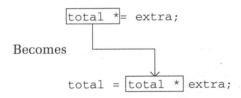

Becomes

The precedence and associativity of the accumulation operators are the same as the assignment operator—last on our list and right to left. If *total* is 100, *extra* is 5, and *old* is 3, *total* becomes 108.

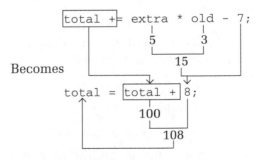

Becomes

Notice that the whole effect of the accumulation operator comes after the multiplication and subtraction. The copy of the *total* variable is not made before the expression is evaluated, but during the evaluation, when the accumulation operator is reached.

Let us put an accumulation operation to use in Program 5–6 to keep track of the total bill and print out its value after finishing the loop.

Program 5–6

```
#include <iostream>
#include <iomanip>
using namespace std;

int main(void)
{   float price;
    float total = 0;                                          // Initialize accumulator
    short quantity;

    cout << setiosflags(ios::fixed) << setprecision(2);        // Remains set
    cout << "Enter price of 0 to quit.\n";
    cout << "Enter price and quantity: ";
    cin >> price;
    while (price)
    {   cin >> quantity;
        cout << "The total for this item is $" << (price * quantity) << endl;
        total += price * quantity;
        cout << "Enter price and quantity: ";
        cin >> price;
    }
    cout << "Your total is $" << total << "." << endl;
    return 0;
}
```

Output

```
Enter price of 0 to quit.
Enter price and quantity: 6.35 8
The total for this item is $50.80
Enter price and quantity: 2.50 10
The total for this item is $25.00
Enter price and quantity: 0
Your total is $75.80.
```

To work correctly, the accumulator variable, *total*, was initialized to zero at the time of its declaration. Without that initial assignment, the first value of *total* would have been whatever was lying around in memory. Accumulating on top of that would not have been very productive.

The accumulation statement,

```
total += price * quantity
```

is exactly equivalent to

```
total = total + price * quantity
```

so *price* and *quantity* are multiplied, and that result is added to *total*, replacing the previous value of *total*.

Counting is specialized, simplified accumulation. Instead of adding a different value to the accumulation variable each time the statement is executed, the counting process adds the same value—1 or 9 or 2.8 or whatever we are counting by. The statement

```
count += 5;
```

counts by fives.

HEADS UP!

Counting is accumulating the same value each time.

Program 5–7

```cpp
#include <iostream>
#include <iomanip>
using namespace std;

int main(void)
{   float price;
    float total = 0;                                    // Initialize accumulator
    short quantity;
    short items = 0;                                    // Initialize counter

    cout << setiosflags(ios::fixed) << setprecision(2);     // Remains set
    cout << "Enter price of 0 to quit.\n";
    cout << "Enter price and quantity: ";
    cin >> price;
    while (price)
    {   cin >> quantity;
        cout << "The total for this item is $" << (price * quantity) << endl;
        total += price * quantity;                      // Accumulate
        items += 1;                                     // Count
        cout << "Enter price and quantity: ";
        cin >> price;
    }
    cout << "Your total is $" << total << " for "
         << items << " different items." << endl;
    return 0;
}
```

Output

```
Enter price of 0 to quit.
Enter price and quantity: 22.95 3
The total for this item is $68.85
Enter price and quantity: 7.29 8
The total for this item is $58.32
Enter price and quantity: 15 4
The total for this item is $60.00
Enter price and quantity: 0
Your total is $187.17 for 3 different items.
```

If we wanted to know how many purchases were made, we could count by one at each purchase and, after exiting the loop, display that total, as in Program 5–7.

COUNTER-CONTROLLED LOOPS

In some cases we want to execute a set of statements a certain number of times—10, 100, 416, or whatever—or we want to look, for example, at every fifth instance of an event. We can use a counter to control our loop. Program 5–8 prints out the numbers 1 through 3. We will use it to illustrate the elements needed for a **counter-controlled loop**.

Program 5-8

```cpp
#include <iostream>
using namespace std;

int main(void)
{   int count;

    count = 1;                                              // Initialization
    while (count <= 3)                                              // Test
    {   cout << count << endl;                                      // Body
        count += 1;                                            // Counter
    }                                                             // End
    cout << "Finished, but why is the count " << count << "?" << endl;
    return 0;
}
```

Output

```
1
2
3
Finished, but why is the count 4?
```

The following elements are necessary for a successful counter-controlled loop:

- **Initialization** A counter, like any accumulator, must start with some initial value.

- **Test** This is a pretest. The loop will continue until the counter is greater than 3.

- **Body.** The statement(s) that the loop was set up to repeat.

- **Counter.** Adds one to the counter variable each time through the loop.

- **End** Sends the program back to the test at the beginning.

Since counting and counter-controlled loops are so common in programming, C++, like many other languages, has a special form for them, the **for** statement:

```
for (initialization; test; counter) statement;
```

or more commonly

```
for (initialization; test; counter)
{   statement;
    statement;
        . . .
}
```

HEADS UP!

A for statement is just an easy way to set up a counter-controlled loop.

HEADS UP!

For readability, use the for statement only for loops controlled by counters.

Program 5-9 executes exactly as did Program 5-7.

To answer the question at the end of the program, when the count was less than or equal to 3, the loop continued. The counter had to go beyond 3 (to 4) to make the loop condition false and exit the loop.

Program 5–9

```
#include <iostream>
using namespace std;

int main(void)
{  int count;

   for (count = 1; count <= 3; count += 1)
   {  cout << count << endl;                          // Braces not required
   }
   cout << "Finished, but why is the count " << count << "?" << endl;
   return 0;
}
```

Output

```
1
2
3
Finished, but why is the count 4?
```

HEADS UP!

Counting occurs at the end of the for loop.

For the most part, the actions caused by a statement occur at the location of the statement within the program. The for statement is the exception; its actions are spread around the loop. As shown in Figure 5–2, the first action, the initialization, occurs only once before the repeating parts of the loop. The second, the test, is the first repeated action in the loop. The third, the counter, actually occurs at the end of the body of the loop—in some cases, hundreds of statements away from the for statement.

Using Floating-Point Counters

C++ will accept any simple data type as a counter, but floating-point counters can sometimes lead to unexpected results. Remember from Chapter 2 that floating-point values are stored in binary E notation and that conversion to this notation involves approximating the decimal value. Consider Program 5–10.

FIGURE 5–2
Counter-Controlled Loops

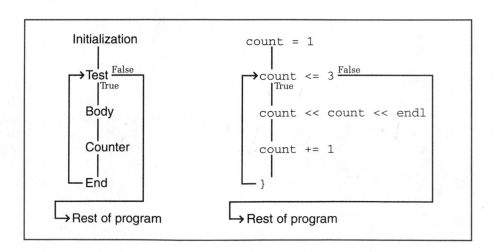

Program 5–10

```
#include <iostream>
#include <iomanip>
using namespace std;

int main(void)
{  float count;

    cout << setiosflags(ios::fixed) << setprecision(1);
    cout << "Values from 0 to 1.0 in steps of 0.1\n";
    for (count = 0; count <= 1; count += 0.1)
        cout <<  count << "   ";
    cout << "\nFinal count: " << count << endl;
    return 0;
}
```

Output

```
Values from 0 to 1.0 in steps of 0.1
0.0  0.1  0.2  0.3  0.4  0.5  0.6  0.7  0.8  0.9
Final count: 1.0
```

This loop should have printed 1.0 within the loop, with the final count being 1.1—greater than 1.0. From the output we can see no evidence of the problem, but it involves the conversion to binary E notation. In the approximations made in the counting process, the accumulated number that we see as 1.0 is actually slightly larger than 1.0 in its approximated binary form, forcing the loop to exit at that point.

The moral here is to avoid floating-point loop counters if at all possible. Program 5–10 could be written as Program 5–11, and the correct results obtained.

Expecting a floating-point counter to behave.

Increment and Decrement Operators

Counting, especially by 1, is a common computer operation. We can add 1 to a variable by the process of accumulation as used above. For example,

NUTS'N BOLTS

MORE ON `for`

We have identified the parameters of the `for` statement as an initialization, a test, and a counter. Internally, C++ makes no such distinctions. Any statements can be used in the position we have identified for the initialization and counter, and any expression can be used in the test position. C++ will simply execute whatever statement is in the initialization position, test whatever expression is in the test position, perform any statements in the body, execute whatever statement is in the counter position, and then go back to the test position.

C++ is very loose about what we put in these various positions, but *we* probably shouldn't be. If we are not specifically writing a counting loop—with initialization, test, and counter—we should probably use a `while` or `do` loop.

Program 5–11

```
#include <iostream>
#include <iomanip>
using namespace std;

int main(void)
{   int count;                                    // Use an integer as a counter

    cout << setiosflags(ios::fixed) << setprecision(1);
    cout << "Values from 0 to 1.0 in steps of 0.1\n";
    for (count = 0; count <= 10; count += 1)
        cout <<  (count / 10.0) << "  ";           // Force double calculation
    cout << "\nFinal count: " << (count / 10.0) << endl;
    return 0;
}
```

Output

```
Values from 0 to 1.0 in steps of 0.1
0.0  0.1  0.2  0.3  0.4  0.5  0.6  0.7  0.8  0.9  1.0
Final count: 1.1
```

HEADS UP!

Increment and decrement operations perform assignments.

whatever = whatever + 1;   or   whatever += 1;

adds 1 to the value of *whatever*.

C++ provides us with the ++ operator to **increment**, add 1 to, a variable as well as the -- operator to **decrement**, subtract 1 from, a variable. In precedence and associativity, they are unary operators, but they actually perform assignments—change the values of variables. They can only be used with variables (it wouldn't make sense to change a constant value or the value of an expression) and they can only add 1 to or subtract 1 from the variable—not 2, 9, or 46. If *rabbit* is 17, it will be 18 after this statement:

++rabbit;

Program 5–12 shows increment and decrement in action.

NUTS'N BOLTS

INCREMENT AND DECREMENT

The increment and decrement operators are not just gimmicks to save a little typing; they actually do make a program operate more efficiently. Most CPUs, as part of their machine language, have direct integer increment and decrement instructions. They can add or subtract 1 from the contents in a memory location.

A typical accumulation—var = var + 1—usually requires many CPU instructions. The value of *var* must be brought into the CPU, 1 must be added to it, and the result must be written to the original location of *var*. If it is available in the target CPU, the C++ compiler will translate the ++ and -- operators into the direct increment and decrement instructions rather than the more roundabout accumulation. These operators are more efficient only with integers, and they are limited to the value 1, but they can make faster programs.

Program 5–12

```cpp
#include <iostream>
using namespace std;

int main(void)
{   int rabbit = 17;

    cout << "Rabbit is " << rabbit << ".\n";
    ++rabbit;
    cout << "Now, rabbit is " << rabbit << ".\n";
    —rabbit;
    cout << "Rabbit is back to " << rabbit << "." << endl;
    return 0;
}
```

Output

```
Rabbit is 17.
Now, rabbit is 18.
Rabbit is back to 17.
```

 HEADS UP!

Increment and decrement operators are commonly used in `for` loops.

One common place to find increment and decrement operators is in counter-controlled loops, incrementing or decrementing the loop counter variable. In the loop example in Program 5–11, our `for` statement looked like this:

```cpp
for (count = 0; count <= 10; count += 1)
```

It could have just as easily been written like this:

```cpp
for (count = 0; count <= 10; ++count)
```

Or, for that matter, like this:

```cpp
for (count = 0; count <= 10; count++)
```

Increment and Decrement in Expressions (Optional)

The increment and decrement operators become more interesting because they can be used in arithmetic expressions, changing the values of the variables they are attached to as the expression is being evaluated. The operator may appear as a prefix, before the variable that it changes, or as a postfix, after the variable. If it appears before, then the variable is changed before its value is used in the expression. If it appears after, the value of the variable is used in the expression, and then the variable is changed.

In this example, if *quantity* is 2 and *price* is 3.5, after the following statement is performed, *totalSales* is 7.0 and *quantity* is 3.

```
totalSales = price * quantity++;
                       3.5        2
                            7.0
                                  3
```

If the increment operator is put in front of the variable, *quantity* still ends up being 3, but *totalSales* is 10.5.

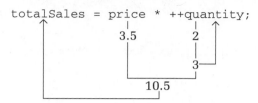

```
totalSales = price * ++quantity;
             3.5        2
                        3
             10.5
```

In Program 5–11, it doesn't matter whether we increment *count* before or after we use it in the expression because we are not using its value in the expression—only changing it.

1. How does accumulation work? ~some algebraic thing to value & variable then replaces new value in variable.~
2. Why is initialization of an accumulator variable important? ~if it contains garbage before accumulation, it will after~
3. How does counting differ from accumulation? How are they the same? ~same, but counting adds same value instead of different values.~
4. What five elements are necessary in a counter-controlled loop? ~initialization, test, body, counter, end.~
5. At what point in the loop does each parameter of a `for` statement execute? ~init → before   counter → end   test → body.~
6. Why is using a floating-point loop counter not advised? ~approximate can lead to errors.~
7. What is the difference between `++x` and `x++` when used in an arithmetic expression? ~before used   after used.~

NESTED LOOPS

Any valid statement or set of statements may be included within a loop. For example, the following program segment is a loop that prints the numbers 1 to 4.

Program Segment

```
for (inner = 1; inner <= 4; ++inner)
{   cout << inner << "  ";
}
```

Output

```
1   2   3   4
```

There is no reason why this could not be inside another loop:

Program Segment

```
for (outer = 1; outer <= 3; ++outer)
{   cout << "Line " << outer << ":   ";
    for (inner = 1; inner <= 4; ++inner)
    {   cout << inner << "  ";
    }
    cout << endl;
}
```

Output

```
Line 1:   1   2   3   4
Line 2:   1   2   3   4
Line 3:   1   2   3   4
```

A loop within another loop is referred to as a **nested loop**. Nesting may be as deep as needed—a loop within a loop within a loop . . . as long as you make sure of the following two things:

Program 5–13

```cpp
#include <iostream>
using namespace std;

int main(void)
{   int n, count, factorial;

    cout << "Enter a positive integer: ";
    cin >> n;
    cout << "Integer  Factorial\n";
    for ( ; n >= 1; --n)                                   // n initialized by cin
    {   cout << "        " << n << "   ";
        factorial = 1;                                       // An accumulator
        for (count = 1; count <= n; ++count)
            factorial *= count;                // Only 1 statement, no braces needed
        cout << factorial << endl;
    }
    return 0;
}
```

Output

```
Enter a positive integer: 5
Integer  Factorial
      5  120
      4  24
      3  6
      2  2
      1  1
```

HEADS UP!

Properly nest loops.

HEADS UP!

Have separate loop counters.

- An inner loop must be entirely contained within an outer loop. This simply follows our rules of combining structures. With proper indenting, as in the example above, violation of this rule will be obvious.

- If the loops are counter controlled, each loop that is operating simultaneously (nested within another) must have a different loop counter variable, such as *x* and *y* above. If you violate this rule, one loop will be modifying the other loop's counter, yielding a mess!

Program 5–13 allows the user to enter a positive integer and prints a table of all integers from the one entered back to 1. The second column of the table is the product of all integers from 1 to the integer in the first column—mathematically, the factorial of the value in the first column.

HEADS UP!

Typically, the outer loop controls the row and the inner loop the column.

Rows and Columns

One common use for nested loops is row and column applications. We use the outer loop to set the row, and then use the inner loop to vary across the columns. Returning to the outer loop sets up the next row, and the inner loop varies across the columns, and so forth.

Program 5-14

```cpp
#include <iostream>
#include <iomanip>
using namespace std;

int main(void)
{   int num, den;

    //--------------------------------------------------- Print Numerator Heading
    cout << "               Numerator\n          ";
    for (num = 1; num <= 10; ++num)
        cout << setw(6) << num;
    cout << "\nDenominator\n";

    //--------------------------------------------------------- Print Table
    cout << setiosflags(ios::fixed) << setprecision(2);
    for (den = 1; den <= 10; ++den)                    // Establish denominator
    {   cout << "          " << setw(2) << den;        // Print denominator heading
        for (num = 1; num <= 10; ++num)                // Numerators from 1 to 10
            cout << setw(6) << (1.0 * num / den);      // Force double
        cout << endl;                                  // Drop down to next row
    }                                                  // Go to the next denominator
    return 0;
}
```

Output

```
              Numerator
              1     2     3     4     5     6     7     8     9    10
Denominator
           1  1.00  2.00  3.00  4.00  5.00  6.00  7.00  8.00  9.00 10.00
           2  0.50  1.00  1.50  2.00  2.50  3.00  3.50  4.00  4.50  5.00
           3  0.33  0.67  1.00  1.33  1.67  2.00  2.33  2.67  3.00  3.33
           4  0.25  0.50  0.75  1.00  1.25  1.50  1.75  2.00  2.25  2.50
           5  0.20  0.40  0.60  0.80  1.00  1.20  1.40  1.60  1.80  2.00
           6  0.17  0.33  0.50  0.67  0.83  1.00  1.17  1.33  1.50  1.67
           7  0.14  0.29  0.43  0.57  0.71  0.86  1.00  1.14  1.29  1.43
           8  0.12  0.25  0.38  0.50  0.62  0.75  0.88  1.00  1.12  1.25
           9  0.11  0.22  0.33  0.44  0.56  0.67  0.78  0.89  1.00  1.11
          10  0.10  0.20  0.30  0.40  0.50  0.60  0.70  0.80  0.90  1.00
```

For example, we might use a program like Program 5-14 to set up a table showing the decimal equivalent of fractions with numerators and denominators varying from 1 to 10. The numerators make up the columns in the table and the denominators the rows. Accordingly, we have used the variable *num* to control the columns, across the table, and *den* to control the rows, down the table. Let us follow a row through. The denominator is set to 1 in the outer loop, and the value of the denominator is printed. Then, still within the denominator loop, the numerator is varied from 1 to 10 and the fraction printed in an inner loop. At the end of the numerator loop, after all 10 fractions have been printed, we drop down to the beginning of the next row to get ready for the next denominator.

1. What is a nested loop? *1 loop contained w/in another.*
2. What two rules must be followed for the correct formation of a nested loop? *inner must be entirely contained in other; if both counter controlled; counter variables must be diff.*
3. Why, in a table situation, does the outer loop typically control the row and the inner loop the column? *moves row to row, colums inside; hence row outer & colums inner*

PUTTING IT TOGETHER

T. Farthington Gotbucks IV is looking into alternative interest-bearing investments for all the money he has inherited. The investments he is considering are all interest bearing and compounded quarterly (the interest is calculated and added back to the balance four times a year), and all extend for three years.

TASK

Write a program for T. Farthy that will allow him to input the rate for a prospective investment, and show him how that investment would progress over three years.

ANALYSIS

The output should be a chart showing the investment's history—starting amount, interest, and ending amount—for each quarter of each year. It should also show the total interest earned in each year as well as over the three years. So that any investment possibility can be compared on equal ground, the program should start with $1,000 for each. The form should be similar to the following:

```
        Start Interest      End
Year 1
     1  ####.##      ##.##  ####.##
     2  ####.##      ##.##  ####.##
     3  ####.##      ##.##  ####.##
     4  ####.##      ##.##  ####.##
   Total interest for the year: $###.##

        [Same for years 2 and 3.]

Ending balance: $####.##.   Interest earned: $###.##.
```

The input will consist of an interest rate to be analyzed. Anything less than 5 percent or greater than 20 percent will be deemed an unreasonable rate and should be rejected.

The interest is calculated by multiplying the current balance by the rate by the time period, one quarter of a year in this case. A new balance is calculated by adding that interest to the current balance.

Overall, Farthy's program should perform these behaviors:

Enter interest rate
Produce chart

Since he wants to perform many analyses, the behaviors should be in a loop. We will use a typical sentinel-value-controlled loop with the interest rate as the sentinel variable.

Enter interest rate
while new analysis desired
    Produce chart
    Enter interest rate

If the interest input is outside the reasonable range, the program should ask for another input.

Enter interest rate
while new analysis desired
    if input out of range
        Print error message
    else
        Produce chart
    Enter interest rate

To make the chart show each quarter's activity with a yearly summary of the balance and total interest, we can expand the **Produce chart** section:

[Produce chart]
Initialize balance and total interest
Yearly for three years
    Initialize yearly interest
    Quarterly for four quarters
        Print quarter and beginning balance
        Figure interest and add to yearly interest and balance
        Print interest and new balance
    Add year's interest to total
Display final totals

Looking at the object summary, we notice that we have a number of nested objects—objects within objects. Also, many of the properties are

OBJECT SUMMARY		
Object Name	**Behavior**	**Properties**
Analysis	ProduceAnalysis by year and quarter.	rate (req) low (con) high (con)
Error	Display Error Message.	
Chart	Calculate and display analysis chart for three years.	balance total interest year
Yearly	Chart for single year.	yearly interest quarter
Quarterly	Chart for single quarter	interest

Program 5–15

```cpp
         #include <iostream>
         #include <iomanip>
         using namespace std;

         const float low = 5.0;                          // Bottom of interest range
         const float high = 20.0;                        // Top of interest range

         int main(void)
 1       {  float rate;

            cout << setiosflags(ios::fixed) << setprecision(2);
            cout << "Enter interest rate (zero to quit): ";
 2          cin >> rate;
 3          while (rate)                                        // or (rate != 0.0)
 4          {  if (rate < low || rate > high) //----------------------------- Error
 5                cout << "   Out of the reasonable range.\n";
             else //----------------------------------------------------- Chart
 6           {  float balance = 1000.0;                  // Initialize for new chart
 7              float totalInterest = 0.0;               // Total accumulated interest

 8              cout << "\n            Start Interest      End\n";
 9              for (int year = 1; year <= 3; ++year)
10              {  float yearlyInterest = 0.0; //------------------------ Yearly

11                 cout << "Year " << year << endl;
12                 for (int quarter = 1; quarter <= 4; ++quarter)
13                 {  float interest; //----------------------------- Quarterly

14                    cout << "        " << quarter << setw(9) << balance;
15                    interest = balance * rate / 100 * 0.25;
16                    yearlyInterest += interest;
17                    balance += interest;
18                    cout << setw(9) << interest << setw(9) << balance << endl;
19                 } // End quarter loop
20                 cout << "    Total interest for the year: $"
                        << yearlyInterest << endl;
21                 totalInterest += yearlyInterest;                 // Accumulate
22              } // End year loop
23              cout << "\nEnding balance: $" << balance
                     << ".  Interest earned: $" << totalInterest << "\n\n";
             }
            cout << "Enter interest rate (zero to quit): ";
24          cin >> rate;
         } // End while loop
         return 0;
      }
```

Output

```
Enter interest rate (zero to quit): .125
   Out of the reasonable range.
Enter interest rate (zero to quit): 12.5

        Start Interest      End
Year 1
     1  1000.00    31.25  1031.25
     2  1031.25    32.23  1063.48
     3  1063.48    33.23  1096.71
     4  1096.71    34.27  1130.98
   Total interest for the year: $130.98
Year 2
     1  1130.98    35.34  1166.33
     2  1166.33    36.45  1202.77
     3  1202.77    37.59  1240.36
     4  1240.36    38.76  1279.12
   Total interest for the year: $148.14
Year 3
     1  1279.12    39.97  1319.09
     2  1319.09    41.22  1360.32
     3  1360.32    42.51  1402.83
     4  1402.83    43.84  1446.66
   Total interest for the year: $167.54

Ending balance: $1446.66.  Interest earned: $446.66

Enter interest rate (zero to quit): 0
```

strictly internal—used only within that object or its component objects. The *balance* property, for example, is established in the *Chart* object, and used there and in the *Yearly* and *Quarterly* subobjects. It is neither input into nor output from the *Chart* object.

IMPLEMENTATION

The Gotbucks investment program is shown in Program 5–15. Note that the declarations of the variables for internal properties are made within the objects that contain those properties, and the declarations of the loop counters *year* and *quarter* are made as part of the initialization statement within the for statement. Since the initialization step, that of *year*, for example, is done before the loop starts, the *year* variable is part of the *Chart* object.

TEST

The tests should include representative rates within the acceptable range as well as tests to reject rates outside the range. The tests should be compared with results obtained by hand. The following test did not actually agree with the hand-calculated results. It was determined, however, that there was a mistake in the hand calculation for quarter two of year three.

EXECUTION CHART

Line	Explanation	rate	balance	total Interest	year	yearly Interest	quarter	interest
1	Declare variable used throughout program	??						
2	Enter interest rate.	.125						
3	*rate* not the sentinel value; perform loop.	.125						
4	*rate* less than 5, condition true.	.125						
	Error object:							
5	Display out of range message.	.125						
	Main program:							
24	Enter new *rate*.	12.5						
3	Still not sentinel value, perform loop.	12.5						
4	*rate* neither <5 nor >20, condition false.	12.5						
	Chart object:							
6, 7	Declare variables for object.	12.5	1000.00	0	--			
8	Display table heading.	12.5	1000.00	0	--			
9	Declare and initialize *year*, test *year*, enter loop.	12.5	1000.00	0	1			
	Yearly object:							
10	Declare variable for object.	12.5	1000.00	0	1	0	--	
11	Display *year*.	12.5	1000.00	0	1	0	--	
12	Declare, initialize, and test *quarter*, enter loop.	12.5	1000.00	0	1	0	1	
	Quarterly object:							
13	Declare variable for object.	12.5	1000.00	0	1	0	1	??
14	Display *quarter* and starting *balance*.	12.5	1000.00	0	1	0	1	??
15	Calculate interest for quarter.	12.5	1000.00	0	1	0	1	31.25
16	Accumulate *yearlyInterest*.	12.5	1000.00	0	1	31.25	1	31.25
17	Accumulate *balance*.	12.5	1031.25	0	1	31.25	1	31.25
18	Display *interest* and ending *balance*.	12.5	1031.25	0	1	31.25	1	31.25
	Yearly object:							
19	Increment *quarter*.	12.5	1031.25	0	1	31.25	2	
12	Test, *quarter* <= 4, continue loop.	12.5	1031.25	0	1	31.25	2	
12–19	After 4 times through the loop and the *Quarterly* object.	12.5	1130.98	0	1	130.98	4	
19	Increment *quarter*.	12.5	1130.98	0	1	130.98	5	
12	Test, *quarter* not <= 4, exit loop.	12.5	1130.98	0	1	130.98	5	
20	Display *yearlyInterest*.	12.5	1130.98	0	1	130.98	5	
21	Accumulate *totalInterest*.	12.5	1130.98	130.98	1	130.98	5	
	Chart object:							
22	Increment *year*.	12.5	1130.98	130.98	2			
9	Test, *year* <= 3, continue loop.	12.5	1130.98	130.98	2			
9–22	After 3 times through *year* loop and *Yearly* object (and 4 times through the *quarter* loop and *Quarterly* object for each time through the *year* loop).	12.5	1446.66	446.66	3			
22	Increment *year*.	12.5	1446.66	446.66	4			
9	Test, *year* not <= 3, exit loop.	12.5	1446.66	446.66	4			
23	Display *balance* and *totalInterest*.	12.5	1446.66	446.66	4			
	Main program:							
24	Enter interest rate.	0						
3	*rate* is sentinel value, exit loop.	0						

- **KEY TERMS** (in order of appearance)

Iteration structure	Counter-controlled loop
Loop	Initialization
Pretest loop	Test
Posttest loop	Body
Sentinel value	Counter
Sentinel-value-controlled loop	End
Accumulating	Increment
Initialize	Decrement
Accumulation operator	Nested loop
Counting	

- **NEW STATEMENTS** (in order of appearance)

```
while (condition) statement;
do statement; while (condition);
for (initialization; test; counter) statement;
```

- **CONCEPT REVIEW**

  - The **iteration structure** or **loop** repeats a set of statements. The condition for repeating the statements is given in a `while` statement. If it is a **pretest** loop, the `while` appears at the beginning of the loop. If it is a **posttest** loop, it starts with a `do` statement and the `while` appears at the end of the loop.

  - Often the condition for a loop involves a **sentinel value**, a special value for a variable that is being used in the loop and that is tested for each time through the loop. When the sentinel value of the variable is found, the loop is exited. The **sentinel-value-controlled loop** is one of the most common types of loops.

  - Two other concepts that are commonly used with loops are **accumulating**, keeping a running total, and **counting**, adding some fixed value to a variable each time through the loop. Since both operations modify the value of an existing variable, that variable must be **initialized** before the first of either operation is performed.

  - Accumulation is so common in programming that C++ has a number of **accumulation operators** that provide us with a simpler notation.

  - In the case of a **counter-controlled loop**, a counter is the determining factor for exiting the loop. This loop has five important ingredients: an **initialization** of the counter; a **test** to determine if the loop should repeat; a **body** of statements to repeat; a **counter** statement that adds to the counter; and an **end** of the loop that sends the execution back to the test. The parameters for initialization, test, and counter can all be stated in a `for` statement.

  - Floating-point counters sometimes give us unexpected results because of the rounding in storing floating-point numbers.

- **Increment** and **decrement** operators, which also make assignments, are often used in counting loops.

- Since any valid statement or structure can be included within any other, we often encounter **nested loops**, one loop within another. We can nest loops (and other structures) as deep as we need to as long as the nesting is complete, and as long as each counting loop has a different counter variable.

- Row and column formations are common applications of nested loops. Typically, the outer loop controls the row and the inner loop, the column.

• HEADS UP: POINTS OF SPECIAL INTEREST

- Loops must have conditions.
- True conditions continue the loop.
- Choose pretest or posttest according to the situation.
- A sentinel value should be something weird.
- An assignment statement is not an equation.
- Initialization can be by any kind of assignment.
- Any of the arithmetic operators can be part of an accumulation.
- Like any other assignment, accumulation is low in precedence.
- Counting is accumulating the same value each time.
- A `for` statement is just an easy way to set up a counter-controlled loop.
- For readability, use the `for` statement only for loops controlled by counters.
- Counting occurs at the end of the `for` loop.
- Increment and decrement operations perform assignments.
- Increment and decrement operators are commonly used in `for` loops.
- Properly nest loops.
- Have separate loop counters.
- Typically, the outer loop controls the row and the inner loop the column.

• TRAPS: COMMON PROGRAMMING ERRORS

- Putting a semicolon after the condition in a pretest loop.
- Testing a variable containing garbage at the beginning of a loop.
- Not putting a semicolon after the condition in a posttest loop.
- Not testing for the sentinel value until after it is used in a normal situation.
- Not initializing an accumulator.
- Expecting a floating-point counter to behave.

• YOUR TURN ANSWERS

• 5–1

1. An iteration structure repeats a set of operations.

2. A true condition in a C++ iteration structure continues the execution of the loop.

3. A pretest loop tests for continuation of the loop at the beginning of the loop. In C++ it begins with a `while` key word followed by the condition in parentheses. It ends at the end of the statement or block of statements following the condition. A posttest loop tests at the end of the loop. In C++ it begins with the key word `do`, followed by a statement or a block, and ends with `while` and a condition terminated with a semicolon.

4. A variable used in the normal course of operations is tested each time through the loop. If it contains the sentinel value, then the loop quits.

• 5–2

1. An accumulation process adds (or multiplies, or whatever) the value of a variable to some other value and stores the result in the original variable.

2. Initialization of the accumulator variable is important because if it contains garbage before the accumulation, it will contain garbage after it.

3. Counting is accumulation, but it adds the same value each time instead of different values.

4. Any counter-controlled loop must contain an initialization, a test, a body, a counter, and an end.

5. The initialization in a `for` statement occurs before the loop; the test occurs at the beginning of the loop; and the counter occurs at the end of the loop.

6. Floating-point numbers are approximated when they are calculated and stored; so successive approximations may lead to erroneous results.

7. If the operator falls before the variable, the variable is incremented before it is used in the expression. If the operator falls after, the variable is incremented after being used.

• 5–3

1. A nested loop is one loop contained with another loop.

2. For the correct formation of a nested loop, the inner loop must be entirely contained in the outer and, if they are both counter controlled, the counter variables must be different.

3. In a table situation, the outer loop typically controls the row and the inner loop the column because the typical output machinery, whether screen or printer, moves across the columns in a row, then down to the next row, across the columns, then down, and so forth. The columns are generated within the rows, hence the column loop within the row loop.

1. Rewrite the following program statements using acceptable, readable form.

   ```
   cout << "Input a number ";cin >> numb;while (numb !=
   0){cout << "That's not zero. Another ";cin >>
   numb);}cout << "Finally a zero." << endl;
   ```

2. Fill in an execution chart for the following program segment with the given execution.

   ```
   { int quiz, total = 0, quizzes = 0;

      cout << "Quiz score? ";
    cin >> quiz;
    do
    { total += quiz;
       ++quizzes;
      cout << "Quiz score? ";
      cin >> quiz;
    }while (quiz > 0);
      cout << setiosflags(ios::fixed) << setprecision(1);
      cout << "Average quiz: " << (1.0 * total / quizzes) << endl;
      return 0;
   }
   ```

   Quiz score? **16**
   Quiz score? **19**
   Quiz score? **-1**
   Average quiz: 17.5

3. Rewrite the following `while` loops using the `for` statement.

   ```
   x = 14;                  y = 65;
   while (x >= 3)           while (y <= 85)
   {  cout << x << endl;    {  cout << y << endl;
      x -= 5;                  y += 5;
   }                        }
   ```

4. Rewrite the following `for` statements using `while` loops.

   ```
   for (x = 250; x >= 100; x -= 50)
      cout << x << endl;


   for (y = 1226; y <= 1426; y += 2)
      cout << y << endl;
   ```

5. What will the output be from the following program segment?

   ```
   for (x = 16; x >= 4; --x);
      cout << "Hello\n";
   for (x = 16; x >= 4; --x)
      cout << "Hello" << endl;
      cout <<"How are you" << endl;
   ```

6. What will the output be from this program segment?

   ```
   for (a = 1; a <= 5; ++a)
   {  cout << a;
      for (b = a; b >= 1; --b)
         cout << b;
      cout << endl;
   }
   cout << a << " " << b;
   ```

PROGRAMS

1. Write a program that prints the smallest of five numbers input. Use an `if` statement to see if the new number input should replace the current minimum.

Variables

`input`	Number input at keyboard
`min`	To keep track of smallest
`count`	Loop counter

Output

```
Enter number 1: 59.2
Enter number 2: -3.789
Enter number 3: 42.5
Enter number 4: -28
Enter number 5: 12.6
The smallest is -28
```

2. You have found some cockroaches in your apartment. Rather than call the exterminator, you decide to perform an experiment. You count the number of roaches and then wait a week and count them again to determine their breeding rate. Print out the estimated roach population from that point on, assuming the breeding rate remains constant. Stop at the week that shows over a million roaches. You need not actually continue the experiment to validate your computer results—call the exterminator.

Variables

```
initialRoaches
roaches
breedingRate
week
```

Output

```
Roaches at beginning of week: 6
Roaches at end of week: 38

Week      Roaches
   2           38
   3          240
   4         1520
   5         9626
   6        60964
   7       386105
   8      2445331
```

3. A Pythagorean triple is three integers that make up the sides of a right triangle; for example, 3, 4, and 5. The sides may be calculated according to the formulas given as long as a is greater than b. Write a program that shows possible triples for a and b varying from 1 to 5.

Formulas

$side1 = a^2 - b^2$
$side2 = 2ab$
$hypotenuse = a^2 + b^2$

Variables

```
a, b
side1, side2, hypotenuse
```

Output

Side1	Side2	Hypotenuse
3	4	5
8	6	10
5	12	13
15	8	17
12	16	20
7	24	25
24	10	26
21	20	29
16	30	34
9	40	41

4. The game *Totals* can be played by any number of people. It starts with a total of 100 and each player in turn makes an integer adjustment between −20 and 20 to that total. The winner is the player whose adjustment makes the total equal to 5. Use only the three variables given.

Suggested Variables

```
total
adjustment
counter      Number of adjustments
decimal      Test for decimal point in input
```

Output

```
WE START WITH 100. WHAT IS
YOUR ADJUSTMENT? -20
    THE TOTAL IS 80
YOUR ADJUSTMENT? 4.6
    NOT AN INTEGER BETWEEN -20 AND 20
YOUR ADJUSTMENT? -35
    NOT AN INTEGER BETWEEN -20 AND 20
YOUR ADJUSTMENT? -20
    THE TOTAL IS 60
YOUR ADJUSTMENT? -15
    THE TOTAL IS 45
        .

        .

        .

YOUR ADJUSTMENT? -6
    THE TOTAL IS 5
THE GAME IS WON IN 14 STEPS
```

5. Write a program to assign a letter grade given a numeric score: 90 or above is an A; 80, B; 70, C; 60, D; and below 60, F. The program should continue to accept values until a negative number is input. The program should print how many of each letter grade were assigned after the input is completed. Use the `else if` construct in your program.

Variables

`score`	Score input
`aS, bS, cS, dS, fS`	Counters for letter grades

Output

```
SCORE? 92
  THE GRADE IS A
SCORE? 70
  THE GRADE IS C++

  .

  .

  .

SCORE? -1

2 A'S
2 B'S
4 C++'S
0 D'S
1 F'S
```

6. Modify Program 5 to use the `switch` statement.

7. Specific points on a compass may be expressed in general directions. For example, 130° is in an easterly direction. Write a program that will take directions in degrees and give them one of four general-direction titles: 315° up to but not including 45° is north, 45°–135° is east, 135°–225° is south, and 225°–315° is west. The program should reject invalid readings and end when a negative compass reading is input.

Variable

`degrees`	Direction in degrees input at keyboard

Output

```
COMPASS READING? 104
  EAST
COMPASS READING? 370
INVALID, ENTER ANOTHER COMPASS READING? 242
  WEST
COMPASS READING? -1
```

8. Write a program that converts feet to meters. Use a `for` loop. It should go from 1 to 10 feet in half-foot steps. One meter equals 3.28083 feet. To avoid approximation problems in fractional counting, use an integral loop counter and calculate the proper figures on output.

Variable

```
feet        Integral loop counter
```

Output

```
FEET TO METERS CONVERSION TABLE
FEET      METERS
 1.0      0.30480
 1.5      0.45720
 2.0      0.60960
           .
           .
           .
 9.0      2.74321
 9.5      2.89561
10.0      3.04801
```

9. Write a program to show the area of a circle (πr^2) and the volume of a sphere ($^4/_3 \pi r^3$) for all radii between 100 and 150 cm in increments of 5 cm ($\pi = 3.1416$).

Variable

```
radius
```

Output

RADIUS	AREA	VOLUME
100	31416.0	4.18880E+06
105	34636.1	4.84906E+06
110	38013.4	5.57530E+06
115	41547.7	6.37064E+06
120	45239.0	7.23825E+06
125	49087.5	8.18125E+06
130	53093.1	9.20280E+06
135	57255.7	1.03060E+07
140	61575.4	1.14941E+07
145	66052.1	1.27701E+07
150	70686.0	1.41372E+07

10. Write a program to create a multiplication table for all combinations of two numbers from 1 to 8.

Variables

```
multiplier
multiplicand
```

Output

	1	2	3	4	5	6	7	8
1	1	2	3	4	5	6	7	8
2	2	4	6	8	10	12	14	16
3	3	6	9	12	15	18	21	24
4	4	8	12	16	20	24	28	32
5	5	10	15	20	25	30	35	40
6	6	12	18	24	30	36	42	48
7	7	14	21	28	35	42	49	56
8	8	16	24	32	40	48	56	64

11. Write a program that allows you to input a desired total, after which it prints all possible combinations of three nonnegative integers that add up to that total. Set up nested loops to generate the three numbers and then test each combination to see whether its total equals the input total. The individual numbers never have to be greater than the desired total.

Variables

total	The desired total
c1, c2, c3	Counters to generate the three numbers
count	To count the number of valid combinations

Output

```
Desired total: 4
  0  0  4
  0  1  3
     . . .
  3  1  0
  4  0  0
15 number combinations total 4.
```

12. Write a program to produce the following output. Use nested `for` loops.

Output

```
1
1  2
1  2  3
1  2  3  4
1  2  3  4  5
1  2  3  4  5  6
1  2  3  4  5  6  7
1  2  3  4  5  6  7  8
1  2  3  4  5  6  7  8  9
1  2  3  4  5  6  7  8
1  2  3  4  5  6  7
1  2  3  4  5  6
1  2  3  4  5
1  2  3  4
1  2  3
1  2
1
```

13. The value of e^x can be calculated by expansion of Taylor's series,

$$1 + x + \frac{x^2}{2}! + \frac{x^3}{3}! + \ldots + \frac{x^n}{n}!$$

The expansion stops when the final term,

$$\frac{x^n}{n}!$$

is less than some value *epsilon*. Write a program that defines *epsilon* as an appropriately small value and allows input of the value for x. Remember, C++ does not have an exponentiation or a factorial operator, so you will have to calculate x^n and the various factorials in loops. Use appropriate variables and an effective output form.

Chapter 6

FUNCTIONS

PREVIEW

Some of the most important facets of objects are the behaviors they can exhibit. When we build completely self-contained objects, we will see that their behaviors are implemented as functions. In this chapter we will closely examine the principles of function use, and learn how we can create functions for our own purposes. You will learn:

- How functions are set up and included in programs.
- How to send values to functions to be processed.
- How to get processed values back from functions.
- Reasons for using functions in programs.
- Some of the functions that already exist in ANSI C++.

Objects exhibit behaviors and we use these behaviors to perform tasks for us. In C++ these behaviors are expressed in the form of **functions**—pieces of code written to perform specific operations. The elegance and sophistication of the C++ language is largely due to its free use of objects and their behaviors, and indeed to its virtual dependence on them. The language itself has very few statements, but along with your C++ compiler you will undoubtedly receive a wealth of different objects—not only the standard ANSI set but also others, many of which address the unique capabilities of your particular hardware. If the language still doesn't do what you want it to, you can make up your own objects with their own functions.

In fact, making up your own objects and functions is a desired objective. Top-down modular designs are easily implemented by translating each module into a separate object. If you set up these objects carefully, making sure they are totally self-contained and do not affect processes outside of them, you can use the objects you have designed for one program as objects in another.

We have already used a number of functions with standard objects; for example, the `setw()` (or `setiosflags()` or `setprecision()`) function with the `cout` object. When we included the name of the function, `setw`, for example, with the `cout` object and gave it something to work with, such as `setw(4)`, it performed its intended operation at that point in the program, that is, it set the width of the next output field to four. Here we will look at the mechanisms by which these functions operate.

HOW FUNCTIONS WORK

Let's look at an example process and see how we might set up some of its behaviors as functions. A company figures and writes its employees' paychecks by hand, a process its accounting personnel find cumbersome. They have called on us to help them.

TASK

Provide a program to calculate the data for employees' paychecks.

ANALYSIS

Each paycheck and check stub must contain the following information:

    Employee number
    Employee department
    Number of other dependents claimed by the employee
    Hours worked
    Pay rate
    Gross pay
    Total deductions
    Net pay

The employee number and department are derived from the employee identification code. The last digit is a department code, and the preceding digits are the employee number. The department codes are:

1   Information Systems
2   Accounting
3   Manufacturing and others

The employee's gross pay is the number of hours worked times the pay rate.

Taxes consist of federal income tax and state income tax. Both taxes are the gross pay times the appropriate tax rate. The federal income tax rate is reduced by 1 percent for every dependent, including the employee. Net pay is the gross pay minus the taxes minus a deduction for health insurance for each dependent beyond the employee.

To operate, then, the program must be given the employee ID, total number of dependents claimed, hours worked, pay rate, federal and state tax rates, and health-insurance deduction. The tax rates and health-insurance deduction change infrequently enough that they can be set up as constants in the program.

DESIGN

To reach the desired output from the inputs listed, the program must:

Input dependents
Decode employee ID
Calculate gross pay
Calculate taxes
Calculate net pay

IMPLEMENTATION and TEST

Let's set up each of these steps as different modules and show various methods of handling the modules. The first module, Input dependents, we will handle as we have done with our other programs up to this point—as inline code in the main() function.

```
int main(void)
{   int dependents;

    cout << "Dependents (including employee)? ";
    cin >> dependents;
}
```

We will add this module to our code when the value of *dependents* is needed.

The second module will require some expansion:

[Decode employee ID]
    Input employee ID
    Separate employee number
    Print employee number
    Separate department code
    Decode and print department code

Instead of putting it in the main() function, let's put it in its own function, *info()*.

```
    void info(void)  //*********************************** Decode employee info
    {   int empId, empNum, dept;

        cout << "Employee ID? ";
        cin >> empId;
        empNum = empId / 10;              // Separate empNum by deleting last digit
        cout << "Employee #" << empNum << " in the ";
        dept = empId % 10;               // dept - remainder is last digit of empId
        switch (dept)
        {   case 1:
                cout << "Information Systems";
                break;
            case 2:
                cout << "Accounting";
                break;
            default:
                cout << "Manufacturing or other";
        }
        cout << " department." << endl;
    }
```

Program 6–1

```
    #include <iostream>                            // Remember .h if needed
    using namespace std;                           // Use it if you need it

    void info(void);                                      // Function declaration

    int main(void) ///////////////////////////////////////////// Main Program
    {
        cout << setiosflags(ios::fixed) << setprecision(2);
4   info();                                                // Function call
8   cout << "Write the check!" << endl;
9   }
                                                       // Function definition
    void info(void)  //*********************************** Decode Employee Info
i1  {   int empId, empNum, dept;

        cout << "Employee ID? ";
i2      cin >> empId;
i3      empNum = empId / 10;              // Separate empNum by deleting last digit
i4      cout << "Employee #" << empNum << " in the ";
i5      dept = empId % 10;               // dept - remainder is last digit of empId
i6      switch (dept)
i7      {   case 1:
i8              cout << "Information Systems";
i9              break;
i10         case 2:
i11             cout << "Accounting";
i12             break;
i13         default:
i14             cout << "Manufacturing or other";
        }
i15     cout << " department." << endl;
i16 }                                               // End of function definition
```

HEADS UP!

The function definition is all the statements in the function.

The Function Definition

This code is a **function definition**. It defines the function's operation—tells C++ what actions to take in the function.

If this were the `main()` function and we ran the program, a sample test would produce:

```
Employee ID? 8471
Employee #847 in the Information Systems department.
```

In other words, this section of code could operate by itself.

The Function Call

Since we want this mini-program, the *info()* function, to be part of a larger program, let's have our `main()` function **call** it—set it in operation as part of the `main()` function code. Program 6–1, on the preceding page with the Output and Execution Chart shown below, adds the call to the `main()` function.

Output

```
Employee ID? 8471
Employee #847 in the Information Systems department.
Write the check!
```

EXECUTION CHART				
Line	Explanation			
4	Call *info()*.			
	info():	empId	empNum	dept
i1	Declare variables in *info()*.	??	??	??
i2	Input *empId*.	8471	??	??
i3	An integer division by 10 deletes last digit.	8471	847	??
i4	Print the employee number.	8471	847	??
i5	The remainder of a division by 10 will be the last digit.	8471	847	1
i6	`switch` on *dept*.	8471	847	1
i7	Matching `case`.	8471	847	1
i8	Print department name.	8471	847	1
i9	Go beyond end of `switch`.	8471	847	1
i15	Print "department."	8471	847	1
i16	End of function, return to call point in `main()`.	8471	847	1
	`main():`			
4	Statement completed, go to next statement.			
8	Final printout.			
9	Program execution ends at the end of the `main()` function.			

The Function Declaration

The **function declaration**, before the main() function, informs C++ of the *info()* function so that it can be called from some subsequent point in the program. The declaration is nothing more than the first line of the function definition (often called a *function header*) copied to a point near the top of the program with a semicolon added to the end. The semicolon is important here. The function declaration, like any other declaration, is a statement and must end in a semicolon.

A function declaration must appear before the function is called. We have put it near the top of the program so that we can call the function from anywhere in the program—from within main(), or perhaps from within some other function. The function definition also acts as a declaration and, in fact, if we had put the definition before main(), we would not have needed the separate declaration. It is common in structured programming, however, to put the controlling module, main() in C++, first, and all the submodules, other C++ functions, after it. This allows the overall process to be described in relatively simple terms near the beginning of the code. The detail is expanded after the overall process is shown.

The Function Return

The function call transfers execution to the function. In our example we set our output manipulators, and the next statements to execute are the declarations in the *info()* function. Execution continues with the statements in the function until the function runs out of statements—the program reaches the closing brace in the function. At that point execution will **return**—go back to where it left off at the call. The next statement to execute, then, is cout << "Write the check!" << endl; in the main() function. When the program reaches the closing brace of the main() function there is nowhere to return, so the program quits.

Let's add the next module, Calculate gross pay, to our program in a *grossPay()* function. With this module we made more sophisticated use of the function return. We will need the value of the gross pay later in the program, so we designed the *grossPay()* function with a **return value**—a value that substitutes for the function call after the function finishes execution. We call the *grossPay()* function from the main() function as follows:

```
int main(void) ///////////////////////////////////////////// Main Program
{
    cout << setiosflags(ios::fixed) << setprecision(2);
    info();                                         // Decode employee info
    gross = grossPay();                     // Function call and assignment
    cout << "Write the check!" << endl;
}
```

We declared *gross* as a double variable; therefore, we want the return value of *grossPay()* to be of data type double, because it will be assigned to *gross*. Following is the declaration of the *grossPay()* function:

```
double grossPay(void); //***************************** Calculate Gross Pay
```

The declaration of *grossPay()* function, and the first line of its definition (without the semicolon), begins with the key word `double`. This first element of a function declaration is the data type of the return value of the function. We refer to *grossPay()* as a `double` function, the type of its return value, because we can call the function anywhere in the program that we can use a `double` expression. The function's value will be a `double` after it has executed. For example, we might have included the *grossPay()* function call after the `cout`:

```
cout << "Write the check for " << grossPay();
```

Or we might add a bonus to an employee's pay like this:

```
cout << "Write the check for " << (grossPay() + bonus);
```

Because of our declaration, we can be assured that *grossPay()* will be a `double` value.

The key word **void** at the beginning of a function declaration, such as that in the *info()* function, means that the function returns no value. No value is substituted for the function call after the function executes.

A function may have only one return value, because the value substitutes for the call. If a function could return two values (which it can't), where would the extra value go?

Let's see how we will generate this `double` return value. Following is the function definition:

```
double grossPay(void) //******************************** Calculate Gross Pay
{  double hours, rate, gross;                          // Local variables

    cout << "Hours? ";
    cin >> hours;
    cout << "Rate? ";
    cin >> rate;
    gross = hours * rate;
    cout << "Gross pay:  " << setw(7) << gross << endl;
    return gross;
}                                    // hours, rate, and gross cease to exist
```

Local Variables

The second line of the *grossPay()* function definition declares three `double` variables: *hours*, *rate*, and *gross*. Because these variables were declared within this function, they are **local** to the function. Their **lifetime**, the part of the program in which C++ has allocated memory for them, begins when they are declared and ends when the function execution ends. When C++ finishes executing the *grossPay()* function, the memory space for these three variables will be deallocated—made available for C++ to use for some other purpose.

All the variables we have used in the `main()` function have been local to `main()`. Of course, since that has been the only function, the variables have "lived" throughout the program's execution. The variable *hours* will exist from the execution of its declaration, at the entry to the *grossPay()* function, until the function is finished executing. If the function is called again, an entirely new *hours* will be created, with an entirely new garbage value, and it will be destroyed again at the function's end.

HEADS UP!

The return value will always be the data type declared for the function.

HEADS UP!

A function can have only one return value.

HEADS UP!

Each call to a function sets up new local variables.

FIGURE 6–1

Local Variables

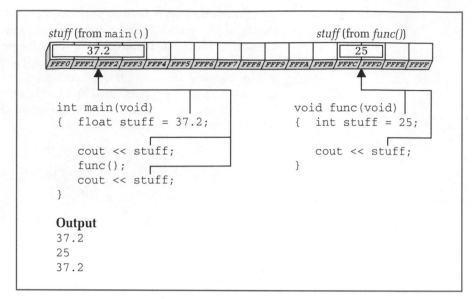

Output
37.2
25
37.2

Two local *stuff* variables are declared in this program. The lifetime of the one at memory address FFF0 extends to the end of the `main()` function, but its visibility is only during execution of statements from `main()`. The one at FFFC exists and is visible only during execution of the *func()* function. When execution returns to `main()`, it ceases to exist and the *stuff* at FFF0 is once again visible.

But what about the variable *gross*? It has been declared in both the `main()` and *grossPay()* functions. They are actually two different variables with two different places in memory. They might as well have been named *apples* and *petunias*, for all C++ cares. The *gross* declared in `main()` exists from its declaration to the closing brace at the end of the `main()` function, essentially throughout the program. However, its **visibility** (or *scope*), the part of the program in which we can access the variable by name, is also local to the `main()` function. That means that when C++ is not executing statements from `main()` it cannot "see," or access, the *gross* declared in `main()`. Therefore, when it is executing statements from *grossPay()*, the only *gross* it can see is the one declared in *grossPay()*.

As shown in Figure 6–1, local variables make it possible for us to write a function without having to worry about the function's variables having the same name as the variables in some other function. This property is especially handy if we make use of the function in some other program. We can simply copy the function without having to check inside it for conflicts.

HEADS UP!

Local variables make our functions more portable.

The `return` Statement

The statements in *grossPay()* execute until C++ encounters the **return statement**,

```
return expression;
```

where the value of `expression` is the return value of the function that substitutes for the call. In our example, the value of *gross* is returned to substitute for the `grossPay()` call in `main()`.

A function with a `void` return type, such as *info()*, may have a `return` statement, but that statement should have no *expression* after it. It can't because no value is to be substituted for the function. The `return` in that situation simply indicates that the process transfers back to the calling point. A function with a declared return type, such as *grossPay()*, must have a `return` statement; it must return a value of the stated type.

The `return` need not be physically the last statement in the function. In fact, there can be more than one `return` in a function. When a `return` is encountered, execution leaves the function and returns back to the calling point. The *info()* function does not return a value, but it could possibly have a number of `return` statements. The following segments execute equivalently:

No Return	Many Returns

```
switch (dept)                      switch (dept)
{  case 1:                         {  case 1:
     cout << "Info Systems dept.\n";     cout << "Info Systems dept.\n";
     break;                              return;
   case 2:                           case 2:
     cout << "Accounting dept.\n";       cout << "Accounting dept.\n";
     break;                              return;
   default:                          default:
     cout << "Manufacturing dept.\n";    cout << "Manufacturing dept.\n";
}                                        return;
Function ends                      }
```

HEADS UP!

A strictly structured function has only one return.

Many structured programmers would balk at the program segment on the right because the `switch` structure has not one but many exit points. To be universally accepted, your structure should have no more than one `return`, and it should be at the end of the function.

In Program 6–2, on the following two pages, let's examine our program with the new function added. We won't repeat the *info()* function in the code, but will assume it is there. We can see in the Execution Chart that the variables declared in each function, `main()` and *grossPay()*, are local to that function. They are visible and accessible only within that function. The variable *gross* declared in `main()` still exists while the program is executing the *grossPay()* function, but it cannot be accessed until the program returns to `main()`. We show this in the Execution Chart by putting its values in parentheses.

YOUR TURN 6–1

1. What is a function definition?
2. What does a function call do?
3. What is a function declaration? Where must it appear?
4. What is the function return?
5. Differentiate between the terms *lifetime* and *visibility* (or *scope*).
6. Describe the actions of the `return` statement.
7. What does the return type or declaration `void` mean?

Program 6–2

```
       #include <iostream>
       #include <iomanip>
       using namespace std;

       void info(void);                                      // Decode employee info
       double grossPay(void);                                // Calculate gross pay

       int main(void) ///////////////////////////////////////////// Main Program
 2     {   double gross;                                     // Local variable

           cout << setiosflags(ios::fixed) << setprecision(2);
 4         info();                                           // Decode employee info
 5         gross = grossPay();                               // Calculate gross pay
 8         cout << "Write the check!" << endl;
 9     }

       double grossPay(void) //******************************** Calculate Gross Pay
g1     {   double hours, rate, gross;                        // Local variables

           cout << "Hours? ";
g2         cin >> hours;
           cout << "Rate? ";
g3         cin >> rate;
g4         gross = hours * rate;
g5         cout << "Gross pay:  " << setw(7) << gross << endl;
g6         return gross;
       }                                 // hours, rate, and gross cease to exist
```

PASSING DATA TO FUNCTIONS

We have seen how a function can return the results of its labors, but we can also, as part of the call, **pass** it data—give it values to work with. Here we are not limited to a single value; we may pass it as many values as we need. In our paycheck example, let's set up a *taxes()* function to calculate the taxes, and return the value of the taxes. In the main() function we will assign the return value to a variable.

```
tax = taxes();                                  // Calculate taxes
```

In order to operate, however, the *taxes()* function needs the gross pay and the number of dependents. We can pass these data as **arguments** to the function.

```
tax = taxes(gross, dependents);                 // Calculate taxes
```

To generalize, a function call consists of the following:

functionName(argument, argument, . . . argument)

where an *argument* is an expression identifying data to be sent to the function.

Output

```
Employee ID? 8471
Employee #847 in the Information Systems department.
Hours? 40
Rate? 15
Gross pay:    600.00
Write the check!
```

EXECUTION CHART

Line	Explanation	gross		hours	rate	gross
2	Declare local variable *gross*.	??				
4	Call *info()*.	??				
5	Call *grossPay()*.	??				
	grossPay():			*hours*	*rate*	*gross*
g1	Declare local variables in *grossPay()*.	(??)		??	??	??
g2	Input *hours*.	(??)		40	??	??
g3	Input *rate*.	(??)		40	15	??
g4	Assign *gross*. This has no effect on the *gross* in `main()`; it is still garbage.	(??)		40	15	600
g5	Print *gross*.	(??)		40	15	600
g6	Set return value of *grossPay()* to *gross*, end execution in the function, and return to `main()`.	(??)		40	15	600
	`main():`					
5	Assign return value of *grossPay()* to *gross*.	600				
8	Final printout.	600				

If we are to send this data to the function, there must be something in the function to receive it. We must declare variables in the function to accept the data that we send it. The first line of the *taxes()* function definition might be

```
double taxes(double gPay, int dependents) //*************** Calculate taxes
```

The generalized form of a definition first line (or function header) is

returnType functionName(declaration, declaration, . . . declaration)

where each *declaration*, or **parameter declaration**, is the declaration of a variable to accept the data being passed to the function.

There are a number of ways of passing data to a function; they are differentiated by the types of the arguments passed and by the declarations of the accepting variables in the function. In this chapter we will discuss first the *pass by reference* and then the *pass by value*.

Pass By Reference

A **pass by reference** allows a called function to access a variable in a calling function by declaring another name for the variable in the called function. (This other name is often referred to as an *alias*.) In the *taxes()* function we want to access the *gross* and *dependents* variables from the `main()` function. In defining the *taxes()* function, then, we set up two variable names as references, other names for, *gross* and *dependents*. To show that these variables are references, we precede the variable name in each declaration with the **reference operator**, `&`. Since *gross* is a `double` and *dependents* is an `int`, the *taxes()* function has to declare references to a `double` and an `int`.

```
double taxes(double &gPay, int &dependents) //************* Calculate taxes
```

There must always be a match between the function call and the first line of the function definition. The definition declares a fixed number of variables in a certain order, each with its own particular data type. In the *taxes()* example there are two variables declared, the first a reference to a `double` and the second a reference to an `int`. The call must provide two variables of those data types in that order, and it does—the type of *gross* is `double` and the type of *dependents* is `int`.

```
tax = taxes(gross, dependents);                          // Calculate taxes

double taxes(double &gPay, int &dependents) //************* Calculate taxes
```

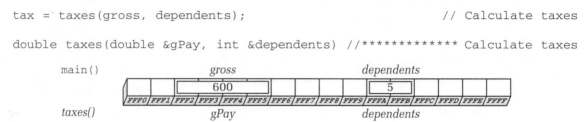

Now we have two names for each variable, one visible in the `main()` function and the other in the *taxes()* function. Two names for each? The names *gross* and *gPay* are certainly different, but the name *dependents* seems to be the same in each place. Only to us though. Remember, the names are only visible in their respective functions, so, in the *taxes()* function, for example, C++ cannot see the *dependents* name in `main()`. Therefore, although they refer to the same place in memory, to C++ they might just as well be two different names.

The Function Prototype

HEADS UP!

The function call not agreeing with the parameter declarations in the function.

The ANSI committee has set some definite standards, referred to as a function **prototype**, for a function declaration. It must state the *returnType*, the *functionName*, and the data types of the variables to be declared for the data passed. It need not include the variable names. The following would be an acceptable prototype for the *taxes()* function we showed above:

```
double taxes(double &, int &);                           // Calculate taxes
```

As noted before, the declaration of the function can be the first line of its definition copied before `main()`, with a semicolon added to it. This makes a perfectly acceptable prototype:

```
double taxes(double &gPay, int &dependents);             // Calculate taxes
```

Most programmers leave the variable names in the prototype for two reasons:

1. With most text editors, it is easy to copy a complete line from one place to another.

HEADS UP!

Prototypes are more readable
with variable names.

HEADS UP!

Make sure your data types
match when calling functions.

2. The declaration is more easily understood with descriptive variable names in it. The C++ compiler will ignore the variable names here in any case.

The function prototype allows the compiler to catch possible errors in the program. Because it knows what to expect, it matches the function call's return type with that of the function, as well as the number and types of passed arguments.

Let's add the *taxes()* function to Program 6–3. In this Execution Chart we have not shown variables that exist but are not visible—the `main()` function's *gross*, *tax*, and *dependents* in the *taxes()* function, for example.

Program 6–3

```
    #include <iostream>
    #include <iomanip>
    using namespace std;

    const float fedRate = 0.2;                         // Federal income tax rate
    const float stateRate = 0.1;                        // State income tax rate

    void info(void);                                    // Decode employee info
    double grossPay(void);                             // Calculate gross pay
    double taxes(double &gPay, int &dependents);        // Calculate taxes

    int main(void) ////////////////////////////////////////////// Main Program
 1  {   double gross, tax;
 2      int dependents;

        cout << setiosflags(ios::fixed) << setprecision(2);
        cout << "Dependents (including employee)? ";
 3      cin >> dependents;
 4      info();                                         // Decode employee info
 5      gross = grossPay();                             // Calculate gross pay
 6      tax = taxes(gross, dependents);                 // Calculate taxes
 8      cout << "Write the check!" << endl;
 9  }

t1  double taxes(double &gPay, int &dependents) //************ Calculate Taxes
t2  {   double fedTax, stateTax;

t3      fedTax = gPay * (fedRate - 0.01 * dependents);
t4      stateTax = gPay * stateRate;
t5      cout << "Taxes:       " << setw(7) << (fedTax + stateTax) << endl;
t6      return fedTax + stateTax;
    }
```

Output

```
    Dependents (including employee)? 5
    Employee ID? 8471
    Employee #847 in the Information Systems department.
    Hours? 40
    Rate? 15
    Gross pay:    600.00
    Taxes:        150.00
    Write the check!
```

Line	Explanation	gross	tax	depend	
3	Input *dependents*.	??	??	5	
4	Call *info()*.	??	??	5	
5	Call *grossPay()*.	600	??	5	
6	Call *taxes()*, passing *gross* and *dependents*.	600	??	5	
taxes():		depend	gPay	fedTax	stateTax
t1	Declare local reference variables *gPay* and *dependents*.	5	600	—	—
t2	Declare local variables *fedTax* and *stateTax*.	5	600	??	??
t3	Calculate federal tax.	5	600	90	??
t4	Calculate state tax.	5	600	90	60
t5	Print total taxes.	5	600	90	60
t6	Set return value of *taxes()* to *fedTax* + *stateTax*, end execution in the function, and return to `main()`.	5	600	90	60
`main():`		gross	tax	depend	
6	Assign return value of *taxes()* to *tax*.	600	150	5	
8	Final printout.	600	150	5	

In the `return` statement, t6, the return value was calculated from an expression, rather than given the value of a single variable. Remember, the `return` statement can contain any expression.

Pass By Value

Another way of getting data to a function is the **pass by value**. Here again, the call will have various arguments and the first line of the function definition will have parameter declarations of variables to receive the arguments. The difference is that in the first line of the function definition we declare actual local variables rather than just new names for other variables. These local variables are initialized by the values of the arguments in the call.

For example, we could have produced the same result in the *taxes()* function by passing by value instead of by reference. The call would have been exactly the same, but the first line of the function definition would have been:

```
double taxes(double gPay, int dependents) //************** Calculate taxes
```

Leaving out the reference operators (&) indicates to C++ that we want these to be local variables initialized by the values of the call arguments, and not just new names for the argument variables.

After executing the call and transferring to the function, memory might look like the following diagram. C++ has allocated space for the *gPay* and *dependents* variables declared in *taxes()* and initialized them with copies of the values of the call arguments. The *gross* and *dependents* variables from the `main()` function still exist, of course, but they are not visible while the program is in the *taxes()* function. Any changes to *dependents* would affect only the *dependents* at AAA1.

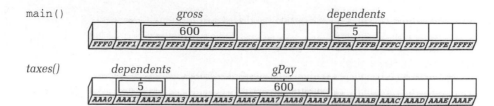

main()

	gross							dependents							

```
                    600                              5
FFF0 FFF1 FFF2 FFF3 FFF4 FFF5 FFF6 FFF7 FFF8 FFF9 FFFA FFFB FFFC FFFD FFFE FFFF
```

taxes()   dependents   gPay

```
         5                          600
AAA0 AAA1 AAA2 AAA3 AAA4 AAA5 AAA6 AAA7 AAA8 AAA9 AAAA AAAB AAAC AAAD AAAE AAAF
```

Let's finish the program by adding a function that calculates and prints the net pay. We want the function to also return the net pay so that we may include it when we write the check. In the calculation of net pay, the health insurance deduction is based on the number of dependents, not including the employee. In the function call, then, we pass one less than the total number of dependents claimed.

```
net = netPay(gross, tax, dependents - 1);                // Calculate net pay
```

For the third argument, `dependents - 1`, we cannot possibly use a pass by reference, because that type of pass simply substitutes one variable name for another. The term `dependents - 1` is not a variable name; it is an expression to be evaluated. We have to use the pass by value, sending a copy of the value of `dependents - 1` to the function and having it initialize a variable there. The other two arguments would work with either type of pass, but let's pass them all by value. The first line of the *netPay()* function definition, then, would be:

```
double netPay(double gPay, double tax, int dependents) //********** Net pay
```

The variable *dependents* in the *netPay()* function is a totally different variable than *dependents* in main(), so the fact that they have different values is no problem. In fact, the variables actually have different names—at least to C++. The same can be said for the variables *net* in *netPay()* and *net* in main(). They end up having the same value, but they are in completely different places in main memory, probably nowhere near each other.

Program 6–4 on the following page shows the revised code.

Let's examine the difference between a variable declared in the first line of a function definition, say *tax* in Program 6–4, and a variable declared within the function, say *net*. There really isn't much! The only difference is that *tax* is initialized by a value passed to the function; *net* is not initialized (unless we change the declaration to something like `double net = 123.45;`). Both are local variables and both will disappear when the program exits the function.

Remember, functions may be called in any place the function's return value is appropriate. For example, we could rewrite our program to combine statements 6 and 7:

```
netPay(gross, taxes(gross, dependents), dependents - 1);       // Net pay
```

In passing values to *netPay()*, C++ will have to evaluate *taxes()* first. The output will be exactly the same.

We would not want to combine 5, 6, and 7:

```
netPay(grossPay(), taxes(grossPay(), dependents), dependents - 1);
```

because that would call *grossPay()* twice—and the operations within *grossPay()* include inputting *hours* and *rate*, then printing the gross pay,

HEADS UP!

A function call is an expression of a declared data type.

Program 6-4

```cpp
     #include <iostream>
     #include <iomanip>
     using namespace std;

     const float fedRate = 0.2;                        // Federal income tax rate
     const float stateRate = 0.1;                      // State income tax rate
     const float health = 10;         // Health insurance for each extra dependent

     void info(void);                                  // Decode employee info
     double grossPay(void);                            // Calculate gross pay
     double taxes(double &gPay, int &dependents);      // Calculate taxes
     double netPay(double gPay, double tax, int dependents);      // Net pay

     int main(void) ///////////////////////////////////////////////// Main Program
1    {   double gross, tax, net;
2        int dependents;

         cout << setiosflags(ios::fixed) << setprecision(2);
         cout << "Dependents (including employee)? ";
3        cin >> dependents;
4        info();                                       // Decode employee info
5        gross = grossPay();                           // Calculate gross pay
6        tax = taxes(gross, dependents);               // Calculate taxes
7        net = netPay(gross, tax, dependents - 1);     // Calculate net pay
8        cout << "Write the check for $" << net << "." << endl;
9    }

n1   double netPay(double gPay, double tax, int dependents) //********   Net Pay
n2   {   double net;

n3       net = gPay - tax - (health * dependents);
n4       cout << "Net pay:     " << setw(7) << net << endl;
n5       return net;
     }
```

TRAP

Depending on a certain order of argument evaluation.

all of which would occur twice. In addition, different implementations of C++ evaluate the arguments in different orders, some from first to last, others from last to first. Our output might be either

Hours? **40**		or	Hours? **40**	
Rate? **15**			Rate? **15**	
Gross pay:	600.00		Gross pay:	600.00
Hours? **40**			Taxes:	150.00
Rate? **15**			Hours? **40**	
Gross pay:	600.00		Rate? **15**	
Taxes:	150.00		Gross pay:	600.00
Net pay:	410.00		Net pay:	410.00

Strings may be passed and returned just as easily as other data types. Let's add a *check()* function (Program 6–5) that writes the check, or at least writes the payee and amount line of the check. We input the payee's *name* in the main() function and pass the value to the *payee* variable in the *check()* function. In this case we could also have passed the string by

EXECUTION CHART

Line	Explanation	gross	tax	net	depend
7	Call *netPay()*, passing values of *gross*, *tax*, and *dependents* – 1.	600	150	??	5
	netPay():	*gPay*	*tax*	*depend*	*net*
n1	Declare and initialize local variables *gPay*, *tax*, and *dependents*.	600	150	4	—
n2	Declare local variable *net*.	600	150	4	??
n3	Calculate net pay.	600	150	4	410
n4	Print net pay.	600	150	4	410
n5	Return value of *net* to call point in `main()`.	600	150	4	410
	`main():`	*gross*	*tax*	*net*	*depend*
7	Assign return value of *netPay()* to *net*.	600	150	410	5
8	Final printout.	600	150	410	5

Output

```
Dependents (including employee)? 5
Employee ID? 8471
Employee #847 in the Information Systems department.
Hours? 40
Rate? 15
Gross pay:    600.00
Taxes:        150.00
Net pay:      410.00
Write the check for $410.00.
```

reference, making *payee* a new name for the *name* variable instead of copying *name*'s value into the *payee* variable. The amount was passed by reference.

Returning More Than One Value

You can't!

A function can return only one value. But we can effectively get more than one value back to the calling function with a pass by reference. Remember, a pass by reference sets up another name in the called function for a variable in the calling function—passing *one* to &*two*, for example. Any change we make to *two* in the called function is a change to *one* in the calling function since they are the same variable. By passing the function references to variables, then, we give the function place to put new values.

Let's illustrate by changing Program 6–5 into Program 6–6. Here we combine the *taxes()* function into the *netPay()* function and change the *check()* function to print out both the net pay and the taxes. Program 6–6 shows `main()` and the changed parts of the program.

We have added another parameter to the *check()* function, `double tax`, so we can print out the taxes withheld in the check. The `main()` function, then, must have a value for *tax* before the call to *check()*. Since taxes are calculated in *netPay()*, there is no call to *taxes()*. Instead, we change the

HEADS UP!

Passing references can overcome the limitation of a single return value.

Program 6-5

```cpp
#include <iostream>
#include <iomanip>
#include <string>
using namespace std;

const float fedRate = 0.2;                          // Federal income tax rate
const float stateRate = 0.1;                        // State income tax rate
const float health = 10;        // Health insurance for each extra dependent

void info(void);                                    // Decode employee info
double grossPay(void);                              // Calculate gross pay
double taxes(double &gPay, int &dependents);        // Calculate taxes
double netPay(double gPay, double tax, int dependents);       // Net pay
void check(string payee, double &amount);           // Check pay line

int main(void) ///////////////////////////////////////////////// Main Program
{   double gross, tax, net;
    int dependents;
    string name;

    cout << setiosflags(ios::fixed) << setprecision(2);
    cout << "Employee name? ";
    cin >> name;
    cout << "Dependents (including employee)? ";
    cin >> dependents;
    info();                                         // Decode employee info
    gross = grossPay();                             // Calculate gross pay
    tax = taxes(gross, dependents);                 // Calculate taxes
    net = netPay(gross, tax, dependents - 1);       // Calculate net pay
    check(name, net);
}

void check(string payee, double &amount) //***************** Check Pay Line
{
    cout << "Pay to the order of " << payee << "  $" << amount << endl;
}
```

Output

```
Employee name? Flitzbargle
Dependents (including employee)? 5
Employee ID? 8471
Employee #847 in the Information Systems department.
Hours? 40
Rate? 15
Gross pay:    600.00
Taxes:        150.00
Net pay:      410.00
Pay to the order of Flitzbargle  $410.00
```

Program 6–6

```
    double netPay(double gPay, double &tax, int dependents); // Net pay and tax
    void check(string payee, double amount, double tax);        // Check output

    int main(void) //////////////////////////////////////////////// Main Program
    {   double gross, tax, net;
        string name;
        int dependents;

        cout << setiosflags(ios::fixed) << setprecision(2);
        cout << "Employee name? ";
        cin >> name;
        cout << "Dependents (including employee)? ";
        cin >> dependents;
        info();                                          // Decode employee info
        gross = grossPay();                              // Calculate gross pay
        net = netPay(gross, tax, dependents - 1); // Calculate net pay and taxes
        check(name, net, tax);
        return 0;
    }

    double netPay(double gPay, double &tax, int dependents) //********* Net Pay
    {   double net, fedTax, stateTax;

        fedTax = gPay * (fedRate - 0.01 * dependents);
        stateTax = gPay * stateRate;
        cout << "Taxes:        " << setw(7) << (fedTax + stateTax) << endl;
        tax = fedTax + stateTax;
        net = gPay - tax - (health * dependents);
        cout << "Net pay:     " << setw(7) << net << endl;
        return net;
    }

    void check(string payee, double amount, double tax) //******** Check Output
    {
        cout << "Pay to the order of " << payee << "  $" << amount << endl;
        cout << "Taxes withheld: " << tax << endl;
    }
```

Output

```
    Employee name? Flitzbargle
    Dependents (including employee)? 5
    Employee ID? 8471
    Employee #847 in the Information Systems department.
    Hours? 40
    Rate? 15
    Gross pay:    600.00
    Taxes:        156.00
    Net pay:      404.00
    Pay to the order of Flitzbargle  $404.00
    Taxes withheld: 156.00
```

double tax parameter in *netPay()* to a reference, double &tax. The value of *tax* in main() before the call is garbage, but *netPay()* will assign it a valid value. After the return from *netPay()*, *tax* has the value needed to send to *check()*.

The *netPay()* function returns only a single value but, because of the reference, main() has two new values after the function executes.

Why Use Functions?

Now that you see how functions operate, let's recap a bit and list the reasons we use functions:

- *Object orientation.* An object's behaviors are expressed in functions. As we start to build more complicated stand-alone objects, the functions we include in these objects can make the objects' behaviors accessible to the rest of the program.

- *Modularity.* Functions are an excellent way of implementing modularity.

- *Readability.* In a modular program, as all of ours should be, the overall process is outlined in the main() function, with all the subprocesses detailed in functions that follow.

- *Debugability.* It is easier to debug—clean out the errors—in a small section of code than in a complicated program. As in our paycheck example, each function was tested and debugged as it was written.

- *Repeatability.* If a process is used more than once during a program (perhaps there are several points at which we must decode an employee ID), the code may be written only once, debugged, and then called any number of times.

- *Reusability.* Most new programs are written by reusing as much code as possible from old programs. For example, tax calculations may have to be done not only in the payroll program but also in the tax-reporting program. The *taxes()* function has already been written and debugged, so we can simply copy it into the tax-reporting program. In fact, we may make a file of the source code for common functions and include the file in a number of programs. By using local variables in the functions, we do not have to worry about the variables in a particular function conflicting with the variables in any other.

EXTERNAL VARIABLES

In Program 6–6, all the variable declarations were **internal**, within some function. The internally declared variables were local to the function. Their visibility (or scope) was limited to code within the function, and their lifetime lasted only until execution of the function's code finished—a return or the closing brace of the function.

When we prototyped the functions, the declarations were **external**, outside of any function. These declarations gave the functions **global**

Program 6-7

```cpp
// Shows use of global variables. Not usually a good idea.
#include <iostream>
#include <iomanip>
#include <string>
using namespace std;

const float fedRate = 0.2;                      // Federal income tax rate
const float stateRate = 0.1;                    // State income tax rate
const float health = 10;        // Health insurance for each extra dependent

void info(void);                                // Decode employee info
double grossPay(void);                          // Calculate gross pay
double taxes(double &gPay, int &dependents);    // Calculate taxes
void netPay(void);                              // Net pay using globals
void check(string payee, double amount);        // Check pay line

double gross, tax, net;                         // Variables used with netPay()
int dependents;

int main(void) ///////////////////////////////////////////////// Main Program
{   string name;

    cout << setiosflags(ios::fixed) << setprecision(2);
    cout << "Employee name? ";
    cin >> name;
    cout << "Dependents (including employee)? ";
    cin >> dependents;
    info();                                     // Decode employee info
    gross = grossPay();                         // Calculate gross pay
    tax = taxes(gross, dependents);             // Calculate taxes
    --dependents;                   // To adjust dependents for function
    netPay();                                   // Calculate net pay
    ++dependents;                   // Return to previous value
    check(name, net);
}

void netPay(void)  //********************************************* Net Pay
{
    net = gross - tax - (health * dependents);
    cout << "Net pay:    " << setw(7) << net << endl;
}
```

visibility—they could be called from anywhere in the program. If we had declared the functions internally, we could only have called the functions from the function that contained the declaration.

We can also declare variables externally, giving them global lifetime (lifetime extending from the declaration to the end of the program) and global visibility (accessibility from within any function in the program). Why bother with all these local variables, passing values, and returns? Why not simply declare our variables externally so that any function can access them? We could rewrite part of our previous example like Program 6–7.

The execution would be the same, but most programmers would shy away from such construction. The *netPay()* function is no longer an independent module; it depends not only on data from another function but also on specific variable names. Making a change in one part of your program may lead to unexpected changes in other parts, and modifications and debugging become difficult.

Our *netPay()* function, which, in a real-world situation, may be called from many different places in many different programs, defines *dependents* as the number of dependents not including the employee. Our previous call, using local variables, adjusted for that by subtracting one from *dependents* in `main()` before sending the value to the function. Our new call, using global variables, must still make the required number of dependents available to the function, so, in `main()`, we had to subtract one from *dependents*, call the function, and then add the one back to *dependents*. Clumsy!

HEADS UP!

Local variables supersede
global variables.

What about the *dependents* variable in *taxes()*? Won't it conflict with the global *dependents*? No. Any local variable will **supersede** or **hide** (or *mask off*) a global variable of the same name. In other words, while the local variable is visible, we cannot "see," or access, the global variable. Once the local variable's visibility is over, we can again access the global variable.

Naming local variables the
same as constants.

Incidentally, notice that all of our constants are declared externally—they are global. We must be careful to not declare local variables with the same names. One handy trick for avoiding the problem is to declare constant names in all uppercase. Since we traditionally use lowercase characters for other variable names, there would be no conflict. This technique is commonly used in C, but has not gained wide acceptance in C++.

The price in execution for using local variables is small compared to the benefits in programming and maintainability. Do yourself and other C programmers (who might have to look at your program) a favor and keep your code as clean and independent as possible.

YOUR TURN 6–2

1. Differentiate between a pass by reference and a pass by value.
2. Why is ANSI prototyping advantageous?
3. List six reasons for using functions.
4. Differentiate between the terms *local* and *global*.
5. Differentiate between the terms *internal* and *external*, specifically as they relate to declarations.
6. How do local variables lead to better modularity within programs?
7. What happens if a local variable has the same name as a global variable?

SOME EXISTING FUNCTIONS

An ANSI C++ compiler will come with a complete stock of functions—certainly all those defined in the ANSI standard, and usually others that work with the specific target computer. To this group you may add an unlimited number of functions that you can buy from third-party vendors and that you write yourself.

Header Files

Under ANSI, all functions should be prototyped—explicitly and completely declared—typically near the beginning of the program. When we use the ANSI functions and usually all the functions provided by third-party vendors, we don't have to write the declarations; they are already written in separate files called **header files**. These files are usually kept in the system in some specific directory or folder, typically named *include*. The file `iostream` is one such file; its name stands for "input/output streams." These files are source code, readable by you and me, and we put them in our source code using the `#include` directive.

```
#include <iostream>
```

We never see the source code because the compiler, when it reaches that directive in our source code, shifts to the header file and copies lines from it. When it runs out of lines from the header file it returns to where it left off in our source file and continues.

We can, however, see the code in the header file by using a text editor and calling up the header file. If you try this, be sure not to make any modifications! You will find that the header files contain prototyped function declarations (among other things) but not function definitions. The definitions are in **libraries** of object code waiting to be combined with your program, if they are needed, during the linking process (refer to the *From Source to Execution* section in Chapter 1).

When you use a library function, then, you must `#include` the proper header file for it; otherwise, C++ will not recognize the function name. When we introduce a library function in this book, we will always put the header-file name in angle brackets to the right of the description.

Terminating a Program

When C++ runs out of statements in the `main()` function, the program quits; this is the normal way of terminating a program. But what if something unexpected happens? The program might receive erroneous or meaningless data; it could get stuck in a loop; the programmer in the office next to yours could stick her finger in a light socket, causing your computer to cough; or whatever. You may want to build other exit points into your program to give the program a "normal" termination instead of printing 147 pages of gibberish and then dying.

Most operating systems are capable of reacting to the termination of a program that has run successfully versus one that has run unsuccessfully. To do that, however, the operating system must receive a signal from the program as it terminates, indicating success or failure. The **exit()** function provides both the termination and the indicator to the operating system.

```
void exit(int status)                              <cstdlib>
```

(We have shown `cstdlib` and the header file for `exit()` and some other functions that we will be examining. This is a relatively new standard for C++. If your program will not compile using it, try its predecessor file, `stdlib.h`.)

HEADS UP!

Header files are source code.

HEADS UP!

The functions themselves are in compiled library files, not header files.

TRAP

Not including the proper header file for a library function.

HEADS UP!

If you can foresee a possible error condition, either handle it in the program or provide an orderly `exit()`.

Program 6–8

```cpp
#include <iostream>
#include <cstdlib>
using namespace std;

int main(void)
{   int ascii;
    char character;

    cout << "Enter an ASCII code and I will show\n"
         << "you the character it represents: ";
    cin >> ascii;
    if (ascii < 32 || ascii > 126)
    {   cout << "Not a printable ASCII code." << endl;
        exit(EXIT_FAILURE);
    }
    character = ascii;
    cout << "The character is '" << character << "'." << endl;
}
```

Outputs

```
Enter an ASCII code and I will show
you the character it represents: 65
The character is 'A'.

Enter an ASCII code and I will show
you the character it represents: 312
Not a printable ASCII code.
[Program ends]
```

The *status* can be any value or expression, but for the operating system to recognize it, we should use the constants EXIT_SUCCESS or EXIT_FAILURE, also defined in cstdlib, to send the proper signal to the operating system.

```cpp
if (result < 0)
    exit(EXIT_FAILURE);
else
    exit(EXIT_SUCCESS);
```

The return value is void because there is no program left to which to return a value! The exit() function is demonstrated in Program 6–8.

The latest proposed ANSI C++ standard includes a concept known as "exception handling" to deal with unexpected problems. Exception handling is really a topic for a more advanced examination of C++; as you become more sophisticated in your C++ programming you may want to look it up.

Some Mathematical Functions

ANSI C++ contains more than two dozen mathematical functions, and most ANSI C++ implementations feature even more. While we will not discuss

Program 6–9

```cpp
#include <iostream>
#include <cmath>
using namespace std;

const float pi = 3.1416;

int main(void)
{   double radius;

    cout << "Enter the radius: ";
    cin >> radius;
    cout << "Volume: " << (4 / 3.0 * pi * pow(radius, 3)) << endl;
}
```

Output

```
Enter the radius: 6.28
Volume: 1037.45
```

HEADS UP!

There are different absolute value functions for different data types.

all of them, a few examples should give you enough to tackle most tasks—and the understanding to research other available functions.

The absolute value of a number is the magnitude of the number irrespective of sign; in other words, expressed without a sign. The absolute value of 5 is 5. The absolute value of –5 is also 5. Three functions, **abs()**, **labs()**, and **fabs()**, return absolute value. The choice of function depends on the data type you are working with.

Function   Library

```
int abs(int expression)                    <cstdlib>
long labs(long expression)                 <cstdlib>
double fabs(double expression)             <cmath>
```

C++ has no exponentiation operator, no way of directly raising a number to a power. Raising values to integer powers can be accomplished by successive multiplication—2^3 is $2 \times 2 \times 2$—but that is certainly insufficient for general exponentiation. C++'s **pow()** function handles the task for us.

```
double pow(double expression, double exponent)     <cmath>
```

The *exponent* can, of course, be anything that evaluates to a number. The return value will be the *expression* raised to the power of the *exponent*, that is, *expression*^{exponent}.

The pow() function follows the usual rules of exponentiation. The *expression* and *exponent* cannot both be zero. If the *exponent* is zero, then pow() returns 1. If the *expression* is negative, the *exponent* must be a whole number.

Program 6–9 prints the volume of a sphere of any radius.

If you want a square root, you can either raise something to the 0.5 power or use the **sqrt()** function:

Program 6–10

```
#include <iostream>
#include <cstdlib>
using namespace std;

int main(void)
{
    cout << "Three random numbers:\n "
         << rand() << " " << rand() << " " << rand() << endl;
}
```

Outputs

```
Three random numbers:          Three random numbers:        Three random numbers:
  10982 130 346                  10982 130 346                10982 130 346
```

double sqrt(double *expression*)   <cmath>

which returns the square root of the expression.

In addition to pow() and sqrt(), there is a full set of logarithmic functions.

The **trigonometric functions** are straightforward in C++. For example, to get the sine of an angle,

double sin(double *angle*)   <cmath>

Expressing angles in degrees.

The *angle* in C++ is represented in radians, not degrees. The following function call would return the sine of *degrees* expressed in degrees.

sin(degrees * pi / 180)   // pi must be assigned before this

There are also functions for the arc sine and hyperbolic sine as well as those for cosine and tangent. All require double arguments and return double values, and all are declared in cmath.

```
sin        asin       sinh
cos        acos       cosh
tan        atan       tanh
```

For a summary of all the ANSI C++ mathematical functions, see Appendix C.

Random Numbers

C++ has three functions that, when used together, generate random numbers (more properly, pseudorandom numbers—mathematically generated random numbers). The first, **rand()**, mathematically generates a pseudo-random number by taking a number, referred to as the **seed**, and applying some monstrous algorithm to it so that the result looks *nothing* like the seed:

int rand(void)   <cstdlib>

There is no argument; not even a seed. C++ maintains the seed number within the system. We don't know where it is but C++ does. The value of the pseudorandom number is always positive and between zero and

Program 6–11

```
#include <iostream>
#include <cstdlib>
using namespace std;

int main(void)
{
    srand(10);
    cout << "Three random numbers:\n "
         << rand() << " " << rand() << " " << rand() << endl;
}
```

Outputs

```
Three random numbers:        Three random numbers:        Three random numbers:
  10345 30957 3463             10345 30957 3463             10345 30957 3463
```

Not setting a seed.

RAND_MAX, a constant defined in cstdlib. To illustrate random numbers, let's run Program 6–10 three times.

All three series of random numbers are exactly the same!

If you start with the same seed (the default seed is 1) and apply the same formula to it, you are bound to get the same results. We must use the **srand()** function to set another seed.

```
void srand(unsigned seed)                                  <cstdlib>
```

Modifying Program 6–10 gets us Program 6–11.

At least the series is different from the earlier one, but we still get the same thing each time we run the program. It's the same problem: same seed, same series. We must have a way of changing the seed with each execution. One way is through the computer system's clock. The **time()** function gives us the computer clock's current time and date. The form of the time and date varies from system to system but at least its value will be different each time we run the program.

```
time_t time(NULL)                                          <ctime>
```

(The previous name for ctime was time.h.)

The data type time_t is defined in the header file ctime, but it is compatible with the unsigned integer required for srand(). In addition to returning the time and date, time() will also store them in a memory location of our choosing. The NULL argument directs the function to just return the value and not store it anywhere else in the system.

Let's try our program again in Program 6–12.

Success! Because each call to rand() returns the next in a series of random numbers, srand() needs to be called only once. Be sure, though, to set the seed—that is, call srand()—before calling rand().

HEADS UP!

You only need one call to srand() in a program.

Typically, we want random numbers in a predetermined range, 1 to 100, or −5 to +5, for example. Numbers between 0 and RAND_MAX, whatever that is, are rarely valuable, so we must convert that range into one that satisfies our requirements.

Take the case of radio station WHEN, which plays only music from the late sixties. At 10 A.M. each day the program director randomly picks a

Program 6-12

```cpp
#include <iostream>
#include <cstdlib>
#include <ctime>
using namespace std;

int main(void)
{
    srand(time(NULL));
    cout << "Three random numbers:\n "
         << rand() << " " << rand() << " " << rand() << endl;
}
```

Outputs

```
Three random numbers:        Three random numbers:        Three random numbers:
 3288 27551 25218             12653 22807 69               527 19141 5956
```

year between 1965 and 1969, and the deejays play only records from that year. Their songs might not be modern but their station is, so they want their computer to pick the random year. To generate an integer in a specific range, as in Program 6–13, we must first know the number of integers in the range. We can determine that by subtracting the bottom of the range from the top and adding 1. There are five integers in the range 1965 through 1969. We can generate integers in a range of 0 through 4, five integers, by dividing the return from `rand()` by 5 and taking the remainder; it must be 0 through 4.

If we then add the starting value for the range to that expression we get exactly the range we want. With this replacement `cout` in Program 6–13, we get the following output:

```cpp
cout << "  " << (rand() % 5 + 1965);
```

New Output

```
Ten random numbers:
 1967  1967  1969  1967  1965  1968  1966  1969  1966  1965
```

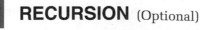

YOUR TURN 6–3

1. What is the purpose of a header file?
2. How is the `exit()` function used?
3. How do `abs()`, `labs()`, and `fabs()` differ from each other?
4. What is the unit of measure of the angles in trigonometric functions?
5. How are random numbers generated in C++?

RECURSION (Optional)

One function may call another function by including the function name in its code. In an earlier example (page 197), the `main()` function called the

Program 6–13

```
#include <iostream>
#include <cstdlib>
#include <ctime>
using namespace std;

int main(void)
{
    srand(time(NULL));
    cout << "Ten random numbers:\n";
    for (int count = 1; count <= 10; ++count)
        cout << "   " << (rand() % 5);
    cout << endl;
}
```

Output

```
Ten random numbers:
    0  1  4  1  4  1  3  3  4  2
```

---

grossPay() function. Control passed to the *grossPay()* function, which returned a value that substituted for the function call in the `main()` function. C++ places no limits on which functions can call which other functions, as long as the called function is visible from the calling function. In fact, a function may call itself—a situation known as **recursion** For purposes of analysis, a recursive call can be treated the same as one function calling another—as if there were two separate functions. In a recursive situation, though, the "two" functions do exactly the same thing.

Many processes lend themselves to recursive solutions, especially those that repeat an operation as some factor moves toward an ending condition. The classic example, and probably the best, is calculating the factorial of a number. The factorial of a number is the number times the number minus 1, times that number minus 1, and so forth until the multiplier becomes 1. For example, 4 factorial (4!) is

$$4 \times 3 \times 2 \times 1 \text{ or } 24$$

We could also say that 4! was $4 \times 3!$

$$4 \times (3 \times 2 \times 1) \text{ or } 4 \times 6 \text{ or } 24$$

and 3! was $3 \times 2!$ and 2! was $2 \times 1!$. The sequence ends when the number gets back to 1, which has a defined factorial of 1.

Summing up:

$$4! = 4 \times 3! = 4 \times 3 \times 2! = 4 \times 3 \times 2 \times 1!$$

A number factorial, then, is that number times the factorial of the number minus 1. It sounds as if we are defining the term in terms of itself—and we are. If we had the proper preexisting *factorial()* function, we could say that

$$4! = 4 * \text{factorial}(3) \quad \text{or} \quad n! = n * \text{factorial}(n - 1)$$

Let's set up that function, then.

```
int factorial(int n)
{
    return = n * factorial(n - 1);
}
```

This, of course, would be infinite; the function would continue to call itself. We need some ending condition. The mathematical definition of the factorial provides us with one: 1! is defined as 1. Therefore, if we send the *factorial()* function a value of 1, we will have it return 1 instead of calling itself again.

```
      int factorial(int n)
      {
f1        if (n <= 1 )              // <= to account for zero and negative arguments
f2            return 1;
          else
f3            return n * factorial(n - 1);
      }
```

To analyze the execution of this function, it is convenient to treat each call as a call to a separate instance of the function—as if there were many, many functions with the name *factorial*. In essence, that is what C++ does. Let's look at the values passed by each call and each return. In the execution chart we show which instance of the function is being examined.

EXECUTION CHART						
Line	Instance	Explanation	n	pass	return
f1	1	*n* not <= 1.	4		
f3	1	Call *factorial()*.	4	3	
f1	2	*n* not <= 1.	3		
f3	2	Call *factorial()*.	3	2	
f1	3	*n* not <= 1.	2		
f3	3	Call *factorial()*.	2	1	
f1	4	*n* is <= 1.	1		
f2	4	Return 1.	1		1
f3	3	Return 2 * 1.	2		2
f3	2	Return 3 * 2.	3		6
f3	1	Return 4 * 6.	4		24

```
factorial(4)
    |                              24
4 * factorial(3)
        |                           6
    3 * factorial(2)
            |                        2
        2 * factorial(1)
                |                    1
                1
```

Recursion or Iteration?

Any situation that could be described recursively could also be described iteratively, that is, using a loop. For example, the *factorial()* function could be rewritten as

```
      int factorial(int n)
f1    {   int fact = n;          // An accumulator to build up the factorial value

                                 for (--n; n > 1; --n)
f5            fact *= n;
f6        return fact;
      }
```

f2, f3, f4

If we pass the function a value of 4, it executes as follows:

Line	Explanation	n	fact
EXECUTION CHART			
f1	Declare and initialize the factorial accumulator.	4	4
f2	Decrement *n*.	3	4
f3	*n* is > 1, execute loop.	3	4
f5	Multiply *n* into the *fact* accumulator.	3	12
f4	Decrement *n*.	2	12
f3	*n* is > 1, execute loop.	2	12
f5	Multiply *n* into the *fact* accumulator.	2	24
f4	Decrement *n*.	1	24
f3	*n* not >1, exit loop.	1	24
f6	Return the value of the *fact* accumulator.	1	24

Which is better? Each could be said to describe the calculation of a factorial. The first follows the theoretical basis of a factorial; the second, the typical hand calculation of it. In general, though, recursive solutions tend to be less efficient. There is a great deal of overhead in a function call. Each call must assign the passed value somewhere in memory and then to the function variable to which it is passed. In addition, the call must store the memory address at which the program will resume when it returns. The return must perform similar operations with the return value as well as find out where to return.

Use recursive algorithms with care. If it makes the program more understandable and the difference in efficiency is not too great, a recursive function may be worth using.

PUTTING IT TOGETHER

The Lucky 13 Car Wash and Casino washes your car while you gamble away the rest of your money on slot machines. They would like to install computers that play "21" (blackjack) with the customers and would like us to write a computer program for them. We are a little busy now, but we said that we will give them a start.

TASK

Write an abbreviated program that will deal just the first hand for the house (the dealer) and the player. It should be set up the way a casino would like it—with an infinite number of decks of cards, making it possible to deal more than one card of the same number and suit.

In the game of blackjack, the initial deal for the house consists of one card face up, so that its value and suit can be seen, and one face down. The player's hand consists of two cards face up. Each card has a suit, a face (2, 5, jack, queen), and a value (face value except for jack, queen, and king, which count as 10; and ace, which can count as either 1 or 11). The object of the game is to keep drawing cards to get as close to 21 as possible. If your hand totals over 21, you lose. In this program we will be concerned with only the initial deal of two cards.

For each hand we should print out the face and suit for the card or cards and, for the player, since we can see both cards, print the total for the hand. Since the house may take more cards later, we may as well also keep track of the house's hand total.

Overall, the program will be organized like this:

    Deal for house
    Deal for player

Expanding the modules above, then, we have:

    [Deal for house]
        Show first card face
        Add to hand total
        Show first card suit

    [Deal for player]
        Show first card face
        Add to hand total
        Show first card suit
        Show second card face
        Add to hand total
        Show second card suit
        Print hand total

Three card faces and three suits are being shown, and three times the card value is being added to the hand total. Instead of writing this code three times, let's consider this dealing process an object with three behaviors. Since we always add the face to the hand total, one behavior is to generate a random face and add it to the total. Another behavior is to generate a random suit. We can implement these behaviors as functions and call them three times.

One function, *card()*, prints out a random card face and adds its value to a hand total passed to it.

    [Card]
        Pick random card
        Show face
        Add to hand total

Since aces can count as 11 or 1, we count them as 11 if the resultant total is not over 21, otherwise as 1.

Another function, *suit()*, can print out a random suit.

```
[Suit]
    Pick random suit
    Show suit
```

The overall design, then, is:

```
[Deal for house]
    [Card]
    [Suit]
[Deal for player]
    [Card]
    [Suit]
    [Card]
    [Suit]
    Print hand total
```

IMPLEMENTATION

The individual functions are expanded in Program 6–14. In the *card()* function, we chose to pass by value—logical enough, since the first thing we passed the function was a value, not a variable. However, we could have accomplished the same result using a pass by reference. Remember, a pass by reference does not make a copy of a value but assigns, in the function, another name for the variable passed it. Any change we make in the variable in the called function will also be reflected in the variable in the calling function, since they are the same variable.

If, in Program 6–14, we change the first line of the *card()* function definition to:

```
void card(int &total) //********* Prints random card and adjusts hand total
```

(don't forget to change the declaration also), and change the following lines, we will be passing by reference to the function.

```
1 {   int player = 0, house = 0;              // Hand totals for both sides

3     card(house);                            // Start with zero total for hand

5     card(player);                           // Start with zero total for hand

7     card(player);                            // Add to previous hand total

c23   total += value;
```

Line 1 starts off both the player and the house at zero. Line 3 passes the *house* variable to *card()*, which, in *card()*, is referred to as *total*. The *card()* function generates a face value, and, instead of returning the *total* plus this *value* in c23, it accumulates the *value* into the *total*, which, of course, is the same variable as *house* in main(). Now when the program returns to the main() function, the value of *house* reflects the new value.

Lines 5 and 7 follow the same process, but with the *player* variable.

Program 6–14

```
        #include <iostream>
        #include <cstdlib>
        #include <ctime>
        using namespace std;

        int card(int total);              // Prints random card and adjusts hand total
        void suit(void);                                    // Prints a random suit

        int main(void)
1    {   int player, house;                          // Hand totals for both sides

2        srand(time(NULL));                               // Set a varying seed

         //***************************************************** Deal for house
         cout << "House has a ";
3        house = card(0);                         // Start with zero total for hand
         cout << " of ";
4        suit();
         cout << " and a down card\n";

         //***************************************************** Deal for player
         cout << "You have a ";
5        player = card(0);                        // Start with zero total for hand
         cout << " of ";
6        suit();
         cout << " and a ";
7        player = card(player);                       // Add to previous hand total
         cout << " of ";
8        suit();
9        cout << " for " << player << endl;           // Player's hand total
     }

     int card(int total) //*********** Prints random card and adjusts hand total
     {   int value;

c1       value = rand() % 13 + 1;                  // Random number between 1 and 13
c2       switch (value)
c3       {   case 1:                // Ace is 11 unless hand over 21, then it is 1
c4             cout << "Ace";
c5             if (total + 11 <= 21)                      // Ace as 11 within 21
c6                value = 11;                             // Set ace value to 11
               else
c7                value = 1;                              // Set ace value to 1
c8             break;
c9           case 11:
c10            cout << "Jack";
c11            value = 10;
c12            break;
c13          case 12:
c14            cout << "Queen";
c15            value = 10;
c16            break;
```

(Continued)

Program 6–14 *(Continued)*

```
c17         case 13:
c18             cout << "King";
c19             value = 10;
c20             break;
c21         default:                                    // 2 through 10
c22             cout << value;
            }
c23     return total + value;
    }

    void suit(void)  //********************************** Prints a random suit
    {
s1      switch (rand() % 4 + 1)                 // Random number between 1 and 4
s2      {  case 1:
s3             cout << "Spades";
s4             break;
s5         case 2:
s6             cout << "Hearts";
s7             break;
s8         case 3:
s9             cout << "Diamonds";
s10            break;
s11        default:
s12            cout << "Clubs";
           }
s13  }
```

Outputs

```
House has a 5 of Spades and a down card
You have a King of Hearts and a Ace of Diamonds for 21

House has a Queen of Diamonds and a down card
You have a Jack of Hearts and a 3 of Spades for 13

House has a Jack of Spades and a down card
You have a 8 of Spades and a 4 of Diamonds for 12
```

TEST

Testing this program could be fun. In any case, a number of tests should be done including those that verify the handling of face cards (jack, queen, and king) and aces. One important test is a hand with two aces to make sure that the second ace is being added as 1 instead of 11. An easy way to do that is to temporarily change the statement that generates a random card value between 1 and 13 to

```
value = 1; // rand() % 13 + 1;          // Random number between 1 and 13
```

to ensure that you get two aces.

This program, of course, is only the start of a complete blackjack game, which, with your current knowledge of C++, you could finish.

The Execution Chart shows values of variables that exist but are not visible in parentheses.

EXECUTION CHART

Line	Explanation	player	house	total	value
2	Set seed for later random numbers. The variables *player* and *house* have garbage values; *total* and *value* do not exist.	??	??	—	—
3	Call *card()*, pass 0.	??	??	—	—
c1	Generate random number between 1 and 13. The variables *player* and *house* still exist but are not visible.	(??)	(??)	0	5
c2	Look for `case 5:`. Doesn't exist, so look for `default:` at c21.	(??)	(??)	0	5
c22	Print card face.	(??)	(??)	0	5
c23	Return previous *total* plus the new *value*.	(??)	(??)	0	5
3	Assign return value to *house*.	??	5	—	—
4	Call suit().	??	5	—	—
s1	Expression evaluates to 1; look for `case 1:`. Find at s2.	(??)	(5)	—	—
s3	Print "Spades".	(??)	(5)	—	—
s4	Jump beyond end of structure.	(??)	(5)	—	—
s13	Return.	(??)	(5)	—	—
5	Call *card()*, pass 0.	??	5	—	—
c1	Generate random number between 1 and 13.	(??)	(5)	0	13
c2	Look for `case 13:`. Find at c17.	(??)	(5)	0	13
c18	Print "King".	(??)	(5)	0	13
c19	Set *value* to 10.	(??)	(5)	0	10
c20	Jump to end of structure.	(??)	(5)	0	10
c23	Return previous *total* plus the new *value*.	(??)	(5)	0	10
5	Assign return value to *player*.	10	5	—	—
6	Call *suit()*, print "Hearts".	10	5	—	—
7	Call *card()*, pass *player*.	10	5	—	—
c1	Generate random number between 1 and 13.	(10)	(5)	10	1
c2	Look for `case 1:`. Find at c3.	(10)	(5)	10	1
c4	Print "Ace".	(10)	(5)	10	1
c5	Test to see if 11 plus the previous *total* would be 21 or less. It would.	(10)	(5)	10	11
c6	Set *value* to 11.	(10)	(5)	10	11
c8	Jump to end of structure.	(10)	(5)	10	11
c23	Return previous *total* plus the new *value*.	(10)	(5)	10	11
7	Assign return value to *player*.	21	5	—	—
8	Call *suit*, print "Diamonds".	21	5	—	—
9	Print *player*.	21	5	—	—

SUMMARY

- **KEY TERMS** (in order of appearance)

Function	Reference operator
Function definition	Prototype
Call	Pass by value
Function declaration	Internal
Return	External
Return value	Global
void	Supersede
Local	Hide
Lifetime	Header file
Visibility	Library
Pass	Trigonometric function
Argument	Seed
Parameter declaration	Recursion
Pass by reference	

- **NEW STATEMENTS AND FUNCTIONS** (in order of appearance)

```
return expression;
```

```
void exit(int status)                                              <cstdlib>
```
    Purpose: Terminate program in orderly fashion indicating *status* of termination.
    Return: None.

```
int abs(int expression)                                            <cstdlib>
```
    Purpose: Obtain absolute value of int *expression*.
    Return: Absolute value of int *expression*.

```
long labs(long expression)                                         <cstdlib>
```
    Purpose: Obtain absolute value of long *expression*.
    Return: Absolute value of long *expression*.

```
double fabs(double expression)                                      <cmath>
```
    Purpose: Obtain absolute value of double *expression*.
    Return: Absolute value of double *expression*.

```
double pow(double expression, double exponent)                      <cmath>
```
    Purpose: Raise *expression* to the power of *exponent*.
    Return: Result of the exponentiation.

```
double sqrt(double expression)                                      <cmath>
```
    Purpose: Obtain the square root of the *expression*.
    Return: Square root of the *expression*.

```
int rand(void)                                                     <cstdlib>
```
    Purpose: Obtain next in a series of random numbers.
    Return: Value between zero and RAND_MAX.

```
void srand(unsigned seed)                                          <cstdlib>
```
    Purpose: Set the *seed* for generation of random numbers.
    Return: None.

```
time_t time(NULL)                                                    <ctime>
```
    Purpose: Used as shown to give a different seed for random-number generation.
    Return: Random-number seed.

• CONCEPT REVIEW

- **Function definition** code is all the operations in the function. The **call** sets this code in operation. Like almost anything else in C++, functions must have a **function declaration** before they are called.

- When a function finishes execution it **returns** to the calling point, often with a **return value** that substitutes for the call. Functions without return values are declared with a **void** data type.

- Variables declared within a function, even in the parameter declarations, have both **local lifetime** and **visibility** within the function.

- If a function has a return value, that value must be assigned to the function call by a **return statement**. The return statement can also be used to terminate a function that does not return a value.

- Values may be **passed** to a function. One pass method is a **pass by reference**, in which variable names stated in the function's **parameter declarations** substitute for variable names in the calling function **arguments**. The **reference operator** is used in the parameter declaration to indicate such a pass. Another method is the **pass by value**, in which variables declared in the parameter declarations are initialized by values sent to the function.

- A function **prototype** is a formalized declaration that tells the compiler what it needs to know to properly error-check (and sometimes type-convert) function calls.

- A function cannot return more than one value, but we can get further values back from a function by sending it references to variables in the calling function and having the called function change those variables.

- There are a number of reasons to use functions. Among them are: object orientation, modularity, readability, debugability, repeatability, and reusability.

- All the variables we have referred to have been declared **internally**, within a function. **External** declarations have **global** visibility and, in the case of variables, global lifetime. Global variables reduce the modularity of a program, however. A local variable with the same name as a global variable will **supersede** or **hide** the global variable.

- Most existing functions are in object-code **libraries** with their declarations in source-code **header files**, which we must #include if we are to use them.

- Some functions reviewed were **exit()**, to terminate a program; **abs()**, **labs()**, and **fabs()**, to return absolute values; **pow()** to raise values to powers; **sqrt()**, to take the square root; various **trigonometric functions** with their arguments all stated in radians; **rand()** and **srand()** to generate pseudorandom numbers; and **time()** to provide a constantly varying **seed** value.

- A function can be called from anywhere in the program, including from a statement within that function—a process known as **recursion**.

• HEADS UP: POINTS OF SPECIAL INTEREST

- The function definition is all the statements in the function.
- Most structured programmers put main() first.

- The return value substitutes for the call.
- The return value will always be the data type declared for the function.
- A function can have only one return value.
- Each call to a function sets up new local variables.
- Local variables make our functions more portable.
- A strictly structured function has only one return.
- Prototypes are more readable with variable names.
- Make sure your data types match when calling functions.
- A function call is an expression of a declared data type.
- Passing references can overcome the limitation of a single return value.
- Use external variables sparingly, if at all.
- Local variables supersede global variables.
- Header files are source code.
- The functions themselves are in compiled library files, not header files.
- If you can foresee a possible error condition, either handle it in the program or provide an orderly `exit()`.
- There are different absolute value functions for different data types.
- You only need one call to `srand()` in a program.

• TRAPS: COMMON PROGRAMMING ERRORS

- Not declaring a function.
- Leaving the semicolon off a function declaration.
- The function call not agreeing with the parameter declarations in the function.
- Depending on a certain order of argument evaluation.
- Naming local variables the same as constants.
- Not including the proper header file for a library function.
- Expressing angles in degrees.
- Not setting a seed.

• YOUR TURN ANSWERS

• 6–1

1. The function definition starts with the declaration of its return type, name, and parameter declarations, and contains all of the code that makes the function operate.
2. The function call passes values or variable names to a function and sets the function in operation.
3. A function declaration informs C++ of the existence of a function. It must appear before the function is called.

4. The function return ends the function and sends execution back to the calling point, possibly with a value to substitute.

5. The lifetime of a variable is the part of the program in which memory is allocated for that variable. The visibility (or scope) of a variable (or function) is the part of the program in which the variable can be accessed (or function called) by name.

6. The `return` statement ceases execution of the function, passes the value of the expression (if any) back to the calling point to substitute for the call, and continues program execution at the calling point.

7. A `void` return type means that no value is being returned by a function. A `void` declaration means that no variables are being declared to be initialized by passed values. In other words, the function call can have no arguments.

● 6–2

1. In a pass by reference, the function uses different names to refer to variables passed to it. A pass by value copies values from the call expressions and initializes new, local variables in the function with those values.

2. An ANSI function prototype allows the compiler to check for mismatched arguments and data types and convert some values to the proper types.

3. Six reasons for using functions are object orientation, modularity, readability, debugability, repeatability, reusability.

4. Global lifetime or visibility is from declaration throughout the entire program. Local is within only a certain section, such as within one function.

5. Internal is within a function; external is outside of any function. Internal declarations are local; external ones are global.

6. By using local variables, we don't have to worry about variable names in the function conflicting with variable names in the rest of the program.

7. A local variable supersedes a global variable with the same name.

● 6–3

1. Header files contain standard definitions of constants and declarations of functions that exist in function libraries.

2. The `exit()` function forces normal termination of a program and returns a status code to the operating system.

3. `abs()`, `labs()`, and `fabs()` all return an absolute value, but of `int`s, `long`s, and `double`s, respectively.

4. The angles sent to trig functions must be in radians.

5. The `rand()` function puts a seed number through a complicated algorithm to generate the next in a series of "random" numbers. To get a different series with each execution of the program, `srand()`, which changes the seed, should be sent the return from a `time()` function call.

1. Given the following `main()` segment, fill in the first line of the function definition. How would the prototyped declaration appear?

```
double t;          ____ func(____ x, ____ y)
float a;
int f;
      . . .
t = func(f, a + 9);
```

2. Given the following function, write a proper call statement to send it the value 16, as well as the values of *a* and *b* + *c*. The result of the function should be stored in *d*.

```
int main(void)  double func(double x, float &y, int z)
{  float a;        {
   int b, c;           return (x + y) / z;
   double d;       }
```

3. Modify the following program so that the marked code is executed in a *milesPerGallon()* function. The main() function should have no *gallons*, or *milesPerGallon* variables, and the function should be called directly from the last cout statement.

```
#include <iostream>

int main(void)
{  int begMiles, endMiles;
   float odoAdjust, gallons, milesPerGallon;

   begMiles = 296;
   endMiles = 513;
   odoAdjust = 1.15;

                                 // This stuff should be in a function
   cout << "How many gallons? ";
   cin >> gallons;
   milesPerGallon = (endMiles - begMiles) * odoAdjust / gallons;
                                      // End of function stuff

   cout << milesPerGallon  << " miles per gallon." << endl;
   return 0;
}
```

4. What is wrong with the function calls in the following cout?

```
int izzy;
long lardo;
float flakey;

cout << labs(izzy) << " " << abs(lardo) << " "
     << fabs(flakey);
```

5. Write a *sine()* function that returns the sine of an angle passed in degrees. Call the `sin()` function from your function.

6. Show an execution chart for the following program, which prints a two-decimal-place random number in a given range.

```cpp
#include <iostream>
#include <iomanip>
#include <cstdlib>
#include <ctime>
using namespace std;

float twoPlace(float &bottom, float &top);

int main(void)
{   float low, high;

    srand(time(NULL));
    cout << "Enter low high for range: ";
    cin >> low >> high;
    cout << setiosflags(ios::fixed) << setprecision(2);
    cout << "Number: " << twoPlace(low, high) << endl;
    return 0;
}

float twoPlace(float &bottom, float &top)
{   int range, begin, rndNum;

    range = (top - bottom) * 100;
    begin = bottom * 100;
    rndNum = rand() % (range + 1) + begin;
    return rndNum / 100.0;
}
```

7. Rewrite the *twoPlace()* function in the program above so that it has no variables other than those declared in the formal parameters and only a `return` statement. (*Hint:* Remember external variables.)

8. Find and examine the `cmath` header file that comes with your compiler. (Most compilers put it in an *include* directory or folder.) See what kind of declaration prototypes and definitions are contained within it. *Be careful to not make any changes to the file!*

PROGRAMS

1. Create a function that prints a page heading. It should print the next page number passed to it. Use the following driver—`main()` function segment—to test your function.

Driver

```cpp
int main(void)
{   int p;

    for (p = 1; p <= 5; ++p)
        page(p);
    return 0;
}
```

Function and Variable

```
page()
 pageNo
```

Output

```
Major Document      Page 1

Major Document      Page 2

Major Document      Page 3

Major Document      Page 4

Major Document      Page 5
```

2. Write a program that accepts any number from the keyboard and tells you whether it is a nonnegative integer. The number should be sent to the function *intTest()*, which returns either the integer value, or −1 if the number is negative, or zero if it is nonnegative but not an integer. Inputs should continue until a zero is input.

Functions and Variables

```
Main()
 input      From keyboard
 integer    Return from function
intTest()
 value      From main()
 result     Value to return
```

Output

```
Your number: 48
The number is 48.
Your number: -14.3
The number is negative.
Your number: 12.345
The number is not an integer.
Your number: 0
```

3. Write a program that shows the maturity value (principal plus accumulated interest) on a deposit at interest rates of 4, 5, 6, and 7 percent. The formula should be calculated in a separate function, but the output should be from `main()`.

Formula

$$maturity\ value = principal\left(1 + \frac{rate}{100}\right)^{years}$$

Functions and Variables

```
main()
 years      Number of years
 rate       Interest rate (percent)
 principal
matVal()     Maturity value function
             Any local variables needed for function
```

Output

```
AMOUNT? 1000
NUMBER OF YEARS? 5

MATURITY VALUES AT VARIOUS INTEREST RATES
4% 1216.65    5% 1276.28    6% 1338.22    7% 1402.55
```

4. The formula for determining the number of possible combinations of *N* things taken *K* at a time is:

$$C = \frac{N!}{K!(N-K)!}$$

Write a program to use this formula. *N*! means "*N* factorial." The factorial of a number is the number times the number minus 1, times that number minus 1, and so forth until the multiplier is 1. 5! (five factorial) = 5 × 4 × 3 × 2 × 1 = 120. The factorial calculations should be done in a separate function. *N* and *K* must be positive integers with *N* >= *K* for the formula to work.

Functions and Variables

```
main()
  c          Combinations
  n          Number of things
  k          Number taken at a time
factorial()
  counter
  fact       Accumulator for factorial
```

Output

```
HOW MANY THINGS? 7
HOW MANY AT A TIME? 4
NUMBER OF POSSIBLE COMBINATIONS IS 35
```

5. Write a program that allows input of two sides of a right triangle and calculates the hypotenuse according to the Pythagorean theorem (). Use no multiplication; use the `pow()` and `sqrt()` functions instead. Use only the variables given.

Variables

```
side1, side2, hypotenuse
```

Output

```
Enter first and second side: 3 4
Hypotenuse: 5
Enter first and second side: 24.75 38.2
Hypotenuse: 45.5171
```

6. Write a program to determine the sides and angles of a right triangle given one side and the adjacent angle. Remember that the angles in the trigonometric functions are expressed in radians.

Variables		Formulas
side	Given side	Hypotenuse = side / cosine
opSide	Opposite side	Opposite side = side × tangent
hypotenuse		Other angle = 90 − given angle
angle	Given angle	Radians = degrees × π / 180
opAngle	Opposite angle	π = 3.1416

Output

```
ENTER ANGLE? 30
ENTER ADJACENT SIDE? 10
OPPOSITE SIDE= 5.77352
HYPOTENUSE= 11.547
OPPOSITE ANGLE= 60
```

7. The pseudorandom numbers generated by C++ should be pretty good, statistically. Write a program to see how good. Generate 1,000 integers between 1 and 5, and keep track of how many of each were produced. Try it with a million. (*Hint:* Don't forget to use longs for your accumulators.) Save as *RANDOM* for modification later.

Functions and Variables

```
main()
  ones, twos, threes, fours, fives    Accumulators
  count                               Loop counter
  rnd()                               Integer between 1 and 5
```

Sample Output

Ones	Twos	Threes	Fours	Fives
220	211	197	204	168

8. Write a guessing game for the computer in which the computer generates a random whole number between 1 and 100 and the player tries to guess that number. The program should allow only ten guesses and should tell the player whether the guess is too low, too high, or correct.

Functions and Variables

```
main()
  secret     The number to be guessed
  guess      The players guess
  guesses    The number of guesses
rnd()        Function for random number between 1 and 100
```

Output

```
THE SECRET NUMBER IS BETWEEN 1 AND 100.

WHAT IS YOUR GUESS? 5
TOO LOW, GUESS AGAIN? 45
TOO LOW, GUESS AGAIN? 92
TOO HIGH, GUESS AGAIN? 46

RIGHT! IT TOOK YOU 4 TRIES.
```

Output

```
THE SECRET NUMBER IS BETWEEN 1 AND 100.

WHAT IS YOUR GUESS? 7
TOO LOW, GUESS AGAIN? 46
    .
    .
    .
TOO HIGH, GUESS AGAIN? 71

YOU LOSE, THAT WAS YOUR LAST GUESS. THE NUMBER WAS 74.
```

9. Write a simple calculator so that you can input an expression with two values separated by an operator and the computer will print out the proper result. Your calculator should include the ^ operator for exponentiation. All calculations should be done in an appropriate function (the functions will be small) and the results printed in main().

Functions and Variables

```
main()
  op                 Operator
  x, y               Values for calculation
add()
subtract()
multiply()
divide()
exponentiate()
  a, b               Local variables for each function
```

Output

```
Enter expression (0 to quit): 34.7+23.5
  58.2
Enter expression (0 to quit): 5.27 * 32.6
  171.802
Enter expression (0 to quit): 1.41414 ^ 2
  1.99979
Enter expression (0 to quit): 657.82 / 0
  Can't divide by  0
Enter expression (0 to quit): 534 & 26
  Invalid operator
Enter expression (0 to quit): 0
```

10. Write a program to make change in coins. The main() function should accept input of the purchase and the amount tendered, and the *change()* function should print the number of quarters, dimes, and so on.

Functions and Variables

```
main()
 purchase
 tendered
change(amount)
  cents            Convert the float amount to the int cents
```

Output

```
Purchase: 3.08
Amount tendered: 4
Quarters: 3
Dimes   : 1
Nickels : 1
Pennies : 2
```

11. In the kids' game "Paper, Rock, Scissors" each player chooses one of the three and the winner is determined by the relationship between the two choices. "Paper covers rock," so paper wins; "rock breaks scissors," so rock wins; and "scissors cuts paper," so scissors wins. If both choose the same, it is a tie and no one wins. Write a program to play the game against the computer until the player enters q instead of a choice.

Functions and Variables

```
main()
  machine                        The machine's choice: p, r, or s
  player                         The player's choice
  result                         Win, lose, or tie
  score                          Accumulated score
char machineChoice(void)         Prints paper, rock, or scissors
  choice                         Random choice
```

Sample Output

```
Choose (p)aper, (r)ock, (s)cissors or (q)uit: p
 The machine chooses scissors.   You lose!   Your
score: -1
Choose (p)aper, (r)ock, (s)cissors or (q)uit: s
  The machine chooses scissors.   It's a tie!   Your
score: -1
Choose (p)aper, (r)ock, (s)cissors or (q)uit: p
  The machine chooses rock.   You Win!   Your score:
0
Choose (p)aper, (r)ock, (s)cissors or (q)uit: r
  The machine chooses scissors.   You Win!   Your
score: 1
Choose (p)aper, (r)ock, (s)cissors or (q)uit: q
```

12. Write a program to display a chart of monthly payments for a car loan at various interest rates over various time periods. The user enters the loan amount, range of years for the chart, and range of interest rates. Choose appropriate variable and function names. The legal formula for monthly payments for a *loan* at an annual interest *rate* for a number of *years* is:

$$loan \frac{\dfrac{rate}{1200}}{1 - \dfrac{1}{\left(1 + \dfrac{rate}{1200}\right)^{years \times 12}}}$$

Output

```
Enter vehicle loan amount> 16543.21
Enter time range in years (low to high)> 2 7
Enter rate range in percent (low to high)> 12 18

MONTHLY PAYMENT CHART
  Rates:     12%      13%      14%      15%      16%      17%      18%
Years
      2     778.75   786.49   794.29   802.12   810.01   817.93   825.90
      3     549.47   557.41   565.41   573.48   581.61   589.81   598.08
      4     435.65   443.81   452.07   460.41   468.84   477.36   485.96
      5     367.99   376.41   384.93   393.56   402.30   411.14   420.09
      6     323.42   332.09   340.89   349.81   358.85   368.02   377.31
      7     292.03   300.95   310.02   319.23   328.58   338.07   347.70
```

Chapter 7

PROGRAMMING WITH CLASS

PREVIEW

We have looked at objects, properties, and behaviors, and at the various processes we can put into behaviors. Now we will gather these concepts into the very heart of object-oriented programming, encapsulating them into stand-alone entities that, once created, we, or other programmers, can simply use without concern for their inner operations. We will examine:

- The principle of abstraction.
- How we create an abstract entity in C++.
- The purposes behind these abstract entities.
- Using these entities in our programs.
- Protecting our entities from improper data or use.

We stressed in Chapter 2 that C++ is a language that can access the computer at a low level—get to the guts of the machine. We have also been exposing that gut-level stuff in subsequent chapters and in the *Nuts 'n' Bolts* boxes. Now we want to develop techniques that hide that low-level mechanical stuff away from us. We want to develop **abstract** things—objects. We know what they do and how to use them, but we don't care how they do it.

Does this sound like we are taking a step backward? Not really. In terms of programming evolution it is a leap forward. Instead of building something from scratch—baking a cake from flour, eggs, baking soda, and so forth—we can use a preassembled object—a cake mix. We will also see that we can take the object, add something to it, squash to the cake mix, for example, and come up with something new. A squash cake? Well, you get the idea.

Since it is we who are designing the objects, we must understand the low-level stuff, but once the object is designed we, or others, can use it without having to look inside it. It becomes abstract.

Of course, we have been using objects since we were born and programming objects since Chapter 2—cin and cout are two good examples. We haven't the foggiest idea how they work, but they get data from the keyboard and display data on the screen. We have also been looking at parts of programs as objects, gathering together code that performs specific behaviors. Now we want to package those objects so they may be picked up and used wherever we happen to need their behaviors.

HEADS UP!

An object can be used without your knowing what is inside it.

OBJECTS AND CLASSES

In Chapter 1 we used a microwave oven as an example of an object. It had properties, some of which were adjustable (such as cooking time and power level), and some of which were not (such as the maximum power and the size of the oven). It also had behaviors, some of which we could initiate from the outside (starting the cooking cycle), and some of which we could not (generating the microwaves). A single oven is a single object, but what if we wanted a bunch of ovens? Would we have to design each one separately, even if they were similar or exactly the same?

The answer C++ provides is again taken from typical human methods. We can create a general description of this type of object, a **class**, outlining the properties and behaviors of a microwave oven. When we actually want an oven, we can create an **instance** of the class, an **object**. If we want two or three or a hundred, we can create two or three or a hundred instances or objects.

If we design the class with some flexibility in mind, we can create objects that differ in some respects. For example, from our microwave-oven class, we might create 600-watt, 800-watt, and 1000-watt ovens by setting an internal property when the object is created.

Notice that the class is intangible; it is only a description, an idea. You can't stuff your leftover macaroni and cheese in a microwave-oven class, because there is nothing there. Similarly, you can't say "I'm thinking of a Corvette, I think I'll hop in it and cruise Main Street." To heat up the mac

HEADS UP!

We create individual objects from class descriptions.

HEADS UP!

Objects of the same class may differ in their properties.

HEADS UP!

Classes are only descriptions. Objects are the real things.

and cheese, you have to create a microwave-oven object (sometimes referred to as *instantiating* an object).

CLASS DECLARATIONS

To show how this process works in C++, let's use a more appropriate object. Let's say that our company has many employees. In our programs dealing with employee information, we treat each employee as an object. Our employees may object to being treated as objects but remember, we are only talking about employee data here, not the actual people. We would not, for example, create walking, talking, and hanging around the coffee machine as behaviors for our employee objects.

There are many pieces of data, **properties**, that describe an employee, but let's keep ours simple, dealing mainly with payroll. The employee object includes the employee's name, pay rate, number of dependents, and the pay that the employee has received so far this year (the year-to-date gross).

We gather all this data together in an employee class using the C++ **class** statement. In this statement we will declare the data (and later, behaviors) that are **members** of the class.

```
class ClassName {member declarations};
```

or in typical structured fashion:

```
class ClassName
{   member declaration;
    member declaration;
    .
    .
    .
};
```

For example,

```
class Employee
{   string name;
    float payRate;
    int dependents;
    double ytdGross;
};                                      // Don't forget this semicolon
```

Leaving off the semicolon after a class declaration.

Punctuation, as usual, is very important here. All the declarations are within a set of braces; each declaration has its own semicolon, and there is a semicolon after the closing brace of the entire class declaration.

In terms of style, the indenting is virtually universal, and lining up the opening and closing braces is a popular style that we have adopted in this book. Many C++ programmers capitalize the first letter of a class name (or the first letter of each word in a class name)—for example, *Employee* or *MicrowaveOven*. This particular style, although certainly not universally followed, makes the various types of names in a program easily identifiable: variables are lowercase, functions are lowercase but followed immediately by parentheses, and classes are initial caps. (Many also put constants in all caps.)

HEADS UP!

Class declarations allocate
no memory space for
variables.

The sample class declaration above seems to define (allocate memory space for) four variables. (Actually, as we shall see, it appears to define three variables and an object of the string class). It does not. It simply declares the properties that an object of that class will contain. Variables are defined and memory space allocated when we declare objects of the class.

We can treat a class as a data type, one that we have made up. This data type is composed of instances of other data types and is often referred to as a **complex data type**.

Public and Private

In Chapter 1 we mentioned public and private properties. **Public** properties are those that we can access from outside the object; **private** properties are those that are accessible only from within the object. By default, all the properties declared in a class are private; we cannot access them from outside the class. We can make all or some of them public by inserting a `public:` key word in our list of *member declarations*. All the properties declared after `public:` will be public.

For example,

```
class Employee
{   string name;                        // Defaults to private
    float payRate;
public:
    int dependents;
    double ytdGross;
};
```

makes *name* and *payRate* private and *dependents* and *ytdGross* public.

`private:` is also a key word. This declaration:

```
class Employee
{   string name;                        // Defaults to private
public:
    float payRate;
    int dependents;
private:
    double ytdGross;
};
```

makes *name* private, *payRate* and *dependents* public, and *ytdGross* private. Most programmers, however, declare the private properties first, then the public ones, as in the earlier example.

For our simple example here we must access all of the properties from outside the object, so we will declare them all public.

```
class Employee
{
public:
    string name;
    float payRate;
    int dependents;
    double ytdGross;
};
```

OBJECT DECLARATIONS

Now that we know what an employee looks like, so to speak, let's create some. Declaring an object is just like declaring a variable of any other data type.

```
ClassName objectName;
```

For example,

```
Employee worker;
```

This declaration defines the *worker* object; memory space is allocated for the *worker* with its properties *name*, *payRate*, *dependents*, and *ytdGross*. We now have an object that we can manipulate.

As with variables, we can declare many objects of the *Employee* class:

```
Employee worker, manager, president, janitor;
```

Each of these is a separate instance of the *Employee* class, each with its own properties and its own space in memory.

Object Properties

We must be able to access each employee's individual properties. Saying `payRate = 9.42;` would be meaningless because it would not tell us whose pay rate. The property, then, must be attached to a particular object with **member operator**, a period.

```
object.property
```

for example,

```
worker.payRate
```

Now we know whose pay rate.

Using the member operator, we can access object properties just as we would any other variables.

```
worker.payRate = 9.42;
cout << worker.payRate;
```

In Program 7–1 on the next page, we use the *Employee* object to write a simple paycheck.

The declaration of the *Employee* class was done externally, before the `main()` function. Like predefined data types such as `int` and `float`, the data types we create by declaring classes should, in most cases, be global, visible throughout the program. Like variables, objects of those data types will typically be local, visible only in the portion of the program in which they are declared.

We can pass an object to a function in the same way we do a variable. In Program 7–2, let's set up a *pay()* function that writes a paycheck and updates the employee's year-to-date gross. We pass a reference to the object so that the function works with the same object (under a different name), not a copy of it. This is necessary because we want the function to change the *ytdGross* property of the object.

HEADS UP!

Typically, class declarations are global and objects are local.

HEADS UP!

Objects are typically passed by reference.

Program 7-1

```cpp
#include <iostream>                                    // .h, if needed
#include <iomanip>
#include <string>
using namespace std;                                          // if needed

class Employee //////////////////////////////////// Declaration of Class
{
public:
    string name;
    float payRate;
    int dependents;
    double ytdGross;
};

int main(void) /////////////////////////////////////////  Main Program
{   Employee worker;                          // Declaration of object
    double hours, gross;

    cout << setiosflags(ios::fixed) << setprecision(2);
    cout << "Name: ";
    cin >> worker.name;        // Input value for name member of worker object
    cout << "Pay rate: ";
    cin >> worker.payRate;
    cout << "Hours: ";
    cin >> hours;
    gross = hours * worker.payRate;
    cout << "Pay " << worker.name << " $" << gross << "." << endl;
    return 0;
}
```

Output

```
Name: Gandalf
Pay rate: 12.63
Hours: 36.2
Pay Gandalf $457.21.
```

Notice that the declaration of the *pay()* function is after the declaration of the *Employee* class. The order is important here because the parameter declarations of the *pay()* function declare a reference to an *Employee* object. The compiler must know what an employee object is at this point.

Object Behaviors

Object **behaviors** are stated in functions, similar to the *pay()* function in Program 7–2, but are declared within the class and becoming part of the class. We refer to a class's properties as data members and its behaviors as **member functions**. When we declare an object of that class, then, we get not only its properties; the object can also access the class's behaviors. In addition, declaring a function within a class allows that function to access all the properties of the class—without having to pass them to the function.

Program 7–2

```cpp
#include <iostream>
#include <iomanip>
#include <string>
using namespace std;

class Employee /////////////////////////////////////// Declaration of Class
{
public:
    string name;
    float payRate;
    int dependents;
    double ytdGross;
};

void pay(Employee &emp);

int main(void) ///////////////////////////////////////////// Main Program
{   Employee worker;                                  // Declaration of object

    cout << setiosflags(ios::fixed) << setprecision(2);
    cout << "Name: ";
    cin >> worker.name;         // Input value for name member of worker object
    cout << "Pay rate: ";
    cin >> worker.payRate;
    cout << "Initial year-to-date gross: ";
    cin >> worker.ytdGross;
    pay(worker);
    cout << "Final year-to-date gross $" << worker.ytdGross << "." << endl;
    return 0;
}

void pay(Employee &emp) //*********************************** Pays Employee
{   double hours, gross;

    cout << "Hours: ";
    cin >> hours;
    gross = hours * emp.payRate;
    cout << "Pay " << emp.name << " $" << gross << "." << endl;
    emp.ytdGross += gross;
}
```

Output

```
Name: Norval
Pay rate: 8.25
Initial year-to-date gross: 5674.82
Hours: 35
Pay Norval $288.75.
Final year-to-date gross $5963.57.
```

HEADS UP!

Object behaviors can always see object properties.

The visibility or scope of the class's properties is the entire class, including the functions within the class. In other words, the behaviors of an object may access the properties of the object.

Program 7–3

```cpp
#include <iostream>
#include <iomanip>
#include <string>
using namespace std;

class Employee /////////////////////////////////////// Declaration of Class
{
public:
    string name;
    float payRate;
    int dependents;
    double ytdGross;

    void pay(void) //****************************Definition of Class Behavior
    {   double hours, gross;

        cout << "Hours: ";
        cin >> hours;
        gross = hours * payRate;                  // Don't need member operators
        cout << "Pay " << name << " $" << gross << "." << endl;
        ytdGross += gross;
    }
};

int main(void) ///////////////////////////////////////////// Main Program
{   Employee worker;                              // Declaration of object

    cout << setiosflags(ios::fixed) << setprecision(2);
    cout << "Name: ";
    cin >> worker.name;        // Input value for name member of worker object
    cout << "Pay rate: ";
    cin >> worker.payRate;
    cout << "Initial year-to-date gross: ";
    cin >> worker.ytdGross;
    worker.pay();                                 // Call member function
    cout << "Final year-to-date gross $" << worker.ytdGross << "." << endl;
    return 0;
}
```

The *pay()* function that we set up as an independent function would more properly be a member function, a behavior, of *Employee*. It deals with an object of the *Employee* class, and its properties are either internal to the function (*hours* and *gross*) or members of the *Employee* class (*name*, *payRate*, and *ytdGross*). In Program 7–3 we make the appropriate changes:

- The new *pay()* function is defined within the *Employee* class.
- It needs no separate declaration since its definition appears before it is used in the rest of the program.
- Its formal parameters are `void`; nothing is passed to it. It is a member function, so it can see the data members of objects of the *Employee* class.

Behaviors can be public or private, just like properties.

- The function is declared in the public: section of the class because we want to use the function in other parts of the program.

- Because this is a member function, we can use data-member names directly—*payRate* rather than *emp.payRate*. Actually, the latter would be meaningless. It will use the *payRate* property of whatever object calls it—*emp* or *worker* or whatever.

- The call to the function from main() is worker.pay(), meaning that it uses the *pay()* behavior of the *worker* object, and, of course, all the properties of this specific object of the *Employee* class. The previous program used a general *pay()* function and sent it the data members for the *worker* object.

The output of Program 7–3 is exactly the same as that of Program 7–2.

The starting properties, *name*, *payRate*, *dependents*, and *ytdGross*, have to be set for each employee, so let's also set up a function to do that. This action is strictly for employees, so it is reasonable to make it a behavior of each employee—in other words, a member function within the *Employee* class.

In Program 7–4, we pick up the first part of the main() function and move it to the *Employee* behavior stated in a *startData()* function. As with *pay()*, we do not have to pass the function anything because it can see all the variables it needs. We refer to this behavior for the *worker* object by tying it to the object with the member operator. The function call is

```
worker.startData()
```

It is important to realize that a class declaration is a description of a type of object. Stating the properties of a class does not establish anything in memory; creating objects of that class does. Each object will have its own set of properties and can exhibit the class's behaviors. Declaring two *Employee*s, or a hundred, will set up objects with completely separate properties. In Program 7–5 we set up two *Employee*s and show the modified main() function. We also made a slight change to the *pay()* function so that we could see who we were paying:

```
cout << "Hours for " << name << ": ";
```

The rest of the program stays the same.

HEADS UP!

Different objects of a class have separate properties but share the same behaviors.

YOUR TURN 7–1

1. What is the difference between an object and a class?
2. Do all objects of a class have to be exactly the same?
3. What is the difference between a class and a data type?
4. How are public properties different from private ones? Which is the default state?
5. How would we reference the *height* property of a *tree* object?
6. Do object properties have to be public or private to be used by object behaviors?

Program 7–4

```cpp
#include <iostream>
#include <iomanip>
#include <string>
using namespace std;

class Employee ///////////////////////////////////////// Employee Class
{
public:
    string name;
    float payRate;
    int dependents;
    double ytdGross;

    void startData(void) //**************************** Provides Initial Data
    {
        cout << "Name: ";
        cin >> name;
        cout << "Pay rate: ";
        cin >> payRate;
        cout << "Initial year-to-date gross: ";
        cin >> ytdGross;
    }

    void pay(void) //**************************************** Pays Employee
    {   double hours, gross;

        cout << "Hours: ";
        cin >> hours;
        gross = hours * payRate;
        cout << "Pay " << name << " $" << gross << "." << endl;
        ytdGross += gross;
    }
};

int main(void) ///////////////////////////////////////// Main Program
{   Employee worker;                              // Declaration of object

    cout << setiosflags(ios::fixed) << setprecision(2);
    worker.startData();
    worker.pay();
    cout << "Final year-to-date gross $" << worker.ytdGross << "." << endl;
    return 0;
}
```

Output

```
Name: Norval
Pay rate: 8.25
Initial year-to-date gross: 5674.82
Hours: 35
Pay Norval $288.75.
Final year-to-date gross $5963.57.
```

Program 7–5

```
int main(void)  ///////////////////////////////////////////// Main Program
{   Employee worker, loafer;                        // Declaration of objects

    cout << setiosflags(ios::fixed) << setprecision(2);
    worker.startData();
    loafer.startData();
    worker.pay();
    loafer.pay();
    cout << "YTD gross for " << worker.name << " $"
        << worker.ytdGross << ".\n";
    cout << "YTD gross for " << loafer.name << " $"
        << loafer.ytdGross << ".\n";
    return 0;
}
```

Output

```
Name: Stellar
Pay rate: 26.87
Initial year-to-date gross: 34085.81
Name: Slacker
Pay rate: 4.12
Initial year-to-date gross: 126.00
Hours for Stellar: 52
Pay Stellar $1397.24.
Hours for Slacker: 7.2
Pay Slacker $29.66.
YTD gross for Stellar $35483.05.
YTD gross for Slacker $155.66.
```

INITIALIZATION AND CONSTRUCTORS

When an object of a class is declared, it is constructed—built—by C++. The program invokes a default **constructor** function that allocates memory and does whatever else is required to establish the new object. We can define our own constructor to add whatever functionality we want to the creation of an object. C++ will do its own construction and then do ours.

The constructor is similar to any other member function, with three exceptions:

- It is automatically called when an object is declared. The statement

  `Employee worker;`

  calls the constructor function.

- It has the same name as the class. The constructor function for *Employee* is *Employee()*.

- It never has a stated return value, not even `void`. The first line of the *Employee* constructor definition is

  `Employee(void)`

Program 7–6

```cpp
#include <iostream>
#include <iomanip>
#include <string>
using namespace std;

class Employee ////////////////////////////////////////////// Employee Class
{
public:
    string name;
    float payRate;
    int dependents;
    double ytdGross;

    Employee(void) { payRate = 5.15; } //************************ Constructor
    void startData(void) //***************************** Initial Object Data
    {
        cout << "Name: ";
        cin >> name;
        cout << "Initial year-to-date gross: ";
        cin >> ytdGross;
    }
    void pay(void) //***************************************** Pays Employee
    {   double hours, gross;

        cout << "Hours for " << name << ": ";
        cin >> hours;
        gross = hours * payRate;
        cout << "Pay " << name << " $" << gross << "." << endl;
        ytdGross += gross;
    }
};

int main(void) ////////////////////////////////////////////// Main Program
{   Employee worker, loafer;

    cout << setiosflags(ios::fixed) << setprecision(2);
    worker.startData();
    loafer.startData();
    worker.pay();
    loafer.pay();
    cout << "YTD gross for " << worker.name << " $"
         << worker.ytdGross << ".\n";
    cout << "YTD gross for " << loafer.name << " $"
         << loafer.ytdGross << "." << endl;
    return 0;
}
```

We will see where we might have parameter declarations other than void, we might pass values to the constructor, but we will never state a return value.

Other than those points, we can do anything in a constructor that we can do in any other member function. We can put thousands of statements there. We probably won't, though. Since the declaration of an object is also

Output

```
Name: Stellar
Initial year-to-date gross: 34085.81
Name: Slacker
Initial year-to-date gross: 126.00
Hours for Stellar: 52
Pay Stellar $267.80.
Hours for Slacker: 7.2
Pay Slacker $37.08.
YTD gross for Stellar $34353.61.
YTD gross for Slacker $163.08.
```

Trying to initialize in a class
declaration.

a call to the constructor, we usually put in the constructor those things important to the object's creation—things such as initialization values for the object's properties.

In fact, this is the only place we can put initialization values. We cannot put initializations in the class declaration like this:

```
class Employee ///////////////////////////////////////// Employee Class
{
public:
    string name;
    float payRate = 5.15;                                   // Won't work
    int dependents;
    double ytdGross;
```

because no memory is allocated; there is no place to store the 5.15.

To start each employee at a *payRate* of 5.15, we can add this constructor to our class declaration:

```
Employee(void)
{   payRate = 5.15;
}
```

Since the function is so short, it is often written on one line:

```
Employee(void) { payRate = 5.15; }
```

To show our constructor at work, we take the *payRate* assignment out of the *startData()* function, giving us Program 7–6.

In Program 7–6, both the *worker* object and the *loafer* object start at the same *payRate* because the creation of each of them calls the same constructor.

Earlier, in Program 7–2, when we used *pay()* as an independent function, we passed the object of the *Employee* class by reference rather than by value. Remember that passing by value creates a new object and will, of course, call the constructor for that object. If we used our independent *pay()* function in Program 7–6, and defined it as a call by value,

HEADS UP!

Watch constructors with
passes by value.

```
double pay(Employee emp)
```

the constructor would set *emp*'s *payRate* to 5.15 no matter what the passed value was.

Remember, a constructor is very much like any other member function. It can contain any kind of statements. We could move all the statements from the *startData()* function to the constructor.

```
Employee(void)
{   payRate = 5.15;
    cout << "Name: ";
    cin >> name;          // Input value for name member of worker object
    cout << "Initial year-to-date gross: ";
    cin >> ytdGross;
}
```

Each time an object was created the constructor would assign the *payRate* and ask for inputs for *name* and *ytdGross*.

Custom Construction

As we said, we can pass values to the constructor. Let's modify our simple constructor to this:

```
Employee(float rate)
{   payRate = rate;
}
```

or, with such a short function, this:

```
Employee(float rate) { payRate = rate; }
```

When we create an *Employee* object, we pass a value into *rate*, which the function assigns to the *payRate* for that object.

Creating an object with such a constructor makes the declaration of the object look like a combination of a declaration and a function call, which it really is—memory is allocated for the object, and the constructor is called.

```
Employee worker(26.87), loafer(4.12);          // Declaration of objects
```

Now *worker*'s *payRate* will be 26.87, and *loafer*'s 4.12.

YOUR TURN 7–2

1. When is a constructor function called?
2. How do constructors differ from other functions?
3. What can we not do in a constructor?
4. How can we initialize different objects of the same class with different values?

USING CLASSES TO ABSTRACTION

We said that one of the advantages of object-oriented programming is that it allows us to set up abstract objects—program routines that we could use by just knowing their outside interfaces, but not necessarily understanding their inner workings. We have, of course, used such objects: `cin`, `cout`, or any of the C++ statements or functions. Now we want to set up our own abstract objects. Since we are going to write them, we will understand their inner workings, but once they are written we shouldn't have to think about how they work, nor should other people who use our objects.

One abstraction technique is **data hiding**, allowing access to the object's properties only through the object's behaviors. This technique makes it possible for us to ensure that use of properties is consistent with the object's purpose. To use a human analogy, let's access the "Gimme a dollar" behavior. A truly abstract person would somehow produce a dollar bill and hand it to us. A totally nonabstract approach would be for us to grab the person's wallet and remove a dollar bill—or perhaps a five, or a hundred.

What if the person doesn't have a dollar? The abstract person would so inform us. In the nonabstract approach we might rip the lining out of the wallet, take a credit card, steal a picture of the grandchildren, or whatever. Without the protection of abstraction, the object loses control over itself.

Insulating Properties

Let's take Program 7–6 and control the access to the *ytdGross* property. First we make the *ytdGross* variable a `private:` member of the *Employee* class.

```
class Employee /////////////////////////////////////////// Employee Class
{   double ytdGross;                                      // Private data
public:
    string name;
    float payRate;
    int dependents;
```

Now, since the variable is only accessible from within the class, we must provide class functions to access it—**access functions**. We already use the *startData()* function to input its value. Let's add some error checking to this function to ensure that the *ytdGross* figure input is at least reasonable.

```
void startData(void) //***************************** Initial Object Data
{
    cout << "Name: ";
    cin >> name;            // Input value for name member of worker object
    cout << "Initial year-to-date gross: ";
    cin >> ytdGross;
    while (ytdGross < 0 || ytdGross > 100000)
    {   if (ytdGross < 0)
            cout << "The employee can't owe us money!\n";
        else
            cout << "Nobody in this company makes that much!\n";
        cout << "Reenter initial year-to-date gross: ";
        cin >> ytdGross;
    }
}
```

The *startData()* function, rewritten, does not allow us to proceed until *ytdGross* is between 0 and 100,000.

Let's test out *startData()* with a `main()` function that begins like this:

```
int main(void) /////////////////////////////////////////// Main Program
{   Employee worker(26.87), loafer(4.12);        // Declaration of objects

    worker.startData();
    loafer.startData();
```

Depending on what we input, it might produce this:

Name: **Stellar**
Initial year-to-date gross: **3408581**
Nobody in this company makes that much!
Reenter initial year-to-date gross: **34085.81**
Name: **Slacker**
Initial year-to-date gross: **-126**
The employee can't owe us money!
Reenter initial year-to-date gross: **126**

Program 7–7

```cpp
#include <iostream>
#include <iomanip>
#include <string>
using namespace std;

class Employee ////////////////////////////////////////// Employee Class
{   double ytdGross;                                        // Private data
public:
    string name;
    float payRate;
    int dependents;

    Employee(float rate) { payRate = rate; }
    void startData(void) //***************************** Initial Object Data
    {
        cout << "Name: ";
        cin >> name;            // Input value for name member of worker object
        cout << "Initial year-to-date gross: ";
        cin >> ytdGross;
        while (ytdGross < 0 || ytdGross > 100000)
        {   if (ytdGross < 0)
                cout << "The employee can't owe us money!\n";
            else
                cout << "Nobody in this company makes that much!\n";
            cout << "Reenter initial year-to-date gross: ";
            cin >> ytdGross;
        }
    }
};

int main(void) ////////////////////////////////////////// Main Program
{   Employee worker(26.87), loafer(4.12);          // Declaration of objects

    cout << setiosflags(ios::fixed) << setprecision(2);
    worker.startData();
    loafer.startData();
    worker.pay();
    loafer.pay();
    cout << "YTD gross for " << worker.name << " $"
        << worker.getYtdGross() << ".\n";          // Uses access function
    cout << "YTD gross for " << loafer.name << " $"
        << loafer.getYtdGross() << "." << endl;    // Uses access function
    return 0;
}
```

Output

```
Name: Stellar
Initial year-to-date gross: 3408581
Nobody in this company makes that much!
Reenter initial year-to-date gross: 34085.81
Name: Slacker
Initial year-to-date gross: -126
The employee can't owe us money!
Reenter initial year-to-date gross: 126
Hours for Stellar: 52
Pay Stellar $1397.24.
Hours for Slacker: 7.2
Pay Slacker $29.66.
YTD gross for Stellar $35483.05.
YTD gross for Slacker $155.66.
```

TRAP

Trying to access a private property directly from outside the object.

There are still places in the program, however, that attempt to access *ytdGross* directly. They cannot, of course, so we must provide other access functions in the *Employee* class.

The `main()` function displayed the *ytdGross*.

```
cout << "YTD gross for " << worker.name << " $"
     << worker.ytdGross << ".\n";
```

Now that *ytdGross* is `private`, it cannot be accessed from `main()` or anywhere outside an object of the *Employee* class, so let's add this access function to the class:

```
double getYtdGross(void) { return ytdGross; }
```

and change the statements in `main()` to this:

```
cout << "YTD gross for " << worker.name << " $"
     << worker.getYtdGross() << ".\n";          // Uses access function
cout << "YTD gross for " << loafer.name << " $"
     << loafer.getYtdGross() << "." << endl;     // Uses access function
```

Now, the *ytdGross* property is completely insulated from anything outside the class. Program 7–7 shows the entire process.

Insulating Behaviors

Typical functions in a class are *setWhatever()*, to assign a value to a property, and *getWhatever()*, to return the value of that property. In many cases there must be a number of ways of setting (or getting) the value of a property. Any of those behaviors should fulfill certain final requirements before the property is set. We can make the *setWhatever()* function a `private:` member of the class and other access functions within the class will have to call it to assign a value to the property.

HEADS UP!

Private behaviors can set consistent underlying processes.

To fulfill the company's legal requirements, we want to make sure that we do not pay anyone less than the minimum wage, so we will make sure that anything that assigns *payRate* will be checked. To make Program 7–8 from Program 7–7 we add a constant declaration,

```
const float minimumWage = 5.15;
```

move the *payRate* declaration to the `private:` section of the *Employee* class, and add a *setPayRate()* function to the `private:` section.

```
class Employee /////////////////////////////////////////////////// Employee Class
{   double ytdGross;                                        // Private data
    float payRate;

    void setPayRate(float rate)                             // Private function
    {   if (rate < minimumWage)
        {   payRate = minimumWage;
            cout << "Pay rate set to minimum wage.\n";
        }
        else
            payRate = rate;
    }
public:
```

One class function, the constructor, already sets the pay rate. To use our new function, we change the constructor from

```
Employee(float rate) { payRate = rate; }
```

to

```
Employee(float rate) { setPayRate(rate); }
```

When `main()` creates two objects,

```
{   Employee worker(26.87), loafer(4.12);        // Declaration of objects
```

the value for the first object, 26.87, is greater than the *minimumWage*, so it is assigned to *payRate*. The second, 4.12, is less, so *payRate* is set to *minimumWage* and the message printed.

We add another `public:` member function to allow a program to input a new *payRate* for an object, and, since *payRate* is now `private:`, a function to return the *payRate*.

HEADS UP!

A private property may only be accessed through object functions.

```
    void inputRate(void)
    {   float rate;

        cout << "Enter new pay rate for " << name << ": ";
        cin >> rate;
        setPayRate(rate);
    }
    float getPayRate(void) { return payRate; }
```

To show the *inputRate()* function in action, let's add this:

```
loafer.inputRate();
```

to `main()` immediately after the call `loafer.startData();`. Running the program to that point might yield:

```
Pay rate set to minimum wage.
Name: Stellar
Initial year-to-date gross: 34085.81
Name: Slacker
Initial year-to-date gross: 126
Enter new pay rate for Slacker: 1.25
Pay rate set to minimum wage.
```

We obviously don't want to pay Slacker even the minimum wage, but we will have to.

Program 7-8

```cpp
#include <iostream>
#include <iomanip>
#include <string>
using namespace std;

const float minimumWage = 5.15;

class Employee ///////////////////////////////////////////// Employee Class
{   double ytdGross;                                           // Private data
    float payRate;

    void setPayRate(float rate)                              // Private function
    {   if (rate < minimumWage)
        {   payRate = minimumWage;
            cout << "Pay rate set to minimum wage.\n";
        }
        else
            payRate = rate;
    }
public:
    string name;
    int dependents;

    Employee(float rate) { setPayRate(rate); }
    void startData(void) //***************************** Initial Object Data
    {
        cout << "Name: ";
        cin >> name;          // Input value for name member of worker object
        cout << "Initial year-to-date gross: ";
        cin >> ytdGross;
        while (ytdGross < 0 || ytdGross > 100000)
        {   if (ytdGross < 0)
                cout << "The employee can't owe us money!\n";
            else
                cout << "Nobody in this company makes that much!\n";
            cout << "Reenter initial year-to-date gross: ";
            cin >> ytdGross;
        }
    }
    void pay(void) //***************************************** Pays Employee
    {   double hours, gross;

        cout << "Hours for " << name << ": ";
        cin >> hours;
        gross = hours * payRate;
        cout << "Pay " << name << " $" << gross << "." << endl;
        ytdGross += gross;
    }
    double getYtdGross(void) { return ytdGross; } //******* Access Functions
    float getPayRate(void) { return payRate; }
```

(Continued)

```
        void inputRate(void) //***************************** Accept New Pay Rate
        {   float rate;

            cout << "Enter new pay rate for " << name << ": ";
            cin >> rate;
            setPayRate(rate);
        }
    };

    int main(void) ///////////////////////////////////////////// Main Program
    {   Employee worker(26.87), loafer(4.12);        // Declaration of objects

        cout << setiosflags(ios::fixed) << setprecision(2);
        worker.startData();
        loafer.startData();
        loafer.inputRate();
        worker.pay();
        loafer.pay();
        cout << "YTD gross for " << worker.name << " $"
            << worker.getYtdGross() << ".\n";         // Uses access function
        cout << "YTD gross for " << loafer.name << " $"
            << loafer.getYtdGross() << "." << endl;    // Uses access function
        return 0;
    }
```

Output

```
Pay rate set to minimum wage.
Name: Stellar
Initial year-to-date gross: 34085.81
Name: Slacker
Initial year-to-date gross: 126
Enter new pay rate for Slacker: 1.25
Pay rate set to minimum wage.
Hours for Stellar: 52
Pay Stellar $1397.24.
Hours for Slacker: 7.2
Pay Slacker $37.08.
YTD gross for Stellar $35483.05.
YTD gross for Slacker $163.08.
```

YOUR TURN 7–3

1. Why is abstraction important?
2. What is data hiding?
3. What is an access function?
4. Why would we insulate behaviors?

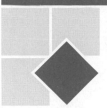

PUTTING IT TOGETHER

Keeping track of time is one of humankind's most common activities, but humans were not very clever in their design of time increments: 60 seconds in a minute, 60 minutes in an hour, 24 hours in a day, and so forth. These odd increments make time calculations difficult. They also make time display difficult. Instead of answering the question "What time is it?" with something like "126.428," we have to say "3:34:27 P.M."

Set up a class to handle common timekeeping functions.

Our time class could include all kinds of behaviors, but let's limit it to a few common ones. It should:

- Keep track of the current time.

- Allow us to set the time.

- Allow us to increment the time (add one second to it).

- Allow us to add any number of hours, minutes, and seconds to the time.

- Display the current time in both standard, 12-hour (H:MM:SS AM/PM) or abbreviated military, 24-hour (HHMM:SS) time.

All of these things should be done with sufficient error-checking so that we don't display some goofy time such as 27:−3:92 PM.

We are designing one object or, more properly, one class from which any number of objects may be created. Let's have an object of this class store the current time in a form that is more convenient for time arithmetic—seconds from midnight rather than hours, minutes, and seconds. Any time we send to the object, in any form, will first be converted to this internal storage format. When we want the object to display the time, the internal format will be converted to the appropriate form, standard or military.

To isolate the internal time from possible outside problems, we will make it a private property of the object; only the object's access functions may use or modify it. We will also design a private behavior to convert to this internal time—not so much to isolate the behavior, but because a number of other access functions will use it.

The private conversion function (implemented in the *Time* function *toInternal()*) should:

```
Receive hours, minutes, and seconds
if in normal ranges (i.e., hours 0–23)
    Convert to internal time
else
    Display error message
    Set internal time to flag for invalid time
Return internal time
```

To set the time (implemented in the *Time* function *set()*) the routine should:

Receive hours, minutes, and seconds
Change internal time to converted internal time
    (using the conversion routine)

The routine for incrementing the time (implemented in the *Time* function *increment()*) should:

if internal time valid
    Add one second to internal time
    if time beyond 23:59:59 (into the next day)
        Set to beginning of next day

For adding to the time (implemented in the *Time* function *add()*) we should:

Receive hours, minutes, and seconds
if internal time valid
    Convert additional time to internal format
    if additional time valid
        Accumulate additional time into internal time
        if time beyond 23:59:59 (into the next day)
            Subtract day to show just time in next day
    else
        Display error message

To display the time (implemented in the *Time* function *display()*) we should:

Receive type of time (standard or military)
if internal time valid
    Calculate seconds
    Calculate leftover time
    Calculate minutes
    Calculate hours
    if military time
        Display hours, minutes, and seconds
    else
        Determine AM or PM suffix
        Adjust hours to 12-hour basis
        Display hours, minutes, seconds, and suffix

When an object is constructed, it should

Receive hours, minutes, and seconds
Set internal time

In our Object Summary, we have one overall class, *Time*, with a number of behaviors and a single property that is accessible from any of the behaviors. Many of the behaviors also have their own properties. Remember, the class is simply a description from which any number of objects can be created.

Class and Functions	Behavior	Properties
Time		internal time
To internal	Converts to internal time	hours, minutes, seconds (req) internal (pro)
Constructor	Creates object, sets internal time	hours, minutes, seconds (req)
Set	Sets internal time	hours, minutes, seconds (req)
Increment	Adds 1 second to internal time	
Add	Adds to internal time	hours, minutes, seconds (req) additional time in internal format
Display	Displays internal time in standard or military form	type, standard or military (req) hours, minutes, seconds temp variable for leftover time suffix, AM or PM

IMPLEMENTATION

The design is implemented in Program 7–9. Wherever possible, routines are called from other routines rather than repeating code in the program. For example, the constructor simply calls the *set()* function; *set()* and *add()* both use the *toInternal()* function. The *increment()* function could have used *add()* by sending it zero hours, zero minutes, and one second, but incrementing is simple compared to adding, so it was more efficient to do the simple incrementing rather than use the more complicated adding routine.

Either adding or incrementing may push the time into the next day, so we test for this by comparing the internal time with the number of seconds in a day ($24 \times 60 \times 60 = 86,400$).

```
if (internal >= 24L * 60 * 60)
```

If the internal time has reached that point in the *increment()* behavior, which adds one second at a time, we can simply set the internal time to zero—the beginning of the next day. If it is in the *add()* behavior, we subtract the number of seconds in a full day, leaving us the seconds in the new day.

We use the notation `24L` in the calculation in case the program is compiled on a system with a 16-bit `int`. Since 86,400 exceeds that `int`'s capacity (32,767), we force the calculation to `long`. Would you have thought of that? Now you will.

In the *display()* function, the simple formula for adjusting hours to a 12-hour format,

```
hours = (hours + 11) % 12 + 1;      // Adjust to 12-hour format
```

is not really so simple. if we took the remainder of a division by 12, we would get hours 0 through 11. Unfortunately, we refer to 0 hours as 12 and need hours 12 through 11. By adding 11 to everything, 0 hours becomes 11, 1 hour becomes 12, and so forth. Our remainder operation still gives us 0 through 11, but everything is one too low—0 hours works out to 11, 1 hour works out to 0—so we add one to the result.

TEST

To test our new class, we write a **driver** routine—code whose only purpose is to exercise our new class. In this case the driver is the `main()`

Program 7–9

```
    #include <iostream>
    #include <iomanip>
    using namespace std;

    class Time ///////////////////////////////////////////////// Time Class
c1  {   long internal;                              // Seconds from midnight

i1      long toInternal(int h, int m, int s) //******************** Internal Time
i2      {   long internal;

i3          if (h >= 0 && h <= 23 && m >= 0 && m <= 59 && s >= 0 && s <= 59)
i4              internal = h * 60L * 60 + m * 60 + s; // Force calculation to long
            else
i5          {   cout << "Time invalid.\n";
i6              internal = -1;                          // Flag for invalid time
            }
i7          return internal;
        }

    public:
T1      Time(int h, int m, int s)
T2      {   set(h, m, s); }
s1      void set(int h, int m, int s)
s2      {   internal = toInternal(h, m, s); }

        void increment(void) //************************* Add One Second to Time
+1      {   if (internal != -1)                       // Internal time must be valid
+2          {   internal += 1;
+3              if (internal >= 24L * 60 * 60)   // Increment may push to next day
+4                  internal = 0;                     // Start at new day
            }
        }

a1      void add(int h, int m, int s) //***************** Add Any Amount of Time
a2      {   long addTime;

a3          if (internal != -1)                        // Internal time must be valid
a4          {   addTime = toInternal(h, m, s);
a5              if (addTime != -1)                     // New time must be valid
a6              {   internal += addTime;
a7                  if (internal >= 24L * 60 * 60)   // Add time may push to next day
a8                      internal -= 24L * 60 * 60;     // Subtract a day
                }
                else
a9                  cout << "Cannot add invalid time.\n";
            }
        }

d1      void display(char type) //*********** Display Standard or Military Time
d2      {   int hours, minutes;
            long seconds,
                 temp;                    // Temporary variable for time calculations
            char suffix;                            // A for AM or P for PM
```
(Continued)

Program 7–9 *(Continued)*

```
d3          if (internal != -1)
d4          {   seconds = internal % 60;               // Remainder leaves seconds
d5              temp = internal / 60;        // Integer division, eliminates seconds
d6              minutes = temp % 60;                   // Remainder leaves minutes
d7              hours = temp / 60;           // Only hours left after integer division
d8              cout << setfill('0');          // Put leading zeros in time display
d9              if (type == 'm' || type == 'M')                      // Military time
d10                 cout << setw(2) << hours << setw(2) << minutes << ":"
                        << setw(2) << seconds;
                else                                                 // Standard time
d11             {   if (hours < 12) suffix = 'A'; else suffix = 'P';
d12                 hours = (hours + 11) % 12 + 1;        // Adjust to 12-hour format
d13                 cout << hours << ':' << setw(2) << minutes << ':'
                        << setw(2) << seconds << ' ' << suffix << 'M';
                }
d14             cout << setfill(' ');                       // Set back to normal fill
            }
            else
d15             cout << "<Invalid time>";
        }
    };
```

Driver Routines

```
    void showTimes(Time &timer);

    int main(void) ///////////////////////////////////////////// Main Program
1   {   int hr, min, sec;
2       Time clock(4, 0, 23);

3       showTimes(clock);
        cout << "Enter hours minutes seconds: ";
4       cin >> hr >> min >> sec;
5       clock.set(hr, min, sec);
6       showTimes(clock);
        cout << "Enter hours minutes seconds: ";
7       cin >> hr >> min >> sec;
8       clock.set(hr, min, sec);
9       showTimes(clock);
10      clock.add(3, 30, 45);
11      showTimes(clock);
12      for (sec = 1; sec <= 10; ++sec)
13      {   clock.increment();
14          showTimes(clock);
        }
        return 0;
    }


t1  void showTimes(Time &timer) //**** Displays Both Standard and Military Time
t2  {   timer.display('s');
        cout << " or ";
t3      timer.display('M');
        cout << endl;
    }
```

EXECUTION CHART

Line	Explanation	hr	min	sec						
1	Declare variables.	??	??	??						
2	Create *clock* object of *Time* class; pass values to constructor.	??	??	??						
	Time.Time():				*internal*	*h*	*m*	*s*		
T1	Declare class variable; initialize local variables.	(??)	(??)	(??)	??	4	0	23		
T2	Call *set()*; pass values.	(??)	(??)	(??)	??	4	0	23		
	Time.set():					*h*	*m*	*s*		
s1	Declare and initialize local variables.	(??)	(??)	(??)	??	4	0	23		
s2	Call *toInternal()*; pass values.	(??)	(??)	(??)	??	4	0	23		
	Time.toInternal():					*h*	*m*	*s*	*internal*	
i1	Declare and initialize local variables.	(??)	(??)	(??)	??	4	0	23	--	
i2	Declare local variable.	(??)	(??)	(??)	??	4	0	23	??	
i3	Test ranges.	(??)	(??)	(??)	??	4	0	23	??	
i4	Calculate internal time.	(??)	(??)	(??)	??	4	0	23	14423	
i7	Return internal time.	(??)	(??)	(??)	??	4	0	23	14423	
	Time.set():					*h*	*m*	*s*		
s2	Assign return value to class variable and return.	(??)	(??)	(??)	14423	4	0	23		
	Time.Time():					*h*	*m*	*s*		
T2	Return.	(??)	(??)	(??)	14423	4	0	23		
	`main():`									
3	Call *showTimes()*; pass *clock* object.	??	??	??	(14423)					
	showTimes():									
t1	Declare *timer* a reference to passed object *clock*.	(??)	(??)	(??)	(14423)					
t2	Call *display()* for object for standard time.	(??)	(??)	(??)	(14423)					
	Time.display():					*type*	*hours*	*minutes*	*seconds*	*suffix*
d1	Declare and initialize local variable.	(??)	(??)	(??)	14423	s	--	--	--	--
d2	Declare local variables.	(??)	(??)	(??)	14423	s	??	??	??	??
d3	Time is valid.	(??)	(??)	(??)	14423	s	??	??	??	??
d4	Assign *seconds*.	(??)	(??)	(??)	14423	s	??	??	23	??
d5	Calculate *temp* (240).	(??)	(??)	(??)	14423	s	??	??	23	??
d6	Calculate *minutes*.	(??)	(??)	(??)	14423	s	??	0	23	??
d7	Calculate *hours*.	(??)	(??)	(??)	14423	s	4	0	23	??
d8	Change output fill character for leading zeros.	(??)	(??)	(??)	14423	s	4	0	23	??
d9	*type* not *m* or *M*.	(??)	(??)	(??)	14423	s	4	0	23	??
d11	*hours* < 12, assign *suffix A*.	(??)	(??)	(??)	14423	s	4	0	23	A
d12	Adjust *hours*.	(??)	(??)	(??)	14423	s	4	0	23	A
d13	Display *hours*, *minutes*, *seconds*, and *suffix*.	(??)	(??)	(??)	14423	s	4	0	23	A
d14	Fill character back to normal.	(??)	(??)	(??)	14423	s	4	0	23	A
	showTimes():									
t3	Call *display()* for object for military time.	(??)	(??)	(??)	(14423)					
	`main():`									
4	Input new time.	20	92	10	(−1)					
5	Call *set()* for *clock* object; pass values. As above *set()* calls *toInternal()*, which passes back −1, which *set()* assigns to *internal*.	20	92	10	(−1)					

	main(): (Continued)	hr	min	sec	internal				
6	Call *showTimes()* which calls *Display* for the *timer* object twice. Since *internal* is –1; pass values.	20	92	10	(–1)				
7–9	Input new time and call *set()* again. Display times.	20	29	10	(73750)				
10	Call *add()* for *clock* object; pass values.	20	29	10	(73750)				
	Time.add():					**h**	**m**	**s**	**addTime**
a1	Declare and initialize local variables.	(20)	(29)	(10)	73750	3	30	45	--
a2	Declare local variable.	(20)	(29)	(10)	73750	3	30	45	??
a3	Time valid.	(20)	(29)	(10)	73750	3	30	45	??
a4	Call *toInternal()*; assign return to *addTime*.	(20)	(29)	(10)	73750	3	30	45	12645
a5	*addTime* valid.	(20)	(29)	(10)	73750	3	30	45	12645
a6	Accumulate into *internal*.	(20)	(29)	(10)	86395	3	30	45	12645
a7	*internal* not greater than seconds in a day.	(20)	(29)	(10)	86395	3	30	45	12645
	main():								
12–14	Call *increment()* 10 times. We look at the 5th, which moves to the next day.	20	29	10	(86399)				
	Time.increment():								
+1	Time valid.	(20)	(29)	(10)	86399				
+2	Add 1 to *internal*.	(20)	(29)	(10)	86400				
+3	*internal* greater than seconds in a day.	(20)	(29)	(10)	86400				
+4	Start new day.	(20)	(29)	(10)	0				
	main():								
	Program ends	20	29	10	(5)				

Output

```
4:00:23 AM or 0400:23
Enter hours minutes seconds: 20 92 10
Time invalid.
<Invalid time> or <Invalid time>
Enter hours minutes seconds: 20 29 10
8:29:10 PM or 2029:10
11:59:55 PM or 2359:55
11:59:56 PM or 2359:56
11:59:57 PM or 2359:57
11:59:58 PM or 2359:58
11:59:59 PM or 2359:59
12:00:00 AM or 0000:00
12:00:01 AM or 0000:01
12:00:02 AM or 0000:02
12:00:03 AM or 0000:03
12:00:04 AM or 0000:04
12:00:05 AM or 0000:05
```

function and the *showTimes()* function that displays the time in both standard and military formats. Our driver should be much more extensive to test all foreseeable possibilities, but this one gives the idea.

Be sure to notice in the Execution Chart when variables exist (when there is something but two dashes), when they are garbage (two question marks), and when they are not visible (the value is in parentheses).

SUMMARY

- **KEY TERMS** (in order of appearance)

Abstract	`public:`
Class	`private:`
Instance	Member operator
Object	Behavior
Property	Member function
`class`	Constructor
Member	Data hiding
Complex data type	Access function
Public	Driver
Private	

- **NEW STATEMENT**

  ```
  class ClassName {member declarations};
  ```

- **CONCEPT REVIEW**

  - A worthy programming objective is to create **abstract** objects—things that we know how to use, but we do not have to know what is in them. We have been using such things in our lives, but now we want to extend the concept to our programs.

  - A **class** is a description of something. An **object** is an **instance** of the class—an actual entity that fits the description.

  - A **class** statement performs a class declaration. It declares the class name and all of the class **members**, each of which has its own declaration within the class. A class may have many **properties**, data members, and really defines a new data type. Since it is made of a combination of other data types, we often refer to it as a **complex data type**.

  - Properties may be either **public**—they can be accessed from outside the class—or **private**—they can only be accessed from within the class. Private is the default, but anything declared after the **public:** key word is public. We can switch back to private declarations with the **private:** key word.

  - Once a class is declared, we may declare objects of the class—actual instances. Properties of a particular object are accessed using the **member operator**, which tells C++ to use the property of that object.

  - Classes are typically declared externally, which makes them global. Objects are typically declared internally, locally. This means that we can declare objects of the class anywhere in the program.

  - We can pass objects to functions, usually by reference, just as we would pass variables.

  - Object **behaviors** are stated as functions and declared within the class declaration. A **member function** can access all the properties of a class, public and private. In calling the function from outside the object, we use the member operator to tell C++ which object properties the function should work with.

- A **constructor** function, with the same name as the class, is automatically called when an object is created. It can never have a stated return value, and none, not even `void`, is ever declared. Constructors are typically used for initializing properties of an object. As with any other function, we can pass values to the constructor.

- One abstraction technique that can be implemented with classes is **data hiding**—allowing the object's properties to be accessed only through class behaviors. Using **access functions**, we can access the properties, but insulate them from uncontrolled use. One common feature of access functions is error checking to ensure that the properties stay within reasonable bounds.

- We can also insulate behaviors by making them private. A common reason for this is to set up some consistent property access or process that many of the object's member functions can use.

- Often for testing purposes, we write **driver** routines that exercise a particular section of code.

• HEADS UP: POINTS OF SPECIAL INTEREST

- An object can be used without your knowing what is inside it.
- We create individual objects from class descriptions.
- Objects of the same class may differ in their properties.
- Classes are only descriptions. Objects are the real things.
- Class declarations allocate no memory space for variables.
- Typically, class declarations are global and objects are local.
- Objects are typically passed by reference.
- Object behaviors can always see object properties.
- Behaviors can be public or private, just like properties.
- Different objects of a class have separate properties but share the same behaviors.
- Watch constructors with passes by value.
- Data hiding allows an object to maintain control of itself.
- Private behaviors can set consistent underlying processes.
- A private property may only be accessed through object functions.

• TRAPS: COMMON PROGRAMMING ERRORS

- Leaving off the semicolon after a class declaration.
- Trying to initialize in a class declaration.
- Trying to access a private property directly from outside the object.

• YOUR TURN ANSWERS

• 7–1

1. A class is a description; an object is an actual instance of what is described.
2. No, all objects of a class do not have to be exactly the same, and they probably shouldn't be. They differ in their properties.
3. A class is a data type that we have defined.

4. Public properties are accessible from outside the object; private properties are accessible only from class behaviors. Private is the default state.

5. We would reference the *height* property of a *tree* object by using the member operator and the notation `tree.height`.

6. To be used by an object behavior, object properties can be either public or private. An object behavior can always see the object's properties.

• 7–2

1. A constructor function is called whenever an object is created.

2. Constructors differ from other functions in that they are automatically called; they have the same name as the class; and they never have a stated return value.

3. Other than return a value, we can do anything in a constructor that we can do in any other function.

4. We can initialize different objects of the same class with different values by passing values to the constructor in the object's declaration.

• 7–3

1. Abstraction allows an object to be used without our having to know its inner workings.

2. Data hiding allows access to an object's properties only through the object itself.

3. An access function provides access to an object's private properties for processes outside the object.

4. We insulate behaviors—make them private—to provide some consistent underlying behavior that other, more general object behaviors can use.

EXERCISES

1. What properties and behaviors would you be interested in if you were evaluating the purchase of the following:

   a. a television   b. a computer
   c. skis   d. a hot dog

2. What are the problems with the following class declarations?

```
a. Class Whatever          b. class WhyNot:
     Public                     {  string words;
        int this              private:
        float that               int numbers = 6;
        double those             float decimals = 32.56;
     }                         };
```

3. Write the declaration for a *JunkFood* class. It should include the *name* and *price* of the product, available to the rest of the program, and the *calories*, available only to *JunkFood* functions.

4. Write a statement that creates a *snack* object from the *JunkFood* class. Write another statement that assigns 0.98 to *snack*'s *price*.

5. What is wrong with the following constructor function?

```
class Clown
{   short stuff;
public:
    void ClownConst(s) { stuff = s };        // Constructor
```

6. Given the declaration in Exercise 5 (and assuming that you have corrected it), what is wrong with these statements in the `main()` function?

```
Clown bozo = 14;
bozo.stuff = 26;
cout << stuff.bozo;
```

7. Given the declaration in Exercise 5, what is wrong with these statements within the *Clown* class declaration?

```
int laughter(float volume)
{   float giggles;
    cin >> Clown.giggles;
    Clown.stuff = volume / Clown.giggles;
```

8. Show a constructor in the *JunkFood* class that initializes each *JunkFood* object with calories of 300. Can you think of an appropriate name for the constructor?

9. Show a constructor in the *JunkFood* class that accepts a name from the object declaration. Show the object declaration that passes the name. Think of a great name for some junk food.

10. Change Program 7–8 to make all of its properties private. You will have to write and use appropriate access functions.

11. Make the *showTime()* function in Program 7–8 a member of the *Time* class.

PROGRAMS

1. Modify Program 7–9 so that the constructor initializes the time from the system clock. To do this, consult your C++ reference manual to investigate the `time()` function (we used it in Chapter 6) to see how to interpret its return value. Also add a *current()* function that, when called, resets the time to the system time. Since both functions set time to the system clock, you should have a private function, *setToSystem()*, that actually sets the time. Modify the driver (`main()`) so that its first few lines are as shown.

Class, Additional Functions, and Variables

```
Time
  Time()            No variables needed
  setToSystem()
    now             Return from time()
  current()         No variables needed
```

Output

```
Initial time: 9:26:41 AM or 0926:41
 .   .   .
Time now: 9:27:08 AM or 0927:08
```

Driver

```
int main(void)
{  int hr, min, sec;
   Time clock;

   cout << "Initial time: ";
   showTimes(clock);
       .  .  .
   clock.current();
   cout << "Time now: ";
   showTimes(clock);
   return 0;
}
```

2. Create the beginnings of a *Rectangle* class that stores a rectangle's width and height as well as the *x* and *y* coordinates for the upper-left corner of the rectangle. You should be able to specify the rectangle's properties either as above or with the *x* and *y* coordinates for both the upper-left and lower-right corners of the rectangle. The function should provide the area and the perimeter (distance around) of the rectangle. Use an isolated function, *set()*, to error-check and, if valid, set the class properties. The *setDimensions()* and *setXy()* functions should keep looping until the *set()* function has valid parameters.

Class, Functions, and Variables

`Rectangle`	The Rectangle class
`x, y`	Coordinates for upper-left corner
`width, height`	
`set()`	Private function to validate and set coordinates
`x1, y1`	Coordinates for upper-left corner
`w, h`	Width and height
`Rectangle()`	Constructor
`x, y`	Coordinates for upper-left corner
`w, h`	Width and height
`setDimensions()`	Set by width and height
`setXy()`	Set by x and y in lower-right corner
`x, y`	Coordinates for upper-left corner
`rx, ry`	Coordinates for lower-right corner
`area()`	Displays area of rectangle
`perimeter()`	Displays length of rectangle perimeter

Driver

```
int main(void)  //////////////////////////////////////////////////Main Program
{  Rectangle box(1, 1, 10, 10);

   cout << "Rectangle area: " << box.area()
        << ", perimeter: " << box.perimeter() << endl;
   box.setDimensions();
   cout << "Rectangle area: " << box.area()
        << ", perimeter: " << box.perimeter() << endl;
   box.setXy();
   cout << "Rectangle area: " << box.area()
        << ", perimeter: " << box.perimeter() << endl;
   return 0;
}
```

Output

```
Rectangle area: 100, perimeter: 40
X and Y for upper left> 6 6
Width and height> 5 7
Rectangle area: 35, perimeter: 24
X and Y for upper left> 6 6
X and Y for lower right> 5 7
Invalid parameters, rectangle not changed.
X and Y for upper left> 6 6
X and Y for lower right> 9 10
Rectangle area: 20, perimeter: 18
```

3. Add to the *Rectangle* class so that it displays the rectangle in *H*s on the screen. Assume that your *x* coordinates and width are in characters and your *y* coordinates and height are in lines. Ensure that when you set the rectangle's properties, the drawn rectangle does not go off the screen. Most displays accommodate 80 characters by 25 lines. Limit yourself to one less each way to avoid line-end turnover problems.

Additional Constants, Function, and Variables

```
screenWidth
screenHeight
Rectangle
 display()
   row, col
```

Driver

```
int main(void) //////////////////////////////////////////////////////Main Program
{  Rectangle box(1, 1, 10, 10);

   box.setDimensions();
   box.display();
   box.setXy();
   box.display();
   return 0;
}
```

Output

```
X and Y for upper left> 10 10
Width and height> 30 16
Invalid parameters, rectangle not changed.
X and Y for upper left> 5 1
Width and height> 10 4
    HHHHHHHHHH
    HHHHHHHHHH
    HHHHHHHHHH
    HHHHHHHHHH
X and Y for upper left> 3 2
X and Y for lower right> 20 5

   HHHHHHHHHHHHHHHHHH
   HHHHHHHHHHHHHHHHHH
   HHHHHHHHHHHHHHHHHH
   HHHHHHHHHHHHHHHHHH
```

4. Refer to the calculator problem (Program 9 at the end of Chapter 6); create a *Calculator* object that exhibits all those behaviors. Create a `main()` driver to test it. The output should be similar to that in the earlier program.

5. Create a *Register* class that stores pennies, nickels, dimes, and quarters. It should be initialized with ten of each. Its *contents()* behavior prints out the current number of each coin in the register. The *sale()* behavior accepts the amount of sale and the coins offered; it then figures out the change, being sure to not give away coins it does not have. If it is impossible to make change, *sale()* should call the *replenish()* behavior that allows the user to add any number of coins of any denomination to the register.

6. Create a *Fraction* class that stores a fraction as a numerator and a denominator. Its constructor should default the fraction to 1/1. Give it a *show()* function to display the fraction. A *mult()* function should multiply two fractions together, returning a resultant *Fraction* object.

Variables, Functions, and Classes

`Fraction`	Class for a fraction
`num, den`	Numerator and denominator of fraction
`Fraction()`	Default *num* and *den* to 1
`n, d`	
`show()`	Display fraction, for example, 3/4
`mult()`	Multiply two fractions together
`f`	*Fraction* object reference

Driver

```
int main(void)
{  Fraction f1(2, 3);
   Fraction f2(3, 4);

   f1.show();          f1.mult (3,4)
   f2.show();
   f1.mult(f2).show();// Use show() behavior of object returned by f1.mult(f2)
   return 0;
}
```

Output

```
2/3
3/4
6/12
```

7. Add a private *reduce()* function in the *Fraction* class in Program 6 to reduce the fraction to its lowest terms. In other words, before 6/12 is stored, it is reduced to 1/2. To keep it simple, use only the prime numbers 2, 3, 5, and 7 to reduce your fraction. (Or, to be robust, generate prime numbers up to the lower of the numerator or the denominator in each case, and use those.)

8. Write the beginnings of a class that models an insect. It should have a constructor that assigns the species name, initial population, and breeding rate. The breeding rate and initial population should default to 4.0 and 100, respectively. Put a *show()* function in your class that prints a line of output as shown in the output below. Include a *breed()* function

that multiplies the current population by the breeding rate. In the `main()` function, create an insect with a breeding rate of 6.5.

Classes, Functions, and Variables

`Insect`	The bug class
`species`	
`pop`	Current size of the population
`breedRate`	
`Insect()`	Defaults *pop* to 100 and *breedRate* to 4.0
`s, p, b`	
`show()`	
`breed()`	
`main()`	
`bug`	An *Insect*

Output

```
Species   Population
Beetle           200

After breeding:
Species   Population
Beetle          1300
```

Chapter 8

ARRAYS

PREVIEW

In this chapter we will look at data in groups called arrays and learn how we can most easily manipulate these arrays in C++. After reading this chapter you should understand:

- What arrays are and what they are composed of.
- How arrays are stored in memory.
- How we declare and initialize arrays.
- How we pass arrays to functions.
- Using arrays of objects.
- Using arrays of arrays.
- Some common applications for arrays.

ata often do not come one piece at a time, but in collections—groups of tens, hundreds, or thousands of values to be processed. We could, possibly, think of tens, hundreds, or even thousands of different variable names, but keeping track of and processing them one after another would require a lot of C++ code. Instead, let's designate a collection of variables with a name for the collection and use a number to designate individual elements of the collection. We will still have tens, hundreds, or thousands of variables with as many names, but the names will be easier to keep track of.

INDEXED VARIABLE NAMES

In algebraic notation we use variables such as X and Y. We can also use subscripted variables such as X_1, X_2, and X_3 (the subscript is the little number following the letter). Subscript notation is typically used for grouping collections of variables. For example, the values of 10 samples in a chemical analysis might be stored in S_1, S_2, on up to S_{10}. Each of the variables is completely separate and has its own value, but we can see that they are all part of a collection because we have given them the same name, S. The different subscripts identify each separate variable in the collection.

We can apply this same concept in C++ using an **array**, which is a collection of individual variables referred to as **elements**. We give the array a name, such as *samples*, and identify each element of the array with an **index** in brackets—*name[index]*—for example, *samples[1]*, *samples[2]*, on up to *samples[10]*. As in algebra, we can refer to the collection of samples as *samples*, but we must remember that the collection is made up of individual variables or elements. Even though we may refer to the collection, we must access each of the individual elements.

In algebra we can choose whatever subscripts we want. In C++ we cannot. The first index value is always zero, and the rest go up from there.

An array element may be used like any other variable; remember, it is only one of a collection of variables. For example, if `samples[4]` is an `int`, it can be treated like any other `int`.

```
samples[4] = 25;
cout << "The value is " << samples[4] << endl;
```

This program segment will print out the value 25.

HEADS UP!

C++ indexes always start with zero.

ARRAY DECLARATIONS

HEADS UP!

An array must be of a single data type.

Like everything else in C++, arrays must be declared. The array can be composed of elements of any data type, but a single array must contain elements of the same type. We can have an array of `int`s or `double`s, but not an array that contains combinations of the two types. A single declaration defines all the elements of the array.

Suppose that we were the proprietors of a muffin stand on the corner and we wanted to keep track of the number of muffins sold each day of the week. We would need seven variables for the seven values. We can establish these in an array of seven elements. The statement

```
short sales[7];
```

declares the array *sales*. In the declaration, the number in brackets is not an index but the number of elements in the array. It must be an expression that has a specific nongarbage value at this point in the program. Constants are often used in array declarations to avoid "magic numbers" (discussed in Chapter 2).

```
const int days = 7;
```

```
int main(void)
{   short sales[days];
```

The elements of an array are always stored contiguously (right next to each other) in memory. This declaration, then, allocates contiguous space in memory for seven elements: *sales[0]*, *sales[1]*, *sales[2]*, on up to *sales[6]*. Using a diagram of main memory similar to that in Chapter 1, we show memory for the *sales* array allocated as follows (we have used hexadecimal notation for memory addresses, a common practice):

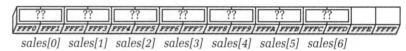

The array *sales* begins at memory address FFF0. (The address was just a guess on our part; C++ stores the array wherever it finds unallocated space.) The element *sales[0]* occupies two memory locations beginning at address FFF0; *sales[1]* begins at FFF2; and so forth. The question marks in the memory spaces indicates that the values of the elements are all garbage—they have no meaningful values yet.

The declaration said `short sales[7];` but there is no space allocated for *sales[7]*. In some other languages the value in the declaration is the highest index, but in C++ it is the number of indexes. Because the first index is always zero, the highest index value will be one less than the number of elements declared.

Initializations

Because array elements are like any other variables, we can assign them in statements such as

```
sales[5] = 47;
sales[0] = 3806;
```

Also, like other variables, we can initialize array elements at the time of their declaration. We do this by putting their values, separated by commas, in braces. Remember, an array declaration establishes a number of elements, so we will have to have a number of values to assign to them.

```
short sales[7] = {3806, 28, 4522, 476, 1183, 47, 12};
```

We do not necessarily have to initialize the entire array. If we initialize any of the elements, the rest are automatically set to zero by C++. For example,

```
short sales[7] = {3806, 28, 4522};
```

NUTS'N BOLTS

HOW MANY ELEMENTS ARE IN YOUR ARRAY?

You have declared your array as `float apples[3]`, and C++ has allocated space in memory for three `float`s, *apples[0]*, *apples[1]* and *apples[2]*. Is that all the elements you have in your array? Yes and no. Yes, that is all the space allocated for the elements in this array, but no, you can access *apples[35]* if you want to. C++ does not keep track of the number of elements in your array, so you are free to use any indexes you want. You are also free to shoot yourself in the foot with your own gun!

When you refer to an array element, such as *apples[1]*, C++ uses the index to count element spaces away from the beginning of the array; *apples[1]* is one `float` from the beginning of the *apples* array. The variable *apples[35]*, then, would be 35 `float`s away from the beginning of the *apples* array. You can actually assign a value there—C++ won't stop you—but the place in memory was not allocated for that element, and may have been allocated for some totally different purpose. What will happen? If you're lucky and the space was unallocated, the program might work. Or it might crash miserably, wiping out everything you've worked on all day.

The moral, here, is that it is up to you to keep your array indexes within the allocated bounds. C++ won't do it for you.

 HEADS UP!

Initializing at least one element sets all the uninitialized elements to zero.

 TRAP

`short sales[7] = {1};` does not initialize all the elements to 1.

assigns those values to *sales[0]*, *sales[1]*, and *sales[2]*, and C++ initializes *sales[3]* through *sales[6]* to zero.

We can easily initialize an array to all zeros like this:

```
short sales[7] = {0};
```

The element `sales[0]` is explicitly set to zero, and all the rest are set to zero by default.

If we initialize the array we can even leave the space within the brackets blank. The C++ compiler will figure out the number of array elements to allocate. The declaration

```
short sales[] = {3806, 28, 4522, 476, 1183, 47, 12};
```

allocates and initializes seven elements, `sales[0]` through `sales[6]`.

THE VARIABLY DEFINED VARIABLE

A major advantage of using arrays is that we can reference different elements—essentially different variables—by changing the index. To make that easier, we can put any expression—anything that evaluates to a numeric value—within the brackets. For example, all of the following are valid:

```
sales[4]
sales[x]
sales[b + q * pow(d, f / 2)]
```

The index is determined by the value of the expression within the brackets. The index must be a nonnegative integral value, so if the expression evaluates to a floating-point value, it is truncated to an integer. The notation `sales[4.9]` refers to the variable *sales[4]*. Be careful of floating-point

Program 8–1

```cpp
#include <iostream>                                    // Need the .h?
#include <iomanip>
using namespace std;                        // If your compiler needs it

const short daysInWeek = 7;

int main(void)
{   short sales[daysInWeek] = {3806, 28, 4522, 476, 1183, 47, 12};
    short day;

    for (day = 1; day <= daysInWeek; ++day)              // day from 1 to 7
        cout << "Sales for day " << day << " = "
             << setw(5) << sales[day - 1] << endl;
    return 0;
}
```

Output

```
Sales for day 1 =   3806
Sales for day 2 =     28
Sales for day 3 =   4522
Sales for day 4 =    476
Sales for day 5 =   1183
Sales for day 6 =     47
Sales for day 7 =     12
```

HEADS UP!

Avoid floating-point indexes.

Going out of the array's range.

indexes, however. Something that evaluates to what looks to be 4.0 may actually be stored in the binary version of 3.99999999, which would truncate to 3.

It is up to you to see that the indexes are within the range allocated in the declaration of the array. The notations `sales[-1]` and `sales[10]` will lead to two values, the first located in the 2 bytes before the array, and the second 20 bytes after the beginning of the array, which is 6 bytes past the end of the array. What is there? Who knows? (See the Nuts 'n' Bolts box, "How Many Elements Are in Your Array?".)

Program 8–1 prints out the muffin sales for each day of the week—the values stored in each element of the *sales* array. The value of *day* determines the index. Notice that the index will be *day* minus one. Because indexes always start with zero, sales for the first day will be found in *sales[0]*, and sales for the seventh day in *sales[6]*.

Let's see how we might use arrays in another example. The shipping clerk at the Acme Widget Company must keep track of each truck that has left the plant and how much weight it was carrying, and, at the end of the day, must produce a shipping report.

TASK

Create a program for Acme to keep track of and report on its trucks.

ANALYSIS

Acme has a fleet of five trucks, conveniently numbered 1 through 5, and any or all of them might be used in any order on a given day. As each truck leaves it is weighed and the truck number and weight are recorded. These data could be input into the computer as follows:

```
Truck? 4
Weight? 312.5
```

At the end of the day, an input of zero for the truck number ends input. At that point the program must produce a report showing the number of each truck that was used and the weight it was carrying, as well as the total number of trucks and total weight.

```
Shipping Report
      Truck  Weight
          1   702.5
          2   816.3
          4   312.5
          5  1124.7
      -----  ------
Total     4  2956.0
```

The principal data requirement is a list of truck weights. A weight of zero should indicate that a truck was not used.

DESIGN

The program consists of two main modules:

    Input weights
    Print report

We want to continue to input weights until the end of the day, when we input a zero truck number—a sentinel-value-controlled loop.

    [Input weights]
        Initialize all weights to zero
        Input truck number
        while truck number not zero
            Input weight
            Input truck number

In "desk testing" this module we see that there is nothing that prevents the shipping clerk from entering a truck number that is not within Acme's range of trucks. We can expand Input truck number to include such a test.

    [Input truck number]
      do
        Input truck number
      while truck number < 0 or > 5

To print the report we have to look at each of the five trucks and, if the number is not zero, print the weight, accumulate it into a total, and count the truck.

    [Print report]
        For 5 trucks
            if weight not zero
                Print truck number and weight
                Accumulate weight
                Add to truck count
        Print truck count and accumulated weight

To store the weight for each of the five trucks, we need five variables. We could make up five—*theBigBlueFord*, *theNissanWithTheDentedFender*, and so forth—but instead, let's use an array with five elements. We can keep track of which truck's weight is in which element by using the index as the truck number. We will have to make a slight adjustment since the truck numbers start at 1 and C++ indexes start at 0, but subtracting 1 from the truck's number should take care of it. The weight for truck 5, then, will be in element 4.

In Program 8–2 on the following page, the weight of each of the trucks is kept in the array *weights[]*, and the truck number, *truckNo*, minus one is the index.

We should test various possibilities, including entry of a wrong truck number. We also see that the shipping clerk can enter the same truck number twice, but this can be a way of correcting a mistaken entry.

YOUR TURN 8–1

1. How is an indexed variable similar to any other variable?
2. How does an indexed variable differ from a normal variable?
3. What is an array?
4. Why do we use arrays?
5. What is the first index value for any indexed variable in C++?
6. How many elements are allocated and what is the index of the last allocated variable in the array declaration float stuff[10];?
7. Given the declaration float stuff[5] = {1.1, 2.2, 3.3};, what will be the value of *stuff[1]*? of *stuff[3]*? of *stuff[5]*?
8. Given the declaration in 7, does *stuff[what]* have a specific value?
9. Of what data type is an index?

NUTS'N BOLTS

THE ZERO ELEMENT

Sometimes having the array indexes start with zero is handy, such as when taking readings of a chemical reaction starting with the time the reaction was initiated—at time zero—and at one-minute intervals after that.

Other times it's a pain in the neck—Acme's trucks, for example. Humans would normally number things starting from 1, not from 0. Therefore, we must accommodate in our program by having the weight for truck 1 in *weights[0]* and using notation such as `weights[truckNo - 1]`.

There are other ways of accommodating for the zero index. One is to train everyone to count from 0 instead of 1—probably not practical! Another is to declare our array one larger than we need and simply not use the zero element. The weight for truck 1 is stored in *weights[1]* and so forth, and we can refer to `weights[truckNo]`. The element *weights[0]* may not be used, but memory for it will still be allocated. If memory is at a premium, this approach will be impractical.

Which approach you choose will depend on your particular situation.

Program 8–2

```cpp
        #include <iostream>
        #include <iomanip>
        using namespace std;

        const int fleet = 5;                        // Number of trucks in the fleet

        int truckIn(void);                                  // Input Truck Number

        int main(void)
   1    {   float weights[fleet] = {0};              // Initialize entire array to zero
            int truckNo;                                        // Truck number
            int totTrucks = 0;                  // Counter for total trucks for report
            float totWeight = 0;                            // Total weight for report

   2        truckNo = truckIn(); //----------------------------------- Input Data
   3        while (truckNo)                         // Exit loop when zero entered
            {   cout << "Weight? ";
   4            cin >> weights[truckNo - 1];
   5            truckNo = truckIn();
            }
            cout << setiosflags(ios::fixed) << setprecision(1);
            cout << "\nShipping Report\n"; //------------------------- Print Report
            cout << "      Truck   Weight\n";
   6        for (truckNo = 1; truckNo <= fleet; ++truckNo)
   7            if (weights[truckNo - 1])                       // If weight nonzero
   8            {   cout << setw(11) << truckNo
                        << setw(8) << weights[truckNo - 1] << endl;
   9                ++totTrucks;
  10                totWeight += weights[truckNo - 1];
                }
            cout << "         -----  ------\n";
  11        cout << "Total " << setw(5) << totTrucks
                << setw(8) << totWeight << endl;
            return 0;
        }

        int truckIn(void)  //*********************************** Input Truck Number
        {   int truckNo;

            do
            {   cout << "Truck (1 to " << fleet << ", 0 to quit)? ";
  t1            cin >> truckNo;
  t2        }while (truckNo < 0 || truckNo > fleet); // Don't let invalid truck past
  t3        return truckNo;
        }
```

Output

```
Truck (1 to 5, 0 to quit)? 7
Truck (1 to 5, 0 to quit)? 4
Weight? 1825.8
Truck (1 to 5, 0 to quit)? 2
Weight? 883.5
Truck (1 to 5, 0 to quit)? 1
Weight? 829.4
Truck (1 to 5, 0 to quit)? 0

Shipping Report
     Truck  Weight
         1   829.4
         2   883.5
         4  1825.8
     -----  ------
Total    3  3538.7
```

EXECUTION CHART

Line	Explanation	weights[5]					tot truckNo	tot Trucks	Weight
1	Initialize entire array to zero.	0.0	0.0	0.0	0.0	0.0	--	--	--
2	Call *truckIn()*.	0.0	0.0	0.0	0.0	0.0	??	0	0
	truckIn():						*truckNo*		
t1	Input truck number.	(0.0)	(0.0)	(0.0)	(0.0)	(0.0)	7	(0)	(0)
t2	Out of range, condition true.	(0.0)	(0.0)	(0.0)	(0.0)	(0.0)	7	(0)	(0)
t1	Input another truck number.	(0.0)	(0.0)	(0.0)	(0.0)	(0.0)	4	(0)	(0)
t2	In range, condition false.	(0.0)	(0.0)	(0.0)	(0.0)	(0.0)	4	(0)	(0)
t3	Return truck number and go back to `main()`.	(0.0)	(0.0)	(0.0)	(0.0)	(0.0)	4	(0)	(0)
	`main():`						*truckNo*		
2	Assign return value to *truckNo*.	0.0	0.0	0.0	0.0	0.0	4	0	0
3	*truckNo* nonzero.	0.0	0.0	0.0	0.0	0.0	4	0	0
4	Input value for *weights[3]*.	0.0	0.0	0.0	1825.8	0.0	4	0	0
5	Input another truck number.	0.0	0.0	0.0	1825.8	0.0	2	0	0
3	*truckNo* nonzero.	0.0	0.0	0.0	1825.8	0.0	2	0	0
4	Input value for *weights[1]*.	0.0	883.5	0.0	1825.8	0.0	2	0	0
5	Input another truck number.	0.0	883.5	0.0	1825.8	0.0	1	0	0
3	*truckNo* nonzero.	0.0	883.5	0.0	1825.8	0.0	1	0	0
4	Input value for *weights[0]*.	829.4	883.5	0.0	1825.8	0.0	1	0	0
5	Input another truck number.	829.4	883.5	0.0	1825.8	0.0	1	0	0
3	*truckNo* zero.	829.4	883.5	0.0	1825.8	0.0	1	0	0
6	Initialize *truckNo* to 1, test for <= 5.	829.4	883.5	0.0	1825.8	0.0	1	0	0
7	Test for *weights[0]* nonzero. It is.	829.4	883.5	0.0	1825.8	0.0	1	0	0
8	Print truck data.	829.4	883.5	0.0	1825.8	0.0	1	0	0
9	Count trucks.	829.4	883.5	0.0	1825.8	0.0	1	1	0
10	Accumulate weight.	829.4	883.5	0.0	1825.8	0.0	1	1	829.4
6–10	Repeat process for all trucks.	829.4	883.5	0.0	1825.8	0.0	6	3	3538.7
11	Print totals.	829.4	883.5	0.0	1825.8	0.0	6	3	3538.7

ARRAYS AND FUNCTIONS

Let's write a function *sumArray()* that returns the sum of the values of all the elements in an array. Our call must pass the array to the function, and the function definition must declare variables to accept the array. Using our *sales* array as an example, one possible call would be

```
sumArray(sales[0], sales[1], sales[2],
        sales[3], sales[4], sales[5], sales[6])
```

meaning that the definition would have to have seven `short` variables to accept those values.

```
short sumArray(short value0, short value1,
              short value2, short value3,
              short value4, short value5,
              short value6)
```

Possible, but ugly!

Rather than passing all the values in the array, let's instead tell the function where the array begins in memory and allow the function to access that memory. The array name without any index, *sales* in our example, references the address of the beginning of the array in memory. In our earlier memory diagram, the address *sales* was FFF0. Let's send that to the function. Using that concept, the call is simpler:

```
sumArray(sales)
```

as is the first line of the definition:

```
short sumArray(short value[])
```

The declaration of the formal parameter in this function definition appears to allocate an array, a collection of contiguous elements. But notice that there is no value in the brackets, nor should there be one. The declaration does not allocate an array, only an array name representing a memory location—the one passed in the function call. In this case, *value* is the same address as *sales*. This is a *pass by pointer*, which is similar to a pass by reference. For our purposes, the principal difference is the bracket notation in the declaration (rather than the &). We shall examine this type of pass more closely and see other examples in Chapter 12.

We can use *value* in the *sumArray()* function just as we used *sales* in the `main()` function. The index refers to an element that is the index number of elements away from the beginning. The element *value[2]* refers to the third element in the array—two away from the beginning.

In Program 8–3 we add the *sumArray()* function to our previous program to print out the total sales.

Because a function that returns a value can be used in any place that data type can be used, we could put the function call directly in the `cout`, eliminating the need for the *total* variable:

```
cout << "Total sales =    " << setw(5) << sumArray(sales) << endl;
```

Where does the *value* array in the *sumArray()* function end? Remember, C++ does not keep track of the ends of allocated arrays, only where they start. We repeat: keeping track of the end of the array is up to *you*. In

HEADS UP!

An array name references the address of an array.

Program 8–3

```cpp
#include <iostream>
#include <iomanip>
using namespace std;

const short daysInWeek = 7;

short sumArray(short value[]);

int main(void)
{   short sales[daysInWeek] = {3806, 28, 4522, 476, 1183, 47, 12};
    short day, total;

    for (day = 1; day <= daysInWeek; ++day)                    // day from 1 to 7
        cout << "Sales for day " << day << " = "
                << setw(5) << sales[day - 1] << endl;
    total = sumArray(sales);
    cout << "Total sales =      " << setw(5) << total << endl;
    return 0;
}

short sumArray(short value[])
{   short count, sum = 0;

    for (count = 0; count < daysInWeek; ++count)          // count from 0 to 6
        sum += value[count];
    return sum;
}
```

Output

```
Sales for day 1 =    3806
Sales for day 2 =      28
Sales for day 3 =    4522
Sales for day 4 =     476
Sales for day 5 =    1183
Sales for day 6 =      47
Sales for day 7 =      12
Total sales =        10074
```

Program 8–3 the function was written specifically for a seven-element array. To make it more general, in addition to the address of the array, we would also have to pass the number of elements,

```cpp
sumArray(sales, daysInWeek)
```

redefine our function to initialize a variable (*elements*) with that value, and then use it to control the summation loop.

```cpp
short sumArray(short value[], int elements)
{   short count, sum = 0;

    for (count = 0; count < elements; ++count)
        sum += value[count];
    return sum;
}
```

Program 8–4

```cpp
#include <iostream>
#include <iomanip>
using namespace std;

short sumArray(short value[]);

int main(void)
{   short sales[] = {3806, 28, 4522, 476, 1183, 47, 12, -1};
    short day = 1;                    // Initialize day at 1 for following loop

    while (sales[day - 1] != -1)
    {   cout << "Sales for day " << day << " = "
            << setw(5) << sales[day - 1] << endl;
        ++day;
    }
    cout << "Total sales =     " << setw(5) << sumArray(sales) << endl;
    return 0;
}

short sumArray(short value[])
{   short count = 0, sum = 0;                      // Initialize count for loop

    while (value[count] != -1)                     // Loop until sentinel reached
    {   sum += value[count];
        ++count;
    }
    return sum;
}
```

Another way to handle the problem is to put a sentinel value at the end of the array, −1 for example. Any operations on the elements of the array would stop when we reached the element with the value −1. This solution is shown in Program 8–4.

Notice that we have eliminated the constant *daysInWeek*. The number of elements in the *sales* array is now controlled by the number of initializers in the array declaration. If we had a month's worth of sales, we could have put all the values, plus the −1, in the declaration and the program would still work. We must be sure, of course, that there is no possibility of sales of −1.

As we have said, *value* in the *sumArray()* function is the same address as *sales* in main(). Memory is allocated as follows:

Using a plausible value for a sentinel.

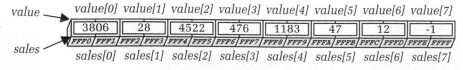

The memory locations are accessed by *sales* in main() and by *value* in *sumArray()*, but they are the same memory locations with the same values. That means if we change the value of *value[2]*, we are also changing the value of *sales[2]*. When we return to the main() function, *sales[2]* will show the new value.

HEADS UP!

An array passed by its name can be modified in a function.

Program 8–5

```cpp
#include <iostream>
#include <iomanip>
using namespace std;

void doubleArray(short value[]);
void showArray(short value[]);

int main(void)
{   short sales[] = {3806, 28, 4522, 476, 1183, 47, 12, -1};

    cout << "Sales array before:";
    showArray(sales);

    doubleArray(sales);

    cout << "Sales array after: ";
    showArray(sales);
    return 0;
}

void doubleArray(short value[])
{   short count = 0;

    while (value[count] != -1)
    {   value[count] *= 2;
        ++count;
    }
}

void showArray(short value[])
{   short count = 0;

    while (value[count] != -1)
    {   cout << setw(6) << value[count];
        ++count;
    }
    cout << endl;
}
```

Output

```
Sales array before:   3806    28  4522   476  1183    47    12
Sales array after:    7612    56  9044   952  2366    94    24
```

To illustrate, let's say that the boss wants us to double our sales. We can create a function *doubleArray()*, which doubles each value of the array passed to it, the *sales* array in this case.

In Program 8–5 we have also added the *showArray()* function, which prints out the array.

YOUR TURN 8–2

1. In what two ways can we effectively "pass an array to a function"?

2. What does the declaration of an array in the formal parameters of a function actually declare?

Program 8–6

```cpp
#include <iostream>
#include <iomanip>
using namespace std;

const int fleet = 5;                                // Number of trucks in the fleet

class Truck /////////////////////////////////////////////////////// Truck Class
{public:
   float weight;
   Truck() { weight = 0; }                  // Initialize each object to zero
};

int truckIn(void)  //*********************************** Input Truck Number
{  int truckNo;

   do
   {  cout << "Truck (1 to " << fleet << ", 0 to quit)? ";
      cin >> truckNo;
   }while (truckNo < 0 || truckNo > fleet); // Don't let invalid truck past
   return truckNo;
}

int main(void)  ///////////////////////////////////////////////// Main Program
{  Truck trucks[fleet];
   int truckNo;                                            // Truck number
   int totTrucks = 0;                 // Counter for total trucks for report
   float weight, totWeight = 0;

   truckNo = truckIn(); //------------------------------------- Input Data
   while (truckNo)                            // Exit loop when zero entered
   {  cout << "Weight? ";
      cin >> trucks[truckNo - 1].weight;
      truckNo = truckIn();
   }
   cout << setiosflags(ios::fixed) << setprecision(1);
   cout << "\nShipping Report\n"; //------------------------- Print Report
   cout << "       Truck  Weight\n";
   for (truckNo = 1; truckNo <= fleet; ++truckNo)
   {  weight = trucks[truckNo - 1].weight;
      if (weight)                                       // If weight nonzero
      {  cout << setw(11) << truckNo
              << setw(8) << weight << endl;
         ++totTrucks;
         totWeight += weight;
      }
   }
   cout << "          -----  ------\n";
   cout << "Total " << setw(5) << totTrucks
        << setw(8) << totWeight << endl;
   return 0;
}
```

Output

```
Truck (1 to 5, 0 to quit)? 7
Truck (1 to 5, 0 to quit)? 4
Weight? 1825.8
Truck (1 to 5, 0 to quit)? 2
Weight? 8835
Truck (1 to 5, 0 to quit)? 1
Weight? 829.4
Truck (1 to 5, 0 to quit)? 0

Shipping Report
      Truck  Weight
          1   829.4
          2  8835.0
          4  1825.8
      -----  ------
Total     3 11490.2
```

3. When we pass an array by pointer to a function, how can we, in the function, determine the end of the array?

4. If we pass an array by name and change some of the elements using the local name in the function, what will happen to the corresponding elements in the calling function?

ARRAYS AND OBJECTS

HEADS UP!

We can have an array of any data type, including classes.

Arrays are simply collections of data of the same type. For example, an array could be a collection of objects, as long as the objects are from the same class. In Program 8–6, let's modify the Acme Widget Company example from Program 8–2 to create a *Truck* object. For now each truck has one property, a *weight*.

The first line within the main() function declares an array of five *Truck* objects, *trucks[0]* through *trucks[4]*. (The value of the constant *fleet* is five.)

```
Truck trucks[fleet];
```

To access the *weight* property of one of the *trucks*, we use normal index notation. The index, of course, refers to the *trucks*, not the *weight*, so it immediately follows *trucks*.

```
trucks[4].weight
```

HEADS UP!

Automatic initialization to zero does not work with objects.

is the weight of the fifth truck.

In Program 8–2 we initialized all the weights to zero in the declaration of the *weights* array. Here, in Program 8–6, we establish a constructor function, *Truck()*, that sets the object's *weight* property to zero when each object is created.

The *truckIn()* function, which ensures that a truck number is within the range, is important to the truck class, but notice that it is not a behavior of the class. Behaviors deal with individual objects of a class, the object

Program 8–7

```cpp
#include <iostream>
#include <iomanip>
using namespace std;

const int fleet = 5;                              // Number of trucks in the fleet

class Truck /////////////////////////////////////////////////////// Truck Class
{   float weight;
public:
    Truck() { weight = 0; }                       // Initialize each object to zero
    void setWeight(float weightIn)
    {   if (weightIn > 0 && weightIn <= 2000)
            weight = weightIn;                              // Assign valid weight
        else
            cout << "   Weight out of range.\n";     // Display error message
    }
    float getWeight(void) { return weight; }
};

int truckIn(void)  //*********************************** Input Truck Number
{   int truckNo;

    do
    {   cout << "Truck (1 to " << fleet << ", 0 to quit)? ";
        cin >> truckNo;
    }while (truckNo < 0 || truckNo > fleet); // Don't let invalid truck past
    return truckNo;
}
```

(Continued)

through which the behavior was called. The *truckIn()* function deals with all the objects of the *Truck* class, not just a single object, so we did not make it a class function. To emphasize its importance to the *Truck* class we have placed the definition of the *truckIn()* function just below the class definition. Because *truckIn()* is now defined (and declared) before it is called in `main()`, it needs no separate declaration.

Looking at the output from Program 8–6, we notice that the user has entered a weight of 8,835 pounds for truck 2. Acme's trucks are not that big; that much weight would crush them. Let's isolate the *weight* property of the *Truck* class, to make sure the entered weight is within reason, and add an access function, *setWeight()*, in Program 8–7 to assign the weight. Because *weight* is now private, we must also provide a function to return the weight, *getWeight()*.

This exactly fits the nature of class functions. Each object has its own properties, but all the objects exhibit the same behaviors. While there are copies of each of the properties for each object, there is only one set of functions for all the objects. When we call the *setWeight()* function, for example

```cpp
trucks[3].setWeight(weight)
```

it uses a common procedure to set the *weight* property for the specific *trucks[3]* object.

HEADS UP!

Objects have their own properties, but share behaviors.

```cpp
int main(void)  ///////////////////////////////////////////// Main Program
{   Truck trucks[fleet];
    int truckNo;                                            // Truck number
    int totTrucks = 0;                  // Counter for total trucks for report
    float weight, totWeight = 0;

    truckNo = truckIn();  //--------------------------------- Input Data
    while (truckNo)                         // Exit loop when zero entered
    {   cout << "Weight? ";
        cin >> weight;
        trucks[truckNo - 1].setWeight(weight);
        truckNo = truckIn();
    }
    cout << setiosflags(ios::fixed) << setprecision(1);
    cout << "\nShipping Report\n";  //------------------------- Print Report
    cout << "       Truck   Weight\n";
    for (truckNo = 1; truckNo <= fleet; ++truckNo)
    {   weight = trucks[truckNo - 1].getWeight();
        if (weight)                                     // If weight nonzero
        {   cout << setw(11) << truckNo
                 << setw(8) << weight << endl;
            ++totTrucks;
            totWeight += weight;
        }
    }
    cout << "          -----   ------\n";
    cout << "Total " << setw(5) << totTrucks
         << setw(8) << totWeight << endl;
    return 0;
}
```

Output

```
Truck (1 to 5, 0 to quit)? 7
Truck (1 to 5, 0 to quit)? 4
Weight? 1825.8
Truck (1 to 5, 0 to quit)? 2
Weight? 8835
    Weight out of range.
Truck (1 to 5, 0 to quit)? 2
Weight? 883.5
Truck (1 to 5, 0 to quit)? 1
Weight? 829.4
Truck (1 to 5, 0 to quit)? 0

Shipping Report
       Truck  Weight
           1   829.4
           2   883.5
           4  1825.8
       -----  ------
Total      3  3538.7
```

CAN'T FIND YOUR CODE?

Have we mentioned readability? A dozen times! And we guarantee we'll mention it again. It is one of the most important aspects of programming. As programs get longer and more complicated, they become harder to read. One of the problems is simply finding a section of code, a class declaration, for example. The `main()` function refers to the *What* class, but with 47 classes, each with 26 properties and 32 behaviors, we have to search through pages of code, line by line, to find `class What`.

Comments can help, but if all the comments look alike, how do we know which set out major code sections and which clarify a single line? Most programmers use a hierarchy of comment forms: a form for showing major sections, another for single-line clarity, and others for situations in between. There are no standards here, but at least your code can exhibit consistency. In this book we use four levels of comments, as outlined below:

```
Major sections: Classes and main ///////////////////////// Class What

    Functions //****************************************** Does This

        Code segments //------------------------------------ Does That

            Single lines                        // Does whatever
```

You can see examples of three of these four in Program 8–6, and of all four in the *Putting It Together* section at the end of the chapter.

Object Array Initialization

Single objects may be initialized by putting the initializers in the declaration of the object. For example, if we established a constructor that would initialize a *Truck* weight with a value passed to it,

```
Truck(float w) { weight = w; }
```

we could create an object and initialize its weight like this:

```
Truck wagon = 123.45;
```

This declaration implicitly calls the constructor when the *wagon* object is created.

We can also explicitly call the constructor in a declaration:

```
Truck wagon = Truck(123.45);
```

Trying to initialize an array of objects without explicitly calling the constructor.

The effect would be exactly the same.

When initializing arrays of objects, we must explicitly call the constructor for each element of the array. For example, if we wanted to create five *Truck* objects using the constructor above, we would have to declare it like this:

```
Truck wagon[5] = {Truck(123.45), Truck(624.3), Truck(45.3), Truck(498.2),
                  Truck(725)};
```

Arrays in Objects

Object properties may be contained in arrays of variables. For example, let's say that each truck is divided into four compartments, each having its own weight. We need four *weights* variables, so why not an array of *weights*?

```
class Truck ///////////////////////////////////////////////// Truck Class
{
public:
    float weights[4];
```

If we then declare an array of five *Truck*s,

```
int main(void) ////////////////////////////////////////////// Main Program
{   Truck trucks[fleet];
```

in a member function, we can refer to the weight in the second compartment of the truck through which we called the function as

```
weights[1]
```

Remember, array indexes start with zero.

Because we declared the *weights* array `public`, in some other function (`main()`, for example) we can refer to the second compartment of the fourth truck as

```
trucks[3].weights[1]
```

If we were to use this with Program 8–7 and wanted to initialize the weights in all the compartments of all the trucks to zero, we might write the constructor as follows:

```
Truck() //****************************** Initialize Each Object to Zero
{   for (int i; i < 4; ++i)            // Initialize each element to zero
        weight[i] = 0;
}
```

YOUR TURN 8–3

1. If we have an array of *gadget* objects, how do we reference the *thing* member of the third *gadget*?
2. How do we initialize all the elements of an array of objects to the same set of values?
3. How do we initialize the elements of an array of objects in the object declaration statement?
4. If we have an array of *gadget* objects with an array of *thing* members, how do we reference the second *thing* of the third *gadget*?

ARRAY APPLICATIONS

Because we can variably define an array element by defining its index, we find there are many processes that lend themselves to array use that would be quite difficult without arrays. Following are a few examples.

Sequential Search

In a **sequential search** (or *linear search*) we start at the beginning of a list of items and look at each in turn until either we find the one we are looking for or we reach the end of the list. The overall pattern is this:

```
Start at beginning of list
while Item not found and still in list
    Go to next item
if item found
    Success condition
else
    Failure condition
```

The search pattern contains a loop that has two different conditions. When either of those conditions is false, the program exits the loop. Once beyond the loop, the program has to determine how it got there and which condition was false, so there is a selection testing for one of the conditions.

Let's go back to Program 8–7, the example of the Acme Widget Company and its five trucks. Each of Acme's five trucks has a license plate with a different number. Let's make the license a property of an object of the *Truck* class. Instead of inputting a truck number, we will enter the license and search through the objects to find it.

For our new program, Program 8–8, we have added a `public:` property, *license*, to the *Truck* class. We made it `public:` so that we can easily access it from `main()`. We could have made it `private:` and written a *getLicense()* access function for it.

In Program 8–7 we initialized each object with zero *weight*. We also want to initialize each object's *license*, so in Program 8–8 we add to our constructor:

```
Truck(int lic) { weight = 0; license = lic; }  // Initialize each object
```

We pass a value for *lic* to the constructor, which is assigned to that object's *license*.

In `main()`, to provide those values, we change the declaration of the array of *Truck* objects to:

```
{  Truck trucks[fleet] = {Truck(312), Truck(47), Truck(555),
                Truck(100), Truck(36)};
```

The creation of each object calls the constructor for that object, passing the value to *lic* in the constructor.

Now we must modify the *truckIn()* function to allow a search for a license number instead of just verifying the truck number. The *truckIn()* function now must see the license property of each of the trucks. We still will not make it a member of the *Truck* class because it deals with all the trucks, not with an individual object of the *Truck* class. Because it must use the *license* member of each of the trucks, however, we will pass it the *trucks* array, receiving it in *trucks[]*.

```
int truckIn(Truck trucks[]);   // Prototyped declaration

truckNo = truckIn(trucks);                     // Call
```

A sequential search that simply returns the truck number with a given license might look like this the code at the top of the next page.

It must be a bit more complicated for our program. A failure condition should send us back for another *license* input, and a *license* of zero, meaning we want to quit, should be treated as a success condition, returning *truckNo* zero. The final code is in Program 8–8 on page 282.

```
int truckIn(Truck trucks[]) //*********************** Match License to Truck
{  int license;                                      // License to search for
   int truckNo; = 1;                        // Start at beginning of list of trucks

   cout << "License? ";
   cin >> license;
   while (license != trucks[truckNo - 1].license        // Item not found
          && truckNo <= fleet)                          // and still in list)
      ++truckNo;                                       // Go to next item
   if (truckNo <= fleet)              // Item found (truckNo still in list)
      cout << "It is truck number " << truckNo << ".\n";        // Success
   else
   {  cout << "No such license.\n";                          // Failure
      truckNo = 0;
   }
   return truckNo;
}
```

HEADS UP!

Data must be in order for a
binary search.

Binary Search

If the items through which we are searching are in order, we can significantly reduce the searching time by using a binary search. With such a
search, each time we consider an item we eliminate half the list of items
rather than just the single item. If we are presented with a number from 1
to 10 and guess the one in the middle, 5, and are told that the number is
too low, we know the number is between 6 and 10. We have eliminated
half the possible range with one guess. We can then repeat the process
with the remaining range and so forth until either we have found the correct value or the range disappears.

To keep track of the range we set up two variables, *low* and *high*, as we
have done in Figure 8–1. The middle of the range, *mid*, is (*low* + *high*) / 2.
If the value at *mid* is too high, we set *high* to *mid* − 1, cutting the range in
half, and repeat the process. The search stops when either the correct value
is found or the *low* is greater than the *high*, indicating that there are no
more numbers in the range.

FIGURE 8–1

A Binary Search

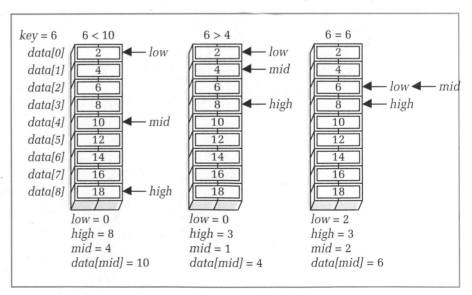

```
#include <iostream>
#include <iomanip>
using namespace std;

const int fleet = 5;                          // Number of trucks in the fleet

class Truck ////////////////////////////////////////////////// Truck Class
{   float weight;
public:
    int license;
    Truck(int lic) { weight = 0; license = lic; }  // Initialize each object
    void setWeight(float weightIn)
    {   if (weightIn > 0 && weightIn <= 2000)
            weight = weightIn;                        // Assign valid weight
        else
            cout << "   Weight out of range.\n";      // Display error message
    }
    float getWeight(void) { return weight; }
};

int truckIn(Truck trucks[]) //********************* Match License to Truck
{   int license;                              // License to search for
    int truckNo;

    do
    {   cout << "License (0 to quit)? ";
        cin >> license;
        if (license)                          // License not zero, don't quit
        {   truckNo = 1;                      // Start at beginning of list of trucks
            while (license != trucks[truckNo - 1].license      // Not found
                    && truckNo <= fleet)                       // and still in list
                ++truckNo;                                     // Go to next item
        }
        else                                              // Set up to quit
            truckNo = 0;
    }while (truckNo > fleet);                 // Failure, truck not 0 or in list
    return truckNo;                                             // Success
}

int main(void) ////////////////////////////////////////////////// Main Program
{   Truck trucks[fleet] = {Truck(312), Truck(47), Truck(555),
                           Truck(100), Truck(36)};
    int truckNo;                                       // Truck number
    int totTrucks = 0;                    // Counter for total trucks for report
    float weight, totWeight = 0;

    truckNo = truckIn(trucks); //------------------------------- Input Data
    while (truckNo)                              // Exit loop when zero entered
    {   cout << "Weight? ";
        cin >> weight;
        trucks[truckNo - 1].setWeight(weight);
        truckNo = truckIn(trucks);
    }
    cout << setiosflags(ios::fixed) << setprecision(1);
```

(Continued)

Program 8–8 *(Continued)*

```
      cout << "\nShipping Report\n"; //------------------------- Print Report
      cout << "    License  Weight\n";
      for (truckNo = 1; truckNo <= fleet; ++truckNo)
      {   weight = trucks[truckNo - 1].getWeight();
          if (weight)                                      // If weight nonzero
          {   cout << setw(11) << trucks[truckNo - 1].license
                  << setw(8) << weight << endl;
              ++totTrucks;
              totWeight += weight;
          }
      }
      cout << "         -----  ------\n";
      cout << "Total " << setw(5) << totTrucks
          << setw(8) << totWeight << endl;
      return 0;
  }
```

Output

```
License (0 to quit)? 10
License (0 to quit)? 100
Weight? 1825.8
License (0 to quit)? 47
Weight? 8835
    Weight out of range.
License (0 to quit)? 47
Weight? 883.5
License (0 to quit)? 312
Weight? 829.4
License (0 to quit)? 0

Shipping Report
    License  Weight
        312   829.4
         47   883.5
        100  1825.8
      -----  ------
Total     3  3538.7
```

Establish low, high, and initial midpoint
while range left and key value not found
   if key < mid value
      Limit search to lower end of range (change high value)
   else
      Limit search to upper end of range (change low value)
   Establish new midpoint

Notice that *low*, *high*, and *mid* keep track of the indexes in the array being searched, not of the values in those elements. Because these indexes are integers, the result of the midpoint division will also be an integer. For example, (0 + 3) / 2 is 1.5 but will be truncated to 1, making the midpoint 1.

For the sake of variety and simplicity let's leave the Acme Widget Company for a while and look at Arrow-Matic Sanitary Construction, which uses odd lengths of sewer pipe in its work. Before anyone cuts a new pipe,

Program 8–9

```cpp
#include <iostream>
#include <iomanip>
using namespace std;

const int pipes = 9;

int main(void)
{   float length[pipes] = {0.8, 1.2, 1.3, 1.9, 2.2, 2.6, 3.1, 3.7, 3.8};
    float key;                                       // Length to search for
    int low = 0,                       // Bottom of the current search range
        high = pipes - 1,              // Top of the current search range
        mid = (low + high) / 2;        // Index at middle of range

    cout << setiosflags(ios::fixed) << setprecision(1);
    cout << "What length pipe? ";
    cin >> key;
    while (low <= high && key != length[mid])
    {   if (key < length[mid])               // Search value lower than midpoint
            high = mid - 1;                  // Limit range to lower half
        else                                 // Search value higher than midpoint
            low = mid + 1;                   // Limit range to upper half
        mid = (low + high) / 2;              // Establish new midpoint
    }
    if (key == length[mid])
        cout << "Pipe " << (mid + 1) << " is " << key << " long." << endl;
    else
        cout << "Pipe length " << key << " not found." << endl;
    return 0;
}
```

Output

```
What length pipe? 2.2
Pipe 5 is 2.2 long.

What length pipe? 3.8
Pipe 9 is 3.8 long.

What length pipe? 1.6
Pipe length 1.6 not found.

What length pipe? 4.1
Pipe length 4.1 not found.

What length pipe? 1.3
Pipe 3 is 1.3 long.
```

they would like to search their stock of pipe pieces for an appropriate length. Program 8–9 uses a binary search to find a length of pipe in stock.

Insert

An insert begins with a collection of values in order and adds one more value to the collection. The new value is added so the collection remains

FIGURE 8–2

An Insert

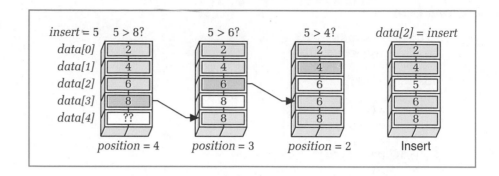

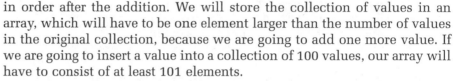

HEADS UP!

When inserting, declare an array one larger than the current collection.

in order after the addition. We will store the collection of values in an array, which will have to be one element larger than the number of values in the original collection, because we are going to add one more value. If we are going to insert a value into a collection of 100 values, our array will have to consist of at least 101 elements.

We know that the new value should be inserted in the collection where it is greater than the number before and less than the number after. Now all we have to do is explain that to the computer. Let's consider a collection of four values—2, 4, 6, and 8—to which we want to add one more—5. As shown in Figure 8–2, we declare an array of five variables, *data[5]*, assign the values to the first four variables in the array, and assign the value we wish to insert to *insert*. We consider each position in the array a possible insert position and use the variable *position* to keep track of it. The element in that position is *data[position]*. We either assign our insert value (*insert*) to that element or go on to the next position.

TRAP

Trying to insert into unordered data.

There will already be a blank position at the end of the array, so let's use that as our first possible insert position. (In Figure 8–2 the possible insert position is represented by a nonshaded area.) If our insert value is greater than the value of the element before our possible insert position (*data[position – 1]*), then it must belong in this position (*data[position]*). (The darker shaded area is the element before the possible insert position.) If it is not greater then it must belong somewhere above, so let's begin to make space for it by moving a value down one position—assigning the value of *data[position – 1]* to *data[position]*. Then we can move our possible insert position up one element by decrementing *position* and repeat the process.

The process stops when we have either found the proper insert position or considered all the positions back to the second. If it doesn't belong in the second position, it must belong in the first. In either case, if we have decremented our *position* correctly, we can simply insert—assign *insert* to *data[position]*. Program 8–10 shows the code.

Also try Program 8–10 with the *insert* values 1 and 9, which should insert at the beginning and the end of the array—the boundary conditions, in this case.

HEADS UP!

Test the boundary conditions when testing any code.

HEADS UP!

In a sort, declare the array with the number of values in the collection.

Sort

A sort arranges a collection of values in order. Unlike those in an insert, the values in a collection to be sorted do not have to start out in any particular order, and no new value is added to the collection. There are a

Program 8–10

```cpp
#include <iostream>
using namespace std;

const int listSize = 5;                         // Size of the list after insert

int main(void)
{   int data[listSize] = {2, 4, 6, 8};
    int insert = 5;
    int position;

    //----------------------------------- Print collection before insert
    cout << "Before: ";
    for (position = 0; position < listSize - 1; ++position)
        cout << "  " << data[position];
    cout << "\nInsert:   " << insert << endl;

    //------------------------------------------------------------ Insert
    position = listSize - 1;        // Start from empty variable at end of set
    while (insert < data[position - 1] && position >= 1)
    {   data[position] = data[position - 1];        // Move next value down
        --position;                                 // Go up the collection
    }
    data[position] = insert;                // Add insert value to collection

    //----------------------------------- Print collection after insert
    cout << "After : ";
    for (position = 0; position < listSize; ++position)
        cout << "  " << data[position];
    cout << endl;
    return 0;
}
```

Output

```
Before:   2  4  6  8
Insert:   5
After :   2  4  5  6  8
```

number of different sort routines—some more efficient at sorting certain types of data, some extremely complicated, some quite specialized. We will use one form of a **bubble sort** here, not because of its great efficiency, but because it is one of the least complicated.

It is called a bubble sort because it makes a number of passes through the collection, and with each pass, smaller numbers "float" like bubbles to the top, while larger numbers "sink." Each pass starts at the beginning of the collection and compares the values of the first and the second elements. If they are in order nothing is done, but if they are out of order, they are **swapped**, their values exchanged, so that at least those two values will be in order. The process continues with the second and third elements, the third and fourth, and so on.

A more appropriate name for this process might be a "sinker sort." While smaller values are bubbling up, larger values are sinking to the bottom in a more ordered fashion. With a single pass through the collection,

FIGURE 8–3

A Swap

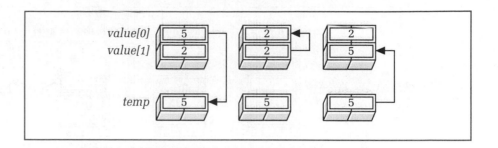

we are assured that the largest value will be at the bottom. We can now make another pass, but this time we will stop a position before the bottom of the collection because we know that the value at the bottom is already in its proper place. With each pass we will move the bottom of the collection up one, stopping after the bottom of the collection is in the second position. With all those values in their proper position, the first must be in place.

Overall, the sort follows this pattern:

Move bottom position from last to second by ones
    Make exchange pass through collection

The exchange pass starts at the top of the collection and compares adjacent values beginning with the first and ending one before the current bottom of the collection—comparing the second to the bottom with the bottom.

Move bottom position from last to second by ones
    Move position from first to one before bottom   [Exchange pass]
        if adjacent element values not in order
            Swap them

The swap requires an extra temporary variable. Graphically, it looks like Figure 8–3.

The whole process, using five short values, looks like Figure 8–4. The lightly shaded areas are adjacent values that are being compared. The darker shaded values are those in their proper positions.

Program 8–11 implements the sort diagrammed in Figure 8–4.

Notice that in the last pass, no swaps were made. If an entire pass is completed and no swaps are made, the entire collection must be in order. This condition may occur well before the last pass, in which case there is no need to continue the process. We can modify our program to test for that condition also.

Set bottom to last element
while bottom > first position and swaps made in last pass
    Move position from first to one before bottom   [Exchange pass]
        if adjacent element values not in order
            Swap them
    Move bottom up one

To keep track of whether swaps were made we use a `bool` **flag** variable, *swaps*. Either we will have made a swap or we won't; therefore the value of *swaps* will either be `true` or `false`—a perfect situation for a variable of the `bool` data type. At the beginning of each pass the value will be set to `false`; if no swaps were made, it will remain `false` after the pass. The following `main()` function segment shows this change:

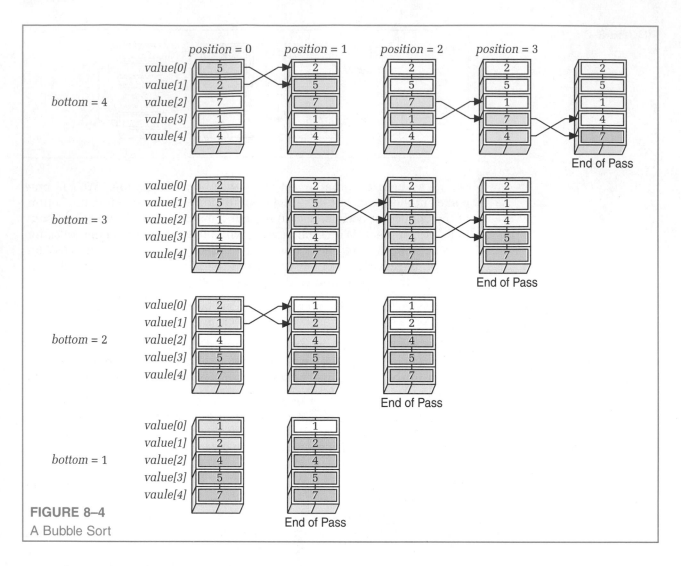

FIGURE 8–4
A Bubble Sort

```
int main(void)
{   short value[values] = {5, 2, 7, 1, 4};
    short position, bottom, temp;
    bool swap = true;                              // Flag indicates swap made
                              // Set true so that loop will execute first time
    cout << "Before sort: ";
    printArray(value);
    //------------------------------------------------------------ Sort
    bottom = values - 1;
    while (bottom > 0 && swap)
    {   swap = false;                              // No swaps made yet
        for (position = 0; position < bottom; ++position)
            if (value[position + 1] < value[position])
            {   temp = value[position];
                value[position] = value[position + 1];
                value[position + 1] = temp;
                swap = true;                       // Swap made
            }
        --bottom;
    }
```

Program 8–11

```
#include <iostream>
using namespace std;
const int values = 5;

void printArray(short arr[]);

int main(void)
{   short value[values] = {5, 2, 7, 1, 4};
    short position, bottom, temp;

    cout << "Before sort: ";
    printArray(value)

    //------------------------------------------------------------------- Sort
                                      // Move bottom from last to second by ones
    for (bottom = values - 1; bottom > 0; --bottom)
                              // Move position from first to one before bottom
      for (position = 0; position < bottom; ++position)
                                    // If adjacent element values not in order
        if (value[position + 1] < value[position])
          {  temp = value[position];                          // Swap them
             value[position] = value[position + 1];
             value[position + 1] = temp;
          }
    cout << "After sort:   ";
    printArray(value);
    return 0;
}

void printArray(short arr[])
{   short index;

    for (index = 0; index <= values - 1; ++ index)
      cout << arr[index] << " ";
    cout << endl;
}
```

Output

```
Before sort: 5 2 7 1 4
After sort:  1 2 4 5 7
```

YOUR TURN 8–4

1. What is a sequential search?
2. What conditions end a sequential search?
3. Why is a binary search more efficient than a sequential search?
4. What special conditions must exist for a binary search to work?
5. In an insert operation, how many elements must the array have?
6. Which is the first possible insert position in the collection? the last?
7. In a sort operation, how many elements must the array have?
8. What is the greatest number of passes that might be made through an array of 10 elements in a bubble sort?

ARRAYS WITH MORE THAN ONE INDEX

Arrays may have more than one index. No matter how many indexes there are, however, we can still view them as separate elements with separate values, but with a more flexible way of referring to them. The following are possible declarations:

```
float axle[7][100], bearing[20][12][25];
int flexus[200][2][4][2];
```

As an example, let's say that our major product, the Finortna, comes in any combination of two models—standard and deluxe—and three colors—red, green, and puce. This gives us six possibilities, but two different criteria: model and color. If we allowed the first index to represent the model and the second the color, we could store the inventories of Finortnas in a double-indexed array *inventory[2][3]*:

```
short inventory[2][3];
```

The typical way of looking at a double-indexed array is as a two-dimensional table, as in Table 8–1. The inventory of deluxe red Finortnas would be stored in *inventory[1][0]*, while standard puce ones would be in *inventory[0][2]*.

A convenient way to view this is as an array of arrays. In fact, this gives us a good insight into how C++ actually allocates memory space for the array. There are three elements in the *inventory[0]* array and three in the *inventory[1]* array. Because C++ guarantees us contiguous storage, if the address, *inventory*, is FFF0, then storage would be like this:

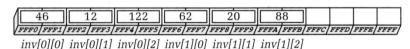

We have contiguous storage of two arrays with contiguous storage of the variables in each array. In essence, the second index (or last index, if there are more than two) varies first.

We saw that the array name was a reference to the address of the array. This also holds true for arrays with more than one index. The name *inventory* references the address FFF0, the address of *inventory[0][0]*. But if this is an array of arrays, then *inventory[0]* must be the "name" of the first three-variable array and *inventory[1]* the "name" of the second. This is indeed the case, with *inventory[0]* a reference to the address of the first, FFF0 (the address of *inventory[0][0]*), and *inventory[1]* a reference to the address of the second, FFF6 (the address of *inventory[1][0]*).

Initializing Multiple-Indexed Arrays

We could initialize the *inventory* array as we did our one-index arrays—by putting enough values in braces in the declaration.

```
short inventory[2][3] = {46, 12, 122, 62, 20, 88};
```

TABLE 8–1 THE FINORTNA TABLE				
inventory	[ ][0]	[ ][1]	[ ][2]	
[0][ ]	46	12	122	(Standard)
[1][ ]	62	20	88	(Deluxe)
	(Red)	(Green)	(Puce)	

HEADS UP!

The last index varies first.

HEADS UP!

Notice how rows and columns make two-index arrays clearer.

Because we are dealing with an array of arrays, the values will be assigned to each major array in turn. If we view the array as a two-dimensional table, the assignments will be in *row-major order*. In other words, 46, 12, and 122 will be assigned to row zero—*inventory[0][0]*, *inventory[0][1]*, and *inventory[0][2]*—and 62, 20, and 88 will be assigned to row one—*inventory[1][0]*, *inventory[1][1]*, and *inventory[1][2]*.

C++ also allows us to separate the arrays-within-the-array by nesting braces:

```
short inventory[2][3] = {{46, 12, 122}, {62, 20, 88}};
```

which we would probably write more illustratively as

```
short inventory[2][3] = {{46, 12, 122},
                         {62, 20,  88}};
```

to maintain the tablelike view of the array.

If we do not supply enough values, the rest of the elements are initialized to zero. But if we use nested braces, this initialization applies to each of the subarrays. For example,

```
short inventory[2][3] = {{46, 12},          // Acceptable
                         {62    }};
```

is equivalent to

```
short inventory[2][3] = {{46, 12, 0},          // Clear
                         {62,  0, 0}};
```

If we supply enough values we can leave the leftmost index blank for the compiler to fill in. Thus,

```
short inventory[][3] = {46, 12, 0, 62, 0, 0};       // Ugly!
```

is equivalent to the previous declaration.

The second-to-last example, showing the values of all the elements in tablelike fashion, is certainly clearer than those before or after it. The one before it would be acceptable if each row had 50 columns and only the first 1 or 2 were to be explicitly initialized. The last example is just plain ugly!

Accessing Multiple-Indexed Arrays

We could print out the values in the *inventory* array by using nested `for` loops; the outer one controls the first index, the row, and the inner one controls the second index, the column. Program 8–12 shows how.

Passing Multiple-Indexed Arrays to Functions

As you know, passing the array name (the address of the array) to a function does not tell the function how many elements are in the array. Nor, of

Program 8–12

```cpp
#include <iostream>
#include <iomanip>
using namespace std;

const int models = 2;
const int colors = 3;

int main(void)
{   short inventory[models][colors] = {{46, 12, 122},
                                       {62, 20,  88}};
    int model, color;

    cout << "                RED   GREEN    PUCE\n";
    for (model = 0; model < models; ++model)
    {   if (model == 0)
            cout << "STANDARD ";
        else
            cout << "DELUXE    ";
        for (color = 0; color < colors; ++color)
            cout << setw(6) << inventory[model][color] << " ";
        cout << endl;
    }
    return 0;
}
```

Output

```
              RED   GREEN    PUCE
STANDARD      46     12     122
DELUXE        62     20      88
```

course, would it tell the function how many indexes the array can safely use or the organization of those indexes. In our declaration of the formal parameters of the array in the function, however, we can fill in some of that information by showing how many index positions there are and stating the number of indexes in each position but the first. The function still will not know the overall size of the array, but its pattern, at least, is evident.

Using Finortnas as an example, viewing the array-within-the-array as the columns within a row, and given our declaration of

`short inventory[2][3];`

in the `main()` function, this function will allocate space for the array that can be viewed as

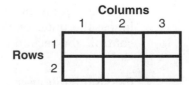

When we pass the array's address to a function,

Program 8–13

```cpp
#include <iostream>
#include <iomanip>
using namespace std;

const int models = 2;
const int colors = 3;

void printInv(short inventory[][colors]);

int main(void)
{   short inventory[models][colors] = {{46, 12, 122},
                                       {62, 20,  88}};

    printInv(inventory);
    return 0;
}

void printInv(short inventory[][colors])                  // No first index!
{   int model, color;

    cout << "              RED   GREEN   PUCE\n";
    for (model = 0; model < models; ++model)
    {   if (model == 0)
            cout << "STANDARD ";
        else
            cout << "DELUXE   ";
        for (color = 0; color < colors; ++color)
            cout <<setw(6) << inventory[model][color] << " ";
        cout << endl;
    }
}
```

```
func(inventory)
```

we are telling the function where the array starts in memory. In the formal parameters of the function we can state how many elements there are in each array-within-the-array, but still not how large the entire array is.

To receive the call above, the *func()* function is declared as

```
func(short inv[][3])
```

and in *func()*, the array is viewed as

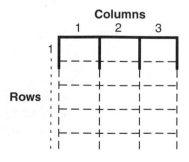

Program 8–14

```cpp
#include <iostream>
#include <iomanip>
using namespace std;

const int models = 2;
const int colors = 3;

short sumArray(short value[], short elements);

int main(void)
{   short inventory[models][colors] = {{46, 12, 122},
                                       {62, 20,  88}};

    cout << "Standard: "
         << setw(6) << sumArray(inventory[0], colors) << endl;      // First
    cout << "Deluxe  : "
         << setw(6) << sumArray(inventory[1], colors) << endl;      // Second
    return 0;
}

short sumArray(short value[], short elements)
{   short count, sum = 0;

    for (count = 0; count < elements; ++count)
        sum += value[count];
    return sum;
}
```

Output

```
Standard:    180
Deluxe  :    170
```

Program 8–13 is Program 8–12 rewritten to print out the inventory in a function. The output is exactly the same.

We can send an array-within-the-array to the function separately by passing its address—array notation without the second index. The formal parameters of the function, of course, will have to receive the address of a single-indexed array.

Let's write a program that shows the total inventories for standard and deluxe Finortnas. In the program we want the sum of each array-within-an-array. Earlier in this chapter we developed the *sumArray()* function (in three versions), which returned the sum of the elements in an array. We can use this function (the second version) to total each of the subarrays in Program 8–14.

The notation *inventory[0]* is the address of the first array-within-the-array—a single-indexed array with three (*colors*) variables. Sending it to *sumArray()* totals the values of those three variables. We follow the same process with *inventory[1]*.

1. Can we set up an array of arrays?
2. Given the declaration `stuff[4][3];`, what does the notation `stuff[2]` signify?
3. How can we use the array-of-arrays concept in initializing arrays?
4. When we pass a multiple-indexed array to a function, how many indexes do we provide values for in the function's formal parameters?
5. How can we pass an array-within-an-array to a function?

PUTTING IT TOGETHER

Professor Fassbinder maintains a strict seating chart in her classes; her students are known to her principally by their row and seat numbers. For administrative purposes, however, she is also forced to refer to her students by name. She needs a system that will allow her to access her students in her favorite way while also listing them alphabetically by name. We told her that we had to spend too much time studying for her darned tests to give her a complete system, but that we would get it started and she could con some of her next term's students into adding to it.

TASK

Provide Professor Fassbinder with the beginnings of her grade-keeping program. We will concentrate on the output section: a grade report by seat, a seating chart showing who is in which seat, and an alphabetical listing of students and scores.

ANALYSIS

For this project we will develop some of the functional components for the larger project to be completed later. The first component, the grade report by seat, should show a row-and-column seating chart with the total grade for the student in that seat.

```
Grade Report by Seat
          1    2    3
Row 1    ##   ##   ##
Row 2    ##   ##   ##
```

The second component, the seating chart, should show the name of the student in each seat.

```
Seating Chart
             1         2         3
Row 1     Xxxxx     Xxxxx     Xxxxx
Row 2     Xxxxx     Xxxxx     Xxxxx
```

The third component should show the student names alphabetically and the two grades for each student.

```
Alphabetical Grade Report
Name      Grd1  Grd2
Xxxxx      ##    ##
Xxxxx      ##    ##
Xxxxx      ##    ##
Xxxxx      ##    ##
Xxxxx      ##    ##
Xxxxx      ##    ##
```

The principal data requirements are a name and two grades for each student and a way of identifying which student is in which seat.

DESIGN

The class is made up of individual students, so the program should make use of a *Student* class from which we can create student objects. The student name will, of course, be a string, and the two grades will be an array of two `int`s. For testing, we must be able to initialize a student object with a name and two grades.

Because we are only concerned with output in this partial project, we can have the object directly provide the data to the rest of the program. In other words, we can make the object's properties `public:`.

Row and seat is Professor Fassbinder's principal way of referring to students, so we will set up a two-index array of student objects. The first index will be the row (actually, the row minus one because C++'s indexes start with zero) and the second index the seat (or seat minus one).

Our three output routines will be implemented as separate functions. They will not be part of the actual *Student* object because they do not refer to an individual student but to all the students—the entire array—and the *Student* properties are `public:`. The `main()` function will simply be a driver to initialize the array and call the output functions.

The grade report by seat should:

Print headings
For each row
   Print row
   For each seat
     Print total score

The seating chart should:

Print headings
For each row
   Print row
   For each seat
     Print student name

OBJECT SUMMARY

Object Name	Behavior	Properties
Student		name (pro) grades (pro)
Full initialization	Initialization of new object with full data	name (req) grades (req)
Empty initialization	Initialization of new object with no data	

The alphabetical grade report should:

[Copy data to a temporary list]
    For each row
        For each seat
            Copy object to temporary list element
Sort temporary list (using bubble sort)
[Print list]
    Print headings
    For each element
        Print name and two grades

Next term's programming volunteers will probably add some input routines, isolate the object's properties, and add some access functions to the object.

IMPLEMENTATION

As we see in Program 8–15 the *Student* class has a constructor that accepts initialization for all the properties of a student object. When next term's programmers take over the project, they will add input routines to replace this constructor and its initialization.

In the *alpha()* function that prints out an alphabetical grade listing we use the bubble sort developed earlier in this chapter. We do not want to sort our row-and-seat array of *Student* objects, however, because that would move all the students to different seats. Instead, we copy the data into a single-index array and sort that. The single-index array can be discarded, and indeed will disappear, at the end of the function's execution.

TEST

We are testing the *Student* class and the three functions we have set up to use it. The main() function is merely a driver to exercise those elements.

Program 8–15

```
     #include <iostream>
     #include <iomanip>
     #include <string>
     using namespace std;                              // If your compiler needs it

     const int rows = 2;
     const int seats = 3;

     class Student //////////////////////////////////////////////// Student Class
     {
     public:
S1     string name;
S2     int grade[2];

S3     Student(string n, int g0, int g1)
S4     {  name = n; grade[0] = g0; grade[1] = g1; }
     };

     void report(Student stu[][seats]);                       // Grade Report
     void chart(Student stu[][seats]);                       // Seating Chart
     void alpha(Student stu[][seats]);              // Alphabetical Grade Listing
```
(Continued)

Program 8–15 *(Continued)*

```
     int main(void)  ///////////////////////////////////////////// Main Function
 1 {   Student pupil[rows][seats]           // Initialization of 2 by 3 array
         = {{Student("Gold", 18, 14),
             Student("Nguyen", 15, 19),
             Student("Aziz", 17, 17)},
            {Student("Mboto", 20, 14),
             Student("VanPelt", 19, 18),
             Student("Snarf", 4, 2)}};

 2     report(pupil);
 3     chart(pupil);
 4     alpha(pupil);
       return 0;
   }

   ///////////////////////////////////////////// Functions Using Student Class
r1 void report(Student stu[][seats])  //*************************** Grade Report
   {  int row, seat;

r2     cout << "Grade Report by Seat\n";
       cout << "        ";
       for (seat = 0; seat < seats; ++seat)
          cout << setw(4) << (seat + 1);
       cout << endl;
r3     for (row = 0; row < rows; ++ row)
r4     {  cout << "Row " << (row + 1);
r5        for (seat = 0; seat < seats; ++seat)
r6           cout << setw(4)
                  << (stu[row][seat].grade[0] + stu[row][seat].grade[1]);
r7        cout << endl;
       }
       cout << endl;
   }

c1 void chart(Student stu[][seats])  //*************************** Seating Chart
   {  int row, seat;

c2     cout << "Seating Chart\n";
       for (seat = 0; seat < seats; ++seat)
          cout << "         " << (seat + 1);
       cout << endl;
c3     for (row = 0; row < rows; ++ row)
c4     {  cout << "Row " << (row + 1) << "   " << setiosflags(ios::left);
c5        for (seat = 0; seat < seats; ++seat)
c6           cout << setw(8) << stu[row][seat].name;
c7        cout << endl << resetiosflags(ios::left);
       }
       cout << endl;
   }

a1 void alpha(Student stu[][seats])  //************* Alphabetical Grade Listing
   {  int row, seat;
a2     Student list[rows * seats] = {Student("", 0, 0), // Empty initialization
                                     Student("", 0, 0),     // of 1 by 6 array
                                     Student("", 0, 0),
                                     Student("", 0, 0),
                                     Student("", 0, 0),
                                     Student("", 0, 0)};           (Continued)
```

```
            //----------------------------------- Set Up Temporary Array to Sort
a3      for (row = 0; row < rows; ++ row)
            for (seat = 0; seat < seats; ++seat)
                list[row * seats + seat] = stu[row][seat];


            //---------------------------------------------------------------- Sort
        int bottom, position;
        bool swap = true;
a4      Student temp("", 0, 0);                          // Empty initialization

a5      bottom = rows * seats - 1;
        while (bottom > 0 && swap)
        {   swap = false;                                     // No swaps made yet
            for (position = 0; position < bottom; ++position)
                if (list[position + 1].name < list[position].name)
                {   temp = list[position];
                    list[position] = list[position + 1];
                    list[position + 1] = temp;
                    swap = true;                             // Swap made
                }
            --bottom;
        }


            //------------------------------------------------- Print Alpha Listing
a6      cout << "Alphabetical Grade Report\n";
        cout << "Name      Grd1  Grd2\n";
        for (seat = 0; seat < rows * seats; ++seat)
            cout << setiosflags(ios::left) << setw(8) << list[seat].name
                 << resetiosflags(ios::left) << setw(6) << list[seat].grade[0]
                 << setw(6) << list[seat].grade[1] << endl;
        cout << endl;
    }
```

Output

```
    Grade Report by Seat
            1    2    3
    Row 1   32   34   34
    Row 2   34   37    6

    Seating Chart
            1         2         3
    Row 1   Gold      Nguyen    Aziz
    Row 2   Mboto     VanPelt   Snarf

    Alphabetical Grade Report
    Name      Grd1  Grd2
    Aziz        17    17
    Gold        18    14
    Mboto       20    14
    Nguyen      15    19
    Snarf        4     2
    VanPelt     19    18
```

Line	Explanation	pupil[2][3]			
1	Declare *pupil* array. Call constructor for *pupil[0][0]*. Pass values.	??... ??... ??... ??... ??... ??...			
	Student():		*n*	*g0*	*g1*
S3	Initialize constructor variables. Define variables declared in S1 and S2 for *pupil[0][0]*.	??... ??... ??... ??... ??... ??...	Gold	18	14
S4	Assign class properties for *pupil[0][0]* object.	Go... ??... ??... ??... ??... ??...	Gold	18	14
	main():				
1	Call constructor for *pupil[0][1]*. Pass values.	Go... ??... ??... ??... ??... ??...			
	Student():		*n*	*g0*	*g1*
S3	Initialize constructor variables. Define variables declared in S1 and S2 for *pupil[0][1]*.	Go... ??... ??... ??... ??... ??...	Nguyen	15	19
S4	Assign class properties for *pupil[0][1]* object.	Go... Ng... ??... ??... ??... ??...	Nguyen	15	19
	main():				
1	Construct rest of *pupil* objects.	Go... Ng... Az... Mb... Va... Sn...			
2	Call *report()*. Pass address of *pupil* array.	Same			

Line	Explanation	stu[][3]	row	seat
	report():	*stu[][3]*	*row*	*seat*
r1	Initialize *stu* with same address as *pupil*.	Go... Ng... Az... Mb... Va... Sn...	--	--
r2	Print headings	Same	??	??
r3	Set *row* to 0; test; *row* < 2.	Same	0	3
r4	Print row number.	Same	0	3
r5	Set *seat* to 0; test; *seat* < 3.	Same	0	0
r6	Print total of two grades for that *stu*.	Same	0	0
	End of *seat* loop; increment *seat*.	Same	0	1
r5	Test; *seat* < 3.	Same	0	1
r3–7	Continue through *row* and *seat* loops. Return to `main()`.	Same	2	3

Line	Explanation	pupil[2][3]		
	main():	*pupil[2][3]*		
3	Call *chart()*. Follow similar process to *report()*.	Go... Ng... Az... Mb... Va... Sn...		
4	Call *alpha()*. Pass address of *pupil* array.	Same		

Line	Explanation	stu[][3]	list[6]
	alpha():	*stu[][3]*	*list[6]*
a1	Initialize *stu* with same address as *pupil*.	Go... Ng... Az... Mb... Va... Sn...	-- -- -- -- -- --
a2	Declare *list[6]* as a 1 by 6 array with blanks and zeros.	Same	... ...
a3	Assign data from *stu[][3]* to *list[6]*.	Same	Go... Ng... Az... Mb... Va... Sn...
a4	Set up temporary *Student* object for swap.	Same	Go... Ng... Az... Mb... Va... Sn...
a5	Bubble sort *list[6]* as outlined in chapter.	Same	Az... Go... Mb... Ng... Sn... Va...
a6	Print *list[6]* and return.	Same	Az... Go... Mb... Ng... Sn... Va...

PLUS

SUMMARY

- **KEY TERMS** (in order of appearance)

Array	Insert
Element	Bubble sort
Index	Swap
Sequential search	Flag
Binary search	

• CONCEPT REVIEW

- An **array** is a collection of **elements**, essentially variables, each of which has a different **index**. An indexed variable may be used any place an ordinary variable may be used, and in the same manner.

- Arrays are declared as a set by putting the name and the number of elements in a declaration statement. Initializations can accompany declarations by putting the values in braces. If any of the elements of an array is initialized, those that are not initialized become zero.

- An index may be any expression. The array element referred to is determined by the value of the expression, meaning that the element can be changed by changing the value of the expression.

- Values of array elements may be passed to functions just like values of normal variables, but more commonly we send functions the address of the array, using the name, so that the function can access any element of the array.

- We may create arrays of any data type, including objects of a class. We may also include arrays as properties of a class. The index immediately follows the array name—the object, or property, or both.

- Initialization of arrays of objects cannot be done like that of simple arrays. It must be accomplished by using explicit calls to a constructor instead of simple initialization values.

- A **sequential search** starts at the beginning of a collection of values and continues until a specified value is found or the end of the collection is reached.

- A **binary search** works on an ordered collection of values and eliminates half the values with each comparison.

- An **insert** adds a value to an ordered collection.

- A sort, such as **bubble sort**, puts an unordered collection in order. The operation involves **swapping** values of adjacent array elements. We can make a bubble sort more efficient by setting up a **flag** to tell us whether a swap has been made.

- Variables may have many indexes. They can be viewed as arrays of arrays, stored in an order that reflects the last index varying first.

- A notation that does not include all the indexes indicates the address of that subarray within the array.

- Arrays with more than one index are declared with sets of brackets containing the number of indexes in each position. They can be initialized by putting values in braces in the declaration. By using nested braces we can tell the compiler specifically which values belong to which subarray.

- When multiple indexes are used in the formal parameters of a function declaration, all indexes except the first are explicitly stated.

• HEADS UP: POINTS OF SPECIAL INTEREST

- C++ indexes always start with zero.
- An array must be of a single data type.
- The last valid index is one less than the number in the declaration.

- Initializing at least one element sets all the uninitialized elements to zero.
- Avoid floating-point indexes.
- An array name references the address of an array.
- An array passed by its name can be modified in a function.
- We can have an array of any data type, including classes.
- Automatic initialization to zero does not work with objects.
- Objects have their own properties, but share behaviors.
- There are two possible conditions for ending a search loop.
- Data must be in order for a binary search.
- When inserting, declare an array one larger than the current collection.
- Test the boundary conditions when testing any code.
- In a sort, declare the array with the number of values in the collection.
- Each index must have its own set of brackets.
- A double-indexed array is an array of arrays.
- Array notation with the last index missing is an address.
- The last index varies first.
- Notice how rows and columns make two-index arrays clearer.

• TRAPS: COMMON PROGRAMMING ERRORS

- Declaring an array with a garbage expression.
- `short sales[7] = {1};` does not initialize all the elements to 1.
- Going out of the array's range.
- Using a plausible value for a sentinel.
- Trying to initialize an array of objects without explicitly calling the constructor.
- Trying to insert into unordered data.

• YOUR TURN ANSWERS

• 8–1

1. An indexed variable, like any other variable, has its own name, its own value, and its own place in memory.
2. Using an indexed variable changing the index changes the element or variable referred to.
3. An array is a collection of indexed elements of the same data type. In C++ all the elements will be contiguous in memory.
4. One reason for using arrays is to create a large number of variables. Another is so that we can change the variable name in our program by changing the value of the index.
5. Indexed variable collections in C++ always start with the index zero.
6. In the array declaration `float stuff[10];` 10 variables are allocated, with the last index being 9, that is, *stuff[9]*.

7. Given the declaration float stuff[5] = {1.1, 2.2, 3.3};, *stuff[1]* will be 2.2. Since only *stuff[0]*, *stuff[1]*, and *stuff[2]* have initialization values, *stuff[3]* will be zero; *stuff[5]*, while we can actually access it, is beyond the end of the array, so we should not access it.

8. Given the declaration in 7, *stuff[what]* would have no specific value because the array element is not determined. If *what* was 2, for example, the value of *stuff[what]* would be 3.3.

9. An index is an integral data type. If a floating-point value is given, it is truncated to an integer.

• 8–2

1. We can "pass an array to a function" by passing all the values in the array as separate values, and by passing the array address using the array name.

2. The declaration of an array in the formal parameters of a function declares only an array prefix to hold the address passed to it by the function call.

3. When we pass an array by pointer to a function, we can't directly determine the end of the array. We might also pass the number of elements or put a sentinel value in the last element, however.

4. If we pass an array by name and change some of the elements using the local name in the function, because both names are the same address, changes in the elements in the called function will also change the corresponding elements in the calling function. They are the same memory spaces.

• 8–3

1. If we have an array of *gadget* objects, we reference the *thing* member of the third *gadget* as gadget[2].thing.

2. We would use a constructor to initialize all the elements of an array of objects to the same set of values. As each object (element) was created it would be assigned those values.

3. To initialize the elements of an array of objects in the object declaration statement we must include successive calls to the class constructor function in the declaration.

4. If we have an array of *gadget* objects with an array of *thing* members, we reference the second *thing* of the third *gadget* as gadget[2].thing[1].

• 8–4

1. In a sequential search you step through a list of values, starting from the first, comparing each in turn with the desired value.

2. The sequential search ends when the value from the list matches the desired value or the end of the list is reached, indicating that the desired value is not in the list.

3. A binary search is more efficient than a sequential search because it eliminates half the range of values with each test.

4. For a binary search to work, the values must be in order.

5. In an insert operation, the array must have at least one more element than the number of values in the list before inserting.

6. The first possible insert position in the collection will be the element one beyond the end of the assigned list. The last to be considered is the second position. If the insert isn't completed by that time, the value must belong in the first position.

7. A sort array must have at least as many elements as there are values to sort.

8. The greatest number of passes that might be made through an array of 10 elements in a bubble sort is nine—one fewer than the number of values in the list. At that point the first one must be in the right place.

• 8–5

1. We set up an array of arrays by using more than one index.

2. Given the declaration `stuff[4][3];`, *stuff[2]* signifies the address of the third array—*stuff[2][0]* through *stuff[2][2]*.

3. We can use the array-of-arrays concept in initializing arrays by enclosing the values for each subarray in its own set of braces.

4. When we pass a multiple-indexed array to a function, all but the first index are filled in. The organization of the array is shown but its size is not.

5. Leaving off the last index in the call will pass the address of the array-within-the-array. The function's formal parameters will naturally have to declare the address of an array with one less index.

EXERCISES

1. Write appropriate array declarations for the following:
   a. The *prices* of products 1 through 10.
   b. A *customerData* array that stores heights, weights, and shoe sizes of 10 customers.
   c. A *scores* array for students by row and seat in three different classes.
   d. An array to store *sales* for 10 product numbers sold in four sales regions over a five-year period.

2. Show the declaration for a *things* array of 10 `double` elements that also initializes the first element to 0, the second to 2.5, and all the rest to zero.

3. How many addressable elements has each of the arrays declared in the following?
   a. `int x[5][2];`
   b. `long double f[5][2][4][3];`
   c. `short a[] = {4, 2, 3, 8};`
   d. `float z[5] = {3.1, 2.8};`

4. What is wrong with the following declarations?
   a. `long double x[2][12] = {{25}, {0}};`
   b. `long x[2, 6];`
   c. `float q[2][3] = {2.1, 3.3};`
   d. `char c[3] = {'a', 'b', 'c', 'd'};`

5. Find the error in the following code segment and tell what error indication will be given.

```
int count, array[5] = {1, 2, 3, 4, 5};
for (count = 1; count <= 5; ++count)
    cout << array[count] << endl;
```

6. Given the following declarations, which statements are invalid and why?

```
double one[10], two[5][5], value = 1.0;
```

   a. `two[3][0] = 25;`   b. `value = two[3][5];`
   c. `cout << two[1] << endl;` d. `one[2] = two[3][4];`

7. Given the following declarations, which statements are invalid and why?

```
class Something
{
public:
    int bunch[5];
};
Something more[6];
```

   a. `cout << bunch[2].more;`
   b. `cout << bunch.more[2];`
   c. `bunch[5].more[3] = 22;`
   d. `func(bunch[2]);`   // Function call
   e. `Something lots[6] = {12, 2, 67, -34, 21, 3};`

8. To the declarations in Exercise 7, add the needed statements to declare a four-element *which* array of *Something*s and initialize them all to zero.

9. Why is the following search loop inadequate?

```
while (values[count] != searchValue)
    ++count;
```

10. How would you set up variables for floating-point *pressure* values for each of the integrally numbered *tires* (1 through 5—don't forget the spare) on your car?

11. Rewrite the binary search program from the text so it works with a list in descending (high to low) order rather than its current ascending order. Change the declaration of the array to

```
float length[PIPES] = {3.8, 3.7, 3.1, 2.6, 2.2, 1.9, 1.3, 1.2, 0.8};
```

12. What is the problem with this insert segment?

```
pos = 4;
while (insertValue < val[pos] && pos > 1)
```

13. Given the declaration `float stuff[10];` correct this bubble sort segment.

```
last = valuesToSort;
while (last >= 0 && swap)
{   swap = true;
    for (position = 0; position <= last; ++position)
        if (value[position] < value[position + 1])
        {   temp = value[position];
            value[position + 1] = value[position];
            value[position + 1] = temp;
            swap = false;
        }
    ++last;
}
```

14. Rewrite the sort program from the text (page 289) so that it sorts in descending (high to low) order rather than ascending order.

15. You want to pass the array double array[10]; to the function *func()*, which uses the identifier *arr* to receive the array. Assuming no return value, show the call to *func()* and the first line of the definition of *func()*.

16. Show the output from this program:

```
#include <iostream>
using namespace std;

int main(void)
{   int array[3][2] = {{6, 2},
                        {3, 5},
                        {1, 7}};
    int r, c;

    for (r = 0; r < 2; ++r)
    {   for (c = 0; c < 3; ++c)
            cout << array[c][r] << "   ";
        cout << endl;
    }
    return 0;
}
```

17. Rewrite the program in Exercise 16 so that the display (the nested for loops) is done in a separate function *print()*. Use the same variables in *print()* as were used in main().

PROGRAMS

1. Modify Program 8–1 (page 265) to input the sales values and print out their total. You will no longer need the initialization of the *sales* array.

2. Write a program to input five numbers and print them out in the reverse order of input. Put both the input and printing in loops.

Variables

```
numbers[]
counter
```

Output

```
Input five numbers:
1? 28.47
2? .0021
3? 7492
4? 12.5
5? 6
Here they are: 6   12.5   7492   0.0021   28.47
```

3. Write a program that accepts input of five values from the keyboard and prints out the values and their difference from the mean (average) value.

Variables

```
value[]
mean        Also use for the total
count
```

Output

```
Enter 5 values separated by whitespace.
46.2 12.6 32.654 6 25.44
Number    Value   Difference
     1    46.20        21.62
     2    12.60       -11.98
     3    32.65         8.08
     4     6.00       -18.58
     5    25.44         0.86
```

4. Modify Program 8–2 (page 268) so that the `main()` function contains only declarations and calls to *inputData()* and *printReport()*. Write the appropriate functions.

5. Write a program that adds two four-element arrays together. The first array should be initialized with values 1, 2, 3, and 4; the second with values 5, 6, 7, and 8. Both arrays should be passed to the function *addArrays()*, which adds corresponding variables of each array together and leaves the results in the second array. The second array should then be printed out by the `main()` function.

Functions and Variables

```
main()          addArrays()
 array1[]         a1[], a2[]
 array2[]         counter
 counter
```

Output

```
Resultant array: 6 8 10 12
```

6. Modify Program 7, Chapter 6 (page 221) to replace the accumulators with an array of accumulators. The program should be much shorter, but the output should be similar.

Functions and Variables

```
numbers[]    Accumulators
count        Loop counter
rnd()        Integer between 1 and 5
```

7. Write a function that merges two ordered integer arrays into a third ordered array. The two arrays should be able to contain any number of nonnegative values. The last value in each array should be the sentinel value, –1. This value should also be placed at the end of the merged array. For test purposes, use `main()` driver below. Test again by changing the array initialization values.

Functions and Variables

```
merge()
 array1[], array2[], merged[]
 sub1, sub2, subM                    Subscripts for the three arrays
```

Driver

```
int main(void)
{   int array1[] = {1, 4, 6, -1};        // 2nd test {2, 3, 5, 7, 8, -1}
    int array2[] = {2, 3, 5, 7, 8, -1};       // 2nd test {1, 4, 6, -1}
    int sub = 0, merged[50];

    merge(array1, array2, merged);
    while (merged[sub] != -1)
    {   cout << merged[sub] << " ";
        ++sub;
    }
    cout << endl;
    return 0;
}
```

Output

```
1 2 3 4 5 6 7 8
```

8. Write a program that will initialize an array of characters to *ABCDE* and allow you to shift, in circular fashion, those characters to the right any number of places you specify. The shifting should be done in the function *shift()*, but all the printouts should be from `main()`.

Functions and Variables

```
main()              shift()
 chrs[]              chrs[]
 places              places
 count               count
 temp[]   To store a copy of the array
```

Outputs

```
Before shifting: ABCDE
Shift how many places? 2
After shifting: DEABC

Before shifting: ABCDE
Shift how many places? 8
After shifting: CDEAB

Before shifting: ABCDE
Shift how many places? 5
After shifting: ABCDE

Before shifting: ABCDE
Shift how many places? 41
After shifting: EABCD
```

9. Rewrite the sequential search example so that the search is a separate

function. This function should work with an array of any number of `int` elements, but you will have to pass it the number of elements. It should return the index of the element found, or −1 if the value was not found.

10. Rewrite the binary search program example to allow you to identify the bin number, an integer, of a piece of pipe. Once the pipe is found, the bin number is printed out. To accomplish this, declare a *Pipe* class with appropriate properties and an array of *pipes*.

11. Bargain Benny's Used Car Emporium is having its fourth annual going-out-of-business sale and wants to give its salespeople up-to-the-minute information on cars no longer in stock. To do this Benny posts a list of stock numbers, in numerical order, of cars sold. Write a program for Benny that will allow a stock number to be input and inserted in the list, and a new list printed each time a car is sold. The program should handle up to 20 sales a day. Input stock number 0 to get out of the program.

Variables

`stock[]`	Array of stock numbers
`sold`	Input for stock number sold
`totalSold`	Number of cars sold (and end of *stock* array)
`position`	Insert loop counter variable

Output

```
What number sold? 71132
    Sold: 71132
What number sold? 38814
    Sold: 38814   71132
What number sold? 41825
    Sold: 38814   41825   71132
What number sold? 0
```

12. Write a program that accepts any number of values (up to 100) from the keyboard and sorts them in descending order (highest number first). Use a zero value to end input.

Variables

Choose appropriate variables

Output

```
Input numbers, type 0 to end input
> 27
> 92
> -116
> 41
> .007
> -.007
> 0
HERE THEY ARE IN DESCENDING ORDER
 92   41   27  0.007 -0.007 -116
```

13. To Program 8–8 (page 282) add a function that sorts the array of *trucks*, and change the sequential search to a binary search.

14. A sample of 11 packages from a day's run of a packing machine are weighed and the weights input into the computer. Write a program that figures the mean and median weights. The mean is the total weight divided by 11. The median is the middle (sixth) value of the ordered collection of weights.

Variables

```
weight[]
bottom, position, temp, swap    Sort variables
total                           Total weight accumulator
```

Output

```
Enter 11 weights:
 1> 10.4
 2> 10.2
 3> 10.3
 4> 9.8
 5> 9.8
 6> 10.4
 7> 10.3
 8> 10.3
 9> 10.1
10> 9.9
11> 10.1
The mean is 10.14545
The median is 10.2
```

15. Modify Program 14 to show the mode (the value occurring most frequently). (*Hint:* After ordering the values, compare each with the next and add to a counter if the values are the same. When a different value is reached, start the counter over again.) Assume there is only one mode.

Additional Variables

```
mode
modeOccurrences     Number of times the mode occurs
valueOccurrences    Number of occurrences of a particular value
```

Addition to Output

```
The mode is 10.3
```

16. Modify Program 15 so it works with 12 weights. The median is now the mean of the two middle (sixth and seventh) values.

Output

```
Enter 12 weights:
 1> 10.4
 2> 10.2
 3> 10.3
 4> 9.8
 5> 9.8
 6> 10.4
 7> 10.3
 8> 10.3
 9> 10.1
10> 9.9
11> 10.1
12> 10.2
The mean is 10.15
The median is 10.2
The mode is 10.3
```

17. Write a function, *sortFloat()*, that will sort any array of floats in either ascending or descending order. You will have to pass the function the address of the array, its size, and either the character *A* for ascending order, or any other character for descending order. Show it tested with an appropriate main() driver that declares and initializes an array, prints the unsorted array, sorts it, and prints it after sorting.

18. Write a program that deals a hand of five cards. Set up a *Deck* class for the deck of cards. To make your dealing accurate, you will have to start with a deck (an array) of 52 cards and shuffle the deck. In a *shuffle()* behavior, set up your deck, numbered from 1 to 52, and another deck with numbers randomly assigned. Sort the random deck and, with each swap in the sort, also swap corresponding cards in the real deck. When the random deck is in order, the real deck will be random. Use the behavior *deal()* to print the suit and number of the next card dealt. Do not forget to include a property that keeps track of how many cards were dealt.

Class, Functions, and Variables

Choose them appropriately

Sample Outputs

```
Your hand: Queen-Diamonds Queen-Hearts 8-Clubs 4-Clubs 7-Spades

Your hand: 5-Spades Ace-Hearts 10-Clubs King-Diamonds 4-Hearts
```

19. Skewed Opinion Research, Inc., sent out survey questionnaires with three questions. Each question was to be answered on a 1 to 5 scale, 1 meaning "awful" and 5 meaning "fantastic." Write a program that allows input of the data, stores them in a two-dimensional array, and displays the average response to each question. The program should handle any number of questionnaires (up to 20). Entry of the sentinel value zero should end the input loop.

Suggested Variables

response[ ][ ]   To store responses to the questionnaires
question   Question number (0, 1, or 2)
questionnaire   Questionnaire number
total[ ]   Accumulators for figuring question averages

Output

```
Input three responses for each:
Questionnaire 1? 4 2 5
Questionnaire 2? 1 4 1
Questionnaire 3? 3 5 2
Questionnaire 4? 3 1 2
Questionnaire 5? 3 3 4
Questionnaire 6? 2 2 3
Questionnaire 7? 5 2 1
Questionnaire 8? 3 2 4
Questionnaire 9? 0

Average response for question 1 is: 3.000
Average response for question 2 is: 2.625
Average response for question 3 is: 2.750
```

20. Channel 117's weatherman and cooking commentator has been keeping track of daily high temperatures each day for the last four weeks. Write a program that initializes an array with these data and allows him to put in a temperature range and print out all the days (week number and day number) that have high temperatures in this range.

21. The wackos in the lab, with unlimited government funding, have decided to experiment with growing green slime mold. They started with five samples, carefully identified with distinct sample IDs, each weighing 1.0 gram. The wackos subjected these samples to various conditions over five days, measuring their weights at the end of each day. Write a program that initializes a double-indexed array, *slime*, to their results. Use the first variable in each subarray as the sample ID. If the test results don't match their expectations, naturally they want to be able to change the test results.

    Your program should display a table of their results using the function *displayTable()*, allow them to change any result using the function *changeTable()*, and print a new table. The *changeTable()* function will have to search the table for the correct ID. This search should be in a separate function, *sampleRow()*, that returns the correct row or −1 if the ID could not be found. The *changeTable()* function should display "Invalid day" or "Invalid ID" if either is the case.

Variables and Constants

Choose appropriate ones

Output

```
Sample Days: 1    2    3    4    5
      417    1.2  1.8  2.7  4.0  5.6
      244    1.0  1.0  1.0  3.8  8.2
      106    1.1  1.2  1.3  1.2  0.6
      333    0.9  0.7  0.5  0.2  0.0
      822    0.8  1.2  2.6  4.9  8.8
Change sample ID day: 333 5
Change 0.0 to what? .1
Sample Days: 1    2    3    4    5
      417    1.2  1.8  2.7  4.0  5.6
      244    1.0  1.0  1.0  3.8  8.2
      106    1.1  1.2  1.3  1.2  0.6
      333    0.9  0.7  0.5  0.2  0.1
      822    0.8  1.2  2.6  4.9  8.8
```

Chapter 9

STRINGS

PREVIEW

We have used strings in a relatively simple manner; now we want to look underneath the smooth exterior of strings into the more detailed and useful workings below. After studying this chapter you should know:

- How C++ stores and interprets string values.
- The nature of string "variables" and something about how they are stored.
- Different ways of inputting strings.
- How to access the individual characters within a string.
- How to convert string values into numeric values.
- How to classify characters and convert them from one classification to another.
- How to assemble strings.
- Methods of separating strings into component parts.

A string is a collection of characters—any characters, as long as they are part of the character coding scheme, such as ASCII, used on your computer. The computer itself attaches no special significance to the characters in the string; in fact, we saw in Chapter 2 that the computer can't even tell the difference between characters and numbers. It is only our instructions that tell it how to interpret a set of bits in storage.

We have been using strings since Chapter 2 but have not yet really delved into exactly what they are, how the language works with them, or some of the more sophisticated (and necessary) things we can do with them. As far as strings are concerned, the vacation is over. It's time to get serious.

HOW STRINGS ARE STORED

Allocation of storage for numbers is relatively easy—any numeric value of a certain data type takes up the same amount of storage. For example, any `long` in most C++s is 32 bits, any `double` is 64 bits. The value zero, stored in a `long`, is 32 zeros; it still takes up all 32 bits.

Strings are different. There is no translation of number systems—decimal to binary—because strings are not numbers. In a string, each individual character, in ASCII form, is stored. Some strings, such as "Al," are short and require very little memory space. Others, such as "Four score and seven years ago . . .", are long and require lots of memory space.

String Values

A string value—*Algonquin*, for example—is a contiguous set of characters, just like the characters in the written word. In fact, storage of a string value in memory is quite similar to storing the string on paper. It starts somewhere on the paper, or in the computer's memory, and the characters, or bytes, continue next to each other until the end of the string. "Contiguous storage of data of the same type." Sounds like the definition of an array, doesn't it? It is! A string is an array of `chars`. Putting a string value in our source code directs C++ to allocate memory for those characters—the array of `chars`. "Algonquin" in our source code will cause the C++ compiler to allocate memory like this:

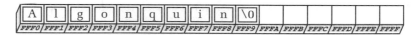

Like any other array, the string is identified by its base address, the address of the first value (character, in this case). Also, like any other array, once the memory is allocated, we are left with the problem of how to tell where the string ends in memory. C++ solves the problem by putting a null character (`'\0'`) in the memory location immediately following the last character of the string. When we ask C++ to perform some process on a string, display it perhaps, it starts at the base address and reads characters until it reaches a null. A **string value**, then, is a null-terminated character array.

HEADS UP!

String values are really arrays of `chars`.

HEADS UP!

String values end in a null character.

But where is this base address? As with variables, we will probably never know; nor do we care, as long as C++ can keep track of it. In our diagram we showed FFF0, but that was just a guess.

The notation for the address of a string value is the string value itself—the characters in double quotation marks. The string value "Algonquin" is the address where C++ has chosen to store the string—it is the address of an array of char values. In our diagram it was FFF0.

String Values Versus Character Values

In Chapter 2 you were introduced to character values such as 'A', 'f', and '\t'. These, we saw, are simply numbers—the ASCII (or EBCDIC) values of the character codes. They are of type char but, as we know, char is an integral numeric data type.

There is a significant difference between the character 'A' and the string "A". The former is an integral number, a char, with the value 65 (*A* in ASCII) that takes up one byte. The latter is the address of an array of two chars, the first with the value 65, and the second with the value zero (the null character, \0).

String Variables

Accurately speaking, there are no string variables in C++. However, there is a **string** class from which we can create string objects, which act enough like variables to allow us to use the term **string variables** without feeling too much guilt.

As with any variable, we can change its value at will by reassigning the string. Problems arise, however, when we want to replace "Al" with "Four score and seven years ago. . . ." C++ has allocated enough memory space for two characters (and the terminating null) and now we want to replace them with hundreds. The problem is solved using **dynamic allocation** of strings. When we assign a value to a string variable, C++ finds enough space in memory to accommodate the value. If we change the value of the string variable to something longer, C++ finds a new space in memory to accommodate the greater number of characters and frees the old space. In other words, it moves the variable in memory.

Problem solved; everything's perfect!

Not quite. We can accommodate virtually any length string (in many C++s the capacity is only limited by the amount of available memory) and can change lengths easily, but the process is inefficient. Changing the int 4 to 18639 is a relatively easy operation: C++ simply writes the binary equivalent of 18639 in the memory space previously occupied by the 4. Changing "Al" to "Four score . . ." requires more operations. C++ must deallocate the memory space dedicated to "Al", search its free memory for a number of contiguous bytes sufficient to store "Four score . . .", and then write the characters there. This is a time-consuming process. Imagine a bubble sort of strings. Each time a swap is made, C++ must find new places in memory to store both strings.

Many implementations of C++ regain some execution efficiency by not reallocating variables when shorter strings are assigned, so a string swap would, at most, reallocate only one variable. This technique is not without cost either. It wastes memory space. Replacing "Four score . . ." with "Al" leaves a lot of memory space that is allocated but not being used. As we have seen before, this is the typical tradeoff between execution efficiency and memory space. As we shall see later, with C++, unlike some other languages, *we* can decide which objective is most important.

Declaring String Variables

Using the simplest method of declaring string variables:

```
string word;
```

allocates just enough memory space for the current value of the string—that is exactly none. The first time we assign a value to *word*,

```
cin << word;
```

or

```
word = "Flange";
```

C++ must hunt around for a new block of memory. If we change that value to something longer,

```
word = "Supercalifragalisticexpialidocious"          // Is that spelled right?
```

C++ must again change its location in memory.

One way of improving efficiency with most C++s is to anticipate the greatest number of characters that might be stored in the string and then tell C++ to allocate that much space. We can initialize in our declaration by specifying a string value as an initializer:

```
string word = "Supercalifragalisticexpialidocious";
```

or we can tell C++ to allocate a number of *bytes*, all with the same *value*:

```
string stringObject (int bytes, char value)
```

For example

```
string word (20, '\0');
```

will allocate and initialize a 20-character string of all nulls.

In either case we can assign anything shorter to *word* without moving things around in memory. Be warned, however, with most C++s, if the system gets desperate for memory space, it may reallocate without warning you.

YOUR TURN 9–1

1. What are two major differences between storage of numbers and storage of strings?
2. How is a string value like a char array?
3. What is the difference between 'X' and "X"?
4. What do we mean by *dynamic allocation*?
5. What is the disadvantage of dynamic allocation?
6. How can we make string assignment more efficient with many C++s? What is the disadvantage of this technique?

STRING FUNCTIONS

Strings are objects of the `string` class. Declaring what we have been considering a string variable

```
string word = "Crepuscular";
```

declares an object of the `string` class, in this case the *word* object, and calls a constructor, in this case one that allocates space for and assigns the characters *Crepuscular*.

Classes can have behaviors—member functions—and the `string` class has a bunch of them.

String Size and Capacity

The **size** of a *string* is the number of characters currently stored in the string object. The **size()** function returns this value.

```
int string.size(void)                                          <string>
```

(The `int` return data type is really, according to the standards, a defined `size_type` data type, but it is compatible with an `int`, so we will use the more familiar data type.)

The **capacity** of the *string*, returned by the **capacity()** function, is the maximum number of characters that can be stored in the string without forcing C++ to move it to another place in memory.

```
int string.capacity(void)                                      <string>
```

After this program fragment,

```
string word = "doldrum";
word = "drum";
```

the value of `word.size()` should be 4, and `word.capacity()`, 7. Program 9–1 illustrates the size and capacity of a string as its value changes. Whenever reassignment of the string would make its size greater than its capacity, the string is reallocated and the capacity increases. With most C++s, if a smaller string is assigned, as in example *D* in Program 9–1, the capacity remains the same—the string is not moved.

The size of the *string* can be changed with the **resize()** function.

```
void string.resize(int newSize)                                <string>
```

HEADS UP!

resize() may change
capacity().

If the string is made smaller, characters are discarded from the right side; if it is made larger, null characters are added to the right side. If the size is made larger than the string's capacity, the string's capacity will be increased to the new size—in other words, a new string will be established in memory. Examples *F* and *G* in Program 9–1 show the effects of changing a string's size. Notice that in example *G* the capacity was also changed to 16, and 16 characters printed out, the 10 characters after *French* being null.

STRING INPUT

We have been using the `cin` object and the extraction operator (>>) for keyboard input of strings, and will continue to do so, but they have some

Program 9–1

```cpp
#include <iostream>                          // Does your system need the .h?
#include <iomanip>
#include <string>
using namespace std;                         // For those systems that need it

void data(char ex, string &str);

int main(void)
{   string stuff = "Burgers";
    string more = "Hamburgers";

    cout <<"Example String        Size   Capacity\n";
    data('A', stuff);
    data('B', more);
    stuff = more;
    data('C', stuff);
    stuff = "Fries";
    data('D', stuff);
    stuff = "French fries";
    data('E', stuff);
    stuff.resize(6);                                    // Shortens string
    data('F', stuff);
    stuff.resize(16);                     // Nulls added and capacity changed
    data('G', stuff);
    return 0;
}

void data(char ex, string &str) //*********************** Print string data
{
    cout << ex << "          " << setiosflags(ios::left) << setw(12) << str
         << resetiosflags(ios::left) << setw(6) << str.size()
         << setw(10) << str.capacity() << endl;
}
```

Output

Example	String	Size	Capacity
A	Burgers	7	7
B	Hamburgers	10	10
C	Hamburgers	10	10
D	Fries	5	5
E	French fries	12	12
F	French	6	12
G	French	16	16

serious limitations. Each value in the input stream is delimited by whitespace. In other words, whitespace ends the input of the value for a particular variable. Trying to input a book title, *Brain Surgery for Fun and Profit*, for example, would require six string variables:

```cpp
cin << word1 << word2 << word3 << word4 << word5 << word6;
```

A different title, *Cyberquackery*, could not use the same `cin` statement.

Program 9–2

```cpp
#include <iostream>
#include <string>
using namespace std;

int main(void)
{   string name;

    cout <<"Give me a name> ";
    getline(cin, name, '\n');
    while (name.size())                                    // Has characters
    {   cout << "   Name: " << name << "  Size: " << name.size() << endl;
        cout << "Give me another name> ";
        getline(cin, name, '\n');
    }
    return 0;
}
```

Output

```
Gimme a name> Lulu Wiersbowski
   Name: Lulu Wiersbowski   Size: 16
Gimme another name> Fred
   Name: Fred  Size: 4
Gimme another name> Lance Luther Lumpley, Jr
   Name: Lance Luther Lumpley, Jr  Size: 24
Gimme another name>
```

What we need is a single behavior that will allow us to input an entire line (up to the newline) and assign it to a string, spaces and all. The `getline()` function serves this purpose.

```cpp
void getline(cin, string string, char delimiter)    <string>
```

For example,

```cpp
getline(cin, sentence, '\n');
```

takes characters from the keyboard stream object, `cin`, and stores them in the *string*, *sentence*, until it reaches the *delimiter* character, newline, in the input. The delimiter is removed from the input stream, but will not be stored in the string in memory.

Program 9–2 illustrates taking lines from the keyboard and storing them in a string object. It uses a sentinel-value-controlled loop to keep accepting new lines from the keyboard until only the *Enter* or *Return* key is typed. The sentinel value is one for the `size()` of the string, *name*. If just newline is entered, no characters are assigned to *name*—a `size()` of zero. Anything more will continue the loop.

This example is a typical one, in which an entire line, up to where the person at the keyboard hit the *Enter* or *Return* key, is assigned to the string. Any character, however, may be specified as a delimiter.

```cpp
getline(cin, sentence, '.');
```

takes characters from the input stream until it reaches a period. Remember, the period will not become part of the string *sentence*. Characters

 **HEADS UP!**

`getline()` removes, but does not store, the delimiter.

 HEADS UP!

`getline()` can work with any character as a delimiter.

FURTHER CHALLENGES

The `getline()` function for the C++ from the same vendor we mentioned in Chapter 8's *Challenges* does not work properly. The vendor recognizes the problem and is working on it. Maybe next version . . .

Until then we can use one of the great advantages of C++ to work around the problem. We can substitute our own `getline()` function for theirs. This is an example of *overloading*, a most valuable facility of C++ that you will learn about in advanced C++ courses.

Near the top of your program, after the `#includes` and `using` (as shown), insert the following function:

```
#include <string>
using namespace std;

void getline(istream &stream, string &str, char delimiter)
{   char temp[500];

    stream.get(temp, 500, delimiter);
    stream.ignore(500, delimiter);
    str = temp;
}
```

[rest of program]

This will substitute our function for theirs.

Remember, this vendor's `setw()` does not work properly with `string`s either.

beyond the period are left for the next access of the input stream. We can use this feature to separate input lines at points other than spaces.

Program 9–3 accepts a last name, a first name, and an address, separates them by the delimiters, and puts them in different variables. We did not put spaces after the delimiters, such as `Prabatnik, Elvin`. If we had, the *firstName* would have been " `Elvin`" with a leading space.

FLUSHING THE INPUT STREAM

HEADS UP!

cin leaves the newline in the stream.

Whitespace is the default delimiter for the extraction operator (>>) used with the `cin` object. When this operator encounters whitespace it stops taking characters, leaving the whitespace in the input stream. This is not a problem if we are using `cin` and the extraction operator for all our inputs, because it also skips whitespace before each input, so the whitespace left in the stream by the last input is skipped at the next.

At the end of a `cin` statement such as

```
cin >> what >> who >> where;
```

the input stream is left with the newline—whitespace—from the *Enter* key. The next `cin` would skip that newline, find the stream now empty, and wait for us to type in more characters followed by *Enter*.

We used the `getline()` function so that we could include whitespace in strings that we input; it does not skip whitespace. It does not include

Program 9–3

```
#include <iostream>
#include <string>
using namespace std;

int main(void)
{   string lastName, firstName, address;

    cout <<"Enter last name,first name/address> ";
    getline(cin, lastName, ',');
    getline(cin, firstName, '/');
    getline(cin, address, '\n');
    cout << firstName << " " << lastName << " of " << address << endl;
    return 0;
}
```

Output

```
Enter last name,first name/address> Prabatnik,Elvin/12 Dreary Ln.
Elvin Prabatnik of 12 Dreary Ln.
```

the final newline in the string, but it does remove it from the input stream. This is not a problem, either, if we use `getline()` all the time.

The problem arises when we follow a `cin` with a `getline()`. The `cin` statement leaves the newline in the input stream. A following `getline()` takes all the characters from the stream up to the newline. In the stream left by `cin`, `getline()` finds a character, the newline, so it does not wait for more input. It simply takes the characters before the newline, zero characters, and assigns them to the string, creating an empty string. You think the system will wait for you to type something, but it doesn't! Look at Program 9–4.

We can use the input stream behavior **ignore()** to **flush**, empty out, the input stream.

```
void cin.ignore(int characters, char delimiter)   <iostream>
```

This function skips characters in the input stream. It stops skipping until *characters* characters have been skipped or it passes the *delimiter* character. If we set the *characters* argument high and use newline as the delimiter,

```
cin.ignore(500, '\n');
```

it will skip characters until it passes the newline, emptying the input stream.

Adding that statement after the *number* input changes the output significantly. See the New Code and New Output with Program 9–4.

HEADS UP!

`getline()` accepts newline as a valid empty string.

TRAP

Not flushing the input stream.

YOUR TURN 9–2

1. What is the difference between the `size()` and the `capacity()` of a string?
2. What does `resize()` do?
3. How is `getline()` different from `cin` using the extraction operator?
4. What problem arises when following a `cin` with a `getline()`?
5. How can we empty the input stream?

Program 9–4

```cpp
#include <iostream>
#include <string>
using namespace std;

int main(void)
{   string str;
    int number;

    cout << "Enter a string> ";
    getline(cin, str, '\n');
    cout << "Your first string: '" << str << "'." << endl;
    cout << "Enter a number> ";
    cin >> number;                              // Leaves newline in stream
    cout << "Your number: " << number << endl;
    cout << "Enter another string> ";
    getline(cin, str, '\n');
    cout << "Your second string: '" << str << "'." << endl;
    cout << "That's all!" << endl;
    return 0;
}
```

Output

```
Enter a string> Ain't C++ fun?
Your first string: 'Ain't C++ fun?'.
Enter a number> 46
Your number: 46
Enter another string> Your second string: ''.
That's all!
```

New Code

```cpp
cin >> number;                              // Leaves newline in stream
cin.ignore(500, '\n');                      // Flush input stream
cout << "Your number: " << number << endl;
```

New Output

```
Enter a string> Ain't C++ fun?
Your first string: 'Ain't C++ fun?'.
Enter a number> 46
Your number: 46
Enter another string> This works now!
Your second string: 'This works now!'.
That's all!
```

ACCESSING INDIVIDUAL CHARACTERS OF STRINGS

We saw that a string value is a contiguous set of characters starting at some address in memory and ending in a null character (\0). A `string` object stores a string in the same fashion. It finds a place in memory long enough to accommodate the string, stores the characters followed by a trailing null there, and keeps track of the beginning address.

Program 9–5

```cpp
#include <iostream>
#include <string>
using namespace std;

int main(void)
{   string word = "Crepuscular";
    int index;

    cout << "The string as a single object> " << word << endl;
    cout << "The string character by character> ";
    for (index = 0; index < word.size(); ++index)
        cout << word[index];
    cout << endl;
    return 0;
}
```

Output

```
The string as a single object> Crepuscular
The string character by character> Crepuscular
```

HEADS UP!

Array notation works with strings.

HEADS UP!

Many string functions require addresses.

HEADS UP!

Ampersand has different meanings in different contexts.

We can use a behavior of the `string` class to access any single character of the string. It looks just like array notation with an index inside brackets. Given the declaration

```cpp
string word = "Crepuscular";
```

the value of *word[0]* is *C* (a `char` data type); the value of *word[2]* is *e*.

Program 9–5 accesses a string as a single `string` object, and then as a set of individual `char` objects using subscript notation.

The `string` data type is relatively new in the C++ language. Many of the functions we use for manipulating strings were developed to be used with what C++'s predecessor, C, used to store strings; that is, a null-terminated array of `char`s. Because this early "string" was stored in an array, it was referred to like most other arrays—by its base address.

We can still use most of these functions with `string` objects, but we typically have to pass them a base address—the address where the `string` object has chosen to store the first character of the string. If the first character of *word*, for example, is the `char` *word[0]*, then we must pass the function the address of this `char`.

Another symbol, the ampersand, &, in front of the variable (yes, it is the same symbol we use to designate a reference, but in a different context) means "the address of," or where that variable is stored in memory. The notation `&word[0]`, then, means the address of the first character of the data in the *word* object. It is this notation that we will use for many of the string functions to follow.

CONVERTING STRINGS TO NUMBERS

Numbers are often expressed in characters, strings, but we must process them as numbers. For example, we might be faced with a string, *Price:*

Program 9–6

```
#include <iostream>
#include <cstdlib>
#include <string>
using namespace std;

int main(void)
{   string str = "Price: $19.95 each";
    int intvar;
    long longvar;
    double doublevar;

    intvar = atoi(&str[8]);        // Conversion start at first chr of number
    longvar = atol(&str[8]);
    doublevar = atof(&str[8]);
    cout << "The string: " << str << endl;
    cout << "Int: " << intvar << ", long: " << longvar
        << ", double: " << doublevar << endl;
    return 0;
}
```

Output

```
The string: Price: $19.95 each
Int: 19, long: 19, double: 19.95
```

$19.95 each, and must add the price to a total. The 19.95 part of the string must be converted to a number.

There are a number of ANSI functions that do the job; we will concentrate on three. The **atof()** function, pronounced "a to f" and standing for "alpha to floating-point," converts a string to type `double`; the **atoi()** function ("alpha to integer") converts a string to an `int`; and **atol()** ("alpha to long") to a `long`.

`double atof(address character)`	`<cstdlib>`
`int atoi(address character)`	`<cstdlib>`
`long atol(address character)`	`<cstdlib>`

(Remember, some C's may declare these functions in `stdlib.h`.)

In each case we pass the function the address of the *character* at which we want the conversion to begin. The function starts at that character, skips any leading whitespace, converts, and ends its conversion at the first inappropriate character for that data type or the end of the string. We will use the notation for a character address that we introduced earlier—the ampersand and indexes. In the example above, 19.95 would begin at `&str[8]`.

Program 9–6 illustrates these conversion functions.

If the number represented by the characters in the string is larger than the data type can accommodate, the resulting assignment is meaningless.

TRAP

Using the wrong conversion function for the data type.

HEADS UP!

Conversion stops at the first inappropriate character.

TRAP

Exceeding the limits of a data type.

Program 9–7

```
#include <iostream>
#include <cctype>
using namespace std;

int main(void)
{   char in;

    do
    {   cout << "Type a letter and <enter>: ";
        cin >> in;                                  // Assign the character to in
    }while ( !isalpha(in));                         // Loop while not zero
    cout << "Finally, an alpha character!" << endl;
    return 0;
}
```

Output

```
Type a letter and <enter>: 4
Type a letter and <enter>: 8
Type a letter and <enter>: /
Type a letter and <enter>: g
Finally, an alpha character!
```

CHARACTER CLASSIFICATION

Often we are presented with a string of characters and must look inside it to interpret it. Is it a complete sentence? Does it present parameters for our program to work with? If so, what are the parameters? To examine it we must look at the individual characters. We can easily test to determine whether a particular character is an *A* or a comma, but usually we want to look at the type of character rather than at its individual value. Is it an uppercase alpha character? Is it a punctuation character?

ANSI C++ provides us with a number of functions to classify individual characters. They all have the same format:

```
int function(int character)                                     <cctype>
```

(The previous name for the cctype header file was ctype.h. If your program does not compile with the first, try the other.)
For example,

```
int isalpha(int character)                                      <cctype>
```

returns a nonzero value if the *character* is a letter, that is, *A* through *Z* or *a* through *z*, or returns zero if it is not a letter. The argument for each of these functions is an int data type, but a char data type will work just as well.

Program 9–7 asks for a letter from the keyboard and will loop until it gets one.

We can examine the individual characters of a string by sending each of the character values to the isalpha() function as in Program 9–8.

Program 9–8

```
#include <iostream>
#include <cctype>
#include <string>
using namespace std;

int main(void)
{  string str = "23 skidoo.";
   int chr = 0;                               // Character position in string

   while(chr < str.size())                    // Loop to the end of the string
   {  if (isalpha(str[chr]))
         cout << "'" << str[chr] << "' is alpha" << endl;
      else
         cout << "'" << str[chr] << "' is not alpha" << endl;
      ++chr;                                   // Go to next character
   }
   return 0;
}
```

Output

```
'2' is not alpha
'3' is not alpha
' ' is not alpha
's' is alpha
'k' is alpha
'i' is alpha
'd' is alpha
'o' is alpha
'o' is alpha
'.' is not alpha
```

The complete list of ANSI classification functions follows. These functions are similar to isalpha() in that their declarations are found in cctype and they return a nonzero int if their conditions are satisfied, or zero if they are not.

isalnum() Returns nonzero if the character is alphanumeric: *0–9*, *A–Z*, or *a–z*.

isalpha() Returns nonzero if the character is alphabetic: *A–Z* or *a–z*.

iscntrl() Returns nonzero if the character is a control code: ASCII 1–31.

isdigit() Returns nonzero if the character is a decimal digit: *0–9*.

isgraph() Returns nonzero if the character is printable, not including space.

islower() Returns nonzero if the character is lowercase: *a–z*.

isprint() Returns nonzero if the character is printable, including space.

ispunct() Returns nonzero if the character is punctuation.

isspace() Returns nonzero if the character is whitespace: space, form feed (\f), newline (\n), return (\r), horizontal tab (\t), or vertical tab (\v).

isupper() Returns nonzero if the character is uppercase: *A–Z*.

isxdigit() Returns nonzero if the character is a hexadecimal digit: *0–9*, *A–F*.

Program 9–9

```cpp
#include <iostream>
#include <cctype>
#include <string>
using namespace std;

int main(void)
{   string str = "mYRnA H. bALthAZaR, III";
    int chr;                                 // Character position in string

    cout << "Before: " << str << endl;
    str[0] = toupper(str[0]);                // Make first character uppercase
    for (chr = 1; chr < str.size(); ++chr)   // Second chr to end of string
       if (str[chr - 1] == ' ')              // Chr after space, uppercase
          str[chr] = toupper(str[chr]);
       else                                  // Not after space, lowercase
          str[chr] = tolower(str[chr]);
    cout << "After : " << str << endl;
    return 0;
}
```

Output

```
Before: mYRnA H. bALthAZaR, III
After : Myrna H. Balthazar, Iii
```

CHARACTER CONVERSIONS

There are two simple functions, `toupper()` and `tolower()`, that convert lowercase characters to uppercase and vice versa. Their forms are:

```
int toupper(int character)                              <cctype>
int tolower(int character)                              <cctype>
```

If the *character* is not alpha, *A–Z* or *a–z*, it will be returned unchanged.

To illustrate both functions let's take a sloppily written name and clean it up by putting it in caps/lowercase in Program 9–9.

mYRnA H. bALthAZaR, III, was a combination of upper- and lowercase letters, as well as punctuation and spaces. All the characters were sent to one function or the other, but `toupper()` changed only the lowercase letters, and `tolower()` changed only the uppercase letters. All the others were returned unchanged. Our trick did not work very well on *III*.

HEADS UP!

Case conversion does not affect nonletters or letters in the proper cases.

YOUR TURN 9–3

1. How do we access single characters of strings?
2. How do we reference the address of a string?
3. Name three functions that convert strings to numbers.
4. At what character does numeric conversion start, and where does it stop?
5. The text introduces 11 functions used to classify characters. Name them and tell which classifications they determine.

6. What is the return value for the classification functions if the character fits the classification? if it doesn't?

7. Which two functions convert a letter between upper- and lowercase?

8. What effect do the conversion functions in 7 have on characters that are nonletters or on letters that are already in the proper case?

PUTTING STRINGS TOGETHER

Suppose that you had a first name, *Mortimer*, and a last name, *Grebble*, in two string variables, and you wanted to put the full name, *Mortimer Grebble*, in one string. You would **concatenate** them—put one at the end of another—with the **concatenation operator**, the plus sign (+).

The value of

```
"Mortimer" + "Grebble"
```

is

```
"MortimerGrebble"
```

We could make it a little cleaner by concatenating a space between the strings.

```
"Mortimer" + " " + "Grebble"
```

is

```
"Mortimer Grebble"
```

HEADS UP!

The plus sign has different meanings.

Mixing data types.

The concatenation operator, +, looks suspiciously like the addition operator, +. It is, of course, the same symbol; C++ determines which operation to use according to the context. If it is between two numbers, C++ adds; between two strings, C++ concatenates. If it is between a string and a number, hopefully your compiler will give you an error message; otherwise you will get some pretty strange results because you cannot combine data types that way.

Program 9–10 shows concatenation in action.

TAKING STRINGS APART

Unlike numbers, each character of a value assigned to a string object is stored as a separate, identifiable entity in main memory. We saw earlier in this chapter that we can access each individual character as a `char` data type using array notation and indexes—*string[2]* and *string[4]* for the third and fifth characters of the *string*. We can also access groups of characters within the string. For example, if we assigned the value *MARTIN* to a string variable, we can refer to any piece of that string, such as *MARTI*, *TIN*, *ART*, or whatever. Such a piece of a string is called a **substring**.

The **substr()** behavior of the `string` object returns pieces of strings.

```
string string.substr(int start, int characters)        <string>
```

Program 9–10

```
#include <iostream>
#include <string>
using namespace std;

int main(void)
{   string city = "Foam Lake", province = "Saskatchewan";
    string location;

    cout << (city + ", " + province + ".") << endl;
    location = city + ", " + province + ", " + "Canada";
    cout << ("Here we are in " + location) << "." << endl;
    return 0;
}
```

Output

```
Foam Lake, Saskatchewan.
Here we are in Foam Lake, Saskatchewan, Canada.
```

Without the optional argument (underlined), the function returns a substring of the *string* object beginning from the *start* character position (where zero is the first position) to the end of the string. With this declaration:

```
string str = "MARTIN";
```

the statement

```
cout << str.substr(3);
```

produces

```
TIN
```

With the second argument, it returns a substring starting from *start* and extending for *characters* characters. The statements

```
cout << str.substr(1, 3) << endl;
cout << str.substr(0, 5) << endl;
cout << str.substr(3, 6) << endl;
```

would produce

```
ART
MARTI
TIN
```

HEADS UP!

The number of characters argument in a substring is unlimited.

TRAP

Using an invalid start argument in a substring.

The third statement specified starting at position 3 and extending for 6 characters. There were not 6 characters in the string from position 3 on, so the function returned characters from position 3 to the end of the string. This is not a problem. But having a *start* position that is beyond the end of the string (6 for *MARTIN*) or a negative *start* or *characters* argument is. Heaven only knows what your C++ compiler will do with those (it varies with the compiler), but it probably will not be pretty!

FINDING STRINGS WITHIN STRINGS

Often we are faced with the task of disassembling a string into component parts, a process referred to as **parsing** a string. Perhaps an input contains several parameters and we must separate them; or we are examining the individual words in a sentence; or a name must be divided into first name, middle initial (if one exists), and last name. To do this we must look for clues that tell us where one part ends and another begins. The first part ends in a space; the second comes before a third, which is enclosed in parentheses; or whatever.

Keep your parsing arguments flexible.

To accomplish this disassembly, we must know what the clues are and have C++ find them for us. The more flexible our algorithm, the more useful it will be. For example, making it immaterial how many spaces there are between parameters allows the program to handle some possibly sloppy parameters.

The **find()** behavior

```
int string.find(string search, int start)                <string>
```

Interpreting the return from `find()` as characters from the start.

returns the position of the first occurrence of the *search* string in the *string* object. If there is a *start* argument, the search for the *search* string starts at the *start* position. The returned result is still the position within the entire *string* object, not the number of characters from the *start* position.

The **rfind()** behavior

```
int string.rfind(string search, int start)                <string>
```

is similar, except that the search starts at the end (right side) of the string and works backward, finding the last occurrence of the *search* string within the *string* object.

Given the declaration

```
string str = "Mississippi";
```

these statements produce the output shown next to them (remember, the first position is position 0).

Statements	Output
```cout << str.find("Miss") << endl;```	0
```cout << str.find("is") << endl;```	1
```cout << str.find("is", 2) << endl;```	4
```cout << str.rfind("is") << endl;```	4
```cout << str.rfind("is", 2) << endl;```	1
```cout << str.find("nuts") << endl;```	-1

The last of the previous statements asked to find *nuts* in *Mississippi*, which, of course, is not there. According to the ANSI standard, the return

Program 9–11

```
#include <iostream>
#include <string>
using namespace std;

int main(void)
{   string location = "Des Moines, Iowa";
    int comma;

    comma = location.find(", ");
    if (comma >= 0 && comma <= location.size() - 1)
        cout << "State: " << location.substr(comma + 2) << "." << endl;
    else
        cout << "There is no \", \" in " << location << "." << endl;
    return 0;
}
```

Output

```
State: Iowa.
```

HEADS UP!

Test for an out-of-range return rather than –1.

should be as presented, –1. Experience has again shown, however, that some C++ vendors have not yet had enough experience with strings. Some C++s return a number that is outside the possible range of indexes for the string object. For the *Mississippi* example, this would be anything less than 0 or greater than 10.

When searching for strings within strings, it is important to know whether the string has been found. Most situations call for a test of the `find()` (or `rfind()`) and a selection structure such as that shown in Program 9–11.

PLUS

OTHER FIND FUNCTIONS

The `find()` and `rfind()` functions find a specific string within another string. But what if you are looking for any one of a number of different characters in a string—a comma, a semicolon, or a colon, for example? We can use one of the following `string` behaviors:

```
int stringObject.findFirstOf(string characters)       <string>
int stringObject.findLastOf(string characters)        <string>
int stringObject.findFirstNotOf(string characters)    <string>
int stringObject.findLastNotOf(string characters)     <string>
```

which will find the first (or last) of any of the `characters` listed.

For example,

```
vowel = str.findFirstOf("AaEeIiOoUu");
```

finds the position of the first vowel.

```
unvowel = str.findFirstNotOf("AaEeIiOoUu");
```

finds the position of anything but a vowel.

All four of these functions may optionally have the second argument of the `find()` function—a `start` position.

Program 9–12

```cpp
#include <iostream>
#include <string>
using namespace std;

int main(void)
{   string name = "Clyde Pringle";
    int space;

    space = name.find(" ");
    if (space >= 0 && space <= name.size() - 1)
    {   name = name.substr(space + 1) + ", " + name.substr(0, space);
        cout << "The restructured name is " << name << "." << endl;
    }
    else
        cout << "Can't work with this name." << endl;
    return 0;
}
```

Output

```
The restructured name is Pringle, Clyde.
```

The test is for `location.size() - 1` because a five-character string—
Hello, for example—will have valid indexes of 0 through 4.

Our work with strings often involves taking a string apart and assembling it in some other way—taking a name such as *Clyde Pringle* and showing it as *Pringle, Clyde*. We can disassemble it using substrings and the `find()` behavior, and reassemble it using concatenation, as in Program 9–12.

YOUR TURN 9–4

1. What is meant by *concatenation* and how do we do it with strings?
2. What is a substring, and how do we reference it in C++?
3. What is parsing, and how do we do it in C++?
4. If a start position is stated in `find()`, is the return value counted from that position or from the beginning of the string?

PUTTING IT TOGETHER

The Flab to Fab Fitness Club keeps height and weight statistics on all its members. The people who type the data into the computer have been directed only to put in the full name, first name first, followed by a colon, the height, a comma, and then the weight. The files are sloppy because everyone inputs the data differently. Some use feet and inches and pounds, others use meters and centimeters and kilograms, some use a combination of the two; some leave spaces, others don't . . . it's a mess.

Set up a mechanism that will keep member information in a consistent form.

There are a few bright spots in this input debacle. The name is always first name first and is always followed by a colon, the height is always followed by a comma, and the weight is always last. Other than that, our program must be able to handle different units of measure and almost anyone's guess as to spacing.

We want our mechanism to keep data in a universal and easy-to-use form. Keeping the names last name first is a commonly accepted form and makes names a lot easier to sort. Being somewhat optimistic, the F. to F. F. C. feels that sometime in the next millennium, the world will standardize on the metric system, so height should be stored in meters and weight in kilograms.

Following are some samples of possible inputs and an indication of how they might be stored in the computer:

Samples

As entered: **Abner Troy Brindle: 6 ft 2 in, 192 lbs**
As stored: Brindle, Abner Troy: 1.88 meters, 87.27 kg.

As entered: **Sheila Shirley Schildkin:1m46cm,115pds**
As stored: Schildkin, Sheila Shirley: 1.46 meters, 52.27 kg.

As entered: **Rocky Q. Flowers: 161 cm, 85 kg**
As stored: Flowers, Rocky Q.: 1.61 meters, 85.00 kg.

For this project we will design a *Person* class from which we may create objects for the members of FlabCo (the staff is not allowed to use this abbreviation in public). Each object must store the name, height, and weight of a person. It must be able to accept entry of those data in various forms and convert them to the standard forms. It should also provide the standard data to other processes using simple access functions.

The entry behavior of the object should determine whether the entry fits the required pattern (we will keep it simple in this example, just finding the colon and the comma) and, if it fits, extract each of these elements, send them to the appropriate adjustment behavior, and assign the result to the stored property of the person.

```
[Entry]
    Get input
    Look for pattern elements
    if pattern correct
        Extract, adjust, and store name
        Extract, adjust, and store height
        Extract, adjust, and store weight
    else
        Display error message
```

Putting It Together **335**

To adjust the name we would have to:

[Adjust name]
    Find dividing point between first and last names
    Build new name with last name first

To adjust the height we would have to:

[Adjust height]
    [Convert first part]
        Find digits
        Find units
        Convert digits according to units
    if any second part, convert it
        Find digits
        Find units
        Convert digits according to units

To adjust the height we would have to:

[Adjust height]
    [Convert first part]
        Find value
        Find units
        Adjust value according to units
    [Add second part]
        Look for digits
        if digits exist
            Find value
            Find units
            Add value according to units

To adjust the weight we would have to:

[Adjust weight]
    Find value
    Find units
    Adjust value according to units

The name, height, and weight properties are isolated from processes outside the object. These properties are set by the entry behavior and provided by access functions.

IMPLEMENTATION

Our real objective in this project is to set up a meaningful *Person* class, so our `main()` function will simply be a driver to create an object of this class, *member*, and will test the class's public behaviors, *entry()*, and the access functions.

In the *entry()* function we will enter the listing using `getline()` and then send the component parts of the input to the proper adjustment functions. The name begins at the beginning of the input and ends at the colon; the height begins there and ends at the comma; and the weight goes from there to the end of the input. First we find the colon and the comma, and then we divide the line with substrings.

The *adjustName()* function finds the dividing point between the first and middle names and the last. That point is the second space in the name.

OBJECT SUMMARY

Name	Behavior	Properties
Person Class		name height weight
Entry	Accept keyboard input of data, adjust them, and assign object properties.	input existence of comma existence of colon height string (pro) weight string (pro)
Adjust Name	Change name from first first to last first.	where last name starts temp name to work with
Adjust Height	Change height from almost any form to meters.	height string (req) position in height string second part of height
Adjust Weight	Change weight from almost any form to meters.	weight string (req) position in weight string

To find the first space, we use the `find()` behavior:

```
name.find(" ")
```

The second space will be after the first, so we can start our search for it at

```
name.find(" ") + 1
```

giving us

```
lastStart = name.find(" ", name.find(" ") + 1);                  // Second space
```

Once we find the second space, we can take a substring consisting of the characters after that—the last name—concatenate a comma to it, and then concatenate a substring consisting of the part of the original string up to the second space—the first and middle names.

In *adjustHeight()* we make use of the `atof()` function and how it skips leading whitespace and converts to the first inappropriate character—either a space or the first character of the units. Because `atof()` does not tell us where it left off, we find the units by starting at the first character of the string and move until the character at *pos* is alpha. The kinds of units we might encounter are such that we only need the units' first character.

The height might have a second part, so we look for more digits beyond the units in the first part. Notice that the search continues only until

```
pos < heightStr.size() - 1
```

the position in the string is one before the end of the string. Fortunately, if there is a digit there will always be at least one more character—units, if nothing else. If we went to the end of the string, the loop would not end until *pos* was beyond the end of the string, and we would send a nonexistent character to `isdigit()` in the second part of the test,

```
!isdigit(heightStr[pos])
```

C++'s reaction to that might crash the program.

Adjusting the weight is similar to adjusting the height, except that there can be no second part. We convert the digits, find the units, and adjust accordingly.

The completed project is shown in Program 9–13.

Testing this program could begin with the sample output we presented in the analysis stage. We should try to think up all possible combinations of names, units, spaces, and whatever else someone might enter, and see if the program works. In this program there are obviously lots of input possibilities we have not accounted for. For example, if someone has no middle name, the process blows up. As you can see, foolproofing inputs can be a programming nightmare!

Program 9–13

```
#include <iostream>
#include <iomanip>
#include <string>
#include <cctype>
#include <cstdlib>
using namespace std;

class Person /////////////////////////////////////////////// Person Class
{   string name;
    double height, weight;

    void adjustName(void)  //***************** First name first to last first
    {   int lastStart;              // Position in name where last name starts
```
n1
```
        lastStart = name.find(" ", name.find(" ") + 1);        // Second space
```
n2
```
        name = name.substr(lastStart + 1) + ", "        // Last name, comma
            + name.substr(0, lastStart);                       // First name
    }
```

h1
```
    void adjustHeight(string &heightStr) //******** Changes height to meters
    {   double height2;                         // For second part of height
        int pos;                                // Current position in string

        //------------------------------- Find value of first part of height
```
h2
```
        height = atof(&heightStr[0]);      // Convert until inappropriate chr

        //------------------------------------------------------- Find units
```
h3
```
        for (pos = 0; !isalpha(heightStr[pos]); ++pos);        // Beg of units
```
h4
```
        heightStr[pos] = toupper(heightStr[pos]);        // First chr needed
```
(Continued)

Program 9–13 *(Continued)*

```
                  //------------------------------- Adjust value according to units
h5        switch (heightStr[pos])                    // Value at heightStr
h6        {  case 'F':                                          // Feet
h7             height *= .3048;
h8             break;
h9          case 'I':                                           // Inches
h10            height /= 39.37;
h11            break;
h12         case 'C':                                        // Centimeters
h13            height /= 100;
          }

          //------------------------------- Add second part of height, if any
            //------------------------------------------------- Find digits
h14        for (++pos;
h15            pos < heightStr.size() - 1 && !isdigit(heightStr[pos]);
h16            ++pos); // Move until digit found or at end of string
h17        if (pos < heightStr.size() - 1)        // If there is a next digit
h18        {  height2 = atof(&heightStr[pos]);     // Convert until inapp. chr

            //------------------------------------------------- Find units
h19         for (++pos; !isalpha(heightStr[pos]); ++pos);   // Beg of units
h20         heightStr[pos] = toupper(heightStr[pos]);   // First chr needed

            //-------------------------- Adjust value according to units
h21         switch (heightStr[pos])                  // Value at heightStr
h22         {  case 'I':                                      // Inches
h23             height += height2 / 39.37;
h24             break;
h25           case 'C':                                     // Centimeters
h26             height += height2 / 100;
            }
          }
        }

w1      void adjustWeight(string &weightStr) //*********** Changes weight to kg
        {  int pos;                          // Current position in string

          //----------------------------------------------------- Find value
w2        weight = atof(&weightStr[0]);        // Convert until inappropriate chr

          //----------------------------------------------------- Find units
w3        for (pos = 0; !isalpha(weightStr[pos]); ++pos);        // Beg of units
          weightStr[pos] = toupper(weightStr[pos]);      // First chr neeeded

          //------------------------------- Adjust value according to units
w4        if (weightStr[pos] == 'L' || weightStr[pos] == 'P')        // If pounds
w5          weight /= 2.2;
        }
```

(Continued)

Program 9–13 *(Continued)*

```cpp
   public:
      void entry(void)  //***************************** Enter a Member Listing
e1    {  string input;
         int colon, comma;              // Positions of colon and comma in input

         cout << "Enter listing: ";
e2       getline(cin, input, '\n');                      // Input entire line
e3       colon = input.find(":");
e4       comma = input.find(",");
e5       if (colon >= 0 && colon < input.size()          // Colon exists
             && comma >= 0 && comma < input.size())      // Comma exists
e6       {  name = input.substr(0, colon);
e7          adjustName();
e8          adjustHeight(input.substr(colon + 1, comma - colon - 1));
e9          adjustWeight(input.substr(comma + 1));
         }
         else
e10      {  cout << "Input could not be decoded." << endl;
e11         exit(EXIT_FAILURE);
         }
      }

      //******************************************************* Access Functions
      string getName(void) { return name; }
      double getHeight(void) { return height; }
      double getWeight(void) { return weight; }
   };                                         // Don't forget this semicolon!

   int main(void) ///////////////////////////////////////////// Main Program
1  {  Person member;

2     member.entry();
      cout << setiosflags(ios::fixed) << setprecision(2);
3     cout << member.getName() << ": " << member.getHeight() << " meters, "
           << member.getWeight() << " kg." << endl;
      return 0;
   }
```

Outputs

```
   Enter listing: Abner Troy Brindle: 6 ft 2 in, 192 lbs
   Brindle, Abner Troy: 1.88 meters, 87.27 kg.

   Enter listing: Sheila Shirley Schildkin:1m46cm,115pds
   Schildkin, Sheila Shirley: 1.46 meters, 52.27 kg.

   Enter listing: Rocky Q. Flowers: 161 cm, 85 kg
   Flowers, Rocky Q.: 1.61 meters, 85.00 kg.
```

EXECUTION CHART

Line	Explanation	member. name	member. height	member. weight			
1	Create *member* object.	(??.......)	(??)	(??)			
2	Call *entry()* behavior.	(??.......)	(??)	(??)			
	member.entry():				*input*	*colon*	*comma*
e1	Declare empty string.	??.......	??	??	....	--	--
e2	Input line: Abner Troy Brindle: 6 ft 2 in, 192 lbs	??.......	??	??	Abner ...	??	??
e3,4	Find colon and comma.	??.......	??	??	Abner ...	18	29
e5	Colon and comma are within string.	??.......	??	??	Abner ...	18	29
e6	Assign first 18 chrs to *name*.	Abner Troy Brindle	??	??	Abner ...	18	29
e7	Call *adjust.name()*.	Abner Troy Brindle	??	??	Abner ...	18	29
	member.adjustName():				*lastStart*		
n1	Find second space beginning one after first space (5).	Abner Troy Brindle	??	??	10		
n2	Build new string with end of *name* + ', ' + beginning of name.	Brindle, Abner Troy	??	??	10		
	member.entry():				*input*	*colon*	*comma*
e8	Call *adjustHeight()*; send portion of *input* between colon and comma.	Brindle, Abner Troy	??	??	Abner ...	18	29
	member.adjustHeight():				*heightStr*	*pos*	*ht2*
h1	Initialize *heightStr*.	Brindle, Abner Troy	??	??	6 ft 2 in	--	--
h2	Skip initial space; convert to space.	Brindle, Abner Troy	6	??	6 ft 2 in	??	??
h3	Move *pos* until at alpha character.	Brindle, Abner Troy	6	??	6 ft 2 in	3	??
h4	Shift chr there to uppercase.	Brindle, Abner Troy	6	??	6 Ft 2 in	3	??
h5	Find *F* at h6.	Brindle, Abner Troy	6	??	6 Ft 2 in	3	??
h7	Convert height to meters.	Brindle, Abner Troy	1.829	??	6 Ft 2 in	3	??
h8	Exit `switch`.	Brindle, Abner Troy	1.829	??	6 Ft 2 in	3	??
h14	Start 1 beyond last *pos*.	Brindle, Abner Troy	1.829	??	6 Ft 2 in	4	??
h15	Look for digit (as described in text).	Brindle, Abner Troy	1.829	??	6 Ft 2 in	4	??
h16	Go to next *pos*.	Brindle, Abner Troy	1.829	??	6 Ft 2 in	5	??
h15, 16	Continue until digit located.	Brindle, Abner Troy	1.829	??	6 Ft 2 in	6	??
h17	*pos* within *heightStr*.	Brindle, Abner Troy	1.829	??	6 Ft 2 in	6	??
h18	Skip initial space; convert to space.	Brindle, Abner Troy	1.829	??	6 Ft 2 in	6	2
h19	Move *pos* until at alpha character.	Brindle, Abner Troy	1.829	??	6 Ft 2 in	8	2
h20	Shift chr there to uppercase.	Brindle, Abner Troy	1.829	??	6 Ft 2 In	8	2
h21	Find *I* at h22.	Brindle, Abner Troy	1.829	??	6 Ft 2 In	8	2
h23	Convert *height2*; add to *height*.	Brindle, Abner Troy	1.879	??	6 Ft 2 In	8	2
h24	Exit `switch` and function.	Brindle, Abner Troy	1.879	??	6 Ft 2 In	8	2
	member.entry():				*input*	*colon*	*comma*
e9	Send part of *input* beyond comma to *adjustWeight()*.	Brindle, Abner Troy	1.879	??	Abner ...	18	29
	member.adjustWeight():				*weightStr*	*pos*	
w1	Initialize *weightStr*.	Brindle, Abner Troy	1.879	??	192 lbs	--	
w2	Skip initial space; convert to space.	Brindle, Abner Troy	1.879	192	192 lbs	??	
w3	Find alpha, shift to uppercase.	Brindle, Abner Troy	1.879	192	192 Lbs	5	
w4	Character is *L*.	Brindle, Abner Troy	1.879	192	192 Lbs	5	
w5	Convert to kilograms.	Brindle, Abner Troy	1.879	87.273	192 Lbs	5	
	member.entry():				*input*	*colon*	*comma*
e9	Exit function.	Brindle, Abner Troy	1.879	87.273	Abner ...	18	29
	`main():`						
3	Print results using access functions.	(Brindle, Abner ...)	(1.879)	(87.273)			

SUMMARY

- **KEY TERMS** (in order of appearance)

String value	Flush
string	Concatenate
String variable	Concatenation operator
Dynamic allocation	Substring
Size	Parsing
Capacity	

- **NEW FUNCTIONS** (in order of appearance)

(Optional parts shown underscored.)

int *string*.size(void)   <string>
> **Purpose:** Determine number of characters in the *string*.
> **Return:**   Number of characters in the *string*.

int *string*.capacity(void)   <string>
> **Purpose:** Determine capacity of *string* without reallocation.
> **Return:**   Capacity of *string*.

void *string*.resize(int *newSize*)   <string>
> **Purpose:** Shorten or lengthen (with nulls) a *string*.
> **Return:**   None.

void getline(cin, string *string*, char *delimiter*)   <string>
> **Purpose:** Assigns characters from input stream to *string*. Stops at *delimiter*.
> **Return:**   None.

void cin.ignore(int *characters*, char *delimiter*)   <iostream>
> **Purpose:** Passes *characters* in input stream unless *delimiter* reached first.
> **Return:**   None.

double atof(address *character*)   <cstdlib>
> **Purpose:** Convert from address of *character* to double.
> **Return:**   Success: Converted number. Error: Meaningless assignment.

int atoi(address *character*)   <cstdlib>
> **Purpose:** Convert from address of *character* to int.
> **Return:**   Success: Converted number. Error: Meaningless assignment.

long atol(address *character*)   <cstdlib>
> **Purpose:** Convert from address of *character* to long.
> **Return:**   Success: Converted number. Error: Meaningless assignment.

int isalnum(int *character*)   <cctype>
> **Purpose:** Test if *character* is alphanumeric: 0–9, A–Z, or a–z.
> **Return:**   True: Nonzero. False: Zero.

int isalpha(int *character*)   <cctype>
> **Purpose:** Test if *character* is alphabetic: A–Z or a–z.
> **Return:**   True: Nonzero. False: Zero.

int iscntrl(int *character*)   <cctype>
> **Purpose:** Test if *character* is a control code: ASCII 1–31.
> **Return:**   True: Nonzero. False: Zero.

```
int isdigit(int character)                                             <cctype>
     Purpose:  Test if character is a decimal digit: 0–9.
     Return:   True: Nonzero. False: Zero.
int isgraph(int character)                                             <cctype>
     Purpose:  Test if character is printable, not including space.
     Return:   True: Nonzero. False: Zero.
int islower(int character)                                             <cctype>
     Purpose:  Test if character is lowercase: a–z.
     Return:   True: Nonzero. False: Zero.
int isprint(int character)                                            <cctype>
     Purpose:  Test if character is printable, including space.
     Return:   True: Nonzero. False: Zero.
int ispunct(int character)                                            <cctype>
     Purpose:  Test if character is punctuation.
     Return:   True: Nonzero. False: Zero.
int isspace(int character)                                            <cctype>
     Purpose:  Test if character is whitespace: space, \f, \n, \r, \t, or \v.
     Return:   True: Nonzero. False: Zero.
int isupper(int character)                                            <cctype>
     Purpose:  Test if character is uppercase: A–Z.
     Return:   True: Nonzero. False: Zero.
int isxdigit(int character)                                           <cctype>
     Purpose:  Test if character is a hexadecimal digit: 0–9, A–F.
     Return:   True: Nonzero. False: Zero.
int toupper(int character)                                           <cctype>
     Purpose:  Convert lowercase character to upper.
     Return:   If character lowercase letter, uppercase equivalent, otherwise no change.
int tolower(int character)                                           <cctype>
     Purpose:  Convert uppercase character to lower.
     Return:   If character uppercase letter, lowercase equivalent, otherwise no change.
string string.substr(int start, int characters)                     <string>
     Purpose:  Get piece of string from start to end of string or number of characters.
     Return:   string object containing those characters.
int string.find(string search, int start)                           <string>
     Purpose:  Find search characters, beginning at start position, in string.
     Return:   Success: Position of search in string. Failure: Value out of range.
int string.rfind(string search, int start)                          <string>
     Purpose:  Find search characters from end, beginning at start position, in string.
     Return:   Success: Position of search in string. Failure: Value out of range.
```

• CONCEPT REVIEW

- A **string value** is an array of chars in memory. It begins at a particular address and extends to the first null character. A quoted string value represents the address where C++ has chosen to store those characters.

- A character value such as 'A' is a number. A string value such as "A" is a set of character values beginning at an address and stored with a trailing null.

- What we have called **string variables** are really objects of the **string** class. Assignment of these "variables" is done by **dynamic allocation**, a process that can conserve memory space, but that is also less efficient in terms of execution. Most C++s will not reallocate memory space when replacing a string with a shorter one.

- String variables may also be declared by stating the number of a specific character to allocate space for the string.

- The `string` class has a number of behaviors. The `size()` function returns the **size** of the string in characters. The `capacity()` function returns the **capacity** of the string before forced reallocation. The `resize()` function shortens a string from the right, or lengthens it with nulls.

- The `getline()` function allows us to set our own input delimiter. It is commonly used with newline to input an entire line from the keyboard. Using `getline()` after `cin` and the extraction operator is hazardous because that combination leaves the newline in the input stream. We can **flush** the input stream with `cin.ignore()`.

- We can access individual characters of strings using index notation. We can reference the address of a string, or any part of a string, by preceding the individual character with an ampersand.

- The `atof()`, `atoi()`, and `atol()` functions convert characters starting at an address to `double`, `int`, or `long`. The conversion stops at the first inappropriate character for the data type.

- The `isalnum()`, `isalpha()`, `iscntrl()`, `isdigit()`, `isgraph()`, `islower()`, `isprint()`, `ispunct()`, `isspace()`, `isupper()`, and `isxdigit()` functions test characters to determine whether they fit into various classifications.

- The `toupper()` function converts a lowercase alpha character to uppercase; `tolower()` does the opposite.

- Strings may be **concatenated**—one put at the end of another—using the **concatenation operator**, the plus sign. **Substrings** of a string are returned by the `substr()` function. We can **parse** a string using the `find()` and `rfind()` functions to find characters within the strings and then take substrings based on the character positions returned.

• HEADS UP: POINTS OF SPECIAL INTEREST

- String values are really arrays of `chars`.
- String values end in a null character.
- To C++, a string value is an address.
- String variables are really objects of the `string` class.
- For efficiency, many C++s do not reallocate for shorter strings.
- `resize()` may change `capacity()`.
- `getline()` removes, but does not store, the delimiter.
- `getline()` can work with any character as a delimiter.
- `cin` leaves the newline in the stream.
- `getline()` accepts newline as a valid empty string.
- Array notation works with strings.
- Many string functions require addresses.
- Ampersand has different meanings in different contexts.

- Conversion stops at the first inappropriate character.
- Case conversion does not affect nonletters or letters in the proper cases.
- The plus sign has different meanings.
- The number of characters argument in a substring is unlimited.
- Keep your parsing arguments flexible.
- Test for an out-of-range return rather than −1.

· TRAPS: COMMON PROGRAMMING ERRORS

- Using ' ' instead of " ".
- Not flushing the input stream.
- Using the wrong conversion function for the data type.
- Exceeding the limits of a data type.
- Mixing data types.
- Using an invalid start argument in a substring.
- Interpreting the return from find() as characters from the start.

· YOUR TURN ANSWERS

• 9–1

1. There are two major differences between storage of numbers and storage of strings: (1) there is no numeric conversion with strings, and (2) memory space is not fixed—it is allocated according to the number of characters to be stored.

2. A string value and a char array are really the same—contiguous storage of char data types.

3. The difference between 'X' and "X" is that the first is a char—one byte in memory; the second is the address of an array of chars—two bytes, X and \0, in memory.

4. Dynamic allocation allocates memory at the time of assignment, allowing different memory allocations for each assignment.

5. The disadvantage of dynamic allocation is that C++ must find a new place in memory for each assignment.

6. We can initialize a string with a large number of characters so C++ will not have to reallocate memory, but that wastes memory space.

• 9–2

1. The size() is the number of characters stored in the string; the capacity() is the number of characters it can hold without reallocation.

2. resize() shortens or lengthens (with nulls) the stored string. It will cause a reallocation if necessary.

3. The getline() function can use any delimiter, such as newline; cin always treats whitespace as a delimiter.

4. When we follow a cin with a getline(), cin leaves the newline in the input stream. To the getline() function, newline is a valid but empty string.

5. The `ignore()` function, using a high number for the characters argument and newline as the delimiter, will flush the input stream.

● **9–3**

1. We access single string characters by using a `string` behavior that looks just like array index notation.

2. We reference the address of a string with "the address of" (`&`) the first character of the string (`string[0]`)—`&string[0]`.

3. Three functions that convert strings to numbers are `atof()`, which converts strings to `double`s; `atoi()`, which converts to `int`s; and `atol()`, which converts to `long`s.

4. Numeric conversion starts at the character at the address passed to the function and stops at the first inappropriate character for the data type.

5. The 11 functions used to classify characters and the classifications they determine are: `isalnum()`, alphanumeric; `isalpha()`, alphabetic; `iscntrl()`, control code; `isdigit()`, decimal digit; `isgraph()`, printable, not including space; `islower()`, lowercase; `isprint()`, printable, including space; `ispunct()`, punctuation; `isspace()`, whitespace; `isupper()`, uppercase; `isxdigit()`, hexadecimal digit.

6. The return values for the classification functions are nonzero if the character fits the classification and zero if it doesn't.

7. The `toupper()` and `tolower()` functions convert letters between upper- and lowercase.

8. The functions in 7 have no effect on nonletters or on letters that are already in the proper cases.

● **9–4**

1. Concatenation puts one string at the end of another. It is done with the concatenation operator (`+`).

2. A substring is a piece of a string that we can access using the `substr()` function.

3. Parsing is the process of disassembling a string into component parts. In C++ we use the `find()` and `rfind()` functions.

4. The return values of `find()` and `rfind()` always count from the beginning of the string.

EXERCISES

1. Which of the following are correct declarations and initializations for strings?

   a. `string str;`
   b. `string str[5];`
   c. `string str = "Mortimer";`
   d. `string str = (30, "\0");`
   e. `string str = (30, "Mortimer", '\0');`

2. Given this declaration, which will execute without error messages, and which will produce valid data?

```
string s1, s2 = "Rita", s3 = "Al";
a. s1 = s3;
b. s3 = s1;
c. s1 = s2 + 14;
d. s3.size(7);
e. cout << s2.capacity() + 14;
f. s1 = s3.resize(14)
```

3. What problem might be encountered with the following section of code, and how might we fix it?

```
cin >> a_float >> an_int;
getline(cin, a_string, '\n');
```

4. What output will the following program produce?

```cpp
#include <iostream>
#include <string>
#include <cctype>
using namespace std;

int main(void)
{   string s = "Algernon";

    cout << s[2] << endl;
    cout << s.size() << endl;
    cout << s.capacity() << endl;
    cout << s.find('n') << endl;
    cout << s.find('n', 7) << endl;
    cout << s.rfind('n') << endl;
    cout << s.substr(2, 4) << endl;
    cout << (s.substr(5) + "sense") << endl;
    cout << islower(s[2]) << endl;
    s[2] = toupper(s[2]);
    cout << s << endl;
    return 0;
}
```

5. What output will the following program produce?

```cpp
#include <iostream>
#include <cstdlib>
#include <string>
using namespace std;

int main(void)
{   string s = "123.456 and so forth";

    cout << atoi(&s[0]) << endl;
    cout << atof(&s[0]) << endl;
    cout << atoi(&s[3]) << endl;
    cout << atof(&s[3]) << endl;
    cout << atoi(&s[4]) << endl;
    cout << atoi(&s[7]) << endl;
    return 0;
}
```

6. What output will the following program produce?

```
#include <iostream>
#include <string>
using namespace std;

int main(void)
{   string s= "Steven C. Lawlor: Author, Raconteur & Scholar";
    int space;

    cout << s.substr(0, s.find(" ") - 1);
    space = s.find(" ", s.find(" ") + 1);
    cout << " " << s.substr(space + 1, s.find(":") - space - 1) << ",";
    space = s.find(" ", s.find(" ", space + 1) + 1);
    cout << s.substr(space, s.rfind("&") - space - 1) << endl;
    return 0;
}
```

PROGRAMS

1. After giving us functions like `isalpha()` and `islower()`, how could the ANSI C++ committee forget the *isvowel()* function? Redeem them by writing the function to work similarly to the others mentioned. It should return nonzero if the character is a vowel (*a*, *e*, *i*, *o*, or *u*, upper- or lowercase), or zero if it is not a vowel. Test the function in a program that allows both input of a string and single character output of the characters in the string with the vowels highlighted as shown.

Functions and Variables

```
main()                                  isvowel()
  str                                     character
  pos    Character position in string     result
```

Output

Aloysius Washington
`<A>l<O>ys<I><U>s W<A>sh<I>ngt<O>n`

2. In the ASCII code, an uppercase letter has a value 32 less than the corresponding lowercase letter. Write a program that will allow you to input any string and print it entirely in uppercase. The function *caps()* should make the actual changes in the string. Do not use any string functions. The program should stop when just the *Enter* key is pressed.

Functions and Variables

```
main()      caps()
  str         str, index
```

Output

```
Your input? What? It isn't I!
The output: WHAT? IT ISN'T I!
Your input? The cost: $2,345.67.
The output: THE COST: $2,345.67.
Your input?
```

3. Program 2 will work on either an ASCII or an EBCDIC machine, but not on both. Rewrite it using string functions so the same program will work on either machine.

4. Write a program to compare two strings. The program should print out which string is greater or that they are equal.

Variables

```
string1
string2
```

Outputs

```
FIRST STRING ? ABNER          FIRST STRING ? ZELDA
SECOND STRING? CRUMP           SECOND STRING? BEULAH
CRUMP IS GREATER THAN ABNER    ZELDA IS GREATER THAN BEULAH

FIRST STRING ? NORBERT         FIRST STRING ? ROSE
SECOND STRING? Nancy           SECOND STRING? ROSE
Nancy IS GREATER THAN NORBERT  ROSE EQUALS ROSE
```

5. Rewrite Program 4 so it is not case-sensitive. In other words, *NORBERT* should be greater than *Nancy*.

6. Generate 10 random characters in the ASCII range (0 to 127). For each, if it is printable, print it and tell whether it is an upper- or a lowercase character, a decimal digit, or punctuation. If it is not printable, print its ASCII code and whether or not it is a whitespace character.

Sample Output

```
Q us an uppercase character.
<SPACE> is whitespace.
ASCII 18 is not printable.
ASCII 13 is not printable but is whitespace.
6 is a decimal digit.
f is a lowercase character.
```
[and so forth]

7. How many 9s can you depend on in a `double` in your C++? Write a program that keeps adding 9s to a string and, to see if they are accurately held in a `double`, converts the string to a `double` and displays it. Experiment by adjusting the constant *nines* until you find the point at which the string does not match the display.

Variables

```
nines    Number of nines
digits   String
number   String converted to number
count    Loop counter
```

Output (in a typical C++)

```
              9  9
             99  99
            999  999
           9999  9999
          99999  99999
         999999  999999
        9999999  9999999
       99999999  99999999
      999999999  999999999
     9999999999  9999999999
    99999999999  99999999999
   999999999999  999999999999
  9999999999999  9999999999999
 99999999999999  99999999999999
999999999999999  999999999999999
9999999999999999  10000000000000000
```

8. Write a function *wordAnalysis()* that receives a string and counts the number of words and sentences in the string, making these available to the calling function. A word ends in a space (or at the end of the string) and a sentence ends in a period, question mark, or exclamation point. Test the function by sending it a string such as:

```
"What language?  Why, C++ of course!"
```

Functions and Variables

```
main()          wordAnalysis()
 line             line
 words            words
 sentences        sentences
```

Output

```
What language?  Why, C++ of course!
  has 6 words and 2 sentences.
```

9. The Farfel Corporation has made a list of its salespeople and their weekly sales. Create a *SalesPerson* class with behaviors that display the data sorted by either name or sales, depending on your input. Your `main()` function should initialize an array of *SalesPerson*s with the data shown.

Class, Functions, and Partial Variable List   **Data**

```
SalesPerson                          Jones   8604
 name                                Smith   3716
 sales                               Brown   7071
 display()                           Hill    12336
   Choose appropriate variables      Green   5004
```

Outputs

```
Sort by? name           Sort by? sales
Brown      7071         Hill       12336
Green      5004         Jones      8604
Hill       12336        Brown      7071
Jones      8604         Green      5004
Smith      3716         Smith      3716
```

10. A company is writing form letters to a list of people. Each listing has a last name, a first name, and sometimes a middle initial. Variations of the name will appear in three places. The envelope will have the first initial and last name, the heading in the letter will have the full name (first name first), and the greeting will have only the first name. Write a program to input a name into an object and call object behaviors that will return it in each of three forms. All the display should be done from main().

Class, Functions, and Partial Variable List

```
Person
 name                Name input
 references()
  space1             Location of the first space
  space2             Location of second reference point (second space or the
                     end of the string plus one)
 envelope()          Return name for envelope
 heading()           Return name for heading
 greeting()          Return name for greeting
```

Sample Outputs

```
Name: Vanderklunk Ophelia T.
      O. Vanderklunk
      Ophelia T. Vanderklunk
      Ophelia

Name: Nisblinger Ted
      T. Nisblinger
      Ted Nisblinger
      Ted

Name: Phurd Agnes Q.
      A. Phurd
      Agnes Q. Phurd
      Agnes
```

Chapter 10

FILES

PREVIEW

Data that we want to store permanently must be kept in files in secondary storage. After reading this chapter, you should have a working understanding of:

- How files are identified, and how we work with sections of them at a time.
- How C++ establishes its connection between a program and a file.
- Working with files using human-readable characters.
- Putting data in a file and retrieving data from a file.
- Keeping track of the program's position in a file.

Most of computing is manipulating data—often large volumes of data. These data must be stored permanently, be called up when needed, have changes made to them, be stored again, and so forth. We have, of course, used data in our previous programs. Typically we have entered them with the keyboard, processed them, and output them on the screen. Because of the nature of main memory, the data were temporary. Now we will look at the permanent retention of data in secondary storage.

Anything kept in secondary storage is considered by the operating system to be a **file**. We often separate files into two categories, program files and data files. To C++ it makes no difference; both are collections of bytes stored on disk. To us, though, the category will probably determine how we organize and access the files. The concentration here will be on data files, although the same rules and techniques apply to everything in secondary storage.

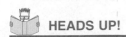

HEADS UP!

To C++ files are simply bytes in secondary storage.

FILE IDENTIFIERS

Every block of data in secondary storage must have a unique identifier. We can't just ask the computer, "Remember that stuff I put on the disk last week?" Different operating systems have different rules for file identifiers. We will look at some general rules that will work with most systems, but you will have to get the particulars from the documentation for your own operating system.

In most operating systems a file identifier can consist of a name and an extension. The **name** usually can be at least eight characters long, and if you stick with the alpha (*A* through *Z*) and numeric (*0* through *9*) characters, you should be safe. (Many operating systems now allow "long file names" that can even include spaces, but the rules given here will still work.) Some operating systems are case-sensitive; some are not. For example, UNIX treats an uppercase *A* as a different character from a lowercase *a*, whereas DOS and Windows do not. Your file might have a name like *PAYROLL* or *lt930412*.

An **extension** is typically up to three characters of the same kinds as those allowable in a name. Extensions are often used to group files together in categories. C++ program source files usually have the extension *CPP*; executable programs often have *EXE* or *COM* (for "command"). All of a company's payroll files might have the extension *PAY* and its employee files *EMP*. Extensions are not usually required, but if they exist, they follow the name and are separated from it by a dot (.). Here are some typical file identifiers:

HEADS UP!

Is your operating system case-sensitive?

PROGRAM.CPP	0396Actg.Qtr
PROGRAM.EXE	X
a.out	Agnes.WHO

In addition to the identifier, most operating systems allow their secondary storage to be divided into logical storage areas called folders or directories and subdirectories. To work with such a system, we must give the system not only the identifier but also a **path** to follow to find its way to the proper folder, directory, or subdirectory. In our directions to C++ we can give not only the file identifiers but also the path directions if they are required or allowed in the operating system.

FIGURE 10–1
File Buffer

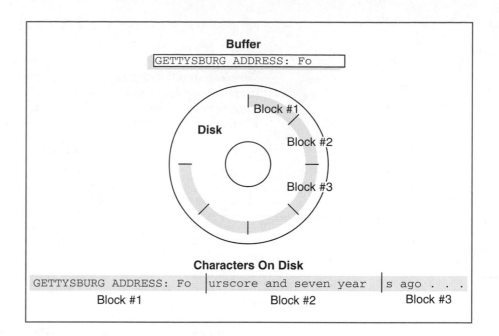

BUFFERED INPUT AND OUTPUT

As we saw in Chapter 1, we cannot access secondary storage a single byte at a time, only in blocks of bytes—perhaps hundreds or thousands of bytes per block. Our program, however, has to work with single bytes. The solution to this apparent contradiction is to bring a block of bytes into main memory, where we can access each byte separately. We call the area in main memory where we temporarily store a block a **buffer**, as illustrated in Figure 10–1.

To access the bytes in a disk block, that particular block must be copied into a buffer in main memory. If our next access takes us into another disk block, the first one is written back to secondary storage and the new one copied into the buffer. We may do the buffering process ourselves, but ANSI C++ has a number of functions that set up and use a file **stream**—a connection to the file that handles buffering. This makes the buffering "transparent" to us—we don't even realize that it is happening. We can access the file as if we are calling for bytes from a continuous collection of them on the disk. With the help of the operating system, C++ keeps track of the byte position in the disk file by maintaining the **file position**, and automatically moves things in and out of buffers when it needs to.

 **HEADS UP!**

File buffering should be transparent to us.

OPENING FILES

To use a file, we must ask C++ to establish a stream and then connect the stream to that particular file. The file stream is an object of the **fstream** class, so our first operation is to declare an fstream object:

```
fstream stream;                                    <fstream>
```

(The previous name for fstream was fstream.h.)

For example, if we were going to use a payroll file, we might declare

```
fstream payfile;
```

We can name the `fstream` object almost anything we want to. In fact, at this point we have only established the mechanism to use a file; we have not actually connected it to a specific file.

We connect to a file using the **open()** behavior of `fstream`.

```
void fstream.open(address fileId, int mode)              <fstream>
```

for example,

```
payfile.open("\\acctg\\payroll.d5", ios::in);
```

The *fileId* is the path (if any), file name, and extension (if any) of the file we intend to use. It is given in the form of an address of a set of characters. Remember that anything in quotation marks *is* the address of that set of characters. If we used a string object for the file identifier, the *fileId* in the `open()` function would be the address of the first character of the file identifier:

```
string pay = "\\acctg\\payroll.d5";

payfile.open(&pay[0], ios::in);
```

Notice that for this operating system, the *fileId* in the `open()` function includes backslashes. The actual *fileId* above is really "\acctg\payroll.d5". We used double backslashes in the string to represent a single backslash because the single backslash is the beginning of a special character. The `'\a'`, for example, is the audible alarm—it makes the computer beep!

If for any reason the stream cannot be connected to the file—in other words, the `open()` fails—the stream object is set to zero. Often we want to check for this after an attempt to `open()` a file:

```
if (payfile == 0)
    cout << "File could not be opened." << endl;
else
    whatever
```

Because the value zero is considered false in C++, we usually substitute

```
if ( !payfile)    for    if (payfile == 0)
```

File Modes

The file *mode* tells C++ how we are going to use the file. It is one or a combination of defined constants that look and work similarly to the flags we used with `setiosflags()`. The available *mode* flags are:

ios::in Opens an existing file with the file position at the beginning of the file. In the absence of further *mode* flags, this file can only be read from (we can get data from the file). If the file does not exist, the stream object is set to zero.

Using a single backslash in a string.

`ios::out` Opens a file with the file position at the beginning of the file. In the absence of further *mode* flags, this file can only be written to (we can put data in the file). If the file does not exist, a new file is created. In most systems (although not part of the standard) `ios::out` alone implies `ios::trunc`—you start with an empty file. If the file cannot be opened or created (no disk space or an invalid path, perhaps), the stream object is set to zero.

`ios::ate` Opens the file with the file position at the end rather than at the beginning of the file.

`ios::app` Ensures that writes are appended to the file, that is, added to the end of the file. This mode will not allow any writes before the original end of the file. In other words, we cannot change anything that was in the file when we opened it.

`ios::trunc` Truncates the file when it is opened. In other words, when the file is opened, everything after the file position is deleted. This would be reasonably used with a mode that placed the file position at the beginning of the file to ensure that, when the file is opened, it is empty. Be careful with this. If you have the secrets of the world on a file and you opened it, for example, with modes `ios::out` and `ios::trunc`, those secrets would be lost.

`ios::binary` States that the file will be interpreted as a binary rather than a text file.

Binary Versus Text Files

Programmed correctly, C++ will work with almost any type of file you can dream up. However, for its own workings it divides files into two types, binary and text, the principal differences being in the line endings in the file and the detection of the end of the file. The mode that we select tells C++ which type we will work with.

Text files, the default type, try to match the internal storage of data in C++ to the typical formatting of text for the operating system being used. The possible adjustments are in the line endings and the end-of-file indications. Internally, C++ stores line endings with the single newline character (\n), typically referred to as a *line feed* (\f, ASCII 10). A text file in UNIX uses the same character at the end of a line, so no change is made when going between main memory and secondary storage.

MS-DOS, Windows, and some other operating systems, however, consider a line ending to be the combination of a return (\r, ASCII 13) and a line feed—a two-character combination. Single-character newlines in main memory, then, are translated into two-character return/line-feed combinations when written to a file, and vice versa when going from a file to main memory. (Whether this is really typical of MS-DOS and Windows text files might be questionable; many DOS and Windows text editors and most word processors use just the line-feed character. It is up to you to find out what is in your files and how to treat them in your programs.)

Some MS-DOS and Windows files use a control-Z character (ASCII 26) as an end-of-file indicator. If this character is encountered in a text file, the

HEADS UP!

Text files differ with different operating systems.

program will get an end-of-file indication. UNIX and many other operating systems (MS-DOS and Windows included) track the end of a file by knowing where the file position is and the number of bytes in the entire file. The control Z is treated like any other character by a UNIX C++ implementation, but it is interpreted as the end of a text file by a C++ for MS-DOS or Windows.

Binary files are the most straightforward. They assume nothing about the operating system and don't make any special adjustments or translations. What is in the program or main memory will be written to the file verbatim, and vice versa. Because text files are the default, we must specify `ios::binary` in the file mode.

What all this really means is that you must know the makeup of the file you are trying to access and whether it fits the standard for your operating system. Many files won't have line endings in them at all, making the difference between the types moot. We will work with these files as binary. In fact, it is always safe to use binary. You can work with the return character (\r) as just another character if it exists at the end of the line.

HEADS UP!

When in doubt, use binary.

Combining File Modes

As in `setiosflags()`, file mode flags can be combined using the pipe symbol (|). Each mode should include either `ios::in` or `ios::out`, or both of them. For example

```
payfile.open("\\acctg\\payroll.d5", ios::in | ios::out);
```

opens a text file that we can both read and write.

```
payfile.open("\\acctg\\payroll.d5", ios::in | ios::out
              | ios::app | ios::binary);
```

opens a binary file that we can read and write, but the writes will always be at the end of the file. We cannot overwrite (replace) data in the file.

CLOSING A FILE

The act of closing a file writes the contents of the current buffer, if it has changed, into the appropriate place in secondary storage, making changes permanent. It also deallocates the memory space for the file buffer and some other space C++ requires to keep track of the file stream. The **close()** function closes a file.

```
void  fstream.close()                                    <fstream>
```

We would close \acctg\payroll.d5 with:

```
payfile.close();
```

Files are automatically closed at a normal program termination, including the execution of an `exit()` function, but they are not closed when the program crashes. An abnormal ending to the program, then, leaves the buffers forgotten in main memory, not updating secondary storage, and possibly losing data.

HEADS UP!

A crash does not automatically close files.

Most programmers are careful to close any file they open as soon as the file is no longer required by the program. The practice saves memory space and prevents possible data loss if something unexpected should happen.

YOUR TURN 10–1

1. What are the rules for file identifiers on your system?
2. What is file buffering?
3. What is a file stream?
4. What does the declaration of an `fstream` object do?
5. Name the behavior that attaches a file to an `fstream` object.
6. Which file modes work with existing files? Which create new files?
7. Which file modes allow read access and which allow write?
8. What is the difference between binary and text files?
9. What does closing a file do and what function does it serve?

CHARACTER ACCESS TO FILES

We will look at two different ways of accessing files. One, **character access** (or *formatted access*), reads and writes files much as we did with the keyboard and the screen—strictly in characters. If we printed a floating-point number, for example, we used `cout` to convert the E-notation storage into the characters that represent its value. The second is **byte access** (or *unformatted* or *binary*), in which we store sets of bytes on the file without regard to what they represent. The E-notation floating-point number, for example, would be copied from its location in memory and written to the file in exactly the same form—virtually unreadable to humans using a text editor. We assume, however, that when we read it back from the file, our program will again store it in a floating-point variable so it makes sense to C++.

Writing Characters to Files

We have used the `cout` object to display characters on the screen, which, as far as C++ is concerned, is simply an output stream. Whatever we can do with the `cout` object, we can do with an `fstream` object. For example,

```
cout << "Hello world!\n";
```

displays *Hello world!* on the screen. Given these statements:

```
fstream file;

file.open("STUFF", ios::out);
```

this,

```
file << "Hello world!\n";
```

puts *Hello world!* in the file *STUFF*.

Program 10–1 accepts any number of inputs from the keyboard and writes them to a file.

Program 10–1

```
#include <iostream>                          // What about the .h?
#include <cstdlib>
#include <string>
#include <fstream>
using namespace std;                         // Do you need this?

int main(void)
{   fstream employee;                        // Create fstream object
    int dependents;
    float payRate;
    string name;

    //----------------------------------------- Go from keyboard to file
    employee.open("c:\\system\\temp\\EMP.DAT", ios::out);
    if ( !employee)                          // Check for error
    {   cout << "Cannot open file" << endl;
        exit(EXIT_FAILURE);
    }

    cout << "Names should be Last, First or <Enter> key to quit.\n";
    cout << "Enter name: ";
    getline(cin, name, '\n');
    while (name.size())                      // Loop while name string not empty
    {   cout << "Enter pay rate, dependents: ";
        cin >> payRate >> dependents;
        cin.ignore(500, '\n');               // Flush input stream
        employee << name << "/" << payRate << "/" << dependents << endl;
        cout << "Enter name: ";
        getline(cin, name, '\n');
    }

    employee.close();
    return 0;
}
```

Output

```
Names should be Last, First or <Enter> key to quit.
Enter name: Quibble, Marvin
Enter pay rate, dependents: 12.34 2
Enter name: Jones, Hatshepset
Enter pay rate, dependents: 9.38 8
Enter name: Montmorrissey, Clyde
Enter pay rate, dependents: 23.98 1
Enter name:
```

File Contents

```
Quibble, Marvin/12.34/2
Jones, Hatshepset/9.38/8
Montmorrissey, Clyde/23.98/1
```

After opening the file we immediately test the *employee* object to see
if the opening was successful. If *employee* is zero there must have been a

problem, so we print the error message and make an orderly exit from the program. The test in the `while` loop checks the size of *name*. If it is zero, false, it means that we pressed only the *Enter* key and the string is empty. Therefore, we would exit the loop.

After inputting *payRate* and *dependents*, we flush the input stream because our input would have left the newline in the stream. Remember, the `getline()` function does not skip whitespace, so it would accept the newline as a valid empty string and not wait for a new input.

When deciding how to put the data in the file, we were careful to think of how we would get data from the file. If the file were simply

```
Quibble, Marvin12.342Jones, Hatshepset9.388Montmorrissey, Clyde23.981
```

we would have a heck of a time separating names from pay rates from dependents. Instead we used delimiters—the specific characters / and newline—to separate the data.

HEADS UP!

When designing a file, think about how you will have to get data from it.

Finding the End of the File

With keyboard input we often set up some sentinel, such as just hitting *Enter* or *Return*, to tell us when to end the process that contains the input. Program 10–1 is a good example of that, where the process of inputting and writing to the file continues

```
while (name.size())      // Loop while name string not empty
```

We can, and often do, put such a sentinel at the end of a file—a character that could not be mistaken for data. More often, however, a file is set up like *EMP.DAT*, which has a number of lines and then just stops.

C++ allows us to make use of such files by setting up a special condition that becomes true when we attempt to read at the end of a file. We can test for this condition using the `fstream` behavior **eof()**,

HEADS UP!

The `eof()` behavior is true only after an attempted read at the end of the file.

```
int fstream.eof(void)                                    <fstream>
```

which returns nonzero, true, if the program has attempted to read while the file position was at the end and zero, false, if it has not. For example,

```
while ( !file.eof())                     // while eof() is false
```

continues the loop until the program *has* attempted to read at the end of the file (eof() is not `false`).

The `eof()` behavior also returns nonzero if a write at the end of the file was unsuccessful. This might happen if the disk was full.

It is important to recognize that `eof()` does not tell you when you are at the end of a file, only when you have attempted an operation at the end of a file. The attempted read must occur before the `eof()` is nonzero. We would not want to set up a loop like this:

TRAP

Thinking `eof()` tells us we are at the end of a file.

```
while ( !file.eof())
{   Read from the file
    Do something with the data
}
```

The last read would be the attempted read at the end of the file, followed by an attempt to do something with the data. What data? We should set up the loop like the classic sentinel-value-controlled loop, where the sentinel, `eof()` becoming nonzero, is tested for immediately after it has the chance of occurring:

```
Read from the file
while ( !file.eof())
{   Do something with the data
    Read from the file
}
```

The end-of-file condition does not go away by itself—even if we move the file position to somewhere within the file. We must specifically get rid of it using the **clear()** behavior for the `fstream` object.

void *fstream*.clear(void)   <fstream>

For example, if we wanted to work with the file connected to *file* again, we could reset its position (we will see how in just a bit) and use

```
file.clear();
```

to reset the end-of-file condition.

Once cleared, the end-of-file condition will not be reset until there is an unsuccessful operation at the end of the file. Do not clear it if you have not moved the position away from the end.

Reading Characters from Files

If an `fstream` object can write to a file, it would make sense that it could also read from a file—and it can. The same things that govern keyboard input with `cin` govern file reading with an `fstream` object. If the *WHAT* file contained *23 Skidoo!*, the following program segment would assign *23* and *Skidoo!* to *number* and *word*.

```
int number;
string word;
fstream file;

file.open("WHAT", ios::in);
file >> number >> word;
```

Inputting Lines from a File

As with `cin`, whitespace is the default delimiter. A more common case, however, is like that in the *EMP.DAT* file, where whitespace is not the desired delimiter. One way to handle such situations is with the `getline()` function, reading an entire line, and then parsing, separating it into its component parts. The function looks and works the same way with file stream as it does with the keyboard stream. For example, to read a newline-delimited set of characters (a line) from the file connected to the *file* stream into the string *str*, we would use

```
getline(file, str, '\n');
```

Let's use this function in Program 10–2, which reads the data from *EMP.DAT* and displays them on the screen.

HEADS UP!

The `eof()` condition must be cleared if we want to use it again.

Clearing `eof` without moving the file position.

Program 10-2

```cpp
#include <iostream>
#include <iomanip>
#include <cstdlib>
#include <string>
#include <fstream>
using namespace std;

int main(void)
{   fstream employee;                                   // Create fstream object
    int dependents;
    float payRate;
    string name;
    string line;                                        // To read line from file
    int slash1, slash2;

    //-------------------------------------------- Go from file to screen
    employee.open("c:\\system\\temp\\EMP.DAT", ios::in);
    if ( !employee)                                     // Check for error
    {   cout << "Cannot open file" << endl;
        exit(EXIT_FAILURE);
    }

    cout << setprecision(2) << setiosflags(ios::fixed);
    cout << "Name                 Pay Rate  Dependents\n";
    getline(employee, line, '\n');
    while ( !employee.eof())                            // Not at end of file
    {   slash1 = line.find("/");                        // Parse line
        slash2 = line.find("/", slash1 + 1);
        name = line.substr(0, slash1);
        payRate = atof(&line[slash1 + 1]);
        dependents = atoi(&line[slash2 + 1]);
        cout << setiosflags(ios::left) << setw(20) << name
             << setiosflags(ios::right) << setw(8) << payRate
             << setw(12) << dependents << endl;
        getline(employee, line, '\n');
    }
    employee.close();
    return 0;
}
```

Output

```
Name                 Pay Rate  Dependents
Quibble, Marvin         12.34           2
Jones, Hatshepset        9.38           8
Montmorrissey, Clyde    23.98           1
```

Let's examine another option for reading the file line using `getline()`. Remember, `getline()` allows us to state any delimiter we want. We know the name ends with a slash, the pay rate also ends with a slash, and the dependents end with a line ending. Let's read a single file line with three `getline()`s, each calling for the appropriate delimiter. Program 10-3 does exactly the same as Program 10-2.

Program 10–3

```cpp
#include <iostream>
#include <iomanip>
#include <cstdlib>
#include <string>
#include <fstream>
using namespace std;

int main(void)
{   fstream employee;                              // Create fstream object
    int dependents;
    float payRate;
    string name;
    string temp;                                   // To read line from file

    //--------------------------------------------- Go from file to screen
    employee.open("c:\\system\\temp\\EMP.DAT", ios::in);
    if ( !employee)                                // Check for error
    {   cout << "Cannot open file" << endl;
        exit(EXIT_FAILURE);
    }

    cout << setprecision(2) << setiosflags(ios::fixed);
    cout << "Name              Pay Rate  Dependents\n";
    getline(employee, name, '/');                           // Read up to slash
    while ( !employee.eof())                                // Not at end of file
    {   getline(employee, temp, '/');                       // Read to next slash
        payRate = atof(&temp[0]);                           // Convert to float
        getline(employee, temp, '\n');                      // Read rest of line
        dependents = atoi(&temp[0]);                        // Convert to int
        cout << setiosflags(ios::left) << setw(20) << name
             << setiosflags(ios::right) << setw(8) << payRate
             << setw(12) << dependents << endl;
        getline(employee, name, '/');                       // Read next name
    }
    employee.close();
    return 0;
}
```

YOUR TURN 10–2

1. What is the difference between character and byte access to files?
2. How is file access similar to cin and cout?
3. Why are delimiters important in a file?
4. How can we tell if we are at the end of a file?
5. Can we use eof() again after moving the position away from the end of a file?
6. What is the file equivalent of getline()?

MOVING THE FILE POSITION

HEADS UP!

A file access always moves
the file position.

The data we want from a file are not always at the beginning. We may have to reach into the middle or go toward the end to get them. One method of moving the file position is by accessing the file. Whenever we read or write, the file position is moved to a position just beyond our last access. However, there are more efficient ways of moving the file position.

The fstream **seekg()** behavior can move the file position anywhere within the file. (The underlined is optional.)

```
void fstream.seekg(long offset, int origin)          <fstream>
```

In its simpler form, the seekg() behavior moves the file position to the *offset* byte position in the file. For example,

```
file.seekg(10);
```

moves the position in the file connected to *file* to the eleventh byte (the first byte, the beginning of the file, is *offset* zero). It is not important where the file position was before the seekg(); after the seekg(), the file position will be the eleventh byte.

TRAP

Attempting to move the file
position out of the bounds of
the file.

What *does* matter, though, is that you move the position to somewhere within the actual file. C++ will not prevent you from forming a statement that would move the position somewhere before the beginning of the file or after the end of the file. The statement certainly will not work properly, but its effects depend on the C++ you are using. Whatever happens will not be pleasant!

In its complete form, seekg() moves the file position *offset* bytes from the *origin* position. The *origin* position is always stated using one of three defined constants:

    ios::beg   The *origin* position is the beginning of the file.

    ios::cur   The *origin* position is the current position in the file.

    ios::end   The *origin* position is the end of the file. Obviously, the *offset* from here must be zero or negative.

The statements below have the following effects:

Statement	Effect
file.seekg(0)	Moves the position to the beginning of the file.
file.seekg(0, ios::beg)	Moves the position to the beginning of the file.
file.seekg(20, ios::cur)	Moves the position forward 20 bytes.
file.seekg(-20, ios::cur)	Moves the position back 20 bytes.
file.seekg(-20, ios::end)	Moves the position 20 bytes from the end of the file.
file.seekg(20, ios::end)	Disaster!

Program 10–4 uses seekg() to simply move the position back to the beginning of the file, but the program illustrates other file techniques. We will look at using seekg() in more sophisticated ways in Chapter 11.

A teacher has a file of questions, *QUIZ.QST*. When a student runs a program with the *giveTest()* function in it, the function administers the test from whatever file is passed to it. The function stores both the questions

QUIZ.QST File

```
What is C++?
How big is a byte?
Who was Babe Ruth?
```

Program 10–4

```cpp
#include <iostream>
#include <cstdlib>
#include <string>
#include <fstream>
using namespace std;

void giveTest(fstream &quest, fstream &ans);
void reviewTest(fstream &ans);

int main(void)
{   fstream questions, answers;

    questions.open("c:\\system\\temp\\QUIZ.QST", ios::in);
    if ( !questions)
    {   cout << "Can't open file of questions." << endl;
        exit(EXIT_FAILURE);
    }
    answers.open("c:\\system\\temp\\QUIZ.ANS",          // Open empty file for
                 ios::in | ios::out | ios::trunc);       // read and write
    if ( !answers)
    {   cout << "Can't open file for answers." << endl;
        exit(EXIT_FAILURE);
    }
    giveTest(questions, answers);
    questions.close();
    answers.seekg(0);
    reviewTest(answers);
    answers.close();
    return 0;
}
```

(Continued)

and the answers in another file, whose `fstream` object is also passed to the function.

The teacher can then run a program with the *reviewTest()* function in it and it will print out the questions and the answers.

The `main()` function in Program 10–4 is a driver to test the functions. It opens *QUIZ.QST* for reading and *QUIZ.ANS* for reading and writing. The `ios::trunc` mode flag assures us that *QUIZ.ANS* will be empty when it is opened. After calling *giveTest()*, `main()` closes *QUIZ.QST*, sets *QUIZ.ANS* back to the beginning, calls *reviewTest()*, and then closes the *QUIZ.ANS* file.

Where Are We?

Often we want to know our current position in a file. C++ tells us if we call the `tellg()` function.

Program 10-4 *(Continued)*

```
void giveTest(fstream &quest, fstream &ans)
{  string question, answer;

   cout << "Answer each question carefully:\n";
   getline(quest, question, '\n');
   while ( !quest.eof())
   {  cout << question << ' ';
      getline(cin, answer, '\n');
      ans << question << ' ' << answer << endl;
      getline(quest, question, '\n');
   }
}

void reviewTest(fstream &ans)
{  string answer;

   cout << "\nHere are this student's wild guesses:\n";
   getline(ans, answer, '\n');
   while ( !ans.eof())
   {  cout << answer << endl;
      getline(ans, answer, '\n');
   }
}
```

Output

```
Answer each question carefully:
What is C++? A grade very close to B.
How big is a byte? No bigger than you can chew.
Who was Babe Ruth? The inventor of a candy bar.

Here are this student's wild guesses:
What is C++? A grade very close to B
How big is a byte? No bigger than you can chew.
Who was Babe Ruth? The inventor of a candy bar.
```

QUIZ.ANS File (After Program)

```
What is C++? A grade very close to B.
How big is a byte? No bigger than you can chew.
Who was Babe Ruth? The inventor of a candy bar.
```

```
long fstream.tellg(void)
```
                                                                    `<fstream>`

For example,

```
position = file.tellg();
```

assigns the current byte position in the file connected to *file* to *position*. If we wanted to return to that position some time later, we could use

```
file.seekg(position);
```

Let's look at Program 10–5, which changes the number of dependents of one of the employees in our *EMP.DAT* file. Here we input the name of a person whose dependents we wish to *change*, but our input may be just

Program 10–5

```cpp
#include <iostream>
#include <iomanip>
#include <cstdlib>
#include <string>
#include <fstream>
using namespace std;

int main(void)
{   fstream employee;                              // Create fstream object
    int dependents;
    float payRate;
    string name, change, temp;
    long currentPosition = 0;              // To save position of last line read

    //------------------------------------------------------------- Open file
    employee.open("EMP.DAT", ios::in | ios::out);
    if ( !employee)                               // Check for error
    {   cout << "Cannot open file" << endl;
        exit(EXIT_FAILURE);
    }
    //------------------------------------------------ Get name to change
    cout << "Whose dependents do you want to change? ";
    getline(cin, change, '\n');

    //----------------------------------------- Search for name in file
    getline(employee, temp, '\n');
    while (temp.substr(0, change.size()) != change       // First chrs match
           && !employee.eof())                           // Or end of file
    {   currentPosition = employee.tellg();              // Beginning of line
        getline(employee, temp, '\n');
    }
    //----------------------------------------- Make change if needed
    if (employee.eof())                           // Hit end of file, no change
    {   cout << "Employee not on file.\n";
        employee.clear();                         // Reset end-of-file condition
    }
    else                                          // Found employee, make change
    {   cout << "New dependents? ";
        cin >> dependents;
        employee.seekg(currentPosition + temp.size() - 1);    // Last byte of
                                                          // previous record
        employee << dependents;                       // Write dependents
    }
```

(Continued)

the first few characters of the name. Then we search through the file, line by line, comparing the characters in the *change* string to the same number of characters at the beginning of each line of the file,

```cpp
temp.substr(0, change.size()) != change
```

We continue the process while they are not equal and we are not at the end of the file,

```cpp
&& !employee.eof()
```

Program 10–5 *(Continued)*

```
        //------------------------------- Go from file to screen (as in 10-3)
        employee.seekg(0);
        cout << setprecision(2) << setiosflags(ios::fixed);
        cout << "Name              Pay Rate  Dependents\n";
        getline(employee, name, '/');             // Read up to slash
        while ( !employee.eof())                  // Not at end of file
        {   getline(employee, temp, '/');         // Read to next slash
            payRate = atof(&temp[0]);             // Convert to float
            getline(employee, temp, '\n');        // Read rest of line
            dependents = atoi(&temp[0]);          // Convert to int
            cout << setiosflags(ios::left) << setw(20) << name
                 << setiosflags(ios::right) << setw(8) << payRate
                 << setw(12) << dependents << endl;
            getline(employee, name, '/');// Read next name
        }
        return 0;
}
```

Output

```
Whose dependents do you want to change? Jones
New dependents? 3
Name                Pay Rate  Dependents
Quibble, Marvin       12.34         2
Jones, Hatshepset      9.38         3
Montmorrissey, Clyde  23.98         1
```

Once out of that loop, we test to see which condition got us out of the loop, and either display *Employee not on file* and reset the end-of-file condition, or make the change in the file. We know where to make the change because before each read from the file, we stored the *currentPosition* in the file. The dependents is always the last character in the line, so we move from that *currentPosition* to the last character, one character less than the size of the line:

```
employee.seekg(currentPosition + line.size() - 1);
```

Let's use this program to take a hard look at reality—there are a number of problems that surface. If there were more than one employee whose name started with *Jones*, this program would stop only at the first. We could fix that by displaying the entire name and asking for confirmation before exiting the search loop.

You may also wonder why, when we have assumed that dependents is the last character of the line, we couldn't move the file position there by stepping back one byte from the current position (where it was left after the last read),

```
employee.seekg( -1, ios::cur);          // Move back one byte
```

This would not take the line ending into account. So move it back two bytes . . . or is it three? Remember, different operating systems use different

line endings. To make our code portable we chose the safe, but more complicated way.

Finally, changing the dependents was an easy operation because that value was always one character. But what if we wanted to change Quibble's dependents to 125 (large family)? That would change the number of characters in that line, overwriting the line ending and resulting in this output:

```
Whose pay rate do you want to change? Qui
New dependents? 125
Name                  Pay Rate  Dependents
Quibble, Marvin         12.34          125
Montmorrissey, Clyde  23.98            1
```

and a file that looks like this (in this operating system, a line ending is return, line feed—two characters):

```
Quibble, Marvin/12.34/125Jones, Hatshepset/9.38/3
Montmorrissey, Clyde/23.98/1
```

Changing the name could cause even larger problems. For example, what if we wanted to change *Jones, Hatshepset* to *Ng, An*? Or the other way around? As you might imagine, the files would be a mess!

A viable solution to that problem is to make everyone's name the same number of characters by **padding** it—adding extra spaces to it. We would also have to do the same for the pay rate and the dependents. Then, if dependents was always four characters, for example, we could set the file position and write

```
employee << setw(4) << dependents;
```

We will look at this technique more fully in Chapter 11, but it has the disadvantage of filling secondary storage with a lot of empty spaces.

We will also look at a technique for changing files, such as *EMP.DAT*, in which not all lines are the same length, but first we must learn some *file housekeeping*.

FILE HOUSEKEEPING

There are a number of little chores that we must perform to keep our files clean and up to date. One of these is deleting files from secondary storage, which we do with the **remove()** function.

```
int remove(address fileId)                                    <cstdio>
```

(The previous name for `cstdio` was `stdio.h`.)

The *fileId* is the file identifier, including any path names necessary to find it in secondary storage. For example, in an MS-DOS system,

```
remove("C:\\RECORDS\\STUDENT.DAT")
```

deletes the file *STUDENT.DAT* from the *RECORDS* folder on the *C* disk. Or, if that path was in the `string` variable *path*,

```
remove(&path[0])   // Use the address of the first character
```

UNIX does not typically use the `remove()` function, because a single file in that system can be referenced in several directories via links to the file. These UNIX systems use the related function, **unlink()**,

```
int unlink(address fileId)                                    <cstdio>
```

which removes the file from the directory. For example,

```
unlink("/records/student.dat")        // Assumes file id was actually lowercase
```

When there are no more surviving links to the file, the file will actually be removed.

The file must exist to be deleted, and it must not be open. A successful deletion returns zero. The return is nonzero otherwise.

We can change the name of a file in secondary storage with the **rename()** function.

```
int rename(address oldId, address newId)                       <cstdio>
```

This function will change the *oldId* to the *newId*. The *oldId* file must exist and must not be open, and there may not already be a file in the current folder or directory with the *newId*.

```
rename("STUFF", "JUNK")
```

will rename the file *STUFF* in the default directory to *JUNK*.

As in `remove()`, full path names may be included, and a successful operation returns zero, whereas a nonzero indicates failure.

TRAP

Attempting to remove a file that is open.

YOUR TURN 10–3

1. What function moves the file position? How can we move the position to the beginning of the file.

2. Name the defined constants for the `seekg()` *origin* for the beginning, the current position, and the end of the file.

3. Can the file position be moved before the file's beginning or after its end?

4. What function returns the current file position?

5. How can we delete a file from secondary storage?

6. What function changes the name of a file in secondary storage?

CHANGING FILES

As promised, we will now write another function to Program 10–4, the quiz program, that makes changes in *QUIZ.QST*, a file with variable-length records. Because we cannot simply write over the record we want to change, we must copy the data from one file to another, making changes as we copy.

FIGURE 10–2
Changing Files

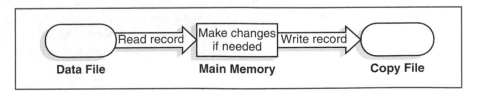

Program 10–6

```cpp
#include <iostream>
#include <string>
#include <fstream>
#include <cctype>
#include <cstdio>
using namespace std;

void changeQuiz(string qstFile);                        // Changes Quiz File

int main(void)
{
    changeQuiz("QUIZ.QST");
    return 0;
}

void changeQuiz(string qstFile) //*********************** Changes Quiz File
{   fstream quest, temp;                        // Temporary file to copy to
    string question;
    char answer;

    quest.open(&qstFile[0], ios::in);                    // Open original file
    if ( !quest)
        cout <<"Could not open file, no changes made." << endl;
    else
    {   temp.open("TEMP.$TM", ios::out);                 // Open temporary file
        cout << "Which question do you want to change?\n";
        getline(quest, question, '\n');             // Read from original
        while ( !quest.eof())                   // Until end of original file
        {   cout << question << " (Y/N)? ";
            cin >> answer;
            cin.ignore(500, '\n');                       // Flush stream
            if (toupper(answer) == 'Y')         // Anything starting with Y or y
            {   cout << "New question: ";
                getline(cin, question, '\n');
            }
            temp << question << endl;     // Write to temporary, changed or not
            getline(quest, question, '\n');              // Read from original
        }
        quest.close();
        temp.close();
        remove(&qstFile[0]);             // unlink(&qstFile[0]); in a UNIX system
        rename("TEMP.$TM", &qstFile[0]);
    }
}
```

HEADS UP!

Changing files with variable-length records requires copying from one file to another.

We will need two files, then—the original and another to which to copy the data. As shown in Figure 10–2, copying involves reading the data, one record at a time, into variables in main memory and then writing the values of those variables to the other file. While the data for a record are in main memory we can examine them to see if we want to make a change.

QUIZ.QST File Before

```
What is C++?
How big is a byte?
Who was Babe Ruth?
```

Output

```
Which question do you want to change?
What is C++? (Y/N)? n
How big is a byte? (Y/N)? y
New question: How many bits in a nybble?
Who was Babe Ruth? (Y/N)? n
```

QUIZ.QST File After

```
What is C++?
How many bits in a nybble?
Who was Babe Ruth?
```

HEADS UP!

Put the original name on the changed file.

In Program 10–6 we set up a function *changeQuiz()* and pass it the name of the file to change. It sets up a temporary file and makes needed changes as it copies. Before it returns, the function gets rid of the original file and changes the name of the temporary file to the original name.

Deleting from a File

The method for deleting data from a file is similar to that for changing a file. You will see that Program 10–7, which deletes a question from the *QUIZ.QST* file, is similar to Program 10–6. To delete data, we simply do not write them to the temporary file; all other data are written.

Adding to a File

HEADS UP!

Adding to the end of a file requires no copying.

There are any number of ways to add data to a file. We can add data to the beginning, somewhere in the middle, or at the end. The first two situations require copying a file, as we did in changing it. The third, adding at the end, is the easiest; we open the file with the position at the end and write the new data there—one file, no copying. Program 10–8 shows that method, and an example of the more complicated addition is contained in the *Putting It Together* section at the end of this chapter.

YOUR TURN 10–4

1. How do we change files that have variable-length records?
2. How do we delete data from a file?
3. How do we add data to a file?

Program 10–7

```cpp
#include <iostream>
#include <string>
#include <fstream>
#include <cctype>
#include <cstdio>
using namespace std;

void deleteQuiz(string qstFile);            // Deletes Question from Quiz File

int main(void)
{
   deleteQuiz("QUIZ.QST");
   return 0;
}

void deleteQuiz(string qstFile) //********* Deletes Question from Quiz File
{  fstream quest, temp;                         // Temporary file to copy to
   string question;
   char answer;

   quest.open(&qstFile[0], ios::in);                    // Open original file
   if ( !quest)
      cout <<"Could not open file, no changes made." << endl;
   else
   {  temp.open("TEMP.$TM", ios::out);                 // Open temporary file
      cout << "Which question do you want to delete?\n";
      getline(quest, question, '\n');                   // Read from original
      while ( !quest.eof())                       // Until end of original file
      {  cout << question << " (Y/N)? ";
         cin >> answer;
         cin.ignore(500, '\n');                             // Flush stream
         if (toupper(answer) != 'Y')   // Anything not starting with Y or y
            temp << question << endl;                // Write to temporary
         getline(quest, question, '\n');            // Read from original
      }
      quest.close();
      temp.close();
      remove(&qstFile[0]);            // unlink(&qstFile[0]); in a UNIX system
      rename("TEMP.$TM", &qstFile[0]);
   }
}
```

Output

```
Which question do you want to delete?
What is C++? (Y/N)? n
How many bits in a nybble? (Y/N)? y
Who was Babe Ruth? (Y/N)? n
```

QUIZ.QST File After

```
What is C++?
Who was Babe Ruth?
```

Program 10–8

```cpp
#include <iostream>
#include <string>
#include <fstream>
#include <cstdio>
using namespace std;

void addQuiz(string qstFile);                               // Adds to Quiz File

int main(void)
{
    addQuiz("QUIZ.QST");
    return 0;
}

void addQuiz(string qstFile) //*************************** Adds to Quiz File
{   fstream quest;                                   // Only original file
    string question;

    quest.open(&qstFile[0], ios::out | ios::app);        // Open original file
    if ( !quest)
        cout <<"Could not open file, no changes made." << endl;
    else
    {   cout << "New question: ";
        getline(cin, question, '\n');
        quest << question << endl;                   // Write at end of file
    }
    quest.close();
}
```

Output

New question: **Compare video games and virtual unreality.**

QUIZ.QST File After

```
What is C++?
Who was Babe Ruth?
Compare video games and virtual unreality.
```

PUTTING IT TOGETHER

Sheldon Diefendorfer has an immense collection of movies on videotape. Right now they are stored on shelves in no particular order, and whenever Shelly wants to watch a video, it takes him an hour to locate the tape. While Shelly's tastes in movies may be a little strange, he's basically a nice guy and has done some favors for us in the past, so we volunteered our computer expertise to help him out.

Develop a cataloging system to help Shelly keep track of and locate his videos on the shelves.

Shelly has some specific data requirements for his video collection. For each movie, he wants to keep track of the title, the year it was released, the length, and its position on his shelves. His shelf positions are labeled from 1 to 5,000 (he will have to add more soon).

He needs total flexibility with the system to allow him to make any type of change to his video file. We propose that the program start off with a menu of choices like this:

```
Do you want to:          Change:
  [A]dd a video?           A [T]itle?
  [D]elete a video?        A [Y]ear?
  [P]rint the list?        A [L]ength?
  [Q]uit?                  A [S]helf position?
Take your pick:
```

He would type in the bracketed letter, in caps or lowercase, to make his choice.

The [P]rint option would display the data on the file in the following form:

```
YEAR    LEN SHELF    TITLE
####    ##  ####     The complete title
```

The length is in minutes, and the title was put last because its number of characters can vary greatly and the columns would look neater that way. The listing is alphabetically by title.

To add a video, Shelly would type in the title, date, length, and shelf position, and the program would put it in its proper place in the file. The dialog would be as follows:

```
New title: Killer Tomatoes Strike Back
Year, length, shelf position: 1990 88 4180
```

To delete a video, he would type in a few of the first characters of the title; the computer would find the first match and ask for confirmation before deleting. If he responded that he did not want to delete, the computer would find each subsequent match until either he responded that he did want to delete or the computer ran out of matches, in which case no deletions would be made. That dialog might be as follows:

```
Delete title: Frank
Delete Frankenstein? n
Delete Frankenstein Meets the Space Monster? y
```

He should be able to change any part of any record. The change dialog would be similar. The computer asks for confirmation on the title, prints out the current value, and waits for the new value. For example, changing the shelf position of a video might look like this:

```
Change position of title: R
Change Rock'N'Roll High School Forever? y
Change 2615 to: 4403
```

Normally these steps would be done in order—the entire design completed before coding and testing—but because the program, Program 10–9, is designed with an object with distinct, encapsulated behaviors, we will look at the three processes for each behavior. We hope this will save you, the reader, a lot of page flipping.

The one factor that is consistent within all the behaviors is the format of the file—all the functions have to work with the same data file. In designing this file, two factors are of prime importance. First, the printouts should be in alphabetical order by title, so we will maintain the file in the same order. Second, Sheldon has spent a fortune on videotapes, and therefore cannot afford much in the way of floppy disks, so storage space must be kept to a minimum.

As we shall see when we look at record-based data in Chapter 11, having files with fixed-length records offers many advantages. One disadvantage, however, is typically a lot of wasted space on the file to make the records even. For example, consider *Hud* and *Incredibly Strange Creatures Who Stopped Living and Became Mixed-Up Zombies, The.* (Yes, it's a real movie! In fact, it was later released as *Teenage Psycho Meets Bloody Mary*, maybe because the first name was too long.) Each title would have to be at least 81 characters, meaning that we would have to pad *Hud* with 78 trailing blanks or nulls—a tremendous waste of file space. Therefore, we will make our file with unequal length records. *Hud* will be stored with just three characters followed by some delimiter to show where the title ends.

The choice of delimiter characters is important. It obviously cannot be a character that might be part of the data. Space is usually the most obvious delimiter, especially because it is the default delimiter for input stream objects such as `cin`. However, video titles usually have spaces in them. Shelly assures us that none of his video titles include a pipe symbol (|), so we will use that to delimit the title. The numbers—year, length, and shelf

OBJECT SUMMARY		
Name	**Behavior**	**Properties**
Movies Class		title data[year] data[length] data[shelf]
Write Movie	Write one object to file.	File (req)
Read Movie	Read one listing from file into object.	File (req) Success or failure (pro)
Constructor	Initialize title string.	
Print File	Displays the video file.	
Add	Adds a listing in alphabetical order to the file.	
Delete	Deletes a listing from the file.	
Change	Changes the title, year, length, or shelf position of a listing in the file.	
New File	Creates a videos file for testing purposes.	

position—will not have spaces within them, so space is an ideal delimiter for them. The entire listing will end in a newline.

A sample file might look like this:

```
Blob, The|1958 95 4265
Cannibal Women in the Avocado Jungle of Death|1988 90 3328
Frankenstein Meets the Space Monster|1965 75 1005
Rock'N'Roll High School Forever|1990 94 2615
```

The *Movies* Class

DESIGN

Each video is treated as an object in the program, with properties common to the entire object, and behaviors that affect the properties. Some of these behaviors affect not just a single video, one *Movies* object, but the entire collection of objects, the whole file. These behaviors are integral in handling *Movies* objects, so they are included in the *Movies* class and called through an object of the *Movies* class. In addition to keeping all the functions dealing with *Movies* together, this technique allows us to set up and access `private` member functions to isolate some critical behaviors.

The properties for an object are the title of the video, a `string`, and three numbers: the year the movie was made, its length in minutes, and its shelf position. These last three values will all fit within `short` variables, so we store them in an array of `shorts` and assign the constants *year*, *length*, and *shelf* as the indexes (0, 1, and 2) for the array.

We will look at the object summary for the *movie* class, including two of its behaviors in detail. We mention its other behaviors, but will discuss them in detail later.

Many of the behaviors either write a listing to a file or read a listing from a file. These behaviors can be `private`, because only *Movies* member functions access them. To write a *Movies* object to a file, we must

> State which file
> Write title, year, length, and shelf position

To read a movie from a file to a *Movies* object, we must:

> State which file
> Read title line
> if read successful
> > Read year, length, and shelf position
> > Return true
> else
> > Return false

The return of true or false will tell the process that uses the function whether it has reached the end of the file.

IMPLEMENTATION

Along with the object properties and the behaviors mentioned, Class *Movies* shows the beginning of the program code, including the `#includes`, and `const` declarations.

Class *Movies*

```
        #include <iostream>
        #include <iomanip>
        #include <cstdio>
        #include <cstdlib>
        #include <string>
        #include <cctype>
        #include <fstream>
        using namespace std;

        const int items = 3;              // Number of data items kept for each video
                                          // Indexes for data array for each video
           const short year = 0;                          // movie.data[0] is year
           const short length = 1;                                  // In minutes
           const short shelf = 2;                         // Position on the shelves

        class Movies ///////////////////////////////////////////////// Movies Class
        {   string title;
            short data[items];                   // Year, length, and shelf position

w1          void writeMovie(fstream &video) //********* Writes Single Movie to File
w2          {   video << title << '|' << data[year] << ' ' << data[length] << ' '
                    << data[shelf] << endl;
            }
r1          bool readMovie(fstream &video) //********* Reads Single Movie From File
r2          {   getline(video, title, '|');
r3              if ( !video.eof())                                  // Not at end of file
r4              {   video >> data[year] >> data[length] >> data[shelf];
r5                  video.ignore(500, '\n');              // Dump trailing newline
r6                  return true;
                }
                else
r7                  return false;
            }
        public:
            void printFile(void) //****************** Displays the Data in the File
            void add(void) //***************************** Adds a Record in Order
            void del(void) //*********************** Deletes a Record from the File
            void change(int index) //********************* Changes Part of a Record
            void newFile(void) //************* Creates New File for Testing Purposes
        };
```

TEST

It would be difficult to test this section of the program without writing some of the subsequent program. Therefore, we will defer actual testing for now, but we will show the execution charts for the *writeMovie()* and *readMovie()* functions. Each function must be passed a reference to an `fstream` object connected to an open file. The *readMovie()* function returns a boolean value of `true` if the read was successful or `false` if not (the end of the file was encountered, for example). The *writeMovie()* function assumes that the write will be successful.

We show *writeMovie()* writing *The Blob* to the file *VIDEOS.DAT* and *readMovie()* reading *The Blob* from the file *VIDEOS.DAT*.

EXECUTION CHART — *writeMovie()*

Line	Explanation	movie.title	movie.data[]		
w1	Receive reference to open file *VIDEOS.DAT.*	Blob, The	1958	95	4265
w2	Write *title*, pipe, and data followed by newline to file.	Blob, The	1958	95	4265

EXECUTION CHART — *readMovie()*

Line	Explanation	movie.title	movie.data[]		
r1	Receive reference to open file *VIDEOS.DAT.*	??	??	??	??
r2	Read *title* up to pipe from file.	Blob, The	??	??	??
r3	Not at end of file.	Blob, The	??	??	??
r4	Read three numeric values into *data* array.	Blob, The	1958	95	4265
r5	Flush input stream.	Blob, The	1958	95	4265

Creating a File for Testing

DESIGN

Before releasing this program to Shelly we want to test it thoroughly, so we will create a dummy file for testing. Our file-creation segment starts by opening the *VIDEO.DAT* file. Then, four times it assigns values to the *Movies* properties and calls *writeMovie()*. Finally, it closes the file.

IMPLEMENTATION

Function *newFile()* shows the code.

TEST

Line 1 in `main()` calls the *newFile()* function for the *Movies* object *movie.*

```
1    // movie.newFile();          // Used only for the first run of the test
```

The line is shown in its normal condition, that is, "commented out." We have put a double slash (//) at the beginning of the line so it won't compile. If we want to create a new file for testing, we can remove the slashes at the beginning, recompile, and run the program.

The *movie* object has no value, it is simply a vehicle for accessing the *Movies* member function, which will assign values and write them to the file.

We can see whether the function works by looking at the resulting file with a word processor or text editor—the editor you use to write your C++ programs would probably be appropriate. This file should be similar to our design, with the title, a pipe, number, space, number, space, number, and line end for each listing.

Function *newFile()*

```
        void newFile(void) //************* Creates new File for Testing Purposes
        {  fstream video;
n1          video.open("VIDEOS.DAT", ios::out | ios::binary);
n2          title = "Blob, The";
n3              data[year] = 1958; data[length] = 95; data[shelf] = 4265;
n4              writeMovie(video);
n5          title = "Cannibal Women in the Avocado Jungle of Death";
                data[year] = 1988; data[length] = 90; data[shelf] = 3328;
                writeMovie(video);
n6          title = "Frankenstein Meets the Space Monster";
                data[year] = 1965; data[length] = 75; data[shelf] = 1005;
                writeMovie(video);
n7          title = "Rock'N'Roll High School Forever";
                data[year] = 1990; data[length] = 94; data[shelf] = 2615;
                writeMovie(video);
n8          video.close();
        }
```

VIDEOS.DAT File

```
Blob, The|1958 95 4265
Cannibal Women in the Avocado Jungle of Death|1988 90 3328
Frankenstein Meets the Space Monster|1965 75 1005
Rock'N'Roll High School Forever|1990 94 2615
```

The `main()` Function

DESIGN

The principal role of the `main()` function is to provide the menu of choices for maintaining the video file. Before the user is offered the menu, though, we check to see that the *VIDEOS.DAT* file actually exists. The structure is:

```
if file does not exist
    Quit
do as many operations as desired
    Print menu
    Input choice
    React to choice
while choice not to quit
```

The expansion of this can easily be done in the code.

The data requirements are a *Movies* object, *movie*, which is mainly used as a vehicle for calling the *Movies* behaviors, and a variable for the menu choice. The reaction to the choice is to call a function to service that choice. In addition, the test for the existence of the file needs an `fstream` object to attempt to open the file.

Program 10–9

```
    int main(void) ///////////////////////////////////////////// Main Program
    { Movies movie;
      char choice;

1 //    movie.newFile();                // Used only for the first run of the test

      //--------------------------------------------- Test to see if file exists
2     fstream video;
3     video.open("VIDEOS.DAT", ios::in);
4     if ( !video)
5     { cout << "Video file missing." << endl;
6         exit(EXIT_FAILURE);
      }
7     video.close();

8     do //------------------------------------------------------------- Menu
9     { cout << "Do you want to:      Change:\n";
        cout << "  [A]dd a video?      A [T]itle?\n";
        cout << "  [D]elete a video?   A [Y]ear?\n";
        cout << "  [P]rint the list?   A [L]ength?\n";
        cout << "  [Q]uit?             A [S]helf position?\n";
        cout << "Take your choice: ";
10      cin >> choice;
11      cin.ignore(500, '\n');                              // Move past newline
12      switch (toupper(choice))
        { case 'A':
13          movie.add();
            break;
          case 'D':
14          movie.del();
            break;
          case 'T':
15          movie.change(-1);
            break;
          case 'Y':
16          movie.change(year);
            break;
          case 'L':
17          movie.change(length);
            break;
          case 'S':
18          movie.change(shelf);
            break;
          case 'P':
19          movie.printFile();
        }
20    }while (toupper(choice) != 'Q');
      return 0;
    }
```

Line	Explanation	movie.title	movie.data[]		
1	Uncomment if we want a new *VIDEOS.DAT* for testing.	(??)	(??)	(??)	(??)
2	Create `fstream` object.	(??)	(??)	(??)	(??)
3	Open *VIDEOS.DAT* for input. The file must exist for a successful open.	(??)	(??)	(??)	(??)
4	if `fstream` object zero, file could not be opened.	(??)	(??)	(??)	(??)
5, 6	Display error message and quit.	(??)	(??)	(??)	(??)
7	If file opened successfully, close it. Other processes will open it as needed.	(??)	(??)	(??)	(??)
8	Menu loop so that we may do as many operations on the file as we want.	(??)	(??)	(??)	(??)
9	Display menu.	(??)	(??)	(??)	(??)
10	Input menu choice.	(??)	(??)	(??)	(??)
11	Menu choice must be followed by a newline (the *Enter* key) to be processed, so flush input stream.	(??)	(??)	(??)	(??)
12	Base menu selection on uppercase character so either lower- or uppercase works.	(??)	(??)	(??)	(??)
13–19	Call appropriate function.	(??)	(??)	(??)	(??)
20	If *choice* was *Q* or *q*, quit.	(??)	(??)	(??)	(??)

IMPLEMENTATION

In Program 10–9, line 1 is shown "commented out." In other words, the line will not execute unless we remove the // from the beginning and recompile.

TEST

To test our test for the existence of the *VIDEOS.DAT* file, we can run the program before creating the new file, and then run it after.

Printing the File

DESIGN

Printing the file involves reading the data from the file and displaying them on the screen. We must continue these two operations until we get to the end of the file. To read a *Movies* object from the file we use our *readMovie()* function, which returns `true` if the read is successful. That return value, then, controls the read-and-display loop.

Function *printFile()*

```
        void printFile(void) //******************** Displays the Data in the File
        {  fstream video;
           short index;                                // Index for data array

p1         video.open("VIDEOS.DAT", ios::in | ios::binary);
p2         cout << "\n YEAR   LEN SHELF   TITLE\n";
p3         while (readMovie(video))
p4         {  for (index = 0; index < items; ++index)
p5               cout << setw(6) << data[index];
p6           cout << "    " << title << endl;
           }
p7         cout << endl;
p8         video.close();
        }
```

Output

```
Do you want to:        Change:
   [A]dd a video?         A [T]itle?
   [D]elete a video?      A [Y]ear?
   [P]rint the list?      A [L]ength?
   [Q]uit?                A [S]helf position?
Take your choice: p

   YEAR   LEN SHELF    TITLE
   1958    95 4265     Blob, The
   1988    90 3328     Cannibal Women in the Avocado Jungle of Death
   1965    75 1005     Frankenstein Meets the Space Monster
   1990    94 2615     Rock'N'Roll High School Forever
```

Line	Explanation	movie.title	movie.data[]			index
EXECUTION CHART — *printFile()*						
p1	Open *VIDEOS.DAT* for input.	??	??	??	??	??
p2	Print heading.	??	??	??	??	??
p3	Call *readMovie()*. Read successful, returns `true`.	Blob, The	1958	95	4265	??
p4	Initialize and test *index*.	Blob, The	1958	95	4265	0
p5	Print value for *data[0]*.	Blob, The	1958	95	4265	0
p4, 5	Do same for *data[1]* and *data[2]*.	Blob, The	1958	95	4265	3
p6	Print *title*.	Blob, The	1958	95	4265	3
p3–6	Do same for other 3 listings.	Rock'N' ...	1990	94	2615	3
p3	At end of file; *readMovie()* returns `false`.	Rock'N' ...	1990	94	2615	3
p7	Print blank line.	Rock'N' ...	1990	94	2615	3
p8	Close file.	Rock'N' ...	1990	94	2615	3

```
Open file
Print heading
Read object while not at the end of the file
    Print numbers
    Print title
Close file
```

The coding for the Function *printFile()* closely follows the design. The argument for the `while` statement is a call to *readMovie()*. When it returns `false` we exit the loop.

The test is for the proper appearance of the output. This will also test the *newFile()* function. If there are problems, we must do a little digging to ascertain which function is at fault.

Adding to the File

Because of the unequal record lengths we must copy the data from one file to another, making changes as we copy.

When adding a record, we have to maintain the file in alphabetical order, so we look for a record that is alphabetically greater than the one we wish to add, and then insert the new record before it. Once we have made the insertion, we want to make sure we do not insert again, so we change the value we have already inserted to something greater than the greatest possible record. That way, our insertion criteria will not be met again as we copy the rest of the records. In our case we have chosen to make the *title* a tilde (~), the greatest printable character, ASCII 126. Nothing will be greater than that.

The pattern of our function is as follows:

```
Open the original data file
Create the new file for copy
Input new title, year, length, and shelf position into new object
Read video object while not at the end of the original file
    if new title < file title
        Write new object to copy file
        Change new title so that it will not be found again
    Write file object to copy file
if new object not added
    Add new object to end of copy file
Close files
Delete original data file
Rename new file with original file name
```

Function *add()* shows the coding for this section.

Function *add()*

```
          void add(void) //****************************** Adds a Record in Order
          { fstream video;
            fstream temp;
a1          Movies newMovie;                                      // Movie to add

a2          video.open("VIDEOS.DAT", ios::in | ios::binary);
a3          temp.open("TEMP.$TM", ios::out | ios::binary);

            cout << "New title: ";
a4          getline(cin, newMovie.title, '\n');
            cout << "Year, length, shelf position: ";
a5          cin >> newMovie.data[year] >> newMovie.data[length]
                >> newMovie.data[shelf];
a6          cin.ignore(500, '\n');                               // Dump trailing newline
a7          while (readMovie(video))
a8          { if (newMovie.title < title)            // Should compare all ucase
a9            { newMovie.writeMovie(temp);
a10             newMovie.title = "~";        // Highest chr, won't find it again
              }
a11           writeMovie(temp);
            }
a12         if (newMovie.title != "~")                 // New listing not added
a13           newMovie.writeMovie(temp);                  // Add to end of file

a14         video.close();
a15         temp.close();
a16         remove("VIDEOS.DAT");
a17         rename("TEMP.$TM", "VIDEOS.DAT");
          }
```

TEST

In testing the *add()* routine, we should be sure to test adding a record at both the beginning and the end of the file, as well as in the middle. In our testing we notice that our titles are case-sensitive, which would make the title *Machine . . .* come after the title *MacTavish . . .* instead of the other way around. The usual solution to this is to make strings into all upper-case characters before any comparisons.

Deleting from the File

DESIGN

Deleting from the file is similar to adding to the file, except that we copy all the records but the one we want to delete. To make it easier to use, we will allow Shelly to type in only a few characters of the title he wants to delete. We will print the full title and ask for confirmation before we delete. Once the program makes a deletion, we set the delete title to a tilde (~) so there will be no more matches.

Output

```
New title: Buffy, the Vampire Slayer
Year, length, shelf position: 1992 100 4180

Take your choice: p

    YEAR  LEN  SHELF   TITLE
    1958   95  4265    Blob, The
    1992  100  4180    Buffy, the Vampire Slayer
    1988   90  3328    Cannibal Women in the Avocado Jungle of Death
    1965   75  1005    Frankenstein Meets the Space Monster
    1990   94  2615    Rock'N'Roll High School Forever
```

EXECUTION CHART — add()

Line	Explanation	movie.title	movie.data[]			newMovie.title	newMovie.data[]		
a1	Create *newMovie* object. This becomes an object within the *add()* behavior of the *movie* object. We refer to the *movie* title as *title*, and the new movie title as *newMovie.title*.	??	??	??	??	??	??	??	??
a2	Open existing *VIDEOS.DAT* for input.	??	??	??	??	??	??	??	??
a3	Open new *TEMP.$TM* to copy to.	??	??	??	??	??	??	??	??
a4, 5	Input data for *newMovie* object.	??	??	??	??	Buffy, …	1992	100	4180
a6	Flush input stream.	??	??	??	??	Buffy, …	1992	100	4180
a7	*readMovie()* returns true.	Blob, The	1958	95	4265	Buffy, …	1992	100	4180
a8	New title not less than file title.	Blob, The	1958	95	4265	Buffy, …	1992	100	4180
a11	Write file object on *TEMP.$TM*. **TEMP**: Blob …	Blob, The	1958	95	4265	Buffy, …	1992	100	4180
a7	*readMovie()* returns true.	Cannibal …	1988	90	3328	Buffy, …	1992	100	4180
a8	New title is less than file title.	Cannibal …	1988	90	3328	Buffy, …	1992	100	4180
a9	Write new object on *TEMP.$TM*. **TEMP**: Blob … Buff …	Cannibal …	1988	90	3328	Buffy, …	1992	100	4180
a10	Change new title so that it will never be less than a file title.	Cannibal …	1988	90	3328	~	1992	100	4180
a11	Write file object on *TEMP.$TM*. **TEMP**: Blob … Buff … Cann …	Cannibal …	1988	90	3328	~	1992	100	4180
a7–11	Repeat process until *readMovie()* returns false. **TEMP**: Blob … Buff … Cann … Fran … Rock …	Rock'N' …	1990	94	2615	~	1992	100	4180
a12, 13	If new movie title not changed, it must not have been inserted. In that case, write new object at end of file.	Rock'N' …	1990	94	2615	~	1992	100	4180
a14	Close *VIDEOS.DAT*.	Rock'N' …	1990	94	2615	~	1992	100	4180
a15	Close *TEMP.$TM*.	Rock'N' …	1990	94	2615	~	1992	100	4180
a16	Eliminate outdated *VIDEOS.DAT* file.	Rock'N' …	1990	94	2615	~	1992	100	4180
a17	Put *VIDEOS.DAT* name on *TEMP.$TM* file.	Rock'N' …	1990	94	2615	~	1992	100	4180

Function *del()*

```
        void del(void) //************************* Deletes a Record from the File
        {   fstream video;
            fstream temp;
d1          string delTitle;                                   // Title to delete
            char answer;                          // Confirm yes or no on deletion

d2          video.open("VIDEOS.DAT", ios::in | ios::binary);
d3          temp.open("TEMP.$TM", ios::out | ios::binary);

            cout << "Delete title: ";
d4          getline(cin, delTitle, '\n');
d5          while (readMovie(video))
d6          {   answer = 'N';                            // Default to don't delete
d7              if                              // Test as many characters as typed in
                    (delTitle == title.substr(0, delTitle.size()))
d8              {   cout << "Delete " << title << "? ";
d9                  cin >> answer;
d10                 cin.ignore(500, '\n');              // Dump newline from stream
                }
d11             if (toupper(answer) != 'Y')             // If not delete, write
d12                 writeMovie(temp);
                else                                    // Have made deletion
d13                 delTitle = "~";                     // Don't find it again
            }
d14         video.close();
d15         temp.close();
d16         remove("VIDEOS.DAT");
d17         rename("TEMP.$TM", "VIDEOS.DAT");
        }
```

Open the original data file
Create the new file for copy
Input title to delete
while not at the end of the original file, read video object
  Default to not deleting unless changed later
  if delete title = file title
   Print full title
   Input Y or N for delete
  if not delete
   Write file object to copy file
  else   [Have made deletion]
   Set delete title so it won't be found again
Close files
Delete original data file
Rename new file with original file name

IMPLEMENTATION

Function *del()* deletes a record. When comparing the few characters of the file to delete with the title from the file, the process compares the delete title with a substring of the file title that has the same number of characters (Line d7).

Output

```
Delete title: Frank
Delete Frankenstein Meets the Space Monster? y

Take your choice: p

    YEAR  LEN SHELF   TITLE
    1958   95  4265   Blob, The
    1992  100  4180   Buffy, the Vampire Slayer
    1988   90  3328   Cannibal Women in the Avocado Jungle of Death
    1990   94  2615   Rock'N'Roll High School Forever
```

EXECUTION CHART — *del()*

Line	Explanation	*movie.title*	*movie.data[]*			*delTitle*	*answer*
d1	Create `string` to hold title to delete.	??	??	??	??	??	--
d2	Open existing *VIDEOS.DAT* for input.	??	??	??	??	??	??
d3	Open new *TEMP.$TM* to copy to.	??	??	??	??	??	??
d4	Input first few characters of title to delete.	??	??	??	??	Frank	??
d5	*readMovie()* returns true.	Blob, The	1958	95	4265	Frank	??
d6	Default to not deleting this listing.	Blob, The	1958	95	4265	Frank	N
d7	Test delete title against first 5 characters of title from file. They are not equal.	Blob, The	1958	95	4265	Frank	N
d11	Don't delete this listing.	Blob, The	1958	95	4265	Frank	N
d12	Write listing on *TEMP.$TM*. **TEMP**: Blob …	Blob, The	1958	95	4265	Frank	N
d5	*readMovie()* returns true.	Buffy, …	1992	100	4180	Frank	N
d6–12	Don't delete next 2 listings; write on *TEMP.$TM*. **TEMP**: Blob … Buff … Cann …	Buffy, …	1992	100	4180	Frank	N
d5	*readMovie()* returns true.	Franken, …	1965	75	1005	Frank	N
d6	Default to not deleting this listing.	Franken, …	1965	75	1005	Frank	N
d7	Test delete title against first 5 characters of title from file. They are equal.	Franken, …	1965	75	1005	Frank	N
d8	Print out full title.	Franken, …	1965	75	1005	Frank	N
d9	Input confirmation.	Franken, …	1965	75	1005	Frank	y
d10	Flush input stream.	Franken, …	1965	75	1005	Frank	y
d11	Delete this listing by not writing it to *TEMP.$TM* in d12. **TEMP**: Blob … Buff … Cann …	Franken, …	1965	75	1005	Frank	y
d13	Set delete title so it won't be found again.	Franken, …	1965	75	1005	~	y
d5–13	Repeat process until *readMovie()* returns false. **TEMP**: Blob … Buff … Cann … Rock …	Rock'N' …	1990	94	2615	~	N
d14	Close *VIDEOS.DAT*.	Rock'N' …	1990	94	2615	~	N
d15	Close *TEMP.$TM*.	Rock'N' …	1990	94	2615	~	N
d16	Eliminate outdated *VIDEOS.DAT* file.	Rock'N' …	1990	94	2615	~	N
d17	Put *VIDEOS.DAT* name on *TEMP.$TM* file.	Rock'N' …	1990	94	2615	~	N

As in adding, it is important to test deletions at the beginning and the end, as well as in the middle of the file.

Changing a Listing

Changing any part of a listing is similar to the other two types of changes—the file must be copied and the listing changed in the process. Again we will allow Shelly to input only a few characters of the title whose data are to be changed.

```
Open the original data file
Create the new file for copy
Input title to change
while not at the end of the original file, read video object
        Default to not changing unless changed later
        if change title = file title
            Print full title
            Input Y or N for delete
            if change
                if change title
                    Input new title
                else
                    Display appropriate old data
                    Input new data
                Set change title so it won't be found again
        Write file object to copy file
Close files
Delete original data file
Rename new file with original file name
```

Function *change()* follows the file-copying pattern for changing file data. Depending on the *index* sent to the function, we will change either the *title* or the appropriate *data* item as determined by the *index*.

Again, testing changes at both the beginning and the end of the file is imperative. Also, we show two tests with Outputs and Execution Charts: *change()* a title and *change()* a number.

Our thorough testing of this routine has pointed up a flaw: the changed title is always placed in the same position in the file as the original title. That means the new title might not remain in alphabetical order. For example, if we changed *Incredibly Strange Creatures Who Stopped Living*

Function *change()*

```
             void change(int index) //*********************** Changes Part of a Record
            {  fstream video;
               fstream temp;
c1             string chTitle;                             // Title in record to change
               char answer;                               // Confirm yes or no on change

c2             video.open("VIDEOS.DAT", ios::in | ios::binary);
c3             temp.open("TEMP.$TM", ios::out | ios::binary);

               cout << "Change title: ";
c4             getline(cin, chTitle, '\n');
c5             while (readMovie(video))
c6             {  answer = 'N';                            // Default to don't change
c7                if                          // Test as many characters as typed in
                     (chTitle == title.substr(0, chTitle.size()))
c8                {  cout << "Change " << title << "? ";
c9                   cin >> answer;
c10                  cin.ignore(500, '\n');               // Dump newline from stream
c11                  if (toupper(answer) == 'Y')
c12                  {  if (index == -1)                          // Change title
                        {  cout << "To: ";
c13                        getline(cin, title, '\n');  // Change the title in record
                        }
                        else                               // Change other data
c14                     {  cout << "Change " << data[index] << " to: ";
c15                        cin >> data[index];
c16                        cin.ignore(500, '\n');         // Dump end of input stream
                        }
c17                     chTitle = "~";                    // Don't find title again
                     }
                  }
c18               writeMovie(temp);                        // Write record
               }
c19            video.close();
c20            temp.close();
c21            remove("VIDEOS.DAT");
c22            rename("TEMP.$TM", "VIDEOS.DAT");
            }
```

---

and Became Mixed-Up Zombies, The, to *Teenage Psycho Meets Bloody Mary*, it would undoubtedly not be in the right place. One way to correct the problem would be to make the change a combination of a deletion and an addition.

For our next test we have chosen the shelf position as the number to change. Any of the numbers, however, would follow the same pattern, but to be sure, we should test them all.

Output — *change()* a title

```
Take your choice: t
Change title: Bl
Change Blob, The? y
To: Blob the Sequel, Part VIII, The

Take your choice: p

YEAR  LEN SHELF   TITLE
1958   95  4265   Blob the Sequel, Part VIII, The
1992  100  4180   Buffy, the Vampire Slayer
1988   90  3328   Cannibal Women in the Avocado Jungle of Death
1990   94  2615   Rock'N'Roll High School Forever
```

Line	Explanation	*movie.title*	*movie.data[]*			*chTitle*	*answer*	*index*
c1	Create `string` to hold title to change.	??	??	??	??	??	--	−1 (title)
c2	Open existing *VIDEOS.DAT* for input.	??	??	??	??	??	??	−1 (title)
c3	Open new *TEMP.$TM* to copy to.	??	??	??	??	??	??	−1 (title)
c4	Input first few characters of title to change.	??	??	??	??	Bl	??	−1 (title)
c5	*readMovie()* returns true.	Blob, The	1958	95	4265	Bl	??	−1 (title)
c6	Default to not changing this listing.	Blob, The	1958	95	4265	Bl	N	−1 (title)
c7	Test delete title against first 2 characters of title from file. They are equal.	Blob, The	1958	95	4265	Bl	N	−1 (title)
c8	Print out full title.	Blob, The	1958	95	4265	Bl	N	−1 (title)
c9	Input confirmation.	Blob, The	1965	75	1005	Bl	y	−1 (title)
c10	Flush input stream.	Blob, The	1965	75	1005	Bl	y	−1 (title)
c11	Change this listing.	Blob, The	1965	75	1005	Bl	y	−1 (title)
c12	*index* says title change.	Blob, The	1965	75	1005	Bl	y	−1 (title)
c13	Input new title.	Blob the …	1965	75	1005	Bl	y	−1 (title)
c17	Set change title so it won't be found again.	Blob the …	1965	75	1005	~	y	−1 (title)
c18	Write object on *TEMP.$TM.*.	Blob the …	1965	75	1005	~	y	−1 (title)
c5–18	Repeat process until *readMovie()* returns false.	Rock'N' …	1990	94	2615	~	N	−1 (title)
c19	Close *VIDEOS.DAT*.	Rock'N' …	1990	94	2615	~	N	−1 (title)
c20	Close *TEMP.$TM*.	Rock'N' …	1990	94	2615	~	N	−1 (title)
c21	Eliminate outdated *VIDEOS.DAT* file.	Rock'N' …	1990	94	2615	~	N	−1 (title)
c22	Put *VIDEOS.DAT* name on *TEMP.$TM* file.	Rock'N' …	1990	94	2615	~	N	−1 (title)

EXECUTION CHART — *change()* a title

Output — *change()* a number

```
Take your choice: s
Change title: C
Change Cannibal Women in the Avocado Jungle of Death? y
Change 3328 to: 4403

Take your choice: p

     YEAR   LEN  SHELF   TITLE
     1958    95  4265    Blob the Sequel, Part VIII, The
     1992   100  4180    Buffy, the Vampire Slayer
     1988    90  4403    Cannibal Women in the Avocado Jungle of Death
     1990    94  2615    Rock'N'Roll High School Forever
```

EXECUTION CHART — *change()* a number

Line	Explanation	*movie.title*	*movie.data[]*			*chTitle*	*answer*	*index*
c1	Create `string` to hold title to change.	??	??	??	??	??	--	2 (shelf)
c2	Open existing *VIDEOS.DAT* for input.	??	??	??	??	??	??	2 (shelf)
c3	Open new *TEMP.$TM* to copy to.	??	??	??	??	??	??	2 (shelf)
c4	Input first few characters of title to change.	??	??	??	??	C	??	2 (shelf)
c5	*readMovie()* returns true.	Blob, The	1958	95	4265	C	??	2 (shelf)
c6	Default to not changing this listing.	Blob, The	1958	95	4265	C	N	2 (shelf)
c7	Test delete title against first character of title from file. They are not equal.	Blob, The	1958	95	4265	C	N	2 (shelf)
c18	Write object on *TEMP.$TM*..	Blob, The	1958	95	4265	C	N	2 (shelf)
c5–18	Repeat until delete title = first character of title from file.	Cannib …	1988	90	3328	C	N	2 (shelf)
c8	Print out full title.	Cannib …	1988	90	3328	C	N	2 (shelf)
c9	Input confirmation.	Cannib …	1988	90	3328	C	y	2 (shelf)
c10	Flush input stream.	Cannib …	1988	90	3328	C	y	2 (shelf)
c11	Change this listing.	Cannib …	1988	90	3328	C	y	2 (shelf)
c12	*index* says shelf change.	Cannib …	1988	90	3328	C	y	2 (shelf)
c14	Display current shelf position.	Cannib …	1988	90	3328	C	y	2 (shelf)
c15	Input new shelf position.	Cannib …	1988	90	4403	C	y	2 (shelf)
c16	Flush input stream.	Cannib …	1988	90	4403	C	y	2 (shelf)
c17	Set change title so it won't be found again.	Cannib …	1988	90	4403	~	y	2 (shelf)
c18	Write object on *TEMP.$TM*..	Cannib …	1988	90	4403	~	y	2 (shelf)
c5–18	Repeat process until *readMovie()* returns false.	Rock'N' …	1990	94	2615	~	N	2 (shelf)
c19	Close *VIDEOS.DAT*.	Rock'N' …	1990	94	2615	~	N	2 (shelf)
c20	Close *TEMP.$TM*.	Rock'N' …	1990	94	2615	~	N	2 (shelf)
c21	Eliminate outdated *VIDEOS.DAT* file.	Rock'N' …	1990	94	2615	~	N	2 (shelf)
c22	Put *VIDEOS.DAT* name on *TEMP.$TM* file.	Rock'N' …	1990	94	2615	~	N	2 (shelf)

SUMMARY

- **NEW FUNCTIONS** (in order of appearance)

void *fstream*.open(address *fileId*, int *mode*)   <fstream>
   Purpose: Attach an *fstream* object to the *fileId* in a specific *mode*.
   Return: None.

void *fstream*.close()   <fstream>
   Purpose: Write leftover buffers to and detach *fstream* object from file.
   Return: None.

int *fstream*.eof(void)   <fstream>
   Purpose: Detect unsuccessful operation at end of file.
   Return: Zero if unsuccessful operation; nonzero if not.

void *fstream*.clear(void)   <fstream>
   Purpose: Clears end-of-file-condition.
   Return: None.

void *fstream*.seekg(long *offset*, int *origin*)   <fstream>
   Purpose: Set the position *offset* bytes from the beginning, or from the *origin*.
   Return: None.

long *fstream*.tellg(void)   <fstream>
   Purpose: Determine current byte position in file.
   Return: Current byte position in file.

int remove(address *fileId*)   <cstdio>
   Purpose: Delete *fileId* file from secondary storage.
   Return: Success: Zero. Error: Nonzero.

int unlink(address *fileId*)   <cstdio>
   Purpose: Remove link to *fileId* or delete file if last link.
   Return: Success: Zero. Error: Nonzero.

int rename(address *oldId*, address *newId*)   <cstdio>
   Purpose: Change file identification from *oldId* to *newId*.
   Return: Success: Zero. Error: Nonzero.

- **CONCEPT REVIEW**

  - Any entity in secondary storage is referred to as a **file**. It must be iden-
    tified by a combination of a **name**, an optional **extension**, and possibly
    a **path**.

  - A program cannot work directly with individual bytes in a file, so a
    portion of the file is brought into main memory in a **buffer**. To use the

file we have to set up a **stream** and connect it to the file. C++ will keep track of its byte position in a file by maintaining a **file position**.

- To use a file we create an object of the **fstream** class and connect it to an actual file stream with the **open()** behavior. To this function, we send the file identification and mode. The mode is stated as one or a combination of defined constants that tell how the file is to be used. One important mode is the file type: **binary** or **text**.

- The **close()** behavior of the fstream object writes the contents of the current buffer, if it has changed, into the appropriate place in secondary storage, making changes permanent, and deallocates memory space.

- **Character access** to a file refers to storing all data on the file in readable characters (converting numbers to strings) and converting back to the proper data types when reading, whereas **byte access** copies bytes from main memory (storing numbers in binary numeric form) and reads them back the same way.

- We write characters to a file with the same methods we use to display characters on the screen, but instead of using the cout object, we use the fstream object we connected to the file stream.

- The **eof()** behavior of the fstream object, when nonzero, tells us that we have attempted an operation at the end of the file. This condition must be cleared using the **clear()** behavior if we want to use the test again after resetting the file position.

- Characters can be read from a file using the same methods as for cin. The getline() works the same if we substitute the fstream object for cin.

- The **seekg()** behavior moves the file position a specified number of bytes from either the beginning of the file, the current position, or the end of the file. The **tellg()** behavior return the current byte position in the file. We notice that we can make changes to files using these two behaviors, but if the replacement does not contain a number of characters equal to the original, we can have problems. One solution is **padding** data to reserve enough characters for different types of data.

- A file may be deleted from secondary storage by **remove()** (or the related **unlink()** for some UNIX systems) or may have its name changed by **rename()**.

- Changing files with variable-length data requires that one file be copied to another, with changes made during the copy process. The old file must then be removed and the new file's name changed to that of the old file.

- Deleting from such a file requires the copying process, but the deleted record is not copied. Adding to the beginning or the middle of a file requires copying, but adding to the end requires only writing to the end of the one file.

- **HEADS UP: POINTS OF SPECIAL INTEREST**

  - To C++ files are simply bytes in secondary storage.
  - Is your operating system case-sensitive?
  - File buffering should be transparent to us.
  - Text files differ with different operating systems.

- When in doubt, use binary.
- A crash does not automatically close files.
- It's good practice to explicitly close any file you open.
- Files written using character access are readable with ordinary text editors.
- When designing a file, think about how you will have to get data from it.
- The `eof()` behavior is true only after an attempted read at the end of the file.
- The `eof()` condition must be cleared if we want to use it again.
- A file access always moves the file position.
- Text files may not be portable.
- Changing files with variable-length records requires copying from one file to another.
- Put the original name on the changed file.
- Adding to the end of a file requires no copying.

• TRAPS: COMMON PROGRAMMING ERRORS

- Using a single backslash in a string.
- Thinking `eof()` tells us we are at the end of a file.
- Clearing `eof` without moving the file position.
- Attempting to move the file position out of the bounds of the file.
- Attempting to remove a file that is open.

• YOUR TURN ANSWERS

• 10–1

1. A typical file identifier can consist of a path, a file name, and an extension, using at least the alpha and the numeric characters.
2. File buffering is moving blocks of a file in and out of a buffer in main memory so as to be able to access the data one byte at a time.
3. The file stream is the connection that C++ establishes to the file to handle file buffering.
4. Declaring an `fstream` object simply provides a mechanism to which we can later attach a file.
5. The `open()` function connects a file to an `fstream` object.
6. The `ios::trunc` mode and `ios::out` mode, when not used with another mode except `ios::binary`, create new files. All other modes work with existing files.
7. Mode `ios::in` allows read access, whereas `ios::out` allows write.
8. The difference between binary and text files is that for the latter, C++ may possibly translate line endings and look for special end-of-file indications, depending on the operating system. C++ makes no translations for binary files.
9. The `close()` function returns the buffered data to secondary storage and deallocates the buffer and other file-related memory.

• 10-2

1. Character access treats the file as we have done with the screen and keyboard—translating everything to and from human-readable characters. Byte access simply copies bytes to and from the file.

2. `cin` and `cout` are stream objects connected to the keyboard and the screen. `fstream` objects are connected to files by `open()`. Whatever we can do with the former, we can do with the latter.

3. Delimiters in a file are important to our ability to separate the data when we retrieve them.

4. We can tell we're at the end of a file because the `eof()` behavior will return true *after* an attempted read.

5. We can use `eof()` again after moving the position away from the end of a file only if we `clear()` the `eof()` condition.

6. `getline()` works with file streams just as it does with `cin`.

• 10-3

1. The `seekg()` function moves the file position. `seekg(0)` will move to the beginning of the file.

2. The defined constants for the `seekg()` *origin* for the beginning, the current position, and the end of the file are `ios::beg`, `ios::cur`, and `ios::end`, respectively.

3. The file position can't realistically be moved before the file's beginning or after its end, but C++ will not stop you from executing a statement that attempts it.

4. `tellg()` returns the current file position.

5. The `remove()` function deletes a file from secondary storage. (The `unlink()` function breaks a link to the file in UNIX systems, deleting the file if the last link has been broken.)

6. The `rename()` function changes the name of a file in secondary storage.

• 10-4

1. To change files that have variable-length records we have to copy the data from one file to another, making changes during the copying process.

2. We delete data from a file by copying the file but not copying the data we want to delete.

3. Adding data to the beginning or the middle of a file requires copying the file. Adding data to the end requires only opening the file with the position at the end and writing the new data.

EXERCISES

1. Show the statements needed to open the file *C:\JUNK\STUFF.DAT* in a stream called *whatever*.

2. Show how you might test for an unsuccessful opening of the file in Exercise 1.

3. Investigate the file identification rules for your operating system.
   a. How many characters are allowed in a file name?
   b. Are file identifiers case-sensitive?
   c. Are spaces allowed in file identifiers?
   d. Are extensions allowed and, if so, how many characters may they contain?
   e. What kinds of "paths" are allowed—disk designations, folders, directories, subdirectories, and so forth?

4. Show the proper file mode for opening a file in each of the following instances.
   a. Read from an existing text file but ensure that the program can make no changes.
   b. Create a new binary file for both read and write access.
   c. Read and write any part of an existing text file.
   d. If a file doesn't exist, create it; otherwise, allow reads and writes anywhere beyond the end of the original binary file.

5. What are the differences between binary and text files in your operating system?

6. Write a generalized function, *openFile()*, that opens a file whose identifier is passed to it, in the mode passed to it, in the stream passed to it. If it is opened successfully, the function should return `true`; otherwise, `false`.

7. Point out the problems in the following program segment.

```
string str;
fstream stuff;

open(stuff, C:\MYFILE, ios::output && ios::bin)
if (stuff)
{   cout << "Can't open file." << endl;
    exit(EXIT_FAILURE);
}
stuff.cin >> str;
stuff.getline(cin, str, '\n');
close(C:\MYFILE);
```

8. The file is positioned at the beginning of the following characters. Show the `cin` statement control string needed to read the data into a string, *str*, and two `float`s, *float1* and *float2*.

   ```
   Farley 46.5  7.1
   ```

9. What will the following program segment produce on the screen? If it is not the output below, change the program so that it is.

```
fstream file;
string words;
int integer;
float real;

file.open("Data", ios::in | ios::out | ios::trunc
          | ios::binary);
file << 123 << 45.67 << "Two words" << endl;
file.seekg(0);
file >> integer >> real >> words;
cout << integer << real << words << endl;
file.close();
```

Output

```
123 45.67 Two words
```

10. Show the statement needed to move the file position as indicated in each of the following instances.

   a. To the beginning of the file.
   b. To the twentieth byte position of the file.
   c. Twenty bytes beyond the current position.
   d. Twenty bytes before the current position.
   e. Twenty bytes before the end of the file.
   f. Twenty bytes after the end of the file.

11. Put statements before and after the following that will return the file position to where it was before the read.

```
getline(file, string, '\n');
```

12. Why won't this stop correctly at the end of the file?

```
while ( !file.eof())
{  getline(file, data, '\n');
   statements
}
```

13. Correct the following program segment.

```
file1.open("DATA", ios::in |ios::trunc | ios::binary);
file2.open("TEMP", ios::out);
    [Copy from one file to the other]
rename("DATA", "TEMP");
```

PROGRAMS

1. Write a program that allows the input of names and ages from the keyboard and stores them, in characters, in the file *PEOPLE.DAT*. After the input is finished, the program should print out what is in the file as well as the average age. Enter the names in alphabetical order so that the file may be used in later programs.

   Variables

   ```
   people           File stream object
   name
   age
   total, count     To calculate average age
   ```

   Output

   ```
   Enter name/age: Freebisch, Lance/72
   Enter name/age: Jones, Abner/45
   Enter name/age: Smith, Melvin/26
   Enter name/age:
   Name        Age
   Freebisch, Lance  72
   Jones, Abner      45
   Smith, Melvin     26
   Average age: 47.67
   ```

2. Write a program that searches the file *PEOPLE.DAT* (from the problem above) sequentially for a name (last name only) input from the keyboard.

Variables

```
people      File stream object
nameIn, lastName, firstName
age
```

Output

```
Enter last name: Smoth
Don't have a Smoth
Enter last name: Smith
Melvin Smith  26
Enter last name:
```

3. Write a program that will allow you to input a last name and change any last or first name or age in the file *PEOPLE.DAT* referred to in Program 1.

4. Write a program that will allow you to add a record, in alphabetical order, to the file *PEOPLE.DAT* referred to in Program 1.

5. Write a program that will allow you to input a last name and delete the record with that last name from the file *PEOPLE.DAT* referred to in Program 4.

6. Rewrite Program 10–4 (pages 366–367) so that the *QUIZ.ANS* file contains only the answer, rather than the question followed by the answer. The output should be the same.

7. Rewrite Programs 10–4 (pages 366–367) and 10–6 (pages 372–373) so you have a *Test* class with behaviors *give()*, *review()*, and *change()*. Write a `main()` driver to test it. The outputs should be the same as for Programs 10–4 and 10–6.

8. A real estate firm uses a computer to keep track of houses on the market. They regularly publish two sets of listings, one of houses less than 2,000 square feet and one of houses 2,000 square feet and over. The individual listing contains the listing date, address, price, and square footage. The date should be in six-digit fashion with year, month, and day (for example, May 4, 1998, would be 980504). Write a program that will accept listings from the terminal and enter them in either of two files, *SMALL* or *LARGE*. After entry is complete, both sets of listings should be printed out.

Variables

```
small, large    File stream objects
date
address
price
sqFeet
```

Output

```
Date, address, price, sq. feet?
980122,14 Walnut,174550,2250
Date, address, price, sq. feet?
980128,345 Oak,143990,1450
```

(Continued)

(Continued)

```
Date, address, price, sq. feet?
980205,22 Elm,156450,1700
Date, address, price, sq. feet?
980213,988 Maple,204550,3300
Date, address, price, sq. feet?
980301,76 Apple,172500,1900
Date, address, price, sq. feet?


HOUSES LESS THAN 2000 SQ. FT.
List date    Address      Price     Sq. Feet
980128       345 Oak      143990    1450
980205       22 Elm       156450    1700
980301       76 Apple     172500    1900


HOUSES 2000 SQ. FT. OR MORE.
List date    Address      Price     Sq. Feet
980122       14 Walnut    174550    2250
980213       988 Maple    204550    3300
```

9. Write a program that works with two files (*EMPLOY* and *WEEKLY*). *EMPLOY* should store the employee name, wage, retirement, and tax rate, and should be filled by input from the terminal. Input is stopped by pressing just the Enter key, at which time the user is asked for the hours worked for each employee. Hours worked and net pay are stored in *WEEKLY*. After all the data are input, a payroll report is generated using data from both files. If *EMPLOY* is filled, the program should sense that this file has data in it and the user should not be prompted for those data. Instead, the user will enter just the *WEEKLY* data, overwriting the *WEEKLY* file, and get a payroll report. Save the program as *PAY* for use later.

Suggested Variables

emp, week	File stream objects
name	Employee name
wage	
ret	Retirement
tax	Tax rate
hours	
net	Net pay (*hours* × *wage* − *hours* × *wage* × *tax* − *ret*)

Output

```
Employee name, wage, ret, tax? Jones 3.5 5.5 .16
Employee name, wage, ret, tax? Smith 4.75 6.35 .21
Employee name, wage, ret, tax? Brown 4.25 5.75 .17
Employee name, wage, ret, tax?

Hours worked for Jones? 34.5
Hours worked for Smith? 38
Hours worked for Brown? 45

NAME      WAGE       RET        TAX       NET PAY
Jones     $3.50      $5.50      16%       $ 95.93
Smith     $4.75      $6.35      21%       $136.25
Brown     $4.25      $5.75      17%       $152.99
```

10. Write a program that will allow input and maintenance of the company's employee file (*EMPLOY*) as described in the *PAY* program in Program 9. Your program should allow you to add or delete employees or change any part of an employee's record.

11. Write a program that keeps track of student grades. It builds a new *GRADE* file by asking for a name for each of three students and three grades for each student. After all the grades are input a grade report is printed, giving the total points and the average.

Variables

Choose appropriate variables

Output

```
Name and grades? Jones 68 97 24
Name and grades? Smith 76 94 78
Name and grades? Brown 91 56 78

NAME     GRD    GRD    GRD    TOT    AVERAGE
Jones    68     97     24     189    63.0
Smith    76     94     78     248    82.7
Brown    91     56     78     225    75.0
```

12. Write a class that analyzes a text file. It should have a *fileOpen()* behavior that opens a specified file, an *analyze()* behavior that examines the file, a *report()* behavior that prints the analysis, and a *fileClose()* behavior that closes the file opened in *fileOpen()*. The analysis should count the number of words, sentences, and paragraphs in a text file. Words end at a space or punctuation; sentences end at periods, exclamation points, and question marks; and paragraphs end at newlines. You can use a text editor or your C++ environment to type in a sample text file.

Output

```
File to scan: WORDS.TXT
WORDS.TXT has 173 words, 19 sentences, and 4 paragraphs.
```

13. The BraneDed Corporation has run out of storage space, so the president, N. O. Smarts, has directed you to implement a new file-compression scheme he has cooked up—it eliminates every other character in the file. Write the *Compress* class to implement it and an appropriate `main()` driver to test it. Now, as long as you don't have to write the program to decompress the files . . .

Output

```
File to compress? JUNK
Now is the time for all good men to come to the aid of their party.
After compression is:
Nwi h iefralgo e ocm oteado hi at.
```

Chapter 11

DIRECT-ACCESS FILES

PREVIEW

When data are manipulated in records that group individual but related values, it is useful to have a mechanism that holds each record together. In this chapter we will look at such a mechanism. At its conclusion you should understand:

- How data are organized into records.

- How these records are stored for efficient access.

- Methods of copying records between main memory and files.

- How to handle the special case of records that include strings.

- How to change—including adding and deleting data—files made of these records.

W have all used a phone book—a telephone directory—at one time or another, probably not giving much thought to what a simple and marvelous piece of organization it is. We flip through the pages, scan down the columns, and *bingo!* there are the name, address, and phone number we wanted. Each listing in the phone book is a complete unit, but a unit made up of distinct parts. We will now examine such units and their parts, how we store them in files, and how we can best manipulate them with the computer.

RECORD-BASED ORGANIZATION

The phone book is a good example of **record-based data**. Let's clean up the phone book a bit—make it easier to see its component parts by putting spaces between each and getting rid of the dots.

Name	Address	Phone
Balderdash, Swoozie J.	46a Finch Dr.	123-4567
Geek, Nerdly Q.	1247 Buzzard Blvd.	555-1212
Klowann, Bozoe T.		987-6543
Trembly, Thaddeus Toadmann	12 Swallow Ct., #5	333-4444

HEADS UP!

Consistency makes record-based data work.

TRAP

Leaving out a field that is empty.

HEADS UP!

Rows and columns are records and fields.

In record-based data, consistency is important. Each listing has a name, an address, and a phone number. We refer to a single phone listing as a **record**, the description of an entity, such as *Swoozie J. Balderdash, 46a Finch Dr., 123-4567*. Each listing has individual characteristics, **fields**. Swoozie has a name, an address, and a phone. Geek's phone is 555-1212; Trembly's address is 12 Swallow Ct., #5. What about Bozoe T. Klowann? Since he (she?) has declined to list an address, we have left it blank. It is there—it is just empty.

We have shown the data in a table format. In fact, this is such a common way of visualizing record-based data that records are often referred to as *rows* and fields as *columns*—in Trembly's row, the value of the phone column is *333-4444*.

One field (or possibly a combination of fields) is often designated a **key**—an identifier for that record. The records are often organized, alphabetically or numerically, by that key. In a phone book the key is usually the name, although there are street directories that are organized by address.

Fixed-Length Records

To be useful to computer programs, the phone book will have to be stored in a file. As we have seen, a file is simply a long series of bytes on a computer disk. It doesn't have neat rows and columns; it is up to our programs to show some order in the file. If we used backslashes at the end of each field and pipes at the end of the record, the phone book in the file would look like this:

```
Balderdash, Swoozie J.\46a Finch Dr.\123-4567|Geek, Nerdly Q.\1247 Buz
zard Blvd.\555-1212|Klowann, Bozoe T.\\987-6543|Trembly, Thaddeus Toad
mann\12 Swallow Ct., #5\333-4444|
```

We have divided the lines only to keep the characters within the boundaries of the printed page; it is really just one line.

We must provide the mechanisms to separate data in a file.

We can find things by searching for the delimiters and testing the values that follow. For example, to find Klowann's phone number, we would look at the set of characters between the beginning of the file and the first backslash and compare it with Klowann. That's not it, so we would move, byte by byte, to the next pipe, and then compare the characters between that pipe and the next backslash. We would continue to do this until we found Klowann. Finally we would move, byte by byte, past two backslashes, and from there to the next pipe would be Klowann's phone number.

It works, but think of a phone book with a million records—slow, even at today's computer speeds.

This is a **sequential-access file**—one in which we must start at the beginning and move through toward the end. Most people, unless they are the weird ones who can't stand the suspense, read a novel sequentially—starting at the beginning and reading toward the end. A cassette tape is also accessed sequentially.

What if Bozoe wanted to list his (her?) address? As we saw in the last chapter, to change such a file we would have to copy the entire file to a temporary one—really slow!

In Chapter 10 we saw how easy it is to move a file position (using `seekg()`). Instead of moving byte by byte in the file, why not just jump from record to record? Because with the file as we now have it organized we do not know where the records start without searching, byte by byte, for the delimiters.

Let's make all the records the same number of bytes, say 60. To get to the beginning of the tenth record we would pass nine records—move the file position 9×60, or 540, bytes. Let's go even further and make each particular field the same number of bytes in all records—the name will be 30 bytes; the address, 22; and the phone number, 8. Now our file in secondary storage looks like this (again, with arbitrarily added line endings):

```
Balderdash, Swoozie J.        46a Finch Dr.         123-4567Geek, Nerd
ly Q.            1247 Buzzard Blvd.      555-1212Klowann, Bozoe T.
                 987-6543Trembly, Thaddeus Toadmann
12 Swallow Ct., #5     333-4444
```

We won't change the file in secondary storage, but it will make it easier to see on the printed page if we put our arbitrary line endings every 60 characters:

```
Balderdash, Swoozie J.        46a Finch Dr.         123-4567
Geek, Nerdly Q.               1247 Buzzard Blvd.     555-1212
Klowann, Bozoe T.                                    987-6543
Trembly, Thaddeus Toadmann    12 Swallow Ct., #5     333-4444
```

Voila! Rows and columns!

To find the phone number of the tenth record in such a file, we move past the first nine records (9×60 bytes), past the name (another 30 bytes), and past the address (22 bytes)—a total of 592 bytes—to the beginning of the phone number. Changing records is also relatively easy. Because all records are the same length, we just replace one with another—no need to copy entire files.

This is a **direct-access file**, meaning we can jump to specific places in the file—we do not have to start in the beginning and move toward them. We access a phone book or dictionary directly. If we are looking up *mutant* in the dictionary, we do not start at the beginning, the *A*s, and run our finger down each page until we come to *mutant*, we open directly to the *M*s. A compact disc (CD) can likewise be accessed directly.

As mentioned in Chapter 10, the advantage is access speed. The disadvantage is the storage space required for all the padding characters, spaces in this example.

YOUR TURN 11–1

1. In record-based data, what are other names for rows and columns?
2. What is a key?
3. Contrast a sequential-access file with a direct-access file.
4. What is the major advantage of fixed-length records?
5. What is the major disadvantage of fixed-length records?

BYTE ACCESS TO FILES

Many of our files are made up of combinations of character and numeric data. The *EMP.DAT* file we used in Chapter 10 is a good example.

EMP.DAT File

```
Quibble, Marvin/12.34/2
Jones, Hatshepset/9.38/8
Montmorrissey, Clyde/23.98/1
```

To store the employee data we converted the numbers into characters with the `fstream` object and the insert operator (`<<`), and filled the file with characters. A distinct advantage of this approach is that we humans, using a text editor, can read both the character and the numeric data in the file.

If only our programs and not humans were going to read the file, we would probably want to store the data in the most efficient form in terms of both the amount of storage space and the processing required for reading and writing. Converting the numeric data to characters and vice versa takes processing time and usually requires more bytes for storage. For example, the value 12345 stored as characters takes five bytes. Stored as a `short` it takes only two. Instead, let's take a direct copy of the bytes in memory and put it in the file—no translation, minimal storage.

 **HEADS UP!**

Copying data, rather than converting them to characters, saves time and storage space.

Data Types: Sizes and Address

Before we tackle that subject, we need to know a little more about data types. For example, how many bytes are there in an `int`? We saw in Chapter 2 that the answer depends on which C++ we are using. If the answer is important to our program—and it will be shortly—we can have our program find out by using the **`sizeof` operator**. This word, `sizeof`, does not look like an operator such as `*` or `+` or `=`, but it is. In fact, it is a unary operator, on the same level of precedence as logical *not* (`!`), increment (`++`), or negate (`-`) (see Appendix B).

Program 11–1

```cpp
#include <iostream>                      // How about the .h?
#include <iomanip>
using namespace std;                     // Do you need this?

int main(void)
{  int array[5];

   cout << "Data Type    Bytes\n";
   cout << "char         " << setw(5) << sizeof(char) << endl;
   cout << "int          " << setw(5) << sizeof(int) << endl;
   cout << "bool         " << setw(5) << sizeof(bool) << endl;
   cout << "short        " << setw(5) << sizeof(short) << endl;
   cout << "long         " << setw(5) << sizeof(long) << endl;
   cout << "float        " << setw(5) << sizeof(float) << endl;
   cout << "double       " << setw(5) << sizeof(double) << endl;
   cout << "long double " << setw(5) << sizeof(long double) << endl;
   cout << "array        " << setw(5) << sizeof(array) << endl;
   cout << "char*        " << setw(5) << sizeof(char*) << endl;
   return 0;
}
```

Output

```
Data Type    Bytes
char             1
int              4
bool             1
short            2
long             4
float            4
double           8
long double     10
array           20
char*            4
```

Leaving the data type out of parentheses after `sizeof`.

The `sizeof` operation evaluates to the number of bytes in whatever data type follows. The data type must be in parentheses. For example,

```cpp
sizeof(char)
```

is one, because there is always one byte in a `char` data type. Program 11–1 shows the `sizeof` operator in action by displaying the number of bytes in the data types in one particular C++. Try running this program with your C++ to see the sizes of your data types.

The second-to-last line

```cpp
cout << "array        " << setw(5) << sizeof(array) << endl;
```

bears explanation. The `sizeof` operator treats an array as a complex data type (much like an object), so the `sizeof` an array evaluates to the total number of bytes allocated for the entire array. In this case it was an array of five four-byte `int`s, or 20 bytes.

We already know that variables (and values, too) are stored in memory at specific addresses. We rarely know what those addresses are, but C++

HEADS UP!

Addresses are data types too.

keeps track of them. We have often referred to the address of the beginning of a string as &string[0]. The address is, of course, some value—data—and it is of some data type. So data types, when stored, have addresses, which are also data types.

This leads us to a whole new set of data types, the addresses of other data types. Putting an asterisk (*) at the end of the name of a data type makes it the data type of that data type's address. char is a data type, and char* is also a data type—the data type of the address of a char. The last line of Program 11–1 shows the sizeof that data type.

```
cout << "char*        " << setw(5) << sizeof(char*) << endl;
```

In this C++ there are four bytes in a char*. Actually, the address of any data type in a particular C++ will have the same number of bytes. It is the number of bytes that the operating system uses to keep track of a memory location. We specify the address of a particular data type because C++ will have to treat the contents at that address differently for different data types. It will certainly treat a char differently from a float or a long double.

Functions that require addresses as arguments usually require addresses of specific data types. Often we wish to use these functions with addresses of other data types, so we will have to **cast**—change one data type to another. The **cast operator** is the data type we want in parentheses. If *what* is a char data type,

```
(int)what
```

is of data type int (*what*, of course, is still data type char). Casting to smaller data types may be a problem if significant bits are lost in the process. For example, if the value of *integer* is 500, the value of

Losing significant digits in a cast.

```
(char)integer
```

would be meaningless because a char data type can hold a numeric value up to only 255.

If *word* is a string, then &word[0] is the address of the first char in the string.

```
(int*)&word[0]
```

results in a data type of an int address.

Remember from Chapter 8 that an array name is the address of the beginning of an array. Given the declaration

```
double stuff[20];
```

stuff is the address of the beginning of the array—data type address-of-double.

```
(char*)stuff
```

results in a data type address-of-char.

Why would we want to do that? Hang in there—we're about to get to it.

Writing Bytes

The fstream **write()** behavior takes a number of bytes beginning at an address in main memory and copies them directly, with no translation, to a file. We tell it the memory *location* and the number of *bytes*, and it writes the contents to a file connected to an *fstream* object.

```
void fstream.write(char* location, int bytes)        <fstream>
```

For example, given the declaration

```
string words = "Hello world!"
```

the statement

```
verbiage.write(&words[0], words.size());
```

would put the entire string *Hello world!* on the file connected to *verbiage*.

The write() function's prototype specifies using the address of a char, but since this function simply copies bytes (any bytes) beginning at an address in memory to a file, why not use it to copy the bytes in a long or a double, or perhaps even an array of doubles? We can do just that if we cast the address as the address of a char. In the following code segments, first we copy the value of *peas* to the file connected to *veggies*. Next we copy the entire *beans* array to the file. The values, both in memory and in the file, are in binary numeric form, unreadable to us, of course.

TRAP

Forgetting to cast the address in a write().

```
long peas;
double beans[10];

veggies.write((char*)peas, 4);                  // Copy bytes in peas to file
veggies.write((char*)beans, 80);                // Copy entire beans array to file
```

To write these statements, we had to know that a long was four bytes and a double eight. We could make the statements more portable using the sizeof operator:

```
veggies.write((char*)peas, sizeof(long));        // Copy bytes in peas to file
veggies.write((char*)beans, 10 * sizeof(double));  //Copy entire beans array
```

Remember we said that the sizeof an array name was the number of bytes allocated for the entire array. Using that concept, we could rewrite the second statement above as:

```
veggies.write((char*)beans, sizeof(beans));  // Copy entire
beans array
```

Reading Bytes

The **read()** function does exactly the opposite of the write() function; it takes a number of bytes from a file and writes them at an address in main memory. You must be certain that there is enough allocated space at that memory location; C++ gives you no help there.

```
void fstream.read(char* location, int bytes)        <fstream>
```

The arguments are exactly the same.

With the same declarations, these statements would copy four bytes from the file stream to *peas*, and 80 bytes to the *beans* array.

```
veggies.read((char*)peas, sizeof(long));         // Copy bytes in file to peas
veggies.read((char*)beans, sizeof(beans));            // Copy to beans array
```

Program 11–2

```cpp
#include <iostream>
#include <cstdlib>
#include <fstream>
#include <iomanip>
using namespace std;

const int maxDays = 60;                                    // No more than 60 days

int main(void)
{   fstream goo;
    float grease[maxDays];
    short count, day = 0;

    //--------------------------------------------------------- Open file
    goo.open("PRODUCT", ios::in | ios::out | ios::trunc | ios::binary);
    if ( !goo)
    {   cout << "Can't open PRODUCT file." << endl;
        exit(EXIT_FAILURE);
    }
    //--------------------------------------------------------- Input values
    do
    {   ++day;                                  // Next day (started with zero)
        cout << "Tons for day " << day << " (-1 to quit): ";
        cin >> grease[day - 1];
    }while (grease[day - 1] != -1);
    --day;                                      // Last input (-1) doesn't count

    //--------------------------------------------------------- Write to file
    goo.write((char*)&day, sizeof(short)); // Number of values to be written
    goo.write((char*)grease, sizeof(float) * day);        // The values

    //--------------------------------------------------------- Read from file
    goo.seekg(0);                              // Reset position to beginning
    goo.read((char*)&day, sizeof(short));            // Number of values
    goo.read((char*)grease, sizeof(float) * day);         // The values
    if (goo.eof())                             // Check for end of file
    {   cout << "Error, end of file reached." << endl;
        exit(EXIT_FAILURE);
    }
    //--------------------------------------------------------- Print report
    cout << setprecision(1) << setiosflags(ios::fixed);
    cout << "\nDay   Tons\n";
    for (count = 1; count <= day; ++count)
        cout << setw(3) << count << setw(7) << grease[count - 1] << endl;
    goo.close();
    return 0;
}
```

HEADS UP!

C++ doesn't care what we copy. We must make it make sense.

Wouldn't it be embarrassing if those 80 bytes in the file (`sizeof(beans)`) did not represent `doubles`? Only to you, though, not to C++.

We can test whether the `read()` was successful or attempted a read at the end of the file by examining `eof()` immediately after the `read()`.

Output

```
Tons for day 1 (-1 to quit): 36.4
Tons for day 2 (-1 to quit): 25
Tons for day 3 (-1 to quit): 42.38
Tons for day 4 (-1 to quit): -1

Day   Tons
 1    36.4
 2    25.0
 3    42.4
```

PRODUCT File

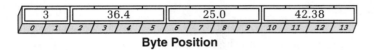

| 3 | 36.4 | 25.0 | 42.38 |

```
0 / 1 / 2 / 3 / 4 / 5 / 6 / 7 / 8 / 9 / 10 / 11 / 12 / 13
```
Byte Position

```
veggies.read((char*)beans, sizeof(beans));                // Copy to beans array
if (veggies.eof())
   cout << "No more file left!" << endl;
```

Or we can use `eof()` to control a file-access loop. For example, if we were reading sets of *beans* arrays:

```
veggies.read((char*)beans, sizeof(beans));                // Copy to beans array
while ( !veggies.eof())                                    // Not at end of file
{  cout << "More beans.\n";
   veggies.read((char*)beans, sizeof(beans));              // Copy to beans array
}
cout << "We're out of beans!" << endl;
```

Program 11–2 allows input of any number of days' production of axle grease in tons and stores the data in a file. Then it prints the data from the file on the screen.

The number of items to be written on the file, *day*, was put on the file first, followed by the items themselves by specifying the number of bytes in the part of the *grease* array that was filled. In the *PRODUCT File* graphic, we showed the numbers in human-readable form. They would, of course, be in strictly binary numeric form—unreadable by humans.

Reading from the file was in exactly the same order—the integer *day* first and then *day* sets of bytes for the array *grease*.

HEADS UP!

If you `write()` it to the file, you must `read()` it from the file.

YOUR TURN 11–2

1. What is an advantage of character access to files?
2. What are advantages of byte access to files?
3. What does the `sizeof` operator tell us?
4. How does putting an asterisk after the name of a data type, such as `int*`, change the data type?
5. What is a cast?
6. Why do we use the `fstream` behaviors `write()` and `read()`?

BYTE ACCESS AND PORTABILITY

Byte access to files may be fast, but it limits the portability of both the files and the programs. We have already mentioned that most of the ANSI standard data types are not standard in the number of bytes in the data type. If an `int` were put on a file as two bytes, but then the program was recompiled on another system that used four-byte `int`s, the data coming back from the same file would be garbage. Systems also differ in the order in which they store bits. Some put the most significant bit on the left, others on the right. Be sure you know the system particulars before you try to move either programs or files from system to system.

FILES AND OBJECTS

HEADS UP!

Objects maintain the fixed-length, consistent data concept of direct-access files.

A class has both properties and behaviors. An object of a class has its own set of property values, but it shares behaviors with all other objects of the class. We can say, then, that an object really has only properties. It has access to behaviors, but the only things actually stored in the object are its properties.

Because the object consists only of properties—data—we should be able to `write()` the contents of an object to a file and `read()` a number of bytes from a file to fill an object. The object is a fixed-length entity with a number of fixed-length properties. This concept is exactly the same as a fixed-length record with a number of fixed-length fields. It would seem natural, then, to read file records into memory objects, and vice versa.

As an example, let's look at daily statistics for our Internet access port. We want to keep track of the number of connections made; the bytes sent; the bytes received; and the minutes, to the thousandth, of connect time. Program 11–3 creates a class with those properties, *Internet*, and an object of that class, *port*. We would probably have some fancy automatic way of gathering the appropriate data directly from our Internet software, but for now, let's just input the data for the *port* object. Once the data are in the *port* object, the program copies the object, byte by byte, to the file *NetStats*.

Those bytes on the file are virtually meaningless unless we have a way of interpreting them. If we copy the bytes back to a *port* object, they will fill the spaces reserved for an `int`, two `long`s, and a `double`—data we can work with.

The program also displays the bytes on the file interpreted as characters—in other words, what we would see if we looked at the file with a text editor. They are truly meaningless to the human eye. (We actually had to fudge the characters a bit; some of the characters on the file drove the word processor nuts! Run the program on your system and see what you get. You might be wise to save all your work to secondary storage first.)

Object with Strings

Let's expand on our employee example from Chapter 10, putting our employee data in a directly accessible file. To enforce fixed-length records, we set up an employee object and copy bytes from the object to the file, and vice versa. We will set up Program 11–4 as a test of the employee object and print out the number of bytes in the object.

Program 11–3

```cpp
#include <iostream>
#include <cstdlib>
#include <fstream>
#include <iomanip>
#include <string>
using namespace std;

class Internet
{
public:
    int connects;
    long sent;
    long rcvd;
    double time;
};

int main(void)
{   Internet port;
    fstream net;
    string data;

    cout << "Connects, bytes sent, bytes received, time> ";
    cin >> port.connects >> port.sent >> port.rcvd >> port.time;
    net.open("NetStats", ios::in | ios::out | ios::trunc | ios::binary);
    net.write((char*)&port, sizeof(port));  // Write object contents to file
    net.seekg(0);                            // Set file back to beginning
    net.read((char*)&port, sizeof(port));   // Read object contents from file
    cout << "Connects: " << port.connects << ", bytes sent: " << port.sent
         << ", bytes received: " << port.rcvd
         << ", time: " << port.time << ".\n";
    net.seekg(0);                            // Set file back to beginning
    getline(net, data, '\n');                // Read characters from file
    cout << "Characters on file:\n";
    cout << data << endl;                    // Display characters
    net.close();
    return 0;
}
```

Output

```
Connects, bytes sent, bytes received, time> 22 43703 26770 5507.31
Connects: 22, bytes sent: 43703, bytes received: 26770, time: 5507.31.
Characters on file:
Fš  œ+¬M¾Æhéð-¥0â¦@
```

HEADS UP!

A string object does not
contain the actual characters.

There being only 13 bytes in the *employee* object does not make sense; there are 18 bytes in the name alone!

The problem here is that a `string` object, such as *employee.name*, contains only information about the string, not the actual characters. It contains the address of the string's location in memory so its behaviors can access the string, but the actual characters are not part of the object. The standard `read()` and `write()` functions will not work because it would do us no good to write memory addresses on the file; we must write the

Program 11–4

```
#include <iostream>
#include <string>
using namespace std;

class EmployeeRec
{
public:
    string name;
    float payRate;
    int dependents;
};

int main(void)
{   EmployeeRec employee;

    employee.name = "Neena Nanna Norney";
    cout << "Bytes in employee: " << sizeof(employee) << endl;
    return 0;
}
```

Output

```
Bytes in employee: 13
```

Copying an object with strings to a file.

actual characters. We will have to create our own *read()* and *write()* functions as behaviors of the class.

Program 11–5 asks for keyboard input of employee records and writes them to the file *EMPLOYEE.DAT*. Then it reads the records from the file and displays them.

The *write()* function is fairly straightforward; it uses the ANSI `write()` behavior to copy the maximum characters for a *name* from its address (`&name[0]`) to the file connected to *file*. There is no need to cast the `&name[0]` because it *is* the address of a `char`. This will actually write the *name* plus a bunch of garbage characters to the file. As we saw in Chapter 9 C++ stores the characters in a `string` object with a trailing null to maintain compatibility with string values. When the characters are copied to the file, the null is too. We will see that when we read the name back to main memory, everything after the null is ignored.

After copying the *name*, the function copies, from the address of *payRate*, enough bytes for a `float` (*payRate*) and an `int` (*dependents*).

HEADS UP!

Read a string into a char array, then assign it to a string.

The *read()* function is a little trickier. We cannot read directly into the address of the first character of a `string` (`&name[0]`) because we cannot be sure how many characters are allocated there; nor will the `string` object know how to `size()` the string. To overcome these problems, we first read the characters, including the trailing null and following garbage, into a `char` array. Then we assign the characters in that array to the `string` *name*. When a character array is assigned to a `string`, C++ knows to stop assigning characters at the trailing null and sets the size appropriately.

Copying into *payRate* and *dependents* is the exact opposite of what we did in *write()*. As we did with similar functions in Chapter 10, this *read()* returns `false` if it is not successful, such as at the end of the file.

Program 11–5

```cpp
#include <iostream>
#include <iomanip>
#include <fstream>
#include <string>
using namespace std;

const int maxName = 30;

class EmployeeRec ///////////////////////////////////// EmployeeRec Class
{
public:
   string name;
   float payRate;
   int dependents;

   void write(fstream &file) //---------------------------- Write a Record
   {  file.write(&name[0], maxName);
      file.write((char*)&payRate, sizeof(float) + sizeof(int));
   }
   bool read(fstream &file) //----------------------------- Read a Record
   {  char str[maxName];                            // Temporary character array

      file.read(str, maxName);                      // Read into character array
      name = str;                                         // Assign to string
      file.read((char*)&payRate, sizeof(float) + sizeof(int));
      if (file.eof())
         return false;
      else
         return true;
   }
};

int main(void) ///////////////////////////////////////////// Main Program
{  EmployeeRec employee;
   fstream employ;

   employ.open("EMPLOYEE.DAT", ios::in | ios::out
               | ios::trunc | ios::binary);
   cout << "Employee name: "; //------------------- Input and Write to File
   getline(cin, employee.name, '\n');
   while (employee.name.size())                              // Empty string
   {  cout << "Pay rate, dependents: ";
      cin >> employee.payRate >> employee.dependents;
      cin.ignore(500, '\n');
      employee.write(employ);
      cout << "Employee name: ";
      getline(cin, employee.name, '\n');
   }
```

(Continued)

 HEADS UP!

Typically, objects written to files make little sense if we look at the file.

Showing the file contents as a result of this program would make little sense. We could see the characters in the strings, but the numbers were written just as they were stored in memory, in binary notation, so those bytes translated as characters would be meaningless.

```
        employ.seekg(0);//-------------------------- Read from File and Display
        cout << setiosflags(ios::fixed) << setprecision(2);
        cout << "\nName                        Pay Rate  Dep\n";
        while (employee.read(employ))
            cout << setiosflags(ios::left) << setw(30) << employee.name
                << resetiosflags(ios::left) << setw(8) << employee.payRate
                << setw(5) << employee.dependents << endl;
        employ.close();
        return 0;
    }
```

Output

```
    Employee name: Maynard Freebisch
    Pay rate, dependents: 10.83 2
    Employee name: Gilda Garfinkle
    Pay rate, dependents: 15.25 4
    Employee name: Beulah Barzoom
    Pay rate, dependents: 12.63 4
    Employee name: LeRoy LaRue
    Pay rate, dependents: 9.5 0
    Employee name:

    Name                        Pay Rate  Dep
    Maynard Freebisch               10.83   2
    Gilda Garfinkle                 15.25   4
    Beulah Barzoom                  12.63   4
    LeRoy LaRue                      9.50   0
```

Program 11–6

```
    #include <iostream>
    #include <iomanip>
    #include <fstream>
    #include <string>
    using namespace std;

    const int maxName = 30;
    const double taxRate = .16;                    // Current income tax rate
    const double depAdjust = .02;         // Adjust tax rate for each dependent

    class EmployeeRec ////////////////////////////////////// EmployeeRec Class
    {
    public:
        string name;
        float payRate;
        int dependents;

        void write(fstream &file) //---------------------------- Write a Record
        {   file.write(&name[0], maxName);
            file.write((char*)&payRate, sizeof(float) + sizeof(int));
        }
```

(Continued)

Program 11–6 *(Continued)*

```
    bool read(fstream &file) //----------------------------- Read a Record
    {   char str[maxName];                      // Temporary character array

        file.read(str, maxName);                // Read into character array
        name = str;                                    // Assign to string
        file.read((char*)&payRate, sizeof(float) + sizeof(int));
        if (file.eof())
            return false;
        else
            return true;
    }
    int size(void) //-------------- Size of Data in Object, Including String
    {   return maxName + sizeof(float) + sizeof(int); }
};

int main(void) /////////////////////////////////////////////// Main Program
{   EmployeeRec employee;
    fstream employ;
    int position;                                  // Byte position in file
    double hours, gross, tax, net;

    employ.open("EMPLOYEE.DAT", ios::in | ios::binary);

    cout << setiosflags(ios::fixed) << setprecision(2);
    employ.seekg(0, ios::end);                        // Move to end of file
    for (position = employ.tellg() - employee.size();  // Beg of last record
         position >= 0;                            // First record or beyond
         position -= employee.size())                 // Back up one record
    {   employ.seekg(position, ios::beg);         // File to proper position
        employee.read(employ);
        cout << "Hours for " << employee.name << ": ";
        cin >> hours;
        gross = hours * employee.payRate;
        tax = (taxRate - depAdjust * employee.dependents) * gross;
        net = gross - tax;
        cout << "   Pay to: " << employee.name << "   $**" << net << "**" <<
endl;
    }
    return 0;
}
```

Output

```
Hours for LeRoy LaRue: 3
    Pay to: LeRoy LaRue    $**23.94**
Hours for Beulah Barzoom: 39
    Pay to: Beulah Barzoom    $**453.16**
Hours for Gilda Garfinkle: 44
    Pay to: Gilda Garfinkle    $**617.32**
Hours for Maynard Freebisch: 36
    Pay to: Maynard Freebisch    $**343.09**
```

STRUCTURES

Before there was C++ there was C, and before there were classes, there were structures. The C++ class is an extension of the C structure, which is still valid in C++. The class definition in Program 11–1 could have been stated as a structure definition:

```
struct Internet
{   int connects;
    long sent;
    long rcvd;
    double time;
};
```

and the rest of the program would remain the same.

The differences between structures and classes are that structure properties default to public—notice that there is no `public` key word—and a C structure did not have behaviors (although they are possible with C++ structures).

We could do this week's payroll by reading the employee data from the file, inputting the number of hours for each, and printing the results. Unfortunately, the way our printer is configured, the first check to print will end up on the bottom of the stack, rather than on top. We, the programming geniuses, will accommodate for that in Program 11–6 by going through the file backward.

To the *EmployeeRec* class we have added a *size()* function to return not the `sizeof` the object but the number of bytes in the data represented by the object. In other words, the maximum number of characters in the *name* plus the `sizeof` the other data.

In `main()`, the `for` loop that goes through the file adjusts a *position* that starts at the beginning of the last record—the end of the file minus the *size()* of a record—and steps backward one record at a time to the beginning of the file. The first operation within the loop—before reading, of course—is to set the file at that *position*.

YOUR TURN 11–3

1. If characters in a byte-access file are meaningless, what good are they?
2. Why can't we simply `write()` a `string` object or an object with a string in it to a file?
3. What character is at the end of every string?
4. How do we `read()` a string from a file?

CHANGING A DIRECT-ACCESS FILE

In Program 11–7 we change the pay rate of one of the people in the *EMPLOYEE.DAT* file using both sequential and direct access to the file. We use sequential access to find the employee in the file. Once we have found the employee's record—matched the name from the file record with the one input from the keyboard—the file position is beyond that record in

Program 11–7

```cpp
#include <iostream>
#include <iomanip>
#include <cstdlib>
#include <fstream>
#include <string>
using namespace std;

const int maxName = 30;

class EmployeeRec ////////////////////////////////////// EmployeeRec Class
{
public:
    string name;
    float payRate;
    int dependents;

    void write(fstream &file) //---------------------------- Write a Record
    {   file.write(&name[0], maxName);
        file.write((char*)&payRate, sizeof(float) + sizeof(int));
    }
    bool read(fstream &file) //------------------------------ Read a Record
    {   char str[maxName];                         // Temporary character array

        file.read(str, maxName);                   // Read into character array
        name = str;                                // Assign to string
        file.read((char*)&payRate, sizeof(float) + sizeof(int));
        if (file.eof())
            return false;
        else
            return true;
    }
    int size(void) //-------------- Size of Data in Object, Including String
    {   return maxName + sizeof(float) + sizeof(int); }
};

int main(void) ////////////////////////////////////////////// Main Program
{   EmployeeRec employee;
    fstream employ;
    string name;                                   // Name in record to change
```

(Continued)

the file. We use direct access to return the file to the byte position of the beginning of the record so we may rewrite the record to the file. The record, of course, is stored in memory in an object.

In this program we have added a section that tests for the successful opening of the file. Also, if the name could not be found (employ.eof() was true) we had to clear the end-of-file condition, because the eof() test is used in the *read()* behavior and that function is used later, in the part of the program that displays the file. If the condition was not cleared, even though the file position was returned to the beginning of the file, eof() would still be true, and the next call to *read()* would think it was at the end of the file and return false.

Program 11–7 *(Continued)*

```
        //------------------------------------------------------------ Open File
        employ.open("EMPLOYEE.DAT", ios::in | ios::out | ios::binary);
        if ( !employ)
        {   cout << "Can't open file" << endl;
            exit(EXIT_FAILURE);
        }
        cout << "Employee's name: ";  //---------- Input Name in Record to Change
        getline(cin, name, '\n');

        employee.read(employ);  //-------------------------------------- Search File
        while (name != employee.name                    // Names don't match
              && !employ.eof())                         // Not at end of file
            employee.read(employ);
        if (employ.eof())                               // Input name could not be found
        {   cout << name << " not on file.\n";
            employ.clear();  // Clear eof condition so eof test can be used again
        }
        else                                            // Change pay rate and rewrite
        {   cout << "Pay rate for " << employee.name << ": ";
            cin >> employee.payRate;
            employ.seekg( -employee.size(), ios::cur);  // To beginning of record
            employee.write(employ);
        }
        employ.seekg(0);//------------------------- Read from File and Display
        cout << setiosflags(ios::fixed) << setprecision(2);
        cout << "\nName                        Pay Rate  Dep\n";
        while (employee.read(employ))
            cout << setiosflags(ios::left) << setw(30) << employee.name
                 << resetiosflags(ios::left) << setw(8) << employee.payRate
                 << setw(5) << employee.dependents << endl;
        employ.close();
        return 0;
    }
```

Outputs

```
    Employee's name: LeRoy LaRue
    Pay rate for LeRoy LaRue: 5.35

    Name                        Pay Rate  Dep
    Maynard Freebisch               10.83   2
    Gilda Garfinkle                 15.25   4
    Beulah Barzoom                  12.63   4
    LeRoy LaRue                      5.35   0

    Employee's name: Ebenezer Bargle
    Ebenezer Bargle not on file.

    Name                        Pay Rate  Dep
    Maynard Freebisch               10.83   2
    Gilda Garfinkle                 15.25   4
    Beulah Barzoom                  12.63   4
    LeRoy LaRue                      5.35   0
```

Program 11–8 *(Change in Program 11–5)*

```
employ.open("EMPLOYEE.DAT", ios::in | ios::out
            | ios::app | ios::binary);
```

Output

```
Employee name: Bertrand Balfarge
Pay rate, dependents: 15.45 3
Employee name:
```

Name	Pay Rate	Dep
Maynard Freebisch	10.83	2
Gilda Garfinkle	15.25	4
Beulah Barzoom	12.63	4
LeRoy LaRue	5.35	0
Bertrand Balfarge	15.45	3

Adding Records

The easiest way to add records to a file is to add them to the end, as we did in Chapter 10. The *EMPLOYEE.DAT* file is in no particular order, so adding to the end of it is as good as anything else. All we have to do is to open the file for writing with the position at the end—ios::app—and write the new records to the file.

Program 11–8 is a more complete program, adding records to the end of the file and then displaying the file's contents. That is exactly what we did in Program 11–5, except that there we started with an empty file— ios::trunc. To make Program 11–8, then, we simply change one statement, the file's open() behavior, from

```
employ.open("EMPLOYEE.DAT", ios::in | ios::out
            | ios::trunc | ios::binary);
```

to

```
employ.open("EMPLOYEE.DAT", ios::in | ios::out
            | ios::app | ios::binary);
```

One of the more common situations is to have the file in order—perhaps alphabetically by name. To add a record to such a file, we have to insert it using the insert process we developed in Chapter 8. The *Putting It Together* section (pages 424–435) shows a good example of that technique.

Deleting Records

If adding records can be so simple, deleting records must be as well. It isn't! When a record is truly deleted, the file becomes shorter by that amount. We can extend files by simply writing to the end of them. There is no easy way to shorten a file. Even if we could maneuver it so that the end record was the one to be deleted, there is no convenient way of telling the system "OK, the file is now this much shorter," so that dead record still hangs around at the end of the file.

One method of deleting a record is to "logically delete" it—identify the record and replace it with some significant character set—all nulls, for

Program 11–9

```cpp
#include <iostream>
#include <iomanip>
#include <cstdlib>
#include <fstream>
#include <cstdio>
#include <string>
using namespace std;

const int maxName = 30;

class EmployeeRec //////////////////////////////////// EmployeeRec Class
{
public:
   string name;
   float payRate;
   int dependents;

   void write(fstream &file) //--------------------------- Write a Record
   {  file.write(&name[0], maxName);
      file.write((char*)&payRate, sizeof(float) + sizeof(int));
   }
   bool read(fstream &file) //---------------------------- Read a Record
   {  char str[maxName];                        // Temporary character array

      file.read(str, maxName);                  // Read into character array
      name = str;                               // Assign to string
      file.read((char*)&payRate, sizeof(float) + sizeof(int));
      if (file.eof())
         return false;
      else
         return true;
   }
   int size(void) //-------------- Size of Data in Object, Including String
   {  return maxName + sizeof(float) + sizeof(int); }
};

int main(void) //////////////////////////////////////////////// Main Program
{  EmployeeRec employee;
   fstream employ, temp;                        // Temporary file for copy
   string name;                                 // Name in record to change

   //----------------------------------------------------------- Open File
   employ.open("EMPLOYEE.DAT", ios::in | ios::binary);
   if ( !employ)
   {  cout << "Can't open file" << endl;
      exit(EXIT_FAILURE);
   }
   temp.open("TEMP.$TM", ios::out | ios::binary);   // Open temporary file
   cout << "Employee's name: "; //---------- Input Name in Record to Delete
   getline(cin, name, '\n');
```

(Continued)

Program 11–9 *(Continued)*

```
      employee.read(employ);  //---------------------------------- Search File
      while ( !employ.eof())                          // Not at end of file
      {  if (name != employee.name)         // Names don't match, don't delete
            employee.write(temp);                        // Write on temp file
         employee.read(employ);                   // Next record from data file
      }
      employ.close();
      temp.close();
      remove("EMPLOYEE.DAT");       // unlink("EMPLOYEE.DAT"); in a UNIX system
      rename("TEMP.$TM", "EMPLOYEE.DAT");

      employ.open("EMPLOYEE.DAT",//--------------- Read from File and Display
               ios::in | ios::binary);
      cout << setiosflags(ios::fixed) << setprecision(2);
      cout << "\nName                            Pay Rate  Dep\n";
      while (employee.read(employ))
         cout << setiosflags(ios::left) << setw(30) << employee.name
              << resetiosflags(ios::left) << setw(8) << employee.payRate
              << setw(5) << employee.dependents << endl;
      return 0;
}
```

Output

Employee's name: **LeRoy LaRue**

Name	Pay Rate	Dep
Maynard Freebisch	10.83	2
Gilda Garfinkle	15.25	4
Beulah Barzoom	12.63	4
Bertrand Balfarge	15.45	3

example. All other programs that use that file will have to be programmed to "understand" that all nulls means that the record has been deleted.

The way to truly delete a record is to revert to the methods we used for variable-length records in Chapter 10; that is, to copy all the records in the file, except for the deleted one, to a temporary file. We show that in Program 11–9.

YOUR TURN 11–4

1. Why can changing a direct-access, fixed-length-record file be easier than changing a variable-length-record file?

2. What was the significance of the *size()* behavior in Program 11–7?

3. How is adding data to the end of a fixed-length-record file different from adding data to the end of a variable-length-record file?

4. How do we add records, in order, to a fixed-length-record file?

5. How is deleting data in a fixed-length-record file different from deleting data in a variable-length-record file?

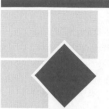

PUTTING IT TOGETHER

Let's go back to Sheldon Diefendorfer's video collection from Chapter 10. One of the criteria we were faced with was that, because of Shelly's shortage of money, storage space had to be kept to a minimum. Recently Shelly's Great Aunt Grizzenda passed on and left him a minor fortune. This was fortunate for Shelly (although not particularly for Aunt Grizzenda) because now he could concentrate on speed of execution instead of minimal storage space.

He wants us to do some rewriting. We are going to charge him for it this time; he can afford it.

TASK

Rewrite Shelly's video system with rapid execution speed rather than minimal storage space in mind.

ANALYSIS

The program should operate exactly as it did in Chapter 10. Heaven forbid that Shelly should have to learn new procedures!

DESIGN, IMPLEMENTATION, AND TEST

Again we will look at individual sections of the program but, as in the Chapter 10 program, all the behaviors will use the same file. However, since our emphasis has shifted to execution speed, we will change the file from one that uses variable-length records to one that uses fixed-length records. The numbers—year, length, and shelf position—were already in fixed-length format because they were direct copies of the numbers in memory.

The titles in the old file were variable-length, delimited by the newline character. In the new file we will make them all 50 characters long. (Remember the *Incredibly Strange Creatures* movie? Shelly has agreed to list it under its *Teenage Psycho* title.) The title will no longer need a delimiter because the next record will always start at the fifty-first character. This will leave a lot of extra space in the file, but remember, Shelly has lots of money now.

The *Movies* Class

DESIGN

The *Movies* class will have the same properties and behaviors as before. Some of the details within the behaviors will change; in fact, many will be simplified because of the use of the fixed-length file.

Let's look at both *readMovie()* and *writeMovie()* in the `private` section of the *Movie* class. Their processes remain the same, so the pseudocode will not change, but the details of their implementation changes because of the fixed-length format, and because we are no longer using the newline delimiter.

Class *Movies*

```
#include <iostream>
#include <iomanip>
#include <cstdio>
#include <cstdlib>
#include <string>
#include <cctype>
#include <fstream>
using namespace std;

const int maxChrs = 50;                          // Maximum length for a title
const int items = 3;                 // Number of data items kept for each video
                                     // Indexes for data array for each video
   const short year = 0;                          // movie.data[0] is year
   const short length = 1;                                  // In minutes
   const short shelf = 2;                          // Position on the shelves


class Movies //////////////////////////////////////////////////// Movies Class
{   short data[items];                      // Year, length, and shelf position
    string title;

    bool readMovie(fstream &video) //********** Reads Single Movie From File
    {   char str[maxChrs];                       // Temporary character array

        video.read(str, maxChrs);                // Read into character array
        title = str;                                  // Assign to string
        video.read((char*)data, sizeof(data));
        if ( !video.eof())
            return true;
        else
            return false;
    }
    void writeMovie(fstream &video) //********** Writes Single Movie to File
    {   video.write(&title[0], maxChrs);
        video.write((char*)data, sizeof(data));
    }
public:
    void printFile(void) //******************** Displays the Data in the File
    void add(void) //****************************** Adds a Record in Order
    void del(void) //*********************** Deletes a Record from the File
    void change(int index) //********** Changes One of the Other Parameters
    void newFile(void) //************* Creates New File for Testing Purposes
};
```

r1	(bool readMovie line)
r2	(char str line)
r3	(video.read str line)
r4	(title = str line)
r5	(video.read data line)
r6	(if !video.eof line)
r7	(return true line)
r8	(return false line)
w1	(void writeMovie line)
w2	(video.write title line)
w3	(video.write data line)

EXECUTION CHART — *readMovie()*

Line	Explanation	str	movie.title	movie.data[]		
r1	Receive reference to open file *VIDEOS.DAT*.	--	??	??	??	??
r2	Declare character array *str*.	??	??	??	??	??
r3	Copy 50 characters from file *VIDEOS.DAT* to address *str*.	Blob, The\0 …	??	??	??	??
r4	Assign characters at *str* to *title*.	Blob, The\0 …	Blob, The	??	??	??
r5	Read next 6 bytes (`sizeof` *data* array) from file to *data*.	Blob, The\0 …	Blob, The	1958	95	4265
r6	If not at the end of file, return `true` in r7, otherwise return `false` in r8. It is `true` in this case.	Blob, The\0 …	Blob, The	1958	95	4265

Line	Explanation	movie.title	movie.data[]		
w1	Receive reference to open file *VIDEOS.DAT*.	Blob, The	1958	95	4265
w2	Write 50 characters from address of beginning of *title* to file.	Blob, The	1958	95	4265
w3	Copy 6 bytes (`sizeof` *data* array) from *data* to file.	Blob, The	1958	95	4265

IMPLEMENTATION

Our new implementation, Program 11–10, can no longer use `getline()` in *readMovie()*; it looks for a specific delimiter and takes only that number of characters from the file stream. We must always take 50 characters from the stream, moving the file position accordingly. The `fstream` behavior `read()` seems like the obvious solution but, as we pointed out earlier in this chapter, strings require special handling. We will use the method we developed earlier to treat strings.

The *writeMovie()* function is somewhat more straightforward, requiring only two `writes()`.

As in Chapter 10, Class *Movies* shows the beginning of the program code, including the `#includes`, `const` declarations, the details of *readMovie()* and *writeMovie()*, and a summary of the rest of the class.

Function *newFile()*

```
       void newFile(void) //************* Creates New File for Testing Purposes
       {   fstream video;
n1         video.open("VIDEOS.DAT", ios::out | ios::binary);
n2         title = "Blob, The";
n3            data[year] = 1958; data[length] = 95; data[shelf] = 4265;
n4            writeMovie(video);
n5         title = "Cannibal Women in the Avocado Jungle of Death";
              data[year] = 1988; data[length] = 90; data[shelf] = 3328;
              writeMovie(video);
n6         title = "Frankenstein Meets the Space Monster";
              data[year] = 1965; data[length] = 75; data[shelf] = 1005;
              writeMovie(video);
n7         title = "Rock'N'Roll High School Forever";
              data[year] = 1990; data[length] = 94; data[shelf] = 2615;
              writeMovie(video);
n8         video.close();
       }
```

VIDEOS.DAT File (Actual)

```
    Blob, The                                       ¦Ð²©»Cannibal Women ...
```

VIDEOS.DAT File (Easier to Read)

```
    Blob, The                                       ¦Ð²©»
    Cannibal Women in the Avocado Jungle of Death   ÄçZœ÷¥
    Frankenstein Meets the Space Monster            -µK¾íš
    Rock'N'Roll High School Forever                 Æ‰^§7¿
```

The Execution Charts show *readMovie()* reading *The Blob* from the file *VIDEOS.DAT*, and *writeMovie()* writing *The Blob* to the file *VIDEOS.DAT*.

Creating a File for Testing

DESIGN

This section fills the *VIDEO.DAT* file with four movies to facilitate testing.

IMPLEMENTATION

The *newFile()* function is completely unchanged from its Chapter 10 version. It works with the new file format because it calls the rewritten *writeMovie()* function. Function *newFile()* shows the code, copied straight from Chapter 10.

TEST

The test produces slightly different results than in Chapter 10 because of the fixed-length records. We have shown the resultant *VIDEOS.DAT* file in two versions. The first is the beginning of it as it would actually be stored—with no line endings. The second is easier to read because we have added line endings at the end of each record in the printout. Remember that although the second may be easier to read, the file is not actually stored that way.

The `main()` Function

DESIGN

Shelly said he did not want to learn any new procedures to use the new program. Because `main()` controls many of those procedures, its design is the same as before; the pseudocode still applies.

IMPLEMENTATION

The `main()` function is shown in Program 11–10, but it is unchanged from Chapter 10.

TEST

The `main()` function runs the same as in Chapter 10.

Printing the File

DESIGN

Printing the file is also unchanged from Chapter 10. As we said, the file is somewhat different, but the changed *readMovie()* function accommodates the differences.

Program 11-10

```cpp
      int main(void) ///////////////////////////////////////// Main Program
      {  Movies movie;
         char choice;

1  //    movie.newFile();            // Used only for the first run of the test

         //------------------------------------------ Test to see if file exists
2        fstream video;
3        video.open("VIDEOS.DAT", ios::in);
4        if ( !video)
5        {  cout << "Video file missing." << endl;
6           exit(EXIT_FAILURE);
         }
7        video.close();

8        do //------------------------------------------------------------- Menu
9        {  cout << "Do you want to:        Change:\n";
            cout << "   [A]dd a video?      A [T]itle?\n";
            cout << "   [D]elete a video?   A [Y]ear?\n";
            cout << "   [P]rint the list?   A [L]ength?\n";
            cout << "   [Q]uit?             A [S]helf position?\n";
            cout << "Take your choice: ";
10          cin >> choice;
11          cin.ignore(500, '\n');                        // Move past newline
12          switch (toupper(choice))
            {  case 'A':
13             movie.add();
               break;
            case 'D':
14             movie.del();
               break;
            case 'T':
15             movie.change(-1);              // Index of -1 signals title change
               break;
            case 'Y':
16             movie.change(year);
               break;
            case 'L':
17             movie.change(length);
               break;
            case 'S':
18             movie.change(shelf);
               break;
            case 'P':
19             movie.printFile();
            }
20       }while (toupper(choice) != 'Q');
         return 0;
      }
```

Function *printFile()*

```
        void printFile(void) //******************* Displays the Data in the File
        {  fstream video;
           short index;                                    // Index for data array

p1         video.open("VIDEOS.DAT", ios::in | ios::binary);
p2         cout << "\n  YEAR   LEN SHELF   TITLE\n";
p3         while (readMovie(video))
p4         {  for (index = 0; index < items; ++index)
p5               cout << setw(6) << data[index];
p6            cout << "    " << title << endl;
           }
p7         cout << endl;
p8         video.close();
        }
```

Output

```
Do you want to:          Change:
  [A]dd a video?           A [T]itle?
  [D]elete a video?        A [Y]ear?
  [P]rint the list?        A [L]ength?
  [Q]uit?                  A [S]helf position?
Take your choice: p

    YEAR  LEN SHELF   TITLE
    1958   95  4265   Blob, The
    1988   90  3328   Cannibal Women in the Avocado Jungle of Death
    1965   75  1005   Frankenstein Meets the Space Monster
    1990   94  2615   Rock'N'Roll High School Forever
```

IMPLEMENTATION

The coding for the Function *printFile()* is simply copied from Chapter 10.

TEST

The test should produce the same output as Chapter 10. Remember, this also tests the *newFile()* function, so if there are problems, we must look at both functions.

Adding to the File

DESIGN

Adding to the file will be significantly different from Chapter 10. With the unequal-record-length file in Chapter 10 we had to copy from one file to another. Here, since all the records are the same length, any one can replace any other. We will use an insert, as we did with arrays in Chapter 8. We do not need to copy from one file to another; it can all be accomplished with one file.

The insert process starts at the end of the file, the first possible insert position being the record after the current last record. As we did with arrays, we will match the record we want to insert with the record before the possible insert position in the file. If the insert record is greater, we exit the loop and write the record at the possible insert position; otherwise, we move the previous record down, move the possible insert position up, and try again.

The process stops when we have either found the proper position or get back to the first record in the file, in which case we simply write the new record there.

Unlike in Chapter 10, there is no need to mark the insert title with a tilde (~) so as to not find it again, because as soon as we insert, the process stops. If the file contained 10,000 records and the insert happened to fall at the end, our new process would require reading only one record and writing only one record. The Chapter 10 method would require us to read and write 10,000 records.

In pseudocode the process looks like this:

```
Open the data file
Input new title, year, length, and shelf position into new object
Set first possible insert position (end of file)
while new title < previous file title and beyond first record
    Move previous record to possible insert position
    Move possible insert position to previous record
Insert at possible insert position
Close file
```

IMPLEMENTATION

Function *add()* shows the coding for this section.

TEST

As in Chapter 10, we should be sure to test adding a record at both the beginning and the end of the file, as well as in the middle.

Deleting from the File

DESIGN

You would think that deleting from the file could be done as a kind of an opposite insert, using just a single file. The problem is that this would leave a superfluous record at the end of the file, and there is no easy way to tell the system to shorten the file by so many bytes. Lengthening the file? Easy! Shortening the file? Not so easy!

The most straightforward method of deleting from the file is the same way we did it in Chapter 10—copying from one file to another. Using the updated *readRecord()* and *writeRecord()*, the *del()* function is unchanged from Chapter 10.

IMPLEMENTATION

Function *del()* is copied directly from Chapter 10.

Function *add()*

```
        void add(void) //******************************** Adds a Record in Order
        {   fstream video;
a1          Movies newMovie;                                        // Movie to add
a2          int recLen = maxChrs + sizeof(data);           // Bytes in one record
a3          long pos;                                      // Possible insert position

a4          video.open("VIDEOS.DAT", ios::in | ios::out | ios::binary);

            cout << "New title: "; //-------------------------- Input new data
a5          getline(cin, newMovie.title, '\n');
            cout << "Year, length, shelf position: ";
a6          cin >> newMovie.data[year] >> newMovie.data[length]
                >> newMovie.data[shelf];
a7          cin.ignore(500, '\n');                       // Dump trailing newline
a8          video.seekg(0, ios::end);                       // End of file is . . .
a9          pos = video.tellg();                   // first possible insert position

a10         video.seekg( -recLen, ios::end);         // Look at previous record
a11         readMovie(video); //----------------------------- Insert into file
a12         while (newMovie.title < title          // Title still too small
a13                 && pos > 0)                          // 2nd record or higher
a14         {   writeMovie(video);                        // Move record down
a15             pos -= recLen;          // Possible insert position back up one record
a16             if (pos > 0)           // Don't allow move before beginning of file
a17             {   video.seekg(pos - recLen, ios::beg);     // Look at prev record
a18                 readMovie(video);           // Puts file position at insert record
                }
            }
a19         video.seekg(pos, ios::beg);                   // At insert position
a20         newMovie.writeMovie(video);                          // Insert

a21         video.close();
        }
```

Output

```
    New title: Buffy, the Vampire Slayer
    Year, length, shelf position: 1992 100 4180

    Take your choice: p

        YEAR   LEN  SHELF    TITLE
        1958    95  4265     Blob, The
        1992   100  4180     Buffy, the Vampire Slayer
        1988    90  3328     Cannibal Women in the Avocado Jungle of Death
        1965    75  1005     Frankenstein Meets the Space Monster
        1990    94  2615     Rock'N'Roll High School Forever
```

TEST

We should do the same tests—deletions at the beginning and the end, as well as in the middle of the file—that we did in Chapter 10.

Line	Explanation	newMovie.title	movie.title	pos [in records]	File Position [in records]
a1	Create *newMovie* object. This becomes an object within the *add()* behavior of the *movie* object. We refer to the *movie* title as *title*, and the new movie title as *newMovie.title*.	??	??	-- [--]	-- [--]
a2	Calculate bytes in each record. There are 56—50 for the string and 6 for the array of `shorts`.	??	??	-- [--]	-- [--]
a3	*pos* keeps track of possible insert position in bytes, we will also show it in records [*pos* / *recLen*].	??	??	?? [??]	-- [--]
a4	Open existing *VIDEOS.DAT* for reading and writing. **File:** Blob … Cann … Fran … Rock …	??	??	?? [??]	0 [1]
a5, 6	Input data for *newMovie* object.	Buffy, …	??	?? [??]	0 [1]
a7	Flush input stream.	Buffy, …	??	?? [??]	0 [1]
a8	Move file position to end of file.	Buffy, …	??	?? [??]	224 [5]
a9	Assign byte number there to *pos*.	Buffy, …	??	224 [5]	224 [5]
a10	Move file to previous position (back one record).	Buffy, …	??	224 [5]	168 [4]
a11	*readMovie()* there. This moves file position to end of read.	Buffy, …	Rock'N' …	224 [5]	224 [5]
a12	New title less than file title.	Buffy, …	Rock'N' …	224 [5]	224 [5]
a13	Possible insert position beyond first record.	Buffy, …	Rock'N' …	224 [5]	224 [5]
a14	Write movie from previous record to current one. **File:** Blob … Cann … Fran … Rock … Rock …	Buffy, …	Rock'N' …	224 [5]	224 [5]
a15	Move possible insert position back one record.	Buffy, …	Rock'N' …	168 [4]	224 [5]
a16	Be sure *pos* > 0, otherwise `seekg()` in next statement would attempt to set file position before the beginning of the file.	Buffy, …	Rock'N' …	168 [4]	224 [5]
a17	Set file position to previous record.	Buffy, …	Rock'N' …	168 [4]	112 [3]
a18	*readMovie()* there. This moves file position to end of read.	Buffy, …	Franken …	168 [4]	168 [4]
a11–18	Repeat process until previous title is *Blob, The*. **File:** Blob … Cann … Cann … Fran … Rock …	Buffy, …	Blob, The	56 [2]	56 [2]
a12	New title not less than file title.	Buffy, …	Blob, The	56 [2]	56 [2]
a19	Needed in case insert is at first record.	Buffy, …	Blob, The	56 [2]	56 [2]
a20	Write the new movie there. **File:** Blob … Buff … Cann … Fran … Rock …	Buffy, …	Blob, The	56 [2]	112 [3]
a21	Close *VIDEOS.DAT*.	Buffy, …	Blob, The	56 [2]	-- [--]

Changing Records

DESIGN

Any changes we make to a record in a fixed-record-length file can be done with only a single file because any record can replace any other. The

Function *del()*

```
        void del(void)  //*********************** Deletes a Record from the File
        {   fstream video;
            fstream temp;
d1          string delTitle;                                    // Title to delete
            char answer;                            // Confirm yes or no on deletion

d2          video.open("VIDEOS.DAT", ios::in | ios::binary);
d3          temp.open("TEMP.$TM", ios::out | ios::binary);

            cout << "Delete title: ";
d4          getline(cin, delTitle, '\n');
d5          while (readMovie(video))
d6          {   answer = 'N';                                   // Default to don't delete
d7              if                                  // Test as many characters as typed in
                    (delTitle == title.substr(0, delTitle.size()))
d8              {   cout << "Delete " << title << "? ";
d9                  cin >> answer;
d10                 cin.ignore(500,'\n');               // Dump newline from stream
                }
d11             if (toupper(answer) != 'Y')                 // If not delete, write
d12                 writeMovie(temp);
                else                                        // Have made deletion
d13                 delTitle = "~";                         // Don't find it again
            }
d14         video.close();
d15         temp.close();
d16         remove("VIDEOS.DAT");
d17         rename("TEMP.$TM", "VIDEOS.DAT");
        }
```

Output

```
    Delete title: Frank
    Delete Frankenstein Meets the Space Monster? y

    Take your choice: p

        YEAR   LEN SHELF    TITLE
        1958    95  4265    Blob, The
        1992   100  4180    Buffy, the Vampire Slayer
        1988    90  3328    Cannibal Women in the Avocado Jungle of Death
        1990    94  2615    Rock'N'Roll High School Forever
```

change() function always rewrites an entire record, with the changed data in the appropriate field.

The process is similar to the *change()* function in Chapter 10. To signal a title change we use an *index* of −1, which could not be an array index, as mentioned before. When the change is made we back up the file position an entire record, rather than just six bytes, and write the entire changed record, no matter what the change was.

Function *change()*

```
c1    void change(int index) //****************** Changes One of the Parameters
      {  fstream video;
c2       string chTitle;                                   // Title to change
         char answer;                           // Confirm yes or no on change

c3       video.open("VIDEOS.DAT", ios::in | ios::out | ios::binary);

         cout << "Change title: ";
c4       getline(cin, chTitle, '\n');
c5       while (readMovie(video))
c6       {  if                              // Test as many characters as typed in
               (chTitle == title.substr(0, chTitle.size()))
c7          {  cout << "Change " << title << "? ";
c8             cin >> answer;
c9             cin.ignore(500,'\n');                  // Dump newline from stream
c10            if (toupper(answer) == 'Y')
c11            {  if (index == -1)                            // Change title
                  {  cout << "To: ";
c12                  getline(cin, title, '\n');        // Change title in record
                  }
                  else                                 // Change other data
c13               {  cout << "Change " << data[index] << " to: ";
c14                  cin >> data[index];
c15                  cin.ignore(500, '\n');            // Dump end of input stream
                  }
c16               video.seekg(-(maxChrs + sizeof(data)), ios::cur);   //Back 1
c17               writeMovie(video);                        // Write record
c18               video.seekg(0, ios::end);                // Force loop exit
               }
            }
         }
c19      video.close();
      }
```

Output

```
Change title: Bl
Change Blob, The? y
To: Blob the Sequel, Part VIII, The

Take your choice: p

   YEAR   LEN SHELF   TITLE
   1958    95  4265   Blob the Sequel, Part VIII, The
   1992   100  4180   Buffy, the Vampire Slayer
   1988    90  3328   Cannibal Women in the Avocado Jungle of Death
   1990    94  2615   Rock'N'Roll High School Forever
```

EXECUTION CHART — *change()*

Line	Explanation	movie.title	movie.data[]			chTitle	answer	index
c1	Receive *index* telling what to change.	??	??	??	??	--	--	-1 (title)
c2	Create `string` to hold title to change.	??	??	??	??	??	--	-1 (title)
c3	Open existing *VIDEOS.DAT* for input and output.	??	??	??	??	??	??	-1 (title)
c4	Input first few characters of title to change.	??	??	??	??	Bl	??	-1 (title)
c5	*readMovie()* returns true.	Blob, The ...	1958	95	4265	Bl	??	-1 (title)
c6	Test change title against first 2 characters of title from file. They are equal.	Blob, The ...	1958	95	4265	Bl	??	-1 (title)
c7	Print out full title.	Blob, The ...	1958	95	4265	Bl	??	-1 (title)
c8	Input confirmation.	Blob, The ...	1958	95	4265	Bl	y	-1 (title)
c9	Flush input stream.	Blob, The ...	1958	95	4265	Bl	y	-1 (title)
c10	Change this listing.	Blob, The ...	1958	95	4265	Bl	y	-1 (title)
c11	*index* is −1, title change.	Blob, The ...	1958	95	4265	Bl	y	-1 (title)
c12	Change title in record.	Blob the S...	1958	95	4265	Bl	y	-1 (title)
c16	Back up file position 1 record.	Blob the S...	1958	95	4265	Bl	y	-1 (title)
c17	Write record.	Blob the S...	1958	95	4265	Bl	y	-1 (title)
c18	Set position to end of file.	Blob the S...	1958	95	4265	Bl	y	-1 (title)
c5	*readMovie()* returns false.	Blob the S...	1958	95	4265	Bl	y	-1 (title)
c19	Close *VIDEOS.DAT*.	Blob the S...	1958	95	4265	Bl	y	-1 (title)

```
Receive choice from menu
Open the data file
Input title of record to change
while not at the end of the file, read video object
    if change title = title
        Print full title
        Input Y or N for change
        if change
            if title change
                Input new title
            else
                Print old data
                Input new data
            Back up file position one record
            Write new record to file
            Set position indicator to end of file to force loop exit
Close file
```

IMPLEMENTATION

Function *change()* changes any part of the record.

TEST

We must test this routine with the title, year, length, and shelf position for a variety of titles. We will demonstrate a title change in the Output and the Execution Chart.

SUMMARY

- **KEY TERMS** (in order of appearance)

  Record-based data   Direct-access file
  Record   `sizeof` operator
  Field   Cast
  Key   Cast operator
  Sequential-access file

- **NEW FUNCTIONS** (in order of appearance)

`void` *fstream*`.write(char*` *location*`, int` *bytes*`)`   `<fstream>`
     Purpose: Copy number of *bytes* from *location* to file connected to *fstream*.
     Return: None.

`void` *fstream*`.read(char*` *location*`, int` *bytes*`)`   `<fstream>`
     Purpose: Copy number of *bytes* from file connected to *fstream* to *location*.
     Return: None.

- **CONCEPT REVIEW**

  - **Record-based data** depend on consistently organizing data in **records**, each with specific **fields**. A field or combination of fields that identifies a record is called a **key**.

  - To secondary storage a file is just a bunch of bytes, essentially in a straight line. We must provide some delimiters or other methods to separate the data.

  - **Sequential-access files** require that we start at the beginning of the data and move toward the end. **Direct-access files** allow us to jump from one record to another. One method for implementing direct-access files is to set up fixed-length records and use multiplying and counting to get from record to record. Padding is usually used to make fixed-length records.

  - The **sizeof operator** evaluates to the number of bytes in the data type that follows. The `sizeof` an array is the total number of bytes allocated for the entire array.

  - Addresses are also data types. Any address has the same number of bytes, but we also specify the data type of the data stored at the address so C++ knows how to interpret the data at that address. To signify the address containing a data type we use the asterisk after the name of the data type.

  - The **cast operator**, a data type in parentheses, evaluates to the new data type.

  - The `fstream` **write()** behavior copies bytes from main memory to a file. The location of those bytes must be stated as the address of a `char`, so any other address must be cast. The **read()** behavior does the opposite. What you `write()` to a file, you typically `read()` from the file.

  - An object contains only its properties; it shares it behaviors with all objects of its class. Because an object is a fixed-length entity with a fixed set of properties, it is a good candidate to copy to and from a fixed-length file.

- Objects with strings are a special case because the `string` object contains only data about the string, not the characters themselves. We have to create our own reading and writing behaviors for such objects.

- A change to the data in a direct-access file requires only the one file. We find the record to change, return to its beginning, and write the new record in its place.

- Records may be added to the beginning, middle, or end of a direct-access file. Adding at the end is easiest, done simply by opening the file with its position at the end and writing the record. Other additions require an insert process. Truly deleting a record from a file requires going back to the copying-from-one-file-to-another routine.

• HEADS UP: POINTS OF SPECIAL INTEREST

- Consistency makes record-based data work.
- Rows and columns are records and fields.
- We must provide the mechanisms to separate data in a file.
- Copying data, rather than converting them to characters, saves time and storage space.
- Addresses are data types too.
- C++ doesn't care what we copy. We must make it make sense.
- If you `write()` it to the file, you must `read()` it from the file.
- Objects maintain the fixed-length, consistent data concept of direct-access files.
- A `string` object does not contain the actual characters.
- Read a string into a `char` array, then assign it to a `string`.
- Typically, objects written to files make little sense if we look at the file.

• TRAPS: COMMON PROGRAMMING ERRORS

- Leaving out a field that is empty.
- Leaving the data type out of parentheses after `sizeof`.
- Losing significant digits in a cast.
- Forgetting to cast the address in a `write()`.
- Copying an object with strings to a file.

• YOUR TURN ANSWERS

• 11–1

1. In record-based data, rows are typically referred to as records and columns as fields.

2. A key is some field or combination of fields that identifies a row.

3. In a sequential-access file, we must start from the beginning and move toward the end. In a direct-access file, we can jump directly to points within the file.

4. The major advantage of fixed-length records is that they allow us to identify record positions in a file simply by multiplying and counting. Typically, direct-access records are of a fixed length.

5. The major disadvantage of fixed-length records is the extra storage space needed for padding.

● 11–2

1. An advantage of character access to files is that we can read the files using an ordinary text editor.

2. The advantages of byte access to files are that the storage required, especially of numbers, is usually less, and no numeric conversions need be made.

3. The `sizeof` operator tells us the number of bytes in a data type.

4. An asterisk after the name of a data type tells C++ that we are working with an address data type where a value of the stated type may be stored.

5. A cast, as indicated by the cast operator, results in the data type of the cast. In other words, it changes the data type of data.

6. The `fstream write()` behavior copies a number of bytes from an address in memory to the current position in a file. The `read()` behavior does the opposite.

● 11–3

1. When the seemingly meaningless characters in a byte-access file are read back to appropriate data types in memory, displaying those data will make sense.

2. The `string` object does not contain the characters in the string, only information about where the string is located in memory (plus a couple of other items about the string). Putting the string's address on the file would be useless.

3. A null character is at the end of every string.

4. To `read()` a string from a file we must first copy the appropriate number of bytes to a `char` array and then assign the `char` array to the string.

● 11–4

1. A fixed-length-record file can be changed by simply rewriting one record. The variable-length-record file must be entirely copied to a temporary file.

2. To move the file position in Program 11–7, we could not use the `sizeof` the object because of the `string` in the object. The object's number of bytes was calculated by the *size()* behavior.

3. The processes of adding data to the ends of either fixed-length-record files or variable-length-record files are the same—both use only one file.

4. We add records, in order, to a fixed-length-record file using the insert process.

5. The processes of deleting data in a fixed-length-record file and a variable-length-record file are the same—both must copy the entire file to a temporary one, deleting during the copy.

EXERCISES

1. Design a fixed-length-record file to keep track of your schedule. Decide which fields you will need, what data types they should be, and, for the strings, how long they should be. Which field(s) would be key? Show a sample with four or five entries.

2. In the sample you created for Exercise 1, how much shorter would it have been if it were a variable-length file with delimiters instead?

3. Correct the following statement:

```
length = (sizeof) *char;
```

4. Run Program 11–1 to see the sizes of various data types in your C++.

5. Assuming a two-byte `short` and a four-byte `long`, what would the following program segment produce?

```
short little = 100;
long big = 100000;

cout << sizeof (short) << " " << sizeof ((short)big) <<
endl;
cout << (short)big << " " << sizeof((char*)little) <<
endl;
```

6. Given the following declaration, create a statement that will write the entire array *array* to the file connected to *file*.

```
int array[3][2];
```

7. Given the following declarations, create a statement that will write the entire object *object* to the file connected to *file*. Create a statement that will read it from the file.

```
class Stuff
{   int whatever;
    double whatever;
};
Stuff object;
```

8. Changing the *object* declaration in Exercise 7 to the following, create a statement that will write the entire array of *object*s to the file connected to *file*. Create a statement that will read it from the file.

```
Stuff object[5];
```

9. Given the `cin` statement below, show the proper statement to write the string *words* to the file connected to *file*. It should work with any string input.

```
cin >> words;
```

10. Create *read()* and *write()* behaviors for the *Stuff* class.

```
const int maxChrs = 20;
class Stuff
{   string words;
    int number;
};
```

11. In Exercise 10, if *object.words* was "Hello" and *object.number* was 10, what would the file look like using a text editor?

12. Using fixed-length records, which of the following operations require two files?

    a. Changing data in the file.
    b. Adding data to the file alphabetically.
    c. Adding data to the end of the file.
    d. Deleting data from the file.

13. What is wrong with this code segment, which changes *Trembley* in the file to some new name?

```
object.read(file)
if (object.name = "Trembley")
{   cout << " New name> ";
    cin >> object.name;
    object.write(file)
}
```

14. Assuming *object* is declared and has proper *write()* and *size()* behaviors, show the program statement that will add *object* to the end of the file *Misc.abc*.

PROGRAMS

1. Modify the program in the *Putting It Together* section (pages 424–435) so that if a title is changed, the file will remain in alphabetical order.

2. Combine into one program the set of programs from this chapter that work with the *EMPLOYEE.DAT* file. Instead of manipulating the file from `main()`, make these manipulations behaviors of the *EmployeeRec* class. Besides *read()* and *write()*, your behaviors should be *add()*, which adds a record in alphabetical order; *display()*, which displays the records similar to the display in the text; *change()*, which allows you to change the numerical data in any record; and *delete()*, which allows you to delete a record. The search for the record to change or delete should be a binary search (Chapter 8), not a sequential search.

3. Rewrite Program 8 from Chapter 10 (page 400) so that it uses fixed-length records and byte access to the file. Use the same data to test the program.

4. Rewrite Program 9 from Chapter 10 (page 401) to use fixed-length records and byte access.

5. Rewrite Program 10 from Chapter 10 (page 402) to use fixed-length records and byte access.

6. Set up a *PersonRec* class with the properties and behaviors indicated. Objects of this class should be stored on a direct-access file called *Person.Dat*. The initial data, for testing purposes, are shown below. Initially fill the file with the data as shown. Your program should accept a portion of a name input at the keyboard, find that person in the array, and print out the person's data as shown.

Name	Age	Height
Bilbao Arlo	28	5.92
Dalrymple Herfy	62	6.02
Greezle Eulalia	35	5.4

Partial Classes, Properties, and Behaviors

```
PersonRec
  name
  age
  height
  find()
  newFile()    Creates new file with initial data. Comment out when not
               needed
```

Outputs

```
Enter characters for name: Dal
H. Dalrymple is 62 years old and 6.02 feet tall.

Enter characters for name: Zerch
No such name.
```

7. The Zippee Delivery Company keeps accurate records on all its delivery vehicles. General data on the vehicles are kept in a direct-access *General.Veh* file. Write a program that allows input of new vehicles and automatically assigns the next vehicle ID to a new vehicle. It will have to find the last ID in the file before assigning a new one.

Partial Classes, Properties, and Behaviors

```
VehicleRec          Class for vehicle objects
  id                Sequential vehicle IDs—1, 2, 3, etc.
  brand             Chevrolet, Nissan, Lamborghini, etc.
  year              Year purchased
  displayAll()      Displays a table of all vehicles
  display()         Displays the listing for one vehicle
```

Output

```
Vehicle brand and year> Freightliner 1996
    Vehicle id: 1
Vehicle brand and year> Trabant 1997
    Vehicle id: 2
Vehicle brand and year> Hyundai 1997
    Vehicle id: 3
Vehicle brand and year>

ID  Brand           Year
1   Freightliner    1996
2   Trabant         1997
3   Hyundai         1997
```

8. Add a menu to Program 7 so you can either add a vehicle to the file, display the entire list, or delete a vehicle from the file. The list should now print out alphabetically by brand. (*Hint:* Before displaying the list, read the entire list into an array of objects and sort the array.)

Output

```
[A]dd a vehicle
[D]elete a vehicle
[P]rint the list
Enter to quit
Choice: p
```

(Continued)

```
ID   Brand          Year
1    Freightliner   1996
3    Hyundai        1997
2    Trabant        1997
```

9. Zippee delivery also keeps track of fuel purchases and mileage. Fuel purchases for all vehicles are recorded in a *Fuel.Veh* file. To Program 8, add menu items for fuel purchases and for printing the mileage for a particular vehicle. Mileage should be calculated by adding all the fuel purchases for that vehicle in *Fuel.Veh* and dividing the high minus the low mileage values for that vehicle by this figure. Initialize the *Fuel.Veh* file with dummy fuel purchases of zero gallons and the initial mileage of the vehicle. Be sure to add this initialization step to the process that adds a vehicle, and remove all the fuel purchases for vehicles as they are deleted.

Additional Classes, Properties, and Behaviors

```
FuelRec     A single fuel purchase
 id         Vehicle ID
 Gallons
 Miles
```

Output Samples

```
[A]dd a vehicle . . .
Vehicle brand, year, current miles> Dodge 1997 104
    Vehicle id: 4
[F]uel purchase . . .
Vehicle id> 6
Invalid. reenter Vehicle id> 4
    Gallons and miles> 29.6 12806
[M]ileage display . . .
Vehicle id> 2
    The 1997 Hyundai is currently getting 33.6 MPG.
```

10. Change the *[P]rint* menu item in Program 9 as shown in the following.

Output

```
[P]rint the list . . .

ID   Brand          Year    Miles    MPG
4    Dodge          1997    12806    16.8
1    Freightliner   1996    104366   14.8
3    Hyundai        1997    12115    33.6
2    Trabant        1997    822      53.1
```

11. Zippee, now a worldwide company, has too many vehicles to sort them in memory. Rewrite the *[P]rint* menu item so that the *General.Veh* data are copied into a *Temp.$tm* file and the file itself is sorted. Use a bubble sort as described in Chapter 8, but instead of manipulating array indexes, manipulate record numbers in the file.

12. Somebody at Zippee had a brainstorm—a rare occasion at Zippee. Instead of moving all those data around in files (as in Program 11), why not set up an array of record numbers in memory (it will be much smaller than all the data) and sort by swapping record numbers in the array? Then, when the list is printed, the program can go sequentially through the array and print the file records whose record numbers appear in the array.

Chapter 12

MEMORY ACCESS

PREVIEW

One of the advantages that C++ has over other languages is that it allows access to main memory. Any language can access variables by name in main memory, but in C++ we often access them by referring directly to where they are stored. This is such an important and useful concept in C++ that it is imperative that you fully understand it. This chapter looks at direct memory access as applied to a number of concepts covered in previous chapters, and so is keyed to those chapters. The material in the sections here may be addressed concurrently with, or any time after, coverage of the chapter in parentheses. The sections are:

- Addresses and Pointers (Chapter 2)
- Pointers, References, and Functions (Chapter 6)
- Pointers and Objects (Chapter 8)
- Pointers and Arrays (Chapter 8)
- Allocating Memory (Chapter 8)
- Linked Lists (Chapter 9)

I n Chapter 1 we saw that main memory was made up of thousands or millions of individual storage spaces, or **locations**, each of which has a distinct numeric **address**. In Chapter 8 we saw the importance of addresses to arrays: that the array values were stored in contiguous locations and that an array name was a reference to the address of the array. In Chapter 9 we looked at functions that required addresses to be sent to them. In Chapter 11 we recognized that the value of an address was a specific data type. In this chapter we will examine addresses and variables that store addresses rather than conventional data. We will see how their use adds flexibility and efficiency to the C++ language.

ADDRESSES AND POINTERS

When we declare a variable, C++ calls on the operating system to find an available contiguous set of locations large enough to accommodate that data type and allocates that space to the variable. For example,

```
float grinch;
```

might result in the following memory allocation:

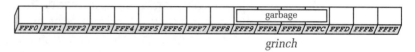

grinch

Assuming that *grinch* is a local variable, its value would be garbage.

C++ allows us to access the variable by name because it keeps track of the address of the first location allocated to the variable. The address of *grinch* is FFF9 (we have used hex notation here as a convenience so we can identify numbers being used as addresses as opposed to those used as other data values). Unless we demand it, C++ does not let us know the addresses of variables we declare; it simply uses its own mechanisms to access them.

If we knew where the variable was, instead of referring to the variable's name, we could tell the computer to access the variable that was in the location with the address 7115 or 24236 or FFF9 or whatever. We call this **pointing** to a variable.

The address of a variable, whether in hex or decimal notation, is just a numeric value and, like any other numeric value, it can be stored in another variable. A variable that contains an address value, rather than a value we would normally think of as regular data, is a pointer variable, or simply a **pointer**.

The Pointer Data Type

Every stored value is of one data type or another, and the variables that store these values must accommodate those data types; they must be declared as the same type. We are familiar with data types such as `short`, `int`, or `double`, and know that types are distinguished by both the number of bytes allocated for them and the type of notation—straight binary or

Program 12–1

```cpp
#include <iostream>                          // Need we mention the .h?
using namespace std;                         // Only if you need it

int main(void)
{   long number = 12345;

    cout << "Number's value is " << number
         << " with size of " << sizeof(number) << " bytes.\n";
    cout << "Number's address is " << &number
         << " with size of " << sizeof(&number) << " bytes." << endl;
    return 0;
}
```

Output

```
Number's value is 12345 with size of 4 bytes.
Number's address is 0xFFFFF4 with size of 3 bytes.
```

HEADS UP!

A pointer is a data type.

exponential. As we saw in Chapter 11, a memory address has its own data type. Although ANSI does not give it an official title, we shall refer to it as the pointer data type.

The pointer data type is integral, similar to `int`. Its size, however, depends on your particular implementation of C++. In most C++s, the size is the number of bytes in which the target computer stores a memory address. For the sake of discussion, let us assume that a pointer has three bytes. It probably doesn't in your C++, but since no other common data type has three bytes, it will help us to distinguish pointers from others in our illustrations here.

We have already had some experience with addresses. The `getline()`, `atof()`, and `remove()` functions, for example, require addresses where they can find sets of character. Remember, the symbol `&` in front of a variable name means "the address of" that variable rather than the value stored in the variable. Using `cout`, we can actually display the address contained in the pointer data type. Program 12–1 offers an example.

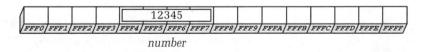

number

HEADS UP!

An address of stored data is always where the data start.

The value of the address is printed in hexadecimal notation (the `0x` tells us that), and the size of the address is three bytes in our imaginary C++. The address is of the location where the variable starts. Here the variable starts at FFF4 (actually, FFFFF4 with a three-byte pointer, but that many characters won't fit on the diagrams!) and spans four bytes, FFF4 through FFF7. Why the specific address FFF4? That address was chosen by C++; we had no control over it. When we declared *number* as a `long`, C++ found an unallocated four bytes somewhere in memory and allocated it to *number*. In fact, the address could change in subsequent executions of the same program.

Pointer Variables

We can declare a variable as pointer data type, but we must do so in a slightly roundabout fashion. The pointer points to something—it contains the address of something—so in addition to declaring it as a pointer data type, we also state the data type to which it points. As with the cast operator we saw in Chapter 11, an asterisk (*) after the data type or, more properly, in front of a variable name in a declaration indicates that it is of type pointer, and the type to which it points is declared in the usual way. In the following declaration *data* is a float and *ptr* is a pointer that we usually describe as being "pointer to float."

```
float *ptr;
float data = 100;
```

We can declare many variables in the same statement this way:

```
int *ptr, things, *stuff, data = 100;
```

The variables *ptr* and *stuff* are pointers to int, and *things* and *data* are ints.

Notice how much more readable the declarations are when stated this way:

```
int *ptr, *stuff;
int things, data = 100;
```

The declarations allocate four bytes (in a typical C++) for *data* and three bytes (in our imaginary C++) for *ptr*. Assuming the declarations were internal, *ptr*'s value is garbage. In other words, it points to a memory space somewhere in the system, but we don't know where it is or what value is stored there—garbage pointing to garbage.

			1.000000E+002						garbage						
FFF0	FFF1	FFF2	FFF3	FFF4	FFF5	FFF6	FFF7	FFF8	FFF9	FFFA	FFFB	FFFC	FFFD	FFFE	FFFF

data   *ptr*

A pointer variable may be assigned and used in the same way any other variable can, but we must remember that its data type is pointer, and its value is an address, not usual data. Saying

```
ptr = 26;
```

might actually work in some C++s (a strict ANSI C++ should recognize that 26 is data type int, not pointer), but using the value could be hazardous, because who knows what is stored at memory location 26 (or 1A in hex)? It could be part of the operating system. We would have a valid pointer, but it would be pointing to garbage.

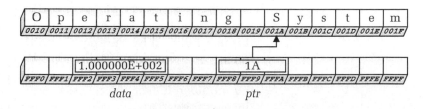

O	p	e	r	a	t	i	n	g		S	y	s	t	e	m
0010	0011	0012	0013	0014	0015	0016	0017	0018	0019	001A	001B	001C	001D	001E	001F

			1.000000E+002						1A						
FFF0	FFF1	FFF2	FFF3	FFF4	FFF5	FFF6	FFF7	FFF8	FFF9	FFFA	FFFB	FFFC	FFFD	FFFE	FFFF

data   *ptr*

If, however, we assign a valid address to *ptr*, an address whose contents we know, then we have something useful.

```
int main(void)
{  float *ptr, data = 100;

   ptr = &data;                // Assign address of data to ptr
```

Now the value of *ptr* is an allocated address, the address of *data*, and it points to a valid value, 100.

This statement,

```
cout <<  ptr << " " << &data << endl;
```

will produce this output:

0xFFF2 0xFFF2   [Actually, 0xFFFFF2 0xFFFFF2 for a three-byte address.]

The addresses, of course, are the same.

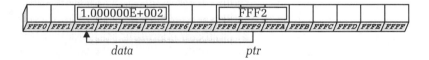

Dereferencing

Often we use pointer variables to access the locations to which they are pointing—using *ptr* to access 100, the value at FFF2, for example. We refer to this process as **dereferencing**. The **dereferencing operator**, *, in front of a variable directs the computer to interpret the value of the variable as an address, to go to the location defined by that address, and to access the value starting there. Declaring the pointer variable as a pointer to a particular data type is important so that C++ will know how many bytes beyond the starting address to access, and whether the storage is in straight binary or E notation.

The dereferencing operator (*) looks suspiciously like the symbol we used to declare a variable as a pointer (*). In fact, one might even mistake it for the one we use for multiplication (*). Although the symbols look the same, their functions are totally different depending on where we find them in the program. In a declaration, the * means pointer variable; in any other statement it means to multiply or to dereference—access the contents at the address contained in the variable.

Both the dereferencing operator and the address operator are unary operators. Like the negate (!), unary minus (-), and increment (++) operators, they have the highest precedence (except for the expression operators such as parentheses), and right-to-left associativity. The multiplication operator is binary; it works with two expressions. In *a, the asterisk means to dereference; in a * b, it means to multiply. (Remember, the spaces around the operator are there for our readability; C++ ignores them.)

We can access the value 100 in three ways, as shown in Program 12–2.

The variable *ptr* is, of course, type pointer, but the notation *ptr is type float because it refers to the value stored at FFF2, the floating-point value of *data*. As we saw, &data is type pointer but *&data is float because

Program 12–2

```
#include <iostream>
using namespace std;

int main(void)
{   float *ptr, data = 100;

    ptr = &data;
    cout << ptr << " " << &data << endl;
    cout << data << " " << *ptr << " " << *&data << endl;
    return 0;
}
```

Output

```
0xFFF2  0xFFF2
100 100 100
```

Data types that don't match.

it refers to the value (*) stored at the address (&) of the variable *data*. To summarize, the value of data is equal to the value of *ptr, which is equal to the value of *&data. All are of type float.

The dereferencing operator can also be used in assignments. If we add these statements to the end of the previous program:

```
*ptr = 200;
cout << data << " " << *ptr << " " << *&data << endl;
```

our output becomes

```
0xFFF2  0xFFF2
100 100 100
200 200 200
```

Our statement told C++ to assign the value 200 to the memory location pointed to by *ptr*. In other words, C++ evaluated the variable *ptr*, found that its value was FFF2, and wrote the value 200 at the location FFF2.

What if our program began with these two statements?

```
{   float *ptr, data = 100;
    *ptr = 200;
```

Both statements are valid, but *ptr*'s value is garbage—it points to nowhere in particular. Assigning 200 there, wherever that is, could potentially be disastrous!

YOUR TURN 12–1

1. What is a *memory location* and what is its address?
2. What does *pointing* to a variable mean?
3. Is there a pointer data type?
4. What is a *pointer variable*?
5. Define *dereferencing*.
6. Name two pointer-related uses for the asterisk.
7. Why is it important to declare a variable as a pointer to something?

Program 12–3

```
    #include <iostream>
    using namespace std;

    void inflate(double *value, double inflator);

    int main(void)
1 {  double cost, inflation = 1.3;

       cout << "Enter the project's cost: ";
2      cin >> cost;
3      inflate(&cost, inflation);
4      cout << "Cost adjusted for inflation is " << cost << endl;
       return 0;
    }

i1  void inflate(double *value, double inflator)
    {
i2     *value *= inflator;                        // *value = *value * inflator
i3  }
```

Output

```
    Enter the project's cost: 100
    Cost adjusted for inflation is 130
```

Line	Explanation	cost	inflation	value	inflator
	EXECUTION CHART				
1	Declare variables in main(). *value* and *inflator* don't exist yet.	??	1.3	--	--
2	Input *cost*.	100	1.3	--	--
3	Call function, pass FFF0 (address of *cost*) and 1.3.	100	1.3	--	--
i1	Allocate and initialize function variables. Variables in main() still exist but are not visible.	(100)	(1.3)	FFF0	1.3
i2	Multiply the value at FFF0 by 1.3, store result at FFF0.	(130)	(1.3)	FFF0	1.3
i3	Transfer execution back to main() at 3.	130	1.3	--	--
4	Display inflated *cost*.	130	1.3	--	--

POINTERS, REFERENCES, AND FUNCTIONS

HEADS UP!

An address, like any other value, can be passed to a function.

All this makes for a diverting mental exercise, but how can we use it?

One valuable way is with functions. Instead of passing data values to functions, we can pass addresses. We saw that in some of the functions we have already examined, but now we will create our own functions that accept addresses.

Once a function knows the address of a variable, the function can change the contents at that location. In other words, without knowing a variable's name, we can change the variable's value.

In Program 12–3 we pass the address of the variable *cost* to the function *inflate* and allow the function to change the value stored there. On entry to the function, that address is assigned to the pointer variable *value*. Within the function, we multiply the contents at the location pointed to by *value*.

Passing a variable address, a pointer, rather than a value is often referred to as a **pass by pointer** (or *pass by address*) as opposed to a **pass by value**. (Before C++, the pass by pointer was referred to as a *pass by reference*, but as we have seen, C++ has a more specific pass by reference.) This program combined both a pass by pointer and a pass by value in one call.

Because we are using the address of *cost* in the `inflate()` call, why not just declare the variable *cost* as a pointer in the first place, and rewrite the `main()` function this way?

```
int main(void)
{   double *cost, inflation = 1.3;

    cout << "Enter the project's cost: ";
    cin >> *cost;                                        // This won't work
    inflate(cost, inflation);
    cout << "Cost adjusted for inflation is " << *cost << endl;
    return 0;
}
```

The problem is that although *cost* is allocated, it is never assigned a value—where it points, no one knows. If we write a value at the location pointed to by *cost*, as we would in the `cin` statement, it might end up in

---

Program 12–4

```
#include <iostream>
using namespace std;

void inflate(double &value, double inflator);

int main(void)
{   double cost, inflation = 1.3;

    cout << "Enter the project's cost: ";
    cin >> cost;
    inflate(cost, inflation);
    cout << "Cost adjusted for inflation is " << cost << endl;
    return 0;
}

void inflate(double &value, double inflator)
{
    value *= inflator;                                   // value = value * inflator
}
```

Output

```
Enter the project's cost: 100
Cost adjusted for inflation is 130
```

FIGURE 12–1

A Swap

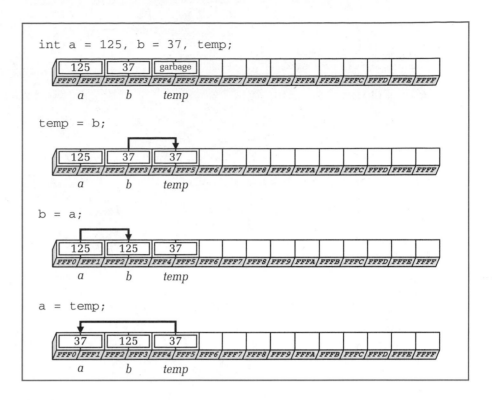

the middle of the operating system, change critical instructions, and crash the computer! We don't want to do that.

We could have achieved the same result using a pass by reference as in Program 12–4. To us the process looks different, because *value* is another name for *cost* rather than an actual variable. To most C++s, though, the process is actually the same. Internally, most C++s translate our pass by reference into a pass by pointer. In most cases the pass by reference notation is easier for us to use, but as we go on, we will see cases in which the pass by pointer notation is the only practical possibility.

Returning More Than One Value

You still can't!

We saw in Chapter 6, however, that we can effectively get more than one value back to the calling function with a pass by reference. We can accomplish the same thing using a pass by pointer. Here we put addresses in the call, have the called function change the values at those locations, and return to the calling function.

Let's swap the values of two variables as an example. A swap is a common operation done in sorting data, inserting into lists, and performing many other tasks. In a swap we want the value that was in *a* to end up in *b* and the value that was in *b* to end up in *a*. To do it we will have to use a temporary variable, *temp*, to hold one of the values while we move the other. Figure 12–1 shows the process.

Because we do swaps so frequently, we want a function, *swap()*, that we can call whenever we need it—swap(a, b). We want the values of both *a* and *b* in the calling function to change, but we cannot return two

Program 12–5

```
#include <iostream>              // Pass By Reference Statements
using namespace std;            // In This Column ************

void swap(int *x, int *y);       // void swap(int &x, int &y);

int main(void)
{   int a = 125, b = 37;

    cout << "Before swap   a: " << a
         << "    b: " << b << endl;
    swap(&a, &b);                //    swap(a, b);
    cout << "After swap   a: " << a
         << "    b: " << b << endl;
    return 0;
}

void swap(int *x, int *y)        // void swap(int &x, int &y)
{   int temp;

    temp = *y;                   //    temp = y;
    *y = *x;                     //    y = x;
    *x = temp;                   //    x = temp;
}
```

Output

```
Before swap   a: 125    b: 37
After swap   a: 37    b: 125
```

---

values from the *swap()* function—so let's pass the addresses of *a* and *b* and have *swap()* manipulate the values at those addresses (or pass references to *a* and *b* and have the function manipulate the variables directly). In Program 12–5 we see both solutions, the pass-by-reference solution in comments next to the pass-by-pointer solution, where the statements are different.

Figure 12–2 examines *swap()* graphically, using a pass by pointer.

Using Returns, References, and Pointers

The Mobile Mud Concrete Company, as part of its sales-invoice program, calculates how many trucks it will take to fill an order and figures the price of the order in the function `price()`. The `main()` function then prints the results. The price is figured at $75 per cubic yard plus $50 per truck; a truck can carry a maximum of 4 cubic yards. The `main()` function needs both the price and the number of trucks from the `price()` function.

One value—in this case the price—can be returned by the function. The other value—the number of trucks—can be obtained either by passing a pointer or by a reference. In the pass-by-pointer solution the value is calculated in the function and assigned at the address contained in the pointer variable *vehicles*. The value of *vehicles* (the address stored there)

FIGURE 12–2

The Swap Function Using
a Pass by Pointer

```
void swap(int *x, int *y)
{  int temp;
```

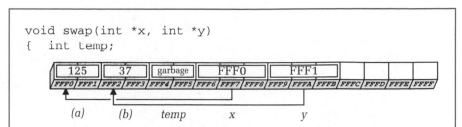

The first line of the definition allocates the variables *x* and *y* and initializes them with the addresses passed from the `main()` function. The variables *a* and *b* still exist, but they are not visible at this time. The local variable *temp* is allocated but has no value yet.

```
temp = *y;
```

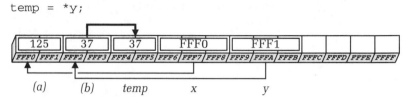

We follow the address stored in *y*, FFF2, to find the value 37. This value is assigned to *temp*. The data type of *temp* is `int`, as is the data type of **y*.

```
*y = *x;
```

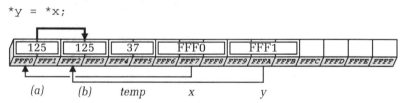

Following the address stored in *x*, FFF0, we find the value 125. This is assigned to the location whose address is stored in *y*, FFF2. The data types of both **x* and **y* are `int`.

```
*x = temp;
```

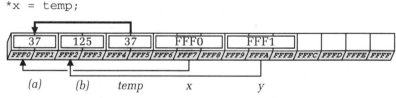

The value of *temp* (37) is assigned to the location whose address is stored in *x*, FFF0.

When the function returns, *x*, *y*, and *temp* disappear, and *a* and *b* are once again visible—but with their values swapped.

was initialized in the function call to the address of *trucks*, a variable visible in the `main()` function. Assigning a value at the location pointed to by *vehicles*, then, assigns a value to *trucks*.

In Program 12–6 we show the pointer solution with the reference solution in comments.

Program 12–6

```
      #include <iostream>                    // Pass By Reference Statements
      using namespace std;

      float price(float yds, int *tks);      // float price(float yds, int &tks);

      int main(void)
      {  float yards;
         int trucks;

         cout << "How many yards? ";
   1     cin >> yards;
   2     cout << "   Price:  "
                 << price(yards, &trucks)     //              << price(yards, trucks)
                 << endl;
   3     cout << "   Trucks: "
                 << trucks << endl;
         return 0;
      }

  p1  float price(float yds, int *tks)        // float price(float yds, int &tks)
      {  float total;

  p2     total = yds * 75;
  p3     *tks = yds / 4;                      //    tks = yds / 4;
  p4     yds -= *tks * 4;                     //    yds -= tks * 4;
  p5     if (yds > 0)
  p6        ++*tks;                           //       ++tks;
  p7     return total + *tks * 50;            //    return total + tks * 50;
      }
```

Outputs

```
      How many yards? 8.2
         Price:  765
         Trucks: 3

      How many yards? 4
         Price:  350
         Trucks: 1

      How many yards? .7
         Price:  102.5
         Trucks: 1
```

YOUR TURN 12–2

1. What are the differences among a pass by value, a pass by pointer, and a pass by reference?
2. What is the problem with declaring a pointer variable and then assigning a value to where it points?
3. Can you return more than one value from a function?

Line	Explanation	yards	trucks	total	yds	tks
1	input *yards*.	8.2	??	--	--	--
2	As part of `cout`, call `price()`, pass value of *yards* and address of *trucks* (FFF2).	8.2	??	--	--	--
p1	Allocate and initialize *yds* and *tks*.	(8.2)	(??)	--	8.2	FFF2
p2	Assign total for yards of concrete.	(8.2)	(??)	615	8.2	FFF2
p3	Assign at FFF4 the number of trucks. Since *tks* is a pointer to `int`, the result is truncated to an integral value.	(8.2)	(2)	615	8.2	FFF2
p4	Subtract yards of concrete carried by the 2 trucks from total yards.	(8.2)	(2)	615	0.2	FFF2
p5	See if any concrete left over. There is.	(8.2)	(2)	615	0.2	FFF2
p6	Leftover concrete requires 1 more truck. Increment value pointed to by *tks*.	(8.2)	(3)	615	0.2	FFF2
p7	Return total for concrete plus total for trucks.	(8.2)	(3)	615	0.2	FFF2
2	Display return value.	8.2	3	--	--	--
3	Display value of *trucks*.	8.2	3	--	--	--

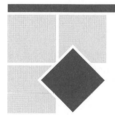

PUTTING IT TOGETHER

Reconciling a bank statement is always a tedious task. Let's have our computer help us.

TASK

Write a program that will use our checking-account information plus outstanding transactions during the current period to perform a reconciliation, telling us whether we are in balance.

ANALYSIS

To perform a manual reconciliation, to the account balance according to our records we add the value of all outstanding checks (those that we have written but the bank has not yet received) and subtract the outstanding deposits. This should equal the balance according to our bank statement.

In our program we will enter the bank-statement balance and the balance according to the checkbook, as well as each outstanding check and deposit; then the program will print a summary of the number of outstanding checks and their total, as well as the number of outstanding deposits and their total. Finally, the program should tell us whether we are in balance or, if not, how far off we are.

A sample run might look like this:

```
Bank statement balance: 465.78
Checkbook balance: 284.22
Enter outstanding checks
  (0 to quit)
  Amount: 182.56
  Amount: 80.35
  Amount: 0
Enter outstanding deposits
  (0 to quit)
  Amount: 50
  Amount: 31.34
  Amount: 0
Outstanding: Number    Amount
     Checks:       2    262.91
   Deposits:       2     81.34
You think you have $0.01 more
than the bank thinks you have.
```

We will have to keep track of both balances, the number and accumulated total of the outstanding checks, and the number and total of the outstanding deposits.

DESIGN

Following the sample run, the overall process is:

Input bank and book balances
Input uncleared checks
Input uncleared deposits
Calculate balance
Print summary and balance

If we expand the Input uncleared checks and Input uncleared deposits modules, we have

Input bank and book balances
while more checks   [Input uncleared checks]
    Input check amount
    Accumulate amount in reconciliation balance
    Count check
while more deposits   [Input uncleared deposits]
    Input deposit amount
    Accumulate amount in reconciliation balance
    Count deposit
Calculate balance
Print summary and balance

The two modules we just expanded are almost alike. The process is the same, but one works with deposits and the other with checks. Because the process is the same, let's have a function—*inData()*—that performs the process and provides the results to the main program. We can return the balance produced in the function and assign it to either a check amount (*checksOut*) or a deposit amount (*depositsOut*). To count the checks or the deposits we will pass the function the address of either the check counter (*noOfChecks*) or deposit counter (*noOfDeposits*), and have the function modify the contents at those addresses.

Program 12-7

```cpp
#include <iostream>
#include <iomanip>
using namespace std;

double inData(short *number);        // Input, accumulate checks or deposits

int main(void)
{   short noOfChecks = 0, noOfDeposits = 0;                      // Counters
    double bankBalance, bookBalance;           // Bank statement & checkbook
    double balance;                  // Checkbook balance after reconciliation
    double checksOut, depositsOut;                     // Amounts outstanding

    //-------------------------------------- Input Bank and Book Balances
    cout << "Bank statement balance: ";
1   cin >> bankBalance;
    cout << "Checkbook balance: ";
2   cin >> bookBalance;

    //---------------------------------------------- Input Uncleared Checks
    cout << "Enter outstanding checks\n";
3   checksOut = inData(&noOfChecks);

    //---------------------------------------------- Input Uncleared Deposits
    cout << "Enter outstanding deposits\n";
4   depositsOut = inData(&noOfDeposits);

    //------------------------------------------------------ Calculate Balance
5   balance = bookBalance + checksOut - depositsOut;

    //-------------------------------------------------------- Print Summary
    cout << setiosflags(ios::fixed) << setprecision(2);
    cout << "Outstanding: Number    Amount\n";
6   cout << "      Checks: " << setw(6) << noOfChecks
         << setw(9) << checksOut << endl;
7   cout << "    Deposits: " << setw(6) << noOfDeposits
         << setw(9) << depositsOut << endl;
8   if (balance == bankBalance)
9      cout << "You are in balance." << endl;
10  else if (balance > bankBalance)
11     cout << "You think you have $" << (balance - bankBalance)
            << " more\n"
               "than the bank thinks you have." << endl;
    else
12     cout << "The bank thinks you have $" << (bankBalance - balance)
            << " more\n"
               "than you think you have." << endl;
    return 0;
}
```

(Continued)

Program 12–7 *(Continued)*

```
//******************************* Enter Data for either Checks or Deposits
     double inData(short *number)
     {  double amount, balance = 0;

         cout << "  (0 to quit)\n";
         cout << "  Amount: ";
i1       cin >> amount;
i2       while (amount)
i3       {  balance += amount;
i4          ++*number;
            cout << "  Amount: ";
i5          cin >> amount;
         }
i6       return balance;
     }
```

Outputs

```
Bank statement balance: 842.39          Bank statement balance: 465.78
Checkbook balance: 377.12               Checkbook balance: 284.22
Enter outstanding checks                Enter outstanding checks
  (0 to quit)                             (0 to quit)
  Amount: 149                             Amount: 182.56
  Amount: 23.87                           Amount: 80.35
  Amount: 106.33                          Amount: 0
  Amount: 305.44                        Enter outstanding deposits
  Amount: 0                               (0 to quit)
Enter outstanding deposits                Amount: 50
  (0 to quit)                             Amount: 31.34
  Amount: 119.37                          Amount: 0
  Amount: 0                             Outstanding: Number    Amount
Outstanding: Number    Amount             Checks:       2    262.91
    Checks:       4    584.64             Deposits:      2     81.34
    Deposits:     1    119.37           You think you have $0.01 more
You are in balance.                     than the bank thinks you have.
```

IMPLEMENTATION

Program 12–7 contains the resulting code.

There could be any number of ways of handling this input while accumulating numbers and balances. The *inData()* function, however, encapsulates the operation and allows it to be used in any application requiring that type of task. We don't have to worry about the variables in the application conflicting with those in the function or, indeed, how the function actually operates once it is tested and debugged.

TEST

As usual, we must test for a number of possible conditions. Among them would be no checks or no deposits, in balance, and out of balance either way.

Line	Explanation	noOf Checks (FFF0)	noOf Deposits (FFF2)	number (inData)	amount (inData)	balance (inData)
1	Enter bank balance (842.39).	0	0	--	--	--
2	Enter book balance (377.12).	0	0	--	--	--
3	Call *inData()*, pass address of *noOfChecks*.	0	0	--	--	--
i1	Enter *amount*.	(0)	(0)	FFF0	149.00	0.00
i2	*amount* nonzero; go into loop.	(0)	(0)	FFF0	149.00	0.00
i3	Accumulate *amount* into *balance*.	(0)	(0)	FFF0	149.00	149.00
i4	Add 1 to location pointed to by *number*.	(1)	(0)	FFF0	149.00	149.00
i5	Enter next *amount*.	(1)	(0)	FFF0	12.37	149.00
i2–5	Continue entering *amounts*, accumulating in *balance*, and incrementing *number*, until *amount* of zero input.	(4)	(0)	FFF0	0.00	584.64
i6	Return *balance*.	(4)	(0)	FFF0	0.00	584.64
3	Assign return to *checksOut*.	4	0	--	--	--
4	Call *inData()*, pass address of *noOfDeposits*.	4	0	--	--	--
i1	Enter *amount*.	(4)	(0)	FFF2	119.37	0.00
i2	*amount* nonzero; go into loop.	(0)	(0)	FFF2	119.37	0.00
i3	Accumulate *amount* into *balance*.	(4)	(0)	FFF2	119.37	119.37
i4	Add 1 to location pointed to by *number*.	(4)	(1)	FFF2	119.37	119.37
i5	Enter next *amount*.	(4)	(1)	FFF2	0.00	119.37
i2	Zero *amount* exits loop.	(4)	(1)	FFF2	0.00	119.37
i6	Return *balance*.	(4)	(1)	FFF2	0.00	119.37
4	Assign return to *depositsOut*.	4	1	--	--	--
5–12	Finish program.	4	1	--	--	--

POINTERS AND OBJECTS

Because the properties of an object are guaranteed to be stored contiguously in memory, pointers to objects can be useful. Borrowing our *EmployeeRec* class from Chapter 11, the definition

```
class EmployeeRec ////////////////////////////////////////        EmployeeRec Class
{
public:
    string name;
    float payRate;
    int dependents;
};
```

and declaration

```
EmployeeRec *empPtr;                                       // Pointer to object
```

declare *empPtr* to be a pointer to the object. In this case, the only memory allocation is the few bytes for the pointer variable *empPtr*. Where it points, no one knows.

To give it a valid location to which to point, we might declare an actual object,

```
EmployeeRec fullTime;
```

in which case we can assign the pointer variable to its address:

```
empPtr = &fullTime;
```

To access an individual member of an object by its pointer, we refer to the contents at the location of the particular member,

```
(*pointer).member
```

For example, to access the *dependents* member of the object pointed to by *empPtr*, we would use the notation

```
(*empPtr).dependents
```

^{TRAP}

Forgetting the parentheses when dereferencing objects.

The parentheses are important because the member operator has precedence over the dereferencing operator, and we want *empPtr* to be evaluated as a pointer first and then direct us to the *dependents* member.

The operation is common but the notation is somewhat clumsy, so C++ also gives us the **member-pointer operator**, ->. This notation:

```
pointer->member
```

means exactly the same thing. The arrow is made of a dash (–) and a greater-than symbol (>) with no space in between. Our example could be rewritten

```
empPtr->dependents
```

HEADS UP!

The member-pointer operator is more intuitive and more commonly used.

meaning the contents of the *dependents* member of the object pointed to by *empPtr*, usually referred to as "empPtr pointer to dependents."

To assign the pay rate we could write the statement

```
empPtr->payRate = 14.25;
```

HEADS UP!

Moving pointers is much quicker than moving objects.

A major advantage of using pointers to objects is that when manipulating the objects, it is often not necessary to copy the entire object from here to there, but only to change pointers—a great saving in the number of operations that the CPU must execute, and a saving in memory. A perfect example is the sorting of an array of objects, with all its required swaps.

Program 12–8 prints an array of employees sorted by name. It uses the bubble-sort algorithm we developed in Chapter 8 that involves swapping array elements until things are in the right order. We can, of course, swap objects, but what if each object were 10,000 bytes long? The execution time for moving all those bytes around would be prohibitive.

HEADS UP!

Manipulating an array of objects by pointer requires an array of pointers.

Instead, let's set up pointers to each of the objects—if we have an array of 500 objects, we need an array of 500 pointers—and swap the pointers instead of the whole objects. Each swap will be of three-byte pointers (imaginary C++) rather than 10,000-byte objects, making it execute more efficiently.

In main(), we start by declaring an array, *emp*, of four *EmployeeRecs*. For testing purposes we initialize the array with data in no particular order.

We added a constructor to the the *EmployeeRec* class to handle the initialization. Recall from Chapter 8 that to initialize an array of objects, we make multiple calls to the constructor in the declaration/initialization.

Following that we declare an array, *empPtr*, of four pointers to *EmployeeRec*. Now, of course, these pointers are garbage; they do not point to anything useful. Our next step, though, is to assign the addresses of the elements of the array *emp* to the elements of the array *empPtr*.

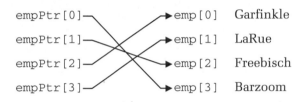

In the swap we swap pointers, elements of *empPtr*. To decide whether to swap, we compare the *name*s in the *emp* element to which the *empPtr* element points. After the sort the *emp* array is unchanged, but the *empPtr* array points to different elements of it.

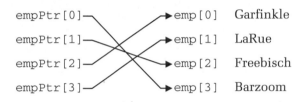

Program 12–8

```
#include <iostream>
#include <iomanip>
#include <string>
using namespace std;

const int totEmployees = 4;

class EmployeeRec ///////////////////////////////////// EmployeeRec Class
{
public:
    string name;
    int dependents;
    float payRate;
    EmployeeRec(string n, int d, float p)             // Initialize objects
    {   name = n; dependents = d; payRate = p; }
};

int main(void) ///////////////////////////////////////////// Main Program
{   EmployeeRec emp[totEmployees] =                   // Initialize array
        {EmployeeRec("Garfinkle Gilda",   5, 15.25),  // Call to constructor
         EmployeeRec("LaRue LeRoy",        0, 9.50 ),
         EmployeeRec("Freebisch Maynard", 3, 10.83),
         EmployeeRec("Barzoom Beulah",    5, 12.63)};
    EmployeeRec *empPtr[totEmployees];                // Array of pointers
```
(Continued)

```
    int c;  //---------------------- Assign Pointers to Locations of Objects
    for (c = 0; c < totEmployees; ++c)
         empPtr[c] = &emp[c];

    //-------------------------------------------------------- Sort Objects
    EmployeeRec *temp;                        // Temporary pointer for swap
    int pos, bottom;                                       // Sort counters
    bool swap = true;                          // Goes to true if swap made

    bottom = totEmployees - 1;
    while (bottom > 0 && swap)
    {   swap = false;                                   // No swaps made yet
        for (pos = 0; pos < bottom; ++pos)
            if (empPtr[pos + 1]->name < empPtr[pos]->name)
            {   temp = empPtr[pos];
                empPtr[pos] = empPtr[bottom];
                empPtr[bottom] = temp;
                swap = true;                                    // Swap made
            }
        --bottom;
    }
    //--------------------------------------------- Print Unsorted Objects
    cout << setiosflags(ios::fixed) << setprecision(2);
    cout << "Unsorted:\n";
    cout << "Name                              Pay Rate  Dep\n";
    for (c = 0; c < totEmployees; ++c)
        cout << setiosflags(ios::left) << setw(30) << emp[c].name
             << resetiosflags(ios::left) << setw(8) << emp[c].payRate
             << setw(5) << emp[c].dependents << endl;

    //--------------------------------------------- Print Sorted Objects
    cout << "\nSorted:\n";
    cout << "Name                              Pay Rate  Dep\n";
    for (c = 0; c < totEmployees; ++c)
        cout << setiosflags(ios::left) << setw(30) << empPtr[c]->name
             << resetiosflags(ios::left) << setw(8) << empPtr[c]->payRate
             << setw(5) << empPtr[c]->dependents << endl;
    return 0;
}
```

Output

```
Unsorted:
Name                          Pay Rate  Dep
Garfinkle Gilda                  15.25   5
LaRue LeRoy                       9.50   0
Freebisch Maynard                10.83   3
Barzoom Beulah                   12.63   5

Sorted:
Name                          Pay Rate  Dep
Barzoom Beulah                   12.63   5
Freebisch Maynard                10.83   3
Garfinkle Gilda                  15.25   5
LaRue LeRoy                       9.50   0
```

To illustrate that point more fully, Program 12–8 prints out the elements of the *emp* array in index order—with the names out of order—using the notation emp[c].name. Then it prints the data in the *emp* array pointing to a particular element with the pointers in the *empPtr* array, using the notation empPtr[c]->name—the name member of the element to which *empPtr[c]* is pointing. The names are in order.

YOUR TURN 12–3

1. What symbol do we usually use to dereference a member of an object described by a pointer variable?
2. What notation would we use to reference the *member* member of an object pointed to by *pointer*?
3. Describe one advantage of referencing objects by address.

POINTERS AND ARRAYS

Like any other declaration, an array declaration allocates memory space for the variables. For array variables, this memory space is guaranteed to be contiguous—one variable follows the next. For our declaration of the *sales* array we used in Chapter 8, C++ would have to find 14 bytes of free memory, say at address FFF0, and allocate them to the variables *sales[0]* through *sales[6]*. The variable *sales[0]*, then, would occupy FFF0 and FFF1; *sales[1]*, FFF2 and FFF3, and *sales[6]*, FFFC and FFFD.

```
short sales[] = {3806, 28, 4522, 476, 1183, 47, 12};
```

3806	28	4522	476	1183	47	12		
FFF0 FFF1	FFF2 FFF3	FFF4 FFF5	FFF6 FFF7	FFF8 FFF9	FFFA FFFB	FFFC FFFD	FFFE	FFFF

sales[0] sales[1] sales[2] sales[3] sales[4] sales[5] sales[6]

You could easily find the address of the beginning of the array, the **base address**, thus:

```
cout "The sales array starts at " << &sales[0];
```

and the statement would print out FFF0. In C++, however, the array name, without any index, is also the base address of the array. It can be used as type pointer or, more specifically, because we declared *sales* as an array of shorts, as a pointer to short. The following,

```
cout "The sales array starts at " << sales;
```

HEADS UP!

An array name is a constant.

would do exactly the same thing.

The prefix *sales*, however, is not a variable but a constant. Once declared, it cannot be changed. This makes a certain amount of sense. Changing the base address of the array would make all the variable names refer to some other locations. Unfortunately, their values would remain at the old addresses! We can assign values, then, to the variable *sales[0]*, but not to the constant prefix *sales*.

Offsets from the Base Address

We human beings can think of *sales[0]*, *sales[1]*, and *sales[2]* as different variables with different names. The concept holds true in C++, but C++'s way of implementing the concept is both simple and elegant. The variables *sales[0]*, *sales[1]*, and *sales[2]* are still different variables with different values, but to C++ the only identifier is the variable's prefix or base address, *sales*. The index, the number in brackets, is an **offset** from that base address. C++ interprets *sales[3]* as an offset of 3, that is, 3 away from the base address *sales*, FFF0.

But three what? Certainly not bytes, because *sales[3]* does not begin at FFF3. The offset is the number of variables from the base address. In bytes it is the index times the size of an individual variable. The variable *sales[3]* begins at FFF0 + (3 × 2) or FFF6. The variable *sales[0]* begins at FFF0 (FFF0 + (0 × 2)).

C++ keeps track of the base address of an array, but it does not keep track of the highest declared index. We could actually assign a value to *sales[7]* and C++ would put that value at memory locations FFFE and FFFF (FFF0 + (7 × 2)). This may well be a location that C++ has allocated for some other purpose, so our assignment will mess things up. Again, it is up to us to see that we do not go out of the bounds of our array.

Pointer Notation

We saw that the prefix for an array is really the base address of the array. Using pointer notation we could refer to the variable *sales[0]*, the first variable of the array, by `*sales`, the contents of the location at the address *sales*. The statement

```
cout <<  *sales;
```

would print the number 3806, the value of *sales[0]*.

To print out all the values in the array, as above, could we simply add 2 to *sales* at each step, having it point to a different location each time? No, because *sales* is not a variable; it is constant. We could, however, use *sales* in an expression such as *sales* + 4 and use dereferencing to access the contents at other addresses. The statement,

```
cout << *(sales + 4);
```

would print out the number 1183, the value of *sales[4]*.

We have illustrated this pointer notation for accessing array variables and it certainly is valid, but in most cases it is not considered good form to mix notations. If you have declared an array using index notation, stick with index notation unless there is some overriding reason to use pointer notation.

Pointer Arithmetic

If *sales* is FFF0, doesn't *sales* + 4 evaluate to FFF4? And why should *sales* + 4 refer to *sales[4]*, whose address is FFF8?

It does indeed refer to the address FFF8 because of **pointer arithmetic**. We declared *sales* as an array of `short`s, which means we are using *sales* as a pointer to `short`. Any time we do arithmetic with pointers, the values

HEADS UP!

The value in brackets is an offset from the base address.

TRAP

Working outside allocated memory.

HEADS UP!

Avoid mixing pointer and index notations.

refer to the number of variables, not the number of bytes. We saw this same phenomenon in calculating offsets from base addresses using bracket ([]) notation. The expression *sales* + 4, since *sales* is a pointer to `short`, is evaluated as *sales* + (4 × 2) or FFF8. If *x* was declared as a `long double` array and allocated the address 7000 (decimal), then *x* + 3 would be interpreted as *x* + (3 × 10) (assuming 10 bytes for a `long double`) or 7030 (decimal).

The parentheses in the expression *(*sales* + 4) are important. The dereferencing operator (*) is higher in precedence than the addition operator. Given the values stored in the *sales* array, look at the difference in evaluation with and without parentheses:

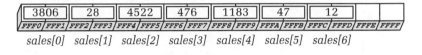

sales[0]   sales[1]   sales[2]   sales[3]   sales[4]   sales[5]   sales[6]

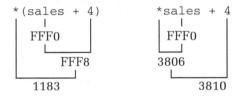

Without the parentheses, the dereferencing operator is applied to *sales*. The address there is FFF0 and the value at that location is 3806. To this we add the 4, not 4 × 2, because we are not dealing with pointers any more, yielding the result 3810, hardly what we were looking for.

The notation *(`sales` + 4), then, is equivalent to `sales[4]`. Both are offsets from the same address. Using index notation, a `for` loop to print out the values in the *sales* array could be written:

```
for (count = 0; count <= 6; ++count)
    cout << "Variable sales[" << count << "] = "
         << sales[count] << endl;
```

Output

```
Variable sales[0] = 3806
Variable sales[1] = 28
Variable sales[2] = 4522
Variable sales[3] = 476
Variable sales[4] = 1183
Variable sales[5] = 47
Variable sales[6] = 12
```

Using pointer notation, the exact same result could be achieved this way:

```
for (count = 0; count <= 6; ++count)
    cout << "Variable sales[" << count << "] = "
         << *(sales + count) << endl;
```

Because *sales* is a pointer, couldn't we just increment *sales* and rewrite the `for` loop like this?

```
short *end, count = 0;

end = sales + 6;              // Ending address of sales array
for (; sales <= end; ++sales)
{   cout << "Variable sales[" << count << "] = "
         << *sales << endl;
    ++count;
}
```

The new variable *end* keeps track of the address of the end of the array. Its value would be *sales* + (6 × 2) or FFFC. The only problem with this approach is that *sales* is constant, and therefore it cannot be changed. The expression ++sales would cause the compiler grief.

We could, however, use a pointer variable and increment it:

```
short *ptr, count = 0;

ptr = sales;                 // Beginning address of sales array
for (; ptr <= sales + 6; ++ptr)
{   cout << "Variable sales[" << count << "] = "
         << *ptr << endl;
    ++count;
}
```

The increment operator (++), which normally adds 1 to the value of a variable, is being applied to a pointer to short; therefore, it adds 2 each time, bringing us to the next variable.

YOUR TURN 12–4

1. What is the significance of the prefix of an array?
2. If *var* is declared as float var[10];, what is the difference between the expressions var[4] and *(var + 4)?
3. Given the declaration float var[10];, if var was F000, would var + 2 be F002?
4. Why can't we put float var[10]; and ++var; statements in the same function?

PUTTING IT TOGETHER

Professor Seligman grades on a curve . . . sort of. He gives hard tests, so no one gets near 100 percent. To make up for that, he takes the difference between the highest score and 100, and adds that to everyone's score. Because his specialty is domestic animal grooming and not computer programming, he has called on us for help.

TASK

Create a function that the professor can add to his grading program to adjust all the grades according to his "curve."

The function should take an existing list of grades, analyze them to figure the amount to be added, and then adjust the grades in their places in memory. To each grade will be added the difference between the highest grade and 100, so that the highest grade will become 100 and the rest will move up.

The data required by the function is the list of grades and the number of grades in the list.

The function should follow the following process:

Accept the scores and number of scores
Determine the high grade
Determine the amount to add
Add that amount to each score

To determine the highest grade we can:

Set up an initial maximum   [Determine the high grade]
For each grade
    if grade > maximum
        Set maximum to grade

We wrote a function called *curve()* that makes the adjustment to everyone's scores. That function calls another, *high()*, that returns the highest score so the professor can figure his "curve."

Program 12–9 works with the array of student scores using two different notations. The main() and *printScores()* functions use index notation, whereas the *curve()* and *high()* functions take advantage of the fact that an array is a set of contiguously stored variables and move a pointer from variable to variable.

The purpose of the main() function is simply to test the *curve()* and *high()* functions. By changing the initialization of the *scores* array, we can perform a number of tests.

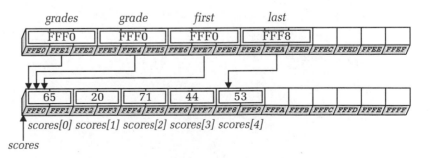

Program 12–9

```cpp
        #include <iostream>
        #include <iomanip>
        using namespace std;

        const int maxScore = 100;
        const int numScores = 5;

        void printScores(int scores[], int students);
        void curve(int *scores, int students);
        int high(int *scores, int *score);

        int main(void) ///////////////////////////////////////////// Main Program
        {   int scores[numScores] = {65, 20, 71, 44, 53};      // Initialize for test

1           printScores(scores, numScores);
2           curve(scores, numScores);
3           printScores(scores, numScores);
            return 0;
        }

        void printScores(int scores[], int students) //********* Display the Scores
        {   int student;

            cout << "Scores: ";
            for (student = 0; student < students; ++student)
                cout << setw(4) << scores[student];
            cout << endl;
        }

c1      void curve(int *grades, int students) //******** Adjust the Scores to Curve
        {   int *grade;                  // Address of particular score being worked on
            int add;

c2          add = maxScore - high(grades, grades + students - 1);
c3          for (grade = grades; grade <= grades + students - 1; ++grade)
c4              *grade += add;
c5                                                              // End of loop
        }

h1      int high(int *first, int *last) //******************** Determine High Value
h2      {   int max = *first;            // Set max to first value to be considered

h3          for (++first ; first <= last ; ++first)          // Move from second
                                                             // element to last
h4              if (*first > max)                   // If value of element > current max
h5                  max = *first;                                   // Replace max
h6                                                              // End of loop
h7          return max;
        }
```

Output

```
        Scores:    65  20  71  44  53
        Scores:    94  49 100  73  82
```

EXECUTION CHART

Line	Explanation	scores[]	scores			
1	Print array.	65 20 71 44 53	FFF0			
2	Call *curve()*, pass address of *scores* array and number of scores.	65 20 71 44 53	FFF0			
	curve():		**grades**	**grade**	**student**	
c1	Initialize *grades* to passed address, and *students* to passed value.	(65 20 71 44 53)	FFF0	--	5	
c2	Call *high()*, pass value of *grades*, which is address of *scores* array, and the address of the last variable in the *scores* array—FFF0 + (*students* × 2) − (1 × 2).	(65 20 71 44 53)	FFF0	??	5	
	high():		**first**	**last**	**max**	
h1	Initialize *first* and *last* to addresses passed.	(65 20 71 44 53)	FFF0	FFF8	---	
h2	Initialize *max* to value at *first*, the first value to be considered.	(65 20 71 44 53)	FFF0	FFF8	65	
h3	Increment *first* because we have already used the first value. Test; *first* is <= *last*.	(65 20 71 44 53)	FFF2	FFF8	65	
h4	Content at *first* (20) not > *max*.	(65 20 71 44 53)	FFF2	FFF8	65	
h6	Make *first* point to next element (*scores[2]*).	(65 20 71 44 53)	FFF4	FFF8	65	
h3	Test; *first* is <= *last*.	(65 20 71 44 53)	FFF4	FFF8	65	
h4	Content at *first* (71) > *max*.	(65 20 71 44 53)	FFF4	FFF8	65	
h5	Replace *max*.	(65 20 71 44 53)	FFF4	FFF8	71	
h6	Make *first* point to next element (*scores[3]*).	(65 20 71 44 53)	FFF6	FFF8	71	
h3–6	Continue until *first* not <= *last*.	(65 20 71 44 53)	FFFA	FFF8	71	
h7	Exit function.	(65 20 71 44 53)	FFFA	FFF8	71	
	curve():		**grades**	**grade**	**students**	
c2	Subtract *high* (71) from *maxScore* (100). Assign 29 to *add*.	(65 20 71 44 53)	FFF0	??	5	
c3	Set *grade* to beginning address of *scores* array. It is <= address of last *scores* variable (FFF8).	(65 20 71 44 53)	FFF0	FFF0	5	
c4	Accumulate *add* (29) to content pointed to by *grade*—65, the value of *scores[0]*. It is now 94.	(94 20 71 44 53)	FFF0	FFF0	5	
c5	Move *grade* to next *scores* variable.	(94 20 71 44 53)	FFF0	FFF2	5	
c3–5	Continue until *grade* past the address of last *scores* variable, then exit function.	(94 49 100 73 82)	FFF0	FFFA	5	
	main():	**scores**				
3	Print scores and quit.	94 49 100 73 82	FFF0			

ALLOCATING MEMORY

In Chapter 6 we saw that an object, whether a variable or an instance of a class, has a specific lifetime. Its lifetime starts when it is declared, which defines and allocates memory for the object. Its lifetime ends, if the object is local, at the end of the block in which it was declared or, if it is global, at the end of the program.

While the object lives, it takes up memory that cannot (or, at least should not) be allocated for anything else. In larger programs, memory space is often at a premium. Perhaps we can control that memory allocation more closely—allocating and deallocating memory whenever we choose.

The **new operator**, `new`, allows us to allocate memory.

```
new object
```

or

```
new object[elements]
```

The result of either of these forms of the `new` operation is the address of memory space that C++ has allocated. The first form allocates space for a single object; the second, space for an array of objects.

For example, if we declare

```
double *vision;
```

establishing *vision* as a pointer to `double`,

vision

then

```
vision = new double;
```

now makes *double* point to some allocated memory space the size of a double.

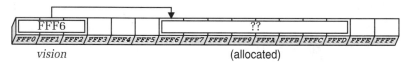

vision   (allocated)

We can assign values to that space using pointer notation:

```
*double = 123.456;
```

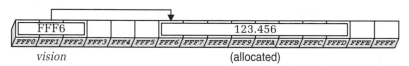

vision   (allocated)

If the `new` operation cannot allocate the required space (the machine is out of free memory, for example) it evaluates to the defined **NULL** address. This might be something we would test for:

```
vision = new double;
if (vision == NULL)                 // Note the uppercase NULL
    cout << "Outta memory!" << endl;
```

To illustrate an array example, let's say that we have declared a *taxReturn* class with all the data, hundreds or thousands of items, that must appear on an individual income tax return. Part of our program might be processing 100 of these at once. We could declare a pointer to a *taxReturn* object,

```
taxReturn *form;
```

THE NULL ADDRESS

The NULL address is the typical error condition set whenever an operation that results in an address fails. The constant, NULL, is defined in a number of header files so that whatever operation might require it will have it. Virtually all C++s (and this has to do with its relationship to the operating system) define the NULL address as zero. Since the zero value is interpreted as false and anything else as true, we often find a statement such as

```
if (vision == NULL)
```

stated as

```
if ( !vision)
```

We also saw this in testing fstream objects after an open() in Chapter 10.

Technically, according to the ANSI C standard and the ANSI C++ working papers (which we have been referring to as ANSI C++), this is shakey practice. If a C++/operating-system combination appeared where the NULL address was not zero, a lot of programs would be junk.

Fortunately, most operating systems are written, at least partially, in C++, so the OS programmers are familiar with the language and the traditional NULL address. Let's hope they continue to protect the shortcuts we C++ application programmers take.

and then allocate as many as we need using new.

```
form = new taxReturn[100];
```

To refer to the *name* on the tenth form, we could use pointer notation,

```
*(form + 9).name
```

Or, since we allocated it as an array, it would be more acceptable to use array notation,

```
form[9].name
```

So what's the big deal about new? C++ allows us to declare objects any time we want without using new. When we want the *vision* variable to come into existence, we can just say

```
double vision;
```

and forget about the pointer notation.

We can do the same with the array of *taxReturn* objects,

```
taxReturn form[100];
```

We would still use the array (or pointer) notation, of course.

One big deal is that the allocated space may be determined at run time instead of when the program is written. C++ allows this code segment:

```
cout << "How many forms do you need? ";
cin >> noOfForms;
form = new taxReturn[noOfForms];                              // No problem
```

but not

```
cout << "How many forms do you need? ";
cin >> noOfForms;
taxReturn form[noOfForms];                       // Can't use variable number of indexes
```

> **HEADS UP!**
>
> Array notation is more acceptable if memory was allocated as an array.

because a declaration must determine memory allocation when the program is compiled, and *noOfForms* does not have a value until the program is run. Using the second concept, we would have to declare enough *taxReturns* to accommodate the largest number we might ever anticipate—probably wasting a lot of memory.

Another big deal is in deallocating the memory space—making that memory space available for other data or processes. Variables do not disappear until the end of the block or the program. Their memory space may not safely be reused until then. Memory space that has been allocated by new can be deallocated with the **delete operator**, `delete`.

```
delete object
```

or

```
delete [] object
```

The first form deletes a single object; the second, an array of objects.

The statement,

```
delete [] form;
```

deallocates the space, the entire array, pointed to by *form*. The statement,

```
delete vision;
```

deallocates the space pointed to by vision. Remember, we have not deallocated the *vision* variable (or the *form* variable), only what it points to. After the statement, in most C++s memory will look like this:

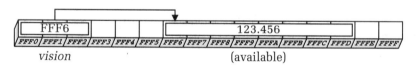

FFF6					123.456		
FFF0	FFF1	FFF2	FFF3	FFF4	FFF5	FFF6	FFF7	FFF8	FFF9	FFFA	FFFB	FFFC	FFFD	FFFE	FFFF

vision   (available)

Isn't that just what it was before the `delete`? Almost. The value is still there, but the space is now "available" rather than "allocated." The next operation may replace that value with something completely different—an array of tax returns, for example.

As with so many things in C++, it is largely up to us to keep things straight. We should be sure that:

- We stay within the bounds of allocated memory space. We would, of course, do this with any array.

- We do not directly access memory space after it has been `delete`d.

- We give the `delete` operator the same address we gave the `new` operator. If, for example, we change the value of *vision* (in other words, where it points) all kinds of crazy things might happen after a subsequent `delete`.

Program 12–10 tests the quality of the random numbers generated by the computer. It generates a set of random numbers in the range 1 through 10, adds them up, and then calculates the average, which should be about 5.5. The user can input the size of the set of random numbers. Because this program will be a small section of a huge program later on, we want it to

Program 12–10

```
#include <time.h>
#include <cstdlib>
#include <iostream>
using namespace std;

int main(void)
{   int *rands;                                // Beginning of the array of random numbers
    int number, numbers, total = 0;

    srand(time(NULL));                                              // Set seed
    cout << "How many numbers for test? ";
    cin >> numbers;
    rands = new int[numbers];                              // Allocate memory
    for (number = 0; number < numbers; ++number)          // Generate numbers
        *(rands + number) =                        // Using pointer notation
                          rand() % 10 + 1;       // Number between 1 and 10
    for (number = 0; number < numbers; ++number)          // Accumulate numbers
        total += rands[number];                    // Array notation instead
    delete [] rands;                               // Deallocate memory
    cout << "The average of " << numbers
         << " random numbers between 1 and 10 is "
         << (total * 1.0 / numbers) << endl;
    return 0;
}
```

Output

```
How many numbers for test? 2000
The average of 2000 random numbers between 1 and 10 is 5.475
```

Accessing deallocated memory.

take up as little memory as possible. Therefore, we allocate the memory for the random numbers after the program is started and we know how much memory we actually need; then we deallocate the memory, using delete, as soon as we are finished with the random numbers.

This program accesses the random numbers using both pointer notation and array notation. This is not a particularly good practice; we have done it for illustrative purposes. Since the variable *rands* is used to keep track of the base address of an array, we might allow ourselves to use array notation in this case. C++, of course, doesn't care.

YOUR TURN 12–5

1. Why would we want to specifically allocate memory rather than use normal declarations?
2. What operator allocates memory? What operator deallocates it?
3. If memory cannot be allocated, what is the result?
4. What is in the allocated memory after executing the delete operator?
5. Show the statement that deallocates space allocated by new array[14];.

LINKED LISTS

If you had a list of your friends' names and telephone numbers you could define a class for the data for a single friend. (We have used the word *pal* in the example instead of *friend* because the latter is a key word in C++.)

```
class Pals
{   string name;
    string phone;
};
```

You could keep the data for all of your friends in an array of *Pal* objects:

```
Pals pal[?];
```

How many friends do you have? After making a fool of yourself at that party last weekend, you're not sure. At any rate, you may have to drop a few from the list, but, since a few people laughed, you might pick up some new ones. So how many variables do we include in the array? It will have to accommodate the maximum number of friends that you might ever have, not just the number you have now. After last weekend, that will mean a lot of wasted memory in blank objects.

How do you add a friend? If you keep them in alphabetical order, you will have to insert into the array as we did in Chapter 8—a routine that may, in some cases, be unavoidable, but one that will take execution time to move all those objects around. You would have to drop a friend by doing the reverse, again moving a lot of objects. Storing lists in arrays, then, has some major disadvantages: allocating a fixed amount of memory, much of which may be wasted, and having to move a number of objects to add and delete.

Let's look at another method of storing lists in which we allocate only the memory we need and no extra. We can allocate a specific block of memory using the new operator and, when we no longer need it, deallocate it using delete. To add a friend, then, we will create a new object and to drop one, we will delete the object. That, however, will not solve the problem of keeping them in order.

Objects Pointing to Objects

We can keep a collection of data in order using a concept called the **linked list**. The list is essentially a chain of objects: the links being created by each object containing a pointer to the next object.

Each object in memory has, as one of its members, a pointer to the next object in the list. To move through the list we start at the **head** of the list, the address of the first object. The first object will contain the address of the second; the second the address of the third; and so forth until the last object, at the **tail** of the list, has a NULL pointer instead of the address of another object.

HEADS UP!

Any data type, including a pointer to an object, can be an object member.

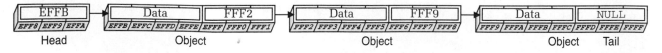

Referring to our example of the list of friends, setting it up as a linked list of objects, we define the class of objects as:

```
class Pals
{   string name;
    string phone;
    Pals *next;
```

The last member of the object, *next*, is a pointer to the data type *Pals*. Its value is the address of the next object in the list. It makes no difference where these objects are in memory, as long as the previous object knows where the next object starts. Assuming that we had allocated space for a number of these objects and properly linked them, our alphabetical list of friends might be as shown:

Address	name	phone	next
CA3A	Deltoid, Bruce	123-456-7890	CB14
CB14	Flowers, May	111-555-1212	NULL
CC0E	Abernathy, Aloysius	111-222-3333	CA3A

All of the pointers are contained in the objects in the list except one: the head of the list. We do not want the head to be a property of the class, because that would create a head property for each object of the class. We want only one head, accessible from any object but not part of any object.

We typically make a class available globally—declaring it externally. Objects may be, and usually are, created locally, but an object may be created from anywhere in the program. Any of the objects that make up our list must be able to access the *head* variable, so that variable should be created globally—externally. Before `main()`, then, we declare the *head* variable.

```
Pals *head = NULL;        // Address of first object in list
```

Initially the list is empty, so the *head* will also be the tail; its value is the NULL address.

Class Declarations

We want our *Pals* class to be truly encapsulated, so we will make the behaviors that manipulate the *Pals* objects members of the class. These functions must refer to the *head* variable, so the declaration of *head* must be before the class definition. But the *head* declaration refers to the *Pals* class, so the *Pals* declaration must be before the *heads* declaration. It sounds like one big impossible circle! Can we satisfy both criteria?

Yes, by using a separate class declaration that simply tells the C++ compiler that we will be using a defined data type but does not tell what is in it.

```
                                    //Declare the existence of the Pals class
                                        // Declare a pointer to Pals
                // Define the Pals class including references to head
```

It's a bit roundabout, but it gets the job done.

Using the class declaration, our friends program looks like Program 12–11. We have shown the *Pals* class properties and the declarations of the behaviors. We will fill in the behaviors as we discuss and run them.

HEADS UP!

Where objects in a linked list fall in memory is unimportant as long as each object knows where the next is.

HEADS UP!

Make the head a global variable.

Leaving out the class declaration.

```
class Pals;
Pals *head = NULL;
class Pals
{   [and so forth]
```

Program 12–11

```cpp
#include <iostream>
#include <iomanip>
#include <cstdlib>
#include <string>
#include <cctype>
using namespace std;

class Pals;                                    // Declare existence of class
Pals *head = NULL;                   // Declare and initialize global variable

class Pals ///////////////////////////////////////////////////// Pals Class
{  string name;
   string phone;
   Pals *next;

   Pals *newpal(void)  //********************************* Set Up New Record

public:
   void print(void)  //*********************************** Print Out List
   void insert(void)  //********************** Insert New Record into List
   void dump(void)  //*************************** Delete Record from List
};

int main(void)  //////////////////////////////////////////////// Main Program
{  Pals pal;
   char choice;

   cout << "(I)nsert, (D)elete, (P)rint, or (Q)uit: ";
   cin >> choice;
   while(toupper(choice) != 'Q')                       // Return ends program
   {  cin.ignore(500, '\n');                           // Dump end of stream
      switch (toupper(choice))
      {  case 'I':
            pal.insert();
            break;
         case 'D':
            pal.dump();
            break;
         case 'P':
            pal.print();
      }
      cout << "(I)nsert, (D)elete, (P)rint, or (Q)uit: ";
      cin >> choice;
   }
   return 0;
}
```

Navigating the List

Let's see how we move from one object in the list to the next. Printing the list in order will require this behavior, so we will examine the expansion of the *print()* Function. We will assume that the data in the previous table are already in the list at the addresses given, and that the value of *head* is CC0E. The process is as follows:

print() Function

```
                void print(void) //*********************************** Print Out List
p1          {   Pals *pal = head;                    // The first value of pal is the head

                cout << setiosflags(ios::left);
p2              while (pal != NULL)                              // The tail is not NULL
p3              {   cout << setw(30) << pal->name << setw(0) << pal->phone << endl;
p4                  pal = pal->next;                         // Set pal to next address
                }
            }
```

Output

```
        Abernathy, Aloysius            111-222-3333
        Deltoid, Bruce                 123-456-7890
        Flowers, May                   111-555-1212
```

EXECUTION CHART — *print()*				
Line	**Explanation**	***pal***	***pal->name***	***pal->next***
p1	Create a pointer to *Pals*; Initialize value with value of global variable *head*.	CC0E	Abernathy,	CA3A
p2	*pal* not NULL, have not reached the tail of the linked list.	CC0E	Abernathy,	CA3A
p3	Print record.	CC0E	Abernathy,	CA3A
p4	Set *pal* to point to next object.	CA3A	Deltoid,	CB14
p2	*pal* not NULL.	CA3A	Deltoid,	CB14
p3	Print record.	CA3A	Deltoid,	CB14
p4	Set *pal* to point to next object.	CB14	Flowers,	NULL
p2	*pal* not NULL.	CB14	Flowers,	NULL
p3	Print record.	CB14	Flowers,	NULL
p4	Set *pal* to point to next object.	NULL	??	??
p2	*pal* is NULL. Exit loop and return.	NULL	??	??

```
            Start pointer at head of list
            while next object not NULL
                Print object
                Set pointer to next object
```

Inserting into a Linked List

To add to our list, we must first create a new object. The *newpal()* function allocates memory for the object and allows the input of data for it. We pass nothing to the function, but the function returns the address of the new object. The *next* member of the object—the pointer to the next object—is set to NULL. When the object is inserted, that will change unless this new one ends up at the end of the list.

We insert the new object in the list by starting from the head and examining each object in the list. When we find the spot to insert—the new name, for example, is less than the name in the current object we are examining—we change the pointer in the previous object to point to the new one and assign the pointer in the new object to the address of the current one.

newpal() Function

```
Pals *newpal(void) //******************************* Set Up New Record
{   Pals *pal;                           // Address of new record

    pal = new Pals;                      // Create memory space for new record
    if (pal != NULL)                     // Be sure memory can be allocated
    {   cout << "Name: ";
        getline(cin, pal->name, '\n');
        cout << "Phone: ";
        getline(cin, pal->phone, '\n');
        pal->next = NULL;
    }
    else
        cout << "Not enough memory!" << endl;
    return pal;
}
```

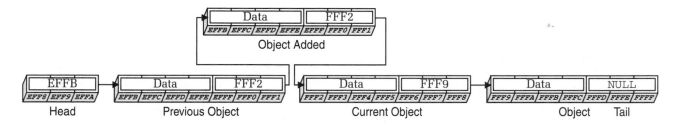

HEADS UP!

The head may change.

The *insert()* function inserts a new listing into the linked list of friends. This function (as well as the rest of the program) has access to the global *head* variable. The function must know where to start on its insert journey, and if the insert position turns out to be the first in the list, *head* has to be changed to point to the new object.

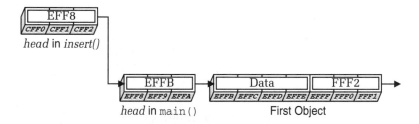

Notice the three pointers to object declared in *insert()*. The first, *pal*, is the address of the new record. It is assigned by a call to the *newpal()* function. If the record is successfully created (the return from *newpal()* is not NULL), the last two pointers are declared. One, *curr*, keeps track of the current record as we move from record to record; it begins at *head*. The other, *prev*, keeps track of the previous one; it starts at NULL. When we find the proper location for the new record, the pointer in the previous record is set to the new one (prev->next = pal), and the pointer in the new record is set to the current one (pal->next = curr).

For the execution example we have chosen the insertion of Ernestine Euforia into the list on page 480.

insert() Function

```
      void insert(void) //*********************** Insert New Record into List
i1    {  Pals *pal;                                  // Address of new record

i2       pal = newpal();
i3       if (pal != NULL)                            // New record created
i4       {  Pals *curr = head,            // Record being examined for input
                 *prev = NULL;                       // Record before curr

i5          while (curr != NULL                      // Not at end of list
                   && pal->name > curr->name)        // Name > record's
i6          {  prev = curr;                   // Save current record address
i7             curr = curr->next;                    // Go to next record
            }
i8          pal->next = curr;            // Insert in front of current record
i9          if (prev == NULL)                        // No previous record
i10            head = pal;                           // First in list
            else
i11            prev->next = pal;             // One before points to this
         }
         else
i12         cout << "Can't create new record." << endl;
      }
```

EXECUTION CHART — insert()

Line	Explanation	pal	pal-> name	pal-> next	prev	prev-> next	curr	curr-> name	curr-> next
i1	Create pointer for new object.	??	??	??	--	--	--	--	--
i2	Call newpal(), assign return to pal. It is not NULL.	CD21	Euforia	NULL	--	--	--	--	--
i3	pal a valid address, insert new record.	CD21	Euforia	NULL	--	--	--	--	--
i4	Make curr pointer the head of the list.	CD21	Euforia	NULL	NULL	??	CC0E	Aberna	CA3A
i5	curr not NULL, pal->name > curr->name.	CD21	Euforia	NULL	NULL	??	CC0E	Aberna	CA3A
i6	Save curr in prev.	CD21	Euforia	NULL	CC0E	CA3A	CC0E	Aberna	CA3A
i7	Set curr to next record.	CD21	Euforia	NULL	CC0E	CA3A	CA3A	Deltoid	CB14
i5	curr not NULL, pal->name > curr->name.	CD21	Euforia	NULL	CC0E	CA3A	CA3A	Deltoid	CB14
i6	Save curr in prev.	CD21	Euforia	NULL	CA3A	CB14	CA3A	Deltoid	CB14
i7	Set curr to next record.	CD21	Euforia	NULL	CA3A	CB14	CB14	Flower	NULL
i5	curr not NULL, pal->name not > curr->name.	CD21	Euforia	NULL	CA3A	CB14	CB14	Flower	NULL
i8	Set new record pointing to curr.	CD21	Euforia	CB14	CA3A	CB14	CB14	Flower	NULL
i9	prev not NULL.	CD21	Euforia	CB14	CA3A	CB14	CB14	Flower	NULL
i11	Set prev record pointing to new one.	CD21	Euforia	CB14	CA3A	CD21	CB14	Flower	NULL

dump() Function

```
           void dump(void)  //***************************** Delete Record from List
d1         {  if (head != NULL)                             // Names exist in list
d2            {  Pals *curr = head,           // Record being examined for deletion
                       *prev = NULL;                     // Record before curr
                 string dumpName;

                 cout << "Name to delete: ";
d3               getline(cin, dumpName, '\n');
d4               while (curr != NULL                      // Not at end of list
                        && dumpName != curr->name)          // Name != record's
d5               {  prev = curr;                        // Save current record address
d6                  curr = curr->next;                     // Go to next record
                 }
d7               if (curr == NULL)                          // Didn't find name
                    cout << "Name not in list." << endl;
                 else                                       // Name found
d8               {  if (prev == NULL)                    // No previous record
d9                     head = curr->next;                // First record dumped
                    else
d10                    prev->next = curr->next;  // Previous rec points to next rec
d11                 delete curr;                      // Deallocate that memory space
                 }
              }                                                  // List empty
           else
d12           cout << "List empty." << endl;
           }
```

Address	*name*	*phone*	*next*
CA3A	Deltoid, Bruce	123-456-7890	CB14
CB14	Flowers, May	111-555-1212	NULL
CC0E	Abernathy, Aloysius	111-222-3333	CA3A

Deleting from a Linked List

An object is deleted by passing the pointers around it. The pointer in the object before is changed to point to the object after the deleted one. The memory space for the deleted object can then be deallocated.

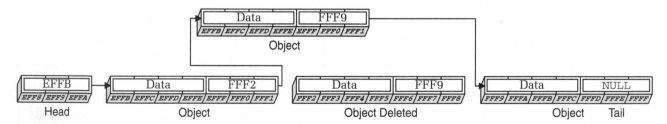

In the friends example, the *dump()* Function deletes a record. As in inserting, we start at the *head* (in this case the *head* will be modified) and examine each record in turn for the one to delete. When we find that one, we assign its pointer to the previous record.

```
prev->next = curr->next;
```

EXECUTION CHART — *dump()*

Line	Explanation	head	dump name	prev	prev-> next	curr	curr-> name	curr-> next
d1	*head* does not point to NULL.	CC0E	--	--	--	--	--	--
d2	The *curr*ent record starts at *head*.	CC0E	--	--	--	CC0E	Aberna	CA3A
d3	Input name to delete.	CC0E	Aberna	NULL	??	CC0E	Aberna	CA3A
d4	*curr* not NULL, *dumpName* =curr->name.	CC0E	Aberna	NULL	??	CC0E	Aberna	CA3A
d7	*curr* not NULL; found delete record.	CC0E	Aberna	NULL	??	CC0E	Aberna	CA3A
d8	*prev* is NULL; delete first record.	CC0E	Aberna	NULL	??	CC0E	Aberna	CA3A
d9	Change *head* to second record.	CA3A	Aberna	NULL	??	CC0E	Aberna	CA3A
d11	Deallocate space at first record and return.	CA3A	Aberna	NULL	??	CC0E	--	--

HEADS UP!

Don't forget to deallocate a deleted object.

We can then deallocate the current record.

```
delete curr;
```

For our execution example we will delete Aloysius Abernathy from this list.

Address	name	phone	next
CA3A	Deltoid, Bruce	123-456-7890	CD21
CB14	Flowers, May	111-555-1212	NULL
CC0E	Abernathy, Aloysius	111-222-3333	CA3A
CD21	Euforia, Ernestine	967-666-7777	CB14

YOUR TURN 12–6

1. How is a linked list linked?
2. What is the head of the linked list? What is the tail?
3. How do we insert an object into a linked list?
4. How do we delete from a linked list?

SUMMARY

- **KEY TERMS** (in order of appearance)

Location	Offset
Address	Pointer arithmetic
Pointing	New operator
Pointer	new
Dereferencing	NULL
Dereferencing operator	Delete operator
Pass by pointer	delete
Pass by value	Linked list
Member-pointer operator	Head
Base address	Tail

• CONCEPT REVIEW

- Main memory is made of millions of **locations**, each of which has a unique **address**.

- Variables can be accessed not only by name but also by address—**pointing** to the variable. Variables that contain addresses are called **pointers**.

- A pointer is a data type, but it is important that we also state to what data type the pointer points. A declaration of a pointer is accomplished by putting an asterisk in front of the variable name in the declaration.

- Like a local variable of any other data type, a pointer's initial value is garbage; it does not point to a valid location.

- Accessing data through pointers is called **dereferencing**, which we indicate using the **dereferencing operator**, the asterisk, in a statement other than a declaration.

- Pointers are often used in conjunction with functions. A **pass by pointer** rather than a **pass by value** passes the address of a variable (or array) to a function, which allows the function to access the location of the variable directly. This can overcome the limitation of allowing only one return value for a function.

- An object's properties are stored contiguously; therefore, pointers to objects can be useful. Accessing a member of an object to which we have a pointer can be accomplished using the dereferencing and member operators, with the proper parentheses, or the **member-pointer operator**, ->, which means the same thing.

- Pointers to objects are often used when a process requires moving objects from here to there—a sort, for example. Instead of moving entire objects we set up an array of pointers to the objects and move the pointers.

- An array index is merely an **offset** from the **base address** of the array. The offset is in variables, not bytes. The offset in bytes is the offset value times the number of bytes in the data type.

- Arrays can also be accessed using pointer notation and **pointer arithmetic**. Array elements can be accessed using calculated offsets from a base address or, if the pointer is a variable rather than the constant prefix to an array, by changing the value of the pointer.

- The **new operator**, `new`, allows us to explicitly allocate at run time memory that can be deallocated using the **delete operator**, `delete`. If `new` cannot allocate memory it evaluates to the defined **NULL** address. We must be sure to `delete` from the same address we used with `new`.

- A linked list is a common application of objects in which order is maintained by having a pointer in each record point to the next record. Using linked lists, we can easily insert into and delete from an ordered list, and the list need not occupy any unused memory.

- A **linked list** starts with a **head**, a pointer to the first object in the list, and ends with a **tail**, the pointer in the last object in the list that points to NULL.

- A class declaration must be used when we want to refer to the class in the definition of the class. This situation typically arises in linked lists.

- Navigating a linked list requires moving from object to object by following the pointers in each object that point to the next object.

- We can insert records into a linked list by putting the address of the new object in the pointer in the object before the insertion spot and making the pointer in the new object equal to what the previous one used to be. We can delete a record by making the previous object point directly to the subsequent one. Once an object has been excluded from the list, it should be deallocated.

- **HEADS UP: POINTS OF SPECIAL INTEREST**

  - A pointer is a data type.
  - An address of stored data is always where the data start.
  - The * in a declaration refers only to the variable immediately following it, not to all the variables.
  - The asterisk has many different meanings.
  - An address, like any other value, can be passed to a function.
  - There are three ways to pass to a function.
  - Passing pointers or references can overcome the limitation of a single return value.
  - The member-pointer operator is more intuitive and more commonly used.
  - Moving pointers is much quicker than moving objects.
  - Manipulating an array of objects by pointer requires an array of pointers.
  - An array name is a constant.
  - The value in brackets is an offset from the base address.
  - Avoid mixing pointer and index notations.
  - Pointer arithmetic is by variables, not bytes.
  - Explicit memory allocation allows us more control over lifetime.
  - Test for successful memory allocation.
  - Array notation is more acceptable if memory was allocated as an array.
  - Memory space allocated by `new` may be deallocated by `delete`.
  - Any data type, including a pointer to an object, can be an object member.
  - Where objects in a linked list fall in memory is unimportant as long as each object knows where the next is.
  - Make the head a global variable.
  - The head may change.
  - Don't forget to deallocate a deleted object.

- **TRAPS: COMMON PROGRAMMING ERRORS**

  - Using pointers that do not point to allocated memory.
  - Data types that don't match.
  - Dereferencing a pointer that points nowhere.
  - Forgetting the parentheses when dereferencing objects.
  - Working outside allocated memory.

- Forgetting the parentheses using pointer notation.
- Not using the all-caps NULL.
- Not giving delete the same address as new.
- Accessing deallocated memory.
- Leaving out the class declaration.

• YOUR TURN ANSWERS

• 12–1

1. A memory location is a physical place in memory capable of storing a byte of data. Its address is the specific numeric identifier for that location.

2. Pointing is referring to a variable by its address rather than its name.

3. Unofficially, there is a pointer data type. A pointer has all the characteristics of a data type—a specific number of bytes and form of storage, integral in the pointer's case.

4. A pointer variable is a variable used to store an address rather than a typical piece of data.

5. Dereferencing is accessing the location to which a pointer is pointing.

6. In a declaration, the asterisk means that the variable following is a pointer. In any other statement, the asterisk means dereferencing—following the address to where it is pointing and accessing there.

7. It is important to declare a pointer variable as a pointer to something because C++ must know how to treat the data in the location to which the pointer points.

• 12–2

1. Passing a value to a function means that the function will work with a copy of the value in the calling function. Passing by pointer means that the calling function tells the called function where a value is, allowing the called function to access the value directly. Passing by reference establishes another name in the function for the passed variable.

2. Declaring the pointer variable allocates space for the pointer variable, but its value, where it points, is garbage. The assigned value will end up in an unallocated location.

3. You can't return more than one value from a function, but you can pass references, or pass addresses to a function and have the function put values there.

• 12–3

1. We can use the dereferencing operator with the proper parentheses to dereference a member of an object described by a pointer variable, but the -> symbol (pointer->member) is more commonly used.

2. The notation pointer->member references the *member* member of an object pointed to by *pointer*.

3. An advantage of referencing objects by address is that if the application involves moving objects, it is quicker to move addresses instead.

• 12–4

1. The prefix is a constant pointer to the beginning of an array—its base address.

2. If *var* is declared as `float var[10];`, `var[4]` and `*(var + 4)` are equivalent.

3. Given the declaration `float var[10];`, if *var* was F000, `var + 2` would not be F002. This calculation would be done using pointer arithmetic, adding two variables to the address. If this C++ had a four-byte `float`, the address would be F008.

4. We can't put `float var[10];` and `++var;` statements in the same function. Because `var` is a constant, it cannot be assigned. If the declaration was `float *var;`, the other statement would be acceptable (although *var* may not point to a valid location).

• 12–5

1. The two usual reasons to specifically allocate memory rather than use normal declarations are (1) to allocate only the memory needed at the time; (2) to have more control over lifetime and, by extension, memory usage, by specifically deallocating the memory.

2. The `new` operator allocates memory, and `delete` deallocates it.

3. If memory cannot be allocated, `new` evaluates to the NULL address.

4. What is in the allocated memory after executing the `delete` operator? Who knows? Accessing there using the pointer set up by `new` is dangerous.

5. `delete [] array;` deallocates space allocated by `new array[14];`.

• 12–6

1. A linked list is linked by having, as a part of each object in the list, a pointer to the next object in the list.

2. The head of a linked list is the address of the first object in the list. The tail is the pointer member of the last object in the list. It is always NULL.

3. We insert an object into a linked list by moving through the list until we find the object in front of which we want to insert. Then we set the pointer in the previous object to point to the new one, and the pointer in the new one to point to the next.

4. We delete from a linked list by finding the record we wish to delete, setting the pointer in the previous object to point to the following object, and deallocating the space for the deleted object.

EXERCISES

1. Given the declarations and statements below, what are the data types (if it's pointer, don't forget to state *pointer to what*) and values of the expressions. Mention any problems that might arise.

```
char *c, *b, a = 'A';          Expressions:
float d, *e;                        &a _____
                                    *c _____
*c = a;                             *b _____
b = c;                              e  _____
e = &d;                             *e _____
d = 1.5;                            *&d _____
```

2. If C++ would allow us to make such an assignment (which it won't), what would be the result of the first assignment below? What about the second, which is a legal assignment?

```
float x = 123.45;
int *y;

y = &x;                    // First assignment
*y = x;                    // Second Assignment
```

3. Fill in the effects of these statements with values and arrows on the following memory diagram.

```
c = &a;
*b = a;
```

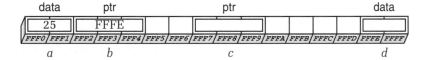

4. Finish the function call and the function that squares both x and y in the main() function.

```
square(_X, _Y);                         // Function call

void square(____A, ____B)               // Squaring function
{   __ *= __;
    __ *= __;
}
```

5. Show an execution chart and the output for the following program.

```
#include <iostream>
#include <iomanip>
using namespace std;

float milesPerGallon(int m, float g, float *c);

int main(void)
{   int miles = 400;
    float mpg, gallons = 20.0, cost = 1.0;

    mpg = milesPerGallon(miles, gallons, &cost);
    cout << setiosflags(ios::fixed) << setprecision(2);
    cout << "The cost of this trip was " << cost
        << " at " << mpg << " mpg." << endl;
    return 0;
}
```

(Continued)

```
float milesPerGallon(int m, float g, float *c)
{
    *c = g * *c;
    return m / g;
}
```

6. Given the following definition and declaration, what notation would you use to access the following?

```
class Rec
{
public:
    string name;
    float salary;
};

Rec item, *temp;
```

   a. The name in the *item* object.
   b. The *salary* in the object pointed to by *temp*.
   c. The address of *salary* in *item*.
   d. The fifth character in the *name* of the object pointed to by *temp*.

7. Referring to the object in Exercise 6, which of the following assignments are valid?

   a. `temp.salary = 1234.56;`
   b. `*temp.name = "Schemp";`
   c. `item.salary = 1234.56;`
   d. `temp->name[4] = 's';`
   e. `temp.salary = 1234.56;`

8. Referring to the object declaration in Exercise 6, show how you would pass the address of *item* to the function *func()* and tell what you would declare in the function to receive it using the identifier *recs*.

9. Referring to the situation in Exercise 8, how would you assign 4256.38 to the *salary* member of the object in the function?

10. Given the following declarations, which statements are invalid and why?

```
double one[10], two[5][5], *ptr, value = 1.0;
```

   a. `ptr = &one;`   b. `ptr = one + 3;`
   c. `ptr = two[2];`   d. `value = two[3][5];`
   e. `cout << two[1];`   f. `one = ptr;`
   g. `*ptr = 14.2;`   h. `*one + 2 = 25.1;`
   i. `*one = *(one + 3);`   j. `++*two;`
   k. `++ptr;`

11. Show the output from this program:

```
#include <iostream>
using namespace std;

int main(void)
{   short *ptr;
    short array[4] = {1,2,3,4};

    for (ptr = array + 3; ptr >= array; --ptr)
        cout << *ptr << "  ";
    cout << endl;
    return 0;
}
```

12. Referring to the declarations in Exercise 6, change the declaration of the *Rec* class so you could have a linked list of records. What other variables would you need?

13. Show the statement that would allocate space for a new record in the linked list in Exercise 12.

14. What is wrong with the following program segment?

```
int *stuff, other;

new stuff[20];
stuff = &other;
delete stuff;
```

15. How would you delete the record allocated in Exercise 14?

16. In Exercise 15 if you were adding this record to the middle of the list, what would you add to the end of the new record, and what would you change in the previous record?

17. How would you change the previous record in Exercise 16 if you were dropping a record in the middle of the list?

18. Why doesn't there need to be any special handling of strings in a linked list as there was using objects on files?

PROGRAMS

1. Write a program that will figure the average of any number of integer values input into the computer. The value zero should be used to signal the end of input. For the main body of the program use only the three pointer variables given. To ensure that they point to usable places in memory, assign them the addresses of the first three variables below. For example, val = &value;. Those three statements (and the declarations) are the only times the variables *value*, *counter*, and *total* should appear in the program.

Variables		Output
value		VALUE? **28**
counter		VALUE? **92**
total		VALUE? **–15**
*val	Number to input	VALUE? **0**
*count	Number of values to average	THE AVERAGE IS 35
*tot	Sum of all the values	

2. Write a program that shows the volumes of all rectangular solids with lengths, widths, and heights varying from 1 to 3. For the main body of the program use only the three pointer variables given. To ensure that they point to usable places in memory, assign them the addresses of the first three variables below. Treat these variables the same as those in Program 1.

Variables

```
length
width
height
*len
*wid
*hgt
```

Output

LENGTH	WIDTH	HEIGHT	VOLUME
1	1	1	1
1	1	2	2
1	1	3	3
1	2	1	2

[And so forth]

3. Write a program that generates five random numbers between 25 and 50 and, after generating each random number, keeps track of the smallest, the largest, and the sum of the numbers. A *rnd()* function should generate each random number in the proper range; a *stats()* function should be used to update the smallest, largest, and sum with each new random number. All printing should be done from main().

Variables and Functions

```
main()                              rnd()    Random number in range
  count
  number    Random number          stats()
  min, max, sum                       num, smallest, biggest
  total
```

Output

Numbers	Minimum	Maximum	Sum
42	42	42	42
35	35	42	77
50	35	50	127
37	35	50	164
27	27	50	191

4. Write a program to prepare an employee's paycheck stub. You should type in the employee's hours, pay rate, and tax rate. All calculations should be done in the function *PayCheck()*, but the resultant information should be printed out in the main() function.

Functions and Variables

```
Main()                payCheck()
  hours                 hrs
  payRate               pRate
  taxRate               tRate
  grossPay              gPay
  tax                   tx
  netPay                nPay
```

Output

```
Hours, pay rate: 30.5, 12.60
Tax rate (%): 15.2

Gross Pay      $384.30
Taxes           58.41
Net Pay        $325.89
```

5. Design a function that calculates the roots of a quadratic equation (the formula is given below). Since there are two roots, have the function return one, and pass the function an address where it can place the second. Test the function by calling it with *a* set to 1, *b* to 5, and *c* to 4. It should produce the given output.

Quadratic Formula

$$\frac{-b \pm \sqrt{b^2 - 4ac}}{2a}$$

Output

```
The roots are -1 and -4.
```

6. Write a program that accepts keyboard entry of five values and prints out the maximum and minimum. Both the maximum and the minimum should be calculated in a separate function and printed in `main()`.

Functions and Variables

```
main()          minMax()
 values[]         array[]
 smallest         min
 largest          max
 count            count
```

Output

```
Enter 5 values separated by whitespace.
5.74 2.6 18 -3.65 14.2
Minimum: -3.65, Maximum: 18.
```

7. Write a program that accepts three integers from the keyboard, puts them in order, and prints out the ordered set as well as the total. The function *order()* should put the values in order. The *swap()* function should perform the swap for sorting order.

Functions and Variables

```
main()          order()          swap()
 n[]              I[]              a, b
 total                             temp
```

Outputs

```
Enter three integers: 35 27 52
27, 35, and 52 add up to 114.

Enter three integers: 9 8 7
7, 8, and 9 add up to 24.

Enter three integers: 16 314 72
16, 72, and 314 add up to 402.
```

8. Modify Program 7–2 (page 231) so the *pay()* function prototype is as below. In other words, the *Employee* object is passed by pointer rather than by reference. The execution should be the same.

```
void pay(Employee *emp);
```

9. Modify Program 12–8 so you can add an employee to the sorted array of *EmployeeRec* objects. The insert should also be done using the array of pointers set up for the sort. Notice the comma after the name in the input.

Output Sample

```
New name, pay rate dependents: Duedropp Elvira, 11.21 2
Name                           Pay Rate  Dep
Barzoom Beulah                    12.63   5
Duedropp Elvira                   11.21   2
Freebisch Maynard                 10.83   3
Garfinkle Gilda                   15.25   5
LaRue LeRoy                        9.50   0
```

10. Write a program with a *backward()* function that prints out a string backward. Use addresses, not array notation.

Functions and Variables

```
main()   backward()
  str       str      Address of the string
            cur      Address of the current character of the string
```

Output

```
Your input? This is a string.
The output: .gnirts a si sihT
Your input? backward?
The output: ?drawkcab
Your input?
```

11. Modify the *backward()* function in Program 10 so the function does not print the string, it actually moves the characters in the string passed from the calling function, so that when the calling function prints the string, it is backward. Use addresses, not array notation. (*Hint:* Swap characters between the front and the back of the string, moving the front and back points toward the center.)

Functions and Variables

main()	backward()	
str	str	Address of the string
	temp	Use for swap of characters from front to back
	front	Address of current front of string
	back	Address of current back of string

Output

```
Your input? This is a string.
The output: .gnirts a si sihT
Your input? backward?
The output: ?drawkcab
Your input?
```

12. Write a program that inserts line breaks in a string. Use addresses, not array notation. The resulting lines should be 16 characters or fewer and should break only on whitespace (spaces, tabs, newlines). Assume that you will not encounter more than one whitespace character at a time. (Or to be more robust, *don't* assume that.) The actual line breaks (insertion of newlines) should be done in the function *split()*.

Functions and Variables

main()	split()	
string	line	
	beginLine	Address of beginning of current line

Output

```
Input a string.
Now is the time for all good people to come to the aid of their party.
Now is the time
for all good
people to come
to the aid of
their party.
```

13. To keep track of your ever-changing collection of CDs, you have decided to set up a linked list. Write the program that will add to the list, delete from it, and print it out.

Objects, Functions, and Variables

AlbumRec	Album class	add()	Add to list
title	Album title	head	
next	Pointer to next record	album	
main()		curr	
head		prev	
option	Add, delete, or print	deleteAlbum()	
print()	Print out list	head	
album		curr	
newAlbum()	Establish new record	prev	
album		delTitle	

14. Write a program to store the entire linked list referred to in Program 13 to the file *ALBUMS.DAT*.

15. Write a program to take the data from *ALBUMS.DAT* created in Program 14 and reform a linked list.

Chapter 13

THE PREPROCESSOR AND

OTHER FEATURES

PREVIEW

The C++ language has a number of additional facilities that make the programming process easier. Many have been compiled in a self-contained unit here, but everything in this chapter can be addressed at some earlier time. Note that each module is followed by a chapter number. That particular module may be addressed concurrently with, or any time after, that chapter.

- Comments (Chapter 2)
- The Preprocessor (Chapter 3)
- The Preprocessor—File Inclusion (Chapter 3)
- The Preprocessor—Code Replacement (Chapter 3)
- The Preprocessor—Macro Replacement (Chapter 3)
- The Preprocessor—Conditional Compilation (Chapter 4)
- The Preprocessor—Error Messages (Chapter 4)
- Renaming Data Types (Chapter 8)
- The Enumeration Data Type (Chapter 4)
- Conditional Expressions (Chapter 4)
- Combining Expressions (Chapter 5)
- Nonstructured Program Flow (Chapter 5)
- Unions (Chapter 12)

C++ and its various implementations have so many features, it would be impossible to cover them all in one book. Even the ANSI standard features are extensive. Here we will look at some of the capabilities of the standard language that you may or may not be required to use at present, but that eventually you should know about.

COMMENTS

In Chapter 2 we introduced C++'s commenting method—that is, putting two slashes with whatever comment we wanted to make at the end of a physical line. It works as a comment because the C++ compiler ignores anything between the two slashes and the line ending. This commenting method did not exist in the predecessor C language, but the old commenting method is still valid—and valuable—in C++.

In C (and C++), the compiler also ignores anything between /* and */. Notice that there is no mention of line endings here; they do not come into play. For example, using this commenting method we could write a line such as

```
taxes = income * /* this is the Federal tax rate */ taxRate;
```

and the compiler would translate it as

```
taxes = income * taxRate;
```

We have never actually seen such a comment in a program; it is not very readable. In fact, it's just plain ugly. However, the old commenting method is handy when a comment spans more than one line:

```
taxes = income * taxRate;    /* Be careful to use the
                                current taxable income
                                and the federal tax
                                rate for the current
                                year.                  */
```

Remember that the */ character combination turns the compiler back on. This means that **nested comments**, comments within comments, are not strictly allowed.

```
taxes = income * taxRate;    /* Be careful to use the
                                current taxable income
                             /* and the federal tax */    Compiler turns back on
                                rate for the current       This stuff is junk
                                year.                  */
```

HEADS UP!

Nested comments restrict portability.

We say "strictly allowed" because some compilers *will* allow nested comments, although it is not part of the ANSI standard. For the sake of portability, you probably should not use nested comments.

Commenting Out

Your program will not compile, or perhaps it runs incorrectly, and you are not sure where the error is. One way to find the error is to remove a section of your program and retest the program. If it performs correctly (minus the removed process, of course), you can be fairly sure that the problem is in the removed section, so you can then examine the removed section.

How? You removed it!

The solution is to remove it as far as the compiler is concerned, but leave it in the source code—**comment out** that section of code—put it between /* and */. In the following program segment, we see a section of the program commented out:

```
    flurp = frazzle(barge + zepple);
/*
    cout << "Creepazoid index is " << reeple(griznek, piffle) << endl;
    rimbage(frazzle(17), reeple(snirts, "Howdy"));
    if ( !dweeb)
        cout << geek(smarkie, 104.6);
    else
        cout << geek(quagle, 13.7);
*/
    cout << "And now, for something completely different." << endl;
```

To make the commenting out obvious we put the opening characters, /*, and closing characters, */, on separate lines starting in the first column. Like so many other style issues in C++, this is personal preference.

Be careful; commenting out can lead to nested comments. If you comment out a section that already contains old-style comments, you will have nested comments. For debugging purposes, because the extra comments will not be part of the final source code anyway, fine!—if your compiler allows it.

THE PREPROCESSOR

We looked at compiler directives and the preprocessor in Chapter 3. In this section we will discuss them more fully. When you compile a program, the first part of the compiler to execute is a segment called the *precompiler* or **preprocessor**. (With some compilers, especially in the UNIX realm, this is actually a separate program, cpp, run first.) This part of the process operates on the source code, making changes in it, but the end result is still source code. The changes, of course, are not made in your source file; they only affect the source code that is passed on to the rest of the compiler.

We will look at a number of preprocessor or compiler **directives**, but no matter what is in the middle, they all start and end in the same way. The beginning of a directive is the # symbol. It must be the first nonwhitespace character on the line. (In some non-ANSI compilers it must be the first character of any kind on the line.) The end of the directive is the first newline character—in other words, the end of the line:

```
#compiler directive
```

An exception to the ending rule is that we are permitted to continue a directive on the next line (after the newline) by putting a backslash (\) at the end of the line:

```
#compiler directive      \
    more directive       \
    more directive       \
    last of directive
```

The preprocessor will strip out the backslash and the newline that follows.

The backslash must be the last thing on the line, including comments. C++-style comments are not allowed in continued directives because they cannot be beyond the backslash and, if they precede it, they will turn off the compiler until the line ending, making the compiler ignore the backslash. Most compilers will choke on this:

```
#compiler directive      \        // Beginning of directive
    more directive
```

or this:

```
#compiler directive              // Beginning of directive   \
    more directive
```

or this:

```
#compiler directive      \    /* Beginning of directive */
    more directive
```

but will have no problem with this:

```
#compiler directive       /* Beginning of directive */   \
    more directive
```

TRAP

Putting C++ comments in a continued directive.

FILE INCLUSION

We looked at file inclusion and the #include directive in Chapter 3. Throughout the text we have used the #include directive to embed the header files provided by C++ into our source code. This freed us from having to define standard constants (ios::fixed, for example) and from having to declare standard objects (cout, for example).

The form of the #include directive can be either

```
#include <fileid>
```

as we have used it to this point, or

```
#include "fileid"
```

TRAP

Using a single backslash in strings.

The *fileid* is the identification of the file to be placed in the source code. In an MS-DOS or Windows system it might be something like *D:\\SYSTEM\\GOODIES.COD* (remember, a double backslash represents a single backslash in a string), which includes not only the file name and extension but also the search path through disks and folders or directories to find the file.

For a UNIX system, make the double backslashes (\\) into single slashes (/) and delete the reference to the disk drive (*D:*), */SYSTEM/ GOODIES.COD*. Be sure to consult your system's reference manual for the correct format.

This difference in the two forms, < > versus " ", is the way in which the C++ compiler searches for the file to include in the absence of a stated path. Both forms are system dependent, so you must find out the particulars of your system. The main difference, though, is that the first form, using the < >, searches a specific directory defined by the compiler (or, in some cases, the operating system). This is typically the directory in which certain standard files, such as iostream, are stored. The other form uses the operating system's default search pattern, typically starting with the directory in which you are currently working.

What can an include file include? Anything, really—the Declaration of Independence, for example. But to be reasonable, it should make some sense to the C++ compiler, which will try to compile it. In other words, it should be C++ source code. The Declaration of Independence made sense to the Founding Fathers, but it won't to the C++ compiler.

#includes may be nested, typically to about five levels. In other words, we may have an include file that has an #include directive in it. The second include file will be embedded in position in the first include file, which is embedded in position in the original source code. For example, our include file might contain #include <iostream>.

You may have written source code—entire functions, for example—that you want to put in a number of programs. Rather than typing or copying it into each program, you can put it in a file—for example, *MYSTUFF.INC* in an *INCLUDE* directory—and include it at the appropriate place in each program with the directive

```
#include "\\INCLUDE\\MYSTUFF.INC"
```

Your *MYSTUFF.INC* may look like the following, with other #includes in it.

```
#include <iostream>
#include <iomanip>
using namespace std;

double maximum(double a, double b)        //********** Returns Highest of 2 Values
{   if (a > b)
       return a;
    else
       return b;
}


double minimum(double a, double b)        //********** Returns Lowest of 2 Values
{   if (a < b)
       return a;
    else
       return b;
}
```

HEADS UP!

Include files can contain commonly used program segments.

HEADS UP!

Thoroughly debug code before putting it in an #include file.

Code should be thoroughly tested and debugged before being put in an include file. Remember, the include file is not part of the source code that is visible to us, it's visible only to the compiler. The inclusion is performed by the preprocessor and used only during the compile process. To fix problems in this section of code, you would have to go back to the include file itself. If you change the include file and then recompile your program, it will compile using the new code in the include file.

1. How does the old-style C commenting method differ from the C++ method?

2. When would you use the C commenting method rather than the C++ method?

3. What are nested comments?

4. What is the function of the preprocessor and when does this function take place?

5. What is the general form of a preprocessor directive and how does it differ from a statement?

6. Can a directive be on more than one line?

7. What does the #include directive do?

8. How can you see what is inserted by the #include directive?

CODE REPLACEMENTS

The **#define** directive replaces a specified set of characters with another piece of code. Near the beginning of the program we #define the *characters* we want to look for and the *code* we want to substitute for it.

```
#define characters code
```

The #define directive has two main uses: replacing one set of characters with another and replacing a short notation with an entire process—referred to as a *macro*.

Character Replacements

Character replacements are fairly straightforward. We #define a set of *characters* and a *replacement* set of characters.

```
#define characters replacement
```

Following the directive, all occurrences of a specific pattern of *characters* in the source code are replaced by the characters in *replacement*. For example,

```
#define PI 3.14
```

will replace each PI in the source code with the characters 3.14. An instance of the specified pattern within quotation marks, of course, will not be replaced (as we see in the cout below). We will not see the replacement; like the #include directive, it works only at the beginning of the compile process.

By tradition, the *characters* are all uppercase, as in PI. This makes the characters slated for replacement easy to spot in the source code and reduces conflict with variables, which are traditionally in caps/lowercase or all lowercase. Remember, C++ is case-sensitive.

Why not just put 3.14 in the source code? We usually use the *characters* as **defined constants**, symbols that represent specific values—*PI* representing the value 3.14, for example. One reason for putting them in the

Source Code	Actual Code to Be Compiled
	[The entire iostream file here]

```
Source Code

        #include <iostream>

        #define PI 3.14

        int main(void)
        {  float radius = 25;
           float circ;

           cout << "The circumference "
                   "formula uses PI\n";
           circ = 2 * PI * radius
        [and so forth]
```

```
Actual Code to Be Compiled

[The entire iostream file here]

        int main(void)
        {  float radius = 25;
           float circ;

           cout << "The circumference "
                   "formula uses PI\n";
           circ = 2 * 3.14 * radius
        [and so forth]
```

#define directive is to have them expressed at the beginning of the program where they may be easy to find if we want to change them. In our example, we may want our *circ* (circumference) or anything else based on π to be more accurate. All we have to do is to change the #define directive to, say,

```
#define PI 3.14159
```

and every occurrence of *PI* will reflect the change.

Another reason for using the #define directive is to enhance program readability. For example, our process may have a high limit of 849.325 and a low limit of −35.769. We often refer to such numbers as "magic numbers." If someone reads those two numbers buried in the source code, it might require some research to find out what they mean. But seeing the words *HIGH* and *LOW* would provide an instant clue.

Remember, directives end at the end of a line. Do not put a semicolon at the end of them, especially the #define, which would include the semicolon as part of the replacement.

const Versus *#define*

Isn't this use of #define the same as the use of a const variable? Yes, the objectives are the same, but the execution is different. The #define works at the preprocessor stage, before compilation begins. It performs only a character replacement. Those replaced characters are what is actually compiled. The disadvantage of a #define is that it has no data type other than what the characters might signify after compilation. A const variable has a data type; the compiler can use it for possible error checking, or calculations can be forced to specific types using it.

The advantage of the #define is that it operates before compilation; it requires no memory space for a variable and no time during execution. Many compilers, however, attempt to **optimize** code; they analyze the situation and introduce shortcuts to increase execution speed or reduce memory requirements. The const variable is one situation that is typically optimized by such compilers. It is treated almost as a #defined constant, but with a data type. Consequently, most C++ programmers use const rather than #define, but you will still find #define in lots of code.

MACRO REPLACEMENT

Basically, the #define directive tells the preprocessor to replace one set of characters with another. However, those replacement characters can be quite complicated. They can even be source code for some computer operation. We refer to such a replacement as a **macro**. The macro is established in the same type of #define directive:

```
#define macroName replacement
```

Whitespace is used to divide the keyword from the *macroName*, and that from the *replacement*.

The *macroName* is nothing more than a set of characters. We usually refer to it as a macro name, however, because it identifies—will be replaced with—program code. This is very much like a function, except that a function operates at execution time and the macro replacement operates at compile (or more properly, precompile) time.

The macro is used by putting the *macroName* in some subsequent spot in the program. Almost any spot will do, except that the *macroName* in a quoted string value or a comment will not be replaced.

Earlier we set up the defined constant *PI*:

```
#define PI 3.14
```

If the statement

```
cout << "Area (PI * r * r) = " << PI * r * r;              // PI defined earlier
```

appeared later in the program, it would be compiled as

```
cout << "Area (PI * r * r) = " << 3.14 * r * r;            // PI defined earlier
```

The *replacement* need not be just a single word, however; it can be anything after the whitespace following the *macroName*. For example,

```
#define PI 3.14                          // See Nuts 'n' Bolts,
#define AREA PI * r * r                  // "Rescanning Macros"

a = AREA;
```

At compile time the statement would become

```
a = 3.14 * r * r;
```

Remember also that C++ concatenates quoted strings that are separated only by whitespace. The code

```
"this " "and " "that."
```

would be compiled as

```
"this and that."
```

By using that feature we can replace strings with macros. For example,

```
#define COMPANY "Ajax Corp"

cout << "The earnings for " COMPANY " are " << earnings << endl;
```

would compile the statement as

```
cout << "The earnings for Ajax Corp are " << earnings << endl;
```

RESCANNING MACROS

When a macro is replaced, the compiler rescans the replacement text to see whether there are any more macros. If there are, it replaces them and rescans again. For example, we might have these definitions at the beginning of our program:

```
#define FOUR 2 * TWO
#define TWO 2
```

At first glance it would appear that the TWO in the first line would not be replaced because TWO was defined after FOUR. This is actually true of the text in the #define directive. If we later put the macro FOUR in a statement, such as

```
cout << FOUR;
```

however, the preprocessor will first translate it to

```
cout << 2 * TWO;
```

and then to

```
cout << 2 * 2;
```

This is useful when using a number of macros from various sources—different include files, perhaps—and the order of the #defines is not evident.

Parameterized Macros

We can define macros with parameters in them that will take on the values of similar parameters in the code when the replacement is made. **Parameterized macros** have one or more parameters in parentheses immediately following the macroName:

```
#define macroName(parameterList) replacement
```

The *parameterList* is any number of identifiers separated by commas. The open parenthesis must immediately follow the *macroName*, with no space in between. The *replacement* should reference those parameters in their desired positions within the *replacement*. For example, given the following:

```
#define area(r) PI * r * r

surface = area(radius);
```

the macro would have substituted radius for r and the statement would be compiled as:

```
surface = PI * radius * radius;
```

When using macros, we must be sure we understand the order in which things are done. The substitution is made before the program is run. If our statement were

```
surface = area(radius + 3);
```

we would get some surprising results because, after translation, our statement would be

```
surface = PI * radius + 3 * radius + 3
```

Because of operator precedence, the order of evaluation would be

```
(PI * radius) + (3 * radius) + 3
```

instead of

```
PI * (radius + 3) * (radius + 3)
```

Not putting arguments in parentheses.

A common way to eliminate that problem is to always put the parameters in the macro definition in parentheses, so that whatever is substituted for them will always be in parentheses.

```
#define area(r) (PI * (r) * (r))
```

when substituted in the statement becomes

```
surface = (PI * (radius + 3) * (radius + 3))
```

Other problems may confront the haphazard macro user. For example, if you set up variable names (other than the macro's parameters), will they conflict with local variables in the code? Will braces, brackets, or other symbols conflict with the control structures in the code? Be sure you are aware of what the final substitution will be with each use of a macro.

 HEADS UP!

Be aware of the final substitution when using macros.

One major advantage of macros is that they can usually be considered typeless. Data of any type can be substituted in the previous macro and it will still work. That carries its own disadvantage, however. The compiler cannot type-check macro code. A further disadvantage is that parameterized-macro code usually does not find its way into the elements used by various external debuggers, making debugging difficult.

 **HEADS UP!**

Macro code is typeless, but it also cannot be type-checked.

We can use any number of parameters in a macro as long as we separate them with commas:

```
#define avg(x, y, z) (((x) + (y) + (z)) / 3.0)      // Parentheses to be safe

average = avg(first, second, third);
```

The macro call in the statement would have `first` substituted for `x`, second for `y`, and `third` for `z`, making the statement (discarding the unneeded parentheses):

```
average = (first + second + third) / 3.0;
```

Both of our example parameterized macros look very much like functions. In fact, they are often used like functions. Many of the things that we introduced as functions were really macros. For example, the string classification "functions" in `ctype.h` are usually macros. We might define `isupper()` this way:

```
#define isupper(c) ((c) >= 'A' && (c) <= 'Z')
```

By tradition, C++ programmers use uppercase names for unparameterized macros (symbolic constants, such as *PI*), but for parameterized macros, they use lowercase or lower/uppercase identifiers to make them look just like functions.

MACRO OR FUNCTION?

Should you define your routine as a macro or a function? If it's long it will probably be a function. But if it's short, you may have a choice. Macros have some advantages. When you call a function, passed values must be copied to the function, return addresses kept, execution moved to another part of memory, return values passed back, execution moved again, and so forth. None of this really accomplishes the task of the routine. It is all *overhead*. A macro, on the other hand, is placed directly in line in the code at compile time, so that at run time this overhead is avoided. As a result, macros execute more quickly.

It should be noted that many optimized compilers automatically take short functions and compile them in line, just like a macro. Check to see whether yours does.

Another advantage of macros is that whereas values passed to functions must be of specific data types, that is not true of macros—the data type is determined in the substitution or the calculations that follow.

For example, with

```
#define square(x) ((x) * (x))
```

the value substituted for *x* could be 4 or 78.2874 or a `char` or `long double` variable. The mathematics will accommodate the data type. If *square()* were a function, a value of a specific data type would have to be passed to it. Different data types would require different functions, as exist with the `abs()`, `labs()`, and `fabs()` functions.

A disadvantage of macros is that if they are used repeatedly in a program, they are copied into the code many times. Function code exists only once. Macros, then, could make the executable program longer and take up much more memory.

Stringizing and Token Pasting

We are writing personalized form letters to people in various towns and we want our greeting to say "Dear whatever-your-name-is of whatever-your-city-is." We can, of course, concatenate these characters together, but there is another way.

Let us set up a macro, *assignGreeting()*, that will put together the name and city with the text of the greeting. We will call the macro giving it the name and the city,

```
assignGreeting(B. Fuddled, Clueless);
```

and #define the macro so that everything is assembled correctly.

To accomplish this, we can using **stringizing**—turning into a quoted string—the replacement, and using C++'s automatic concatenation of adjacent strings to assemble the greeting. The stringizing operator is # and it belongs just before the symbol we want stringized. Following is the #define, the call, and the replacement shown in two steps:

```
#define assignGreeting(name, city) \
        greeting = "Dear " #name " of " #city
```

Call	`assignGreeting(B. Fuddled, Clueless);`
Replacement, step 1	`greeting = "Dear " "B. Fuddled" " of " "Clueless";`
Replacement, final	`greeting = "Dear B. Fuddled of Clueless";`

The **token-pasting** operator, ##, allows us to put together two *tokens* or sets of characters. For example, if in some part of our code we wanted to refer to the variable *factorMin*, or *factorMax*, or *factorAvg*, depending on the situation at that point in the program, we could

```
#define factor(x) factor ##x
```

and call it like this:

```
result = 0.2762 * factor(max);
```

The replacement would be:

```
result = 0.2762 * factorMax;
```

A Macro's Lifetime

Because a macro is replaced before the program is actually compiled, a macro does not have a lifetime during the program execution. It does, however, have an effective range within the source code. Macros are effective from the point at which they are defined in the source code to the end of the source code, or to the line where they are undefined using the **#undef** directive:

```
#undef macroName
```

For example,

```
#undef area
```

Macros may not be redefined unless the redefinition of the macro is the same as the existing definition. This allows, for instance, a macro such as NULL or EOF to be defined in more than one header file without conflict. To change a macro's definition we would have to #undef (undefine) it and #define it again.

```
                  // PI is 3.14 in this section of the program

                       // PI changes to 3.14159 at this point
```

HEADS UP!

Macros are essentially global.

```
#define PI 3.14
. . .
#undef PI
#define PI 3.14159
```

YOUR TURN 13–2

1. Do we see the changed characters when we have a #defined character replacement in our source code?
2. In what parts of a program will a macro or character replacement be made?
3. Why are parentheses important in parameterized macros?
4. Can we use existing variable names as macro parameters?
5. How can we perform a macro replacement in the middle of a string?
6. How can we put two strings together during a macro replacement?
7. What is a macro's effective range?

CONDITIONAL COMPILATION

The compiler doesn't necessarily have to consider all the code that you have written. You can direct the preprocessor to skip some. *Skip some?!* After all the time you spent typing the code, why would you want some skipped? There are a number of valid reasons. Often when debugging a program we put in extra statements to see what is happening at a certain point—some `cout`s, perhaps.

We do not want these executing after the debugging, so we erase them. And when we find a bug or two more, we retype them. Instead, let's just leave them in the code and tell the compiler to ignore them when we are not debugging.

We might be writing a program that will eventually run on more than one type of computer or be destined for a number of slightly different users. A few lines of code will have to be different for each application. We could leave all the code in the source file but tell the preprocessor that if this is the Acme Company, compile these lines; if it's Baker, compile those; and so forth.

To accomplish this we use directives that work much like the `if` and `else` statements—the **#if** and **#else** directives. Because the preprocessor does not use the C++ block structure, we end the #if structure with an **#endif**:

```
#if condition
    Compile these statements
#else
    Compile these statements
#endif
```

The #if, #else, and #endif directives work only with the preprocessor, so the *condition* can only react to those things that are active in the preprocessing stage—the results of other preprocessor directives such as `#define`.

For example, we may want to declare a variable differently depending on how many records the program might process:

```
#define MAXRECORDS 45000
. . .
#if MAXRECORDS <= 32767
    short records;
#else
    long records;
#endif
```

We do not need parentheses around the condition here as we do in the `if` statement. They are, of course, acceptable.

An `#else` branch is not required. We might need an extra variable if we have a lot of records, so we could write

```
#define MAXRECORDS 45000
. . .
int records;
#if MAXRECORDS > 32767
    int recordSet;
#endif
```

We might use a multibranch structure as in Chapter 4. An #if structure may be nested within another #if structure branch or, more commonly, we use the multibranch structure in which we combined the `if` on the same line as the `else` to make a kind of `else if` statement. For the preprocessor, we don't have to make up one; there is one—**#elif**, meaning *else if*. If we had three possibilities for the maximum number of records, we might write

```
#define MAXRECORDS 45000
  . . .
#if MAXRECORDS <= 127
    char records;
#elif MAXRECORDS <= 32767
    short records;
#else
    long records;
#endif
```

We can, of course, use as many #elifs as we need.

The keyword **defined** can be used in a *condition* to test to see whether a symbolic constant has been defined. It is always followed by the constant name being tested.

```
if defined name
```

often written

```
if defined(name)
```

The value of the constant is immaterial. All that counts is whether it has been used in a #define directive.

For example, let us say that we are testing a program and have inserted debugging statements throughout. Near the beginning of the program we can have the directive

```
#define DEBUG
```

The value of *DEBUG* is nonexistent, empty, but as far as the preprocessor is concerned, it has been defined. Later in the program, we can put

```
#if defined(DEBUG)
    [debugging statements]
#endif
```

The **#ifdef** directive combines #if and defined(). We could write the first line of the previous segment as

```
#ifdef DEBUG
```

The only advantage of the long form is in cases in which you need a *condition* with two or more tests, such as

```
#if defined(DEBUG) and MAXRECORDS > 500
```

We can test for a constant not having been defined using either the logical not or the **#ifndef** directive.

```
#if !defined(DEBUG)
```

or

```
#ifndef DEBUG
```

COMMENT OUT OR CONDITIONALLY COMPILE?

We looked at commenting out code for debugging—enclosing the code in /* */:

```
/*
    cout <<"Test value at step 4 is " << test;
    cout << "At iteration " << count << endl;
*/
```

This is fine unless one of the statements also has a comment. Most C++s do not support the nesting of comments (although some are starting to), so in the following, the second statement would be compiled instead of ignored.

```
/*
    cout << "Test value at step 4 is " << test << endl; /* Increase */
    cout << "At iteration " << count << endl;
*/
```

Conditional compilation, such as the following, avoids those problems.

```
#ifdef DEBUG
    cout << "Test value at step 4 is " << test << endl; /* Increase */
    cout << "At iteration " << count << endl;
#endif
```

In addition, using conditional compilation, many sections of code can be turned off or on with a single #define, whereas each commented-out section will have to be dealt with separately.

PREPROCESSOR ERROR MESSAGES

Errors may be introduced just as easily in the preprocessor code as in the rest of the program. You can set up debugging aids in the rest of the program by putting in cout statements at critical points to print out values, error messages, or whatever. You can do a limited amount of that in the preprocessor code with the **#error** directive:

```
#error message
```

where the *message* is any quoted string. The #error directive stops the compile process and prints the *message*.

Because the directive stops the compile if it is encountered, it is typically within an #if structure as a "we shouldn't be here" type of thing. For the error directive to be useful, you must anticipate possible errors and place the directives appropriately. For example,

```
#if PARSNIP = 1
    #define TURNIP 3
#elif PARSNIP = 2
    #define TURNIP 0
#else
    #ifndef PARSNIP
        #error "PARSNIP undefined."
    #else
        #error "PARSNIP must be 1 or 2."
    #endif
#endif
```

HEADS UP!

#error directives stop the compiling process.

RENAMING DATA TYPES

Using **typedef** we can change the name of an existing data type to something else,

```
typedef oldName newName;
```

where the *oldName* is the name of an existing data type—`long double`, `int`, a class name that we had defined earlier, or even a *newName* defined earlier. The *newName* can be used anywhere a data-type name is valid—declaring variables and functions, casts, `sizeof` operations, and so forth. For example,

```
typedef int INTEGER;
typedef float REAL;
typedef long GRADES[MAXSEATS];
```

establishes three new names for data types, the third being a `long` array of *MAXSEATS* length. *MAXSEATS*, of course, must have been `#defined` previously. Later in the program we may declare variables using these new names:

```
INTEGER x, y, z = 45;
REAL ity;
GRADES row;

GRADES rows[10];
```

In the third statement we declared *row* as a *GRADES* array of *MAXSEATS*. The declaration without the `typedef` would have been

```
long row[MAXSEATS]
```

In the fourth statement we declared *rows* as an array of 10 *GRADES* arrays of *MAXSEATS* each. The declaration without the `typedef` would have been

```
long rows[10][MAXSEATS];
```

A convenient way of viewing the `typedef` process is to substitute the declared variable or array for the *newName* in the `typedef`. In our last example, substituting `rows[10]` for `GRADES` in

```
typedef long GRADES[MAXSEATS];
```

yields

```
long rows[10][MAXSEATS];
```

Notice the semicolons after `typedef`. It is a statement and so must have them. Often we put new names for data types in capitals, like defined constants, to make them easily recognizable.

A `typedef`ed name must be a complete data type; it cannot be modified by things like `signed` or `unsigned`. Given the previous `typedef`, this is illegal:

```
unsigned INTEGER q;                                    // Illegal
```

Now that we know how to rename a data type, why do it? One reason is for portability. We know that data types can have different sizes in different implementations of C++. Imagine we are working with a Midget computer as well as a SuperMax. On the Midget, an `int` has 16 bits; a `long`, 32; a `float`, 32; and a `double`, 64. The SuperMax has a 32-bit `int` and a 64-bit `float`. If we want our program to work with 32-bit integers and 64-bit real numbers, no matter which implementation of C++ we use, we can set up the following near the beginning of our code:

```
#define MACHINE 0                      // 0 = Midget, 1 = SuperMax
#if MACHINE = 0
    typedef long INTEGER;
    typedef double REAL;
#else
    typedef int INTEGER;
    typedef float REAL;
#endif
. . .
REAL function(INTEGER this, REAL that);
. . .
INTEGER i, j, k;
REAL x, y, z;
```

By changing the `#define` near the beginning of the code, we can compile the program for either computer.

Another reason to use `typedef` is for readability and consistency. Suppose that we are working with various arrays of pointers to a specific class:

```
class Specific
{   string name;
    int age;
    return 0;
};
. . .
Specific *array1[20], *array2[20];         // Similar declarations elsewhere
```

We could `typedef` the data type to make the declarations both more clear and more consistent.

```
typedef Specific *SPEC_PTR[20]
. . .
SPEC_PTR array1, array2;                    // Similar declarations elsewhere
```

YOUR TURN 13–3

1. Show the pattern, along with the key words, for a three-branch conditional compilation.

2. How is the key word `defined` used in a conditional compilation?

3. How can we test for a constant definition in a conditional compilation without using the `defined` key word?

4. What preprocessor directive do we use to send an error message? What does it do besides display the error message?

5. Can we create a new data type using `typedef`?

6. Can we use modifiers such as `long` or `unsigned` with a `typedefed` data type?

PUTTING IT TOGETHER (The Preprocessor and `typedef`)

Senator Jack S. Bloehardt of the Great State of Confusion would like a quick way to estimate the amount of federal funds needed to cover financial losses from natural disasters—earthquakes in California, volcanic eruptions in the Northwest, blizzards in the Rockies, tornadoes in the Midwest, hurricanes in the East, laryngitis in Washington, D.C.—name your disaster.

TASK

Design a program that will provide the senator and his staff a quick way of estimating federal funds needed.

ANALYSIS

The calculations are quite complicated and the process is huge, but we will concentrate on the final formula:

$$loss = devastation \times population \times percapita \times case$$

where *loss* is the dollar amount of the losses, *devastation* is the percentage of complete loss in the area, *population* is the number of people in the area adjusted by a factor calculated by dividing the number of people registered in the senator's party by the number registered in the other party, *percapita* is the average loss per person if the devastation was total, and *case* is a factor based on whether the disaster is in the senator's home state (worst case, most funds) or someone else's state (best case, least funds).

IMPLEMENTATION

We want to make the program as flexible as possible, so the important parameters are defined in the beginning of the program. The senator wanted the program to work for estimating the need for funds not only in his home state but also in some other state. Naturally, the calculations would be different. We couldn't remember whether the senator was a Republican or a Democrat, so we allowed for stating a party affiliation prior to compiling.

Only a few of the actual statements are shown in Program 13–1, but let's examine the preprocessor manipulations.

TEST

Testing the program would, of course, require that the rest of the program be filled in. The tests should include all possible combinations of factors referred to in the preprocessor directives.

THE ENUMERATION DATA TYPE

The **enumeration data type** (**enum**) sets up a different use of an integral data type. The enum definition establishes a data type that can hold one

Program 13–1

```
 1  #include <iostream>                          // Standard input/output header file
    using namespace std;

 2  #define DEMOCRAT                                   // If Republican, leave this out
 3  #define PERCAPITA 25000         // Loss per person if total devastation
 4  #define DETAIL                              // Print details, not just result
 5  #define HOMESTATE                   // Change to OTHERSTATE if appropriate
 6  #define BESTCASE 0.65                     // Least possible amount of funds
 7  #define WORSTCASE 1.35             // Greatest possible amount of funds

 8  #ifdef OTHERSTATE
 9     #define STATE "your"
10     #define CASE BESTCASE                      // Apply least funds factor
11  #elif defined HOMESTATE
12     #define STATE "my"
13     #define CASE WORSTCASE                  // Apply greatest funds factor
    #else
14     #error "Must define either HOMESTATE or OTHERSTATE."
    #endif

15  #ifdef DEMOCRAT                 // Adjust by percent of population in party
16     #define population(total, demo, repub) ((total) * (demo) / (repub))
    #else
17     #define population(total, demo, repub) ((total) * (repub) / (demo))
    #endif

18  #if PERCAPITA > 20000
19     typedef long double LOSSES;              // Larger data type for most funds
    #else
20     typedef double LOSSES;
21  #endif

    int main(void)
22  {  LOSSES loss, devastation;       // Force final calculation to LOSSES type
       . . .
23     #ifdef DETAIL
24        cout << "Case factor: " << CASE << ".\n";
25        cout << "Adjusted population: " << population(pop, dem, gop)
                  << ".\n";
       #endif
26     loss = devastation * population(pop, dem, gop) * PERCAPITA * CASE;
27     cout << "Funds needed in " STATE " state are " << loss << endl;
       return 0;
    }
```

 **HEADS UP!**

C++ does not enforce enum values.

integer value from a defined set of possible integer values. A group of constants established in this definition are used to represent these values. Variables declared to be of this data type should hold only those values, although C++ does not actually enforce this.

The general form of an enum definition is (optional stuff underlined):

enum *tag* {*constant = value*, *constant = value*, . . .};

EXECUTION CHART	
Line	**Explanation**
1	Insert source file *iostream*.
2–7	Initial defines.
8	*OTHERSTATE* was not defined.
11	*HOMESTATE* was defined in line 5.
12	Define *STATE* as "my".
13	Define *CASE* as *WORSTCASE*, which was defined in line 7 as 1.35.
15	*DEMOCRAT* was defined in line 2.
16	Define *population* macro.
18	*PERCAPITA*, defined in line 3, is greater than 20,000.
19	Set up data type *LOSSES* as long double.
22	Declare 2 variables of type *LOSSES* (long double) as defined in line 19.
23	*DETAIL* was defined in line 4.
24	Print case factor *CASE*, defined in line 13.
25	Print result of *population* macro, defined in line 16.
26	Calculate *loss* using *population*, defined in line 16, *PERCAPITA*, line 3, and *CASE*, line 13.
27	Substitute "my" for STATE giving: "Funds needed in " "my" " state are " and finally: "Funds needed in my state are ".

where the `tag` is the new data type and `constant` is the name of an allowed constant. If a `value` is not stated, the first value is zero and each value is 1 greater than the previous one. For example,

```
enum boolean {false, true, off = 0, on, no = 0, yes};
```

defines the data type *boolean* and its possible values: *false*, *off*, and *no* are zero, and *true*, *on*, and *yes* are one.

A declaration of variables of an enum data type are made following this form:

```
enum tag variable = value, variable = value, . . .;
```

For example,

```
enum boolean status, indicator = false;
```

Definitions and declarations can be made in the same statement; for example:

```
enum
    {sun = 1, mon, tue, wed, thu, fri, sat}
    day, firstWorkDay = mon;
```

In this example of the combination statement, however, no `tag` is defined. We could not set up another variable, *startWeekEnd*, using the same defined values because we cannot define more than one value with the same name.

Defining more than one enum value with the same name.

Program 13–2

```cpp
#include <iostream>
using namespace std;

enum months {JAN = 1, FEB, MAR, APR, MAY, JUN,
             JUL, AUG, SEP, OCT, NOV, DEC};

int main(void)
{   enum months month;

    cout << "Enter number for month: ";
    cin >> month;                       // Or (int)month - see 'More Challenges'
    if (month < JAN || month > DEC)    // C++ doesn't prevent improper values
        cout << "Invalid Month." << endl;
    else
    {   cout << "That is in the ";
        if (month <= MAR)
            cout << "first";
        else if (month <= JUN)
            cout << "second";
        else if (month <= SEP)
            cout << "third";
        else
            cout << "fourth";
        cout << " quarter of the year." << endl;
    }
    return 0;
}
```

Outputs

```
Enter number for month: 4
That is in the second quarter of the year.

Enter number for month: 20
Invalid Month.

Enter number for month: 10
That is in the fourth quarter of the year.
```

```cpp
enum {hot, cold} temp;
enum {hot, cold} degrees;              // This causes an error
```

will not be accepted by the compiler, but

```cpp
enum warmth {hot, cold} temp;
enum warmth degrees;                   // No problem
```

will be accepted.

Program 13–2 sets up enumeration values for the names of the months and uses them to determine the quarter each month is in.

Program 13–2—or any program, for that matter—could be written without enums, but use of the enum data type makes the program more readable.

THE CONDITIONAL EXPRESSION

We examined ways of forming two-branch or multibranch structures using sets of statements in Chapter 4. C++ also gives us the **conditional expression**, using the operators ? and :, which allows us to set up a two-branch situation within an expression. The general form of a conditional expression is

condition ? *trueExpression* : *falseExpression*

C++ first evaluates the *condition* to true or false. If the *condition* is true, then C++ will evaluate the *trueExpression*, which becomes the value of the entire conditional expression. Otherwise C++ will evaluate the *falseExpression*. For example, if the value of *x* is 150, then the value of this expression,

```
x > 100 ? x * 1.1 : x * .9
```

is 165, the value of the *trueExpression*.

This is not like an if statement, where the value of the condition allows the program to go to one set of statements or another. A conditional expression, like any other expression, reduces to a single value. As an example, let's say that salespeople are paid their salary plus a commission of 10 percent on all sales if they sell up to and including $1,000, and 12 percent on all sales plus a bonus of $100 if they sell more than $1,000 worth of merchandise.

```
pay = salary + (sales > 1000 ? sales * 0.12 + 100 : sales * .1);
```

If *sales* was $2,000 then the value of the entire conditional expression, everything within the parentheses, would be $340—*sales* × 0.12 + 100—which would be added to *salary* and the result stored in *pay*.

Program 13–3

```cpp
#include <iostream>
#include <iomanip>
using namespace std;

int main(void)
{  float comm, salary, sales;

   cout << "Input salary and sales> ";
   cin >> salary >> sales;
   if (sales > 1000)
      comm = sales * .12 + 100;
   else
      comm = sales * .1;
   cout << setiosflags(ios::fixed) << setprecision(2);
   cout << "Pay is: " << (salary + comm) << "." << endl;
   return 0;
}
```

Program 13–4

```cpp
#include <iostream>
#include <iomanip>
using namespace std;

int main(void)
{  float salary, sales;

   cout << "Input salary and sales> ";
   cin >> salary >> sales;
   cout << setiosflags(ios::fixed) << setprecision(2);
   cout << "Pay is: "
        << (salary + (sales > 1000 ? sales * .12 + 100 : sales * .1))
        << "." << endl;
   return 0;
}
```

Outputs for Both Programs

```
Input salary and sales> 200 800
Pay is: 280.00.

Input salary and sales> 200 1500
Pay is: 480.00.
```

The parentheses are important in the example above because the precedence of the conditional operator is very low, just above the assignment operators. Its associativity is right to left (refer to Appendix B).

The data type of the entire conditional expression is determined by both the expressions contained within it, not by which is eventually chosen. The usual promotion rules apply. If the true expression evaluates to int and the false to float, then the type of the whole expression is float even if the condition is true.

Program 13–3 and Program 13–4 produce the same results. Both calculate a salesperson's pay by adding salary to commission. Normal commission is 10 percent of sales, but if sales total greater than $1,000, the commission is 12 percent of sales plus a $100 bonus. Program 13–3 uses a conventional selection structure; Program 13–4 uses a conditional expression in the final `cout`.

COMBINING EXPRESSIONS

We can combine two or more expressions into a single one to make programs more compact or, as we shall see here, to allow us to execute and evaluate a number of expressions where a language element allows only one.

If, for example, we were assigning three different but related variables,

```
length = 14;
width = 6;
height = 2;
```

we could use the **comma operator** to combine the three expressions into one:

```
length = 14, width = 6, height = 2;
```

The comma operator is absolutely last in precedence, has left-to-right associativity, and discards the result of the expression to the left of it. In an expression such as the one above, the value of the entire expression will be the value of the last assignment, 2. Notice that the comma operator does not prevent the execution of all the component expressions. All the assignments in the example above are made, but recall from Chapter 2 that the value of an assignment expression is the value of the assignment. It is these values that are discarded.

If we wanted *height* and *depth* assigned the same value, we could write a single expression as follows:

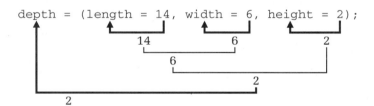

We have used the above expression for illustrative purposes only. Although the expression is correct, we do not advocate such an expression—it's a bit complicated. But let us see how we can apply the comma operator to a sentinel-value-controlled loop. In Program 13–5, the `cout` and `cin` statements have to be repeated because the loop needs something new to test each time through. We can avoid repeating those statements if we include them as expressions in the `while` loop condition, as shown in Program 13–6. The two programs produce identical output.

The prompt, input, and test expressions are all contained within the parentheses following `while`. Each time the program gets to the `while` statement, whether from above or from being sent back from the end of the loop, the condition expression, with all its component parts, is executed. Here the `cout` is executed first and, since it is followed by a comma, its

Program 13–5

```cpp
#include <iostream>
#include <iomanip>
using namespace std;

int main(void)
{   float price;
    short quantity;

    cout << setiosflags(ios::fixed) << setprecision(2);
    cout << "Enter 0 0 to quit.\n";
    cout << "Enter 'price quantity': ";                          // Prompt
    cin >> price >> quantity;                                    // Input
    while (price != 0)                                           // Test
    {   cout << "The total for this item is $" << (price * quantity)
            << ".\n";
        cout << "Enter 'price quantity': ";                      // Prompt
        cin >> price >> quantity;                                // Input
    }
    cout << "Thank you for your patronage." << endl;
    return 0;
}
```

Program 13–6

```cpp
#include <iostream>
#include <iomanip>
using namespace std;

int main(void)
{   float price;
    short quantity;

    cout << setiosflags(ios::fixed) << setprecision(2);
    cout << "Enter 0 0 to quit.\n";
    while (cout << "Enter 'price quantity': ",                   // Prompt
           cin >> price >> quantity,                             // Input
           price != 0)                                           // Test
    {   cout << "The total for this item is $" << (price * quantity)
            << ".\n";
    }                                            // Don't even need these braces
    cout << "Thank you for your patronage." << endl;
    return 0;
}
```

Output for Both Programs

```
Enter 0 0 to quit.
Enter 'price quantity': 6.29 5
The total for this item is $31.45.
Enter 'price quantity': 0 0
Thank you for your patronage.
```

return value (actually, a reference to an object) is discarded. Then the `cin` is executed, assigning the values to *price* and *quantity*. It is followed by a comma, so its return value (another reference to an object) is also discarded. Finally, the test expression is evaluated. It will be either 0 or 1 (false or true), depending on the value of *price* just assigned. That value is not discarded and becomes the value of the entire expression within the `while` parentheses. In other words, it is that last value that determines whether to stay in the loop or exit it.

This use of the comma operator is not universally accepted in structured environments because of its propensity toward abuse. Can you imagine a `while` condition with 47 statements separated by commas? If you use it, *use it carefully*. Do not make it too long (three expressions is almost too long), and use it only to avoid writing a statement twice in a loop situation.

HEADS UP!

Use the comma operator sparingly, if at all.

YOUR TURN 13–4

1. When do we use an enumeration data type?
2. Does C++ check to see that values of `enum` variables are in the list of declared constants?
3. Can a conditional expression alone be a statement?
4. What determines the data type of a conditional expression?
5. What does the comma operator do with the value of the expression immediately preceding it?

NONSTRUCTURED PROGRAM FLOW

HEADS UP!

C++ will allow breaking the rules of structure in many cases.

The C++ language offers the programmer a number of ways to approach programming tasks. C++ is designed to be an all-purpose language and therefore is applicable to the programming style of almost anyone. Structured programming is a style that has been adopted by most programmers, but it is neither universally accepted nor universally followed. C++ makes allowances for this by permitting program flow control that does not demand structure.

The following concepts are not strictly part of structured programming, but are part of the language. Be aware, however, that none of these concepts is absolutely necessary to C++ programming. There are structured solutions that will replace all of them.

Labels

A **label** identifies a specific place in a program. The identifier is a set of characters following the same naming rules as variables. In fact, label names may even duplicate variable names without interference, but it is considered bad form to have the same name for both a label and a variable. The following are legal label names:

```
Here            NewProcedure
instance1       analysisSection
```

The label should always be the first item on a line and is followed by a colon. For example:

```
        cout << "Preliminary analysis completed.\n";
    FinalAnalysis:                                    // Entry point for final analysis
        result += secondSample;
        adjust = result / (1 - fudgeFactor);
```

or

```
        x = y * y * 4.7;
    action: q = x + 9;
        cout << "Percentage: " << (q / 100) << endl;
```

Unconditional Transfers

The `goto` statement causes a computer to transfer execution of the program to some specific location marked by a label. Presumably, this spot in the program is some place other than the next one in line. In other words, using `goto` you can jump around from place to place in a program. This kind of jumping about makes structured programmers shudder because it allows you to jump out of the middle of one section into the middle of another, severely affecting the program's structure. You will *not* find `goto` statements in structured programs, but they are part of the language, so we will address them here:

HEADS UP!

Use `goto` with care, if at all.

```
goto label;
```

When a `goto` statement is encountered in a program, the next statement to execute will be the one immediately following the *label*. The following program segment shows `goto`s in use:

```
{
        . . .
    if (total == 0)
    {   cout << "Error, no total." << endl;
        goto end;                                     // No colon here
    }
    if (total < 0)
    {   cout << "Error, negative total." << endl;
        goto end;                                     // No colon here
    }
        . . .
    exit(EXIT_SUCCESS);                               // Successful program stops here
end:                                                  // Don't forget this colon
    cout << "The program has been terminated because of this error."
         << endl;
    exit(EXIT_FAILURE);
}
```

TRAP

Trying to `goto` a place in another function.

When the *label* is used as a reference in the `goto` statement (as opposed to the label marking a location in the program), there is no colon following the label. The semicolon, of course, denotes the end of the statement.

The `goto` statement must have a place to go to; in fact, the label has to be in the same function as the `goto` statement.

Jumping to the End of a Loop

There are two C++ statements that will disrupt the normal flow of a loop. *Disrupt* is a significant word here because the normal structure of the loop is not maintained. Neither of these statements would be found in a strictly structured program, but sparingly used and well commented, they are often accepted as part of a well-formed C++ program.

The `break` statement was introduced in Chapter 4. It causes execution to jump beyond the end of a `switch` structure. In this instance it is an indispensable part of the structured C++ language. But the `break` statement may also be used in loops—either `while`, `do`, or `for`—for exactly the same purpose. The program segment below would never execute statements 3 or 4; nor would it go through the loop a second time no matter what the value of *x*:

```
while (x > 9)
{   statement 1;
    statement 2;
    break;
    statement 3;
    statement 4;
}
```

HEADS UP!

break does not jump out of
if structures.

It would be reasonable to ask, "Why even write the program with the `break` and statements 3 and 4 in it?" You probably wouldn't. However, the `break` statement can be used rather productively in an `if` statement within a loop, as shown in Program 13–7. Remember, the `break` only jumps out of loops and `switch`es, not `if`s, so when the `if` is within a loop, the `break` will jump beyond the end of the loop.

Program 13–7 is a nonstructured version of the sentinel-value-controlled loop in Program 5–5 (Chapter 5). The statements used to input the *price* and *quantity* did not have to be repeated, but neither the exit point of the loop nor the conditions for the loop are at the beginning or the end of the loop. Instead, the loop conditions are stated in the `if` and the loop is made to continue by setting the `while` condition to `true`. When a *price* of zero is input, the `if` condition is then true and execution jumps to the statement following the closing brace.

If the `while` statement had a condition that might be false, such as `while (quantity > 0)`, the loop would have two possible exit points, the `while` statement and the `break` statement. Remember that in Chapter 1 we stated that in structured programming, any structure should have only one entry point and one exit point.

The `continue` statement is similar to `break` except that `continue` does not work with `switch` and it jumps to the end of the loop, not beyond it. In other words, the loop will continue given that the condition is still true:

HEADS UP!

continue jumps to the end
of a loop; break jumps
beyond it.

```
while (x > 9)
{   statement 1;
    statement 2;
    continue;
    statement 3;
    statement 4;
}
```

This will execute differently from the last example with the `break` statement. Statements 3 and 4 will still be skipped, but `continue` will send the execution to the end of the loop, from which point it will go back to the test in `while` and perhaps back through the loop again.

Program 13–7

```cpp
#include <iostream>
#include <iomanip>
using namespace std;

int main(void)
{   float price;
    float total = 0;
    short quantity;

    cout << setiosflags(ios::fixed) << setprecision(2);
    cout << "Enter 0 0 to quit.\n";
    while (true)                          // Always true, loop exit at break below
    {   cout << "Enter 'price quantity': ";
        cin >> price >> quantity;
        if (price == 0) break;                        // Exit point for the loop
        cout << "The total for this item is $" << (price * quantity)
            << ".\n";
        total += price * quantity;
    }
    cout << "Your total is $" << total << "." << endl;
    return 0;
}
```

Output

```
Enter 0 0 to quit.
Enter 'price quantity': 6.35 8
The total for this item is $50.80.
Enter 'price quantity': 2.50 10
The total for this item is $25.00.
Enter 'price quantity': 0 0
Your total is $75.80.
```

Remember that in a `for` loop, the counting operation is at the end of the loop. The `continue`, then, would send execution to the counting operation and then back to the test at the top of the loop.

In Program 13–8 we have modified Program 13–7 to warn the user if the total is getting too high.

YOUR TURN 13–5

1. How do `goto` and labels work together?
2. Why is `goto` not considered entirely proper in a structured program?
3. If a `break` statement is executed from within a loop, where does execution go?
4. If a `continue` statement is executed from within a loop, where does execution go?
5. Why are `break` and `continue` not considered entirely proper in a structured program?

Program 13–8

```
    #include <iostream>
    #include <iomanip>
    using namespace std;

    int main(void)
    {   float price;
        float total = 0;
        short quantity;

        cout << setiosflags(ios::fixed) << setprecision(2);
        cout << "Enter 0 0 to quit.\n";
1       while (true)                                  /* Loop exit at break below */
        {   cout << "Enter 'price quantity': ";
2           cin >> price >> quantity;
3           if (price == 0) break;                    /* Exit point for the loop */
4           cout << "The total for this item is $" << (price * quantity)
                 << ".\n";
5           total += price * quantity;
6           if (total < 100) continue;                /* Goes to end of loop */
7           cout << "Your total is getting high.\n";
            cout << "It now stands at $" << total << ".\n";
8       }
9       cout << "Your total is $" << total << "." << endl;
        return 0;
    }
```

Output

```
    Enter 0 0 to quit.
    Enter 'price quantity': 14.25 6
    The total for this item is $85.50.
    Enter 'price quantity': 9.98 3
    The total for this item is $29.94.
    Your total is getting high.
    It now stands at $115.44.
    Enter 'price quantity': 0 0
    Your total is $115.44.
```

UNIONS

You cannot put two things in the same place at the same time. True, but you can put one thing in that place and call it by two different names. This is the principle behind **unions**—using different identifiers to access the data in one set of memory locations. The definition of a union looks like the definition of a class, except

- The key word is **union** instead of `class`.

- A `union` has no behaviors.

- All the members of a `union` are `public`.

- A `union` may not include a `class` (although it may include a structure, referred to in the C++ Plus, "Structures" [page 418]).

Line	Explanation	price	quantity	total
1	Sets up infinite loop. The test value is always true.	??	??	0
2	Input *price* and *quantity*.	14.25	6	0
3	See if *price* is sentinel value. It isn't.	14.25	6	0
4	Display total for the item.	14.25	6	0
5	Accumulate item total in *total*.	14.25	6	85.50
6	The *total* is less than 100, so jump to end of loop at 8.	14.25	6	85.50
8	Go back to while at 1.	14.25	6	85.50
1	Still true, of course.	14.25	6	85.50
2	Input *price* and *quantity*.	9.98	3	85.50
3	See if *price* is sentinel value. It isn't.	9.98	3	85.50
4	Display total for the item.	9.98	3	85.50
5	Accumulate item total in *total*.	9.98	3	115.4 4
6	The *total* is not less than 100. Don't `continue`.	9.98	3	115.4 4
7	Display the warning message.	9.98	3	115.4 4
8	Go back to while at 1.	9.98	3	115.4 4
1	Still true, of course.	9.98	3	115.4 4
2	Input *price* and *quantity*.	0	0	115.4 4
3	See if *price* is sentinel value. It is, so `break` to beyond loop at 9.	0	0	115.4 4
9	Display *total* and quit.	0	0	115.4 4

The result of the definition, however, is significantly different. A class defines an aggregate data type and states the accessible member variables for it. The union defines a data type, but it is one that accommodates a number of variable names of various data types accessing the same space in memory.

For example, let us say that we sell two different types of products, one in bulk (by the pound or fraction thereof), and one packaged (by the package). The units of the bulk product we would want to keep in a double variable, packaged units in an int. To conserve memory space we could store either of them at a single memory address by defining a union data type like this:

```
union Units
{   double pounds;                          // For bulk products
    int packs;                              // For packaged products
};
```

We could declare a variable (or variables) of that type by putting the name after the definition or, more typically, in a separate declaration as in Program 13–9. C++ will allocate enough space to accommodate the largest data type in the union, in this case the double.

We refer to members of the union just as we refer to members of an object of a class—with the member operator (.). It is important that we use the member of the union with the data type that matches the data stored in

Program 13–9

```
#include <iostream>
using namespace std;

union Units                          // Define the union type
{   double pounds;                       // For bulk products
    int packs;                       // For packaged products
};

int main(void)
{   Units item;                      // Declare the union variable
    char bulk;

    cout << "Bulk Product (y/n)? ";
    cin >> bulk;
    if (bulk == 'Y' || bulk == 'y')          // Cap or lowercase
    {   cout << "Pounds? ";
        cin >> item.pounds;
    }
    else
    {   cout << "Packages? ";
        cin >> item.packs;
    }
    cout << "Pounds: " << item.pounds << ", Packages: " << item.packs
         << endl;
    return 0;
}
```

Output

```
Bulk Product (y/n)? y
Pounds? 12.34
Pounds: 12.34, Packages: 2061584302
```

the union. In Program 13–9 item.pounds is of data type double and item.packs is of data type int.

The *item* Union

The last line of the output bears some examination. The cout statement is syntactically correct, and therefore runs without complaint from the compiler. But the output, at least the packages part, is nonsense! We stored 12.34 as a double value (eight bytes in this C++) in the *item* union. The second part of the cout asked C++ to get a four-byte int from that space. It did, making no sense of course. You can see that keeping track of the data types currently stored in unions is up to us. C++ will not do it.

TRAP

Accessing a union member using the wrong data type.

YOUR TURN 13–6

1. How is a union similar to a class?
2. How is a union different from a class?

SUMMARY

- **KEY TERMS** (in order of appearance)

Nested comment	`#endif`
Comment out	`#elif`
Preprocessor	`defined`
Directive	`#ifdef`
`#define`	`#ifndef`
Defined constant	`#error`
Optimize	Enumeration data type
Macro	`enum`
Parameterized macro	Conditional expression
Stringizing	Comma operator
Token-pasting	Label
`#undef`	Union
`#if`	`union`
`#else`	

- **NEW STATEMENTS** (in order of appearance)

```
typedef oldName newName;
goto label;
break;
continue;
```

- **CONCEPT REVIEW**

  - The old-style C commenting method is still valid in C++. Anything between /* and */ is ignored by the compiler. This commenting style is useful in multiline comments or **commenting out** sections of programs. One must be careful, however, of **nested comments**.

  - The precompiler or **preprocessor** segment of the compiler makes changes in the source code.

  - Preprocessor **directives** start with a # symbol and end at the end of a line (or set of lines if each is continued with a backslash).

  - The #include directive temporarily inserts a file of source code lines at that point in the source code.

  - The **#define** directive tells the preprocessor to replace one set of characters with another. Simple character replacements are typically used for **defined constants**. Defined constants are often used instead of `const` variables. Compiler **optimization** often makes the two methods similar.

  - More complicated replacements are called **macros**. The replacement can be any set of characters—single words, a quoted string, formulas, and the like. Quoted strings are often used to concatenate a set of characters into another quoted string.

- We can also use **parameterized macros**—sets of characters, typically expressions, into which other parameters will be substituted at run time. These macros can act just like functions. In fact, many of those things that were previously presented as functions are actually macros.

- In macro replacement, the **stringizing** operator, #, turns the replacement value into a quoted string, typically so that it can be concatenated into another quoted string. The **token-pasting** operator, ##, tells the preprocessor to attach the sets of characters on each side of the operator directly together. This is typically used to create a single word, such as a variable name, out of a combination of tokens.

- Macros exist from the point in the source code in which they are defined to the end of the code, or until they are **#undef**ined. A macro must be undefined before it can be defined again unless the new definition is exactly the same as the old.

- Not all of the source code need be compiled. We often write statements in our programs that we use only for special purposes such as debugging or compiling for different implementations. Using the **#if**, **#elif**, **#else**, and **#endif** directives, we can test for certain conditions, and only those statements in the indicated branches will be compiled.

- The condition often includes a test to see whether a constant has been defined. For this purpose, we can use the key word **defined** after the #if, or the key word **#ifdef**. To test if a constant has not been defined, we can use the key word **#ifndef**.

- We can direct the preprocessor to stop the compile process and print an error message by sending the process to a branch with an **#error** directive.

- Using the **typedef** statement, we can change the name of an existing data type to a name of our own choosing. This is often done to make a program listing clearer, to enhance portability, or to simplify the description of complex data types.

- The **enum** key word establishes an **enumeration data type** that can hold any one of a number of predefined integer values.

- A **conditional expression** evaluates to the value of one of two expressions depending on whether its test is true or false. The condition is followed by a ?, then the true expression, a :, and the false expression.

- Expressions can be combined using the **comma operator**, which evaluates but discards the value of the previous expression, and goes on to the next.

- A number of statements in C++ allow program flow that does not strictly follow the rules of structure but, given the proper situation, can be handy in programming.

- The **goto** statement directs the computer to jump the processing to a place in the program identified by a **label**.

- Two unstructured but valid statements can be used with loops. The **break** statement sends execution beyond the end of the loop; the **continue** statement sends execution to the end of the loop but keeps the execution within the loop.

- A **union** allows a single place in memory to be accessed by different identifiers with different data types. It is defined and declared using the **union** key word.

• HEADS UP: POINTS OF SPECIAL INTEREST

- Nested comments restrict portability.
- Commenting out can help you debug.
- Commenting out can create nested comments.
- The preprocessor affects source code.
- Include files can contain commonly used program segments.
- Thoroughly debug code before putting it in an `#include` file.
- Be aware of the final substitution when using macros.
- Macro code is typeless, but it also cannot be type-checked.
- Macros are essentially global.
- Conditional compilation is handy for debugging.
- Conditional compilation is handy for development for different platforms.
- `#error` directives stop the compiling process.
- Defining data types can enhance portability.
- `typedef`s can improve clarity.
- C++ does not enforce `enum` values.
- Use the comma operator sparingly, if at all.
- C++ will allow breaking the rules of structure in many cases.
- Use `goto` with care, if at all.
- `break` does not jump out of `if` structures.
- `continue` jumps to the end of a loop; `break` jumps beyond it.

• TRAPS: COMMON PROGRAMMING ERRORS

- Putting a comment before a directive.
- Putting C++ comments in a continued directive.
- Using a single backslash in strings.
- Not putting arguments in parentheses.
- Using something other than preprocessor elements with `#if`.
- Defining more than one `enum` value with the same name.
- Trying to `goto` a place in another function.
- Accessing a `union` member using the wrong data type.

• YOUR TURN ANSWERS

• 13–1

1. The C comment method directs the compiler to ignore everything between /* and */, line endings included. The C++ method directs the compiler to ignore everything between // and the end of the physical line.

2. The C method makes it easy to write multiline comments or comment out sections of the program and in that respect is preferable to the C++ method.

3. Nested comments are comments within comments. They can occur in the old-style commenting method, and are not allowed by standard compilers.

4. The preprocessor makes modifications in source code in response to directives, just prior to the actual compilation of the program.

5. A preprocessor directive begins with any amount of whitespace, a # and the directive key word, and the arguments for the directive. It ends at the end of the physical line. A directive acts at compile time, whereas a statement acts at run time.

6. A directive may be on more than one line by ending the current physical line with a backslash.

7. The #include directive inserts a file of source code into the program just prior to compilation.

8. You can't see what is inserted by the #include directive in your program. You must access the included file with a text editor.

- **13–2**

1. The character replacement is part of the preprocessor operation that is typically followed immediately by a compile. We do not see the result of a preprocessor operation in source code.

2. A macro or character replacement will be made after the directive, any place but inside quotation marks or in a comment.

3. Parentheses are important in parameterized macros because they isolate the replacement expressions when the substitution is actually performed.

4. We can't use existing variable names as macro parameters because after the replacement, the names will conflict, causing the compiler problems.

5. We can't perform a macro replacement in the middle of a string.

6. We can put two strings together during a macro replacement with stringizing and C++'s normal concatenation of adjacent strings.

7. A macro's effective range begins where it is defined and ends at the end of the program or at the line where it is specifically undefined.

- **13–3**

1. The pattern for a three-branch conditional compilation is

```
#if
    . . .
#elif
    . . .
#else
    . . .
#endif
```

2. In a conditional compilation the key word defined tests to see whether a symbolic constant has been set in a #define directive.

3. We can test for a constant definition in a conditional compilation without using the defined key word by using #ifdef or #ifndef.

4. The #error directive sends an error message. It also stops compilation.

5. We can't create a new data type using typedef. We can only rename an existing one.

6. We can't use modifiers such as `long` or `unsigned` with a `typedefed` data type. The data type must be fully defined in the `typedef` statement, including any modifiers.

• 13–4

1. We use an enumeration data type when we want to use a variable that should take on only certain values, such as true or false; red, green, blue, and purple; off or on; and so forth.

2. C++ does not check to see that values of `enum` variables are in the list of declared constants.

3. A conditional expression alone could be a statement, but since the conditional expression evaluates—reduces to a single value—presumably something should be done with that value, such as assigning it to a variable, sending it to a function, or whatever.

4. The data type of a conditional expression is determined by the highest data type of either component expression, whether or not that expression was chosen.

5. The value of the expression immediately preceding the comma operator is discarded.

• 13–5

1. The `goto` statement sends execution to the location of the label in the program.

2. The `goto` statement allows the programmer to go into and out of structures at other than the designated entry and exit points, and so is not considered entirely proper in a structured program.

3. If a `break` statement is executed from within a loop, the execution goes beyond the end of the loop.

4. If a `continue` statement is executed from within a loop, the execution goes to the end of the loop, but remains in the loop.

5. The `break` and `continue` statements are not considered entirely proper in a structured program for the same reason as the `goto` statement; they allow the programmer to go into and out of structures at other than the designated entry and exit points.

• 13–6

1. A union is similar to a class in that it defines a data type; the form of its definition and declaration are alike, and it uses the member operator to address different members.

2. A union is different from a class because it defines a single memory space that can be accessed using different names and data types.

EXERCISES

1. Correct the following code segment.

```
cout << "This stuff ain't working right!" << endl;
/*
    riparian = watersEdge(birds, bugs);          /* These things live there */
    floods = renew(riparian);
*/
    cin >> howsomever;
```

2. What will be the output from the program below?

```cpp
#include <iostream>
using namespace std;

#define SQUARE(x) ((x) * (x));

int square(int x)
{
    return x * x;
}

int main(void)
{   int SQ, a = 2, b = 2;

    SQ = SQUARE(a + 1);
    cout << "SQUARE " << SQ << ", square " << square(b + 1) << endl;
    return 0;
}
```

3. Why won't the following program provide the desired results?

```cpp
#include <iostream>
using namespace std;

#define volume(length, height, width) length * height * width

int main(void)
{   float a = 1, b = 2, c = 3;

    cout << "The volume is " << volume(a + 1, b - 1, c - 2) << endl;
    return 0;
}
```

4. Show the statements after substitution using the following defined macro:

```cpp
#define cost(a, b) (a + (b) / 6 * 100)
a. result = cost(z + 25, 100)
b. result = cost(f, b * 5)
```

5. Given the following macro definitions, show the substitutions made for the following macro calls:

```cpp
#define output(a) cout << "At " # a ": << a << endl;
#define str(a) str ## a
```

```cpp
a. output(46);
b. str(ing);
```

6. Rewrite a previously written program (or several) so that if *DEBUG* is defined, the program prints out the name and value of each variable as soon as it is assigned or reassigned.

7. Define the data type *fourByte* as a four-byte, unsigned integral data type in your C++.

8. Using `typedef`, define a single data type, *INFO*, that is a class consisting of an array of three product names, each with an array of sales for the last four quarters. Information for each product should be `typedef`ed as *PRODUCT*, and sales for each product should be `typedef`ed as *SALES*.

9. Show the definition of an enumeration data type tagged *Size* with constants *small*, *medium*, and *large* having values of 1, 2, and 3, and *Unsized* having the value 9. Declare variables *shirt* and *pants* of this type.

10. Replace the following program segment with one statement using a conditional expression.

```
if (x > 10)
    x = x + y + 150;
else
    x = x + y + 50;
```

11. Replace the following program segment with a `while` statement that performs both the input and the test.

```
cout << "Gimme a number ";
cin >> number;
while (number > 0)
{   [process the number]
    cout << "Gimme a number ";
    cin >> number;
}
```

12. Rewrite Program 5–4 (page 148) using the `break` and/or `continue` statements.

13. Show the declaration of a union *Stuff* that consists of an array of 12 `doubles` and a `string`. Choose your own member names. Declare a variable *things* of that type.

14. Write the statement that assigns "Calabash" to the `string` member of the union in Exercise 13.

PROGRAMS

1. Refer to Chapter 3, Program 4 (page 102): the Ajax Company plans to use the defined constants in other programs as well. Write an include file, *PAYCONST.INC*, that contains those constants, properly commented. Test the include file by using it in the program.

2. Write a macro that will swap the values of two variables of a specified type. The call should be similar to `swap(a, b, float)`. Your macro will have to declare a temporary variable of the appropriate type. Put it in a program that initializes two variables and displays their values before and after the swap.

Output

```
Before: a=5.3. b=3.6.
After:  a=3.6. b=5.3.
```

3. Write a macro, *abso()*, that will return the absolute value of any value, given the value and its data type. Test it in a short program.

4. Write a macro the gives the smallest of three values. Test it in a short program.

5. Write a *trace* macro that will allow you to print out the name and value of a variable or expression during the debugging of your program. It should work with any data type—remember casts! Validate it with the following program.

```
#include <iostream>
using namespace std;

// Your macro

int main(void)
{   int a = 15;
    float b = -3.123;

    trace(a);
    trace(b);
    trace(a + b);
    return 0;
}
```

Output

```
a: 15
b: -3.123
a + b: 11.877
```

6. Depending on certain conditions, a calculation in your program might use one of a number of different variables (*var0a*, *var0b*, *var1a*, and so forth with the number and the last letter varying independently). Write a VAR macro with two parameters that specify the number and letter. Validate it in the following program.

```
#include <iostream>
using namespace std;

// Your macro

int main(void)
{   float x1a = 1.1, x2d = 2.4;

    cout << "x1a: " << VAR(1, a) << ", x2d: " << VAR(2, d) << endl;
    return 0;
}
```

Output

```
x1a: 1.1, x2d: 2.4
```

7. Write a macro, *concat(string, number)*, that will concatenate a given number of strings to the first string.

8. Set up a partial program that conditionally compiles according to the defined constant *DEBUG*. It should show the following outputs with various values of this constant:

```
DEBUG on.
DEBUG level 1, a = 1

DEBUG on.
DEBUG level 2, a = 1, b = 2

DEBUG on.
DEBUG level > 2, a = 1, b = 2, c = 3
```

9. Rewrite Program 2 in Chapter 4 (page 138) so it uses a conditional expression rather than an `if` statement.

10. Rewrite Program 5 (or 6) in Chapter 5 (page 173) so the loop is controlled by a set of statements including prompt, input, and test.

11. Rewrite Program 4 in Chapter 5 (page 172), which plays the game Totals, using `break` and/or `continue`.

12. Using `break` and/or `continue`, rewrite Program 5 (or 6) in Chapter 5 (page 173), which translates numeric scores into letter grades.

13. A firm uses two types of containers: boxes and cans. A box's dimensions are its height, width, and length; its volume is the product of the three. A can's dimensions are its diameter and height; its volume is

$$\pi \times radius^2 \times height$$

where the *radius* is half the diameter. Write a program that uses the *inPack()* function to input the type of container and *outPack()* to display the type of container and its volume.

Appendix A

ASCII TABLE

Dec	Hex	Ctrl	Code
0	00	^@	NUL
1	01	^A	SOH
2	02	^B	STX
3	03	^C	ETX
4	04	^D	EOT
5	05	^E	ENQ
6	06	^F	ACK
7	07	^G	BEL
8	08	^H	BS
9	09	^I	HT
10	0A	^J	LF
11	0B	^K	VT
12	0C	^L	FF
13	0D	^M	CR
14	0E	^N	SO
15	0F	^O	SI
16	10	^P	SLE
17	11	^Q	CS1
18	12	^R	DC2
19	13	^S	DC3
20	14	^T	DC4
21	15	^U	NAK
22	16	^V	SYN
23	17	^W	ETB
24	18	^X	CAN
25	19	^Y	EM
26	1A	^Z	SIB
27	1B	^[	ESC
28	1C	^\	FS
29	1D	^]	GS
30	1E	^^	RS
31	1F	^_	US

Dec	Hex	Char
32	20	sp
33	21	!
34	22	"
35	23	#
36	24	$
37	25	%
38	26	&
39	27	'
40	28	(
41	29	)
42	2A	*
43	2B	+
44	2C	,
45	2D	-
46	2E	.
47	2F	/
48	30	0
49	31	1
50	32	2
51	33	3
52	34	4
53	35	5
54	36	6
55	37	7
56	38	8
57	39	9
58	3A	:
59	3B	;
60	3C	<
61	3D	=
62	3E	>
63	3F	?

Dec	Hex	Char
64	40	@
65	41	A
66	42	B
67	43	C
68	44	D
69	45	E
70	46	F
71	47	G
72	48	H
73	49	I
74	4A	J
75	4B	K
76	4C	L
77	4D	M
78	4E	N
79	4F	O
80	50	P
81	51	Q
82	52	R
83	53	S
84	54	T
85	55	U
86	56	V
87	57	W
88	58	X
89	59	Y
90	5A	Z
91	5B	[
92	5C	\
93	5D	]
94	5E	^
95	5F	_

Dec	Hex	Char
96	60	`
97	61	a
98	62	b
99	63	c
100	64	d
101	65	e
102	66	f
103	67	g
104	68	h
105	69	i
106	6A	j
107	6B	k
108	6C	l
109	6D	m
110	6E	n
111	6F	o
112	70	p
113	71	q
114	72	r
115	73	s
116	74	t
117	75	u
118	76	v
119	77	w
120	78	x
121	79	y
122	7A	z
123	7B	{
124	7C		
125	7D	}
126	7E	~
127	7F	DEL

Operator	Symbol	Explanation	Example
Expression Left-to-right associativity			
Parens	`( )`	To change the order of evaluation.	`4 * (6 + 2)`
Subscript	`[ ]`	Subscript of array. Offset in variables from base address.	`array[4]`
Member	`.`	Identifies member of an object.	`object.member`
Member pointer	`->`	Content at location of member of a pointer to an object.	`ptrToObject->member`
Unary Right-to-left associativity			
Negate	`-`	Reverse the sign of an expression.	`-4`
Add	`+`	Specify a positive value. (This is the default, anyway.)	`+4`
Increment	`++`	Add 1 to variable in expression.	`++var or var++`
Decrement	`--`	Subtract 1 from variable in expression.	`--var or var--`
Complement	`~`	Change 1 bits to 0 and 0 to 1.	`~var`
Logical NOT	`!`	Make false expression (0) true or true (nonzero) false.	`!(time > present)`
Dereferencing	`*`	Contents of location in expression.	`*(array + 3)`
Address	`&`	Address of variable.	`&var`
Size	`sizeof`	Size of expression or (data type) in bytes	`sizeof (int)`
Cast Right-to-left associativity			
	`(type)`	Convert to data `type`.	`(int)4.2`
Multiplicative Left-to-right associativity			
Multiply	`*`	Multiply expressions on either side.	`6 * 4`
Divide	`/`	Divide expressions on either side.	`6 / 4`
Remainder	`%`	Remainder of first divided by second.	`6 % 4`
Additive Left-to-right associativity			
Add	`+`	Add expressions on either side.	`6 + 4`
Subtract	`-`	Subtract expressions on either side.	`6 - 4`
Relational Left-to-right associativity			
Greater	`>`	First greater than second?	`x + y > z - 19`
Less	`<`	First less than second?	`cost < maximum - 10`
Greater or equal	`>=`	First greater than or equal to second?	`load >= limit`
Less or equal	`<=`	First less than or equal to second?	`TestValue <= Norm`
Equality Left-to-right associativity			
Equal	`==`	First equals second?	`Count + 1 == End`
Not equal	`!=`	First not equal to second?	`CheckSum != NewSum`
Logical AND Left-to-right associativity			
	`&&`	First and second true?	`val1 && val2`
Logical OR Left-to-right associativity			
	`||`	First or second or both true?	`val1 || val2`
Conditional Right-to-left associativity			
	`? :`	If test true, perform first expression, otherwise second.	`x > 4 ? p + 9 : p - 4`
Assignment Right-to-left associativity			
Simple	`=`	Assign value of expression on right to variable on left.	`x = y * 22.4`
Accumulation	`*= /=` `%= +=` `-=`	Perform arithmetic operation on variable to left and value of expression on right. Assign result to variable on left.	`a *= x`
Sequential Evaluation Left-to-right associativity			
Comma	`,`	Dump value of previous operation, perform next.	`while(cin >> x, x>0)`

Appendix C

FUNCTION REFERENCE

CHARACTER CLASSIFICATIONS

`int isalnum(int character)` `<cctype>`
> **Purpose:** Test if `character` is alphanumeric: *0–9*, *A–Z*, or *a–z*.
> **Return:** True: Nonzero. False: Zero.

`int isalpha(int character)` `<cctype>`
> **Purpose:** Test if `character` is alphabetic: *A–Z* or *a–z*.
> **Return:** True: Nonzero. False: Zero.

`int iscntrl(int character)` `<cctype>`
> **Purpose:** Test if `character` is a control code: ASCII 1–31.
> **Return:** True: Nonzero. False: Zero.

`int isdigit(int character)` `<cctype>`
> **Purpose:** Test if `character` is a decimal digit: *0–9*.
> **Return:** True: Nonzero. False: Zero.

`int isgraph(int character)` `<cctype>`
> **Purpose:** Test if `character` is printable, not including space.
> **Return:** True: Nonzero. False: Zero.

`int islower(int character)` `<cctype>`
> **Purpose:** Test if `character` is lowercase: *a–z*.
> **Return:** True: Nonzero. False: Zero.

`int isprint(int character)` `<cctype>`
> **Purpose:** Test if `character` is printable, including space.
> **Return:** True: Nonzero. False: Zero.

`int ispunct(int character)` `<cctype>`
> **Purpose:** Test if `character` is punctuation.
> **Return:** True: Nonzero. False: Zero.

`int isspace(int character)` `<cctype>`
> **Purpose:** Test if `character` is whitespace: space, \f, \n, \r, \t, or \v.
> **Return:** True: Nonzero. False: Zero.

`int isupper(int character)` `<cctype>`
> **Purpose:** Test if `character` is uppercase: *A–Z*.
> **Return:** True: Nonzero. False: Zero.

`int isxdigit(int character)` `<cctype>`
> **Purpose:** Test if `character` is a hexadecimal digit: *0–9*, *A–F*.
> **Return:** True: Nonzero. False: Zero.

CHARACTER CONVERSIONS

```
int tolower(int character)                                    <cctype>
```
    Purpose: Convert uppercase *character* to lower.
    Return: If *character* uppercase letter, lowercase equivalent, otherwise no change.

```
int toupper(int character)                                    <cctype>
```
    Purpose: Convert lowercase *character* to upper.
    Return: If *character* lowercase letter, uppercase equivalent, otherwise no change.

DATA CONVERSIONS

```
double atof(address character)                                <cstdlib>
```
    Purpose: Convert from address of *character* to double.
    Return: Success: Converted number. Error: Meaningless assignment.

```
int atoi(address character)                                   <cstdlib>
```
    Purpose: Convert from address of *character* to int.
    Return: Success: Converted number. Error: Meaningless assignment.

```
long atol(address character)                                  <cstdlib>
```
    Purpose: Convert from address of *character* to long.
    Return: Success: Converted number. Error: Meaningless assignment.

FILES

```
void fstream.clear(void)                                      <fstream>
```
    Purpose: Clears end-of-file-condition.
    Return: None.

```
void fstream.close()                                          <fstream>
```
    Purpose: Write leftover buffers to and detach *fstream* object from file.
    Return: None.

```
int fstream.eof(void)                                         <fstream>
```
    Purpose: Detect unsuccessful operation at end of file.
    Return: Zero if unsuccessful operation; nonzero if not.

```
void fstream.open(address fileId, int mode)                   <fstream>
```
    Purpose: Attach an *fstream* object to the *fileId* in a specific *mode*.
    Return: None.

```
void fstream.read(char* location, int bytes)                  <fstream>
```
    Purpose: Copy number of *bytes* from file connected to *fstream* to *location*.
    Return: None.

```
int remove(address fileId)                                    <cstdio>
```
    Purpose: Delete *fileId* file from secondary storage.
    Return: Success: Zero. Error: Nonzero.

```
int rename(address oldId, address newId)                      <cstdio>
```
    Purpose: Change file identification from *oldId* to *newId*.
    Return: Success: Zero. Error: Nonzero.

```
void fstream.seekg(long offset, int origin)                   <fstream>
```
    Purpose: Set the position *offset* bytes from the beginning, or from the *origin*.
    Return: None.

```
long fstream.tellg(void)                                      <fstream>
```
    Purpose: Determine current byte position in file.
    Return: Current byte position in file.

```
int unlink(address fileId)                                    <cstdio>
```
    Purpose: Remove link to *fileId* or delete file if last link.
    Return: Success: Zero. Error: Nonzero.

```
void fstream.write(char* location, int bytes)                                        <fstream>
```
    Purpose: Copy number of `bytes` from `location` to file connected to `fstream`.
    Return: None.

MATH

```
int abs(int expression)                                                              <cstdlib>
```
    Purpose: Obtain absolute value of `int` `expression`.
    Return: Absolute value of `int` `expression`.

```
double fabs(double expression)                                                       <cmath>
```
    Purpose: Obtain absolute value of `double` `expression`.
    Return: Absolute value of `double` `expression`.

```
long labs(long expression)                                                           <cstdlib>
```
    Purpose: Obtain absolute value of `long` `expression`.
    Return: Absolute value of `long` `expression`.

```
double pow(double expression, double exponent)                                       <cmath>
```
    Purpose: Raise `expression` to the power of `exponent`.
    Return: Result of the exponentiation.

```
int rand(void)                                                                       <cstdlib>
```
    Purpose: Obtain next in a series of random numbers.
    Return: Value between zero and RAND_MAX.

```
double sqrt(double expression)                                                       <cmath>
```
    Purpose: Obtain the square root of the `expression`.
    Return: Square root of the `expression`.

```
void srand(unsigned seed)                                                            <cstdlib>
```
    Purpose: Set the `seed` for generation of random numbers.
    Return: None.

```
time_t time(NULL)                                                                    <ctime>
```
    Purpose: Used as shown to give a different seed for random-number generation.
    Return: Random-number seed.

PROGRAM CONTROL

```
void exit(int status)                                                                <cstdlib>
```
    Purpose: Terminate program in orderly fashion indicating `status` of termination.
    Return: None.

STRINGS

```
int string.capacity(void)                                                            <string>
```
    Purpose: Determine capacity of `string` without reallocation.
    Return: Capacity of `string`.

```
int string.find(string search, int start)                                            <string>
```
    Purpose: Find `search` characters, beginning at `start` position, in `string`.
    Return: Success: Position of `search` in `string`. Failure: Value out of range.

```
void string.resize(int newSize)                                                      <string>
```
    Purpose: Shorten or lengthen (with nulls) a `string`.
    Return: None.

```
int string.rfind(string search, int start)                                           <string>
```
    Purpose: Find `search` characters from end, beginning at `start` position, in `string`.
    Return: Success: Position of `search` in `string`. Failure: Value out of range.

```
int string.size(void)                                                                <string>
```
    Purpose: Determine number of characters in the `string`.
    Return: Number of characters in the `string`.

```
char *strcat(char *cString, char *add)                              <string.h>
    Purpose:    Put add string at the end of cString.
    Return:     cString.
int strcmp(char *cString1, char *cString2)                          <string.h>
    Purpose:    Compare two strings.
    Return:     Positive value if cString1 greater, negative if cString2, zero if equal.
char *strcpy(char *destination, char *source)                       <string.h>
    Purpose:    Copy source string to destination.
    Return:     destination.
size_t strlen(char *cString)                                        <string.h>
    Purpose:    Find number of characters at cString.
    Return:     Number of characters at cString.
char *strncat(char *cString, char *add, size_t max)                 <string.h>
    Purpose:    Put up to max characters of add string at the end of cString.
    Return:     cString.
int strncmp(char *cString1, char *cString2, size_t max)             <string.h>
    Purpose:    Compare up to max characters of two strings.
    Return:     Positive value if cString1 greater, negative if cString2, zero if equal.
char *strncpy(char *destination, char *source, size_t max)          <string.h>
    Purpose:    Copy up to max characters of source string to destination.
    Return:     destination.
string string.substr(int start, int characters)                    <string>
    Purpose:    Get piece of string from start to end of string or number of characters.
    Return:     string object containing those characters.
```

TERMINAL INPUT/OUTPUT

```
stream& cin.get(char *cString, int max, char delimiter)            <iostream>
    Purpose:    Assigns characters from input stream until delimiter or max - 1 reached.
    Return:     Reference to input stream object.
void getline(cin, string string, char delimiter)                   <string>
    Purpose:    Assigns characters from input stream to string. Stops at delimiter.
    Return:     None.
void cin.ignore(int characters, char delimiter)                    <iostream>
    Purpose:    Passes characters in input stream unless delimiter reached first.
    Return:     None.
stream& resetiosflags(flags)                                       <iomanip>
    Purpose:    Set flags back to default condition.
    Return:     Reference to stream.
stream& setiosflags(flags)                                         <iomanip>
    Purpose:    Set various output formatting flags.
    Return:     Reference to stream.
stream& setprecision(digits)                                       <iomanip>
    Purpose:    Set number of digits for floating-point or decimal places for integral output.
    Return:     Reference to stream.
stream& setw(minimumWidth)                                         <iomanip>
    Purpose:    Specify minimumWidth for next output field.
    Return:     Reference to stream.
```

Appendix D

C STRINGS

PREVIEW

The "old" method of storing strings—developed under the predecessor C language—is still valid and, indeed, sometimes preferable to the C++ string object covered in Chapter 9. This appendix will cover "C strings." It may be used in addition to or in place of Chapter 9. Here you will learn:

- How C strings are stored and interpreted.
- Ways to input and output C strings.
- Different ways of manipulating C strings.
- How we store arrays of C strings.
- Methods of converting between strings and numbers.
- How to classify characters and convert from one classification to another.
- Methods of separating C strings into component parts.

When we looked at the `string` class in Chapter 9, we said that it was a relatively new addition to the C++ language. The major advantage of the `string` class is that dynamic allocation of strings and a wealth of string behaviors make it easier for the programmer. As usual, there is a trade-off for such an advantage. In this case it is the efficiency of the program when it is executing. The `string` class typically makes it faster for the programmer but slower for the computer. Also, because the `string` class is new, not all compilers have implemented it yet.

So, to be compatible with older compilers and to examine more efficient (for the computer) ways of handling strings, this appendix covers the traditional treatment of strings as defined under the C language. For lack of a better term, we will call these concepts "C strings." All of these concepts have been absorbed into C++, and so should be available in new compilers as well. Much of this appendix will be a repetition of Chapter 9; some readers will substitute it for that chapter.

STRING VALUES

The C-string concept of a string value is exactly the same as that using the `string` class. A string value is a null-terminated character array. We have used string values in our programs before; they are collections of characters enclosed in quotation marks. Let's examine how these characters are actually stored in memory. We know that the characters are stored as sets of bits, and that each character takes up one byte (eight bits). Each character, then, is data type `char`. Putting a string value in our source code directs C++ to allocate memory for those characters—an array of `chars`. `"Algonquin"` in our source code will cause the C++ compiler to allocate memory like this:

Like any other array, the string is identified by its base address, the address of the first value (character, in this case). Also like any other array, once the memory is allocated, we are left with the problem of how to determine where the string ends in memory. C++ solves the problem by putting a null character (`'\0'`) in the memory location immediately following the last character of the string. When we ask C++ to perform some process on a string, displaying it perhaps, it starts at the base address and reads characters until it reaches a null.

But where is this base address? As with variables, we will probably never know—nor do we care, as long as C++ can keep track of it. In our diagram we showed FFF0, but that was just a guess.

The notation for the address of a string value is the string value itself—the characters in double quotation marks. The string value `"Algonquin"` is the address where C++ has chosen to store the string—it is the address of a set of `char` values. In our diagram it was FFF0.

HEADS UP!

Strings in C++ end in a null character.

HEADS UP!

To C++, a string value is an address.

HEADS UP!

Λ character in single quotation marks is a numeric value.

Using ' ' instead of " ".

String Values Versus Character Values

In Chapter 2 we looked at character values such as `'A'`, `'f'`, and `'\t'`. These, as we saw, are simply numbers—the ASCII (or EBCDIC) values of the character codes. They are of type `char` but, as we know, `char` is an integral numeric data type.

There is a significant difference between the character `'A'` and the string `"A"`. The former is an integral number, a `char`, with the value 65 (*A* in ASCII) that takes up one byte. The latter is the address of an array of two `char`s, the first with the value 65 and the second with the value zero (the null character, `\0`).

C-STRING VARIABLES

There aren't any!

If you read Chapter 9 you saw how we used an object of the `string` class much as we have used other variables but, strictly speaking, there are no string variables. We have seen, however, that a string value is stored as an array of `char`s—that is, beginning at some address in memory, continuing in contiguous memory locations, and terminated by a null. Let's follow that pattern, then, and store our string in an array of `char` variables.

Declaration and Initialization

Not allocating enough space for C strings.

In deciding on a declaration of a `char` array, we must consider the largest string we might have to store in it because C++ will allocate the space and then probably allocate something else right next to it. Also, C++ will not prevent us from overwriting what we consider to be the end of the string; in other words, writing into the space allocated for the next variable or whatever.

If we are declaring a `char` array for names and most of them are "John," "Maria," "Edna," and such, but one person might be named "Cadwallader," then we must allocate at least 12 characters of space for the string. Twelve? There are only 11 characters in "Cadwallader." Remember that C++ considers a C string as starting at some memory address and ending in a null character. We must leave an extra space for the null character.

HEADS UP!

Don't forget the null character when allocating C strings.

```
char name[12];
```

This allocates 12 variables, *name[0]* through *name[11]*. They have no meaningful values yet, but we can initialize them at the time of their declaration.

```
char name[12] = {'Z', 'e', 'l', 'd', 'a'};
```

We have assigned values to the first five variables of the array. Because we have initialized the first few, the rest of the variables in the array will be assigned the value zero, which, not entirely coincidentally, is the null character.

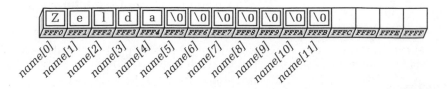

Remember from Chapter 8 that the name of an array refers to its address in memory. We now have a string value in memory beginning at the address *name*, FFF0 in the example, and ending at the first null at FFF5. We can refer to it as the *name* array or, since we are using it to store a set of characters, the *name* string.

The same declaration could have been accomplished this way:

```
char name[12] = {90, 101, 108, 100, 97};
```

using the ASCII values for the characters, but it is a bit easier to understand using the former method.

The same declaration and initialization could also be accomplished this way:

```
char name[12] = "Zelda";
```

C++ would interpret the quoted string as five character values and store them in the first five variables of *name*, setting the rest to null.

We should mention that a declaration could also be made this way:

```
char name[] = "Zelda";
```

leaving out the number of variables in brackets. This would differ from the previous declaration of *name* because only six variables, *name[0]* through *name[5]*, would be allocated (remember the null; C++ does).

C-STRING ASSIGNMENTS

Because C strings are sets of separate variables for each character, we can assign them one character at a time.

```
int main(void)
{   char name[12];

    name[0] = 'Z';
    name[1] = 'e';
    name[2] = 'l';
    name[3] = 'd';
    name[4] = 'a';
    name[5] = '\0';
    return 0;
}
```

We have been careful to explicitly assign the null character at the end of the string. Without it, a typical string operation would start with *Z* and continue until some garbage character in memory happened to be the null character.

We could not have done this:

```
name = "Zelda";
```

Even though the statement is similar to that in our earlier declaration, it is interpreted quite differently. In this case, `"Zelda"` refers to the address where the string is stored in memory, and not to the individual characters. The notation `name` also refers to an address—the address of the 12-variable `char` array—but `name` is not a variable; it cannot be assigned.

In essence, assigning a string must be done one character at a time. We will see, however, that there are a wealth of ANSI C++ functions that we can call on to do this for us.

YOUR TURN D–1

1. If we do not use the `string` class in C++, in what data type do we store strings?
2. Where does a string value stored in memory begin and end?
3. How does the string value `"A"` differ from the character value `'A'`?
4. In what kind of variables do we store C strings?
5. How does C++ ensure that we do not assign C strings to unallocated locations?
6. What are the differences among the following four declarations?
   ```
   char name[12] = {'Z', 'e', 'l', 'd', 'a'};
   char name[12] = {90, 101, 108, 100, 97};
   char name[12] = "Zelda";
   char name[] = "Zelda";
   ```
7. How are C strings assigned?

C-STRING INPUT

We have used the `cin` object to input numbers and individual characters. We can also use it to input C strings:

```
cin >> name;
```

The function takes a set of characters from the input stream (from the current position to the next whitespace) and writes them beginning at the address *name*. It also adds a null at the end of the characters to maintain C++'s concept of a string. If our previous assignment to *name* had been *Zelda* and we typed in *Al*, memory would look like this:

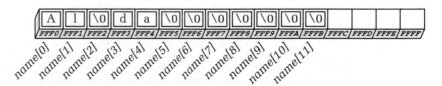

Part of *Zelda* is still lying around, but it makes no difference because the C string ends at the first null, at FFF2.

Program D–1

```cpp
#include <iostream>                                   // Same old question about .h
#include <iomanip>
using namespace std;                                     // Again, same old question

const int length = 10;

int main(void)
{   char product[length];
    float price;

    cout << setiosflags(ios::fixed) << setprecision(2);
    cout << "Enter price and product: ";
    cin >> price >> product;
    cout << "The price of a " << product << " is " << price << endl;
    return 0;
}
```

Outputs

```
Enter price and product: 12.98 widget
The price of a widget is 12.98.

Enter price and product: 12.98, widget
The price of a , is 12.98.
```

HEADS UP!

Know how `cin` works.

Assigning characters beyond the space allocated for the string.

In Program D–1 `cin` is used to input both a number and a string.

In the second execution we tried to use the comma as a delimiter between the two values input. Comma, an inappropriate character for a number, ended that conversion, but the comma was left in the input stream. Since comma is appropriate for a string, C++ started the string at the comma and went to the next whitespace, including only the comma in the string.

The *product* array has 10 elements, meaning that we can effectively store only 9 characters. What if we type in a 15-character product name? It will be assigned, overflowing the memory space allocated for the *product* array and messing up something else in memory.

Inputting Lines

Whitespace is the default delimiter for `cin` and the extraction operator (>>), which means that inputting a single string with whitespace in it is not possible. If there might be two-word product names, such as *red shoes*, we would have to use something other than `cin >>`, as presented here, to input the product. We can, however, use the **get()** behavior of the `cin` object to input complete lines. This is similar in concept and appearance to the `getline()` function in the `string` class.

```cpp
stream& cin.get(char *cString, int max, char delimiter)                    <iostream>
```

For example,

```cpp
cin.get(sentence, 30, '\n');
```

Program D–2

```cpp
#include <iostream>
using namespace std;

const int length = 10;

int main(void)
{   char cString[length];
    double number;

    cout << "Enter a string> ";
1   cin.get(cString, length, '\n');              // Leaves newline in stream
2   cout << "Your first string: '" << cString << "'." << endl;
    cout << "Enter a number> ";
3   cin >> number;                               // Leaves newline in stream
4   cout << "Your number: " << number << endl;
    cout << "Enter another string> ";
5   cin.get(cString, length, '\n');              // Leaves newline in stream
6   cout << "Your second string: '" << cString << "'." << endl;
    cout << "That's all!" << endl;
    return 0;
}
```

Output D–2A

```
Enter a string> Hi there
Your first string: 'Hi there'.
Enter a number> 34.95
Your number: 34.95
Enter another string> Your second string: ''.
That's all!
```

Output D–2B

```
Enter a string> Phone # 555-1212
Your first string: 'Phone # 5'.
Enter a number> Your number: 55
Enter another string> Your second string: '-1212'.
That's all!
```

HEADS UP!

cin.get() does not remove, nor does it store, the delimiter.

takes characters from the keyboard stream object, cin, and stores them in the char array *sentence*. The behavior stops taking characters from the input stream when either of two conditions is reached:

- It reaches the delimiter character, the newline in the example. Unlike the getline() behavior of the string class, the delimiter is not removed from the input stream (nor is it stored in the string in memory). In this way it acts like cin with the extraction operator.

- It reaches *max* – 1 characters. This allows us to limit the number of characters assigned at the address of the *cString* to ensure that we do not overflow the allocated space. Why *max* – 1? Remember, a string always ends in a null. This saves room for cin.get() to add the null at the end. In our example we limit the assignment to

Program D–3

```
#include <iostream>
using namespace std;

const int length = 10;

int main(void)
{   char cString[length];
    double number;

    cout << "Enter a string> ";
    cin.get(cString, length, '\n');                 // Leaves newline in stream
    cout << "Your first string: '" << cString << "'." << endl;
    cout << "Enter a number> ";
    cin >> number;                                  // Leaves newline in stream
    cin.ignore(500, '\n');                          // Flushes the input stream
    cout << "Your number: " << number << endl;
    cout << "Enter another string> ";
    cin.get(cString, length, '\n');                 // Leaves newline in stream
    cin.ignore(500, '\n');                          // Flushes the input stream
    cout << "Your second string: '" << cString << "'." << endl;
    cout << "That's all!" << endl;
    return 0;
}
```

Output

```
Enter a string> Phone # 555-1212
Your first string: 'Phone # 5'.
Enter a number> 34.95 dollars
Your number: 34.95
Enter another string> What now?
Your second string: 'What now?'.
That's all!
```

 HEADS UP!

cin.get() could leave characters in the input stream.

 HEADS UP!

cin.get() does not skip leading whitespace.

29 characters plus the trailing null. If *max* – 1 is reached, whatever characters are left in the input stream remain there, ready to mess up the next input.

Unlike cin and >>, cin.get() does not skip leading whitespace. Whitespace is considered by cin.get() as a valid character for a string.

The return value of cin.get() is a reference to the stream object, cin. At this level, we will not use its return value. Program D–2 shows cin.get() in action, along with a couple of problems associated with the behavior.

As shown by Output D–2A, we have solved the problem of inputting spaces, but why were we not able to enter a second string? We did; it was the newline at the end of *34.95*. Remember, cin >> (line 3) leaves the delimiter, the newline in this case, in the stream. The cin.get() in line 5 saw a stream with valid characters (the newline) and took characters up to but not including the newline—no characters. Subsequent cin.get()s would find the stream in the same condition and also skip inputs.

Let's use the same program to highlight another problem. In Output D–2B we entered 16 characters. Line 1 assigned the first 9 characters to *string*, leaving *55-1212* still in the stream. Line 3 converted to the first inappropriate

numeric character (the '−' is not appropriate in this position), assigned 55 to *number*, leaving *-1212* in the stream. Line 6 assigned those characters to *string*.

Flushing the Input Stream

Our problems seem to stem from leaving characters in the input stream for one reason or another. Let's use the input stream behavior **ignore()** to **flush**—empty out—the input stream.

```
void cin.ignore(int characters, char delimiter)  <iostream>
```

This function skips characters in the input stream. It stops skipping until *characters* characters have been skipped or it passes the *delimiter* character. If we set the *characters* argument high and use newline as the delimiter,

```
cin.ignore(500, '\n');
```

Not flushing the input stream.

it will skip characters until it passes the newline, emptying the input stream.

Program D–3 shows this statement in action.

Our previous examples of inputting strings are typical, in which an entire line, up to where the person at the keyboard hit the *Enter* or *Return* key, is assigned to the string. Any character, however, may be specified as a delimiter.

 HEADS UP!

`cin.get()` can work with any character as a delimiter.

```
cin.get(sentence, 50, '.');
```

takes characters from the input stream until it reaches a period. Remember, the period will not become part of the string *sentence*, and characters from the period on are left for the next access of the input stream. We can remove the delimiter (the period in our example), and any characters left over before the delimiter if *max* − 1 was reached, using `cin.ignore()`.

```
cin.ignore(500, '.');
```

Program D–4 accepts a last name, a first name, and an address, separates them by the delimiters, and puts them in different variables. We did

Program D–4

```cpp
#include <iostream>
using namespace std;

const int nameLen = 20;
const int addLen = 30;

int main(void)
{   char lastName[nameLen], firstName[nameLen], address[addLen];

    cout <<"Enter last name,first name/address> ";
    cin.get(lastName, nameLen, ',');
    cin.ignore(500, ',');
    cin.get(firstName, nameLen, '/');
    cin.ignore(500, '/');
    cin.get(address, addLen, '\n');
    cin.ignore(500, '\n');
    cout << firstName << " " << lastName << " of " << address << endl;
    return 0;
}
```

Output

```
Enter last name,first name/address> Prabatnik,Elvin/12 Dreary Ln.
Elvin Prabatnik of 12 Dreary Ln.
```

not put spaces after the delimiters, such as `Prabatnik, Elvin`. If we had, the *firstName* would have been " `Elvin`", with a leading space.

YOUR TURN D–2

1. What character delimits strings when inputting with `cin >>`?
2. How can we input entire lines, including embedded spaces?
3. How can we ensure that we do not assign characters beyond the allocated space for a string when we input?
4. What is left in the input stream after a `cin >>` or a `cin.get()`?
5. How can we get rid of characters in the input stream?

STRING MANIPULATIONS

Now that we know how C strings are stored, we can perform all kinds of operations on them—print them out, assign values to them, take them apart, reassemble them, and so forth. To make life easier for us, ANSI C++ includes a group of functions to do many of these manipulations for us. Common to all these functions is C++'s concept of a string—a group of contiguous characters starting at some address and ending with a null character. Also common to most of them is that C++ does nothing to stop you from assigning characters beyond the memory locations allocated for an individual string. You must take care of that yourself.

HEADS UP!

Most C++ functions will allow you to write beyond the space allocated for a string.

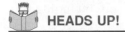

Using a C-string function that changes the size of a string object.

C-string functions refer to the string by its base address—the name of the character array. Many of these functions can also be used with string objects. The characters within a string object are also contiguously stored; C++ also puts a null at the end of the characters; and we can refer to the base address of the characters using the notation &string[0]. However, we often cannot be sure of the capacity of the string object; C++ is free to change that. Also, if we change the number of characters in the string using a C-string function, the return value of the size() behavior (or the capacity() behavior) will not be changed. For those reasons we should avoid using C-string functions that might change the number of characters in a string object.

We could determine the length of a C string, the number of characters in it, by starting at its base address and moving one character at a time until we found the null character. That is what the ANSI **strlen()** function does.

```
size_t strlen(char *cString)                          <string.h>
```

The required header file is string.h. For many of our C++ functions there is a shift toward header files without the *.h* at the end. That is not the case here. There are two distinct header files: string, which contains the declarations for the string class, and string.h, which contains the declarations for C strings.

The return value of strlen() is the number of characters in the *cString*, not including the null at the end. The size_t data type is implementation dependent—typically, but not always, an unsigned int. At least it will always be compatible with an int.

The notation char *cString, with the asterisk (*), declares that *cString* is the address of a char, where it is stored in memory, rather than the value of a char. For strlen() to count the number of characters, we must send it a string. Remember, a C string is a char array beginning at some address and ending at the first null. If we declare

```
char name[12] = "Zelda";
```

memory might be allocated like this:

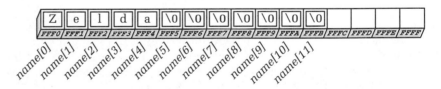

The term *name* is the address of the beginning of the string—FFF0.

If we say

```
cout << strlen(name) << endl;
```

we send *name*, FFF0, to the strlen() function. It can start counting characters there until it gets to the null at FFF5, and return the number of characters, 5, in the string. cout will print the value 5.

The **strcpy()** function copies a C string from one location to another.

```
char *strcpy(char *destination, char *source)        <string.h>
```

This function copies the string at the address *source*, including the terminating null character, to the location of the *destination*. It is up to you to see that there is enough allocated room at the *destination* to accommodate the entire *source* string. The return value is the address of the *destination* string.

The `strcpy()` function has many uses, but one is to just assign a string value to an array. Remember, a string value is the address of a null-terminated string in memory, so, given the declaration, the following statement will assign *Algonquin* at the location *cString*.

```
char cString[20];

strcpy(cString, "Algonquin");
```

A way to be sure that you do not overflow the space allocated at the *destination* is to use the **strncpy()** function, which copies up to a stated maximum of characters.

```
char *strncpy(char *destination, char *source, size_t max)          <string.h>
```

Not copying a terminating null with `strncpy()`.

This function can be tricky, though. If C++ encounters a null in the *source* string before it reaches *max* characters, it copies all the characters up to and including the null, leaving the *destination* string with an exact copy of the *source*. Otherwise, C++ copies the first *max* characters from the *source* string. If those characters include the terminating null, fine. If not, no null is added. Program D–5 shows an example of the latter situation.

You could ensure that your string was properly terminated by assigning a null character to the fifth character position of the first string (*name1[4]*).

```
strncpy(name1, name2, 4);

name1[4] = '\0';
cout << name1 << endl;
```

The **strcat()** function concatenates C strings—puts one string at the end of another.

```
char *strcat(char *cString, char *add)          <string.h>
```

Not enough allocated space at the end of the string to be lengthened.

This function copies the string at *add* to the location of the null in *cString*. It overwrites the null in *cString* and includes the terminating null at the end of *add*. Be sure there is enough allocated space at the location *cString* for all the characters in both strings plus the terminating null. The return value is the address of the combination string, *cString*.

```
char first[20] = "Arlo ", last[] = "Bilbao";

cout << strcat(first, last) << endl;
```

will print

```
Arlo Bilbao
```

and *first* will contain the value *Arlo Bilbao* with a terminating null. The string *Bilbao* is still at the location *last*, of course. Because the return value

Program D–5

```
#include <iostream>                              // Do you need .h here?
#include <string.h>                              // Be sure the .h is here!
using namespace std;

int main(void)
{   char name1[12] = "Albemarle", name2[12] = "Ferdy";

    strncpy(name1, name2, 4);
    cout << name1 << endl;
    return 0;
}
```

Output

```
Ferdmarle
```

Before Function

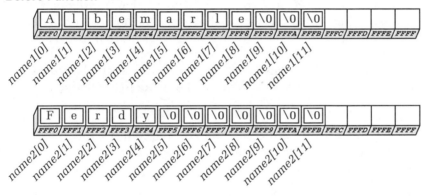

After Function

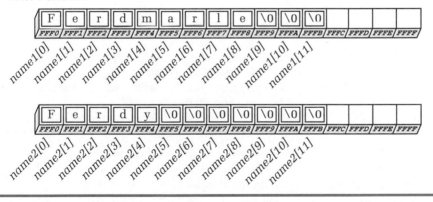

of strcat() is the address of the concatenated string, it is used as the argument in the cout.

We can limit the number of characters copied from the add string with **strncat()**.

```
char *strncat(char *cString, char *add, size_t max)                    <string.h>
```

The `strncat()` function does not have the problem associated with `strncpy()`; a terminating null is always added at the end of the concatenated string.

Often we must compare two strings to see which is greater. But how do we know whether *Murgatroyd* is greater than *Stella*? Let's examine how C++ makes the comparison. Each character value is nothing more than a number—the numeric value of its ASCII (or EBCDIC) code. C++ will compare these individual values character by character, beginning with the first character position (variable) in each string and moving toward the end. C++ makes the greater-than, less-than decision the first time it finds a difference in the character position it is currently comparing.

Murgatroyd and *Stella* are easy. C++ compares an *M* (ASCII 77) with an *S* (ASCII 83). The *S* is greater, so *Stella* is greater than *Murgatroyd*. Notice that the number of characters in each string is not significant. The first difference ends the comparison.

How about *Aaron* and *Aardvark*? The first three character positions in each string are the same, but in the fourth position are *o* and *d*. The *o* (111) is greater than the *d* (100) so *Aaron* is greater than *Aardvark*. But *aardvark* is greater than *Aaron* because, in the first character position, *a* (97) is greater than *A* (65). *Bytes* is greater than *Byte* because the *s* in *Bytes* is greater than the null at the end of *Byte*.

Again, ANSI C++ has saved us from the necessity of writing the C-string comparison ourselves by providing the **strcmp()** function.

```
int strcmp(char *cString1, char *cString2)          <string.h>
```

The two strings are compared and the return value set to a positive value if *cString1* is greater, to zero if they are equal, or to a negative value if *cString1* is less.

```
if (strcmp(name, "Muleford") == 0)
    cout << "We have found him!" << endl;
```

The following statement does us no good at all:

```
if (name == "Muleford")
    cout << "We have found him!" << endl;
```

because we are simply comparing two addresses, both of which the C++ compiler assigned based on available space.

Like `strncpy()` and `strncat()`, the **strncmp()** function compares only up to *max* characters in each string.

```
int strncmp(char *cString1, char *cString2, size_t max)          <string.h>
```

Program D–6 uses a number of the functions just presented. It combines two C strings together with the greatest first. Notice that the *combined* C string has only 25 characters allocated to it, making its effective length 24 characters. To ensure that we do not overflow the allocated space, we limited the number of characters we can concatenate to the end of the string to 24 less the number of characters already in the string. If the strings are equal, we copy a message to the *combined* string. But again, we do not want to overflow the allocated space, so we used `strncpy()`. Because that function may not copy the terminating null, we specifically put one in the last byte of *combined*.

Program D–6

```cpp
#include <iostream>
#include <string.h>
using namespace std;

const int length = 20;
const int combo = 25;                          // Not enough room for 2 full strings

int main(void)
{   char cString1[length], cString2[length], combined[combo];

    cout << "Give me two strings and I will put them together\n"
            "with the greatest first and a space in between.\n"
            "Your first string? ";
    cin.get(cString1, length, '\n');
    cin.ignore(500, '\n');
    cout << "Your next string? ";
    cin.get(cString2, length, '\n');
    cin.ignore(500, '\n');
    if (strcmp(cString1, cString2) > 0)              // First string greater
    {   strcpy(combined, cString1);
        strcat(combined, " ");                                  // Add space
        strncat(combined, cString2, combo - 1 - strlen(combined));
                                                            // Don't overflow
    }
    else if (strcmp(cString1, cString2) < 0)         // Second string greater
    {   strcpy(combined, cString2);
        strcat(combined, " ");                                  // Add space
        strncat(combined, cString1, combo - 1 - strlen(combined));
                                                            // Don't overflow
    }
    else
        strncpy(combined, "They're equal. Which is first?", combo);
    combined[combo - 1] = '\0';                      // In case null not copied
    cout << "The result: " << combined << endl;
    return 0;
}
```

Output

```
Give me two strings and I will put them together
with the greatest first and a space in between.
Your first string? Hi there, pal.
Your next string? What's cookin'?
The result: What's cookin'? Hi there
```

YOUR TURN D–3

1. What function returns the number of characters in a string?

2. What two functions will copy characters from one location to another? How do they differ?

3. What two functions concatenate one string to another? How do they differ?

4. What two functions compare two strings? How do they differ? How are the comparisons made?

ARRAYS OF STRINGS

We said that a C string is an array of characters and that a double-indexed array is an array of arrays, so we could store an array of C strings in a double-indexed `char` array.

```
char words[4][6] = {"zero", "one", "two", "three"};
```

The braces around the string values are necessary because they enclose a block of values. We could also declare it as

```
char words[][6] = {"zero", "one", "two", "three"};
```

leaving the first index out. Because of the initialization values, C++ knows how many arrays to set up.

This array takes up 24 bytes of memory, organized like this:

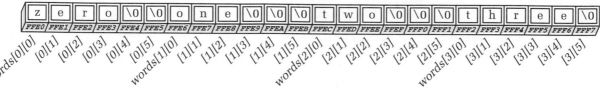

HEADS UP!

Index notation without the last index(es) becomes an address.

Exceeding the boundaries of your allocated array within the array.

Remember, when we leave the last index off an array identifier, it becomes the address of that array-within-an-array. In other words, *words[2]* is the address of *words[2][0]*, or *two*. Using that concept, we can access the *words* array as in Program D–7.

As always, staying within the boundaries of the arrays is up to you. Let's see what happens if we change the value of `words[1]` to something greater than five characters.

The `strcpy()` function wrote *singular\0* beginning at the address *words[1]*. The `cout` statement printed the string beginning at *words[1]* and then the string beginning at *words[2]*—hence the strange, but explainable, output. In memory, it looks like this:

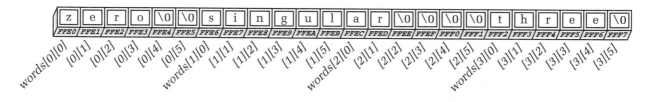

YOUR TURN D–4

1. What is an array of strings?
2. Given the declaration `char s[4][10]`, what is `s[2]`?
3. Given the declaration in Question 2, how would you print the third string in the array?

Program D–7

```
#include <iostream>
using namespace std;

const int strings = 4;
const int size = 6;

int main(void)
{   char words[strings][size] = {"zero", "one", "two", "three"};
    int count;

    for (count = 0; count < strings; ++count)
        cout << "Digit: " << count << ". Word: " << words[count] << endl;
    return 0;
}
```

Output

```
Digit: 0. Word: zero
Digit: 1. Word: one
Digit: 2. Word: two
Digit: 3. Word: three
```

New Program Segment

```
#include <string.h>
   . . .
    strcpy(words[1], "singular");
    for (count = 0; count < strings; ++count)
        cout << "Digit: " << count << ". Word: " << words[count] << endl;
```

Output

```
Digit: 0. Word: zero
Digit: 1. Word: singular
Digit: 2. Word: ar
Digit: 3. Word: three
```

CONVERTING STRINGS TO NUMBERS

HEADS UP!

Use the appropriate function
for the data type.

Numbers are often expressed in characters, strings, but we must process them as numbers. For example, we might be faced with a string, *Price: $19.95 each*, and must add the price to a total. The *19.95* part of the string must be converted to a number.

There are a number of ANSI functions that do the job; we will concentrate on three. The `atof()` function, pronounced "a to f" and standing for "alpha to floating-point," converts a *cString* to type `double`. The `atoi()` function ("alpha to integer") converts a *cString* to an `int`; and `atol()` ("alpha to long") to a `long`.

```
double atof(char *cString)                          <cstdlib>
int atoi(char *cString)                             <cstdlib>
long atol(char *cString)                            <cstdlib>
```

Program D–8

```cpp
#include <iostream>
#include <cstdlib>
using namespace std;

int main(void)
{   char cString[] = "123.456 is a number.";
    int intvar;
    long longvar;
    double doublevar;

    intvar = atoi(cString);
    longvar = atol(cString);
    doublevar = atof(cString);
    cout << "The string: " << cString << endl;
    cout << "Int: " << intvar << ", long: " << longvar
         << ", double: " << doublevar << endl;
    return 0;
}
```

Output

```
The string: 123.456 is a number.
Int: 123, long: 123, double: 123.456
```

Exceeding the limits of your data type.

In each case the conversion begins at the address *cString*, skips any leading whitespace, and ends at the first inappropriate character for that data type or the end of the string (the null). Program D–8 illustrates these conversion functions.

If the number represented by the characters in the string is larger than the data type can accommodate, the resulting assignment will be meaningless.

CHARACTER CLASSIFICATION

Often we are presented with a string of characters and must look inside it to interpret it. Is it a complete sentence? Does it present parameters for our program to work with? If so, what are the parameters? To examine it we must look at the individual characters. We can easily test to see if a particular

OTHER ANSI CONVERSION FUNCTIONS

The ANSI functions strtod(), strtol(), and strtoul() allow you to do some extra things with string-to-number conversions including returning the address where the conversion stopped (the inappropriate character) and, in the latter two, allowing you to state the radix (base) of the string representation.

Program D–9

```cpp
#include <iostream>
#include <cctype>
using namespace std;

int main(void)
{  char in;

   do
   {  cout << "Type a letter and <enter>: ";
      cin >> in;                              // Assign the character to in
   }while ( !isalpha(in));                    // Loop while not zero
   cout << "Finally, an alpha character!" << endl;
   return 0;
}
```

Output

```
Type a letter and <enter>: 4
Type a letter and <enter>: 8
Type a letter and <enter>: /
Type a letter and <enter>: g
Finally, an alpha character!
```

character is an *A* or a comma, but usually we want to look at the type of character rather than at its individual value. Is it an uppercase alpha character? Is it a punctuation character?

ANSI C++ provides us with a number of functions to classify individual characters. They all have the same format:

```
int function(int character)                          <cctype>
```

For example,

```
int isalpha(int character)                           <cctype>
```

returns a nonzero value if the `character` is a letter—that is, *A* through *Z* or *a* through *z*—or returns zero if it is not a letter. The data type of the argument is `int` because under the old C standards, a character value (such as `'A'`) was actually stored in an `int`, wasting a number of bytes of memory. The functions work fine when sent `char` data types; the extra bytes are just ignored.

Program D–9 asks for a letter from the keyboard and will loop until it gets one.

We can examine a string, character by character, by sending the character values to the `isalpha()` function, as in Program D–10.

The complete list of ANSI classification functions follows. These functions are similar to `isalpha()` in that their declarations are found in `cctype`, and they return a nonzero `int` if their conditions are satisfied or zero if they are not.

isalnum() Returns nonzero if the `character` is alphanumeric: *0–9*, *A–Z*, or *a–z*.

isalpha() Returns nonzero if the `character` is alphabetic: *A–Z* or *a–z*.

Program D–10

```
#include <iostream>
#include <cctype>
using namespace std;

int main(void)
{   char cString[] = "23 skidoo.";
    int chr = 0;                                // Character position in string

    while(cString[chr] != '\0')                 // Loop to the end of the string
    {   if (isalpha(cString[chr]))
            cout << "'" << cString[chr] << "' is alpha" << endl;
        else
            cout << "'" << cString[chr] << "' is not alpha" << endl;
        ++chr;                                   // Go to next character
    }
    return 0;
}
```

Output

```
'2' is not alpha
'3' is not alpha
' ' is not alpha
's' is alpha
'k' is alpha
'i' is alpha
'd' is alpha
'o' is alpha
'o' is alpha
'.' is not alpha
```

---

iscntrl() Returns nonzero if the character is a control code: ASCII 1–31.

isdigit() Returns nonzero if the character is a decimal digit: 0–9.

isgraph() Returns nonzero if the character is printable, not including space.

islower() Returns nonzero if the character is lowercase: a–z.

isprint() Returns nonzero if the character is printable, including space.

ispunct() Returns nonzero if the character is punctuation.

isspace() Returns nonzero if the character is whitespace: space, form feed (\f), newline (\n), return (\r), horizontal tab (\t), or vertical tab (\v).

isupper() Returns nonzero if the character is uppercase: A–Z.

isxdigit() Returns nonzero if the character is a hexadecimal digit: 0–9, A–F.

CHARACTER CONVERSIONS

There are two simple functions, **toupper()** and **tolower()**, that convert lowercase characters to uppercase and vice versa. Their forms are:

Program D–11

```cpp
#include <iostream>
#include <cctype>
using namespace std;

int main(void)
{   char cString[] = "mYRnA H. bALthAZaR, III";
    int chr;                                    // Character position in string

    cout << "Before: " << cString << endl;
    cString[0] = toupper(cString[0]);           // First character uppercase
    for (chr = 1; cString[chr] != '\0'; ++chr)  // 2nd chr to end of string
        if (cString[chr - 1] == ' ')            // Chr after space, uppercase
            cString[chr] = toupper(cString[chr]);
        else                                    // Not after space, lowercase
            cString[chr] = tolower(cString[chr]);
    cout << "After : " << cString << endl;
    return 0;
}
```

Output

```
Before: mYRnA H. bALthAZaR, III
After : Myrna H. Balthazar, Iii
```

```
int toupper(int character)                                          <cctype>

int tolower(int character)                                          <cctype>
```

If the *character* is not alpha, *A–Z* or *a–z*, or if the character is already in the desired case, it will be returned unchanged.

To illustrate both functions in Program D–11, let's take a sloppily written name and clean it up by putting it in caps/lowercase.

mYRnA H. bALthAZaR, III was a combination of upper- and lowercase letters, punctuation, and spaces. All the characters were sent to one function or the other, but `toupper()` changed only the lowercase letters and `tolower()` changed only the uppercase letters. All the others were returned unchanged. Our trick did not work very well on *III*.

YOUR TURN D–5

1. What three functions are commonly used to convert strings to numbers?
2. The text introduces 11 functions used to classify characters. Name them and tell which classifications they determine.
3. What is the return value for the classification functions if the character fits the classification? if it doesn't?
4. Which two functions convert letters between upper- and lowercase?
5. What effect do the conversion functions in Question 4 have on characters that are nonletters or letters that are already in the proper case?

Program D–12

```
#include <iostream>
using namespace std;

int main(void)
{   char cString1[] = "Daisy";
    char cString2[] = "Rose";
    char *anyString;

    cout << "anyString is now  " << anyString << endl;
    anyString = cString1;
    cout << "anyString is now  " << anyString << endl;
    anyString = cString2;
    cout << "anyString is now  " << anyString << endl;
    return 0;
}
```

Output

```
anyString is now  @j!}`~t
anyString is now  Daisy
anyString is now  Rose
```

POINTERS—A BRIEF GLANCE

HEADS UP!

A pointer variable contains an address.

We said that the asterisk in front of a variable in a function's formal parameter declaration means that the variable contains the address of some data rather than the data themselves. This address variable is referred to as a **pointer**—it points to, contains the address of, some other value in memory. We have also seen that most of the formal parameters of the string functions we have examined contained such declarations. Since a string starts at a specific address and ends at the first null, the function needs only the beginning address to access the string, so we send such addresses to the functions.

We can declare pointer variables as part of our own programs. In fact, many of the string functions we will be examining return pointers, and we may want to store those pointers in variables. The declaration

```
char *ptr;
```

Accessing or copying characters to a meaningless address.

allocates memory for a pointer variable. It contains an address, which at this time (assuming it is a local variable) is garbage—it doesn't point to anything in particular. We refer to the variable as a "pointer to char." Because of the data type specified in the declaration, C++ knows that it points to—contains the address of—a char data type.

We also said that the prefix of an array was an address, or a pointer, using that terminology. The prefix, remember, is constant. Its value may not be changed. In other words, we may not make it point to somewhere else in memory. We could, however, assign that address to a pointer variable, as Program D–12 shows.

After the declarations, memory might have been organized something like the following. (We are assuming a pointer variable takes up three bytes. It probably doesn't in your C++, but it makes illustration easier.)

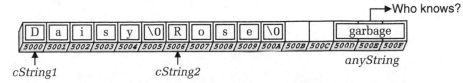

The pointer *anyString* does not have a valid value. When we printed it in the first cout, it pointed to a place in memory that happened to have the characters shown followed by a zero byte—a null. That memory area, before it reached a zero byte, might have contained the Gettysburg Address, machine language for a picture of Donald Duck, or something that might have locked up the screen!

After assigning the value of *cString1* to *anyString* memory would look like this:

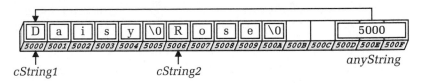

and *anyString* points to the same place as *cString1*. The second cout shows this.

Assigning the value of *cString2* to *anyString* makes it point to *Rose*, as the last cout shows.

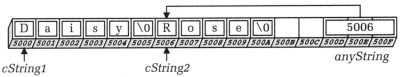

HEADS UP!

The asterisk means different things in different places.

In a declaration, the asterisk means that the variable following it is a pointer—in our case, a pointer to char. Anywhere else, the asterisk in front of a pointer variable means that we are referring to the data to which the pointer points—in our case, a char. In our example, *anyString* is the address of *R* in memory. The notation **anyString*, however, refers to data at that address; in other words, the char value *R*.

In fact, using that notation, we can change the data at that address. This statement,

```
*anyString = 'H';
```

puts the character *H* at the memory location to which *anyString* points— where the *R* used to be. Now if we printed the string starting at the address *anyString* it would be *Hose*. Since *anyString* points to the same place as *cString2*, printing *cString2* would also produce *Hose*. The name *cString2* is a constant; it cannot be changed; *anyString*, however, is a variable; it can be changed, as we have already done. Changing it, of course, makes it point to a different place in memory with different data in it.

We have added to Program D–12 to show the asterisk notation and how it works. The while loop at the end of Program D–13 starts with

Program D–13

```
#include <iostream>
using namespace std;

int main(void)
{   char cString1[] = "Daisy";
    char cString2[] = "Rose";
    char *anyString;

    cout << "anyString is now  " << anyString << endl;
    anyString = cString1;
    cout << "anyString is now  " << anyString << endl;
    anyString = cString2;
    cout << "anyString is now  " << anyString << endl;
    cout << "The data at anyString is " << *anyString << endl;
    *anyString = 'H';                          // Change the value at anyString
    cout << "anyString is now  " << anyString << endl;
    cout << "and cString2 is now " << cString2 << endl;  // cString2 is same
    cout << "Moving the pointer along to the first null, we get ";

    while (*anyString != '\0')                 // Data at anyString not null
    {   cout << *anyString;                    // Print individual character values
        ++anyString;                           // Move anyString to next address
    }
    cout << endl;
    return 0;
}
```

Output

```
anyString is now  @j!}`~t
anyString is now  Daisy
anyString is now  Rose
The data at anyString is R
anyString is now  Hose
and cString2 is now Hose
Moving the pointer along to the first null, we get Hose
```

---

anyString pointing to *H* and adds to *anyString*, moving the pointer, until it points to a null—the end of the string. Character by character, it prints *Hose*.

YOUR TURN D–6

1. What does an asterisk mean in a declaration such as `char *what;`?
2. What is the difference in the meanings of *what* and *that* in these two declarations: `char what[10];` and `char *that;`?
3. Given the declaration `char *that, what[] = "Flower";` and the statement `that = what + 1;`, to which string does *that* point?
4. Given the declaration and statement in Question 3, if we added the statement `*that = 'P'`, to which string would *that* point? To which string would *what* point?

TAKING STRINGS APART

Often we are faced with the task of disassembling a string into some component parts, a process referred to as **parsing** a string. Perhaps an input contains several parameters and we must separate them; we are examining the individual words in a sentence; or a name must be divided into first name, middle initial (if one exists), and last name. To do this we must look for clues that tell us where one part ends and another begins. The first part ends in a space; the second comes before a third, which is enclosed in parentheses; or the like.

To accomplish this disassembly, we must know what the clues are and have C++ find them for us. The more flexible our algorithm is, the more useful it will be. For example, making it immaterial how many spaces there are between parameters allows the program to handle some possibly sloppy parameters.

The **strstr()** function (usually referred to as "string string") returns the address of the beginning of a *search* string within a *reference* string.

```
char *strstr(char *reference, char *search)        <string.h>
```

If the *reference* string does not contain the *search* string, the function returns the NULL address constant. The code segment

```
char location[] = "Des Moines, Iowa";
cout << "State: " << (strstr(location, ", ") + 2) << endl;
```

would print out *Iowa*. The strstr() returns a pointer. In this case it is the address of the beginning of the comma/space combination within *location*—the address of the comma. The name of the state begins two characters after the comma, so adding 2 to the return value of strstr() gives us the address of *I*. The cout prints from there to the terminating null—*Iowa*.

Notice that if the comma were not in the *location[]* array, we would be asking cout to print what was at the NULL address—probably nothing we

---

Program D–14

```cpp
#include <iostream>
#include <string.h>
using namespace std;

int main(void)
{   char location[] = "Des Moines, Iowa";

    if (strstr(location, ", ") == NULL)
        cout << "There is no \", \" in " << location << endl;
    else
        cout << "State: " << (strstr(location, ", ") + 2) << endl;
    return 0;
}
```

Output

```
State: Iowa
```

Program D–15

```
#include <iostream>
#include <string.h>
using namespace std;

int main(void)
{  char *comma, location[] = "Des Moines, Iowa";

   comma = strstr(location, ", ");
   if (comma == NULL)
      cout << "There is no \", \" in " << location << endl;
   else
      cout << "State: " << (comma + 2) << endl;
   return 0;
}
```

would want to see displayed on our screen. We test for this condition in Program D–14 on the previous page.

Because we are calling the strstr() function twice in this program, in Program D–15 we will assign its return value to a pointer variable with a single call and use that pointer for the rest of the program.

The strstr() function is probably the most basic of the functions that find specific characters within a string. The **strchr()** function is similar except that it finds the first occurrence of a single character instead of an entire string.

HEADS UP!

strchr() searches for a specific single character.

```
char *strchr(char *reference, int character)      <string.h>
```

If the *character* is not found in the *reference* string, the function returns the NULL address constant. In the strchr() function, the null character at the end of the string is a possible search character. A search for it provides a pointer to the position one beyond the last character in the string.

We could use this to find and display the dollar amount in the string given:

Program Segment

```
char cString[] = "Widgets cost $49.95";
cout << "Cost: " << strchr(cString, '$') << endl;
```

Output

```
Cost: $49.95
```

In this case the return from strchr() is the address of the $, so the string printed by cout extends from the $ to the first null—the end of the string.

The **strrchr()** function is similar to strchr() except that it searches in reverse order, starting from the end of the *reference* string, finding the last occurrence of the *character*.

HEADS UP!

strrchr() searches backward for a specific single character.

```
char *strrchr(char *reference, int character)      <string.h>
```

Program D–16

```cpp
#include <iostream>
#include <string.h>
using namespace std;

int main(void)
{   char date[] = "12/6/1492";

    cout << "Date: " << date << endl;
    strtok(date, "/- ");                        // Null inserted at delimiter
    cout << "Month: " << date << endl;
    return 0;
}
```

Output

```
Date: 12/6/1492
Month: 12
```

HEADS UP!

strpbrk() searches for any
of a set of characters.

Another similar function is **strpbrk()**, which finds the first occurrence of any one of the characters of the *search* string in the *reference* string.

```cpp
char *strpbrk(char *reference, char *search)      <string.h>
```

For example, if we were not quite sure whether two items in a *string* were separated by a comma, a space, a dash, or a slash, we could find the separator with:

```cpp
separator = strpbrk(cString, ", -/");
```

where *separator* is a pointer variable.

The **strtok()** function is particularly useful in extracting **tokens**, sets of characters, from strings. It searches a *reference* string for any character from a string of *delimiters* (separating characters) and replaces that delimiter with a null, effectively ending the string there. The return value is the address of the *reference* string. The token, then, is the string at the returned address.

```cpp
char *strtok(char *reference, char *delimiters)   <string.h>
```

For example, Program D–16 extracts the characters representing the month from the date given. Notice that it would not matter whether we expressed the dates as *12/6/1492*, *12-6-1492*, or *12 6 1492*, or, for that matter, if we had a date like *9/17/92*.

After the call to strtok(), *date* still points to the same place, but the string is shortened because the null was inserted where the first slash was.

HEADS UP!

strtok() searches for any
of a set of characters, and
then moves its starting point.

The strtok() function, however, remembers where the null was inserted. A subsequent call to strtok() with NULL (the defined NULL pointer) as the *reference* string argument is a signal to the function to make the *reference* argument the address of the character after the inserted null from the previous call. In other words, strtok() will start where it left off last time. The returned value will be the new *reference* address. We can illustrate this with Program D–17, which divides a date into *month*, *day*, and *year* strings.

Program D–17

```
#include <iostream>
#include <string.h>
using namespace std;

int main(void)
{   char date[] = "12/6/1492";
    char *month, *day, *year;

    cout << "Date:   " << date << endl;
    month = strtok(date, "/- ");              // Null inserted at delimiter
    cout << "Month: " << month << endl;
    day = strtok(NULL, "/- ");                // Start where last left off
    cout << "Day:     " << day << endl;
    year = strtok(NULL, "\0");                // Null will be replaced with null
                                              // in other words, no change
    cout << "Year:    " << year << endl;
    return 0;
}
```

Output

```
Date:   12/6/1492
Month: 12
Day:    6
Year:   1492
```

Before

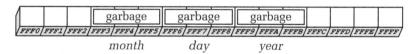

After

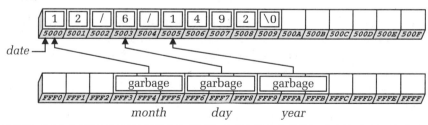

YOUR TURN D–7

1. What does it mean to *parse* a string?

2. Which function searches for a particular set of characters in a string? for a single character? for the last occurrence of a single character? for any of a set of characters?

3. How does `strtok()` differ from `strpbrk()`?

PUTTING IT TOGETHER

The Flab to Fab Fitness Club keeps height and weight statistics on all its members. The people who type the data into the computer have been directed only to put in the full name, first name first, followed by a colon, the height, a comma, and then the weight. The files are sloppy because everyone inputs the data differently. Some use feet and inches and pounds, others use meters and centimeters and kilograms, some use a combination of the two; some leave spaces, others don't . . . it's a mess.

TASK

Set up a mechanism that will keep member information in a consistent form.

ANALYSIS

There are a few bright spots in this input debacle. The name is always first name first and is always followed by a colon, the height is always followed by a comma, and the weight is always last. Other than that, our program must be able to handle different units of measure and almost anyone's guess as to spacing.

We want our mechanism to keep data in a universal and easy-to-use form. Keeping the names last name first is a commonly accepted form and makes names a lot easier to sort. Being somewhat optimistic, the F. to F. F. C. feels that sometime in the next millennium, the world will standardize on the metric system, so height should be stored in meters and weight in kilograms.

Following are some samples of possible inputs and an indication of how they might be stored in the computer:

Samples

```
As entered: Abner Troy Brindle: 6 ft 2 in, 192 lbs
As stored:  Brindle, Abner Troy: 1.88 meters, 87.27 kg.

As entered: Sheila Shirley Schildkin:1m46cm,115pds
As stored:  Schildkin, Sheila Shirley: 1.46 meters, 52.27 kg.

As entered: Rocky Q. Flowers: 161 cm, 85 kg
As stored:  Flowers, Rocky Q.: 1.61 meters, 85.00 kg.
```

DESIGN

For this project we will design a *Person* class from which we may create objects for the members of FlabCo (the staff is not allowed to use this abbreviation in public). Each object must store the name, height, and weight of a person. It must be able to accept entry of those data in various forms and convert them to the standard forms. It should also provide the standard data to other processes using simple access functions.

The entry behavior of the object should determine whether the entry fits the required pattern (we will keep it simple in this example, just finding the colon and the comma) and, if it fits, extract each of these elements, send them to the appropriate adjustment behavior, and assign the result to the stored property of the person.

```
[Entry]
    Get input
    Look for pattern elements
    if pattern correct
        Extract, adjust, and store name
        Extract, adjust, and store height
        Extract, adjust, and store weight
    else
        Display error message
```

To adjust the name we would have to:

```
[Adjust name]
    Find dividing point between first and last names
    Build new name with last name first
```

To adjust the height we would have to:

```
[Adjust height]
    [Convert first part]
        Find digits
        Find units
        Convert digits according to units
    if any second part, convert it
        Find digits
        Find units
        Convert digits according to units
```

To adjust the height we would have to:

```
[Adjust height]
    [Convert first part]
        Find value
        Find units
        Adjust value according to units
    [Add second part]
        Look for digits
        if digits exist
            Find value
            Find units
            Add value according to units
```

To adjust the weight we would have to:

```
[Adjust weight]
    Find value
    Find units
    Adjust value according to units
```

The name, height, and weight properties are isolated from processes outside the object. These properties are set by the entry behavior and provided by access functions.

IMPLEMENTATION

Our real objective in this project is to set up a meaningful *Person* class, so our main() function will simply be a driver to create an object of this

Name	Behavior	Properties
Person Class		name height weight
Entry	Accept keyboard input of data, adjust them, and assign object properties.	input existence of comma existence of colon height string (pro) weight string (pro)
Adjust Name	Change name from first first to last first.	where last name starts temp name to work with
Adjust Height	Change height from almost any form to meters.	height string (req) position in height string second part of height
Adjust Weight	Change weight from almost any form to meters.	weight string (req) position in weight string

class, *member*, and will test the class's public behaviors, *entry()*, and the access functions.

In the *entry()* function we enter the listing using `cin.get()` and then send the component parts of the input to the proper adjustment functions. The name begins at the beginning of the input and ends at the colon; the height begins there and ends at the comma; and the weight goes from there to the end of the input. First we find the colon and the comma, and then we divide the line into tokens.

The *adjustName()* function finds the dividing point between the first and middle names and the last. That point is the second space in the name. First we copy the name into a temporary string, then we reassemble it into *name*. To find the first space, we use the `strchr()` function:

```
strchr(temp, ' ')
```

The second space will be after the first, so we can start our search for it at

```
strchr(temp, ' ') + 1
```

giving us

```
lastStart = strchr(strchr(temp, ' ') + 1, ' ');                    // Second space
```

Once we find the second space, we can build a new *name* by copying the last name (from beyond the second space to the end of the string) from *temp*. To that we concatenate a comma and a space. Finally, we concatenate from the beginning of *temp* the number of characters up to the second space (the first and middle names).

In *adjustHeight()* we make use of the `atof()` function and how it skips leading whitespace and converts to the first inappropriate character—either a space or the first character of the units. Because `atof()` does not tell us where it left off, we find the units by starting at the first character of the string and move until the character at *pos* is alpha. The kinds of units we might encounter are such that we only need the units' first character.

The height might have a second part, so we look for more digits beyond the units in the first part. Notice that if the `strpbrk()` function does not find a digit, it returns NULL.

Adjusting the weight is similar to adjusting the height, except that there can be no second part. We convert the digits, find the units, and adjust accordingly.

The completed project is shown in Program D–18.

Testing this program could begin with the sample output we presented in the analysis stage. We should try to think up all possible combinations of names, units, spaces, and whatever else someone might enter, and see if they work. In this program there are obviously lots of input possibilities we have not accounted for. For example, if someone has no middle name, the process blows up. As you can see, foolproofing inputs can be a programming nightmare!

Program D–18

```
       #include <iostream>
       #include <iomanip>
       #include <string.h>
       #include <cctype>
       #include <cstdlib>
       using namespace std;

       const int chars = 60;              // Maximum number of characters for a string

       class Person ///////////////////////////////////////////////// Person Class
       {   char name[chars];
           double height, weight;

           void adjustName(void) //***************** First name first to last first
n1     {   char *lastStart;                       // Address where last name starts
           char temp[chars];                      // Temporary name while adjusting

n2         strcpy(temp, name);                           // copy name to temp
n3         lastStart = strchr(strchr(temp, ' ') + 1, ' ');       // Second space
n4         strcpy(name, lastStart + 1);                  // Last name to name
n5         strcat(name, ", ");                                     // Comma
n6         strncat(name, temp, lastStart - temp);     // First and middle names
       }

h1     void adjustHeight(char heightStr[]) //********* Changes height to meters
       {   double height2;
h2         char *pos;                             // Current position in string

           //----------------------------- Find value of first part of height
h3         height = atof(heightStr);         // Convert until inappropriate chr

           //--------------------------------------------------- Find units
h4         for (pos = heightStr; !isalpha(*pos); ++pos);      // Beg of units
h5         *pos = toupper(*pos);                     // First chr needed

           //--------------------------------- Adjust value according to units
h6         switch (*pos)                            // Value in heightStr
h7         {   case 'F':                                          // Feet
h8             height *= .3048;
h9             break;
h10            case 'I':                                        // Inches
h11            height /= 39.37;
h12            break;
h13            case 'C':                                    // Centimeters
h14            height /= 100;
       }
```

(Continued)

```
                //----------------------------- Add second part of height, if any
                    //---------------------------------------------------- Find digits
h15                 pos = strpbrk(pos, "0123456789");            // Next digit
h16                 if (pos != NULL)                      // If there is a next digit
h17                 {   height2 = atof(pos);              // Convert until inapp. chr

                        //---------------------------------------------------- Find units
h18                     for ( ; !isalpha(*pos); ++pos);          // Beg of units
h19                     *pos = toupper(*pos);                    // First chr needed

                        //--------------------------- Adjust value according to units
h20                     switch (*pos)                            // Value at pos
h21                     {   case 'I':                                  // Inches
h22                             height += height2 / 39.37;
h23                             break;
h24                         case 'C':                            // Centimeters
h25                             height += height2 / 100;
                        }
                    }
                }

w1      void adjustWeight(char weightStr[]) //************* Changes weight to kg
w2      {   char *pos;                          // Current position in string

            //---------------------------------------------------- Find value
w3          weight = atof(weightStr);           // Convert until inappropriate chr

            //---------------------------------------------------- Find units
w4          for (pos = weightStr; !isalpha(*pos); ++pos);        // Beg of units
w5          *pos = toupper(*pos);                    // First chr neeeded

            //--------------------------- Adjust value according to units
w6          if (*pos == 'L' || *pos == 'P')               // If pounds
w7              weight /= 2.2;
w8      }
    public:
        void entry(void) //**************************** Enter a Member Listing
e1      {   char input[chars];

            cout << "Enter listing: ";
e2          cin.get(input, chars, '\n');                    // Input entire line
e3          cin.ignore(500, '\n');
e4          if (strchr(input, ':') != NULL                  // Colon exists
                && strchr(input, ',') != NULL)              // Comma exists
e5          {   strcpy(name, strtok(input, ":"));           // Input to colon
e6              adjustName();
e7              adjustHeight(strtok(NULL, ","));            // Past colon to comma
e8              adjustWeight(strtok(NULL, "\0"));           // Rest of input
            }
            else
e9          {   cout << "Input could not be decoded." << endl;
e10             exit(EXIT_FAILURE);
            }
        }

        //**************************************************** Access Functions
        char *getName(void) { return name; }
        double getHeight(void) { return height; }
        double getWeight(void) { return weight; }
    };                                          // Don't forget this semicolon!
```
(Continued)

Program D–18 *(Continued)*

```
      int main(void) ///////////////////////////////////////////// Main Program
1  {  Person member;

2     member.entry();
      cout << setiosflags(ios::fixed) << setprecision(2);
3     cout << member.getName() << ": " << member.getHeight() << " meters, "
          << member.getWeight() << " kg." << endl;
      return 0;
   }
```

Output

```
      Enter listing: Abner Troy Brindle: 6 ft 2 in, 192 lbs
      Brindle, Abner Troy: 1.88 meters, 87.27 kg.

      Enter listing: Sheila Shirley Schildkin:1m46cm,115pds
      Schildkin, Sheila Shirley: 1.46 meters, 52.27 kg.

      Enter listing: Rocky Q. Flowers: 161 cm,85 kg
      Flowers, Rocky Q.: 1.61 meters, 85.00 kg.
```

EXECUTION CHART

Line	Explanation	member. at *name*	height	weight	
1	Create *member* object.	(??......)	(??)	(??)	
2	Call *entry()* behavior.	(??......)	(??)	(??)	
	member.entry():				**at input**
e1	Declare 60-chr, empty string.	??......	??	??	??......
e2	Input line.	??......	??	??	Abner Troy Brindle: 6 ft 2 in, 192 lbs
e3	Flush stream.	??......	??	??	Abner Troy Brindle: 6 ft 2 in, 192 lbs
e4	Colon and comma within string.	??......	??	??	Abner Troy Brindle: 6 ft 2 in, 192 lbs
e5	Put null at colon, copy to name.	Abner Troy Brindle	??	??	Abner Troy Brindle\0 6 ft 2 in, 192 lbs
e6	Call *adjustName()*.	Abner Troy Brindle	??	??	Abner Troy Brindle\0 6 ft 2 in, 192 lbs
	member.adjustName():				**at lastStart** / **at temp**
n1	Pointer variable.	Abner Troy Brindle	??	??	??...... / --
n2	Copy chrs from *name* to *temp*.	Abner Troy Brindle	??	??	??...... / Abner Troy Brindle
n3	Inner strchr() finds space after *r*, outer strchr() starts search 1 after that (at *T*) and finds second space after *y*. Assign address to *lastStart*.	Abner Troy Brindle	??	??	Brindle / Abner Troy Brindle
n4	Copy from 1 beyond *lastStart* to *name*.	Brindle	??	??	Brindle / Abner Troy Brindle
n4	Add comma and space to *name*.	Brindle,	??	??	Brindle / Abner Troy Brindle
n3	Add chrs between *temp* and *lastStart*.	Brindle, Abner Troy	??	??	Brindle / Abner Troy Brindle
	member.entry():				**at input**
e7	strtok() starts beyond null, replaces comma with another null, sends address after first null to *adjustHeight()*.	Brindle, Abner Troy	??	??	Abner Troy Brindle\0 6 ft 2 in\0 192 lbs

(Continued)

EXECUTION CHART *(Continued)*

Line	member.adjustHeight():	member. at *name*	*height*	*weight*	at *heightStr*	at *pos*	*height2*
h1	Initialize *heightStr*.	Brindle, Abner Troy	??	??	6 ft 2 in	--	--
h2	Pointer variable.	Brindle, Abner Troy	??	??	6 ft 2 in	??......	??
h3	Skip initial space; convert to space.	Brindle, Abner Troy	6	??	6 ft 2 in	??......	??
h4	Move *pos* until at alpha character.	Brindle, Abner Troy	6	??	6 ft 2 in	ft 2 in	??
h5	Shift chr there to uppercase.	Brindle, Abner Troy	6	??	6 Ft 2 in	Ft 2 in	??
h6	Find *F* at h7.	Brindle, Abner Troy	6	??	6 Ft 2 in	Ft 2 in	??
h8	Convert height to meters.	Brindle, Abner Troy	1.829	??	6 Ft 2 in	Ft 2 in	??
h9	Exit `switch`.	Brindle, Abner Troy	1.829	??	6 Ft 2 in	Ft 2 in	??
h15	Look for digit starting at *pos*.	Brindle, Abner Troy	1.829	??	6 Ft 2 in	2 in	??
h16	Digit found.	Brindle, Abner Troy	1.829	??	6 Ft 2 in	2 in	??
h17	Convert to *height2*.	Brindle, Abner Troy	1.829	??	6 Ft 2 in	2 in	2
h18	Find first alpha chr.	Brindle, Abner Troy	1.829	??	6 Ft 2 in	in	2
h19	Shift chr there to uppercase.	Brindle, Abner Troy	1.829	??	6 Ft 2 In	In	2
h20	Find *I* at h21.	Brindle, Abner Troy	1.829	??	6 Ft 2 In	In	2
h22	Convert *height2*; add to *height*.	Brindle, Abner Troy	1.879	??	6 Ft 2 In	In	2
h23	Exit `switch` and function.	Brindle, Abner Troy	1.879	??	6 Ft 2 In	In	2

Line	member.entry():	member. at *name*	*height*	*weight*	at *input*		
e8	Send last part of *input* to *adjustWeight()*.	Brindle, Abner Troy	1.879	??	Abner Troy Brindle\0 6 ft 2 in\0 192 lbs		

Line	member.adjustWeight():	member. at *name*	*height*	*weight*	at *weightStr*	at *pos*	
w1	Initialize *weightStr*.	Brindle, Abner Troy	1.879	??	192 lbs	--	
w2	Pointer variable.	Brindle, Abner Troy	1.879	??	192 lbs	??......	
w3	Skip initial space; convert to space.	Brindle, Abner Troy	1.879	192	192 lbs	??......	
w4	Find alpha chr.	Brindle, Abner Troy	1.879	192	192 lbs	lbs	
w5	Shift to uppercase.	Brindle, Abner Troy	1.879	192	192 Lbs	Lbs	
w6	Character is *L*.	Brindle, Abner Troy	1.879	192	192 Lbs	Lbs	
w7	Convert to kilograms.	Brindle, Abner Troy	1.879	87.273	192 Lbs	Lbs	
w8	Return to *entry()* and `main()`.	Brindle, Abner Troy	1.879	87.273	192 Lbs	Lbs	

Line	`main():`	member. at *name*	*height*	*weight*			
3	Print using access functions.	(Brindle, Abner ...)	(1....)	(87...)			

SUMMARY

- **KEY TERMS** (in order of appearance)

  Flush
  Pointer

  Parse
  Token

• NEW FUNCTIONS (in order of appearance)

stream& cin.get(char *cString, int max, char delimiter)   <iostream>
> **Purpose:** Assigns characters from input stream until *delimiter* or *max* - 1 reached.
> **Return:** Reference to input stream object.

void cin.ignore(int characters, char delimiter)   <iostream>
> **Purpose:** Passes *characters* in input stream unless *delimiter* reached first.
> **Return:** None.

size_t strlen(char *cString)   <string.h>
> **Purpose:** Find number of characters at *cString*.
> **Return:** Number of characters at *cString*.

char *strcpy(char *destination, char *source)   <string.h>
> **Purpose:** Copy *source* string to *destination*.
> **Return:** *destination*.

char *strncpy(char *destination, char *source, size_t max)   <string.h>
> **Purpose:** Copy up to *max* characters of *source* string to *destination*.
> **Return:** *destination*.

char *strcat(char *cString, char *add)   <string.h>
> **Purpose:** Put *add* string at the end of *cString*.
> **Return:** *cString*.

char *strncat(char *cString, char *add, size_t max)   <string.h>
> **Purpose:** Put up to *max* characters of *add* string at the end of *cString*.
> **Return:** *cString*.

int strcmp(char *cString1, char *cString2)   <string.h>
> **Purpose:** Compare two strings.
> **Return:** Positive value if *cString1* greater, negative if *cString2*, zero if equal.

int strncmp(char *cString1, char *cString2, size_t max)   <string.h>
> **Purpose:** Compare up to *max* characters of two strings.
> **Return:** Positive value if *cString1* greater, negative if *cString2*, zero if equal.

double atof(address character)   <cstdlib>
> **Purpose:** Convert from address of *character* to double.
> **Return:** Success: Converted number. Error: Meaningless assignment.

int atoi(address character)   <cstdlib>
> **Purpose:** Convert from address of *character* to int.
> **Return:** Success: Converted number. Error: Meaningless assignment.

long atol(address character)   <cstdlib>
> **Purpose:** Convert from address of *character* to long.
> **Return:** Success: Converted number. Error: Meaningless assignment.

int isalnum(int character)   <cctype>
> **Purpose:** Test if *character* is alphanumeric: *0–9*, *A–Z*, or *a–z*.
> **Return:** True: Nonzero. False: Zero.

int isalpha(int character)   <cctype>
> **Purpose:** Test if *character* is alphabetic: *A–Z* or *a–z*.
> **Return:** True: Nonzero. False: Zero.

int iscntrl(int character)   <cctype>
> **Purpose:** Test if *character* is a control code: ASCII 1–31.
> **Return:** True: Nonzero. False: Zero.

int isdigit(int character)   <cctype>
> **Purpose:** Test if *character* is a decimal digit: *0–9*.
> **Return:** True: Nonzero. False: Zero.

```
int isgraph(int character)                                              <cctype>
     Purpose:  Test if character is printable, not including space.
     Return:   True: Nonzero. False: Zero.
int islower(int character)                                              <cctype>
     Purpose:  Test if character is lowercase: a–z.
     Return:   True: Nonzero. False: Zero.
int isprint(int character)                                             <cctype>
     Purpose:  Test if character is printable, including space.
     Return:   True: Nonzero. False: Zero.
int ispunct(int character)                                             <cctype>
     Purpose:  Test if character is punctuation.
     Return:   True: Nonzero. False: Zero.
int isspace(int character)                                             <cctype>
     Purpose:  Test if character is whitespace: space, \f, \n, \r, \t, or \v.
     Return:   True: Nonzero. False: Zero.
int isupper(int character)                                             <cctype>
     Purpose:  Test if character is uppercase: A–Z.
     Return:   True: Nonzero. False: Zero.
int isxdigit(int character)                                            <cctype>
     Purpose:  Test if character is a hexadecimal digit: 0–9, A–F.
     Return:   True: Nonzero. False: Zero.
int toupper(int character)                                             <cctype>
     Purpose:  Convert lowercase character to upper.
     Return:   If character lowercase letter, uppercase equivalent, otherwise no change.
int tolower(int character)                                             <cctype>
     Purpose:  Convert uppercase character to lower.
     Return:   If character uppercase letter, lowercase equivalent, otherwise no change.
char *strstr(char *reference, char *search)                         <string.h>
     Purpose:  Find a search string in a reference string.
     Return:   Success: Address of search string in reference string. Error: NULL.
char *strchr(char *reference, int character)                        <string.h>
     Purpose:  Find the first occurrence of a character in a reference string.
     Return:   Success: Address of the character in the reference string. Error: NULL.
char *strrchr(char *reference, int character)                       <string.h>
     Purpose:  Find the last occurrence of a character in a reference string.
     Return:   Success: Address of the character in the reference string. Error: NULL.
char *strpbrk(char *reference, char *characters)                    <string.h>
     Purpose:  Find first occurrence of any of characters in reference.
     Return:   Success: Address of occurrence. Error: NULL.
char *strtok(char *reference, char *delimiters)                     <string.h>
     Purpose:  Extract and mark end of delimited tokens in reference string.
     Return:   Success: Address of beginning of reference string. Error: NULL.
```

- **CONCEPT REVIEW**

  - A string is an array of chars in memory. It begins at a particular address and extends to the first null character. A quoted string value represents the address at which C++ has chosen to store those characters.

  - A character value such as 'A' is a number. A string value such as "A" is a set of character values beginning at an address and stored with a trailing null.

- C strings are not stored in single variables but in arrays of `chars`. C strings may be declared and initialized in the same manner as other arrays, but we may also state the initializing characters in quotation marks rather than as separate values.

- Strings must be assigned one character at a time. There are ANSI C++ functions that help with this.

- The `cin` object can input strings as well as numbers. Like most ANSI objects, it automatically assigns the trailing null at the end of the string.

- The `cin` behavior `get()` can be used to input strings with spaces within them—entire lines, for example. In this function we state a maximum number of characters allowable for the string (including the trailing null) and the behavior will not assign more than that to the string. This may leave unexpected characters in the input stream, however.

- To get rid of the newline and any other unexpected characters in the input stream we can **flush** the stream using `cin.ignore()`. Both `cin.get()` and `cin.ignore()` can be used with any delimiters.

- ANSI C++ has a number of functions that aid us in manipulating both C strings and `string` objects. `strlen()` returns the number of characters in a string (as a `size_t` data type); `strcpy()` and `strncpy()` copy a string to another location; `strcat()` and `strncat()` copy one string to the end of another; and `strcmp()` and `strncmp()` compare one string to another.

- Arrays of C strings may be set up by declaring an array of arrays—a double-indexed array. An array notation without the last index(es) is the address of an array within the array.

- The `atof()`, `atoi()`, and `atol()` functions convert strings to `doubles`, `ints`, and `longs`.

- The `isalnum()`, `isalpha()`, `iscntrl()`, `isdigit()`, `isgraph()`, `islower()`, `isprint()`, `ispunct()`, `isspace()`, `isupper()`, and `isxdigit()` functions test characters to see whether they fit into various classifications.

- The `toupper()` function converts a lowercase alpha character to uppercase; `tolower()` does the opposite.

- A **pointer** is an address. We may use pointer variables, declared with asterisk notation, to store addresses. In other parts of the program the asterisk notation accesses the data being pointed to. A pointer variable differs from an array prefix in that the prefix is a constant and points to an allocated address in memory whereas the variable, unless initialized or otherwise assigned, points to nowhere in particular.

- There are a number of functions that help us in **parsing** strings. The `strstr()` function finds one string within another, whereas `strchr()` and `strrchr()` find a specific character within a string. The `strpbrk()` function finds the first occurrence of any of a number of characters in the string. The `strtok()` function helps us to extract series of **tokens** from strings.

• HEADS UP: POINTS OF SPECIAL INTEREST

- Strings in C++ end in a null character.
- To C++, a string value is an address.

- A character in single quotation marks is a numeric value.
- Don't forget the null character when allocating C strings.
- An array name cannot be assigned.
- Know how `cin` works.
- `cin.get()` does not remove, nor does it store, the delimiter.
- `cin.get()` could leave characters in the input stream.
- `cin.get()` does not skip leading whitespace.
- `cin.get()` can work with any character as a delimiter.
- Most C++ functions will allow you to write beyond the space allocated for a string.
- Many C-string functions can be used with `string` objects.
- String comparisons are done one character position at a time.
- In ASCII, all lowercase characters are greater than any uppercase character.
- Index notation without the last index(es) becomes an address.
- Use the appropriate function for the data type.
- A pointer variable contains an address.
- The asterisk means different things in different places.
- Make your routines as error-proof as possible.
- `strstr()` searches for a specific set of characters.
- `strchr()` searches for a specific single character.
- `strrchr()` searches backward for a specific single character.
- `strpbrk()` searches for any of a set of characters.
- `strtok()` searches for any of a set of characters, and then moves its starting point.

• TRAPS: COMMON PROGRAMMING ERRORS

- Using `' '` instead of `" "`.
- Not allocating enough space for C strings.
- Attempting to assign a string value (address) to an array prefix.
- Assigning characters beyond the space allocated for the string.
- Not flushing the input stream.
- Using a C-string function that changes the size of a `string` object.
- Including `string` when you want `string.h`.
- Not copying a terminating null with `strncpy()`.
- Not enough allocated space at the end of the string to be lengthened.
- Comparing two string addresses instead of using `strcmp()`.
- Exceeding the boundaries of your allocated array within the array.
- Exceeding the limits of your data type.
- Accessing or copying characters to a meaningless address.

• YOUR TURN ANSWERS

• D–1

1. Strings are stored as arrays of `chars` if we do not use the `string` class in C++.

2. A string value stored in memory begins at some base address—wherever C++ has chosen to put it—and ends with a null.

3. The string `"A"` is stored as an array of two `chars`, the ASCII code for *A* followed by null. The notation in quotation marks refers to its base address in memory. `'A'` is a single `char` and simply the numeric value of its character code—65.

4. We store C strings in arrays of `char` variables.

5. C++ doesn't ensure that we do not assign C strings to unallocated locations—that's up to us.

6. The first three are identical. Each allocates 12 `chars`, sets the first 5 to *Zelda*, and makes the rest null. The fourth allocates only 6 `chars`, enough for *Zelda* and null.

7. C strings are assigned a single character at a time.

• D–2

1. As with numbers, whitespace delimits strings with `cin >>`.

2. The `cin.get()` behavior allows us to set our own delimiter. For an entire line, including embedded spaces, we would use newline as a delimiter.

3. Using `cin` and the extraction operator, we cannot ensure that we do not assign characters beyond the allocated space for a string. Using `cin.get()` we can state the maximum allowable space (including the trailing null) to be assigned.

4. After a `cin >>` or a `cin.get()`, both will leave the newline, and `cin.get()` leaves any characters beyond the maximum − 1 stated in the behavior.

5. We can flush the input stream using `cin.ignore()`.

• D–3

1. The `strlen()` function returns the number of bytes from the address sent to it to the first null.

2. `strcpy()` copies a string from one address to another, including the terminating null. `strncpy()` does the same, but will not exceed a maximum number of bytes, even if the null is not copied.

3. `strcat()` copies a string from one address to the end of a string at another address. `strncpy()` does the same, but will not copy more than a maximum number of bytes.

4. `strcmp()` and `strncmp()` compare bytes a position at a time from each address given. The comparison is made according to the numeric value of the ASCII codes. The comparison stops at the first difference or, in the case of `strncmp()`, at a maximum number of bytes.

• D–4

1. Because a string is an array of `chars`, an array of strings is an array of arrays of `chars`.

2. Given the declaration char s[4][10], s[2] is the address of the beginning of the third string—the address of *s[2][0]*.

3. Given the declaration in Question 2, the third string in the array would be printed with cout << s[2];.

• D–5

1. The atof(), atoi(), and atol() functions convert strings to double, int, or long data types.

2. The 11 functions used to classify characters are: isalnum(), alphanumeric; isalpha(), alphabetic; iscntrl(), control code; isdigit(), decimal digit; isgraph(), printable, not including space; islower(), lowercase; isprint(), printable, including space; ispunct(), punctuation; isspace(), whitespace; isupper(), uppercase; isxdigit(), hexadecimal digit.

3. The return value for the classification functions is nonzero if the character fits the classification and zero if it doesn't.

4. The toupper() and tolower() functions convert letters between upper- and lowercase.

5. The functions in Question 4 have no effect on nonletters or letters that are already in the proper case.

• D–6

1. An asterisk in a declaration such as char *what; means that *what* is an address variable, a pointer, that can contain the address of a char.

2. There is little difference in meaning between *what* and *that* in the declarations char what[10]; and char *that;. Both are pointers to char, but *what* is constant and points to 10 bytes of allocated space, whereas *that* is a variable and points to no place in particular.

3. Given the declaration char *that, what[] = "Flower";, the statement that = what + 1; makes *that* point to an address one beyond *what*, which makes it point to *lower*.

4. Because *that* points to the *l* in *lower*, changing the data at that address to *P* makes *that* point to *Power*. The variable *what* points to *FPower*, whatever that means.

• D–7

1. Parsing a string means separating it into its component parts—words or special codes, for example.

2. The strstr() function searches for a particular set of characters in a string, strchr() for a single character, strrchr() for the last occurrence of a single character, and strpbrk() and strtok() for any of a set of characters.

3. The strtok() function replaces the character with a null and remembers its address. Future calls with a NULL reference argument will start where it left off the last time. The strpbrk() function simply returns the address of the character.

EXERCISES

1. Which are correct declarations and initializations for C strings?

   a. `char a[10] = "Alice";`
   b. `char a[] = "Alice";`
   c. `char a[10] = 'A', 'l', 'i', 'c', 'e';`
   d. `char a[10] = {0};`
   e. `char a[5] = "Alice";`

2. Given the following declaration and statement, which will execute without error messages, and which will produce valid data?

   ```
   char s1[16] = "Rita", *s2, s3[] = "Al";
   s2 = s3;
   ```

   a. `cin >> s1;`
   b. `cin >> s2;`
   c. `s2 = "Farley";`
   d. `s1 = "Fred";`
   e. `s1 = s2;`
   f. `s2 = s1;`
   g. `strcpy(s1, s2);`
   h. `strcat(s1, s2);`
   i. `strcat(s2, s1);`
   j. `*s2 = 'L';`
   k. `++s2;`

3. What problem might be encountered with the following section of code, and how might we fix it?

   ```
   cin >> aFloat >> anInt);
   cin.get(aString, 500, '\n');
   ```

4. What output will the following program produce?

   ```cpp
   #include <iostream>
   #include <string.h>
   #include <cctype>
   using namespace std;

   int main(void)
   {   char s[] = "Algernon";

       cout << &s[2] << endl;
       cout << strcmp(s, "Farley") << endl;
       cout << strncmp(s, "Algeria", 5) << endl;
       cout << *strchr(s, 'g') << endl;
       cout << strlen(s) << endl;
       cout << islower(s[2]) << endl;
       cout << strstr(s, "ger") << endl;
       cout << *strpbrk(s, "nle") << endl;
       return 0;
   }
   ```

5. What output will the following program produce?
```cpp
#include <iostream>
#include <cstdlib>
using namespace std;

int main(void)
{   char s[] = "123.456 and so forth";
    double f;

    cout << s << endl;
    cout << atoi(s) << endl;
    cout << atof(s) << endl;
    f = atof(&s[4]);
    cout << f << endl;
    s[2] = 'Q';
    cout << atof(s) << endl;
    return 0;
}
```

6. What output will the following program produce?
```cpp
#include <iostream>
#include <string.h>
using namespace std;

int main(void)
{   char s[] = "Steven C. Lawlor: Author, Raconteur & Scholar";

    cout << strtok(s, " .:");
    cout << (strtok(NULL, ":") + 2) << endl;
    cout << (strtok(NULL, "&") + 1) << endl;
    return 0;
}
```

PROGRAMS

1. Do Program 1 in Chapter 9 (page 348) using C strings instead of the string class.

2. Do Program 2 in Chapter 9 (page 348) using C strings instead of the string class.

3. Do Program 3 in Chapter 9 (page 349) using C strings instead of the string class.

4. Do Program 4 in Chapter 9 (page 349) using C strings instead of the string class.

5. Do Program 5 in Chapter 9 (page 349) using C strings instead of the string class.

6. Do Program 6 in Chapter 9 (page 349) using C strings instead of the string class.

7. Do Program 7 in Chapter 9 (page 349) using C strings instead of the `string` class.

8. Do Program 8 in Chapter 9 (page 350) using C strings instead of the `string` class.

9. Do Program 9 in Chapter 9 (page 350) using C strings instead of the `string` class.

10. Do Program 10 in Chapter 9 (page 351) using C strings instead of the `string` class.

11. Write a function, *stringcmp()*, that works like `strcmp()` but is not case-sensitive. In other words, *NORBERT* would be greater than *Nancy*. Test it with an appropriate `main()` function driver.

12. Expand Program D–7 (page 559) so it sorts the strings and then prints out the sorted result. Of course, the digits and words will not match. The output should be as below:

Output

```
Digit: 0. Word: zero
Digit: 1. Word: one
Digit: 2. Word: two
Digit: 3. Word: three

Digit: 0. Word: one
Digit: 1. Word: three
Digit: 2. Word: two
Digit: 3. Word: zero
```

INDEX

H

Hard disk 10
Hardware **7**
Head **474**
Header, function 182, 187
Header file **47**, 83, **199**
hex **89**
Hexadecimal number system **17**
Hide **198**
High-level language 21, **22**
Hollerith, Herman 4

I

IBM 5, 6, 13
IC 6
IDE **22**
Identifier, variable 51
if **114**
#if **505**
#ifdef **506**
#ifndef **506**
ignore() **323**, **551**
Implementation **27**
#include 83, 199, 496
Increment operator **157**
Index **262**
    Floating-point 264
Initialization
    Array 263
    Counter-controlled loop **154**
    Multiple-index array 290
    Object 237
    Object array 278
    String 318
    Variable **53**
Insert **284**
Insertion operator **46**
Instance **226**
Instantiate 227
Instruction register **11**
int **55**
Integer arithmetic **62**
Integral
    Data type **54**
    Number **48**
    Value 55
Integrated circuit 6
Integrated development environ-
    ment (IDE) **22**
Interface **24**
Internal **196**
iomanip 89
iomanip.h 89
ios::fixed **90**
ios::left **91**
ios::right **91**

Ios flag **90**
iostream 47, 83, 323, 548, 551
iostream.h 47
isalnum() **328**, **561**
isalpha() 327, **328**, **561**
iscntrl() **328**, **562**
isdigit() **328**, **562**
isgraph() **328**, **562**
islower() **328**, **562**
isprint() **328**, **562**
ispunct() **328**, **562**
isspace() **328**, **562**
isupper() **328**, **562**
isxdigit() **328**, **562**
Iteration structure 106, **142**, 206

J

Jacquard, Joseph Marie 3
Jacquard loom 3

K

K&R **42**, 80
Kernighan, Brian 42
Key **404**

L

Label **518**
labs() **201**
Language
    Assembly **21**
    High-level 21, **22**
    Machine **21**
Large-scale integration 6
Library **199**
Lifetime **183**
Line feed 357
Linear search 279
Link **22**
Linked List **474**
Literal 48
Local **183**, 196, 229
Location **9**, **444**
Logical
    Operation 7, **8**
    Operator **112**
    Plan **27**
long **55**
long double **56**
Loop **142**
    Counter-controlled **153**
    Nested **159**
    Posttest **143**
    Pretest **143**
    Sentinel-value-controlled **148**
Lovelace, Countess of 4

M

Machine Language **21**
Macintosh 13
Macro **500**
    Parameterized **501**
Magic number 263
main() 43, 46
Main memory **9**
Manipulator 50, **89**
Mantissa **56**
Mask off 198
math.h 201
Mathematical function 200–204
Member **227**
    Function **230**
    Operator **229**, 523
Member-pointer operator **460**
Method 24
Mode 356
Modifiable lvalue 65
Modular design **23**, 80, 106, 178,
    196
Module **23**
Modulo 62
Modulus 62
MS-DOS 13, 354, 357, 370, 496

N

Name
    File **354**
    Variable **51**
Nested **109**
    Comment **494**
    #include 497
    Loop **159**
new **470**
New operator **470**
Newline **46**
not operator **112**
NULL 203
Null character 316
Number
    Integral **48**
    Real **48**
Number system
    Binary **15**
    Decimal **14**
    Hexadecimal **17**

O

Object **24**, 45, 178, **226**
    Array 275
    Behavior **230**
    Class 227
    Code **22**
    Comma **516**